PATERNOSTER BIBLICAL MONOGRAPHS

On the Road Encounters in Luke-Acts

Hellenistic Mimesis and Luke's Theology of the Way

Octavian Baban

Foreword by Karl Olaf Sandnes

Eugene, Oregon

Wipf and Stock Publishers
199 W 8th Ave, Suite 3
Eugene, OR 97401

On the Road Encounters in Luke-Acts
Hellenistic Mimesis and Luke's Theology of the Way
By Baban, Octavian D.
Copyright©2006 Paternoster
ISBN 13: 978-1-59752-999-0
ISBN: 1-59752-999-0
Publication date 3/15/2004
Previously published by Paternoster, 2006

This Edition Published by Wipf and Stock Publishers
by arrangement with Paternoster

Paternoster
9 Holdom Avenue
Bletchley
Milton Keyes, MK1 1QR
Great Britain

Series Preface

One of the major objectives of Paternoster is to serve biblical scholarship by providing a channel for the publication of theses and other monographs of high quality at affordable prices. Paternoster stands within the broad evangelical tradition of Christianity. Our authors would describe themselves as Christians who recognise the authority of the Bible, maintain the centrality of the gospel message and assent to the classical credal statements of Christian belief. There is diversity within this constituency; advances in scholarship are possible only if there is freedom for frank debate on controversial issues and for the publication of new and sometimes provocative proposals. What is offered in this series is the best of writing by committed Christians who are concerned to develop well-founded biblical scholarship in a spirit of loyalty to the historic faith.

Series Editors

I. Howard Marshall, Honorary Research Professor of New Testament, University of Aberdeen, Scotland, UK

Richard J. Bauckham, Professor of New Testament Studies and Bishop Wardlaw Professor, University of St Andrews, Scotland, UK

Craig Blomberg, Distinguished Professor of New Testament, Denver Seminary, Colorado, USA

Robert P. Gordon, Regius Professor of Hebrew, University of Cambridge, UK

Tremper Longman III, Robert H. Gundry Professor and Chair of the Department of Biblical Studies, Westmont College, Santa Barbara, California, USA

This book is dedicated to my spouse, Daniela, and to our two children, Raluca and Vlad, who graciously helped me to find the time to write it.

Contents

Foreword	xi
Preface	xiii
Acknowledgements	xv
Abbreviations	xvii
INTRODUCTION	1
THE SIGNIFICANCE OF THE *HODOS* SETTINGS	2
THE SIGNIFICANCE OF THE ENCOUNTER EVENTS	11
HELLENISTIC LITERATURE AND LUKE'S STYLE	18
CHAPTER 1 A REVIEW OF LUKAN SCHOLARSHIP	27
FORM CRITICISM AND THE WAY METAPHOR	27
The Journey Motif in Tales, Legends, Itineraries	28
The Idealisation of the Way Setting	32
REDACTION CRITICISM AND LUKE'S *REISENOTIZEN*	56
Mark's Journeying Motif and Luke's Reisenotizen	56
New Ways of Interpreting Luke's Reisenotizen	63
CHAPTER 2 THE WAY AND HELLENISTIC *MIMESIS*	73
MIMESIS AND ITS ALTERNATIVE MEANINGS	73
Definition and Different Types of Mimesis	74
Plato's Mimesis and Its Social Effects	91
Aristotle's Mimesis as Creative Representation	99
Hellenistic Historians and Mimesis	109
HELLENISTIC MIMESIS AND LUKE'S JOURNEY MODELS	118
The Journey Motif in Hellenistic Novels	118
The Journey Motif in Jewish Literature	123
The Journey Motif and Its Greco-Roman Models	127
Mimesis, Journeying and Ideology	136
CHAPTER 3 THE WAY AND SYNOPTIC MIMESIS	141
LUKE'S REPRESENTATION OF MARK AND MATTHEW	142
Mark's Use of the Way Motif	142
Matthew's Use of the Way Motif	153
Luke's Representation of the Way Motif	158
LUKE'S JOURNEY MOTIF IN LUKE-ACTS	173
The Journey Motif and the Infancy Narratives	174
Jesus' Journey to Jerusalem and Its Hodos Stories	176
The Emmaus Story: A Journey Beyond Jerusalem	186

CHAPTER 4 THE POST-EASTER PARADIGM — 195

LITERARY UNITY AND TRANSITION IN LUKE 24 - ACTS 1 — 195
   The Narrative Context of Luke 24 - Acts 1 — 198
   Narrative Unity and Transition in Luke 24 — 202
LITERARY UNITY AND TRANSITION IN ACTS 8:26-9:31 — 207
   Literary Coherence and Unity in Acts 8:26-9:31 — 207
   Saul's Encounter as Narrative Landmark — 213
   Hodos Encounters and Narrative Transitions — 225
THE ANATOMY OF LUKE'S ON THE ROAD PARADIGM — 227
   The Emmaus Meal as Sacramental Ending — 227
   The Hodos Paradigm — 231
   The Reversal and Restoration Act — 256

CONCLUSIONS — 273

THE RELEVANCE OF MIMESIS FOR LUKE'S JOURNEY MOTIF — 273
THE NARRATIVE COHERENCE OF LUKE'S JOURNEY STORIES — 278

BIBLIOGRAPHY — 280

PRIMARY RESOURCES — 280
SELECTIVE BIBLIOGRAPHY — 283

INDEXES — 317

INDEX OF GENERAL TERMS — 317
INDEX OF AUTHORS — 327

FOREWORD

I met Dr. Octavian Baban in Cambridge in 1999, when he was about to finish his doctoral thesis and I was enjoying my Sabbatical at Tyndale House. By late evenings, when we were tired of reading and writing, we walked along the streets of Cambridge, and discovered that we shared the same interest in how New Testament writers drew on Hellenistic philosophy and literature. It is, therefore, a pleasure to see that my Cambridge-friend has now revised his thesis and is making it available to the New Testament exegetes who share similar concerns and favour the literary approaches to the NT.

In the present work Dr. Baban approaches a well-known topic, that of Luke's theology of journeying, in a new way. He argues that key passages in Luke-Acts have been "storied" according to certain Hellenistic models, some of them being found in Aristotle's *Poetics*, where one can find a special focus on the ancient compositional patterns of mimesis. Baban shifts the perspective from the traditional view that Luke imitates the Septuagint to the NT mimesis of Hellenistic storytelling. Luke appears, thus, as an educated writer, a clever storyteller and an evangelistic theologian who "stories" the idea of meeting the risen Christ "in a life changing encounter, during one's journey through life" (p. 279).

Karl Olav Sandnes,
The Norwegian Lutheran School of Theology, Oslo
October 2005

PREFACE

This book represents a revised form of my PhD thesis, submitted at The London School of Theology in the Spring of 1999. The ideea of this research, focused on Luke's theology of journeying and on his art of literary representation, has occured first during a NT seminar with Dr. C. Gempf, at LST (LBC – at that time), when the main topic in discussion was Jesus' appearances in Luke 24, and, in relation to it, the issue of Luke's style and the meaning of the disappearance or appearance stories in the NT (appearances during a storm, walking on the sea, post-Easter appearances – or disappearances, missionary stories in Acts, etc.). The question arised, then, whether these narratives are a sort of ghost stories told for the sake of their own spectacular nature, or / and as a testimony for Jesus' and his disciples' ministry, or valued, as well, as good and meaningful literature, reflecting certain literary patterns of the time. The thought of referring to Aristotle's *Poetics* and his views on mimetic composition, as influential for the NT authors, and, in particular, for Luke, has come considerably later, during a study weekend at Tyndale House, Cambridge.

In its attempt to answer these stylistic and theological issues, the present book focuses on three Lukan post-Easter encounters: the two disciples' encounter with resurrected Jesus on the Emmaus road (Lk. 24:13–35), Philip's evangelisation of the Ethiopian on the Gaza road (Acts 8:25–40), and Saul's encounter with Christ on the Damascus road (Acts 9:1–31). In essence, it argues that the right context for interpreting Luke's post-Easter 'on the road' encounters is Luke's general motif of Journeying, rather than his series of post-Easter glorious visions of the resurrected Jesus. It suggests that one needs a different approach to Luke's theology of the Way, as well, complementary to the common focus on Jesus' journey to Jerusalem (Lk. 9-19). In order to make this need more clear, the first chapter reviews the main results and emphases of form-critical and redactional studies of Luke's Journey motif.

Then, the second chapter looks at the Hellenistic perspectives on the art and the techniques of literary representation (mimesis), as seen in Plato's works, in Aristotle's treatises, and in the work of Hellenistic historians such as Duris, Theopompus and Phylarchus, which prove to be surprisingly relevant for understanding the composition of Luke's 'on the road' paradigm.

The third chapter attempts and assessment of Luke's paradigmatic redaction of the Synoptic journey stories, as a testimony of his more general compositional tendencies and choices in source representation. The relation between Luke's and Mark's journeying motifs is interpreted as a form of mimetic-redactional representation and a similar approach is attempted, as well, in relation to Luke's and Matthew's motifs of the Way, although this would implay a more thorough and nuanced discussion of Luke's possibility to interract with Matthew's gospel in its final variant, and a more complex consideration of the Synoptic hypotheses, than this book format would allow. This assessment emphasizes in the end the evidence that Luke had his own theological agenda and literary preferences in many of these journey stories, especially so in his 'journey within journey' narratives, in Luke 9-19, and in the resurrection stories (Luke 24 – Acts 1).

Chapter four focuses on this journey paradigm, as such, in Luke-Acts, highlighting its narrative function and its literary 'anatomy'. Through its characteristics and emphases this paradigm corresponds well to the literary and theological transition present in Luke 24 – Acts 1 and in Acts 8–9. Its literary structure corresponds to Aristotle's plot model.

In conclusion, Luke's post-Easter 'on the road' encounters reflect his artistic representation of sources or events displaying unity of action, of time and space, a special emphasis on recognition scenes (divinely ordained encounters), on ethical and theological choices (the theme of individual testing at the crossroads), on reversals of destiny in the context of suffering and restoration. Luke builds a complex plot in these stories communicating, thus, his interest for special revelations 'on the road', for a challenging and life-changing adventure of a journeying individual (a perspective that supplements the usual emphasis on a collective journeying paradigm in Luke-Acts).

On the whole, this book's argument intends to add a new perspective to the current assessment of Luke's theology and artistic skills, to the study of Luke's style as a Hellenistic historian. It attempts to throw fresh light on the early transmission of the Easter kerygma, seen as a process that involved both the transmission of the apostolic message and the issue of the NT evangelists' specific literary taste and narrative choices, of their representational philosophy. In particular, Luke appears to have presented his encounter stories not as an increasingly spiritualised type of divine man narratives or as 'visions' of Jesus' heavenly glory, yet more as an early, fashionable and evangelistically effective, series of significant encounterings with Jesus while journeying amidst one's own adventure in life.

Octavian Baban
The Baptist Theological Institute, Bucharest
The University of Bucharest, Romania
February 2006

Acknowledgements

I would like to acknowledge, with gratitude and the best of memories, that I have greatly benefited from the friendly academic environment at the London School of Theology (known, also, as LBC). I owe much, in particular, to Dr. Conrad Gempf and Dr. Max Turner, my supervisors, who passed on to me their enthusiasm for the theology of Luke-Acts, and to Dr. Loveday C.A. Alexander, for her kind and precious academic guidance in matters of NT cultural environment. I would like to mention, as well, my fellow researchers Dr. Volker Rabens, Dr. Robert Goodwin, and Dr. Alexandru Neagoe for sharing their time, thoughts and insights on NT issues. I have also benefited from the encouragement and mature wisdom of Dr. Ian Randall, whom I admire both as a scholar and as a pastor. Finally, I would like to express my warm thanks to Dr. Jeremy Mudditt and Dr. Anthony R. Cross for their constant support, advice, and patience in preparing this book for publication.

Octavian Baban
The Baptist Theological Institute, Bucharest
The University of Bucharest, Romania
February 2006

Abbreviations

AJA	*The American Journal of Archaeology*
AnBib	Analecta Biblica
AJPh	*The American Journal of Philology*
ASTI	*Annual of the Swedish Theological Institute*
Bib	*Biblica*
BTB	*The Biblical Theology Bulletin*
Bib.Td.	*The Bible Today*
BZ	*Biblische Zeitschrift*
CBQ	*The Catholic Biblical Quarterly*
CPh	*Classical Philology*
EstB	*Estudios Bíblicos*
ExpTim	*The Expository Times*
EvT	*Evangelische Theologie*
HerKor	*Herder-Korrespondenz*
HSCPh	*The Harvard Studies in Classical Philology*
Int	*Interpretation*
HTR	*The Harvard Theological Review*
JAAR	*Journal of the American Academy of Religion*
JAF	*Journal of American Folklore*
JBL	*The Journal of Biblical Literature*
JEChS	*The Journal of Early Christian Studies*
JSNT	*The Journal for the Study of the New Testament*
JSS	*The Journal of Semitic Studies*
JR	*The Journal of Religion*
JTS	*The Journal of Theological Studies*
LCL	The Loeb Classical Library Series
LTP	*Laval Théologique et Philosophique*
LumV	*Lumen Vitae*
LXX	The Septuagint
Neot	*Neotestamentica*
NIDNTT	*The New International Dictionary of NT Theology*
NJBC	*The New Jerome Bible Dictionary*
NovT	*Novum Testamentum*
NTS	*New Testament Studies*
NRT	*Nouvelle Revue de Theologie*
PRS	*Perspectives of Religious Studies*

QJS	The Quarterly of Jewish Studies
RCatT	Revista Catalana de Teologia
RHPR	Revue de l'Histoire et de Philosophie Religieuses
RHR	Revue de l'Histoire des Religions
RB	Revue Biblique
RevExp	Review and Expositor
REL	Revue des Études Latines
RSR	Reserches de Science Religieuse
SBL	The Society for Biblical Literature
SBT	Studia Biblica et Theologica
ScE	Science et Esprit
TvT	Tijdschrift voor Theologie
TDNT	The Theological Dictionary of the NT
EDNT	The Exegetical Dictionary of NT
TLZ	Theologische Literaturzeitung
TQ	Theologische Quartalschrift
TR	Theologische Revue
TU	Texte und Untersuchungen
TynB	Tyndale Bulletin
TWNT	Theologisches Wörterbuch zum Neuen Testament
TZ	Theologische Zeitschrift
ZNW	Zeitschrift für die neuetestamentlische Wissenschaft und die Kunde des Urchristentums
VigChr.	Vigilae Christianae
ZTK	Zeitschrift für Theologie und Kirche.

Introduction

The present study of Luke-Acts represents an attempt to understand Luke's theology of journeying in relation to his literary style. One of the main issues in discussion is whether contemporary scholarship constructs Luke's theology of the Way, or his Journey motif, in a comprehensive manner, by taking into consideration the entire variety of Luke's journey accounts in Luke-Acts, not only the last journey of Jesus to Jerusalem (Lk. 9-19, *cf.* Mk. 8-10).[1] The reason for such an assessment is the observation that, in these accounts Luke's stylistic and theological preferences betray a complex understanding of literary representation, a philosophical depth and literary awareness that seem to go deeper than is commonly acknowledged.

To illustrate these points, the argument of this book focuses on three important journey stories in Luke-Acts: the Emmaus road encounter, Luke 24:13-35; Philip's evangelisation of the Ethiopian on the Gaza road, Acts 8:26-40; and Saul's encounter with the risen Christ on the Damascus road, Acts 9:1-31 (the three of them being placed in pivotal sections of Luke-Acts and displaying a similar literary structure: a special encounter, a setting 'on the road' - ἐν τῇ ὁδῷ, an evangelistic dialogue, a sacramental ending).[2]

---

[1] Few would argue against the importance of the Way theme or of the journey motif in Luke-Acts. Luke builds his narratives on certain famous journeys such as Jesus' journey from Galilee to Jerusalem, together with his disciples, and the missionary journeys to Samaria, Damascus, Asia Minor, Macedonia, Greece, and, finally, Rome, in Acts. The issue is whether, apart from these, one could highlight other important journey stories and emphases which contribute in a significant way to Luke's overall theology of journeying.

[2] During these journeys Luke is constantly referring to 'the Way' (Gk. *he hodos*, ἡ ὁδός) both as a setting and as a messianic metaphor, often stressing the ideea of religious challenge and obedience to God. These references to the way manifest a clustering tendency as in Luke 1-3, 9, 24, Acts 8-9 (*cf.* W. F. Moulton and A. S. Geden, *Concordance to the*

Surprisingly, although their literary correspondences have been noted by various commentators, these stories have not yet been assessed as three related journey accounts, nor as part of Luke's general motif of the Way, or as evidence for Luke's literary style. Therefore, the following introduction will present the significance of these correspondences, advocating the need for a more detailed assessment of Luke's art of literary representation.

The Significance of the *Hodos* Settings

The *hodos* setting (ἡ ὁδός, 'the way') is a common, prominent feature of all these three accounts. It occurs in the double report of the Emmaus story, ὡς ἐλάλει ἡμῖν ἐν τῇ ὁδῷ (Lk. 24:32) and ἐξηγοῦντο τὰ ἐν τῇ ὁδῷ (Lk. 24:35), in the repeated reference to the encounter setting in the Ethiopian's conversion story (Acts 8:26, ἐπὶ τὴν ὁδὸν τὴν καταβαίνουσαν ἀπὸ Ἰερουσαλὴμ εἰς Γάζαν, αὕτη ἐστὶν ἔρημος, 8:36, ὡς δὲ ἐπορεύοντο κατὰ τὴν ὁδόν, 8:39, ἐπορεύετο γὰρ τὴν ὁδὸν αὐτοῦ χαίρων), and in Saul's conversion account, as well: the Way metaphor in Acts 9:2, ἐάν τινας εὕρῃ τῆς ὁδοῦ ὄντας (*cf.* also Acts 19:9, 23; 24:14, 22) in Ananias' and Barnabas' summaries of the event (Acts 9:17, ὁ κύριος ἀπέσταλκέν με, Ἰησοῦς ὁ ὀφθείς σοι ἐν τῇ ὁδῷ ᾗ ἤρχου, and Acts 9:27, διηγήσατο αὐτοῖς πῶς ἐν τῇ ὁδῷ εἶδεν τὸν κύριον καὶ ὅτι ἐλάλησεν αὐτῷ).

Such an emphasis has suggested the possibility of a Lukan 'on the road' paradigm and the need to study it further, the more only a few NT scholars have referred to it clearly, among them E. H. Scheffler[3] and C. H. Lindijer,[4] for whom the 'way' setting had a major hermeneutical value.[5]

Greek Testament: According to the Texts of Westcott and Hort, Tischendorf and the English Revisers (Edinburgh: T&T Clark, 1993), pp. 226-227; A. Schmoller, *Pocket Concordance to the Greek New Testament: Based on the Text of the Nestle-Aland Novum Testamentum Graece and The Greek New Testament* (Stuttgart: Deutsche Bibelgesellshaft, 1994), p. 355; see H. Balz and G. Schneider (eds.), 'ὁδός', *EDNT* (Grand Rapids, MI: Eerdmans, 1991), vol. 2, 491-492).

3 E. H. Scheffler, 'Emmaus - a Historical Perspective', *Neot* (23) 1989, 251-267.

4 C.H. Lindijer, 'Two creative encounters in the work of Luke. Luke 24:13-35 and Acts 8:26-40', in T. Baarda, F. F. Lijn, and W. C. van Unnik (eds.), *Miscellanea Neotestamentica*, supp. to *Novum*

Introduction 3

These parallelisms, in particular the correspondences between the Emmaus account and the Ethiopian's conversion, led to the conclusion that Luke is the source of this literary phenomenon, not his sources.[6] Thus, Dupont writes that 'ce n'est pas dans ses sources que Luc a trouvé le schème de ses récits, il les a construits lui-même'.[7] For Dillon, as well 'it

---

    Testamentum, XLVIII (Leiden: Brill, 1978), 77-86; idem, *Handelingen van de Apostolen*, vol. 1: *Van Jerusalem naar Antiochië (hfsk 1-12)* (Nijkerk: Callenbach, 1975), p. 225.

5 See also J. A. Fitzmyer and R. J. Dillon, *cf.* Fitzmyer, *The Gospel According to Luke X-XXIV* (Garden City, NY: Doubleday, 1985) and R. J. Dillon, *From Eye-Witnesses to Ministers of the Word: Tradition and Composition in Luke 24* (Rome: PBI, 1978). Fitzmyer acknowledges the similarity, yet cautions against 'overinterpreting' it (*op.cit.*, p. 1560).

6 At the origin of this discussion stands a series of articles of J. Dupont, *e.g.*, 'Le Repas d'Emmaüs', *LumV* 31 (1957), 77-92 (English transl. as 'The Meal at Emmaus', in J. Delorme, P. Benoit, M. E. Boismard (eds.), *The Eucharist in the New Testament* (London: Chapman, 1964), 105-121); 'Les pèlerins d'Emmaüs (Luc 24:13-35)', in R. M. Diaz (ed.), *Miscellanea Biblica B Ubach, Scripta et documenta* 1 (Montrat: Benedictine Abbey, 1953), 349-374, esp. pp. 361-364. The similarity has been noted by others, as well, such as J. A. Grassi, 'Emmaus revisited (Luke 24:13-35 and Acts 8:36-40)', *CBQ* 26 (1964), 463-465; J. Kremer, *Die Osterbotschaft der vier Evangelien: Versuch einer Auslegung der Berichte über das leere Grab und die Erscheinungen des Auferstandenen* (Stuttgart: Katholisches Bibelwerk, 1969); J. Wanke, '"... wie sie ihn beim Brotbrechen erkannten", Zur Auslegung der Emmauserzählung Lk. 24:13-35', *BZ* 18 (1974), 181-192, esp. p. 192; also, Wanke, *Die Emmauserzählung: eine redaktionsgeschichtliche Untersuchung zu Lk. 24:13-35* (Leipzig: St. Benno, 1973); D. McBride, *Emmaus: The Gracious Visit of God According to Luke* (Dublin: Dominican, 1991), p. 129; J.-M. Guillaume, *Luc interprète des anciennes traditions sur la résurrection de Jésus* (Paris: Gabalda, 1979), pp. 80-81; *cf.* also, I. H. Marshall, *The Gospel of Luke: A Commentary on the Greek Text* (Exeter: Paternoster, 1992), p. 890; J. Roloff, *Das Kerygma und der irdische Jesus: Historische Motive in den Jesus-Erzählungen der Evangelien* (Göttingen: Vandenhoeck, 1970), pp. 256-258; J. B. Polhill, *Acts* (Nashville, TN: Broadman, 1992); A. A. Just, Jr., *The Ongoing Feast: Table Fellowship and Eschatology at Emmaus* (Collegeville, MN: Liturgical, 1993), p. 71, etc. Guillaume provides a detailed scheme of their correspondences (*Luke interprète*, pp. 80-81).

7 J. Dupont, 'Les pèlerins d'Emmaüs (Luc 24:13-35)', in *Miscellanea Biblica B Ubach, Scripta et Documenta (1)*, (Montserrat: Benedictine Abbey, 1953), 349-74, p. 352.

would be hard to deny that the composing hand in both these passages is the same',[8] and, independently, J.-M. Guillaume points out that 'les idées générales sont les mêmes dans les deux péricopes'.[9] As Lindijer notes this series represents 'a conception of Luke'.[10]

Therefore, the major issue is 'how Luke came to creating this series of motifs',[11] and equally so, what are his particular emphases in these accounts, and how does he emphasize his interests, redactionally (in terms of literary art, or theological discussion).

Theological literature hosts a great variety of answers, in this respect, some of them favourable to a literary approach of Luke's accounts, some dominated by other perspectives. For example, Dillon regarded this *hodos* pattern as a 'topos of charismatic lore' in the early Christian Church.[12]

Scheffler saw in them evidence of 'fictitiousness, or at least heavy Lukan redaction'.[13] For him, Luke relates history and theology in a relevant and transparent manner for his social context dominated by religious persecution, poverty, and ostracism.[14]

Lindijer argued that in the Emmaus encounter and in Philip's evangelism of the Ethiopian, Luke highlights Philip's *creative continuation of Jesus' ministry*[15] (Saul's encounter is

---

8   Dillon, *Eye-Witnesses*, p. 112.
9   Guillaume, *Luc interprète*, p. 80.
10 Lindijer, 'Creative', p. 81.
11 Lindijer, 'Creative', p. 82.
12 Dillon, *Eye-Witnesses*, p. 153; There is a strong correspondence between Lk. 24 and Acts 8, and, in particular, Lk. 24:31 and Acts 8:39-40 suggests 'a topos of charismatic mission lore' (*op.cit.*, p.153, n.239).
13 Scheffler, 'Emmaus', pp. 257, 260.
14 Scheffler, 'Emmaus', p. 262. Scheffler's discussion refers to van Aarde's and Schmithals' reconstructions of the persecution context in which lived the Christians of Asia Minor, at the end of the reign of Emperor Domitian from AD 81 to AD 96 (A. van Aarde, 'Narrative point of view: an ideological reading of Luke 12:35-48', *Neot* 22 (1988), 235-252, p. 244; W. Schmithals, *Einleitung in die drei ersten Evangelien* (Berlin: Gruyter, 1985), pp. 358-365).
15 Lindijer, 'Creative', p. 80. He echoes Marxsen's 'Die Sache Jesu geht weiter' (W. Marxsen, 'Die Auferstehung als historisches und als theologisches Problem', in W. Marxsen (ed.), *Die Bedeutung der Auferstehungsbotschaft für den Glauben an Jesu Christus* (Gütersloh:

Introduction

thought to reflect a similar concern).[16] In particular, these two stories share several common features, such as[17]

(a) a divinely planned meeting on the road
(b) a dialogue[18]
(c) the use of the proof from Scriptures[19]
(d) a turning point in the journey[20]
(e) the sight theme (as seeing, understanding, disappearing)
(f) a final sacrament.[21]

Lindijer wants to include Paul's conversion in the post-Easter encounter series, as well, and regards this series as a general motif of particular significance in Luke-Acts

> Another pericope written by Luke is related to our stories: the description of the conversion of Paul. The affinity between our stories and that of Saul's conversion certainly fortifies the impression that the series of motifs was important to Luke.[22]

Despite this important insight, however, his article remains focused on two stories, only, that is, on the Emmaus encounter and on the Gaza 'on the road' encounter.[23] This is a good illustration of an interesting, more general tendency in NT

Delling, 1968), p. 29; cited in Lindijer, 'Creative', p. 84). F. S. Spencer notes that: 'by so modelling the Emmaus and eunuch narratives after a common pattern, Luke no doubt betrays his customary concern to demonstrate continuity between the experiences of Jesus and the early church' (*The Portrait of Philip in Acts* (Sheffield: Sheffield Academical, 1992), p. 142).

16 Lindijer includes Paul's encounter in this series, as well ('Creative', p. 85).
17 Lindijer, 'Creative', pp. 77, 78-81.
18 Lindijer notes that 'a dialogue begins, questions are put and answered to, problems are expressed' ('Creative', p. 83), suggesting the idea of a dialectic nature and compositional origin of these Lukan dialogues.
19 As Lindijer notes 'the element of interpreting the Scriptures is wanting' in Saul's case (Lindijer, 'Creative', pp. 82, 83-84).
20 Lindijer, 'Creative', pp. 80, 85.
21 Lindijer, 'Creative', pp. 81-83 (*cf.* the final meal in Gen. 28).
22 Lindijer, 'Creative', p. 82.
23 Focused on the same two stories are the studies of J. Dupont, 'Meal', pp. 105-121; *idem*, 'Les pèlerins', pp. 349-374; Guillaume, *Luc interprète*; Dillon, *Eye-Witness*, etc.

scholarship. These accounts have been studied rather as pairs of related stories and very rarely considered as a triad or as stories integrated in a larger motif of Luke – such as the Journey motif, the post-Easter appearance motif, the report to the apostles motif, etc. (among the few exceptions is J. Drury who does not elaborate more on his observations, though).[24] This pairing up has remained the dominant approach to Luke's post-Easter encounters and there could be adduced quite a number of examples.

R. C. Tannehill highlights, for instance, the similarity between Luke's presentation of Philip's ministry and that of Saul, in Acts.[25] In Samaria Philip 'was proclaiming (ἐκήρυσσεν) the Messiah' (Acts 8:5), and in Damascus Saul 'was proclaiming (ἐκήρυσσεν) Jesus as the Son of God' (Acts 9:20). In both stories the final lines include the sacramental act of baptism (Acts 9:18; 10:47-48; 11:16-17). Both end with a report to the Twelve in Jerusalem (Acts 9:27; 11:1-18).

Boismard and Lamouille note, as well, an interesting linguistic similarity between the Emmaus' 'road' encounter (Acts 24:29, 32) and Lydia's conversion (Acts 16:13-15). Both mention the opening of mind or heart to the message (Acts 16:14 has ὁ κύριος διήνοιξεν τὴν καρδίαν, and Luke 24:32 has οὐχὶ ἡ καρδία ἡμῶν καιομένη ἦν... ὡς διήνοιγεν ἡμῖν τὰς γραφάς), also both mention an insistent prayer to stay (Acts 16:15, παρεκάλεσεν λέγουσα... εἰς τὸν οἶκόν μου μένετε· καὶ παρεβιάσατο ἡμᾶς, and Luke 24:29, καὶ παρεβιάσαντο αὐτὸν λέγοντες, μεῖνον μεθ' ἡμῶν).[26]

L. T. Johnson has found, in a further example, that the most similar sequence to the Emmaus episode is the story of Cornelius' conversion (Acts 10-11) with its emphasis on community decisions (Acts 12-15).[27] The two stories display

---

24 J. Drury notes a common format for Luke's parables and his journey stories: a crisis situation placed in the middle of the story (not at the end, as in Matthew) and greater attention payed to human characters, to the details of their existence (*The parables in the Gospels: history and allegory* (London: SPCK, 1985), pp. 112-113, 114-115).

25 R. C. Tannehill, *The Narrative Unity of Luke-Acts: A Literary Interpretation* (Philadelphia, PA: Fortress, 1990), vol. 2, p. 113.

26 M.-É. Boismard and A. Lamouille, *Les Actes des deux apôtres: analyses littéraires* (Paris: Gabalda, 1990), vol. 3, pp. 18-19.

27 L. T. Johnson, *The Gospel of Luke* (Collegeville, MN: Liturgical, 1991), p. 399.

Introduction 7

the same marks of Lukan vocabulary and style (Lk. 24:13, ἧ ὄνομα᾽ Ἐμμαοῦς, 24:18 εἰς ὀνόματι Κλεοπᾶς, Acts 10:1, ὀνόματι Κορνήλιος; Lk. 24:19, ἀνὴρ προφήτης δυνατὸς ἐν ἔργῳ καὶ λόγῳ ἐναντίον τοῦ θεοῦ καὶ παντὸς τοῦ λαοῦ, Acts 10:1-2, Ἀνὴρ δέ... εὐσεβὴς καὶ φοβούμενος τὸν θεόν, 10:22, ἀνὴρ δίκαιος καὶ φοβούμενος τὸν θεόν, etc.).

There are certain correspondences, as well, between the Ethiopian's encounter with Philip, on the Gaza road, and Cornelius' evangelisation by Peter, in Caesarea. It has been suggested that at the root of this similarity is the fact that both had initially represented a 'simple', thus popular, account of a leader's evangelistic exploits, a similar tradition of the first-ever God-fearer believer,[28] an evangelistic story 'innocent of any deeper meaning'.[29] For the first Christians the Ethiopian represented a first-ever 'symbolic convert',[30] and Cornelius represents a 'prototypical "God-fearer" or "semi-proselyte,"' a 'most typical, and most likely kind of person to convert to the Christian faith'.[31]

---

28 M. Dibelius, 'The Conversion of Cornelius', in M. Dibelius, *Studies in the Acts of the Apostles* (London: SCM, 1956), 108-122, esp. pp. 121-122.

29 The Ethiopian's story is seen as the Hellenistic version of a first Gentile convert ever 'a rival story to the later account about Cornelius' (H. Conzelmann, *The Acts of the Apostles* (Philadelphia, PA: Fortress, 1963), p. 67, 80; see E. Haenchen, *The Acts of the Apostles* (Oxford: Blackwell, 1971), p. 315, etc.). For Barrett, both the Ethiopian and Cornelius 'are described as neither born Jews nor proselytes but sympathetically interested in Judaism' and both illustrate, similarly, the progress of mission (C. K. Barrett *The Acts of the Apostles* (Edinburgh: T&T Clark, 1994), vol. 1, p. 421).

30 B. R. Gaventa, *From Darkness to Light: Aspects of Conversion in the New Testament* (Philadelphia, PA: Fortress, 1986), pp. 103, 106. For F. F. Bruce he is a typical convert (*The Acts of the Apostles: The Greek Text with Introduction and Commentary* (Leicester: Apollos, 1990), pp. 174-179). J. Roloff notes as well the paradigmatic character of this story in Luke-Acts in *Die Apostelgeschichte* (Göttingen: Vandenhoeck), vol. 1, p. 139. Similarly, G. Schille, *Die Apostelgeschichte des Lukas* (Berlin: Evangelische Verlaganstalt, 1984), p. 215.

31 M. Turner, *Power from on High: The Spirit in Israel's Restoration and Witness in Luke-Acts* (Sheffield: Sheffield Academical, 1996), p. 386, and he mentions, as well, P. F. Esler, *Community and Gospel in Luke-Acts: The Social and Political Motivations of Lucan Theology* (Cambridge: Cambridge UP, 1987), chapters two to five; J. Jervell, 'The

In terms of sources, the similarity can be explained, in part, by the literary transmission of popular traditions.[32] Story telling has selectively highlighted similar elements, many being picked up and even more emphasized by Luke, such as the presence of an angel as an initiator of the event (Acts 8:26; 10:3), the Spirit's instruction concerning the encounter (Acts 8:29; 10:19-20), the similarity of Philip's preaching to that of Peter, ἀνοίξας δε ὁ Φίλιππος [Πέτρος] τὸ στόμα (Acts 8:35; 10:34). In Acts 8:36 and 10:47 the baptism of the foreigner is introduced by a question phrased with the verb κωλύω (what or who could prevent the baptism of the Gentiles?).[33] The interpretation of Scripture plays an important role in the eunuch's conversion (Acts 8:32-33), and also occurs in Cornelius' evangelisation, although in a much shorter form (Acts 10:43). Both stories display a joyful, positive ending, a recurrent feature of Luke's evangelistic episodes (Acts 8:39; *cf.* 8:8; 10:44-46).[34]

Church of Jews and Godfearers', in J. B. Tyson (ed.), *Luke-Acts and the Jewish People* (Minneapolis, MN: Augsburg, 1988), 11-20.

32   This subject has come to the forefront of theological debate due to the important contributions of K. E. Bailey, 'Informal Controlled Oral Tradition and the Synoptic Gospels', *Themelios* 20/2 (1995) 4–11; *idem*, 'Middle Eastern Oral Tradition and the Synoptic Gospels', *ExpTim* 106/12 (1995) 363-7; J. D. G. Dunn, *Christianity in the Making, Jesus Remembered*, vol. 1 (Grand Rapids, MI: Eerdmans, 2003), etc.

33   Tannehill, *Narrative*, vol. 2, p. 111. On the LXX character of κωλύω and ἀνάστηθι καὶ πορεύου, see W. C. Unnik, 'Der Befehl an Philippus', *ZNW* 47 (1956), 181-191, pp. 188-189, 190-191). The use of κωλύω could indicate an early Christian baptismal rite.

34   J. Zmijewski, *Die Apostelgeschichte* (Regensburg: Pustet, 1994), p. 366; *cf.* Acts 2:46; 5:41; 13:52; 15:3; 16:34, etc. The similarity does not include a *special* receiving of the Spirit (J. D. G. Dunn, *The Acts of the Apostles* (Peterborough: Epworth, 1996), p. 115). Turner considers that the 'rejoicing' (Acts 8:39) should be taken as 'adequate ongoing evidence of the Spirit earlier received' (Turner, *Power*, p. 449). Bruce does not elaborate on this point, although he mentions the manuscript variant of the δ text, πνεῦμα ἅγιον ἐπέπεσεν ἐπι τὸν εὐνοῦχον, ἄγγελος δὲ κυρίου ἥρπασεν τὸν Φίλιππον (the Holy Spirit fell on the eunuch, and an angel of the Lord caught up Philip), and comments that 'the point of this expansion is to show that (as in 2:38) baptism was followed by the gift of the Holy Spirit' (Bruce, *Acts*, p. 230; *cf.* its witnesses in A 36a. 94. 103. 307. 322. 323. 385. 453. 467. 610. 945. 1678. 1739. 1765. 1891. 2998. *l* 1178 *p* 1 p (w syh**) itar, l, p, (w) vgmss copmeg arm geo slav

Insofar as journeying is concerned, while it is true that Peter travels to Caesarea with the messengers, at the prompting of the Spirit (ὁδοιπορούντων, Acts 10:12; τῇ πόλει ἐγγιζόντων, at 10:9; cf. ἐγγίζειν τῇ Δαμασκῷ, 9:3; at noon, 10:9, τῇ δὲ ἐπαύριον, cf. 8:26, κατὰ μεσημβρίαν), this account does not include any special revelation *on the road*. Accordingly, nothing special about journeying and no *hodos* encounter appear in the final report (Acts 11:11-12). The vision feature retains its central place in the story, Luke's interest in Gentile evangelism and in the post-Easter kerygma is present here as in other Lukan accounts, yet the road is no longer a *locus of revelation and evangelism*. Thus, despite all these narrative correspondences, Cornelius' conversion cannot be seen as part of the post-Easter encounter series, the subject-matter of the present study, although it might be studied as part of Luke's more general fondness for encounters and visions.

In his analysis of the influent role of the Emmaus story in Luke-Acts, B. P. Robinson has suggested that this account constitutes Luke's model not only for Acts 8:26-40, but also for Acts 12:6-17,[35] the account of Peter's escape from prison (one should note how frequently the Emmaus story is mentioned as a first element of comparison in a series of stories, as a paradigm; its literary qualities seem to have inspired Luke to re-use its emphases). Robinson notes that in both cases the narratives are dated at Passover-time. Herod is involved and shares responsibility. The opening of the prison gates corresponds with the rolling away of the stone from the tomb on Easter morning. Just as Rhoda's message is reckoned as madness (Acts 12:15), so the women's story of the empty tomb is thought by the apostles to be nonsense (*cf.* λῆρος, Lk. 24:11). Both stories include recognition scenes (*cf.* Acts 12:14, 17), and

---

Eph Jer Aug Hier Did Cyr, *cf.* B. M. Metzger, *A Textual Commentary on the Greek New Testament* (London: UBS, 1975), pp. 360-361). Conzelmann has suggested the possibility of a late, anti-Gnostic motivation for this variant (Conzelmann, *Acts*, pp. 69-70). The overwhelming evidence for the actual reading (P45,74 ℵ A* B C E Ψ 33vid 81 181 614 1175 1409 2344 *Byz* [L P] *Lect* itc,dem,e,gig,ph,r,ro,t vg syrp copsa,bo eth Did Chrys), however, indicates that this narrative format, without any mention of the Spirit's special manifestation, has been largely acknowledged by the first Christian copyists and readers.

35 B. P. Robinson, 'The Place of the Emmaus Story in Luke-Acts', *NTS* 30 (1984), 481-497, esp. pp. 483.

refer to the action of a divine messenger. The joy of Rhoda (Acts 12:14) parallels the joy of the Emmaus disciples (Lk. 24:32) and of the Eleven (24:41). Both accounts end with a sudden departure of the messenger (Acts 12:17, *cf.* Lk. 24:31).[36] Although it includes an encounter 'in the jail' (or a vision), and an appearance 'at the door', and makes good use of this element of surprise (recognition and reversal of fate), Peter's escape from prison does not use the paradigm of journeying or of the *hodos* setting, in a clear manner, and its connection with Jesus' resurrection is rather loose.

Summing up, several commentators have emphasized the existence in Luke-Acts of a number of narrative parallels based, to a degree, on the Emmaus story as a model. Although the vision motif itself is present in many of them not all share the *hodos* or the journey setting, the Easter connections and the ethical-evangelistic focus found in the Emmaus story, the Ethiopian's conversion and the account of Saul's call. Rather than pairing them up as separate cases of narrative parallelism, these three pericopes should probably be seen as a special coherent series integrated into Luke's more general motif of the Way, which represents an overarching theme in Luke-Acts (*cf.* the Infancy narratives, the messianic preaching of John the Baptist, Jesus' journey to Jerusalem, to his Passion; the missionary journeys of the Church, in Acts, Christianity seen as a Way, *cf.* Acts 9:2; 19:9, 23; 24:14, 22, etc.). At the same time, they are part of Luke's geographical motif which includes theological connotations of localities, settings and movements.[37]

---

36   The shared Passover setting and the existence of narrative patterns have been emphasized by M. D. Goulder, as well (*Type and History in Acts* (London: SPCK, 1964), pp. 44-45). He, however, has not focused on this particular parallel between Emmaus and the imprisoned Peter.

37   *Cf.* A. H. W. Curtis, 'Theological Geography', in R. J. Coggins and J. L. Houlden (eds.), *A Dictionary of Biblical Interpretation* (London: SCM, 1990), 687-689, esp. p. 688. The idea seems basic to D. J. Bosch, *Transforming Mission: Paradigm Shifts in Theology of Mission* (Maryknoll, NY: Orbis), 1996, p. 88; D. Senior, 'The Foundations for Mission in the New Testament', in D. Senior and C. Stuhlmueller (eds.), *The Biblical Foundations for Mission* (Maryknoll, NY: Orbis), 1983, 141-132, p. 255; H. E. Dollar, *A Biblical-Missiological Exploration of the Cross-Cultural Dimensions in Luke-Acts* (Lewiston, NY: Mellen, 1993); D. J. Dillon, 'Easter Revelation and Mission Program in Luke

The Significance of the Encounter Events

If literary correspondences such as the common *hodos* setting, the teaching *in via*, the evangelistic dialogue and the sacramental ending play an unifying role for the three selected post-Easter accounts, the appearance event (appearance or disappearance, recognition, vision) led the NT scholars to different classifications and interpretations.

For example, Alsup and others chose to overlook the literary and theological prominence of the Emmaus encounter and suggest another perspective according to which the model for all the appearance reports in the NT was Saul's encounter with the risen Jesus. Its δόξα emphasis was seen to pre-date the later emphasis on Jesus' physical appearance (*cf.* 1 Cor. 15:3ff.) and, thus, all the NT appearances were considered to have been, at first, visions of Jesus' heavenly glory, of his heavenly radiance.[38] The rationale behind this hypothesis is that the initial testimony on Jesus' resurrection was based on

---

24:46-48', in D. Durken (ed.), *Sin, Salvation and the Spirit* (Collegeville, MN: Liturgical, 1979), 240-270, pp. 241, 246. For the synoptists, in particular, the topographical element appears to be of crucial importance (G. Strecker, *Theologie des Neuen Testaments* (Berlin: Gruyter, 1996), pp. 397-438). For example, H. Conzelmann's study *Die Mitte der Zeit: Studien zu Theologie des Lukas* (Tübingen: Mohr, 1953), *cf.* English transl., *The Theology of St. Luke* (London: Faber, 1960), posits that Luke adapted Mark's early topography and historical scheme to his own theological agenda (W. W. Gasque, *A History of the Criticism of the Acts of the Apostles* (Peabody, MA: Hendrickson, 1989), p. 291).

38 J. E. Alsup provides a comprehensive discussion of the characteristics and history of these approaches (*The Post-Resurrection Appearance Stories of the Gospel Tradition: A History-of-Tradition Analysis with Text-Synopsis* (London: SPCK, 1975), pp. 31-36, 54-55, 60). This unitary view on the Easter and post-Easter appearance reports, based on Saul's encounter and its vision-like features, is also supported by M. Albertz, L. Brun, U. Wilckens, H. Graß, E. Hirsch, W. Michaelis (*cf.* M. Albertz, 'Zum Formgeschichte der Auferstehungsberichte', *ZNW* 21 (1922), 259-269; U. Wilckens, 'The Tradition-history of the Resurrection of Jesus', in C. F. D. Moule (ed.), *The Significance of the Message of the Resurrection for Faith in Jesus Christ* (Naperville, IL: Allenson, 1968), 51-76, *idem*, *Resurrection, Biblical Testimony to the Resurrection: An Historical Examination and Explanation* (Atlanta, GA: Knox, 1978); H. Graß, *Ostergeschehen und Osterberichte* (Göttingen: Vandenhoeck, 1962), etc.).

the 'apocalyptic vision' model which, later, was in danger of being misrepresented by pharisaic Judaism; thus, it was replaced by accounts which emphasized the physical aspect of Jesus' resurrection and localised the appearance scenes in significant public places like Jerusalem (the 'Jerusalem-type' appearances).[39] Christian apologetics, indeed, has developed in time a stronger stance in favour of Jesus' bodily resurrection, yet the idea that early witnesses have labelled their accounts as mere 'visions', be they 'objective visions', at first, and only later thought of them as 'appearances' seems to lack internal NT evidence.[40] The NT contrast is rather a stylistic one, not one of essence: Mark's early emphasis on the disciples' emotional reactions at the resurrection news (fear, haste, etc.) and his paucity of detail in favor of narrative dynamism, is contrasted with the elaborate, doubt-and-proof descriptions provided later by Luke, Matthew, and John.

For others, the Emmaus account seen as an appearance story highlights through its unique features its lack of connection with the other appearance accounts, and with Luke 24, in general. A. Ehrhardt argued, for example, that Luke 24 represents a fragmentary, composite work and it is 'a serious error of modern theologians that they try to treat the recorded events of the first Easter as forming a coherent historical report'.[41] In particular, he wanted to disengage the Emmaus story from all such collective studies, as well as from their OT theology, in favour of a general Hellenistic approach (whilst an early Hellenistic understanding of Christ is quite appropriate to consider, the thought of not acknowledging the literary and theological unity of Luke 24 and the narrative and theological centrality of the Emmaus account is rather unusual).[42]

---

39 P. Seidensticker, *Der Auferstehung Jesu in der Botschaft der Evangelisten* (Stuttgart: Katholisches Bibelwerk, 1967), pp. 56, 71, 104, 150, as cited in Alsup, *Post-Resurrection*, p. 40.
40 Alsup, *Post-Resurrection*, p. 35; R. H. Fuller, *The Formation of the Resurrection Narratives* (Philadelphia, PA: Fortress, 1980), p. 33.
41 A. Ehrhardt, 'The Disciples of Emmaus', NTS 10 (1963), 182-201, p. 193.
42 Ehrhardt, 'Disciples', pp. 194-198, vs. H. Gunkel, *Genesis, translated and interpreted by H. Gunkel*, M. E. Biddle (tr.) (Macon, GA: Mercer UP, 1997), in German, *Die Genesis, übersetzt und erklärt von H. Gunkel* (Göttingen: Vanderhoeck, 1977); idem, *Zum religionsgeschichtlichen Verständnis des Neues Testaments* (Göttingen: Vanderhoeck, 1903), etc.

Introduction

The 'vision'-based arguments have caused further damage to the unitary interpretation of Luke's *hodos* series. From such a perspective C. H. Dodd pointed out that it is impossible to count Jesus' appearance to Saul as belonging to the group of the resurrection appearances

> Outside the canonical Gospels there is little that we can bring into comparison [with the post-Easter appearances]. We have three accounts of the appearance of Christ to Paul, but none of the three constitutes a narrative unit comparable with those which provide the material of the Gospels. The narrative, in all its forms, resembles those of the Gospels in so far that the word of Christ initiates the transaction, that the recognition is the central feature, and that the scene ends with a command of Christ. But the whole situation is so different that the comparison is of little significance.[43]

He proceeded to divide the Easter appearances into two form-historical categories, one group of 'concise' accounts - the early kerygmatic stories (class I accounts), and a second group of later 'circumstantial' accounts, represented by better developed, more complex narratives (class II accounts).[44] The kerygmatic accounts tend, according to Dodd, to be short, proclamative and indirect, while the circumstantial stories are longer, including debates, details, etc., and indicate a higher degree of interpretation.[45] For example, passages such as Matthew 28:8-10; 28:16-20; John 20:19-21 would represent good illustrations of the concise class I resurrection narratives, and Dodd stresses that they have a similar literary format (their correspondences reminding of the *hodos* accounts)

---

43 C. H. Dodd, 'The Appearances of the Risen Christ: an Essay in Form-Criticism of the Gospels', in D. E. Nineham (ed.), *Studies in the gospels: essays in memory of R.H. Lightfoot* (Oxford: Oxford UP, 1957), 9-35 (also in Dodd, *More New Testament Studies* (Grand Rapids, MI: Eerdmans, 1968), 102-133, esp. pp. 20-21).

44 Dodd, 'Appearances', pp. 9-35; *cf.* Alsup, *Post-Resurrection*; A. W. Zwiep, *The Ascension of the Messiah in Lukan Christology* (Leiden: Brill, 1997).

45 *Cf.* L. Goppelt, 'Das Osterkerygma heute', in L. Goppelt, *Christologie und Ethik: Gesamte Aufsatze zum Neuen Testament (Göttingen:* Vandenhoeck, 1968), 79-101, esp. p. 87 (Alsup, *Post-Resurrection*, pp. 54-55, 60, n. 196).

A. The crisis situation: Christ's followers bereft of their Lord.
B. The appearance of the Lord.
C. The Greeting.
D. The Recognition.
E. The Word of Commandment.[46]

In particular, the Emmaus account stands out as an elaborate appearance story, of the second, circumstantial type of Easter accounts (class II)

> The Walk to Emmaus is a highly-finished literary composition, in which the author, dwelling with loving interest upon every detail of his theme, has lost no opportunity of evoking an imaginative response in the reader.[47]

Dodd, therefore, notes the paradigmatic nature of the Emmaus account, as well as its more complex composition

> It is clear, then, that we have no mere expansion of the general pattern, but a carefully composed statement, which, in the framework of a narrative of intense dramatic interest, includes most of what needs (from this evangelist's point of view) to be said about the resurrection of Christ.[48]

Specifically, and remarkably, he emphasizes, further, the importance of the *recognition* feature

> Here, as elsewhere, the story begins with the disciples feeling the loss of their Lord, that Jesus takes the initiative, and that the dramatic centre of the whole incident is the ἀναγνώρισις - for it seems proper in this case to use the technical term applied by ancient literary critics to the recognition-scene which was so often the crucial point of a Greek drama.[49]

---

46 Dodd, 'Appearances', p. 11. Alsup acknowledges, as well, these similarities, although he dismisses Dodd's approach to the NT appearances, *cf.* Alsup, *Post-Resurrection*, pp. 211; 269, also pp. 28-29.
47 Dodd, 'Appearances', p. 13.
48 Dodd, 'Appearances', p. 14.
49 Dodd, 'Appearances', p. 14. As Dillon notes (*Eye-Witnesses*, pp. 75-76), here Dodd builds on the earlier insights on 'recognition' of M. Albertz, who suggested the existence of a separate category of christophany labelled as *scenes of personal recognition*, and of L. Brun, who

Introduction 15

This acknowledgement that 'Aristotle's distinctions of various methods of recognition may be aptly applied to the New Testament material', can be counted as one of Dodd's major contributions to the later study of NT mimesis.[50] He recommends Greek parallels as an important hermeneutical tool for the NT stories, along with rabbinic traditions and OT references

> For some other forms of tradition which enter into the Gospels the form-critics have been able to adduce analogies from other fields, as, for instance, the Epidaurus inscriptions for some of the healing-stories, and rabbinic aphorisms and dialogues for didactic pericopae.
>
> It is more difficult to find any such analogies for the post-resurrection narratives. In certain respects the more circumstantial narratives recall accounts of theophanies in the Old Testament and in profane literature, especially those in which at first the Visitant is not recognized for what He is, but when recognized imparts some solemn instruction, promise or command (e.g. Gen. 18, Jud. 6, 13). But the points of difference are more numerous and striking than the points of resemblance. In particular, in theophany stories proof is usually offered of the supernatural or divine character of the Visitant: in the Gospel stories the proofs tend to show His real humanity (He has flesh and blood, bears wounds in His body, even eats human food). In some ways we might find a nearer analogy in the ἀναγνώρισις - scenes [recognition - scenes] of Greek drama, but again the analogy is by no means close.[51]

---

    remarked the presence of auxiliary motifs (the use of the OT argument for understanding Jesus' Passion and the reenactment of meals, as a double focal point). For Dillon the series of events in Lk. 24:13-35 includes a 'delayed recognition, [a] remembrance process, then recognition at a point coinciding with the completion of the argumentum of the author' (*Eye-Witnesses*, p. 76). For a more recent discussion, *cf.* C. Hickling, 'The Emmaus Story and its Sequel', in S. Barton and G. Stanton (eds.), *Essays in Honour of Leslie Houlden* (London: SPCK, 1994), 21-33, esp. p. 29, n. 1.

50 Dodd, 'Appearances', pp. 14, 18; Aristotle, *Poetics*, 1454b.19 - 1455a.21 (critical text by R. Kassel (ed.), *Aristotelis. De Arte Poetica Liber* (Oxford: Clarendon, 1965); *cf.* Aristotle, *Poetics*, S. Halliwell (tr.) (Cambridge, MA: Harvard UP, 1995); previous LCL translation by W. H. Fyfe).

51 Dodd, 'Appearances', p. 34.

This was a daring line of argument at a time when Hellenistic literature was not accepted as a primary resource for NT criticism. In fact, by and large, NT scholarship ignored Dodd's suggestion and chose to consider the gospel appearance *Gattung* as first and foremost an imitation of the OT appearance accounts (an interesting case of an eminently Greek concept used exclusively with LXX connotations). In particular, the Emmaus story was seen as an illustration of an OT-inspired anthropomorphic theophany.[52]

The alternative of Hellenistic influences from stories involving appearances or disappearances of a θεῖος ἀνήρ, and with it, the idea of NT parallels with Hellenistic drama, has been regarded as a cause of 'inner tensions', since it is 'impossible to consider these accounts as analogous in any essential sense'. Alsup takes a firm stand that 'contrary to popular opinion... the Hellenistic background offers little help *in making precise* the actual origins of the gospel story *Gattung*'.[53]

One consequence of this rejection was an increasingly firm exclusion of Saul's encounter from any series of resurrection appearances of Jesus, on the grounds that it represents a post-Ascension appearance with parallels in the later Jewish Hellenistic stories of conversion (the legends of Heliodorus, 2 Macc. 3:8, 13; of Joseph and Aseneth, etc.), rather than in the OT material, proper.[54] For such reasons, G. Lohfink wrote that the appearance on the Damascus road 'simply does not belong to the Easter appearances of Jesus'.[55] Alsup considers, as well, that there is a strong separation line between the gospel appearances of Jesus and the appearance to Saul (Acts 9) or, later, to Stephen (Acts 7)

> Chapters 9, 22, 26 contain accounts of the appearance to Paul on the road to Damascus... its type as Gattung is that of the heavenly

---

52 Alsup, *Post-Resurrection*, p. 265.
53 Alsup, *Post-Resurrection*, pp. 239, 270. For him, against Dodd, instead of unifying the accounts, formally, the recognition event is precisely 'the point at which the stories' variance from one another is the strongest' (p. 211).
54 The Lukan Paul refers to it as οὐράνιος ὀπτασία, a 'heavenly vision', at Acts 26:19.
55 G. Lohfink, *The Conversion of St. Paul* (Chicago, IL: Franciscan Herald, 1976), p. 25.

radiance appearance, not unlike Acts 7 noted above, and as such is to be held separate from the gospel type... The differences in concept and form existing between this type and that of the gospels are so categorical that two distinct traditional origins are undoubtedly to be sought... The gospel stories were formulated within the special context of the gospel genre, the heavenly radiance type by and large was not.[56]

The Ethiopian's conversion, as well, has been regarded as an odd story, impossible to integrate with the other *hodos* accounts, since it corresponds only in part and superficially to the appearance paradigm illustrated by the Emmaus account,[57] and tells the story of an unusual evangelistic encounter combined with a miraculous disappearance of a human, not divine, character.[58]

This emphasis on the *appearance* event, seen as an OT-related genre (OT epiphany), with a specific development from 'visions' to 'appearances' and from 'concise' to 'circumstantial',

---

56   Alsup, *Post-Resurrection*, p. 84.
57   For Alsup the Emmaus account and the Ethiopian's conversion have little in common 'outside of this one formal element [the disappearance event that occurs after baptism]' (*Post-Resurrection*, p. 196, n. 560). His argument seems to be based on an *a priori* principle, the primacy of OT as a source and the superficial nature of the similarity. Thus, he mentions and rejects the views of J. Kremer, for whom both stories represent a similar type of *religiöse Unterweisung* story, that is, a story of religious instruction (*cf. Osterbotschaft*, p. 69), and of H. D. Betz, for whom Lk. 24:31, 51 and Acts 8:39 represent an *Entrückungs- und Versetzungstopos*, a type of rapture story (*cf. Lukian von Samosata und das Neue Testament religionsgeschichtliche und paränetische Parallelen: Ein Beitrag zum Corpus Hellenisticum Novi Testamenti* (Berlin: Akademie, 1961), p. 168). Similar views are held by P. Schubert, A.J. Dupont, G. Bouwman and J. Mouson. Labelling the appearances as a literary 'topos' is reminiscent of Dillon's 'charismatic topos' (or 'charismatic lore'), an assessment not mentioned by Alsup (*cf.* Dillon, *Eye-Witnesses*, p. 153). One is surprised by Alsup's hasty dismissal of Dodd's arguments in favour of a Hellenistic interpretation of the appearances: 'Dodd has seen correctly that it is necessary to approach the gospel appearance texts literarily' yet 'it is never clear just why this pattern should have shown such tenacity in the oral tradition other than perhaps ostensibly to have preserved succinctly and most accurately the "facts" of appearance encounters' (*op.cit.*, pp. 28-29, *cf.* p. 269).
58   Alsup, *Post-Resurrection*, p. 84

draws attention to the nature and history of the appearance stories at the expense of their form and literary relation, and places them in distinct, separate groups. In the process, the importance of the *plot elements* is disregarded, as well as the NT authors' art of representation

> Not isolated story elements gave rise to a more or less fixed pattern, but a unified story form with more or less constant motifs and themes appears to have been the warp and woof of this vehicle of expression from the very beginning. In short, they were *stories* and not story-constructs and as such they participated in a particular story *Gattung*.[59]

In conclusion, the history-of-tradition approach has encouraged *a global NT perspective* on the Lukan *hodos* stories, dismissing their correspondences and emphasizing themes or interests related to the larger context of the NT. In its attempt to counter-balance this perspective, the present study will focus rather on their own Lukan narrative context, where formal and theological correspondences are more meaningful as an expression of Luke's authorial involvement. Instead of seeing them as post-Easter appearances, solely, they will be characterised as post-Easter *encounter* stories, stressing their common genre, structure, narrative and theological function, rather than their contrasting features.

Hellenistic Literature and Luke's Style

In order to interpret this series of formal correspondences in a more coherent way, one could suggest that these three post-Easter 'on the road' encounters of Luke-Acts need to be assessed more consistently from a Hellenistic literary perspective, with reference to the available literary theories and to the narrative models provided by both Jewish and Greco-Roman cultures. This will take the quest for Luke's narrative paradigms into a more detailed consideration of Aristotle's *Poetics*, where a key concept is μίμησις as literary imitation or narrative representation of life.[60] Apart from such

---

59 Alsup, *Post-Resurrection*, p. 269.
60 W. Michaelis virtually ignores this Aristotelian use of mimesis, focusing rather on Plato's philosophical usage (*cf.* Paul's similar use of

Introduction 19

an elevated literary reference, by chosing to re-consider certain parallels between Luke's accounts and the Greco-Roman appearance stories, of which some were, probably, too easily dismissed,[61] this analysis argues that Luke's style should be understood in a contextualized way, embedded in the popular literature of his time which used similar composition rules, addressed similar audiences, and bred similar literary tastes. Mimesis needs, therefore, to be understood rather as cultural contextualization, as imitation of *literary form* and *philosophy*, as composition, an aspect less explored in the NT studies than mimesis as imitation of *content* and *style* (*cf.* Luke and LXX).[62]

Two main objections can be raised in relation to such an approach, however. First, one should account whether literary theories such as Aristotle's analysis of drama and poetry are compatible with the literary genre of the gospels; second, one needs to ask to what extent there is enough evidence that Luke was acquainted with Aristotle works and concepts.

Regarding the first objection, Aristotle himself provides an acceptable response. Although Luke does not write Greek

---

the term in 1 Cor. 9:12, 2 Thes. 3:7, Phil. 3:17, etc.; Michaelis, 'μιμέομαι, μιμητής', *TDNT*, vol. 4, 659-667; *cf.* p. 660, n. 3; and p. 662, n. 5).

61 Alsup is skeptical, for example, of the significance of Romulus' legend as a formal parallel to Luke's encounters (*cf.* Alsup, *Post-Resurrection*, p. 234). The plot of Romulus' legendary appearance, however, displays several correspondences in common with Luke's encounters, cf. Plutarch, *Romulus*, 28.1-7; Dionysius of Halicarnassus, *The Roman Antiquities*, 2.63.1-4.

62 T. L. Brodie is a major advocate of content mimesis in Luke-Acts (*Luke the Literary Interpreter: Luke-Acts as a Systematic Rewriting and Updating of the Elijah-Elisha Narrative in 1 and 2 Kings* (Rome: PBI, 1987). However, G. J. Steyn highlights well the underlying debate: 'Did Luke make use of the *Jewish* hermeneutical methods, or did he make use of the *Greek* methods, e.g. the rhetorical technique, μίμησις, when he used and re-interpreted the material from his Jewish Scriptures?' He notes that 'If T. Brodie is right in identifying this ancient rhetorical technique in Luke's gospel, then it should be present in the *manner* (or form), rather than the *matter* (or contents) of what his source texts contained.' See G. J. Steyn, 'Luke's Use of MIMHΣIΣ? Re-opening the Debate', in C. M. Tuckett (ed.), *The Scriptures in the Gospels* (Leuven: Leuven UP, 1997), 551-557, esp. p. 553), and, *cf.* also, the articles in Dennis R. MacDonald (ed), *Mimesis and Intertextuality in Antiquity and Christianity* (Harrisburg, PA: Trinity International, 2001).

drama, all arts including epic poetry and tragedy, as well as comedy, or music playing, etc., are equally, although in different ways, artistic representations of life, πᾶσαι τυγχάνουσιν οὖσαι μιμήσεις τὸ σύνολον.[63] The study of epic imitation on the basis of Aristotle's *Poetics* is conceivable for 'epic matches tragedy to the extent of being mimesis [imitation] of elevated [serious] matters' (μετὰ μέτρου λόγῳ μίμησις εἶναι σπουδαίων). Thus, 'whoever knows about good and bad tragedy knows the same about epic, as epic resources belong to tragedy',[64] despite differences concerning length, metre, the existence of multiple sections, etc.[65]

In relation to this observation, there is a subsidiary issue, however, namely whether Aristotle's ideas were indeed known and applied to drama or epic works, in Luke's time or after him, since, apparently, his *Poetics* was not much quoted for almost 18 centuries after its composition.[66] As far as we know, the treatise entered its first period of major popularity, as an authoritative work complementary to Horace's *Ars Poetica*, only after its recovery by the Renaissance scholars.[67] One

---

63   Aristotle, *Poetics*, 1447a.13-15.
64   Aristotle, *Poetics*, 1449b.9-20 (Halliwell).
65   Aristotle, *Poetics*, 1459b.15-30, 1462a.15-20.
66   A. Preminger, L. Golden; O. B. Hardison, Jr.; K. Kerrane (eds.), *Classical Literary Criticism: Translations and Interpretations* (N.Y.: Ungar, 1974), 97-139, esp. p. 106.
67   *Cf.* L. Castelvetro, *Poetica d'Aristotele vulgarizzata e sposta* (Basilea: Pietro de Sedabonis (Peter Perna), 1576 (1570)). A recent English version is that of A. Bongiorno, *Castelvetro on the art of poetry: an abridged translation of Lodovico Castelvetro's Poetica d'Aristotele vulgarizzata e sposta*, A Bongiorno (tr.) (Binghamton, NY: State University of New York, 1984). See also the modern Italian version, *Poetica d'Aristotele vulgarizzata e sposta*, W. Romani (tr.) (Roma: Laterza, 1978-1979). Before the Rennaisance, a translation was made into Syriac (end of 9th century), and from the Syriac, Abu Biser made an Arabic version (before AD 940). Averroes produced in Cordova in AD 1174 a commentary on the *Poetics* (available in A. J. Minnis and A. B. Scott (eds.) and D. Wallace (assistent), *Medieval Literary Criticism c.1100 - c.1375* (Oxford: Clarendon, 1988); *cf.* J. Hutton, *Aristotle's Poetics*, transl., introduction and notes, by J. Hutton (N.Y.: W.W. Norton, 1982), p. 24.

Introduction 21

possible explanation of this limited interaction could be its lecture-notes character, its student-oriented origins.[68]

Although direct confirmation of a general knowledge of this book in antiquity is missing, and arguments such as that of A. Rostagni who favours an early widespread influence are debatable,[69] there are a number of indications that the *Poetics*, or its approach of the Greek drama, were still far from being unknown or unfamiliar. For example, Themistius (4th century A.D.) takes from it the reference to the origin of comic plots in Sicily (*Oratio*, 27.337B, from *Poetics* 1449b6). Ammonius and Boethius (5th-6th century) quote chapter twenty on the "parts of speech" in their treatise *On Interpretation*.[70] Olympiodorus (6th century A.D.) analyses the syllogisms present in Aristotle's works (the demonstrative, the dialectical, the rhetorical, the sophistic, and the poetic) and for the last type he refers to the *Poetics*.[71] Other early references are apparently provided by Heraclides of Pontus, Aristotle's contemporary, whose treatise *On Poetics and the Poets* suggests an allusion to Aristotle.[72] Another interesting testimony comes from a papyrus fragment of Satyrus' *Life of Euripides*, that uses the Aristotelian concepts of 'peripety' and 'recognitions'.[73] Porphyrion, an ancient commentator on

---

68   Halliwell, *Aristotle, Poetics*, p. 4; Hutton, *Aristotle's Poetics*, p. 5.
69   A. Rostagni, 'Aristotele e l'aristotelismo nella storia dell'estetica antica', *Studi Italiani di Filologia Classica* 2 (1922), 1-147 (as cited by Hutton, *Aristotle's Poetics*, p. 40, n. 78).
70   I. Bywater, *Aristotle on the Art of Poetry* (Oxford: Oxford UP, 1909), pp. 261-262.
71   Cited by Hutton, *Aristotle's Poetics*, p. 24. One of possible reasons for which the *Poetics* was rarely quoted by the early literary theorists was that it might have been understood as a treatise on logic, together with the *Rhetoric*.
72   H. B. Gottschalk, *Heraclides of Pontus* (Oxford: Clarendon, 1980); also, the recent Aelianus, *Historical Miscellany (Varia Historia)*, translation and notes by N. G. Wilson (London: Harvard UP, 1997 (*cf.* Claudius Aelianus, *Aeliani Varia historia: Heraclides Pontici et Nicolai Damasceni quae supersunt; ad optimorum librorum fidem accurata edita* (Leipzig: Teubner, 1829); F. Wehrli, *Herakleides Pontikos* (Basel: Schwabe, 1969); see Hutton, *Aristotle*, p. 40, n. 74).
73   κατὰ τὰς π[ερι]πετείας... ἀναγνωρισμοὺς διά τε δακτυλίων καὶ διὰ δεραίων, *Oxyr. Pap.* 9, Frg. 39.7, a fragment of Satyrus' *Life of Euripides*, A. S. Hunt (tr.) (London: Egypt Exploration Fund, 1912, no.

Horace (3rd century BC), informs us that Horace has put together the poetic precepts of Neoptolemus of Parum, and he in his turn was influenced by Aristotle's *Poetics*.⁷⁴ Similarly, it has been argued by K. von Fritz that Duris,⁷⁵ and other historians of this school 'could have adopted certain principles under the influence of the *Poetics* in a way not intended by Aristotle'.⁷⁶ The role of poetry in the Greco-Roman city cannot be underestimated, and, for example, Aristophanes has Euripides saying that praiseworthy poets encourage their fellow citizens to be worthier people, and Aeschylus, that boys are taught by their teachers at school, while 'poets are teachers of men'.⁷⁷

The possibility of an implicit wider influence of such a study on composition (or the idea that Aristotle's compositional approach was itself a synthesis of a larger literary tendency) can be contemplated without major objections. This agrees with the fact that mimesis had come to involve, in time, an

---

    1166-1223, vol. 9, p. 149; *cf.* D. W. Lucas, *Aristotle's Poetics* (Oxford: Oxford UP, 1968), p. 159.

74 *Cf.* C. O. Brink, *Horace: On Poetry. The 'Ars Poetica'*, vol. 2 (Cambridge: Cambridge UP, 1971), cited by Hutton, *Aristotle's Poetics*, p. 40, n. 78.

75 Duris of Samos (*ca.* 257 BC), wrote a life of Agathocles of Syracuse, a treatise on tragedy, a history of Macedonia, etc., most of his works being lost now, or surviving in fragments, *cf.* E. Schwartz, 'Duris', in A. F. Pauly, G. Wissowa *et al* (eds.), *Real-Encyclopädie der klassischen Altertumswissenschaft* (RE), vol. 5, 1905, col. 1853-1856; P. Pédech, *Trois Historiens Méconnus: Théopompe-Duris-Phylarque* (Paris: Belles Lettres, 1989), pp. 257-389, etc.

76 K. von Fritz, 'Die Bedeutung des Aristoteles für die Geschichtsschreibung', in *Histoire et historiens dans l'antiquité: Entretiens sur l'antiquité classique* (Geneva: Vandoeuvres, 1956), 85-145, p. 85; *cf.* A. Lesky, *A History of Greek Literature* (London: Methuen, 1966), first published as *Geschichte der Griechischen Literatur* (Bern: Francke, 1957-1958), p. 765; Pédech, *Trois Historiens*, p. 369; L. Torraca, *Duride di Samo: la maschera scenica nella storiografia ellenistica* (Salerno: Laveglia, 1988), pp. 6-9. *Cf.* also, on Aristotle's influence on Dio Chrysostomus, Z. Ritoók, 'Some Aesthetic Views of Dio Chrysostom and Their Sources', in J. G. J. Abbenes, S. R. Slings, I. Sluiter (eds.), *Greek Literary Theory After Aristotle: A Collection of Papers in Honour of D. M. Schenkeweld* (Amsterdam: Amsterdam UP, 1995), 125-134, esp. p. 133.

77 Aristophanes, *Frogs*, 1009, 1054-55.

increasingly larger semantic area,[78] and through its connotations and related terms this concept influenced much of the Greco-Roman discussion of dramatic representation.

At first, mimesis had to do with the intermediary character of artistic performance,[79] and with the special participation of audience's to the act of representation. This could involve a reaction of crying, fear and awe (κλαίοντάς τε... φοβερὸν ἢ δεινόν),[80] or of pleasure (ἡδονή) induced by the narrated fiction (ἀπάτη), the narrative being a source of enjoyment

---

[78] As G. J. Steyn notes, μίμησις terminology includes terms like εἰκάζειν (copy), ὅμοια (resemblances), τύπος (pattern), ἀφομοιοῦσθαι (assimilate), πλάττειν (mold), παραδείγμα (model), εἴδωλον (image), etc. (Steyn, 'Luke's Use of ΜΙΜΗΣΙΣ?', p. 552; cf. Plato, Timaeus, 19d-20b).

[79] Plato, Ion, 533e.4-534d.5. The 'good poets' interpret the divine utterances to the people (Ion, 535a.3-4) and the rhapsodes are 'interpreters of interpreters', interpreters of poets (Ion, 535a.9; in other words 'imitators of the imitators'). Plato, in general, reproaches art that imitates reality 'at a third remove' from the divine essence, as in Republic, 377d-e, 392c-398b, 401b, 597e, 602c, 606c-608b; Timaeus, 30c-d etc. Imitation of great orators, however, is a necessary effort for the aspiring rhetor, as Hyperides, for example is described by Longinus as attempting to imitate Demosthenes [τῆς συνθέσεως μιμεῖσθαι τὰ Δημοσθένεια], and Lysias (Longinus, On the Sublime, 34.2.1-5).

[80] Plato, Ion, 535c.7-8, 535e.1-4. It is in terms of such 'fear' that Longinus stresses the difference between the rhetorical art of Hyperides and that of Demosthenes: "no one feels frightened [οὐδεὶς... φοβεῖται] while reading Hyperides'. But Demosthenes 'takes up the tale' and shows the merits of great genius: 'in their most consummate form, sublime intensity, living emotion, redundance, readiness, speed. [...] You could sooner open your eyes to the descent of a thunderbolt than face his repeated outbursts of emotion without blinking' (Sublime, 34.4.4-16). Artistic "fear" is related to a fundamental concept of Aristotle's Poetics, katharsis (κάθαρσις), referring in principal to the purifying effect of tragedy on the audience's emotions and intellect (Poetics, 1449b.25-30: δι' ἐλέου καὶ φόβου περαίνουσα τὴν τῶν τοιούτων παθημάτων κάθαρσιν). Aristotle mentions also the pair φρίττειν καὶ ἐλεεῖν, horror and pity (Poetics, 1453b.5-10). The poet creates pleasure (ἡδονή) out of these feelings, through mimesis, and educates through indignation (νεμεσᾶν) and mercy, ἔλεος (Poetics, 1453b.13-14). Plato, however, is against any horrifying and frightening details or names in a play or a story, avoiding τὰ δεινὰ τε καὶ φοβερά, things that make the audience shudder, φρίττειν δὲ ποιεῖ πάντας τοὺς ἀκούοντας (Rep. 387b-c).

(ψυχαγωγία), an artistic media bringing together the useful (χρήσιμον) and the delightful (τερπνόν).[81]

Even historians began to use this literary style. For Polybius, for example, reading history enables one 'to make a general survey, and thus derive both benefit and pleasure' (ἅμα καὶ τὸ χρήσιμον καὶ τὸ τερπνὸν ἐκ τῆς ἱστορίας ἀναλαβεῖν).[82] Some commentaries on Acts acknowledge a similar rhetorical approach in Luke's style, as well.[83]

With regard to the second objection, Luke's access to Aristotle's precepts and recommendations needs to be seen in relation to its cultural context and in relation to his own ability to identify the proper rules of composition, the literary forms that correspond to the literary taste of his audience. An interesting illustration is, for example, the way Dionysius of Halicarnassus defended the primacy of Demosthenes among

---

[81] Dion. Hal., *On the Style of Demosthenes*. Demosthenes' style is best, the 'most perfectly adapted to all aspects of human nature', both to the desire for *gravity* and for *pleasure* (*Dem.* 33.1-3); he is most successful at combining the plain, grand and intermediate styles (*Dem.* 33.25, 34.10-15; *cf.* Dionysius' preference for the third "well-blended" style, in Dion. Hal., *On Literary Composition*, 21.18-20; 24.1-10, etc). If *Dem.* 38-39 presents the characteristics of the austere style, with Thucydides as its most famous representative, *Dem.* 40 focuses on the polished, spectacular style whose object 'is euphony and musical effect, and the pleasure [τὸ ἡδύ] they produce' (*Dem.* 40.1-5); *Dem.* 41 is dedicated to the balanced, well adapted style to a given audience. Demosthenes excels at using appropriately 'devices which please and beguile', τὴν ἡδονὴν καὶ τὴν ἀπάτην (*Dem.* 45.45), focusing on the goal of every work, *i.e.* 'pleasure and beauty', τοῦ καλοῦ καὶ τῆς ἡδονῆς (*Dem.* 47.1-8). This goal can be expressed as 'enjoyment' ψυχαγωγία (*Dem.* 44.14; *Letter to Gnaeus Pompeius*, 6.45; *On the Ancient Orators*, 1.1.6, 7.4.13), or 'delight', τερπνόν (*Orators*, 2.1.1), and its literary counterpart is the 'usefulness' of a narrative, χρήσιμον (*Roman Antiquities*, 1.36.3.7, 6.49.5.2, 6.86.2.16, 10.52.2.6, 20.13.2.2; *Composition*, 26.148).

[82] Polybius, *The Histories*, 1.4.11. F. W. Walbank comments that in such passages 'the traditional antithesis between τέρψις and ὠφέλεια is in effect dissolved by the identification of the two' ('Profit or Amusement: Some Thoughts on the Motives of Hellenistic Historians', in H. Verdin, G. Schepens and E. de Keysen (eds.), *Purposes of History: Studies in Greek Historiography from the 4th to the 2nd centuries BC* (Leuven: Leuven UP, 1990), 253-266, p. 262).

[83] B. Witherington III, *The Acts of the Apostles. A Socio-Rhetorical Commentary* (Carlisle: Paternoster, 1998).

the orators on the basis that he need not learn his skill from Aristotle's *Rhetoric*, but discovered and used, by his own genius, the rules of rhetorical excellence.[84] Keeping the proportions and changing the perspective, the present mimetic approach of the 'on the road' encounters in Luke-Acts is based not only on Luke's literary style as a reflection of Hellenistic standards, but also on Luke's own gifts as a story-teller who finds himself in agreement with such rules, independently. He could have used the popular lore regarding the well-told story and the elements of a well devised plot, or equally so, he could have learnt these structures and literary standards from popular legends and novels, from the current works of philosophy, history and medicine, or from Greek drama on the stage. One way or another, his writing came to reflect many such subtle and persuasive figures of style. For example, in Luke 24:28, where Jesus draws near Emmaus, he is, surprisingly, portrayed in theatre-like language, as pretending or playing, or making-believe (προσεποιήσατο) that he were journeying further...[85]

---

84 Dion. Hal., *The First Letter to Ammaeus* in *Critical Essays*, vol. 2, 306-348, esp. pp. 306, 309, 327, 345.

85 προσεποιήσατο (προς-ποιεῖσθαι) means 'make believe, simulate'. Plato uses it often (and even more, still, Dio Cassius, Galenus, Plutarchus, etc.): *Charmides* 155b.5: 'what stops you from pretending to him that you know a cure for headache?' (ἀλλὰ τί σε κωλύει προσποιήσασθαι πρὸς αὐτὸν ἐπίστασθαί τι κεφαλῆς φάρμακον); *Charmides*, 170e.1: τὸν προσποιούμενον ἰατρὸν εἶναι ('he, who pretended to be a doctor'); or *Rep.* 421a.4, 577b.6, etc. Generally, the verb occurs in educated philosophical works, with important theatrical connotations.

CHAPTER 1

A Review of Lukan Scholarship

The specific contribution of the post-Easter 'on the road' encounters to Luke's general Way motif could be more easily understood if one takes the trouble of considering, in a short *resumé*, the main views of NT scholarship on this issue. Thus, it will be shown, first, the extent to which *form-critical* studies such as those of H. J. Cadbury, M. Dibelius, E. Repo, S. V. McCasland, W. Jaeger and others, have explored the semantic range of the Way metaphor. Next, how *redaction-critical* studies have brought into discussion Luke's relation to Mark and to the Old Testament journey themes, as well as the issue of theological continuity of the Way motif in Luke-Acts. H. Conzelmann's époque-making observations have prompted a large number of responses, some emphasizing the continuity of Luke's motif of the Way (W. C. Robinson), the diversified and personalised meaning of this metaphor (R. E. Brown), or the dialectical overlapping of various types of journeys schemes (H. Flender). Finally, the *literary perspectives* on the Way motif have drawn attention to Luke's Christological and missionary emphases based on LXX motifs (C. F. Evans, C.A. Evans, D. P. Moessner, J. Navone, M. L. Strauss, W. M. Swartley, and E. Mayer).[1]

Form Criticism and the Way Metaphor

After a turn of the century (approx. 1895-1915) dominated by 'a far-reaching, multifaceted, high-level debate over the historicity of Acts',[2] the contributions of H. J. Cadbury and of M. Dibelius have been instrumental in introducing the new

---

[1] J. Kodell, 'The Theology of Luke in Recent Study', *BTB* 1 (1971), 115-144; A. Denaux, 'Old Testament Models for the Lukan Travel Narrative: A Critical Survey', in C. M. Tuckett (ed.), *The Scriptures in the Gospels* (Leuven: Leuven UP, 1997), 271-305.

[2] C. J. Hemer, *The Book of Acts in the Setting of Hellenistic History* (Tübingen: Mohr, 1989), p. 3, in a somewhat nostalgic view.

literary emphasis in NT studies.³ Their work has redrawn Luke's portrait as a writer and as a literate preacher of the early kerygma. Jesus' missionary itinerary and his miracles have been discussed, in this context, as representing traditional material in the form of preaching examples (*Predigtbeispiele*), of kerygmatic paradigms (apophthegms), of idealised reports (legends) and interpreted, entertaining stories (tales, *Novellen*).⁴

The Journey Motif in Tales, Legends, Itineraries

Cadbury, in particular, has identified in Luke-Acts a number of *popular literary forms* (as distinct from proper and more skillful *literary* forms),⁵ such as tales of wonder and miracle,

---

3   H. J. Cadbury, *The Style and Literary Method of Luke* (Cambridge: Cambridge UP, 1920); also, Cadbury, *The Making of Luke-Acts* (London: Macmillan, 1927); M. Dibelius, *From Tradition to Gospel* (London: Nicholson, 1934); *idem*, H. Greeven (ed.), *Studies in the Acts of the Apostles* (London: SCM, 1956). Despite their reaction towards historical criticism, the *Formgeschichte* and *Redaktiongeschichte* approaches to the NT preserved an in-built diachronism. Furthermore, the study of the NT texts from the perspective of oriental religions enjoyed a certain priority to the detriment of possible links with classical philology, or with Jewish and non-Jewish rhetorical culture (*cf.* F. Siegert, 'Mass Communication and Prose Rhythm in Luke-Acts', in S. E. Porter and T. H. Olbricht (eds.), *Rhetoric and the New Testament: Essays from the 1992 Heidelberg Conference* (Sheffield: Sheffield Academical, 1993), 42-58, esp. pp. 53-55; H. D. Betz, *Hellenismus und Urchristentum. Gesammelte Aufsätze* (Tübingen: Mohr, 1990), p. 3; see, V. K. Robbins, 'Oral, Rhetorical, and Literary Cultures: A Response', in J. Dewey (ed.), *Semeia 65: Orality and Textuality in Early Christian Literature* (Missoula, MT: Scholars, 1995), 75-91, p. 80; *idem*, *The Tapestry of Early Christian Discourse: Rhetoric, Society and Ideology* (London: Routledge, 1996); *idem*, *Jesus the Teacher. A Socio-Rhetorical Interpretation of Mark* (Minneapolis, MN: Fortress, 1992)).

4   *Cf.* R. I. Pervo, *Profit with Delight: The Literary Genre of the Acts of the Apostles* (Philadelphia, PA: Fortress, 1987), p. 2. D. L. Bock, *Proclamation from Prophecy and Pattern: Lucan Old Testament Christology* (Sheffield: Sheffield Academical, 1987), p. 27.

5   Cadbury, *Making*, pp. 127-139. The difference between a coherent *Kunstliteratur* and a fragmented *Kleinliteratur* such as the NT is difficult to draw (K. L. Schmidt was the first to describe the Gospels as 'popular literature'). This difference would stand more 'in the degree

miraculous releases from prison (Acts 12:6-18; 16:16-25), public competitions between a true and a false prophet (Acts 8:4-25; 13:4-14), parables and various Christian *memorabilia* (tradition, memories, ὑπομνήματα, ἀπομνημονεύματα). Among them one finds, as well, the *travel tale* which takes mainly two forms - the *maritime adventure* along the coasts (περίπλους), and the *journey by land* (usually in the form of journey notes or περιήγησις).[6] In his analysis of Luke's journey stories, however, Cadbury tended to refer mainly to Paul's voyage to Rome, with its impressive shipwreck episode at Malta (Acts 28).

Dibelius' attention was captured by this adventure, as well, for 'the sea-voyage is one of the most literary sections of Acts',[7] and he explicitly noted the influence of certain secular models here: 'a secular description of the voyage and shipwreck served as [its] pattern, basis or source'.[8] Paul's missionary itinerary was seen as 'the basis of the composition' to which Luke 'made his own additions, as well as inserting other traditions'.[9]

They did not discuss Luke's 'on the road' encounters specifically, only noted them in terms of NT *legends, paradigms*, and *Novellen*.[10] For example, with the exception of

---

    rather than in kind' (Cadbury, *op.cit.*, p. 131). Luke's literary standards, in particular 'were more akin to formal literature than were those of the other evangelists' (Cadbury, *op.cit.*, pp. 137, 134). As a definition 'popular literature' is understood as an *aesthetic* characterised by straightforwardness, continuity between life and art, simplicity, and a conglomerate, episodic structure (W. Hansen, 'Introduction', in W. Hansen (ed.), *Anthology of Ancient Greek Popular Literature* (Bloomington, IN: Indiana UP, 1998), xi-xxix, esp. pp. xiv-xxii).

6   Cadbury, *Making*, pp. 143-145.
7   M. Dibelius, 'The Acts of the Apostles in the Setting of the History of Early Christian Literature', in *Studies*, 192-206; p. 205.
8   M. Dibelius, 'Style Criticism of the Book of Acts', in *Studies*, pp. 1-25.
9   Dibelius, 'Style', p. 6.
10   For Dibelius a *Legende* was a piece of kerygmatic tradition: 'religious narratives of a saintly man' with aetiological and biographical information (*Tradition*, p. 104). *Legends* deal with the human characters, *paradigms* are centrad on the proclamation and *novels* (*Novellen*) deal with the works of the divine character (Dibelius, *Tradition*, p. 105). However, Bultmann calls 'miracle stories' what is

Luke 24:21b, 22-24, the Emmaus story is labeled by Dibelius a *legend* in 'pure form'.[11] Under Gunkel's influence, the *formgeschichtlich* school often perceived the Emmaus encounter as a legend imitating the OT stories of heavenly travellers (*cf.* the angels before Abraham, Gen. 16:2ff.; Gen. 18:1ff.; see also Judg. 13:3-21, and Manoah's sacrifice, in Judg. 23:11ff.), and following, as well, the model of 'wisdom stories'.[12] More recently, Guillaume confirmed such OT parallels and suggested a direct borrowing of themes from the LXX.[13] As an alternative, however, Ehrhardt thought that its models are found in Hellenistic literature.[14] In the same vein Betz saw in the Emmaus story a 'cult legend',[15] similar to Hellenistic stories where not a god but a human being appears after his death (*e.g.* Aristeas of Proconnesus, Zalmoxis, Peregrinus Proteus and Apollonius of Tyana, or the Romulus legend).[16] The legendary character of the recognition scene has been noticed by Kurz, also, and echoing Auerbach's comments, he

---

'novels' for Dibelius, 'historical stories' what Dibelius labels as 'legends', and finally, 'legends' what Dibelius calls 'myths'.

11 Dibelius, *Tradition*, p. 191, n. 1; R. Bultmann, *Die Geschichte der synoptische Tradition* (Göttingen: Vandenhoeck, 1967), p. 310. For Bultmann Emmaus as a 'legend' meant that the story had no historical value in spite of being the oldest of the synoptic Easter stories ('Fascher Erich: Die Formgeschichtliche Methode', *TLZ* 50 (1925), 313-318; *cf.* Bultmann, *Geschichte*, p. 314). Marshall acknowledges carefully that it shows 'features of popular legend' (Marshall, *Gospel*, p. 890), yet it 'demonstrates the reality of the resurrection and the identity of the Risen One with Jesus' (p. 891; also, Dodd, 'Appearances', p. 35).

12 Gunkel, *Verständnis*, p. 71; For him, Christ appears in the guise of a wandering deity (like Wotan, the wanderer) *cf.* K. Koch, *Was ist Formgeschichte: Neue Wege der Bibelexegese* (Neukirchen: Neukirchener, 1964), p. 169; Bultmann, *Geschichte*, p. 310.

13 Guillaume, *Luc interprète*, p. 90.

14 Ehrhardt, 'Disciples', pp. 185, 194.

15 H. D. Betz, 'The origin and the nature of Christian faith according to the Emmaus legend (Luke 24:13-32)', *Int* 23 (1969), 32-46, p. 33.

16 Betz, 'Origin', p. 34; *cf.* Lucian of Samosata, *The Death of Peregrinus*, 28; Philostratus, *Apollonius* 7.30-31. See also Ehrhardt, 'Disciples', p. 194; Dillon, *Eye-Witnesses*, pp. 73-74. The *Jesus Seminar* argues that the legend connotations are related to the cultural perspective of the author and the story belongs to Luke (R. W. Funk, R. W. Hoover, and *The Jesus Seminar*, in *The Five Gospels: The Search for the Authentic Words of Jesus* (N.Y.: Macmillan, 1993), p. 399).

stressed the similarity between the recognition of Jesus at Emmaus and Odysseus' disguised return, and the hidden identity of the one causing the plague in *Oedipus the King*.[17] The recognition of Jesus' hidden identity is seen as prefigured, as well, in some LXX texts like Nathan's parable of the slaughtered lamb (2 Sam. 12:1-6) and the final recognition of the angel Raphael in Tobit (Tob. 12).[18]

At its turn, the conversion of the Ethiopian eunuch was characterised, as well, as a legend and 'on the whole without literary embellishment'.[19] In terms of OT parallels, it displays certain parallels with the Elijah-Elisha narratives (1 Kgs 18:12f.).[20] However, its half-biographical, half-kerygmatic character allows, also, for a *Novelle* classification, since the Spirit of the Lord is the miracle working character.

Saul's 'on the road' encounter was discussed mainly as an introduction to Paul's story in Acts.[21] In terms of genre, the account represents either a *legend* (an aetiological story of a

---

17 W. S. Kurz, *Reading Luke-Acts: Dynamics of Biblical Narrative*, Louisville, KY: Westminster, 1993, p. 70; see E. Auerbach, *Mimesis: The Representation of Reality in Western Literature* (Princeton, NJ: Princeton UP, 1953), pp. 3-23. Auerbach's famous parallels between the scene of Odysseus' Scar (*Odyssey*, 19.425-505) and that of Abraham's sacrificing Isaac (Gen. 22:1-20), and between Fortunata's portrait (Petronius, *Satyricon*, 37-38) and Percennius' speech (Tacitus, *Annals*, 1.16-18) and Peter's denial in Mk. 14:67-72, emphasize the contrast between their different style and representation principles (Auerbach, *op.cit.*, pp. 24-49; *cf.* A. Melberg, *Theories of Mimesis* (Cambridge: Cambridge UP, 1995), p. 43).

18 Kurz, *Reading Luke-Acts*, p. 70: Luke uses a 'Raphael typology in Luke 24 and an Elijah typology in Acts 1'. See also J. G. Davies, *He Ascended into Heaven: A Study in the History of Doctrine* (London: Lutterworth, 1958), pp. 53-55; *idem*, 'The Prefigurement of the Ascension in the Third Gospel', *JTS* 6 (1955), 229-233; P. A. van Stempvoort, 'Interpretation of the Ascension in Luke and Acts,' *NTS* 5 (1958), 30-42; C. H. Talbert, *Literary Patterns, Theological Themes and the Genre of Luke-Acts* (Missoula, MT: Scholars, 1974), p. 59, n. 23 (at p. 65); Zwiep, *Ascension*, p. 12.

19 Dibelius, 'Style', p. 15.
20 Alsup, *Post-resurrection*, p. 84.
21 Dibelius, 'Paul in the Acts of the Apostles', in *Studies*, pp. 207-214.

famous missionary),[22] or, for others, a resurrection *novel*[23] centred on a post-Easter epiphany.[24]

The literary genre of these *hodos* encounters is quite a volatile category, apparently. The Emmaus account, as a further example, can be characterized not only as a *legend*, focused on the wonders of Jesus, yet also as a *paradigm* (Dibelius), since Luke stresses the Easter kerygma and the proof-from-prophecy elements, and even as a *Novelle* (the divine Jesus is the character who causes the non-recognition and recognition miracles, the appearance and disappearance events).

The Idealisation of the Way Setting

An important landmark for the literary analysis of the Way metaphor has been, further, E. Repo's monograph, *Der 'Weg' als Selbstbezeichnung des Urchristentums*,[25] focused on the NT *hodos* passages in Luke, John, Hebrews, Matthew, etc. Starting from a unitary-canonical perspective, he tried to highlight the directional, geographical, legal, Christological, eschatological, and ethical connotations of the Way motif,[26]

---

22 The typical features of *legends* are present here: a falling down, a message and / or vision addressed to the elected, a call and a mission (Conzelmann, *Acts*, pp. 72-73; see, also R. Witherup, 'Functional redundancy in the Acts of the Apostles: a Case Study', *JSNT* 48 (1992), 67-86; esp. pp. 67, 70, 81, 83).

23 Dibelius, *Tradition*, p. 71. For K. Löning the Damascus story represents a *Novelle*. The theological meaning of the story, the *metanoia*, is seen as secondary (*Die Saulustradition in der Apostelgeschichte* (Münster: Aschendorff, 1973), p. 90). Not the proclamation (the kerygma, as in a *paradigm*) but the miracle-worker (Wundertäter) lies at the centre of a *Novelle* (Löning, *op.cit.*, pp. 88, 89).

24 Dibelius tends to include among the *Novellen* the *epiphanies*, as well, seen as a work of God (*Tradition*, p. 94, cf. Löning, *Saulustradition*, p. 88). *Cf.* Löning, *Saulustradition*, p. 92, and the presence of the *divine passive* in the Emmaus story.

25 E. Repo, *Der 'Weg' als Selbstbezeichnung des Urchristentums*: *eine Traditionsgeschichtliche und Semasiologische Untersuchung* (Helsinki: Suomalainen Tiedeakatemia, 1964). S. V. McCasland's comprehensive article has preceded Repo's analysis in many respects, though without similar in-depth details ('The Way', *JBL* 77 (1958), 220-230).

26 *Cf.* Repo, Weg, p. 32. F. Bovon, Luke the Theologian: Thirty-three Years of Research (1950-1983) (Allison Park: Pikwick, 1987), p. 322.

setting the research agenda for quite a time. He succeeded in raising the issue of a cultural process of *idealisation* of the Way metaphor, that finally reached a high point in the NT understanding of the Way as a personified concept (Jesus, the Christians). Although it imposed a unitary and limiting view on this motif in the NT (for which he was rightly criticized), Repo's analysis has the merit of having raised the issue of cultural development of the Way's paradigms and meanings.

STAGES OF IDEALISATION

From an initial OT Wandering motif based on the geographical metaphor and on the importance of the divine presence and guidance for Israel (as in Genesis and Exodus, implying a *theologia viatorum*),[27] the Way motif underwent a process of idealisation gaining legalistic and ethical connotations as obedience or disobedience to Yahweh's commandments (*cf.*the typological interpretations of the Way of the Lord, with Deuteronomic nuances, as well as Isaianic, as a New Exodus, a new conquest, a restoration of the land, etc.).[28]

---

27 Repo, *Weg*, p. 7. Similarly, S. Lyonnet had suggested that from an initially general, lay meaning of the Way as 'behaviour' or 'way of life', the *hodos* imagery in the OT had a special meaning as leadership or plan of salvation for God's people ('"La Voie" dans les Actes des Apôtres', *RSR* 69 (1981), 149-164; in J. Delorme and J. Duplacey (eds.), *Études lucaniennes à la mémoire d'Augustin George* (Paris: RSR, 1981), pp. 154, 164). These early meanings prepared the later Christian use of 'the Way of the Lord' (Lyonnet, *op.cit.*, p. 153).

28 Repo, *Weg*, p. 147. For details, see the third chapter of Repo's *Weg* (Die 'Formgeschichte' der Verkürzung 'Weg'), pp. 139-166. As Denaux notes ('OT Models', p. 291), the New Exodus theme, as an idealisation of the Exodus journey, can be linked either to the Deuteronomy (Ringe, Dawsey, Moessner) or to the Deutero-Isaianic imagery (Is. 40-55, *cf.* as well, Ezek. 36-37). *Cf.* M. L. Strauss, *The Davidic Messiah in Luke-Acts: The Promise and its Fulfillment in Lukan Christology* (Sheffield: Sheffield Academical, 1995, pp. 284-297, and his bibliography; also, C. Stuhlmueller, *Creative Redemption in Deutero-Isaiah* (Rome: PBI, 1970); R. E. Watts, 'Consolation or Confrontation? Isaiah 40-55 and the Delay of the New Exodus', *TynB* 41 (1990), 31-59. Also in favour of the wilderness typology is E. Mayer, *Die Reiseerzählung des Lukas (Lk. 9:51-19:10): Entscheidung in der Wüste* (Frankfurt: Lang, 1996), discussed in Denaux, 'OT Models', pp. 293-294.

As W. C. Robinson and H. Conzelmann have noted, this process of idealisation continued in NT times and has affected, in Luke's case, more than the Way metaphor: it transformed the geographical space into a faith symbol, the symbol of humanity's link with the spiritual world.[29] For Conzelmann, in particular, Luke has begun 'the process by which the scene becomes stylized into the "Holy Land"'.[30]

---

29 Cf. W. C. Robinson, *Der Weg des Herrn: Studien zur Geschichte und Eschatologie im Lukas Evangelium. Ein Geschpräch mit Hans Conzelmann* (Hamburg: Bergstedt, 1964), p. 22, 'Lukas hat die Geographie Palästinas als die eines "heiligen Landes" idealisiert, idem "der Berg" der Ort des Gebetes, der esoterischen Epiphanie und der Kommunikation mit der oberen Welt ist'.

30 Conzelmann, *Luke*, pp. 70-71. The subject has been addressed by an ever increasing number of studies: S. MacCormack, 'Loca sancta: The Organization of Sacred Topography on Late Antiquity', in R. Ousterhout (ed.), *The Blessings of Pilgrimage* (Urbana Champaign, IL: University of Illinois, 1990), 7-40; R. A. Markus, 'How on Earth Could Places Become Holy? Origins of the Christian Idea of Holy Places', *JEChS* 3 (1994), 257-271; C. D. Smith, 'Geography or Christianity? Maps of the Holy Land before AD 1000', *JTS* 42 (1991), 143-152; J. Z. Smith, *Drudgery Divine: On the Comparison of Early Christianities and the Religions of Late Antiquity* (Chicago, IL: University of Chicago, 1990); J. Z. Smith, *Map is not territory: studies in the history of religions* (Leiden: Brill, 1978); J. Z. Smith, *To take place: toward theory in ritual* (Chicago, IL: University of Chicago, 1992); J. E. Taylor, *Christians and the Holy Places: The Myth of Jewish-Christian Origins* (Oxford: Clarendon, 1993); P. W. L. Walker, *Holy City, Holy Places? Christian Attitudes to Jerusalem and the Holy Land in the Fourth Century* (Oxford: Clarendon, 1990); P. W. L. Walker (ed.), *Jerusalem Past and Present in the Purposes of God* (Croydon: Deo Gloria, 1992); R. L. Wilken, *The Land Called Holy* (New Haven, CT: Yale UP, 1992), etc. However, in its first three centuries Christianity had not stressed in any remarkable way the importance of holy places (Smith, *To take place*, pp. 1-23). Eusebius argued that in contrast to Moses, who also 'promised a holy land and a holy life therein', Jesus Christ has promised 'a far better land in truth, and a holy and godly, not the land of Judaea, which in no way excels the rest (of the earth), but the heavenly country which suits souls that love God' (Eusebius, *The Proof of the Gospel*, 3.2.91d.8-13; W. J. Ferrar). Christianity is interested not in the 'Jerusalem below' but in the 'new and real City of Heaven' (Eusebius, *Proof*, 2.3.61b.3; 2.3.66d.14-17; 2.3.69a.4-5; 4.12.166c.6-d.1). In spite of this early profession of faith, the sacralisation of places has

At this point it is relevant to ask what is the stage of this idealisation process at the level of Luke's own work and time? Did he use the Way metaphor only as a reference to OT prophets, as the 'Way of the Lord', as an idealisation of the Exodus journey (Ps. 13:3, Is. 40:3, 58:9, etc.),[31] or, also, as a Hellenistic paradigm? How did this idealization influenced the 'way' metaphor in Luke-Acts, as a symbolical setting for important encounters, and as paradigm of transition?

On the whole, Luke had access to two different types of meanings for his journey and *hodos* paradigms: to *internalised* connotations of the Way (*e.g.*, legalistic, ethical, personal) and to *external* symbols (related to itinerary, quality of path, journeying processes, destinations, type of leaders, etc.).

INTERNALISED JEWISH CONNOTATIONS OF THE WAY

The internalised connotations of the Way include the metaphors of the Way that apply to the spiritual, inner life of the believer and are shown outwardly in the form of obedience, behaviour, and character. Among these is the Way understood as the Law of God, and as ethical, personal achievement.

The Way as the Law and Obedience to the Law

Luke's use of ὁδός and αἵρεσις seems to indicate an already fixed usage of these terms, with certain community-related connotations.[32] In Acts 22:4 αἵρεσις is used as 'a term for a manner of behaviour but also for those who adopted the behaviour',[33] and the idiom הדרך was used in a similar way at

---

become a dominant note of popular Christianity (Markus, 'How on Earth', p. 271).

31 The phrase 'the Way of the Lord' (דרך יהוה) and its variations can be found in a larger number of OT texts, as well, like Gen. 18:19; Judg. 2:22; 2 Kgs. 21:22; Jer. 5:4-5; Ezek. 18:25; 33:17 (*cf.* Repo, *Weg*, pp. 161, 166; McCasland, 'Way', pp. 225-226, 230).

32 *Cf.* Conzelmann, *Luke*, p. 227, n. 1; W. Michaelis, 'ὁδός, ὁδηγός, ὁδηγέω', *TDNT*, vol. 5, 42-114, p. 43. Repo emphasizes as well the early character of this usage 'Der hier vorkommende Gebrauch von "hodos" hängt mit der etwas früher Erklärung ὁδός-αἵρεσις zusammen und wird auf dieser Grundlage verständlich, obgleich das Wort absolut angewandt ist' (Repo, *Weg*, p. 26).

33 C. K. Barrett, *The Acts of the Apostles* (Edinburgh: T&T Clark, 1994), vol. 1, p. 448; *Cf.* 'αἵρεσις', in J. P. Louw and E. A. Nida, *Greek-English*

Qumran (from here Christians could have derived it through the agency of John the Baptist).³⁴

For example, one notes that the members of the Qumran community are characterised in relation to the Law as 'those perfect of the way', בתמים דרך, 1QS 8:18; 9:5, 9;³⁵ or 'the chosen of the way', לבחירי דרך.³⁶ The Master of the Community, a messianic figure, guides them 'with knowledge ... so that they may walk perfectly each one with his fellow in everything which has been revealed to them. This is the time to prepare the way to the wilderness', עת פנות הדרך למדבר (1 QS 9:18-20).³⁷ The perfect walking in the Way is related to the preparation of the Messiah's time, and Isaiah 40:3 is central to this paradigm

> They shall separate themselves from the session of the men of deceit in order to depart into the wilderness to prepare there the Way of the Lord (?); as it is written: 'In the wilderness prepare the way of the Lord, make level in the desert a highway for our God'. This (alludes to) the study of the Torah wh[ic]h he commanded through Moses to do, according to everything which has been revealed (from) time to time, and according to that which the prophets have revealed by his Holy Spirit.³⁸

Lexicon of the New Testament Based on Semantic Domains (N.Y.: UBS, 1988-1989), p. 129.

34 The prehistory of the Christian understanding of the Way is in general seen as Essene and Jewish (Conzelmann, *Luke*, p. 227, n. 1). McCasland and E. Repo wrote extensively on this theme (Repo, *'Weg'*, pp. 26, 32, 55-60, etc.; McCasland, 'Way', pp. 239-230, esp. p. 230). The majority of scholars emphasized that at Qumran the 'way' was understood as strict observance of the Mosaic Law, like in 1 QS 9.17, 18; 10.21; 11.3, etc. (Repo, *'Weg'*, p. 173; Barrett, *Acts*, vol. 1, p. 448). H. Schonfield argued that the early Christians identified themselves with the Essene paradigms of the Way as community (*The Essene Odyssey. The Mystery of the True Teacher and The Essene Impact on the Shaping of Human Destiny* (Shaftesbury: Element, 1993), p. 81).

35 J. H. Charlesworth (ed.), *The Dead Sea Scrolls: Hebrew, Aramaic, and Greek Texts with English Translations. Rule of the Community and Related Documents* (Tübingen: Mohr, 1994), vol. 1, pp. 37-41.

36 1 QS 9:18, *cf.* in fragments as well, 4QS Frg.8, Col.1; Frg.3, Col. 2; *Scrolls*, vol. 1, pp. 41, 65, 79.

37 Charlesworth, *Scrolls*, vol. 1, p. 41; In 1 QS 8:13 one finds 'The way of the Lord' or 'His way', דרך הואה, *Scrolls*, vol. 1, p. 37, n. 210.

38 1 QS 8:13-16, *Scrolls*, vol. 1, p. 37.

However, although Luke - as well as the other evangelists - has given special attention to Isaiah 40:3, as a major reference in the preaching of John the Baptist, the earliest Christian tradition did not retain this legalistic meaning of the Law.[39]

The Ethical Significance of the Way

As a metaphorical, internalized concept, the Way contributed to the formation of numerous poetical constructs such as the 'way of light', לדרך אור,[40] the 'ways of true righteousness', דרכי צדק אמת,[41] the 'ways of truth', דרכי אמת,[42] the 'way of wickedness', הרשעה בדרך,[43] the 'way of traitors', בוגדים דרך,[44] the 'ways of prostitutes', דרכי זונות,[45] the 'way of the people', דרך העם.[46] In 4 Q434, 436 (the *Hymns of the Poor*), the Lord God directs 'their foot to *the way*' (יכן לדרב רגלם; Frg. 2, 1.4) and they walk 'in *the way of His heart*' (וילבו בדרך לבו; Frg. 2, 1.10).[47]

These ethical connotations of the Way seem to have encouraged a specialised use of the singular and the plural forms. Repo suggests that this semantic polarization between

---

39 On the legalistic meaning of the Way, Barrett stresses that 'this is not how even the most conservative Jewish Christian groups understood their "Way"' (Barrett, *Acts*, vol. 1, p. 448). The Essene use of the term may have provided the material for the first accusations against the Christians (Schonfield, *Essene Odyssey*, p. 82, 84).
40 1 QS 3:3, 20, *Scrolls*, vol. 1, pp. 13, 15.
41 1 QS 4:2, *Scrolls*, vol. 1, p. 17.
42 1 QS 4:17, *Scrolls*, vol. 1, p. 19.
43 1 QS 5:11, *Scrolls*, vol. 1, p. 23.
44 CD MS A 8:4-5. See J. H. Charlesworth (ed.), The Dead Sea Scrolls: Hebrew, Aramaic, and Greek Texts with English Translations (Damascus Document, War Scroll, and Related Documents) (Tübingen: Mohr, 1995), vol. 2, p. 27.
45 CD *MS A* 8:5 (*Scrolls*, vol. 2, p. 29), or CD 19:17 the same phrase translated as 'ways of unchastity' (*Scrolls*, vol. 2, p. 33).
46 CD 8:16; *Scrolls*, vol. 2, p. 29.
47 R. H. Eisenman and M. Wise, *The Dead Sea Scrolls Uncovered* (Shaftesbury: Element, 1992), pp. 238-240; see also the 1 QH - the *Thanksgiving Hymns*, and 4 Q434 - *Barki, nafshi*, Frg. 1, in G. Vermes, *The Dead Sea Scrolls in English* (Sheffield: JSOT, 1995), pp. 189-236, 280-281.

the negative *ways* (pl.) and the perfect *way* (sing.), reflects in a nutshell the historical process of progressive modifications

> Es ist möglich, dass im früheren Sprachgebrauch der Bewegung die Metapher 'Weg', vor allem in der Bedeutung von Gebot und Gesetz, mehr im Plural als im Singular üblich war.[48]

Such a distinction occurs, for example, in 1 QS, the scroll of the Community Rule. The first part of 1 QS (1.1-7.25) could be called 'The Ways of Light and the Ways of Darkness' (using mainly plural constructs), while, in contradistinction, its second part refers to the theme of The Perfect Way, using preponderently the singular.[49]

The men of holiness are expected to 'walk perfectly', בתמים ההולכים,[50] and the rebellious members of the community need to turn back to 'the perfect way' (or 'perfection of the way', תום הדרך, 1 QS 11:11)

> I [the Master] do not hold anger towards those who turn away from transgression; but I will not have compassion for all those who deviate from the way. I will not console those who are being obstinate until their way is perfect.[51]

The true perfection of the way, however, comes from God, and so the Master acknowledges his own shortcomings

> For my way (belongs) to Adam [לאדם דרכו ואנוש לוא יבין צעדו]. The human cannot establish his righteousness; for to God (alone) belongs the judgement and from him is the perfection of the way [תום הדרך].[52]

This Essenian use of the singular has created an important precedent for Luke's reference to the Way in Luke-Acts. Christians' claim to be seen as 'those belonging to the Way'

---

48 Repo, *Weg*, p. 170.
49 McCasland, 'Way', pp. 225-226; According to him, 1 QS has 33 mentions of the Way; the first 12 are in the plural, and the rest of the 21, from 1 QS 8.1 on, are all in the singular (p. 225; *cf.* Repo, *Weg*, p. 170). This witnesses of a certain *stylistic polarisation*, but it does not amount to a firm and absolute semantic distinction between the two forms.
50 1 QS 9:6, 8, 19, *Scrolls*, vol. 1, pp. 39-41.
51 1 QS 10:20-21, *Scrolls*, vol. 1, p. 47.
52 1 QS 11:10-11, *Scrolls*, vol. 1, p. 49.

would be the equivalent of an absolute claim for true, superlative obedience to the Law of God, and at the same time, a claim that the Church is *the* messianic community.[53]

EXTERNAL JEWISH CONNOTATIONS OF THE WAY
As an external symbol, the Way includes several meanings, the connotations of itinerary, quality of path, journeying processes, destinations, even of types of leadership (overlapping here with the internalised connotations) and has provided important paradigms for the NT narratives, plot lines and historical references. All of these meanings allow, in Repo's analysis, for as many development lines of the concept of the Way.

For example, in terms of journey destination, the process of idealisation has started with the simple reference to walks or visits, pilgrimages or liberation and conquest journeys (*cf.* the Abrahamic journeys, the Exodus, the conquest of Canaan, etc.) and finally led to the idea of an existential journey to heaven, inspiring people to think of their eschatological restoration (Repo's 'der Gedenke vom himmlischen Ziel').[54] The final place of arrival could take the form of a heavenly house or of a heavenly city (*cf.* Jn. 14:2, 4, 5; and Heb. 11:14f.; 12:22; 13:14) and the journey there could turn into a symbolic, apocalyptic journey (one of Repo's merits is that he discusses a number of less common types of destinations, for example, the apocryphal journeys to Heavens or to Hell, or Hades, known in Greek literature as *nekyia*).[55]

---

53   Zmijewski, *Apostelgeschichte*, p. 377. The corresponding connotations for the denotation of the way as 'teaching' could be both positive or negative, in Acts. In the singular, *hodos* has the potential of indicating the good Way or, by unlawful substitution, a false Way (Acts 24:14, κατὰ τὴν ὁδὸν ἣν λέγουσιν αἵρεσιν) (p. 378; also, Haenchen, *Acts*, p. 320, n. 1).
54   Repo, *Weg*, pp. 177, 189, 223.
55   Repo, *Weg*, pp. 189-191; 194, 196; *cf.* R. Bauckham, 'Early Jewish Visions of Hell', *JTS* 41 (1990), 355-385; and M. Himmelfarb, *Tours of Hell: Apocalyptic Form in Jewish and Christian Literature* (Philadelphia, PA: Pennsylvania State University, 1983). Also, see Himmelfarb, *Ascent to Heaven in Jewish and Christian Apocalypses* (Oxford: Oxford UP, 1993). Apocryphal literature emphasizes the link between life as journeying (πορεύεσθαι) and death as rest (ἀνάπαυσις) at destination. The intermediary state is described as a silent repose, as

Destinations are important for this study, in particular, because Palestine - as the homeland, and Jerusalem and the Temple - as the major sites of Israel' religious and political life, are also the most important destinations in Luke-Acts. Jesus' journeying is essentially related to his Passion, Ascension and the inauguration of the time of the Church.[56]

Jerusalem as Journey Destination
Jerusalem as destination is a prominent compositional element in Luke's narrative. The gospel's journeys bring finally together 'the two [main] participants in the drama of the Passion... Jesus and Jerusalem'.[57] In order to stress this development Luke ignores all other traditional reports about Jesus' journeys to Jerusalem and emphasizes only one, last journey that takes the Messiah to the Cross and for him 'there is only one journey, one visitation, one supreme and decisive encounter culminating in Jesus' martyrdom and Jerusalem's destruction'.[58]

The Jerusalem stage of this journey - as a destination announced through many *Reisenotizen* - is so prominent that it can overshadow the dynamics of journeying proper, favouring a static perspective. This effect is strengthened by the massive presence of teaching pericopes in Luke 9-19 (and for such a reason Luke's Central Section has been called the 'Jerusalem

---

in 1 Enoch 49.3; 100.6 (*cf.* 2 Macc. 12:45; Baruch 30:1; see P. Volz, *Die Eschatologie der Jüdischen Gemeinde im Neutestamentlichen Zeitalter* (Hildesheim: Olms, 1966), p. 257, also T. F. Glasson, *Greek Influence in Jewish Eschatology* (London: SPCK, 1961), pp. 8-10; J. J. Collins, *The Apocalyptic Imagination* (N.Y.: Crossroads, 1983), pp. 43-45.

56 Conzelmann, *Luke*, pp. 74, 259.
57 A. Hastings, *Prophet and Witness in Jerusalem, A Study of the Teaching of Saint Luke* (London: Longmans, 1958), p. 120.
58 Hastings, *Prophet and Witness*, pp. 120, 100, 103; also L. Vaganay, *Le Problème Synoptique* (Paris: Desclée, 1954), pp. 106-107. It is not difficult to suppose that there were several journeys (Lk. 9:51-10:42, 17:11-19:41), yet Luke presents them as one major, dominant journey to Jerusalem. The importance of this last journey can be seen from the increasing frequency of the journey markers 'as Jerusalem looms larger on the horizon' (*cf.* Lk. 18:31, 35; 19:1, 11, in J. B. Green, *The Theology of the Gospel of Luke* (Cambridge: Cambridge UP, 1995), p. 104).

Document').[59] At the same time, the motif of Jerusalem's centrality is so intense in Luke-Acts that it tends to obscure the specific contribution of Luke's *hodos* accounts. In particular, however, for the careful reader, these accounts mount an effective challenge to Jerusalem's centrality.

The Temple as Journey Destination

Luke's gospel starts in the Temple (Lk. 1-2), and the journey and pilgrimage pericopes provide enough evidence for making a distinction between Jesus' journey to Jerusalem and a separate journey to the Temple (Conzelmann, Miyoshi, Flender, Davies, etc.).[60] While the core of Jesus' journey to

---

59 K. E. Bailey, *Poet and Peasant: A Literary-cultural Approach to the Parables in Luke* (Grand Rapids, MI: Eerdmans, 1976), p. 82. According to him 'there is no "travelling" done at all and the title "Travel Journey" is a misnomer [...] We prefer to call it the "Jerusalem Document"' (pp. 82, 83). This section is one of the most 'difficult to outline' (C. L. Blomberg, 'Midrash, Chiasmus, and the Outline of Luke's Central Section', in R. T. France and D. Wenham (eds.), *Gospel Perspectives: Studies in Midrash and Historiography*, vol. 3 (Sheffield: JSOT, 1983), p. 217). Its itinerary 'does not move like a river; rather it spreads out like a lake' (F. Stagg, 'The Journey Toward Jerusalem in Luke's Gospel. Luke 9:51-19:27', *RevExp* 64 (1967) p. 499). Similarly, Green notes that Jesus and his disciples 'meander, making little or no progress towards their destination, and few geographical markers are provided to signal what progress is made' (Green, *Theology*, p. 104). As early as 1931, A. Schlatter argued that it would not be appropriate to call this narrative a "journey report" (A. Schlatter, *Das Evangelium des Lukas, aus seinem Quellen erklärt* (Stuttgart: Calwer, 1960), p. 53). In the same vein, wrote Drury (*Tradition and Design in Luke's Gospel: A Study in Early Christian Historiography* (London: DLT, 1976), p. 138), and Bailey (*Poet and Peasant*). Even the moderate I. H. Marshall notes that 'the general themes of the section are hard to define and it is even more difficult to find any kind of thread running through it' (Marshall, *Gospel*, p. 401). The list of scholars sharing this kind of approach includes further J. Blinzler, G. Ogg, E. E. Ellis, J. N. Geldenhuys, V. Taylor, R. P. B. Rigaux, L. Girard, etc. (*cf.* Conzelmann, *Luke*, p. 61; D. P. Moessner, *Lord of the Banquet: The Literary and Theological Significance of the Lukan Travel Narrative* (Minneapolis, MN: Fortress, 1989), p. 23).

60 Jesus 'enters the Temple, and later the city' (Conzelmann, *Luke*, p. 71, 76; A. Denaux, 'The Delineation of the Lucan Travel Narrative within the overall Structure of the Gospel', in C. Focant (ed.), *The Synoptic*

Jerusalem (Lk. 13:33-35) brings a solemn judgement upon the city (*cf.* Lk. 13:35a: 'your house is left to you [desolate]'),[61] the end of the gospel presents the disciples continually blessing God in the Temple (24:53).[62] Jerusalem and its Temple seem to illustrate two different types of destiny, although, in the end, both come under judgement for their failure to welcome Jesus as the Messiah.[63]

Luke's challenge of the Temple's significance, from a journey perspective, is present implicitly in the Ethiopian's encounter with Philip (Acts 8:27), as well as in Paul's relation to the priests prior to his conversion (Acts 9:1-2), and in his final arrest, in Jerusalem, at the end of the third missionary journey (Acts 21:17-37). The theological and geographical perspectives of Luke-Acts leave the Temple behind, although at a later time than Jerusalem, providing thus a centrifugal

---

Gospels: Source Criticism and the New Literary Criticism (Leuven: Leuven UP, 1993), 357-392, esp. p. 388); *cf.* J. H. Davies, 'The Purpose of the Central Section of St. Luke's Gospel', in F. L. Cross (ed.), *Studia Evangelica*, vol. 2 (Berlin: Akademie, 1964), 164-169, esp. p. 168: 'the entry into Jerusalem is the earthly end of the Journey [...] but it is also the prefiguring of the Ascension [...] then, the journey reaches a swift climax in the cleansing of the Temple'.

61 Walker, *Jesus and the Holy City*, p. 61. Luke has a more positive attitude towards the Temple, even if the city and the Temple share, in the end, the same fate (*cf.* M. Bachmann, *Jerusalem und der Tempel: Die geographisch-theologischen Elemente in der lukanischen Sicht des jüdischen Kultzentrums* (Stuttgart: Kohlhammer, 1980); F. D. Weinert, 'Luke, the Temple and Jesus' Saying about Jerusalem's Abandoned House (Luke 13:34-35)', *CBQ* 44 (1982), 68-76; *idem*, 'The meaning of the Temple in Luke-Acts', *BTB* 11 (1981), 85-89). The case of Luke's favourable attitude towards the Law and the atonement at the Temple can be easily overstated, however (*cf.* D. Ravens, *Luke and the Restoration of Israel* (Sheffield: Sheffield Academical, 1995), pp. 167-169, 254).

62 W. M. Swartley, *Israel's Scripture Traditions and the Synoptic Gospels* (Peabody, MA: Hendrickson, 1994), pp. 280-281.

63 Walker, *Jesus and the Holy City*, p. 64. He notes that 'Luke both affirms and denies the Temple, affirming its past status but denying its future' (p. 68). For Green, at the end of the Gospel Luke demonstrates symbolically 'that the holiness-purity matrix embodied in and emanating from the temple has been undermined' ('The Demise of the Temple as 'Culture Center' in Luke-Acts: an Exploration of the Rending of the Temple Veil', *RB* 101/4 (1994), 495-515, esp. p. 515).

movement associated with the expansion of Christianity, a journey of the gospel 'from Temple to Rome', from Jews to Gentiles.[64]

The Way and the Deuteronomic Exodus
The idealisation of Jesus' journeying confers a symbolical significance not only to its destination but also to the actual journeying itself. In this respect, Luke's Central Section has Mosaic and Davidic connotations,[65] a feature shared with the other Synoptic gospels, as well, especially with Mark.[66] One can note, for example, the linguistic connection between Jesus and Moses in Luke 9:31 (Jesus and his ἔξοδος),[67] while Luke 9:1-50 represents a parallel to Moses' mediation on the Sinai mountain.[68] C. F. Evans argued that the order and content of

---

64 Swartley, *Scripture Tradition*, p. 185, n. 86. See, also, P. W. Walaskay, *"And So We Came To Rome": The Political Perspective of St. Luke* (Cambridge: Cambridge UP, 1983); S. Safrai, 'Pilgrimage to Jerusalem at the End of the Second Temple Period', in O. Michel *et al.* (eds.), *Studies on the Jewish Background of the New Testament* (Assen: Gorcum, 1974), 184-215.

65 Among the them the Sinai and Exodus parallels (law and leadership through the desert), the conquering of the promised land (Deuteronomy and Joshua), the Kingship theme; see Swartley, *Scripture Traditions*, pp. 259-292; Denaux, 'OT Models', pp. 275-297. These correspondences stand in contrast with A. D. Baum's observation that, since Luke's geography in the Central Section is vague, the associated *Theologie* must also be vague (Baum, *Lukas als Historiker der letzten Jesusreise* (Zürich: Brockhaus, 1993), p. 380).

66 R. E. Watts, 'The Influence of the Isaianic New Exodus on the Gospel of Mark', Cambridge University (1990), PhD thesis; W. M. Swartley, 'The Structural Function of the Term 'Way' (Hodos) in Mark's Gospel', in W. Klassen (ed.), *The New Way of Jesus: Essays Presented to Howard Charles* (Newton, KA: Faith and Life, 1980), 73-86.

67 ἔξοδος is regarded as a Lukan pun suggesting both death and departure to heaven (*cf.* Lk. 9:51, ἀνάλημψις; see Strauss, *Davidic Messiah*, p. 271). For the linguistic parallels see Fitzmyer, *Luke I-IX*, p. 794; S. H. Ringe, 'Luke 9:28-36: The Beginning of an Exodus', in M. A. Tolbert (ed.), *Semeia 28: The Bible and Feminist Hermeneutics* (Missoula, MT: Scholars, 1983), 83-99, esp. p. 96. D. P. Moessner, 'Luke 9.1-50: Luke's Preview of the Journey of the Prophet Like Moses of Deuteronomy', *JBL* 102 (1983), 575-605, and *idem, Lord*, pp. 45-48.

68 Moessner, *Lord*, pp. 60, 84. Moessner follows O. H. Steck's model of Israel's rejection of the prophets and subsequent exile (Steck, *Israel*

the teaching in Luke 10:1-18:14 corresponds passage by passage with Deuteronomy 1-26;[69] this lectionary-type of correspondence was received with skepticism, however.[70] Moessner suggested, in place, a rather loose correspondence, centred on two pivotal passages, Luke 9:1-50 and Acts 6:1-9:31.[71]

Anticipation of Fulfilment	Fulfilment of Heilsgeschichte	Extension of Fulfilment
Galilee	Jerusalem	Rome
Lk. 1:1——9:1-50————	——Acts 6:1-9:31————	——28:31
Galilee → Jerusalem	Jerusalem → Nations	

Through the Death of
the Prophet like Moses at Jerusalem

However, if the Mosaic pattern is reflected in Jesus' journey to Jerusalem, in the gospel, Acts seems dominated by a different pattern, by the conquest and persecution paradigm

(1) Acts 1:16-5:42 - Celebrating Pentecost (pilgrimage journeys);
(2) Acts 6:1-9:31 - Hellenistic evangelism (and journeying);
(3) Acts 9:32-12:25 - Peter's initiatory journeys to the Gentiles;

---

und das gewaltsame Geschick der Propheten (Neukirchen: Neukirchener, 1967); cf. Strauss, *Davidic Messiah*, pp. 276-84; Turner, *Power*, p. 246). However, Luke's journey and Jesus' role do not correspond flawlessly to a Mosaic model (cf. Strauss, *Davidic Messiah*, p. 246, n. 100; esp., P. F. Feiler, 'Jesus the Prophet: The Lucan Portrayal of Jesus as the Prophet like Moses', Princeton Theological Seminary (1986), PhD thesis, pp. 196-207).

69 C. F. Evans, 'The Central Section of St. Luke's Gospel', in D. E. Nineham (ed.), *Studies in the Gospels* (Oxford: Blackwell, 1957), pp. 37-53.
70 Swartley, *Scripture Traditions*, p. 130; cf. pp. 130-132. For a detailed critique of C. F. Evans, see Blomberg, 'Midrash', pp. 221-228; Strauss, *Davidic Messiah*, pp. 275-276; also, M. Nola, 'Towards a Positive Understanding of the Structure of Luke-Acts', Aberdeen University (1987), PhD thesis, pp. 10-54.
71 Moessner, *Lord*, pp. 294, 296-297, 325; 260; Denaux, 'OT Models', pp. 281-283)

(4) Acts 13:1-15:35 - Paul's first journeying, with Barnabas;
(5) Acts 15:36-19:20 - Paul's missionary journeys, with Silas;
(6) Acts 19:21-28:31 - Paul's imprisonment journey to Rome.

The list above represents, in fact, an alternative structure for Acts, since each of these sections is a thematic whole and ends with a summary description (5:42; 9:31; 12:24-25; 15:35; 19:20; 28:30-31).[72]

On the whole, this Mosaic reading of Luke-Acts based on Jesus-Moses parallelism and on the journey motif, raises a few issues. First, one could note that Luke's *hodos* encounters come with various, different OT emphases, not only with Mosaic connotations: Jesus as the Servant of the Lord, Jesus the Suffering Messiah, the Davidic king, Jesus the Revolutionary, etc. Second, the journey perspective broadens in the Lukan narrative, in contrast to the OT perspectives: Jerusalem or Palestine as destinations are replaced by a more comprehensive agenda that takes the disciples 'to the ends of the earth' (Acts 1:8).

The Isaianic New Exodus and Jesus as the Davidic Messiah

As noted, Luke's journeying theology reflects not only the Deuteronomic paradigm, yet, as well, the New Exodus patterns from Isaiah and the Prophets. This is a line that identifies Jesus not so much as the prophet like Moses, but as the Davidic Messiah.[73]

---

[72] Moessner, *Lord*, pp. 296-297; F. V. Filson has roughly the same journey divisions ('The Journey Motif in Luke-Acts', in W. W. Gasque and R. P. Martin (eds.), *Apostolic History and the Gospel: Biblical and Historical Essays Presented to F. F. Bruce on His 60th Birthday* (Grand Rapids, MI: Eerdmans, 1970), 68-77, pp. 72-73).

[73] Strauss, *Davidic Messiah*, p. 297. With a problematic turn of argument he rejects T. Holtz's claims while still using the latter's hypothesis to argue that 'Luke had a greater interest in the prophecies of Isaiah than in the book of Deuteronomy' (Strauss, *Davidic Messiah*, p. 298; *cf.* T. Holtz, *Untersuchungen über die alttestamentlichen Zitate bei Lukas* (Berlin: Akademie, 1968). In a *SBL* review, Oct. 1996, D. Juel has raised a number of issues regarding this way of assessing Luke's use of OT texts, because it gives an exaggerated role 'to the exegesis of these texts by OT scholars than to the way they were read in post-biblical Judaism, as reconstructed by scholars in that field' (*cf.* D. Juel, review of M. L. Strauss, *The Davidic Messiah in Luke-Acts: The Promise and*

From this perspective, Jesus' messianic journey starts earlier than Luke 9:51 and this New Exodus encompasses the whole 'way' of Jesus (Lk. 1:76; 3:4; 7:27) 'from the commencement of his public ministry, in Nazareth, to its climax in Jerusalem, including Jesus' death, resurrection, ascension and exaltation'.[74] At the same time, the New Exodus imagery goes even *beyond* Jesus' journey to Jerusalem. For example, Boismard is confident that in the Ethiopian's conversion, Acts 8:25-40, the themes of the road, the desert, the water, and the motif of rejoicing, are all imported from Isaiah 35:1-10. The fact that the story of the Ethiopian has three *hodos* mentions in Acts 8:26, 36 and 39c, is not by chance at all ('pas un hasard'), for in Isaiah 35:8 the prophet uses it three times, as well.[75]

Further, it is interesting to note that the New Exodus is associated with the Isaianic motif of judicial blindness and deafness (*cf.* Is. 2:20, 30:22; 31:17. 44:17ff.; in Is. 44:9-19 (20), 44:18 - יבינו ולא; לא ידעו ולא; Ps. 115:4-8 and Ps. 135:15-18)[76] which includes the motif of restoration of sight and of understanding (Yahweh will blind the people - Is. 6:9, Is. 1:3,

---

Its Fulfillment in Lukan Christology, Review of Biblical Literature, http://www.bookreviews.org (2000), see Strauss, *op. cit.*, p. 242; Also J. Jeremias, and W. Zimmerly, 'παῖς θεοῦ', *TDNT*, vol. 5, 654-717, esp. p. 686). The first-century rabbis may have not expounded the passages in context, in contrast with Strauss' assumption (*op.cit.*, p. 242, esp. n. 4). As regards Luke's use of LXX, see also W. D. Litke, 'Luke's knowledge of the Septuagint: A Study of the Citations in Luke-Acts', McMaster University, Canada (1993), PhD thesis; Bock, *Proclamation*, p. 16; W. G. Most, 'Did St. Luke Imitate the Septuagint?', *JSNT* 15 (1982), 30-41, etc.

74 Strauss, *Davidic Messiah*, p. 303. Similarly, E. E. Ellis, *The Gospel of Luke* (London: Marshall, 1974, p. 148; *cf.* J. R. Dongel, 'The Structure of Luke's Gospel', Union Theological Seminary, Virginia (1991), PhD thesis. For É. Samain, the journey section starts with the Nazareth sermon (Lk. 4:29-30), is forcefully re-started at 9:51, to continue as far as Acts 2:1, see 'L'évangile de Luc et le livre des Actes: éléments de composition et de structure', *Foi et Vie* 70 (1971) 3-24; and, *idem*, 'Le récit lucanien du voyage de Jésus vers Jérusalem. Quelques études récentes', in *Foi et Vie* 72 (1973), 3-23, in Denaux, 'Delineation', p. 368).

75 M.-É. Boismard, and A. Lamouille, *Les Actes des Deux Apôtres: Le Sens des Récits* (Paris: Gabalda, 1990), vol. 2, pp. 180-181.

76 Watts, 'Consolation', pp. 44-47.

5:13a; cf. the use of γιγνώσκειν, συνίειν, ἰδεῖν, but he will also restore their sight, Is. 10:10; 30:20ff.; 29:9-16; 28:9-14; 35, etc.).[77] This link introduces the possibility that Luke's post-Easter accounts can be read according to a New Exodus hermeneutical key, a hypothesis with significant implications for Luke's *hodos* paradigm.

Indeed, there is an 'eye and recognition' chiasmus in Luke 24:16, 31a, and the motif of 'seeing' is present in the whole of Luke's gospel (Lk. 2:30; 4:20; 6:39-42; 10:23; 11:34; 18:35-42; 19:42, and Lk. 24:16, 31). Similarly, it occurs in Acts, in the disappearance of Philip; in the story of Saul's conversion – cf. Acts 9, 22, 26; and of Paul's confrontation with Elymas, the sorcerer (Acts 13:4-12) which echoes in a twisted way Paul's own experience on the Damascus road (cf. the association between the sight motif and that of 'making crooked the straight paths of the Lord [διαστρέφων τὰς ὁδοὺς τοῦ κυρίου]').[78]

One of the valid objections, however, against such a reading of Luke's *hodos* encounters, is that *seeing* Jesus and *understanding* the Scriptures do not correspond entirely to all the details of Isaiah's scheme of divine punishment-and-healing (apart from the account of Saul's conversion). Thus, the Ethiopian finds himself in a full process of seeking understanding and finding meaning;[79] he is a victim restaured not a backsliding believer who regains acceptance in the people of God. Further, in the Emmaus story, the two despondent disciples, are not punished for leaving Yahweh, in any way, so that their recovery of sight could be interpreted as a reward for obedience; their journey is not described as a sinful journey that needs to be stopped and reversed, either. Apart from that, the veiling of the eyes, during the journey, coexists with the 'opening' of the νοῦς[80] and preceeds the full disclosure of Jesus' identity at the table.

A number of details suggest, further, that Luke's source in these stories was not the New Exodus paradigm, at least not exclusively. The sight motif suggests a Hellenistic influence,

---

77 Watts, *Influence*, pp. 102-112.
78 Just, *Feast*, pp. 64-68.
79 Johnson, *Luke*, p. 399.
80 Guillaume, *Luc interprète*, p. 78. See Lk. 24:27 (διερμήνευσεν), 24:32 (διήνοιγεν); 24:45 (διήνοιξεν); Acts 16:14 (διήνοιξεν).

as well. Thus, the disappearance mentioned in Luke 24:31, ἄφαντος (a *hapax legomenon* in the NT) is unknown to the Septuagint, and as Ehrhardt notes 'linguistically we are faced in our story with material which is alien to biblical diction'.[81] Here, Luke's Hellenistic environment (Asia Minor and Syria) seems to have encouraged him to use certain paradigms characteristic of the *theios anēr* exploits.[82]

Luke's use of Isaiah seems to emphasise, as well, other messianic themes, distinct from the New Exodus, although associated with it. In the Emmaus 'road' encounter, for example, one notes the motifs of the Suffering Servant, as mentioned earlier, and very probably, that of a Maccabean Messiah (the Messiah as political and military leader). The Ethiopian's conversion includes, similarly, the motif of the Suffering Servant (*cf.* Is. 53:7-8 in Acts 8:32-33). In Saul's encounter one meets again the Davidic theme of persecution and salvation, and, as well, the Mosaic motif of receiving a divine revelation while being 'on the way' (*cf.* the burning bush scene, the Sinai revelation, etc.).

As a conclusion, even if the New Exodus theme shapes the heart of Isaiah 40-55 to an extent that would replace 'the first Exodus as *the* saving event',[83] this does not imply that the 'Exodus motif is *the* controlling theme of Luke's work',[84] and,

---

81   Ehrhardt, 'Disciples', p. 185; *cf.* pp. 183-184. However, similar phrases are found in 2 Macc. 3:32-34, ἐφάνησαν and ἀφανεῖς ἐγένοντο. On divine 'translations' in Hellenistic literature and early charismatic stories, see also Dillon, *Eye-Witnesses*, p. 153; W. Grundmann, *Das Evangelium nach Lukas* (Berlin: Evangelische Verlagsanstalt, 1961), p. 447; Guillaume, *Luc interprète*, p. 89, etc.

82   Repo, *Weg*, pp. 160-166. Parallels from Qumran support this hypothesis (p. 160). John, Luke and Paul ministered among the Christians in that area - they are the main NT authors who use the Way as a 'high' metaphor. If for Matthew the Way has heavy ethical connotations, in Luke's case there are a couple of other aspects, as well, associated with the Hellenistic culture of Syria and Asia Minor. For example, the Way and the geographical perspective (journeying to the ends of the earth, in the Mediterranean area, etc.), plus a theology of *theios anēr* 'who appears and disappears at will' (*cf.* Pervo, *Profit*, p. 71; R. H. Fuller, *The Formation of the Resurrection Narratives* (Philadelphia, PA: Fortress, 1980), p. 106).

83   Watts, 'Consolation', p. 33.

84   Strauss, *Davidic Messiah*, p. 304.

therefore, a more comprehensive assessment of Luke's *hodos* stories needs to take into account other sources, as well.

Christ as the Way: the Emergence of a *Hodos* Christology

Repo's analysis is well-known, in particular, for his suggestion of a comprehensive *hodos* Christology in the NT (esp. in Luke-Acts), which, according to him, reflects an early 'urchristlichen Hodosdenken'. Coordinating the references where Jesus identifies himself with Christians who belong to the Way (Acts 9:1-2, 5; 22:4) with the texts where the Way and (or) Christ are denigrated - κακολογεῖν τὴν ὁδόν and κακολογεῖν με (*i.e.*, Χριστόν) - in Acts 16:17 (*cf.* Mk. 15:29; see οἱ βλασφημοῦντες τὴν ὁδόν, Heb. 13:13), and, further, with texts where Christ is presented as the Way (Heb. 10:20, Jn. 14:4-6), Repo concludes that the whole of the NT displays an early Christian attempt to identify Christ as the Way, which implies an incipient '*hodos* - Christology'

> Die Christologie jener urchristlichen Kreise, in denen die Wegmetapher direkt auf Jesus bezogen wurde, könnte man mit gutem Grund Hodoslogie bzw Hodos-Christologie (vgl. Logos-Christologie) nennen.[85]

Despite the fact that a *hodos* Christology seems to cohere with the synoptic portrait of Jesus as a peripatetic Messiah who performs miracles and teaches 'on the way',[86] as well as with Jesus' own testimony in John 14:6, Repo's suggestion of a developed *hodos* NT Christology, where Christians are the *hodos*-members of the *hodos*-Christ (Acts 9:2), has been regarded with skepticism. For example, S. Brown called it 'pure fantasy',[87] and Bovon was not entirely convinced of his arguments.[88] Repo's study, however, has rightly pointed out that in its process of idealization the Way metaphor developed specific Christian connotations, which appear to coagulate in

---

85 Repo, *Weg*, pp. 183-184, *cf.* pp. 187-189.
86 Repo, *Weg*, p. 185.
87 S. Brown, *Apostasy and Perseverance in the Theology of Luke* (Rome: PBI, 1969), p. 142.
88 Repo, *Weg*, pp. 183-184. Bovon would accept the idea of a primitive *Hodos*-Christology yet with certain objections: 'theologically, we have no doubts, but philologically, a question mark remains' (*Luke the Theologian*, p. 322).

the form of a new Christology. Luke's *hodos* encounters might, thus, be seen as integrated parts of such an emergent theology of the Way, based on both OT and Greco-Roman paradigms and on the specific connotations of the Christ-event.

GRECO-ROMAN CONNOTATIONS OF THE WAY
There is a certain tendency among the NT scholars to consider the Essene use of the Way as the major source or background for Luke's 'way' in Acts.[89] The increasingly persuasive portrait of Luke as a Hellenistic writer, however, makes it plausible that the Greco-Roman use of the Way metaphor could have influenced him, as well.[90] The Hellenistic imagery included external symbols such as roads, journeys, one's course of life, adventure, and, as well, internalised symbols such as mystic initiations, wisdom, happiness, all being able to enrich and inspire Luke's use of journey paradigms.[91]

The Way as Solemn Procession
One of the interesting connotations of the Way, for a Greek mind, was the imagery of an initiatory procession, as in the

---

[89] There is also a Hellenistic Jewish component and an OT specific usage, different from Qumran (Hengel, on Repo in *TLZ* 92 (1967), 361-364, esp. p. 364).

[90] *Cf.* W. Jaeger, *The Theology of the Early Greek Philosophers* (Oxford: Clarendon, 1947); idem, *Early Christianity and Greek Paideia* (Cambridge, MA: Harvard UP, 1961); also, O. Becker, *Das Bild des Weges und verwandte Vorstellung im frühgriechischen Denken* (Berlin: Weidmann, 1937). In spite of referring to these studies, Conzelmann is deeply skeptical of a Greek background for Luke's use of hodos in Acts 9:1, 19:9, 23; 22:4; 24:14, 22; *cf.* Acts, p. 71; Bovon, Luke the Theologian, p. 468, n. 19.

[91] Ø. Andersen and V. K. Robbins, 'Paradigms in Homer, Pindar, the Tragedians and the New Testament', in V. K. Robbins (ed.), *Semeia 64: The Rhetoric of Pronouncement* (Missoula, MT: Scholars, 1994), 3-31, p. 29). They note that 'the way in which they [NT writers] engage in paradigmatic argumentation, however, has amazing similarities with the way in which paradigmatic argumentation was being employed throughout Mediterranean culture' (p. 29). For Luke, *cf.* the case of the sign of Jonah (Lk. 11:14-36; Mt. 12:38-42); the Queen of the South (Lk. 11:31; Mt. 12:12); the Elijah and Elisha references (Lk. 4:16-30); Abraham's exploits (Acts 7:28); the patriarchs' lives (Acts 7:9-16); Moses (Acts 7:17-44); Joshua (Acts 7:45); David (Acts 7:46); Solomon (Acts 7:47), etc.

Eleusinian celebrations.⁹² The sacred objects were brought from Eleusis to the Athens' Eleusinium in a special procession on the first day of initiation. On the second day another special procession went to the sea for purification, followed by two days of sacrifices. The fifth day included a climactic procession starting from Athens in the early morning and bringing back to Eleusis the sacred objects (ιηρα).⁹³ In the sixth, the statue of Iacchus was solemnly carried from Ceramicus to Eleusis. The way they went out from the city was called the 'sacred way', ἱεριε ὁδός, and the multitudes halted for a rest in the place called 'of the sacred fig tree', ἱεριε συκῆ. Finally, they entered Eleusis by a special entrance known as the μυστικὴ εἴσοδος. Such journeys were readily used by Christians as a parallel with the idea of a sacred journey of Jesus to Jerusalem, and of Christ as the true hierophant.⁹⁴

The Motif of the Honored, Journeying Hero
In the earliest examples of Greek literature, in Homer's writings, the Way has various mundane meanings as 'way' or 'street',⁹⁵ 'course', 'journey' or 'military march'.⁹⁶ However,

---

92 M. R. Brown, 'Eleusinian Mysteries', in P. K. Meagher, Th. O'Brien, C. M. Aherne (eds.), *Encyclopedic Dictionary of Religion* (Washington DC: Corpus Publication, vol. A-E, 1979), p. 1179; F. Graf, 'Eleusinian Mysteries', in M. Eliade (ed.), *The Encyclopedia of Religion* (London: Macmillan, 1987), vol. 5, 83-85; M. Eliade, *A History of Religious Ideas* (London: Collins, 1979), vol. 1, p. 294; also J. Lemprière, *Classical Dictionary* (London: Brackens, 1994), pp. 447-448. The casual visitors to the Eleusinian processions were informed at arrival about their significance through guidebooks like *The Sacred Way* of Polemo of Ilium (*ca.* 300 BC) (L. Casson, *Travel in the Ancient World* (Baltimore, MA: John Hopkins UP, 1994), p. 294).
93 Eliade, *Religious Ideas*, p. 294.
94 In his *Protrepticus* 3.1.12.120.11-12, after speaking of Eleusis, Clement of Alexandria refers to Christ as 'the true hierophant' (ὡ τῶν ἁγίον ὡς ἀληθῶς μυστηρίον... ἅγιος γίνομαι μυούμενος ἱεροφαντεῖ δὲ ὁ κύριος), the great priest and demiurgos (οὗτος ᾽Ιησοῦς εἰς ὁ μέγας ἀρχιερεὺς θεοῦ ... ὧν ἐγὼ δημιουργὸς θελήματι πατρός). In *Protrepticus* 3.1.12.120.14-15, Clement points out that all these were illustrations but Christ is the archetype that should be followed, ὡ πᾶσαι μὲν εἰκόνες οὐ πᾶσαι δὲ ἐμφερεῖς· διορθώσασθαι ὑμᾶς πρὸς τὸ ἀρχετύπον βούλομαι, ἵνα μοι καὶ ὅμοιοι γένησθη.
95 Homer, *Iliad*, 7.340: 'a way for the driving of chariots'.

there is a tendency towards metaphor, as well, especially in the description of heroes' adventures. For example, journeying together brings 'unity of thinking', ἥδε δ᾽ ὁδός καὶ μᾶλλον ὁμοφροσύνῃσιν ἐνήσει, and successful heroes don't delay their journeys yet embark on them under divine guidance.[97] In Pindar the idea of journeying occurs in various forms, as well; thus, heroic virtues are sung in 'kingly words and ways' or in 'authoritative speech', as for the descendants of Aegina and Zeus, θρασύ μοι τόδ᾽ εἰπεῖν φαενναῖς ἀρεταῖς ὁδὸν κυρίαν λόγων οἴκοθεν;[98] or, shown to everyone to see them, as for the sons of Iamus, who, by honoring virtue, came to 'pass along a shining road', τιμῶντες δ᾽ ἀρετὰς ἐξ φανερὰν ὁδὸν ἔρχονται.[99] Greek gods grant protection and reward heroes, so that, with them 'there are many paths of prosperity', πολλαὶ δ᾽ ὁδοὶ σὺν θεοῖς εὐπραγίας,[100] and 'swift is the achievement, short are the ways of gods, when bent on speed', ὠκεῖα δ᾽ ἐπειγομένων ἤδη θεῶν πρᾶξις ὁδοί τε βραχεῖαι.[101]

The Path to Ethical Ideals

Particularly worth noting is W. Jaeger's suggestion that the Way represented a coherent religious concept in Hellenistic

---

96   Homer, *Odyssey*, 2.256, 273, 285, 404. In general, the 'way' is used with various meanings and grammatical forms. For example, ὁδοιπορίην: *The Hymn to Hermes*, 85-86 (ἔσπασε Πιερίηθεν ὁδοιπορίην ἀλεείνων, διά τ᾽ ἐπειγόμενος δολιχὴν ὁδόν, αὐτοτροπήσας); or, ὁδοιπορίον, in *Odyssey*, 15.506; or ὁδοιπόρον, in *Iliad*, 24.375; ὁδεύειν, in *Iliad*, 11.568, etc.
97   Homer, *Odyssey*, 2.273: οὔ τοι ἔπειθ᾽ ἁλίη ὁδὸς ἔσσεται οὐδ᾽ ἀτέλεστος, 'So then shall this journey of thine be neither vain nor unfulfilled' - 2.285: σοι δ᾽ ὁδὸς οὐκέτι δηρὸν ἀπέσσεται, ἣν σὺ μενοινᾷς, 'but for thyself, the journey on which thy heart is set shall not be long delayed'; 4.480: καὶ τότε τοι δώσουσιν ὁδὸν θεοί, ἣν σὺ μενοινᾷς, 'Then at length shall the gods grant thee the journey thou desirest';7.30: ἐγὼ δ᾽ ὁδοῦ ἡγερμονεύσω, 'I will lead the way (Athene Pallas) - 8.150: σοι δ᾽ ὁδὸς οὐκέτι δηρὸν ἀπέσσεται, ἀλλά τοι ἤδη, 'Thy journey shall no more be long delayed', etc.
98   Pindar, *Nemean Odes*, 7.50-51 (J. Sandys). Also, H. Maehler (ed.), *Pindari Carmina cum Fragmentis* (pars I-II) (Leipzig: Teubner, 1987-1989); W. J. Slater (ed.), *Lexicon to Pindar* (Berlin: Gruyter, 1969).
99   Pindar, *Olympian Odes*, 6.71-73. φανερὰν ὁδὸν can be translated also as 'public path', or 'a path that is seen by all'.
100 Pindar, *Olympian Odes*, 8.13.
101 Pindar, *Pythian Odes*, 9.68.

thinking.[102] He built his argument on a general assessment of the Greek pairs of opposites in relation to the Way (e.g., the two ways of darkness and light, of truth and lie, etc.)[103] and of Parmenides' references to the way as a 'way of inquiry',[104] 'the right way to truth' and 'the way of god / goddess',[105] which is 'the way [which] leads him who knows unscathed wherever he goes', ὁδὸν βῆσαν πολύφημον ἄγουσαι δαίμονες, ἣ κατὰ πάντ' ἄστη φέρει εἰδότα φῶτα, κτλ.[106]

Apart from that, Plato is known, as well, for a number of famous references to the way imagery, such as the philosopher's journey to light.[107] Christian Gnostic texts described later the human soul and life in similar terms as a journeying from pre-existence in heaven to earthly life, at birth,[108] and from earth to God's heaven, at death.[109]

The way imagery and its links with immortality or death have, in fact, a long tradition in Greek literature. For example, Homer writes about the 'road of the immortals', ἀθανάτων

---

102 Jaeger, *Theology*, pp. 91-108, 134-135. See, also Becker, *Das Bild des Weges*.
103 On the two ways of the good and evil souls, after death, see Plato who speaks of 'judgement in the meadow at the dividing of the road, whence are the two ways leading one to the Isles of the Blest and the other to Tartarus' (*Gorgias*, 524a.3-4; *cf. Rep.* 614c; Pindar, *Olympian Odes*, 2.60-80).
104 Parmenides, *Fragmenta*, 6.10, 7.2, ἀφ' ὁδοῦ ταύτῃ διζήσιος.
105 Parmenides, *Frg.* 8.17-18, οὐ γὰρ ἀληθής ἐστι ὁδός. See *Frg.* 1.8, κατὰ... ὁδὸν τοῦ δαίμονος, *Frg* 1.12, ἐπὶ τὴν ἁπάντων ὁδηγεῖ γνῶσιν, κτλ.
106 Parmenides, *Frg.* 1.26, with a translation by Jaeger (*Theology*, pp. 98-99; also p. 225, n. 20, 23). Parmenides' way metaphors include 'the way to truth' or 'the way to celestial light', as noted by Michaelis, 'ὁδός', p. 47.
107 Plato, *Rep.* 514-518b.
108 *The Naasene hymn*, in Hippolytus, *Ref.* 5.16: τὰς ὁδούς, δι' ὧν εἰσελήλυθεν ὁ ἄνθρωπος εἰς τὸν κόσμον ἀκριβῶς δὲ διδαγμῆνοι, κτλ (as cited by R. Bultmann, 'Die Bedeutung der neuerschlossenen mandäischen und manichäischen Quellen für das Verständnis des Johannesevangeliums', *ZNW* 24 (1925), 100-146, p. 134).
109 *The Naasene hymn*, in Hippolytus, *Ref.* 5.10, with Jesus' proclamation: σφραγῖδας ἔχων καταβήσομαι, αἰῶνας ὅλους διοδεύσω, μυστήρια δ' ἀνοίξω, μορφὰς δὲ θεῶν ἐπιδείξω, τὰ κεκρυμμένα τῆς ἁγίας ὁδοῦ, γνῶσιν καλέσας, παραδώσω (in Bultmann, 'Mandäischen und manichäischen Quellen', p. 134).

ὁδός,[110] and Pindar uses similar metaphors such as 'the way of truth known by the mortal man', εἰ δὲ νόῳ τις ἔχει θνατῶν ἀλαθείας ὁδόν,[111] or σοφίας ὁδόν, 'the way of wisdom'.[112]

The common course of human life was described as a 'way' or 'journey' in various contexts. For Democritus, for example, 'a life without leisure is like a long road without a place for rest', βίος ἀνεόρταστος μακρὴ ὁδὸς ἀπανδόκευτος.[113] Thales of Miletus and Anacharsis, the Scythian, are said to have taught their pupils a Homeric way of life, ὁδόν τινα παρέδοσαν βίου Ὁμηρίκην.[114] Similarly, Isocrates writes about 'those who travelled this life's road', ὅσοι τοῦ βίου ταύτην τὴν ὁδὸν ἐπορεύθησαν.[115]

The imagery of life as a journey or as a road was often accompanied by motifs of ethical choice. For many classical authors the ethical ideal in life was that the 'middle way' (μέση ὁδός). For example, one of Xenophon's characters, Aristippus, favours explicitly such a middle way between living as a ruler (inclined to tyranny) and living as a slave (subject to lack of self-control): 'There is, as I hold, a middle path'.[116] The ideal of the 'middle path' is also characteristically present in

---

110 Homer, *Odyssey*, 13.112: οὐδέ τι κείνῃ ἄνδρες ἐσέρχονται, ἀλλ ἀθανάτων ὁδός ἐστιν, 'not do men enter thereby; it is the way of the immortals'; similarly, Pindar, *Dithyramb*, 4.18.
111 Pindar, *Pythian Ode*, 3.103.
112 Pindar, *Paean Ode*, 7.15; *cf.* 'thou hast perplexed the power of man and the way of wisdom' (a prayer to the sun) ἔθηκας ἀμάχανον ἰσχύν τ' ἄνδρασι καὶ σοφίας ὁδόν (Pindar, *Paean Ode*, 9.4).
113 Democritus, *Fragmenta*, 230.1.
114 Plato, *Rep*. 600a.
115 Isocrates, *To Demonicus*, 5.5. Among the multiple connotations of ὁδός one can mention that of 'conduct' or 'method', or 'measure' of life, as well. καθ' ὁδόν meant 'methodically', *cf.* Plato, *Phaedrus*, 263b: 'he who is to develop an act of rhetoric must first make a methodical division', πρῶτον μεδεῖ ταῦτα ὁδῷ διῃρῆσθαι; or, in Plato, *Rep*. 435a: 'that seems a sound method and that is what we must do', καθ' ὁδόν τε λέγεις καὶ ποιεῖν χρὴ οὕτως (Michaelis, 'ὁδός', p. 43). In a number of papyri of the first and early second century AD ὁδός has a juridical meaning: *P. Lond.* 897.10 (84 AD): εὑρηκὼς τινα ὁδὸν γράψον μοι - 'procedure', 'means'; *P. Tor.* I.6.13 (116 BC): κατὰ νόμους ὁδῶι πορεύμενος - 'taking the legal path' (see, on ὁδός and μέθοδος, Jaeger, *Theology*, p. 98; *cf.* Michaelis, *ad.loc.*).
116 Xenophon, *Memorabilia*, 2.1.1.

Aristotle's *Nicomachean Ethics*, who recommends it both in arts and in virtues.[117]

The way as a setting for ethical choice (or as a manner of life resulting from an ethical choice) provides several parallels to the NT parables of the Two Ways, Two Gates or Two Doors (*cf.* Mt. 17:13-16, Lk. 13:24-25, see chapter three). For example, in the *Cynic Epistles*, Diogenes writes that

> Just as we do toward philosophy, the masses hasten eagerly toward what they think is happiness, whenever they hear of a short cut leading to it. But when they come up to the road [ἐπὶ τὴν ὁδόν] and survey its ruggedness, they draw back as though they were sick.[118]

As illustrated by Plato, one of the recurring Hellenistic stories is that of a young person who has to decide as 'a man who has come to a crossroads and is not quite sure of his way' (καθάπερ ἐν τριόδῳ γενόμενος καὶ μὴ σφόδρα κατειδὼς ὁδόν), be it that he journeys alone or with company (εἴτε μόνος εἴτε μετ' ἄλλων τύχοι πορευόμενος), needing to question others or himself on what is the truly good direction in life (τῆς πορείας).[119] This literary and philosophical *topos* was often visited by the Hellenistic authors, occurring, for example in Prodicus' fable of Heracles at the 'crossroads', and in other legendary moments in the life of Heracles.[120] The Cynic Epistles provide a number of interesting parallels, too.[121] For

---

117 Aristotle, *The Nicomachean Ethic*, 2.6.8-10, 2.6.13-16; 2.7.7, 2.7.12. See, for example, that for Aristotle 'virtue, therefore is a mean state in the sense that it is able to hit the mean', μεσότης τις ἄρα ἐστὶ ἡ ἀρετὴ στοχαστικὴ γε οὖσα τοῦ μέσου (2.6.13-14). The mean is the best amount for humans to experience in any sort of experiences, a mark of virtue, τὸ δ' ὅτε δεῖ καὶ ἐφ' οἷς καὶ πρὸς οὕς καὶ οὗ ἕνεκα καὶ ὡς δεῖ, μέσον τε καὶ ἄριστον, ὅπερ ἐστὶ τῆς ἀρετῆς (2.6.12). See further, on Heracles' paradigm, chapter two of the present study.
118 'Diogenes to Hipparchia', in A. J. Malherbe, *The Cynic Epistles* (Missoula, MT: Scholars, 1977), p. 107. Crates writes to Metrocles the Cynic that 'the way that leads to happiness through words is long', μακρὰ γὰρ διὰ τῶν λόγων ὁδὸς ἐπ' εὐδαιμονίαν ('Crates to Metrocles the Cynic', *Cynic Epistles*, p. 71).
119 Plato, *Laws*, 799c-d.
120 Xenophon, *Memorabilia*, 2.1.22-34; Dio Chrysostomus, *Discourses*, 4.73-75; Epictetus, *Dissertationes ab Arriano digestae*, 2.16.44-45.
121 'Diogenes to Hicetas' and 'Diogenes to Monimus', in Malherbe, *Cynic Epistles*, pp. 131-133, 155-159.

example, in the letter to Hicetas, Diogenes presents Socrates as lecturing on the two ways to happiness, one short, steep and difficult, the other, smooth and easy (the two contrasting pathways to the Acropolis).[122] In Diogenes' letter to Monimus, the author meets 'on the road' (κατὰ τὴν ὁδόν) a certain Lacydes who invites him to his home, and among the subjects discussed at the table is the steep and rugged 'road leading to happiness' (μίαν ὁδὸν προσάντη καὶ τραχεῖαν), a road of choice and determination.[123] In another letter to Monimus, Diogenes warns those who do not prepare themselves for death, that they would labour 'a great deal along the way [ἐν τῇ ὁδῷ]', journeying without a guide, exposed to great dangers.[124]

Redaction Criticism and Luke's *Reisenotizen*

In spite of such rich cultural connotations of the Way, redactional approaches focused mainly on Luke's *Reisenotizen* in Luke 9-19. One of the main reasons for such an emphasis was Mark's use of the Way motif and the prominence of Jesus' journey to Jerusalem in the theology of the third gospel.

Mark's Journeying Motif and Luke's Reisenotizen

The starting point in interpreting Jesus' *Reisenotizen*, as intimated, is the synoptic context, specifically the gospel of Mark.[125] Evolving from strict editorial criticism to a criticism of composition,[126] redactional studies led to the conclusion that Luke also 'reveals his theology by the way in which he organizes, arranges, or structures his gospel'.[127] One of these

---

122 'Diogenes to Hicetas', 5-20, p. 131.
123 'Diogenes to Monimus', 10-25, p. 157.
124 Another letter 'Diogenes to Monimus', 15-20, in Malherbe, *Cynic Epistles*, pp. 165-167.
125 M. A. Tolbert, *Sowing the Word: Mark's World in Literary-Historical Perspective* (Minneapolis, MN: Fortress, 1989), p. 27; E. Haenchen, *Der Weg Jesu: Eine Erklärung des Markus-evangeliums und der kanonischen Parallelen* (Berlin: Gruyter, 1968).
126 J. R. Donahue, 'Redaction Criticism: Has the *Hauptstrasse* Become a *Sackgasse*?', in E. S. Malbon and E. V. McKnight (eds.), *The New Literary Criticism and the New Testament* (Sheffield: Sheffield Academical, 1994), 27-57.
127 Denaux, 'Delineation', p. 358; W. E. Hull, 'A Structural Analysis of the Gospel of Luke', in *RevExp* 64 (1967) 421-425, p. 422, n. 4. See also C.

major structural units is Luke's Central Section, and as early as 1794 J. G. Eichhorn noted that it has a remarkable Lukan character.[128] F. D. E. Schleiermacher was among the first to use the term *Reisebericht* as reference to its redactional, composite nature 'das Ganze nicht ein ursprünglich zusammenhängender Reisebericht [ist]'.[129] W. M. L. de Wette characterised it as a compositional journey, a non-chronological and non-historical theological discourse.[130]

MARK'S AND LUKE'S USE OF THE GEOGRAPHICAL MOTIF

Regarded as a fundamental feature of his gospel, Luke's editing of the Central Section (Lk. 9-19) into a major journey was interpreted as following the journey model of Mark's corresponding section (Mk. 8-10).[131] Mark is the first to give journeying a central place in the gospel narrative, and, in general, he makes extensive use of the geographical motif. For example, he presents Jesus' ministry in a characteristic tree-part structure (the Galilean period - Mk. 1-8:26, Jesus' journey

---
A. Evans, 'Source, Form and Redaction Criticism: The "Traditional" Methods of Synoptic Interpretation', in S. E. Porter and D. Tombs (eds.), *Approaches to the New Testament Study* (Sheffield: Sheffield Academical, 1995), 17-45, p. 18.

128 J. G. Eichhorn, *Allgemeine Bibliothek der biblischen Litteratur* (Leipzig: Weidmann, 1794), vol. 5, p. 992 (cited by Baum, *Lukas*, p. 2); see also, Eichhorn, *Einleitung in das Neue Testament*, vol. 1-5 (Leipzig: Weidmann, 1804-1824).

129 F. D. E. Schleiermacher, *Über die Schriften des Lukas: ein kritischer Versuch* (Berlin: Reiner, 1817), pp. 160-161, as cited in Baum, *Jesusreise*, p. 2; in English, *Luke - A Critical Essay* (Lewiston, NY: Mellen, 1993). The idea of a composite journey has become a matter of consensus (*cf.* L. Girard, *L'Évangile des voyages de Jésus, ou la section 9:51-18:14 de Saint Luc* (Paris: Gabalda, 1951); G. Ogg, 'The Central Section of the Gospel according to St. Luke', *NTS* 18 (1971), 39-53). For further bibliography, see J. L. Resseguie, 'Interpretation of Luke's Central Section (Luke 9:51-19:44) since 1856', *SBT* 1-5 (1971-1975), 3-36; D. Gill, 'Observations on the Lukan Travel Narrative and Some Related Passages', *HTR* 63 (1970), 199-221.

130 W. M. L. de Wette, *Kurzgefasstes exegetisches Handbuch zum Neuen Testament: kurze Erklärung der Evangelien des Lukas und Markus* (Leipzig: Weidmann, 1846), vol. 1, p. 76.

131 K. L. Schmidt, *Der Rahmen der Geschichte Jesu: Literarkritische Untersuchungen zur ältesten Jesusüberlieferung* (Berlin: Trowitzsch, 1919), pp. 246-271, esp. pp. 246, 247, 269; see Robinson, *Weg*, p. 7.

to Jerusalem - Mk. 8:27-11:1, his Passion and Resurrection in Jerusalem - Mk. 11-16), and uses several *topoi* of Christological value,[132] such as the desert - ἔρημος, the way - ὁδός, the mountain - ὄρος, the house - οἶκος, the boat - πλοῖον, etc.[133] Some of these symbols are borrowed and enhanced by Luke (like the mountain and the lake), others are given less prominence (*e.g.*, the wilderness).[134]

However, Luke holds different views of geography than Mark. One example is his 'Jewish particularism' according to which he avoids mentioning Jesus' miracles in Gentile sites such as Caesarea Philippi, Idumaea, Peraea, and puts aside any reference to Phoenicia and Decapolis,[135] focusing only on Jesus' ministry in the Jewish territory (*cf*. Lk. 7:31).[136] On the one hand, he reserves Gentile evangelism for Acts, on the other hand, he is fond, indeed, of progressive presentations, on using discrete, meaningful geographical divisions in his history of the Church. Thus, Luke is characteristically 'tidying up the story' so that Peter ministers in Judaea (*cf*. Acts 9:32-11:18) and never crosses into the Paul's area,[137] and Paul's

---

[132] G. Strecker, *Theologie des Neuen Testaments* (Berlin: Gruyter, 1996), p. 364.

[133] Such *topoi* disclose Jesus' messiahship while many parables hide it (Strecker, *Theologie*, pp. 364-367; W. Wrede, *The Messianic Secret* (Cambridge: Cambridge UP, 1971); *cf*. Mk. 1:34, 44; 3:12; 5:43; 7:36; 8:26, 30; 9:9).

[134] The 'mountain' is a generic place of revelation, in Luke (Conzelmann, *Luke*, pp. 44-45; B. van Iersel, *Reading Mark* (Edinburgh: T&T Clark, 1989), p. 126). On the lake's significance, see Conzelmann, *Luke*, pp. 44-45, and for the wilderness, *cf*. U. Mauser, *Christ in the Wilderness: The Wilderness Theme in the Second Gospel and its basis in the Biblical Tradition* (London: SCM, 1963), pp. 142-148. See also R. W. Funk, 'The Wilderness', *JBL* 78 (1959), 205-214.

[135] Conzelmann, *Luke*, pp. 45-46, 53-54, 71; *cf*. E. Lohmeyer, *Galiläa und Jerusalem* (Göttingen: Vandenhoeck, 1936), p. 42.

[136] Mk. 6:46-8:27 has no parallel in Luke (V. Taylor *Behind the Third Gospel: A Study of the Proto-Luke Hypothesis* (Oxford: Clarendon, 1926), p. 171; S. G. Wilson, *The Gentiles and the Gentile Mission in Luke-Acts* (Cambridge: Cambridge UP, 1973), pp. 25-56; J. Navone, 'Three Aspects of the Lucan Theology of History', *BTB* 3 (1973), 115-132, esp. pp. 115-118; Conzelmann, *Luke*, pp. 52-54, 55).

[137] M. D. Goulder, *Luke: A New Paradigm* (Sheffield: Sheffield Academical, 1989), vol. 1, p. 437.

mission itself is presented as progressively and circularly invading the ancient Greco-Roman world.

CONZELMANN'S INTERPRETATION OF LUKE'S JOURNEY THEME
Conzelmann's assessment of Luke's motif of the Way is indivisibly linked to his views of Luke's redaction of Mark and of Luke's theological 'centre' in the gospel.[138] Based on a careful interpretation of Luke 4:21; 16:16; 22:35-37, he built a static, famous three-stage picture of Luke's history of redemption, divided in three distinct periods of time which are confirmed by a firm caesura between John the Baptist and Jesus: (a) the time of Israel; (b) the time of Jesus (characterised through a significant last journey to Jerusalem); and, finally, (c) the time of the *ecclesia pressa* (of the persecuted church).[139] In the light of Conzelmann's contribution, it became clearer that, if Luke did not create the Way motif but borrowed it from Mark, he was, however, 'the first to develop it into a *scheme*'.[140]

Contradiction and Coherence in Luke's *Reisenotizen*
An instrumental role in highlighting Jesus' journey to Jerusalem and its traditional theology was played by Luke's series of *Reisenotizen* (journey indicators), with its frequent use of πορεύομαι, ἀναβαίνω and ἐγγίζω or ἔρχομαι (*cf.* Lk. 9:51,

---

138 Conzelmann wrote *Die Mitte der Zeit* as a response to O. Cullmann, for whom Jesus represented the centre of time (*The Christology of the New Testament* (London: SCM, 1963; idem, *Salvation in History* (London: SCM, 1967); see the discussion in G. Hasel, *New Testament Theology: Basic Issues in the Current Debate* (Grand Rapids, MI: Eerdmans, 1993), pp. 148-149).
139 Conzelmann's views were anticipated by K. L. Schmidt who writes that 'Lukas *periodisiert* und *psychologisiert* hier also wie in zahlreichen früheren Fällen' (Schmidt, *Rahmen*, p. 260, on Lk. 9:51, italics mine; *cf.* also, Robinson, *Weg*, p. 27). Navone emphasizes three distinctive aspects of the Lucan theology of history: (a) his conception of the Way of the Lord, (b) the role of present time in mediating the salvation in Jesus Christ, (c) the universalism of Luke ('Three Aspects', pp. 115-118; idem, *Themes of Saint Luke* (Rome: Gregorian UP, 1970), pp. 188-198).
140 Conzelmann, *Luke*, p. 61, n. 6; p. 67 (on Lk. 10:38), italics mine.

52, 53, 56, 57; 10:1, 17, 38; 13:22, 31-33; 14:25; 17:11; 18:31, 35; 19:1, 11, 28, 41).[141]

Based on such references, Conzelmann has built his reconstruction of Luke's theology of the Way by emphasising the importance of Jesus' last journey while the possible contribution of Luke's *hodos* stories went largely unnoticed.[142]

Apart from obscuring the presence of the *hodos* stories, this common emphasis on the *Reisenotizen* in Luke's Central Section had another, subtle effect. For example, on their account Luke was charged with a chronic lack of geographical precision.[143] Conzelmann and others have argued that Luke's journey indicators are (a) incoherent and contradictory; (b) infrequent, and hence unable to sustain a real sense of movement; and (c) vague and indefinite in their topographical detail.[144]

Such imprecision and difficulties,[145] combined with Luke's emphasis on static teaching scenes, enhanced the impression

---

[141] Navone notes that 'the Way motif achieves its climax in the Lucan travel narrative (Lk 9:51-18:14), with its repeated references to Jesus' movement in the direction of Jerusalem' ('Three Aspects', p. 117).

[142] Although the common emphasis on Luke's Central Section is, generally, correct, it leads to a very restrictive hermeneutic of the Way motif. Every journey in Luke came to be assessed with reference to it. For example, J. B. Green assessed the Emmaus account 'in light of the importance of the journey motif to the Lukan enterprise... (see above on 9:51-19:48)' (*The Gospel of Luke* (Cambridge: Eerdmans, 1997), p. 843, pp. 396-397).

[143] Conzelmann, *Luke*, p. 19.

[144] *Cf.* Moessner, *Lord*, p. 15.

[145] The classical example is Lk. 17:11, καὶ ἐγένετο ἐν τῷ πορεύεσθαι εἰς Ἰερουσαλὴμ καὶ αὐτὸς διήρχετο διὰ μέσον Σαμαρείας καὶ Γαλιλαίας. C. C. McCown suggested that Luke is 'a study-table geographer who never did any field work' ('Gospel Geography: Fiction, Fact and Truth', *JBL* 60 (1941), 1-25; pp. 15, 17, 18; 'The Geography of Jesus' Last Journey to Jerusalem', *JBL* 51 (1932), 107-129; 'The Geography of Luke's Central Section', *JBL* 57 (1938), 51-56). In a milder approach, stressing the literary role of the journey section, C. H. Talbert notes that 'the geography [of Luke's Central Section] cannot be satisfactorily traced.. This travel section is an editorial framework created by the evangelist' (Talbert, *Reading Luke: A Literary and Theological Commentary on the Third Gospel* (N.Y.: Crossroad, 1982), p. 111). Excessive pessimism, however, has received a number of balanced responses, such as that of M. Hengel, 'The Geography of Palestine in Acts', in R. Bauckham (ed.),

of a 'discrepancy between the material and the scheme' or of a 'dissonance of form from content' (*Spannung zwischen Form und Stoff* - in Conzelmann's words),[146] a feature that threatens to reduce the overall composition to a heterogeneous and 'characterless' collection of stories.[147] The more impressive, therefore, is Luke's success in presenting Jesus' life in the shape of a teaching journey, a 'piece of deliberate editorial work', a meaningful pattern imposed on the biographical and traditional material.[148]

Thematic Support for Luke's Journey Motif

Apparently, Luke's journey scheme survives in the gospel through its conventional value as a literary framework for Jesus' ministry, through its inherent appeal to the reader's imagination, and, as well, through Luke's ability to combine different motifs in order to strengthen the main line of the story.

Conzelmann drew attention, in this context, that Luke juxtaposes the journeying motif and that of the disciples' misunderstanding of the Passion, strengthening the tension of

---

The Book of Acts in Its Palestinian Setting (Carlisle: Paternoster, 1995), 27-78, esp. pp. 28, 50); Hemer, *Acts*; G. E. Sterling, *Historiography and Self-Definition: Josephos, Luke-Acts, and Apologetic Historiography* (Leiden: Brill, 1992). For a review of Lukan historiography, see J. S. Jáuregui, 'Historiografía y teología en Hechos. Estado de la investigación desde 1980', *EstB* 53 (1995), 97-123. Goulder espouses Hengel's geographical optimism, as well 'Luke views Palestine from abroad... The geographical implications of Luke's writings are in fact astonishingly accurate' (Goulder, *Luke*, vol. 1, p. 117).

146 Moessner, *Lord*, p. 14; for Conzelmann, *cf. Mitte*, pp. 54-55.
147 Moessner, *Lord*, p. 15; Bailey, *Poet and Peasant*, p. 79, n. 1. The challenge of this dissonance is at the origin of a large number of articles and essays, and of major monographs, apart from those already mentioned, such as L. Girard, *L'Évangile des voyages de Jesus, ou la Section 9:51-18:14 de Saint Luc* (Paris: Gabalda, 1951) and H. L. Egelkraut, *Jesus' Mission to Jerusalem: A Redaction Critical Study of the Travel Narrative in the Gospel of Luke, Lk 9:51-19:48* (Frankfurt: Lang, 1976).
148 Conzelmann, *Luke*, pp. 73-74, 64. See also p. 73 'the more meagre the [journey] material, the more distinct does the author's intention become' (p. 73).

Jesus' destiny.[149] Jesus' own awareness of the coming Passion is presented by Luke 'in terms of the journey', as well, for Conzelmann (cf. Lk. 13:33).[150] The discipleship motif is developed progressively, further, in connection with journeying, taking the disciples from a low ebb to a state where they are able to imitate their master's way.[151] And, finally, two other major narrative lines contribute to the coherence of the story, the theme of suffering and the theme of kingship.[152]

Lukan scholarship agreed to a great extent that Luke includes here a 'massive' portrayal of Jesus as king,[153] and that the journey to Jerusalem has clear royal overtones, as *der königliche Weg Jesu*.[154] Jesus is portrayed as a heir-apparent journeying to Jerusalem, rejected by his countrymen and deprived of his inheritance until his journey turns into a divine confirmation of his kingship, at the Ascension.[155]

In Acts, however, the journey paradigm is changed. The glory and the reward associated with Jesus' kingship become more distant and Jesus' disciples face persecution and trials.

---

149 Conzelmann, *Luke*, pp. 64-65. Although, as Conzelmann notes 'in Jesus' sayings [in Luke] there is nothing that lends itself to misunderstanding'.
150 Conzelmann, *Luke*, pp. 65; 93-94, and he remarks in this context the important role of the Emmaus story. Strauss disputes, however, the central role of this awareness in Luke's narrative: 'it is not Jesus' awareness of his Passion, as Conzelmann suggests, but his determination to go to Jerusalem which is central' (Strauss, *Davidic Messiah*, p. 274; a determination originating in the Davidic destiny of Jesus, and in his ministry as the Suffering Servant; *op.cit.*, pp. 285, 292).
151 Green, *Theology*, p. 104.
152 Conzelmann, *Luke*, pp. 68, 71, 75-76.
153 Swartley, *Scripture Traditions*, p. 235 (cf. pp. 232-251). F. W. Danker, *Luke* (Philadelphia, PA: Fortress, 1987), p. 13. See also A. George, 'La royauté de Jésus', in A. George (ed.), *Études sur l'oeuvre de Luc* (Paris: Gabalda, 1978), 257-282 (cf. 'La royauté de Jésus selon l'Évangile de Luc', *ScE* 14 (1962), 57-62).
154 M. Miyoshi, *Der Anfang des Reiseberichtes Lk 9:51-10:24: eine redaktionsgeschichtliche Untersuchung* (Rome: PBI, 1974), p. 51 (cf. Lk. 19:11).
155 Miyoshi, *Anfang*, pp. 44, 51. This disinheriting of Jesus comes over pregnantly in Luke 13:31-33 (for many commentators, this represents the centre of the Lukan journey).

Journeying as *following* Jesus is replaced now by journeying as *sharing* in Jesus' *mission and persecution*.[156] According to Conzelmann, the Way in Acts moves in the direction of an ethic of suffering (*cf.* the mention of πειρασμός, at the Last Supper, and the command to arms, *cf.* Lk. 22:35), communicating that 'the Christian life is a *way*' and it 'inevitably leads through many tribulations (Acts 14:22)', requiring patience and perseverance (ὑπομονή, Luke 7:15).[157]

New Ways of Interpreting Luke's Reisenotizen

Conzelmann's elaborate views on Luke's theology of the Way raised a large number of issues and prompted several debates and responses. The scale of the response has confirmed that after Conzelmann's study the issue was no longer whether Luke has a theology of the Way, but, instead, of what it stands for.[158] The hermeneutical potential of this literary theme has been acknowledged; however, this achievement has come at the expense of a more comprehensive perspective on Luke's journeying motif. For example, at the origin of these limitations are the key role given to the hypothesis of Markan priority (while a redactional comparison of Luke with Matthew might lead to further important insights on Luke's purposes with the Journey section) and a certain dismissal of Acts in interpreting the theology of Luke's Journey motif.[159]

According to the theological agenda of the time, NT scholarship has responded to Conzelmann's reconstruction of Luke's theology of the Way by stressing that journeying is an element of theological *continuity* not of discontinuity (W. C. Robinson *versus* Conzelmann's three-stage view on redemption history), a theological vehicle for illustrating the change in the discipleship paradigms of Luke's gospel and of Acts (S. Brown),

---

156 Conzelmann, *Luke*, p. 233.
157 Conzelmann, *Luke*, pp. 233-234, 227. On Conzelmann's exegesis of πειρασμός and on the persecutions of the church, as incumbent to the post-Easter discipleship, see S. Brown, *Apostasy*, chapter one.
158 W. Shepherd, *The Narrative Function of the Holy Spirit as Character in Luke-Acts* (Atlanta, GA: Scholars, 1994), p. 23.
159 Gasque notes in *A History of the Interpretation of the Acts of the Apostles* (Peabody, MA: Hendrickson, 1989 (1975)), p. 291, that Conzelmann 'does not think that Luke's fundamental themes have been developed to quite the same extent in the book of Acts'.

and an elusive, dialectic and literary multiform metaphor that contributes to the general narrative coherence and openness of the text (H. Flender).[160] Characteristically, all these responses have followed to an important extent Conzelmann's own argument, focusing on Jesus' *Reisenotizen*.

W. C. ROBINSON: THE CONTINUITY OF REDEMPTION HISTORY

Robinson agreed that Luke has modified the geographical and chronological data of Mark,[161] but was reluctant to accept Conzelmann's classical scheme of a three part redemption history.[162] Consequently, he reassessed Luke's theology of the Way,[163] and his influential analysis aimed at demonstrating the 'theological *homogeneity* of Luke-Acts', the continuity between Jesus and the Church, and at re-assessing the significance of Luke's geography, a trend picked up by many authors, afterwards.[164] Therefore, he discussed Luke's journey scheme in a more comprehensive, unified manner than Conzelmann, trying to rescue the *geographical* meaning of the Way metaphor from the latter's *temporal* emphasis.

---

160 Kodell, 'Theology', esp. pp. 134-138; E. Richard, 'Luke - Writer, Theologian, Historian: Research and Orientation of the 1970's', *BTB* 13 (1983), 3-15.
161 Robinson, *Weg*, p. 7.
162 Robinson, *Weg*, p. 9. Writing in German, W. C. Robinson made sure that his response travels far and reaches the right destination, the origin of the debate.
163 Robinson, *Weg*, p. 8.
164 Italics mine. Among other contributions, *cf.* P. S. Minear, 'Luke's Use of the Birth Stories', in L. E. Keck and J. L. Martyn (eds.), *Studies in Luke-Acts* (London: SPCK, 1968), 113-130, esp. p. 121; I. H. Marshall, *Luke, Historian and Theologian* (Exeter: Paternoster, 1970); *idem*, *Gospel*, pp. 300-301; or 'Luke and his "Gospel"', in P. Stuhlmacher (ed.), *Das Evangelium und die Evangelien* (Tübingen: Mohr, 1983), 289-308. For G. Braumann persecution is the unifying theological theme of Luke-Acts ('Das Mittel der Zeit', *ZNW* 54 (1963), 117-145). E. Lohse favoured the 'promise and fulfillment' motif ('Lukas als Theologe der Heilsgeschichte', in E. Lohse (ed.), *Die Einheit des Neuen Testaments: exegetische Studien zur Theologie des Neuen Testaments* (Göttingen: Vandenhoeck, 1973), 145-164; *cf.* the discussion in R. P. Menzies, *Empowered for Witness: The Spirit in Luke-Acts* (Sheffield: Sheffield Academical, 1994), pp. 121-122).

Thus, he highlighted that Luke has 'visualized the continuity of the history of salvation as a course (δρόμος) or way (ὁδός)' in all of Luke and Acts (πορεύομαι and ὁδός, in Lk. 9-19, cf. 13:33, etc., δρόμος, Acts 13:25, 20:18; εἴσοδος, Acts 13:24; ἔξοδος in Lk. 9:31, ἡ ὁδός again in Acts 9:2; 19:9, 23; 22:4; 24:14, 22, etc).[165] The journey scheme is rather a combined geographical-temporal scheme in Luke-Acts.[166] And, in Jesus' agenda at Luke 23:5 (cf. Acts 13:31), Robinson identifies three *geographical* stages of the kerygma

(1) the Gospel goes into all of Judaea, καθ' ὅλης τῆς Ἰουδαίας,
(2) after it started in Galilee, ἀρξάμενος ἀπὸ τῆς Γαλιλαίας, and
(3) prior to its arrival everywhere, ἕως ὧδε.[167]

Even the temporal condition for apostleship (that of having been with Jesus ἐν παντὶ χρόνῳ, Acts 1:21) is expressed geographically, spatially, notes Robinson, as the condition of having participated in Jesus' journey from Galilee to Jerusalem (Acts 13:31, ὃς ὤφθη ἐπὶ ἡμέρας πλείους τοῖς συναναβᾶσιν αὐτῷ ἀπὸ τῆς Γαλιλαίας εἰς Ἰερουσαλήμ).[168] In Acts 1:2, Galilee, a spatial symbol, is a landmark for Jesus' ministry, not John the Baptist (as Conzelmann emphasized).[169] Although there is a temporal development in

---

165 W. C. Robinson, 'The Theological Context for Interpreting Luke's Travel Narrative (9:51 ff.)', *JBL* 79 (1960), 20-31, esp. pp. 23, 29. Luke avoids Mark's disjointed collection of episodes by presenting 'a "sort of chain" of events', a 'bridged' history in two-parts ('Travel Narrative', pp. 23-24, 27). As a balanced responce to Conzelmann, Robinson's articulate arguments proved extremely influential. Navone refers to him extensively (cf. 'Three Aspects', pp. 115-132; 'The Way of the Lord', *Script* 20 (1968), 24-30; 'The Journey Theme,' *Bib.Td.* 58 (1972), 616-619; see idem, *Themes*, pp. 188-198, etc.), and so does S. Brown, G. Lüdemann (the latter simply re-iterates Robinson's argument in *Paul Apostle to the Gentiles* (London: SCM, 1984), p. 15).
166 Robinson, *Weg*, p. 33. For him 'the course of the narration is *like a way* [emph.mine]. When one reads through the Gospel of Luke, traces of the ὁδός concept of *Heilsgeschichte* are visible' (Robinson, 'Travel Narrative', p. 23).
167 Robinson, *Weg*, pp. 30-31.
168 Robinson, *Weg*, p. 34.
169 Robinson, *Weg*, pp. 33, 82 (Lk. 23:5; Acts 10:37; Lk. 16:16; Acts 1:21; 10:37; 13:34; 19:4).

Luke-Acts, Luke uses rather the geographical dynamics of the journey motif.

Prefiguring the later literary analysis of Luke's unity of composition (space, time, plot) Robinson noted that space and time cooperate dynamically in Luke-Acts in communicating the plan of salvation by the metaphor of the Way.[170] The plan of bringing together Jews and Gentiles in God's salvation is brought to fulfillment, dynamically, through a *journeying* gospel, through a 'geography on the move'

> Die lukanische Geographie ist nicht primär statisch an spezifische Orte gebunden, wenn auch besondere Orte eine eigene Bedeutung haben, sondern sie ist eine 'Geographie in Bewegung'; sie beschreibt eine Reise, die einem Zeitschema folgt, Gottes Plan entspricht und unter Gottes Leitung fortschreitet, eine Reise, auf der von Zeit zu Zeit das Reich Gottes naht, wenn Gott sein Volk heimsucht, einen Weg des Herrn, der zu den Heiden fürht, 'bis daß die Zeiten der Heiden erfült werden'.[171]

In Acts, the Way of Jesus becomes a model for the Way of the Church, for her mission. Journeying with Jesus represents for the disciples the perfect obedience to God, both in Jesus' lifetime and after his ascension, a divinely guided journey in contrast with the nations' wandering on their own ὁδοί (Acts 14:16). Therefore, Luke's vision of this stage of *Heilsgeschichte* could deservedly be entitled *the Way of the Lord* as a journey from Nazareth to Rome.[172]

Robinson's emphasis on the *literary and theological continuity* of the Way motif and on its temporal and spatial dynamics has explored in greater depth Luke's idealisation of the Way, turning this motif into a major premise for all subsequent literary analysis of Luke's narrative frameworks.

S. BROWN AND H. FLENDER: REDEFINING LUKE'S PARADIGMS

S. Brown, however, went beyond this barrier of Jesus' journey to Jerusalem. First, he regarded the Way motif as a significant one for the whole of Luke-Acts.[173] Then, for him it is Luke's

---

170 Robinson, *Weg*, p. 8.
171 Robinson, *Weg*, p. 67.
172 Robinson, 'Travel Narrative', pp. 26-27; *Weg*, p. 43; also Lüdemann, *Paul*, pp. 15-16.
173 Brown, *Apostasy*, p. 133.

A Review of Lukan Scholarship

second volume which provides the 'norm of interpretation' since its author had 'greater freedom of theological expression in Acts than in the gospel'.[174] Brown, thus, embarks on a reverse approach to the Way theme starting from principles discovered in Acts.

S. Brown and the New Discipleship Paradigms

Characteristically, for Brown the 'Way' in Luke-Acts displays 'unity in diversity'. Therefore, in contrast to Robinson's understanding of the Way motif, he suggests the need for a greater emphasis on the salvation of the individual

> Robinson, it seems to us, has not devoted sufficient attention to the shifts in meaning within Luke's Way theology. Furthermore he has treated this terminology almost entirely in connection with Luke's representation of *salvation history*. We believe that the Way motif also has significance for the Lukan conception of the *salvation of the individual* and in particular for his notion of apostasy and perseverance.[175]

To take further his observation, Luke's motif of the Way is still in need of being assessed as an individual experience, for the majority of journey models have imposed a collective interpretation of the Way, often inspired from the experience of Exodus and from the book of Deuteronomy.

As regards Brown, however, he focused on a particular aspect of individual salvation, the aspect of personal faithfulness in following Christ and later, in following the apostles.

In his comprehensive discussion of *peirasmos* (temptation, perseverance, trials, apostasy) in Luke-Acts, he objected to Conzelmann's 'Satan-free Age of Jesus' (Lk. 4:13-22:3).[176] on

---

174 Brown, *Apostasy*, p. 2.
175 Brown, *Apostasy*, p. 131.
176 Brown, *Apostasy*, pp. 1-3, 5-52; *cf.* Conzelmann, *Luke*, pp. 16, 28, 156; 188, n. 4. For Conzelmann the 'middle of time', or Jesus' period, is also characterised by a departure of Satan 'for a while' (καὶ συντελέσας πάντα πειρασμὸν ὁ διάβολος ἀπέστη ἀπ' αὐτοῦ ἄχρι καιροῦ, Lk. 4:13) and a ministry without temptations (πειρασμός) until the second *caesura* intervenes and the devil returns (εἰσῆλθεν δὲ Σατανᾶς εἰς ' Ιούδαν, Lk. 22:3) and with him the 'trials' (πειρασμοῖς, Lk. 22:28; *cf.* S. Garrett, *The Demise of the Devil: Magic and the Demonic in Luke's*

the grounds that Satan's temptations continued during all of Jesus' ministry, since it is evident in the lives of his disciples. This is why during Jesus' earthly ministry '"standing by" Jesus on his Way represents the *perseverance* of the apostles in their faith in Jesus' messianic dignity, and turning aside from Jesus' Way signifies apostasy from discipleship'.[177]

In Acts, the spatial relation of 'standing by' Jesus (διαμένω, which expressed the relationship of the apostles to Jesus, Lk. 22:28) is replaced by a devotion to the apostles, instead, as representatives of the Way (Acts 1:14; 2:42, 46; 6:4; 8:13; 10:2). This transition in the forms of discipleship and in the understanding of the Way reflects the increasing spiritualisation of the Way metaphor, a 'higher encoding'.[178]

> Now that Jesus is removed from the ordinary laws of time and space, salvation can no longer be associated with a spatial relationship to him, as to an historical personality. Instead it is associated (temporarily) with an historical *place*, with the city of Jerusalem, where alone the disciples can experience the crucial events of the resurrection and the coming of the Spirit. During the period between crucifixion and Pentecost the perseverance of the disciple is visually represented by remaining in Jerusalem.[179]

The two disciples travelling to Emmaus are, for Brown, two 'runaways' brought back by Jesus, in contradistinction to the steadfastness of the apostles.[180] His discussion of the

---

Writing (Minneapolis, MN: Fortress, 1989), etc.). As a response to this view, one needs to see that (a) Satan has not actually left the scene (*cf.* Lk. 10:18; 11:15); and (b) that Jesus does not turn the conflict with Satan into his principal theme, since the proclamation of the kingdom of God has absolute priority, *cf.* J. A. Fitzmyer, *Luke the Theologian: Aspects of His Teaching* (London: Chapman, 1989), pp. 146-169; G. Baumbach, *Das Verständnis des Bösen in den synoptischen Evangelien* (Berlin: Evangelische Verlaganstalt, 1963).

177 Brown, *Apostasy*, p. 133. Discipleship was expressed during the Age of Jesus 'in terms of continuous spatial proximity to him' acquires a double significance in Luke: (a) it guarantees the reliability of the witness and (b) expresses the apostles' continuous faith in Jesus' Messianic dignity (p. 81).
178 Brown, *Apostasy*, pp. 131, 143-144.
179 Brown, *Apostasy*, p. 135.
180 Brown, *Apostasy*, pp. 74-77. For him Cleopas and his companion belong to the group of οἱ λοιποί, distinguished by Luke from the Eleven (see

Interregnum sets the Emmaus account in a comprehensive static scheme, the journey emphasis or the internal literary motifs being given a secondary place. The Emmaus encounter illustrates, thus, the need for perseverance, for obedience, and highlights Jerusalem's centrality.

As regards the changes in the meaning of the Way metaphor, for Brown this is 'no longer connected with an historical person or place', and 'no longer signifies a *geographical journey* made by a human individual, even though the spatial imagery may still be present'.[181] The participation in the geographical journey of Jesus ('the Way of the Lord') is replaced in Acts by the proclamation of 'the Way of the Word'.[182]

Founding his reading of the Way motif on Acts, Brown highlights the tension between Jerusalem's centrality at Jesus' resurrection and Ascension (apart from the Emmaus story, the rest of Jesus' appearances take place in Jerusalem), the initial command to wait in Jerusalem, for the bestowing of the Spirit, and the later missionary change of the journeying pattern.[183]

The new perspective on mission and on Jerusalem changes the journeying paradigm, according to Brown, and this turns from a simple *linear* expansion to become 'a *radiation* in many directions'.[184] After functioning as a *destination* and a scene for Jesus' ἔξοδος, Jerusalem's centrality is 'transfigured', turning into a *source* of missionary journeys (although this role will be challenged by later by Antioch).[185] For this reason, Brown

---

Lk. 24:9). The two travelers are 'unbelieving' (24:21) and leave Jerusalem (p. 75).
181 Brown, *Apostasy*, pp. 135-145, esp. p. 135 (italics mine).
182 Brown, *Apostasy*, pp. 136-137, 145. The disciples' spatial relationship to a minister of the Word is different from their earlier spatial relationship to Jesus (pp. 136-137, 145; *cf.* Acts 8:6, 10; 16:14; 28:24).
183 Brown, *Apostasy*, p. 75. Jerusalem is still at the centre of action, in the first half of Acts (Luke omits the reference to Galilee Lk. 24:6; Mk. 16:7), and Brown notes that 'apart from the scene in Emmaus itself all of Jesus' apparitions to the disciples occur in Jerusalem vv. 34-36'. However, Saul's encounter is arguably a second instance of such a post-Easter appearance outside Jerusalem, and the change in Jerusalem's centrality seems more drastic than Brown would acknowledge.
184 Brown, *Apostasy*, p. 135.
185 Brown, *Apostasy*, p. 75. The referential nature of Jerusalem is stressed by the repeated occurrence of 'they returned to Jerusalem', ὑπέστρεψαν

argues that concomitantly, the Way takes a more independent and metaphorical meaning in Acts

> The Way of the Lord starts to be used more and more in the absolute: the connection with external geographical movement, still present in the metaphorical usage (Acts 1:8) is abandoned.[186]

The Way of the Lord becomes now Christianity itself.[187] On the whole, Brown's analysis raised the issue of a more literary assessment of Luke's motif of the Way. To the interpretative role of well-known series of *Reisenotizen*, he added the importance of Jerusalem and of the *Interregnum* period as the place and time when journeying paradigms are changed.

H. Flender and the Dialectic Nature of Luke's Journeys

Aimed, as well, at providing a theological response to Conzelmann's historicism, H. Flender's approach to the Way theme is characterised by a special emphasis on Luke's use of contrasting perspectives.[188] According to him, Luke-Acts displays a 'dialectical structure' and 'contains a great many parallels of individual texts but also correspondences which run all through the work'.[189]

In principal, his thesis is that Luke has a 'two stage Christology', and Jesus' existence oscillates between two main modes, the heavenly one and the earthly one. As a consequence, against Conzelmann, 'history cannot be treated objectively'.[190] For Flender 'history' and 'salvation' are two opposite concepts and Luke distinguishes between 'a human history' open to observation and the same 'history in its eschatological aspect', which eludes observation.[191]

εἰς Ἰερουσαλήμ (Lk. 2:45; 24:33, 52; Acts 1:12; 8:25; 13:13; 22:17 (*op.cit.*, p. 77, n. 307).

186 Brown, *Apostasy*, p. 138 (Acts 14:22).
187 Brown, *Apostasy*, pp. 139-140.
188 Flender, Saint Luke: Theologian of Redemptive History (London: SPCK, 1967).
189 Flender, *Luke*, p. 8. See the 'rule of two' noted by R. Morgenthaler, *Die lukanische Geschichtsschreibung als Zeugnis: Gestalt und Gehalt der Kunst des Lukas* (Zürich: Zwingli, 1948-1949), vol. 1, p. 96, etc.
190 Flender, *Luke*, pp. 20, 41, 90.
191 Flender, *Luke*, pp. 125, 140; Flender's opposition between history and revelation has been criticised as betraying Luke's thought (W.

These two modes of Jesus' existence are reflected in the multivalent meaning of Jesus' journey to Jerusalem.[192] Flender emphasizes that Jesus journeys towards his Passion as well as towards 'his heavenly exaltation'.[193] There is, furthermore, an earthly messianic journey of Jesus to the temple; an 'earthly' and a 'heavenly' journey of his disciples (one, with Jesus, to his Passion; another one to salvation, continuing after Jesus' resurrection). Following or imitating Jesus' journeying has its limitations, however, for Jesus' manner of death is for him alone.[194] The disciples' journey to salvation continues in Acts through 'unconditional surrender' joined with 'new involvement in the secular order', two things which 'co-exist in tension'.[195]

This review of traditional, mainline Lukan scholarship indicates that, apart from considering the 'way' metaphor, the main discussion of Luke's Way motif has tended to focus on Jesus' journey to Jerusalem and its journey indicators, on its messianic paradigms (the royal Davidic type, the prophet like Moses, the Isaianic New Exodus, the Deuteronomic model, etc.), on the history of redemption and its continuity, on the multiplicity of journeys and the change of journey paradigms (from convergent to Jerusalem to divergent journeying). On the one hand, this points out that the Way motif is a versatile and complex motif, with many nuances to account for. On the other hand, this review emphasized the need to extend the textual basis of the present assessment of the Way motif by considering the whole of Luke-Acts, and to take into account, as well, the shorter journey stories among which are the *hodos* encounters themselves, with their refined literary style and pervasive Hellenistic intertextuality.

Pannenberg and R. Rendtorff *et. al.* (eds.), *Revelation as History* (N.Y.: Macmillan, 1968); C. E. Braaten, *History and Hermeneutics* (Philadelphia, PA: Westminster, 1966); R. A. Edwards, 'The Redaction of Luke', *JR* 49 (1969), 392-405).

192 Flender, *Luke*, p. 32.
193 Flender, *Luke*, pp. 34, 75.
194 Flender, *Luke*, pp. 75, 83; *cf.* p. 74: 'But unlike the disciples, the reader is called in his *post*-Easter situation to understand suffering as sent from God (δεῖ) and to accept it.'
195 Flender, *Luke*, p. 80.

CHAPTER 2

The Way and Hellenistic *Mimesis*

In a perceptive note on Luke's style, E. Haenchen emphasized that Luke has a specific way of reporting stories, reflecting his 'conception of the narrator's calling'. According to him, a narration is, in fact, an *interpreted* account of events

> A narration should not describe an event with the precision of a police-report, but must make the listener or reader aware of the inner significance of what has happened and impress upon him, unforgettably, the truth of the power of God made manifest in it.[1]

Such an understanding represents an implicit reference to selective and interpreted representations of reality, known as *mimesis* (Grk.), or *imitatio* (Lat.), which has been regarded in antiquity as an art involving special techniques and specific philosophies, various trends or fashions, from drama and novels to history, from songs and musical interpretation to painting, sculpture, architecture.

Contemporary NT scholarship has explored surprisingly little how deeply mimesis was ingrained in Hellenistic story-telling, and, hence, in NT writings. As regards the relevance of mimesis for Luke's style, it is essential to ask, with Steyn, not only what kind of stories could have inspired Luke in his accounts (in terms of content and style, as literary sources) but also what narrative models he followed (in terms of form, plot, type of literary representation).[2]

Mimesis and Its Alternative Meanings

Since mimesis and its cognates are recurrent terms in classical philosophy and in art theories (Plato, Aristotle, Dionysius of Halicarnassus, Longinus, etc.), as well as in Hellenistic history writing (Polybius, Theopompus, Ephorus, Duris of Samos, etc.), a first step towards using it in Lukan studies would be to

---

1   Haenchen, *Acts*, p. 110.
2   Steyn, 'Luke's Use of ΜΙΜΗΣΙΣ?', p. 553.

ensure a comprehensive definition of the term. Then, mimesis will be considered from the two main complementary perspectives used in NT studies, as mimesis of *content* or *source* (Luke's imitation of the LXX style; *cf.* Brodie, Cadbury, Plümacher) and mimesis of *form* or *composition* (Luke's representation of events; *cf.* Dodd, Fitzmyer, Dillon, Hedrick).

Definition and Different Types of Mimesis

A complex, versatile term whose precise connotations may vary according to context, mimesis has been translated as "imitation", "representation", "image-making", "reproduction", "expression", or, equally so, as "fiction", "emulation", "make-believe", "impersonation", or even "deception", etc.[3]

Historically, the first meaning of mimesis derives from μῖμος, a word with cultic connotations, referring to the enacting of a myth through dancing or play, often at the Dionysius' celebrations.[4] The second meaning, as the ending in -σις suggests, is that of an action, a process. Phenomenologically, mimesis (μίμησις) is the production of "representations", μιμήματα,[5] and indicates a relation between something which *is* and something *made to resemble* it.[6]

---

3 P. Woodruff, 'Aristotle on mimesis', in A. O. Rorty (ed.), *Essays on Aristotle's Poetics* (Princeton, NJ: Princeton UP, 1992), 73-95, esp. p. 73. T. L. Brodie defines mimesis as a creative process 'a process of inspection, contemplation, wrestling, pioneering, digesting', including techniques of adaptation such as compression, abbreviation, expansion, fusing and dividing ('Luke 7:36-50 as an Internalization of 2 Kings 4:1-37: A Study of Luke's Rhetorical Imitation', *Bib* 64 (1983), 457-485, p. 462). Imitation does not imply 'slavish copying' but rather 'emulation or rivalry', a creative transformation (internalisation) of sources ('Greco-Roman Imitation of Texts as a Partial Guide to Luke's Use of Sources', in C. H. Talbert (ed.), *Luke-Acts: New Perspectives from the Society of Biblical Literature Seminar* (N.Y.: Crossroads, 1984), 17-46, pp. 20-22).

4 H. Koller, *Die Mimesis in der Antike. Nachamung, Darstellung, Ausdruck*, Bern: Francke, 1954), pp. 38, 45, 47, as cited by S. Lücking, *Mimesis der Verachteten: eine Studie zur Erzählweise von Mk. 14:1-11* (Stuttgart: Katholisches Bibelwerk, 1992), p. 18.

5 Woodruff, 'Aristotle on mimesis', p. 73.

6 R. McKeon, 'Literary criticism and the concept of imitation in antiquity', in R. S. Crane (ed.), *Critics and criticism: ancient and modern* (Chicago, IL: University of Chicago, 1952), 147-175, p. 152 (first published in *Modern Philology* 34 (1936), 1-35).

The concept itself has an in-built reference to 'repetition', yet modern literary theorists have often emphasized that mimesis implies both similarity and difference as fundamental traits.[7] According to M. Heidegger and H.-G. Gadamer, for example, mimesis should not be simply understood as 'primitive imitation' (*Nachbilden*) but rather as a 'production which comes after' or follows the initial subject in form and (or) content (*Nachmachung*) involving similarity as well as distance between the imitated model (the 'truth', or the source) and its imitation (the representation).[8] In this sense the subject of mimesis has been approached from two complementary perspectives: (a) a diachronical view, considering the development of narrative representation in the history of literature and the way in which literary fashions (schools) and writers have influenced each other, and (b) a technical, compositional perspective which analyses mimesis as characteristic of a given author, of his style and of his philosophy of representation.[9]

LINGUISTIC AND STYLISTIC MIMESIS

The contemporary discussion of Lukan mimesis has to do rather with a diachronic approach, for NT scholarship has focused mainly on Luke's imitation of the Septuagint, in style, story and vocabulary, emphasizing Luke's interest in giving

---

7 Melberg, *Theories*, p. 1, 3.
8 M. Heidegger, *Nietzsche* (Pfullingen: Neste, 1961), vol. 1, p. 215; H.-G. Gadamer, *Wahrheit und Methode* (Tübingen: Mohr, 1990), vol. 1, p. 118 (as cited in Melberg, *Theories*, p. 4).
9 Auerbach's seminal study has prompted a long series of responses. *Cf.* W. Naumann, 'Mimesis', *Modern Philology* 45 (1947/48), 211-212, and F. Gogarten, 'Das abendländische Geschichtsdenken: Bemerkungen zu dem Buch von Erich Auerbach "Mimesis"', *ZTK* 51 (1954), 270-360. A comprehensive assessment of his contribution is found in S. Lerer (ed.), *Literary History and the Challenge of Philology: The legacy of Erich Auerbach* (Stanford, CA: Stanford UP, 1996). Auerbach's historical perspective on mimesis has been continued by studies such as that of G. Gebauer and C. Wulf, *Mimesis: Culture. Art. Society* (Berkeley, CA: University of California, 1995), the German ed., *Mimesis: Kultur-Kunst-Gesellschaft* (Reinbeck: Rowohlt, 1992), or counterbalanced by analyses such as that of A. Cook, *History Writing: The theory and practice of history in Antiquity and in Modern Times* (Cambridge: Cambridge UP, 1988).

his volumes a 'respectable biblical flavour'.[10] Thus, according to Cadbury, the massive presence of semitisms and archaisms in Luke-Acts is a case of 'biblical imitation' which is understandable for 'Luke belonged to a setting in which imitative style was not uncommon'.[11] Septuagintal mimesis has been one of the main emphases of E. Plümacher's studies in Luke's style, as well.[12]

In fact, the presence of Semitisms allows for a rather nuanced interpretation, since there are three possible sources

---

10 M. Diefenbach, *Die Komposition des Lukasevangeliums unter Berücksichtigung antiker Rhetorikelemente* (Frankfurt: Knecht, 1993), p. 31. On LXX imitation, *cf.* Lk. 3:22; 9:35 as related to Is. 42; Lk. 13:35, 19:38 as related to [LXX] Ps. 117:26, etc. Among the notorious hebraisms of Luke one can mention the use of καὶ ἐγένετο + verb (וַיְהִי); καὶ ἰδού (וְהִנֵּה); ἐν τῷ + inf. (בְּ); ἐνώπιον (לִפְנֵי); ἐπιθυμίᾳ ἐπεθύμησα, 22:15 (Heb. absolute infinitive prefixed to a finite verb); τιθέναι, τίθεσθαι ἐν τῇ καρδίᾳ (peculiar to Luke-Acts: Lk. 1:66; 21:14; Acts 5:4; also Lk. 9:44 θέσθαι εἰς τὰ ὦτα, *cf.* [LXX] 1 Kgs. 21:12; 29:10; 2 Kgs. 13:33). Phrases with πρόσωπον may also be seen as hebraising: Lk. 1:76 (*cf.* 7:27)- 9:52, πρὸ προσώπον; 2:31, κατὰ πρόσωπον; 21:35, ἐπὶ πρόσωπον; 9:51, 53. Similarly, phrases like δοξάζειν τὸν θεόν (8 times), ποιεῖν ἔλεος μετά (Lk. 1:72; 10:37), μεγαλύνειν ἔλεος μετά (Lk. 1:58), ποιεῖν κράτος (Lk. 1:51). Luke transliterates the Hebrew words σίκερα (1:15), βάτος (16:6), κόρος (16:7) like the LXX (J. M. Creed, *The Gospel According to St. Luke* (London: Macmillan, 1930), p. lxxix). However, semitisms cannot be attributed only to Luke's sources. Apart from Lk. and Acts 1-15, they are found also in Acts 16-28, where presumably, the author is writing in a more free style. In both sections semitisms appear to be the same (ἰδού; ἤρξα(ν)το + inf.; ἐν μέσῳ + gen.; ἔθετο τῇ καρδίᾳ (or τῷ πνεύματι, etc.). At the same time, Luke's style is somewhat ambivalent, for he also reduces the number of semitisms. For example, there are 31 *amen* occurrences in Matthew, 14 in Mark and only 6 in Luke (*cf.* NT Greek Text, UBS 3). Luke's attempts to improve his style, however, were probably restricted by his own knowledge of the LXX and by his familiarity with the religious vocabulary of the primitive Church, which must have been 'vilely semitic' (W. L. Knox, *Some Hellenistic Elements in Primitive Christianity* (London: Oxford UP, 1944), pp. 1-29; esp. p. 7).

11 Cadbury, *Making*, p. 122. For the similar views of Busse, Radl, Klauck, see Diefenbach, *Komposition*, pp. 31-39.

12 E. Plümacher, *Lukas als hellenistischer Schriftsteller: Studien zur Apostelgeschichte* (Göttingen: Vandenhoeck, 1972), pp. 38, 51, 57. This type of imitation is characteristic of Philo and Josephus Flavius (Diefenbach, *Komposition*, p. 40).

The Way and Hellenistic Mimesis 77

for these Semitisms: direct translation from Semitic, the use of Semitised Greek translations from Semitic (reflecting his own sources),[13] (and) or his conscious imitation of the Septuagint.[14] As Luke's Semitisms in Acts seem to appear in groups or 'pools', N. Turner has argued that such accumulations might indicate that Luke's own language was itself a variant of Semitic Greek.[15] For this reason it was relatively easy for St. Luke 'to write in what merely looks like a LXX style, because it was Jewish Greek; this was his natural speech, and he was expert enough to make it sound quite classical at times'.[16]

This classical, at times, quality of Luke's language and composition, even if marred by inconsistency, is that of 'a

---

13 R. Riesner, 'Luke's Special Tradition and the Question of a Hebrew Gospel Source', *Mishkan* 20 (1994), p. 44; *idem*, 'James' Speech (Acts 15:13-21), Simeon's Hymn (Luke 2:29-32) and Luke's Sources', in J. B. Green and M. Turner (eds.), *Jesus of Nazareth: Lord and Christ. Essays on the Historical Jesus and New Testament Christology* (Grand Rapids, MI: Eerdmans, 1994), 263-280; E. Schweizer 'Eine hebraisierende Sonderquelle des Lukas?', in *TZ* 6 (1950), 161-185; *idem*, in *Das Evangelium nach Lukas*, Götingen: Vandenhoeck, 1982), pp. 1-4; R. Martin, *Syntactical Evidence of Semitic Sources in Greek Documents* (Missoula, MT: Scholars, 1974), p. 128, etc. For Schweizer, in particular, the phrase τὴν ὁδὸν τοῦ κυρίου in Acts 18:24-26 signals the presence of an OT source (see E. Schweizer, 'Die Bekehrung des Apollos, Apg. 18:24-26', in *Beiträge zur Theologie des neuen Testaments: Neutestamentliche Aufsätze* (Zürich: Zwingli, 1970), 71-79, esp. p. 76, as cited by H.-S. Kim, *Die Geisttaufe des Messias: eine kompositionsgeschichtliche Untersuchung zu einem Leitmotif des lukanischen Doppelwerks* (Frankfurt: Lang, 1993), p. 222).
14 H. F. D. Sparks, 'The Semitisms of Luke's Gospel', *JTS* 44 (1943), 129-138, especially pp. 132-134; *idem*, 'The Semitisms of the Acts', *JTS* ns 1 (1950), 16-28. A. Plummer considers that the specific nature of Luke's Greek derives from his Gentile origins, from his use of sources and of the LXX, and from his relation with Paul, *cf.* A. Plummer, *A Critical and Exegetical Commentary on the Gospel According to Saint Luke* (Edinburgh: T&T Clark, 1981 (1896)), pp. i, xlix).
15 N. Turner, *Style*, vol. 4 in J. H. Moulton (ed.), *A Grammar of New Testament Greek* (Edinburgh: T&T Clark, 1976), pp. 55-57.
16 Turner, *Style*, p. 56. For others, like Creed, the idea of a Lukan Semitic Greek is not acceptable (Creed, *Gospel*, pp. lxxvi-lxxvii).

conscious artist', 'the most versatile of all NT writers',[17] and this is evident both in Luke's style and his vocabulary.

For example, the author removes Aramaic and Latin loan words from his accounts, words which good Hellenistic literary taste would consider barbaric, such as διάβολος for σατανᾶς, διδάσκαλος for ῥαββί or ῥαββουνί, φόρος for κῆνσος (census), ἑκατοντάρχης for κεντυρίων (centurio).[18] Luke's vocabulary complies well with Aristotle's requirements, thus, since excellence of *diction* meant for the latter clarity and avoidance of banality and of barbarisms.[19]

Luke-Acts displays, in fact, many other marks of an educated language.[20] He often uses the *enthymeme* (a syllogism with one of the premises implicit), particularly in Jesus' speeches.[21] He conserves certain classical phrases, 'un certain nombre de tournures classiques, qui avait plus ou moins complètement disparu de la κοινή non littéraire'.[22] And, interestingly, his vocabulary 'is not so far removed from the the literary style of the Atticists' to be beyond comparison with them'.[23] In fact, according to Mealand 'Acts is especially close

---

17 N. Turner, 'The Quality of the Greek of Luke-Acts', in J. K. Elliot (ed.), *Studies in New Testament Language and Text* (Leiden: Brill, 1976, p. 387.
18 H. Koester, *History, Culture, and Religion of the Hellenistic Age* (Philadelphia, PA: Fortress, 1980), p. 108.
19 Aristotle, *Poetics*, 1458a.15-25. According to Pervo's assessment of Acts 8:25-40, Luke's use of elevated diction and *paronomasia* introduces a 'veneer of education', in contrast with the otherwise 'barbarian' character of the story, even elements of a certain racial and cultural superiority (*Profit*, pp. 70-71).
20 Cadbury, *Style*, pp. 4-39, esp. p. 8; E. Trocmé, *Le 'Livre des Actes' et l'Histoire* (Paris: PU de France, 1957), pp. 105-106; Creed, *Gospel*, pp. lxxix-lxxxii; Koester, *History*, p. 108.
21 W. S. Kurz, 'Hellenistic Rhetoric in the Christological Proof of Luke-Acts', *CBQ* 42 (1980), 171-195; R. B. Vinson, 'A Comparative Study of the Use of Enthymemes in the Synoptic Gospels', in D. F. Watson (ed.), *Persuasive Artistry: Studies in NT Rhetoric in Honour of George A. Kennedy* (Sheffield: JSOT, 1991), 119-141, esp. pp. 119-122. Even G. A. Kennedy recognises it in his later studies, *e.g.* in *New Testament Interpretation through Rhetorical Criticism* (Chapel Hill, NC: North Carolina UP, 1984), pp. 7-8, 104.
22 Trocmé, *Livre des Actes*, p. 106.
23 Cadbury, *Style*, p. 8; Creed, *Gospel*, p. lxxxi.

to Attic prose'.²⁴ Such a comparison with the Atticists, however, has its limits. Phrynichus' list of standard Atticist vocabulary shows that Luke has a rather mixed style, for whereas he followed many of the Atticist choices, he also used terms of which Phrynichus disapproves.²⁵

In view of such mixed evidence, Luke-Acts was considered to belong to 'popular' Greek literature.²⁶ NT scholars such as A. Wifstrand and L. Rydberg argued that Luke's language does not aspire towards 'Atticism' or 'Classicism', although it is an educated language distinct from the every day idioms. According to them, Luke's prose an intermediary one, a *Zwischenprosa*, well-used, yet popular written language, a *Schreibtischprodukt* distinct from the literary Greek of that

---

24 D. L. Mealand, 'Hellenistic Historians and the Style of Acts', *ZNW* 82 (1991), 42-66, p. 42. See *idem*, 'The Phrase "Many Proofs" in Acts 1:3 and in Hellenistic Writers', *ZNW* 80 (1989), 134-135; *idem*, 'Luke-Acts and the Verbs of Dionysius of Halicarnassus', *JSNT* 63 (1966), 63-86, etc. The Atticist movement was a return to the pure literary style of the Greek classics, an imitation of their style, and originated either in the early second century BC or later, around 60 BC, with Greeks who worked in Rome; it was quite in vogue in Luke's time. *Cf.* G. Kennedy, *The Art of Persuasion in Greece* (Princeton, NJ: Princeton UP, 1963), p.330; J. Wisse, 'Greeks, Romans, and the Rise of Atticism', in J.G.J. Abbenes, S.R. Slings, I. Sluiter (eds.), *Greek Literary Theory After Aristotle, A collection of papers in honour of D.M. Schenkeweld* (Amsterdam: VU-University, 1995), 65-82; p.72; U. von Wilamowitz-Moellendorff, 'Asianimus und Atticismus, *Hermes* 35 (1900), 1-52; pp.1-8, etc.
25 Creed, *Gospel*, p. lxxxiii. See the list at p. lxxxiv (*cf.* Arabius Phrynichus, *Attistica*, in *New Phrynichus. A revised text of the Ecloga of the grammarian Phrynichus*, W. G. Rutherford (tr.) (London: Macmillan, 1881), pp. lxxii, lxviii, cccli, lvi).
26 K. L. Schmitd's term; *cf.* C. F. Evans, 'Speeches in Acts', in A. Descamps and R. de Halleux (eds.), *Mélanges Bibliques en hommage à R.P. Béda Rigaux* (Gembloux: Duculot, 1970), 287-302. Its language, the 'koine Greek' was a 'complex phenomenon, comprising the actually spoken vernacular as the technical languages of law, science, economy, and administration, the language of school and rhetoric, and *various degrees of influence from classical literary conventions* [italics mine]. There were also a number of writers who wrote in an "elevated Koine", *i.e.*, in a kind of cultivated common language' (Koester, *History*, p. 103).

period.²⁷ L. Alexander has argued in a similar vein, suggesting that the discrepancy between Luke's style in the preface and that of the rest of his work reflects the fact that his prologue had been composed according to the literary 'convention of *autopsia*', a style used in technical and scientific manuals.²⁸

Such arguments emphasize a broad linguistic 'middle zone' to which Luke-Acts might belong as literature, avoiding the extremes of seeing Luke's writing as simply an uneducated *Volkssprache* or as high literature, *Hochliteratur*. His imitative style and representational principles would therefore reflect the extent to which classical mimesis permeated the popular culture of the Mediterranean *oikoumene*.

THEMATIC MIMESIS

T. L. Brodie has specifically developed the argument that Luke's imitation of LXX vocabulary has been accompanied by an imitation of LXX themes and narrative structures, as well.²⁹ Characteristically, he sees Luke as a Greco-Roman

---

27 A. Wifstrand, *L'Eglise ancienne et la culture grécque* (French transl. by L.-M. Dewailly, of *Fornkyrkan och den grekkista Bildningen* (Stockolm: Svenska Kyrkans Diakonistyrelses Bokforlag, 1957), (Paris: Cerf, 1962)), p. 46 (*cf.* also in German, *Die alte Kirche und die griechische Bildung* (Bern: Francke, 1967)); *idem*, 'Lukas och Klassicismen', *Swensk Exegetisk Årsbok* 5 (1940), pp. 139-151; L. Rydberg, *Fachprosa, vermeintliche Volkssprache und Neues Testament: Zur Beurteilung der sprachlichen Niveauunterschiede im nachklassischen Griechisch* (Uppsala: Academia, 1967), pp. 177, 187-190 (as quoted in L. Alexander, *The Preface to Luke's Gospel: Literary Convention and Social Context in Luke 1:1-4 and Acts 1:1* (Cambridge: Cambridge UP, 1993), pp. 169-172, and in D. Dormeyer, *The New Testament Among the Writings of Antiquity* (Sheffield: Sheffield Academical, 1998), pp. 47-48).

28 Alexander, *Preface*, pp. 34-41, 44, 174-175, 208-209. This technical Hellenist style would have involved a 'contrast in style and language between preface and text', a characteristic of Luke (see Alexander, *op.cit.*, p. 175).

29 Brodie, 'Greco-Roman Imitation' and 'Luke 7:36-50 as an Internalization of 2 Kings 4:1-37', cited earlier, and a series of other articles such as 'Towards unravelling Luke's use of the Old Testament: Luke 7:11-17 as an imitation of 1 Kings 17:17-24', *NTS* 32 (1986), 247-267; 'Luke as an Imitation and Emulation of the Elijah-Elisha Narrative,' in E. Richard (ed.), *New Views on Luke and Acts* (Collegeville, MN: Liturgical, 1990), 78-85; 'The Departure for

author who employs rhetorical conventions and as a Christian theologian who interprets the Jewish Scriptures for his own post-resurrection community.[30] He explores in particular Luke's internalization and appropriation of OT texts as Christian spirituality.[31] Thus, in contrast with Talbert or Barr, Brodie considers that 'however much the evangelists drew inspiration from various Greco-Roman literary models, they were particularly indebted to the [OT] biblical histories'.[32]

For this reason Brodie's analysis has a certain hybrid look about it. Luke is supposed to have interacted mainly with the OT, yet formally this interaction is best described in terms of Greco-Roman mimesis. What is being omitted here is the idea of a Lukan Greco-Roman imitation of Greco-Roman models, that is, Luke's mimesis of Hellenistic standards and literary paradigms.[33]

G. Kennedy has justified the OT-oriented approach by arguing that rhetorical mimesis, according to which 'one studied an author and tried to reproduce his style', tended to overshadow the earlier Aristotelian meaning of imitation.[34]

Jerusalem (Luke 9:51-56) as rhetorical imitation of Elijah's departure for the Jordan (2 Kgs. 1:1-2:6)', *Bib* 70 (1989), 96-109. A similar view has G. J. Steyn, 'Intertextual Similarities between Septuagint Pretexts and Luke's Gospel', *Neot* 24 (1990), 229-245.

30 Spencer, *Philip*, p. 137. See H. Gross, 'Motivtransposition als überlieferungs-geschichtliche Prinzip im Altes Testament', *BEthL*, 12-13 (1959), pp. 325-334. R. Alter referred to the same feature under the name of 'type-scenes' (*The Art of Biblical Narrative* (N.Y.: Basic Books, 1981)). For general a discussion of OT paradigms in the NT, see W. Berg, *Die Rezeption alttestamentlicher Motive im Neuen Testament - dargestellt and den Seewandelerzählungen* (Freiburg: Hochschul, 1979); J. Rius-Camps, 'Cuatro paradigmas del Pentateuco refundidos en los Hechos de los apóstoles', *EstB* 53 (1995), 25-54, etc.

31 Brodie, 'Unravelling', p. 44; *idem*, 'Luke 7:36-50 as an Internalization of 2 Kings 4:1-37', p. 457.

32 Brodie, 'Luke as an Imitation and Emulation', p. 78. E. Reinmuth favours the OT connections of the Emmaus story (*Pseudo-Philo und Lukas* (Tübingen: Mohr, 1994), p. 179, *vs.* other approaches which focus on Greco-Roman paradigms (Windisch, Ehrhardt, Betz, Bultmann, Grundmann, Guillaume, etc.). Similar views are held by Alsup, *Post-resurrection*, p. 265; Zwiep, *Ascension*, pp. 159-166; Seidensticker, *Auferstehung*, p. 56.

33 Steyn, 'Luke's use of ΜΙΜΗΣΙΣ?', p. 553.

34 Kennedy, *Persuasion*, p. 332.

Where Plato and Aristotle meant 'imitation of reality or of nature', the rhetoricians meant 'imitation or emulation of a classical literary model'.[35] One can cite, for example, Longinus' emphasis in his treatise *On the Sublime* where the road to sublimity is 'zealous imitation of the great historians and poets of the past' (μίμησίς τε καὶ ζήλωσις) and in their mimesis of the past masters writers contend like athletes to win the crown of excellence.[36] Resting his case on linguistic arguments, Cadbury acknowledges a similar parallel between Lukan biblical imitation and Greek Atticist perfectionism

> Archaism had certainly affected Jewish literature before him [*i.e.*, Luke]... The apocryphal books, the Wisdom of Solomon and First Maccabees... represent an archaizing manner. Indeed all late use of Hebrew was an artificial return to an obsolescent language comparable to the tour de force involved in Greek Atticism [...] imitation, μίμησις of definite authors became a rhetorical practice for young students that finished authors never outgrew. It is therefore not improbable that some of the more obvious Semitisms of the speeches in Acts are Biblical imitation.[37]

It does not seem realistic, however, to restrict the studying of Luke's style only to the issue of LXX imitation.

COMPOSITIONAL MIMESIS AND SOURCE REPRESENTATION

As a new direction of research, compositional mimesis is more easily to follow now, when narrative approaches to the NT focus on theology as a 'discourse about God in the setting of a story', at the centre of this theology being the 'depiction of reality, ultimate and penultimate, in terms of plot, coherence, movement, and climax'.[38] From Auerbach, Frye, Burke, and Wilder, decisively influential authors on this subject, there 'has emerged a general concept of the "fictive" representation

---

35 Kennedy, *Persuasion*, p. 333; *cf.* R. McKeon, 'Literary criticism', p. 147.
36 Longinus, *On the Sublime*, 13.2, 4. See D. C. Innes, 'Longinus: Structure and Unity', in J. G. J. Abbenes, S. R. Slings, I. Sluiter (eds.), *Greek Literary Theory After Aristotle* (Amsterdam: V.U. University, 1995), 111-124.
37 Cadbury, *Making*, p. 122.
38 G. Fackre, 'Narrative Theology. An Overview', *Int* 37 (1983), 340-352, p. 343.

of "reality" whose scope is broad enough to be applied to history writing as well as to fiction".[39]

A discussion of the literary representation of reality, in the context of the first century AD, involves from the beginning the need to assess the contrasting concepts of Plato and Aristotle.[40] While Platonic mimesis has to do mainly with image-creating, with copying reality, and with imitation and dramatic impersonation, Aristotle's is defined by *mythos* and *praxis*, story and action, stressing compositional creativity and the narrative re-creation of facts.[41] Plato's rejection of impersonation as popular and vulgar, his preference for the indirect style creates an interesting context for evaluating Luke's style, since Luke so often represents speeches and dialogues.

More relevant for the present study of Luke's literary paradigms, however, seems to be Aristotle's discussion of mimesis. He emphasizes the paradigmatic nature of plot as an

---

39 P. Ricoeur, 'The Narrative Function', in W. A. Beardslee (ed.), *Semeia 13: The Poetics of Faith: Essays Offered to A. N. Wilder* (Missoula, MT: Scholars, 1978), 177-202, p. 189; N. Frye, *The Anatomy of Criticism: Four Essays* (Princeton, NJ: Princeton UP, 1959); K. Burke, *A Grammar of Motives* (N.Y.: Prentice-Hall, 1945); N. A. Wilder, *The Language of the Gospel: Early Christian Rhetoric* (London: SCM, 1964).

40 The classical opposition between Plato's and Aristotle's views on poetry has been regarded as 'the Ormazd and the Ahriman' of novelistic aesthetics (G. Genette, *Narrative Discourse* (Ithaca, NY: Cornell UP, 1980), p. 163).

41 Melberg, *Theories*, pp. 44-45; G. F. Else, *Aristotle's Poetics: The Argument* (Cambridge, MA: Harvard UP, 1957), p. 322. The Aristotelian pair of *praxis / mythos* has been replaced in modern theories by concepts like story / plot, fibula / sjuzet, histoire / récit (Melberg, *op.cit.*, p. 48). P. Ricoeur in particular has developed the opposition *praxis / mythos* into a full philosophy of narrative representation. The action (praxis; or the 'before-mythos') is characterised by a pre-narrative order, as a prefiguration of 'reality' (mimesis I); the story ('mythos') is a narrative representation of reality, a recreation of its logical connections (of its intrinsic 'order'), as in N. Frye's 'explanation by emplotment' (mimesis II); finally, the 'after-mythos' stage takes the intrinsic order of the story to reshape the 'reality' itself with its perception of 'reality' (refiguration, as the third stage of mimesis, 'mimesis III'; P. Ricoeur, *Time and Narrative* (Chicago, IL: University of Chicago, 1984), vol. 1, p. 74; *idem*, 'Narrative Function', pp. 185-193).

important factor of literary coherence, defining it as the mimesis of an action 'complete, whole, and of magnitude', the 'whole' (ὅλον) having 'a beginning, a middle, and end', so that 'well-constructed plots [συνεστῶτας εὖ μύθους], therefore, should neither begin nor end at an arbitrary point, but should make use of the patterns stated'.[42] Aristotle's definition is both simple and fundamental in its observations, and it has been used almost unchanged in modern narrative studies. For example, W. S. Kurz defines narrative criticism as the study 'of the plot of any narrative, including history, with a beginning, middle, and end'.[43] Consequently, as D. Tracy explains it, one should not limit in NT studies the Aristotelian reference to his *Rhetorics*, but instead, 'we must turn... to the *Poetics* and its insistence that... form and matter are indissoluble, that the disclosive and transformative power and meaning of the story are grasped only in and through the narrative itself'.[44]

Thus, one can note among NT scholars an increasingly emphatic turning to an Aristotelian assessment of NT narratives. For example, according to Dan O. Via 'the primacy of plot in the parables makes the Aristotelian literary approach especially pertinent'.[45] Hedrick also favours the use of mimesis as defined in Aristotle's *Poetics* for the study of Luke's stories, especially if the plot line involves such themes as journeys, miracles, escapes, arrests, etc.[46] Specifically, he applies Aristotle's categories in the analysis of the Good Samaritan parable seen as a mimetic illustration of real life.[47]

---

42 Aristotle, *Poetics*, 1450b.25-35.
43 Kurz, *Reading Luke-Acts: Dynamics of Biblical Narrative*, Louisville, KY: Westminster, 1993), pp. 2-3. According to an actualised definition plot is 'any system of parts that carries over, continuous and changing, from the beginning to the end' (P. Goodman, *The Structure of Literature* (Chicago, IL: University of Chicago, 1964), p. 17, cf. E. M. Forster, *Aspects of the Novel* (London: Clowes, 1974), p. 58).
44 D. Tracy, *The Analogical Imagination* (N.Y.: Crossroads, 1981), p. 275.
45 D. O. Via, *The Parables: Their Literary and Existential Dimension* (Philadelphia, PA: Fortress, 1967), p. 100.
46 C. W. Hedrick, *Parables as Poetic Fictions: The Creative Voice of Jesus* (Peabody, MA: Hendrickson, 1994), pp. 47-50.
47 Hedrick, *Parables*, p. 93. Hedrick regards Luke's parables as 'fictive representations of actions that happened or may have happened' and

For Hedrick the plot imposed on the story data is a major compositional feature, characteristic for novels as well as for history-writing.[48] Reminding one of Luke's style, and implicitly of Aristotle's recognitions and reversals of plot, Ricoeur notes that 'no story without surprises, coincidences, encounters, revelations, recognitions, etc. would hold our attention'.[49]

A comprehensive analysis of a NT text from a composite Platonic-Aristotelian mimetic perspective can be found, in another example, in S. Lücking's study on Mark 14:1-11. Starting from a literary parallel between one passage in Plato's *Republic* and Mark 14:3, *i.e.* the anointing of a foreigner's head as a sign of respect for his talents,[50] Lücking introduces the Markan Jesus as a μῖμος τῶν ἀτιμήτων, one who identifies himself with the destitute and the inferior.[51]

If his starting point is a Platonic text, reflecting the philosopher's dislike of actors and foreign performers, in his actual mimetic analysis of Mark 14:1-11 Lücking turns soon to Aristotle's concepts of diction (λέξις), thought (διανοία), character (ἤθη), and plot (μῦθος), affirming the essential literary unity of this text, its compositional structure, its narrative function (*Schlüsselfunktion*) in the Markan narrative and its historic significance (Mark's *historische Motiv*).[52] In an interesting generalisation, Jesus' Passion, even

---

addresses the issue of 'what is being represented and how true is it to human life' (pp. 80-81).

48 Hedrick, *Parables*, p. 84 (*cf.* Via, *Parables*, p. 100).
49 Ricoeur, 'Narrative Function', p. 182.
50 Plato, *Rep.* 397e.9-398a.8.: 'therefore when any one of these pantomimic gentlemen, who are so clever that they can imitate anything, comes to us, and makes a proposal to exhibit himself and his poetry, we will fall down and worship him as a sweet and holy and wonderful being; but we must also inform him that in our State such as he are not permitted to exist; the law will not allow them. And so when we have anointed him with myrrh, and set a garland of wool upon his head, we shall send him away to another city' (B. Jowett). *Cf.* the similarity of Plato's and Mark's texts, as noted by Lücking: προσκυνοῖμεν ἂν αὐτὸν ὡς ἱερὸν καὶ θαυμαστὸν καὶ ἡδύν... μύρον κατὰ τῆς κεφαλῆς κατὰ χέαντες καὶ ἐρίωι στέψαντες, and Mk 14:3 κατὰ κειμένου αὐτοῦ ἦλθεν γυνὴ ἔχουσα ἀλάβαστρον μύρου νάρδου πιστικῆς πολυτελοῦς, συντρίψασα τὴν ἀλάβαστρον κατέχεεν αὐτοῦ τῆς κεφαλῆς.
51 Lücking, *Mimesis*, p. 14.
52 Lücking, *Mimesis*, pp. 15-16.

the whole argument in Mark, represents for him the equivalent of a great messianic recognition (*anagnorisis*).[53] Such examples as those mentioned above show that compositional mimesis is at present both a necessary and a fashionable perspective in the NT studies, so that a more complex assessment of Luke's theology of the Way from this point of view, will be, probably, more than welcome.

LITERARY DETAILS AND HISTORICAL REFERENCE

Apart from compositional perspectives on mimesis, an important issue in the debate concerning the forms of representation in the NT is that of historical realism or 'representational reference', that is, the reflection in the NT of its historical environment, of life as lived in the first century AD.[54] The issue as such is quite complex. In a way, representational analysis lies 'in the background of all literary and rhetorical approaches'[55] and it allows a 'critical recovery of the traditional conviction that the text and its interpretation deal with the truth and reality of a world of value that can, however imperfectly, be known'.[56] In particular, the quality of this correspondence between narrative and the reality it narrates is the foundation of Luke-Acts as a historical document. At this level, mimesis is a window for testing the author's links with his world, as well as his compositional interests.

Specifically, as regards journeying, Luke-Acts abounds with details highlighting their author's familiarity with journeys in the Hellenistic world, with their customs and itineraries, or with their literary models.[57] The text includes realistic features like journey omens (*cf.* the symbol of the Dioscuri,

---

53 Lücking, *Mimesis*, pp. 108-109, 114-121.
54 W. A. Beardslee, 'What is it about? Reference in New Testament Literary Criticism', in E. S. Malbon and E. V. McKnight (eds.), *The New Literary Criticism and the New Testament* (Sheffield: Sheffield Academical, 1994), 367-386, esp. p. 384.
55 Beardslee, 'Reference', p. 369.
56 Beardslee, 'Reference', pp. 367, 369.
57 B. M. Rapske, 'Acts, Travel, and Shipwreck', in D. W. J. Gill and C. Gempf (eds.), *The Book of Acts in Its Graeco-Roman Setting* (Carlisle: Paternoster, 1994), 1-47; p. 44; Casson, *Travel*, p. 94. See also J. M. Gilchrist, 'The Historicity of Paul's Shipwreck', *JSNT* 61 (1996), 29-51.

Acts 28:11), revelations and dreams at the beginning of journeying (Peter's Confession and the Transfiguration before Jesus' journey to Jerusalem, Peter's vision prior to his visit to Cornelius, Paul's vision of a Macedonian before his journey to Europe, the prophecy of Agabus before Paul's journey to Jerusalem, etc.), sailing details.[58] From this perspective Acts as a record of travel and sea-voyage should be given 'a careful and thorough reading, keeping an eye on the patterns and experience of travel in antiquity'.[59]

The importance of such a realistic reflection of life, thus, seems to reside not only in the assessing of Luke's credibility yet, as well, in the actual selection of events and in their arrangement in the literary plot, in their symbolic value, in the role they play in communicating the author's' intention.[60]

FIGURAL MIMESIS AND PSYCHOLOGICAL MIMESIS

As a cultural phenomenon, mimesis can take different forms and illustrate various principles. Contemporary studies highlighted, for example, that in terms of techniques and perspectives, one could use two major approaches to mimesis: there is a figural, compositional representation of events, which reflects and reconstructs reality at the narrative level, and, also, a philosophical, psychological type of representation which unveils patterns of social behaviour and deeply-rooted inner motivations.

As regards figural mimesis, E. Auerbach is one of its major and most famous literary theorists who provided an excellent and exquisite excursus in the history of literature, emphasizing the differences between the Greco-Roman and the Biblical representational styles.[61] Auerbach's historical and figural analysis of mimesis has been taken further by authors such as G. Gebauer and C. Wulf,[62] and, by turning the

---

58 Rapske, 'Acts, Travel', pp. 43-44; Casson, *Travel*, p. 178; Gilchrist, 'Historicity', pp. 50-51.
59 Rapske, 'Acts, Travel', pp. 46-47.
60 Cook, *History Writing*, p. 206.
61 Auerbach, *Mimesis*, pp. 3-23, on OT and Homer, and 24-49, on Mk. And Petronius and Tacitus (Mk. 14:67-72).
62 G. Gebauer and C. Wulf, *Mimesis*. They continued Auerbach's comparative analysis with the works of Molière, Shakespeare, Racine,

subject into a fashion, the way was soon paved for a second major discussion of literary mimesis, the psychologising approach of R. Girard, often used in Pauline studies.[63]

For R. Girard, mimesis is a complex phenomenon placed at the intersection of several planes: ethical, philosophical, and literary. Reminiscent of Aristotle's views, Girard's mimesis deals with a deeply-rooted human tendency to unconsciously imitate one another, a tendency which leads, according to him, to a culture of discontent and violence. One of the most recognisable patterns of this type of mimesis is the motif of the substitutionary victim sacrificed by a murderous collectivity for the sake of general peace or atonement (the 'scapegoat' motif), a pattern largely reflected in myths and early religious literature, as well as in modern novels.[64] In view of this sacrificial emphasis, Girardian mimesis has been regarded with much interest by many NT scholars.[65] Apart from the

---

Diderot, Lessing, Rousseau, and literary philosophers such as Benjamin, Adorno, and Derrida (cf. Melberg, *Theories*, pp. 2-5).

[63] J. L. Boyce, 'Graceful imitation: "imitators of us and the Lord" (1 Thessalonians 1:6)', *Word & World Supplement* 1 (1992), 139-146; J. A. Brant, 'The place of mimesis in Paul's thought', *Studies in Religion / Sciences religieuses*, 22/3 (1993), 285-300; W. J. Ong, 'Mimesis and the Following of Christ', *Religion and Literature*, 26/2 (1994), 73-77.

[64] R. Girard, *Deceit, Desire, and the Novel* (Baltimore, MA: John Hopkins UP, 1965); idem, *Violence and the Sacred* (Baltimore, MA: John Hopkins UP, 1979); idem, *Things Hidden since the Foundation of the World* (Stanford, CA: Stanford UP, 1987); idem, *A Theater of Envy* (Oxford: Oxford UP, 1991); idem, '"The ancient trail trodden by the wicked": Job as scapegoat', in A. J. McKenna (ed.), *Semeia 33: René Girard and Biblical Studies* (Missoula, MT: Scholars, 1985), 13-41, etc.

[65] *Cf.* R. G. Hamerton-Kelly, 'A Girardian interpretation of Paul: rivalry, mimesis and victimage in the Corinthian correspondence', in A. J. McKenna (ed.), *Semeia 33: René Girard and Biblical Studies* (Missoula, MT: Scholars, 1985), 65-81; R. Detweiler, 'Introduction: from chaos to legion to chance: the double play of apocalyptic and mimesis', in R. Detweiler and W. Doty (eds.), *The Daemonic Imagination: Biblical Text and Secular Story* (Atlanta, GA: Scholars, 1990), 1-26; M. I. Wallace and Th. H. Smith (eds.), *Curing Violence* (Sonoma, CA: Polebridge, 1994); also, W. Schweiker, 'Sacrifice, interpretation, and the sacred: the import of Gadamer and Girard for religious studies', *JAAR* 55 (1987), 791-810; A. J. Levoratti, 'La lectura no sacrificial del evangelio en la obra de René Girard', *Revista Bíblica* 47 (1985), 159-176; *cf.* G. Bailie,

obvious illustrations that can be found in Paul's epistles, the Lukan corpus includes, as well, a number of relevant passages and interests. For example, Luke is a keen observer of the social behaviour of large groups as well as of individuals, and of the way the Gospel stirs passions and fears, opposition or enthusiasm, in its journey to 'the ends of the earth' (*cf.* his description of trials, of crowds psychology, etc.; *cf.* reactions provoked by Paul's addresses in Acts 16:20, 18:12-17, 19:32-33).

Although the present study is not trying to avoid this Girardian type of insights into Luke's stories, and is coming quite close, actually, to such an analysis during the assessment of Plato's social aspects of mimesis and in the study of Luke's use of the suffering motif, *pathos* (discussed at length by Aristotle), it will focus, however, more on the stylistic and compositional significance of mimesis in the NT. This approach is closer to Auerbach's views than that of Girard.

In particular, Auerbach's discussion provides many inspiring observations for the current study of Luke-Acts. For example, he emphasizes the specific roles of 'recognition' in the the OT, NT and in the Greek and Latin narratives. To this end he compares, in one famous instance, Odysseus' recognition by the old Euryclea (Homer, *Odyssey*, 19.415-505) with the story of Isaac's sacrifice (Genesis 22:1-20).[66] He highlights there the presence of a high dramatism in the OT accounts *versus* a peaceful, idyllic representation of reality, in Homer (this contrast is helped, however, by Auerbach's own selection, for Isaac's sacrifice takes place in an unfamiliar context, while Odysseus' story takes place in the familiar surroundings of his home).[67]

Violence Unveiled: Humanity at the Crossroads (N.Y.: Crossroads, 1995), pp. 116-118, etc. For a response, *cf.* B. Levine, 'René Girard on Job: the question of the scapegoat', in A. J. McKenna (ed.), *Semeia 33: René Girard and Biblical Studies* (Missoula, MT: Scholars, 1985), 125-133; W. J. Ong, 'Mimesis and the Following of Christ', *Religion and Literature* 26 (1944), 73-77.

66   Auerbach, *Mimesis*, pp. 3-23, *cf.* p. 8, cf. pp. 22, 28.
67   Auerbach, *Mimesis*, p. 22. As he notes, even the domestic scenes are profoundly dramatic in biblical stories (*cf.* Cain and Abel; Noah and his sons; Abraham, Sarah, and Hagar; Rebekah, Jacob, and Esau, etc.), something 'inconceivable in the Homeric style'.

His further observations on Mark's mimetic style play an important role in contextualizing Luke's manner of literary representation, as well. Thus, he argues that the mimetic style of the NT is popular and unsophisticated, impressive through sincerity and personal witness (*cf.* Fortunata's portrait in Petronius, *Satyricon*, 37-38, and Percennius' speech in Tacitus, *Annals*, 1.16-18, *versus* Peter's repeated denial of Jesus in Mk. 14:67-72).[68] If Petronius and Tacitus display a highly descriptive art, using with great effect the eye-catching details of human life and its predicament, famous retorts or impressing speeches, Mark's style is entirely different betraying 'neither survey and rational disposition, nor artistic purpose', only a natural vivid imitation of reality, the narrator being 'at the core of what goes on; he observes and relates only what matters in relation to Christ's presence and mission'.[69]

The dramatic presentation of Peter's betrayal, in Mark, fits thus 'no antique genre' being placed in an intermediary position: 'too serious for comedy, too contemporary and everyday for tragedy, politically too insignificant for history'. Its form is one of 'such immediacy that its like does not exist in the literature of antiquity'.[70] Its 'seriousness' is not planned or consciously pursued, but rather comes as a consequence of God's own dramatic intervention in history, similar to the dramatism of the Incarnation.[71] By contrast, however, Luke's

---

68   Auerbach, *Mimesis*, pp. 24-49.
69   Auerbach, *Mimesis*, p. 47.
70   Auerbach, *Mimesis*, p. 45. R. Girard objects that Auerbach focused on mimesis as *form* and failed to observe the importance of mimesis as *content* (Girard, 'Peter's denial and the question of mimesis [Mk 14:66-72]', *Notre Dame English Journal* 14 (1982), 177-189). A similar objection is formulated by Melberg who notes that 'Auerbach makes his most interesting observations on the mimetic play of similarity and difference not in terms of representation', that is, in terms of *figura* and figural style and interpretation, not in terms of composition and representation of sources (Melberg, *Theories*, p. 2; J. M. Gellrich, '*Figura*, Allegory and the Question of History', in S. Lerer (ed.), *Literary History*, 107-123: also Auerbach, *Mimesis*, pp. 16, 48, 73, 156, 194-196).
71   Auerbach, *Mimesis*, p. 41. The epic genre and tragedy were seen as 'mimesis of elevated matters [μίμησις εἶναι σπουδαίων]' (*Poetics*, 1449b.9-20). In general, Aristotle holds poetry as more elevated or serious than history (*Poetics*, 1451b.5). On σπουδαῖος, meaning both

narration seems closer to Hellenistic mimesis, since his rhetoric is often characterised by eye-catching descriptions or impressing retorts and speeches, or by elaborate dialogues that have no place in Mark, by a careful mis-en-scéne of the story.[72] A closer look at the mimetic concerns of Greek literary theorists such as Plato, Aristotle and Hellenistic historians, could help us understand better the features of NT mimesis, as well as Luke's own, specific style.

Plato's Mimesis and Its Social Effects

Plato's discussion of art theories (poetry, music, painting, as mimesis)[73] is characteristically placed in the context of his interest in politics.[74] He is not interested simply in stylistic matters but, concomitantly, in the ethical implications of arts, in their social and political role.[75]

Plato's views on mimesis and representative arts are, in general, minimalist and negative. For him mimesis is 'an inferior child born of inferior parents' (φαύλη ἄρα φαύλῳ ξυγγιγνομένη φαῦλα γεννᾷ ἡ μιμητική)[76] and his definition emphasizes the alienating element in imitation, that is, the assimilation of 'oneself to another person in speech or manner' (ὁμοιοῦν ἑαυτὸν ἄλλωι ἢ κατὰ φωνὴν ἢ κατὰ σχῆμα μιμεῖσθαι).[77] He allows, however, ironically, for a certain ambiguity in the definition of mimesis, questioning his own concept, as such,

---

"serious" and "good" see cf. G. F. Ferrary, 'Plato and Poetry', in G. A. Kennedy (ed.), *The Cambridge History of Literary Criticism*, vol. 1: *Classical Criticism* (Cambridge: Cambridge UP, 1995), 92-148, esp. p. 119, n. 29.

72 Direct discourse in the NT gospels indicates a relation with classical rhetoric, cf. Luke's dialogues 'on the road' (Auerbach, *Mimesis*, p. 46).

73 On mimesis and music, cf. *Laws*, 668a, 953a-b; on mimesis and painting: *Rep.* 596d, 598b; on mimesis and poetry: *Rep.* 392d.5, 394-398, etc.

74 J. D. Denniston, *Greek Literary Criticism* (London: Dent, 1924), pp. xiii-xiv. For Plato the planning of an ideal society (ideal city) is in fact a 'mimesis of the fairest and truest life, which is in reality,... the truest tragedy' (*Laws*, 817b.5; cf. Melberg, *Theories*, p. 21).

75 P. Murray, *Plato on Poetry: Ion, Republic 376e-398b, Republic 595-608b* (Cambridge: Cambridge UP, 1996), p. 182; Plato, *Rep.* 393c.1-3, 397d.1-3.

76 Plato, *Rep.* 603b.3-4.

77 Plato, *Rep.* 393c.5-6 (Lee).

when he asks 'could you tell me in general what imitation is? For neither do I myself quite apprehend what it would be at'.[78]

Indeed, Plato's own attitude towards mimesis is ambiguous, dualistic. He can accept mimesis under certain restrictions yet, also, he can go as far as demanding its general and total exclusion from the life of the ideal city.[79] This inconsistency[80] has alternatively been regarded as a two-view theory. According to the first, mimesis bears negative connotations being ontologically separate from reality and harmful to the human soul. According to the second, mimesis has a positive aspect, useful as an approach to the divine truth, in education or social life, although of secondary importance.[81] Fundamental to Plato's approach to mimesis is, however, the discussion of its ethical component.

THE ETHICS OF MIMESIS

Interestingly and representatively, Plato's theory of mimesis starts with the first ever coherent literary critique of Homer. Although Homer is regarded as a leader of tragedians and the first poet of the Greeks,[82] Plato follows Xenophanes and Heraclitus in criticising the rhapsodist's impious portrayal of gods and heroes as something that misleads the young and desecrates their ideals.[83] Homer's alternate use of indirect narration, ἁπλῇ διηγήσει, and *impersonation* or enactment through dialogue (διὰ μιμήσεως) is seen as the root of all this psychological evil.[84] Such a combination is scorned as one

---

[78] Socrates, in Plato, *Rep.* 595c.7. A similar irony is present in *Ion*, 532d.8-10.
[79] Plato, *Rep.*, chs. 2-3, 10; *Laws*, ch. 7. In *Rep.* 595a.4-5 the ideal state is right in excluding all imitation, and in *Rep.* 607a.3-5 he suggests the removing of poetry altogether from Greek culture. *Cf.* A. Nehamas, 'Plato on imitation and poetry in Republic 10', in J. Moravcsik and P. Temko (eds.), *Plato on beauty, wisdom, and the arts* (Totowa, NJ: Rowman and Allanheld, 1982), 47-78, p. 53; also Ferrary, 'Plato and Poetry', p. 120.
[80] Woodruff, 'Aristotle on mimesis', p. 75.
[81] L. Golden, *Aristotle on Tragic and Comic Mimesis* (Atlanta, GA: Scholars, 1992), pp. 41-47.
[82] Plato, *Rep.* 598d, 600e.
[83] Plato, *Rep.* 390-392.
[84] Plato, *Rep.* 392d.4-398a.

bringing delight only to children, nurses, and the general (vulgar and feeble) public.[85]

Mimesis as impersonation (recitation, repetition, acting) is supremely dangerous for it can involve change for the worst for the whole person (voice, thinking, behaviour), it can create habits and encourage indulgence, interfering destructively with the character of the young.[86] Greek education, based on recitation, finds itself, thus, in great danger.[87] Mimesis becomes for Plato a problem of life and death, and behind the rejection of mimetic poetry there is a fear of a 'loss of self' and 'of character';[88] the minimum poets could do, as a safeguard, is to use more of the plain narrative (διήγησις), and less of impersonation.[89]

To these ethical objections against mimesis Plato adds further philosophical arguments. He rejects it entirely, in the end, especially as *image-making*: since mimesis mirrors reality (the ideal, divine form, τὸ εἶδος) only superficially,[90] it deceives its audience with a superficial impression of depth of knowledge.[91]

MIMESIS AS A REFLECTION OF TRUTH

Plato imagines two types of creators: ὁ φυτουργός, the divine creator of essences, ἰδέαι, and ὁ δημιουργός, who, like a workman, creates three dimensional images of these divine essences.[92] By comparison, painters, as well as poets or any

---

85 Plato, *Rep.* 397d.
86 Plato, *Rep.* 395-397; 695-697; *Laws*, 798e.4-8, 817a-e.
87 Woodruff, 'Aristotle on mimesis', p. 76.
88 Melberg, *Theories*, p. 20.
89 Plato, *Rep.* 393e. Plato's antithetical examples include the scene where Chryses, rejected by Agamemnon in his request, starts a vivid series of imprecations (Homer, *Iliad*, 1.15f). Imitation reaches its worst when bad language is joined by vulgar gestures (Plato, *Rep.* 392e-394b). Plato favours, thus, written literature in opposition to 'oral' representation or recitation, called the 'homeric state of mind' (*cf.* E. R. Havelock, *Preface to Plato* (Cambridge, MA: Harvard UP, 1963), p. 41).
90 Plato, *Rep.* 600e.3-7.
91 Plato, *Rep.* 598b-d. Mimesis corrupts the human soul, *cf.* Golden, *Tragic and Comic Mimesis*, p. 41.
92 Plato, *Rep.* 597d. He also classifies the creative techniques in use, manufacture, and representation (χρησομένην, ποιήσουσαν, μιμησομένην, *Rep.* 601d.1-3).

other artists, belong to a third category, as μιμητής, the imitators of images, whose object of imitation is itself an imitation of something else, thus, an appearance (φαντάσματος μίμησις),[93] and a reflection three times removed from the real essence of the world: τὸν τοῦ τρίτου ἄρα γεννήματος ἀπὸ τῆς φύσεως μιμητὴν καλεῖς.[94] Plato reproaches art, then, that it is busy imitating reality 'at a third remove' from the divine originals.[95]

Despite these accusations, mimesis can still be an acceptably accurate reproduction of reality,[96] reflecting a true relationship between the human world and that of the divine essences (ἰδέαι).[97] The state's laws, for example, provide for the people the reflection (μιμήματα) of the truth known by experts.[98] In a certain sense, mimesis is the very formula for the creation of the world.[99] The movements of the stars follow the designs of the Supreme Being, reflecting his eternal nature and intelligence.[100]

Mimesis, therefore, paradoxically, can turn to be acceptable even for Plato if one has got the antidote of a lucid mind[101] (mimesis could act both as a poisonous drug, and as curing medicine, φάρμακον).[102]

SUPERVISED MIMESIS *VERSUS* MIMETIC CORRUPTION

In particular, through his critique of mimesis Plato tried to control and balance public education and social life, by

---

93   Plato, *Rep.* 598b.4.
94   Plato, *Rep.* 597e.3-4.
95   Plato, *Rep.* 596-602.
96   Plato, *Laws*, 668a-b.
97   Plato, *Timaeus*, 47b-c.
98   Plato, *Statesman*, 300c.8-14; *Laws*, 817b-d; *cf.* Woodruff, 'Aristotle on mimesis', p. 77.
99   Plato, *Timaeus*, 29e-30d, on creation.
100 Plato, *Timaeus*, 39d.8-e.2 (*cf.* Melberg, *Theories*, p. 22). Mimesis could function as a means for reaching the truth, valid yet inferior to dialectic and reason (Golden, *Tragic and Comic Mimesis*, pp. 45-47).
101 Plato, *Rep.* 595b.4-6.
102 Plato, *Rep.* 382c.5-10; *cf.* Melberg, *Theories*, pp. 12-14, 32 (see J. Derrida, 'La Pharmacie de Platon', in J. Derrida, *La Dissémination* (Paris: Seuil, 1972), p. 122).

restricting the usual emphasis on pleasure (ἡδονή)¹⁰³ or on artistic fiction (ἀπάτη).¹⁰⁴ His acceptance of mimesis comes with a strong emphasis on the need for state supervision and censorship of mimesis in music, dance and art, education, etc.¹⁰⁵ Even if such supervision was in place, however, Plato preferred the forms of *accurate* imitation of models to *creative* or *innovative* performance which might be open to exaggerations, τὴν ὁμοιότητα τῷ τοῦ καλοῦ μιμήματι,¹⁰⁶ in other words, he prefers 'correctness' to 'pleasure', οὐχ ἥτις ἡδεῖα, ἀλλ' ἥτις ὀρθή.¹⁰⁷

In order to avoid moral ambiguity and the ethical damage caused by mimesis, Plato recommends firm regulations for the education of youth, especially for the young cultural wardens. These, as an elite group invested to watch over the ideological purity of the city and supervise its cultural life should be educated with the greatest care: mimesis was allowed in the form of poetry, acting, recitation, yet only if the youth played or imitated 'suitable' parts, like 'men of courage, self-control, piety, freedom of spirit and similar qualities [ἐὰν δὲ μιμῶνται μιμεῖσθαι τὰ τούτοις προσέκοντα εὐθὺς ἐκ παίδων, ἀνδρείους, σώφρονας, ὁσίους, ἐλευθέρους, καὶ τὰ τοιαῦτα πάντα]'.¹⁰⁸ They were categorically not allowed to play 'the parts of women, young or old (for they are men)'; nor such actions like women 'abusing their husbands or quarrelling with heaven and boasting of their supposed good fortune, or mourning and lamenting in misfortune,... or in sickness or love or childbirth' for these are not worth of men.¹⁰⁹

---

103 Plato, *Rep.* 387b.1-7. Murray notes that for Plato 'poetry is dangerous precisely in the proportion to the pleasure it gives' (Murray, *Plato*, pp. 138, 159). See F. W. Walbank, 'Profit or Amusement: Some Thoughts on the Motives of Hellenistic Historians', in H. Verdin, G. Schepens and E. de Keysen (eds.), *Purposes of History: Studies in Greek Historiography from the 4th to the 2nd centuries BC* (Leuven: Leuven UP, 1990), 253-266, esp. p. 254.
104 Plato, *Rep.* 387b, 397d-e; 602a-c; *cf.* K. Ziegler, 'Tragödia', in *RE*, vol. 6 (1937), cols. 1899-2075, esp. 2017-2022; also, Walbank, 'Profit or Amusement', pp. 253-254.
105 Plato, *Laws,* 654b-657b; 668a-e; 797b-c; 799b; 817a-e.
106 Plato, *Laws,* 668a.8-b.2.
107 Plato, *Laws,* 668b.5-6. See also, *Laws,* 816e.1-3.
108 Plato, *Rep.* 395b.9-d.1 (Lee).
109 Plato, *Rep.* 395d.5-396b.7 (Lee).

The decent man, ὁ μέτριος ἀνήρ, should, therefore, represent only good characters, someone failing only in a few respects and to a limited degree, and should avoid impersonating a man worse than himself.[110] Serious or elevated imitation (σπουδῆι, σπουδαῖος) is here a crucial concept opposed to childish fun (παιδιᾶς χάριν). Otherwise μίμησις is merely a game not a serious entreprise, παιδιάν τινα καὶ οὐ σπουδήν.

PLATO, LUKE, AND THE CHALLENGES OF TRAVELLERS

When this is applied to the NT, Luke, as well as the other NT writers, could not be described as a 'safe' literary authors or safe travelers for Plato's ideal city. In terms of literature, Luke uses both indirect narratives and the direct (mimetic) style, finding place for impersonation, including numerous speeches in his accounts, emulating the most probable style of their authors (semitisms, LXX phrases, higher Greek, various quotations, etc.; *cf.* the dialogues and hymns in the Nativity narratives, Lk. 1-3; Peter's proclamation at Pentecost, Acts 2:14-36; Stephen's defending speech in Jerusalem, Acts 7:2-57; Paul's speech in Athens, Acts 17:22-31, etc.). Generally, though, Luke's imitation tends to be 'elevated' or 'serious' in style and content, reflecting the nature of his subject, the Christ and his Church.

However, Luke's missionary reports confirm that Hellenistic towns often adopted a Platonic type of policy towards the disciples, as foreigners, trying to defend their traditional culture against innovations and external challenges. For example, in Acts 16:20, the rich owners of the slave girl with a spirit of divination are antagonised by Paul's miracle and his preaching of the gospel and use a cultural argument against him: 'these men are disturbing our city [ἐκταράσσουσιν ἡμῶν τὴν πόλιν]; they are Jews and are advocating customs that are not lawful for us as Romans to adopt or observe [ἔθη ἃ οὐκ ἔξεστιν ἡμῖν παραδέχεσθαι οὐδὲν ποιεῖν]'.[111] A similar argument is put forward in Ephesus (Acts 19:26-27).

The imagery of cities with closed gates for strangers is very close to the picture drawn by Plato's tirade against foreign visiting actors (ξένοι)

---

110 Plato, *Rep.* 396c.5-e.2 (Lee).
111 Plato manifests a special care for the city's customs, ἔθη (cf. *Laws*, 817a.1-e.4).

Do not imagine, then, that we will ever thus lightly allow you to set up your stage beside us in the market-place, and give permission to those imported actors of yours, with their dulcet tones and their voices louder than ours, to harangue women and children and the whole populace, and to say not the same things as we say about the same institutions, but, on the contrary, things that are, for the most part, just the opposite.[112]

The casual visitor had to be checked at arrival 'when he comes to the city, at the markets, harbours, and public buildings outside the city', etc., so that none of these strangers should 'introduce any innovation [μὴ νεωτερίζῃ]'.[113]

A different treatment was in view, yet, for the foreign cultural representative (or 'inspector') who journeyed 'to view some noble object which is superior in beauty to anything to be found in other States'.[114] The city leaders should politely assist such a quest for cultural information. By accepting such visitors honour is done to 'Zeus, patron of strangers, instead of expelling strangers by means of meats and ceremonies... or else, by savage proclamations'.[115] In this way, two of Luke's

---

112 Plato, *Laws*, 817c.1-8.
113 Plato, *Laws*, 952e.6-953a.1.
114 Plato, *Laws*, 953c-e. The benefits of knowledge are often associated with journeying, and *theoria* itself 'implies a journey'. In Herodotus' description of Solon's travels *theoria* is used as a 'wishing to see the world', an expression of the passion for seeing and knowing (Herodotus, *History of the Greek and Persian War*, 1.30.11-14: παρ' ἡμέας γὰρ περισέο λόγος ἀπῖκται πολλὸς καὶ σοφίης εἵνεκεν τῆς σῆς καὶ πλάνης, ὡς φιλοσοφέων γῆν πολλὴν θεωρίης εἵνεκεν ἐπελήλυθας). Cf. J. Navone, *Towards a Theology of Story* (Slough: St. Paul, 1977), pp. 96-97. The theorist is a *sophos*, one 'skilled, knowledgeable about the world, people, customs, languages' (p. 96). His journey is 'a voyage of inquiry', and 'theorizing is a voyage to worthy sight' (Navone, *Theology of Story*, p. 97). Plato uses *theoria* as a journey in search of 'divinely inspired men' (Plato, *Laws*, 951b.5-c.4; 952d.4-953e.7). *Rep.* 514-518b opens with a reference to journeying, and, likewise, many of the *Dialogues* (cf. the discussion in Navone, *ad.loc.*).
115 Plato, *Laws*, 953c.3-e.3. R. Bury notes that expelling was possible, as well as forbidding the presence of the foreigners at ceremonial feasts (Plato, *Laws*, 953e, LCL, vol. 2, p. 514, n. 1). Theophilus, if a God-fearer of Hellenistic background, could thus have understood in a special way

main themes in Acts, the status of the visiting evangelist and the cultural significance of meals, can be checked, independently, in the philosophy of life of the first-century Hellenistic town (*cf.* Acts 16:20, 17:16-34, 19:26-27, etc.; yet also in the rest of NT, from a Christian cultural perspective, this time, in 2 Jn. 1:9-11; 3 Jn. 1:10-11, Rom. 14-15).

Greek cultural inspectors (θεωρός), however, were dealt with caution; should they return with corrupted ideas after visiting foreign states in search of best customs and teachers, they could face death for 'being a meddler in respect of education and the laws'.[116]

It is interesting to note that, apart from the status of the evangelist in a foreign city, mentioned before in relation to Acts (Acts 16:20, 17:16-34, 19:26-27) Luke's narrative reflects the unsettling effects of cultural mimesis, in various forms, with Jewish nuances, in his 'on the road' encounters. For example, Saul had the high priests' support in arresting the Christians, who could be seen as cultural innovators who 'belonged to the Way'. Later, he shares the fate of the Greek cultural inspectors who become themselves infected with new, foreign teaching during their visits and faced the condemnation of the state (although, the first Christians were not 'foreign' yet a very Jewish messianic sect).

Similarly, the Emmaus road dialogue between Jesus and Cleopas (Lk. 24:19-21) mentions the violent intervention of the Jerusalem leaders against Jesus, who was arrested and condemned to death on similar grounds, as an innovative preacher, a powerful prophet who challenged the established ways of Jerusalem (Girard's scapegoat mechanism is well illustrated in the four gospels, in the violent, collective, social mimesis that led to Jesus' crucifixion).

Further, the Ethiopian eunuch, as a challenging person, is implicitly presented as a stranger or foreign inspector looking for cultural and religious illumination, yet unable to raise himself up to the standards of Zion (due to his physical condition and his lack of understanding of the Scriptures). After unsettling the established paradigms of worship in Samaria, Caesarea and Azotus, Philip's ministry integrates

---

Luke's stress on meal fellowship in the context of Acts, as a 'cultural exchange' (*cf.* 1 Cor. 10:27).
116 Plato, *Laws*, 951d.1-952d.6.

him into the new people of God, and the Ethiopian eunuch himself would probably unsettle the worshipping paradigms of his native Ethiopia (Acts 8).

Paul's missionary journeys are further evidence that Luke's journeying accounts and the gospel's effect in Luke-Acts can be well understood as cultural interaction between the city-state and the visiting evangelist. His journeys are journeys of challenge and change rather than journeys of perfect integration in the Hellenistic Mediterranean world.

Aristotle's Mimesis as Creative Representation

The majority view is, with certain nuances, that Aristotle has developed his concept of mimesis in dialogue with Plato's correspondent category, if not as a response to him. It is very tempting to frame Aristotle's theory in Platonic terms, especially as mimesis is defined in Plato (*Rep.* 393c.5-6), but has no definition in Aristotle's *Poetics*. Thus, as L. Golden contends, Plato's views on mimesis represents the 'principal point of departure' for Aristotle's aesthetic theories

> Aristotle's theory of art is both a refutation of Plato's negative view of mimesis and a skilled and revolutionary refinement of his great teacher's insight into the positive force of mimesis.[117]

Aristotle's refinement of Plato's mimesis seems to end up 'meaning almost the exact opposite of what Plato had meant by it'.[118] Alternatively, it might simply represent an independent argument since 'there is no good internal evidence that Aristotle was driven in the *Poetics* by the need to answer Plato'.[119] The scale, however, seems to incline towards Aristotle's opposition to Plato: even a formal detail like Plato's famous criticism of Homer, is completely reversed in Aristotle's *Poetics* who praises the famous bard for his use of mimesis

> Homer deserves praise for many other qualities, but especially for realising, alone among epic poets, the place of the poet's own voice. For the poet should say as little as possible in his own voice, as it is not this

---

117 Golden, *Tragic and Comic Mimesis*, pp. 1-3.
118 Else, *Aristotle's Poetics*, p. 12.
119 Woodruff, 'Aristotle on mimesis', p. 72.

that makes him a mimetic artist. The others participate in their own voice throughout, and engage in mimesis only briefly and occasionally, whereas Homer, after a brief introduction, at once brings 'onto stage' a man, woman, or other figure (all of them rich in character).[120]

For Aristotle mimesis, yet, is more than just Homeric impersonation. Primarily, it has to do with literary creativity, with the art of representing reality through a complex story.

ARISTOTLE AND LITERARY IMAGINATION

For Aristotle mimesis is a key term - his 'master concept' as Else put it,[121] which relates *action* and *plot, praxis* and *mythos*, the creative writer and the world of real events. In a surprising move, instead of a definition, Aristotle provides his readers with a rather naturalistic justification of mimesis

> For it is an instinct of human beings, from childhood to engage in mimesis (indeed, this distinguishes them from other animals: man is the most mimetic of all, and it is through mimesis that he develops his earliest understanding).[122]

Imitation reflects, thus, an 'instinctive' cognitive disposition, all its forms originating in mankind's natural desire for knowledge. This desire provides the pleasure (ἡδονή) of learning and inference (μανθάνειν καὶ συλλογίζεσθαι).[123]

Creativity in representation is present at several levels in the artist's work. For example, in his choice of mimetic *media* (rhythm, language, music; τὴν μίμησιν ἐν ῥυθμῷ, καὶ λόγῳ καὶ ἁρμονίᾳ),[124] or of a mimetic *mode* (narrative or dramatic enactment),[125] or of a mimetic *object* like men in action (πράττοντας or δρῶντας).[126] Mimetic representations can have for objects reality or an imagined picture 'things which were or

---

120 Aristotle, *Poetics*, 1460a.6-10 (Halliwell). *Cf. Poetics*, 1448a.20-21.
121 Else, *Aristotle's Poetics*, p. 12.
122 Aristotle, *Poetics*, 1448b.3-17 (Halliwell).
123 Aristotle, *Poetics*, 1450b.3, 1451b.5-10; Golden, *Tragic and Comic Mimesis*, p. 20, 63, 71. It is worth noting that Aristotle recommends, among other types of dramatic recognition, the discovery by reasoning or inferrence, ἐκ συλλογισμοῦ (*Poetics*, 1455a.4; 1455a.20).
124 Aristotle, *Poetics*, chapter one, 1447a.20-23.
125 Aristotle, *Poetics*, chapter three, 1448a.20-21.
126 Aristotle, *Poetics*, 1448a, 1448a.25.

The Way and Hellenistic Mimesis

are the case; the kind of things that people say and think; the kind of things that ought to be the case [ἢ γὰρ οἷα ἦν ἢ ἔστιν, ἢ οἷά φασιν καὶ δοκεῖ, ἢ οἷα εἶναι δεῖ]'.[127] One could add to this list of subjects poetical licence, as well, even 'impossible things', ἀδύνατα.[128]

Quite cleary, thus, Aristotle had in view a different kind of imitation, namely, a creative mimesis.[129] His mimesis is so little reduplication of reality that he emphasizes the need for idealised characters in tragedy, who act as better characters than existing humans (βελτίους μιμεῖσθαι βούλεται τῶν νῦν).[130] In fact, in literary works mimesis re-creates reality.[131] Therefore, as Hedrick notes, according to Aristotle 'the "poet" is an inventor, ποιητής, of plots, or one might say a "maker" of stories'. Poetry constitutes 'the re-presentation or μίμησις of an action'.[132]

Since poetic creativity and imaginative writing are central to Aristotle's mimesis,[133] the making of plots is, also, a complex

---

127 Aristotle, *Poetics*, 1460b.5-10 (Halliwell).
128 Aristotle, *Poetics*, 1460b.20-25.
129 R. McKeon, 'Literary criticism', pp. 146-175.
130 Aristotle, *Poetics*, 1448a.17-18. By contrast, comedy's characters are inferior (χείρους) to existing humans. Mimetic artists represent people in action (πράττοντας), elevated or serious characters (σπουδαίους), or base ones (φαύλους); they can represent people better (βελτίονας) than in normal life, worse (χείρονας), or similar to living persons (τοιούτους), see *Poetics*, 1448a.1-5.
131 Else, *Aristotle's Mimesis*, p. 322. Ricoeur uses for this process the concepts of 'description' and 'redescription' (Ricoeur, 'Narrative Function', p. 194), or 'prefiguration' (the perception of reality), narrative 'figuration' (the account about reality), and 'refiguration' (the recreation of reality) (Ricoeur, *Time*, vol. 1, p. 74). As N. Goodman put it fictions 'reorganize the world in terms of works and works in terms of the world' (*Languages of Art: An Approach to a Theory of Symbols* (Indianapolis, IN: Bobbs-Merrill, 1969), p. 241; as cited by Ricoeur).
132 Hedrick, *Parables*, p. 48; cf. *Poetics*, 1451b.27: 'the poet should be more a maker of plots than of verses, in so far as he is a poet by virtue of mimesis, and his mimesis is of actions [ὅτι τὸν ποιητὴν μᾶλλον τῶν μύθων εἶναι δεῖ ποιητὴν ἢ τῶν μέτρων, ὅσῳ ποιητής κατὰ τὴν μίμησίν ἐστιν, μιμεῖται δὲ τὰς πράξεις]' (Halliwell).
133 Cf. *Poetics*, 1455a.32-34: 'hence poetry is the work of *a gifted person*, or of *a manic*: of these types, the former have versatile imaginations, the latter get carried away' (Halliwell; emph. mine).

artistic endeavour.¹³⁴ The plot line, as such, plays an important part in the overall purifying effect of the dramatic art, through its κάθαρσις or cleansing of the emotions and intellect,¹³⁵ by feelings of fear and pity (δι' ἐλέου καὶ φόβου).¹³⁶

Luke's writing is clearly aiming at such an effect, as it often emphasize the characters' feelings. For example, the two disappointed disciples, Cleopa and his companion, feel, on their journey to Emmaus, that their hearts were 'burning' at Jesus' words (Lk. 24:32, ἡ καρδία ἡμῶν καιομένη ἦν [ἐν ἡμῖν]); Saul is portrayed as 'breathing destruction' (Acts 9:1, ἐμπνέων ἀπειλῆς), and Christians were afraid of him even after his conversion (Acts 9:26); the Ethiopian journeys further 'full of joy' (Acts 8:39, χαίρων), etc. The list of Lukan examples can continue, beyond the 'hodos' stories, and so when Peter is recognized by Rhoda the whole church rejoices (Acts 12:13-16), when Eutichus is brought back to life the whole church is

---

134 μῦθος (story) as 'arrangement', 'structure' of actions (or facts), σύστασις, σύνθεσιν, συνεστάναι (Poetics, 1450a.15, 1451a.30-35, 1452b.30-35).

135 Golden, *Tragic and Comic Mimesis*, p. 26; cf. Poetics, 1449b.25-30: δι' ἐλέου καὶ φόβου περαίνουσα τὴν τῶν τοιούτων παθημάτων κάθαρσιν. *Katharsis* is complex concept, including different meanings: medical (cleansing, purgation), religious (ritual purification), cognitive and emotional one (resolution, intense feelings, etc.) It is difficult to favor only one of these, in Aristotle (Golden, *op.cit.*, p. 18; idem, 'The Clarification Theory of Catharsis', *Hermes* 104 (1967), 443-446; cf. Aristotle's Poetics 1455b.15 and the 'salvation by purification', σωτηρία διὰ τῆς καθάρσεως, in A. Kosman, 'Acting: *Drama* as the mimesis of *Praxis*', in A. O. Rorty (ed.), *Essays on Aristotle's Poetics* (Princeton, NJ: Princeton UP, 1992, 51-72, esp. pp. 51, 67; C. A. Freeland, 'Plot Imitates Action: Aesthetic Evaluation and Moral Realism in Aristotle's Poetics', in A. O. Rorty (ed.), *Essays on Aristotle's Poetics* (Princeton, NJ: Princeton UP, 1992), 111-132).

136 Aristotle, *Poetics*, 1449b.25-30 and 1452b.30-35, etc. At times, Aristotle uses an alternative formula, φρίττειν καὶ ἐλεεῖν, horror and pity (1453b.5-10). The poet creates pleasure (ἡδονή) through mimesis, and educates through the stirring of indignation (νέμεσις) and of mercy (ἐλέος) (1453b13-14; Golden, *Tragic and Comic Mimesis*, p. 92). Cf. that for Plato plays or poems should get rid of horrifying and frightening names, τὰ δεινά τε καὶ φοβερὰ (like Styx, Cocytus, etc.), of things that make 'everyone shudder [φρίττειν]', for the young could become 'more nervous and less tough than they should be [φρίκης θερμότεροι καὶ μαλακώτεροι τοῦ δέοντος γέγνωνται]' (*Rep.* 387b.1-c.2).

comforted (Acts 20:12), when the snake bite has no effect on Paul the Malteans are amazed (Acts 28:2-6), etc.

ARISTOTLE'S UNDERSTANDING OF PLOT

The plot (μῦθος) of story is given special attention by Aristotle, who values highly the plots well-made (τὸν καλῶς ἔχοντα μῦθον) and the well-constructed (συνεστῶτας εὖ μύθους).[137] Of the six components of tragedy (plot - μῦθος, character - ἦθος, diction - λέξις, thought - διανοία, spectacle - ὄψις, and lyric poetry - μελοποιία),[138] the plot is described as the first principle, the soul of tragedy (ἀρχὴ μὲν οὖν καὶ οἷον ψυχὴ ὁ μῦθος τῆς τραγῳδίας).[139] Aristotle calls it 'the goal of tragedy', 'the most important of all things' in a story (ὁ μῦθος τέλος τῆς τραγῳδίας τὸ δὲ τέλος μέγιστον ἁπάντων),[140] and, so, its link with mimesis is of particular value for one's literary style.

Mimesis and Plot Shaping

Indeed, there is a very close relation between the literary plot (*mythos*) and the action (*praxis*) it represents. The plot imitates action, and in the same way action is a succession of real events, the plot is a succession of narrative scenes and a synthesis of real events: 'the plot is the mimesis of the action... the construction [structure] of events [ἔστιν δὲ τῆς μὲν πράξεως ὁ μῦθος ἡ μίμεσις, λέγω γὰρ μῦθον τοῦτον τὴν σύνθεσιν τῶν πραγμάτων]'; μῦθος is a concept of order which makes it possible to view literary works as 'structured wholes'.[141]

The dynamics of plot derives from the dynamics of its object: it coherently portrays 'people in action', 'people on the move' (ἡ γὰρ τραγῳδία μίμησις ἐστιν οὐκ ἀνθρώπων ἀλλὰ πράξεως καὶ βίου)'.[142] The causal connection between the various parts of a

---

137 Aristotle, *Poetics*, 1453a.10-15, and 1450b.25-35. *Cf.* the plot line of successful plots (*Poetics*, 1447a.1-5).
138 Aristotle, *Poetics*, 14450a.5-10.
139 Aristotle, *Poetics*, 1450a.37.
140 Aristotle, *Poetics*, 1450a.23-25.
141 Aristotle, *Poetics*, 1450a.3-5 (Halliwell). *Mythos* involves a structured sequence of *narrated* events, similar to *praxis*, which is a natural sequence of *real* events (Melberg, *Theories*, p. 44).
142 Aristotle, *Poetics*, 1450a.15 (Halliwell). The plot involves the rearranging of events and of temporal-spatial frames in the narrative (*cf.* Melberg, *Theories*, p. 44).

plot reconstructs on the literary level the coherence of the real life action.[143] Outstandingly witty, this concept of Aristotle has encouraged various, further elaborations. For example, D. O. Via attempted to define 'literary themes' or paradigms as a 'plot at a standstill' (a definition well-suited for Luke's paradigms, as well).[144]

Plot Components

Aristotle mentions four main elements of the dramatic plot: 'reversal' (περιπέτεια), 'recognition' (ἀναγνώρισις), 'suffering' (πάθος) and 'character' (ἦθος).[145]

Emphasizing the dynamic structure of a plot, Aristotle notes that 'reversal' and 'recognition' are the two most important elements of plot for the emotional effect of tragedy.[146] They are major factors of *change* (μεταβολή, μετάβασις) in the story line, and in relation to them plots could be 'simple' when 'the change of fortune occurs without "reversal" or "recognition"', or 'complex' when 'the change coincides with a "recognition" or "reversal" or both'.[147]

'Reversal' (περιπέτεια) is 'a change to the opposite direction of events', that is in accord 'with probability and necessity'.[148] 'Recognition' (ἀναγνώρισις, 'discovery' for Fyfe), as its name

---

143 Golden, *Tragic and Comic Mimesis*, p. 73-74: 'The plot must provide persuasive causation and must depict the consequences of that causation in a credible manner'. *Cf.* Aristotle *Poetics*, 1452a.18-21. On narrative causality and history, *cf.* W. B. Gallie, *Philosophy and Historical Understanding* (N.Y.: Schoken, 1958).

144 Via, *Parables*, pp. 100-101. Ricoeur notes that 'every narrative may be seen as a competition between its episodic and its configurational dimensions, between its sequence and its pattern' (Ricoeur, 'Narrative Function', p. 184; *cf.* L. O. Mink, 'History and Fiction as Modes of Comprehension', in R. Cohen (ed.), *New Directions in Literary History* (Baltimore, MA: John Hopkins UP, 1974), 104-124).

145 Aristotle, *Poetics*, chapters 10-15. The primary meanings of ἦθος are 'familiar place', 'abode', 'usage', 'manners', 'customs'; by extension it may also mean 'disposition', 'delineation of character', or *dramatis persona* (*cf.* H. G. Liddell and R. Scott, *A Greek-English Lexicon, A New Edition, Revised and Augmented Throughout by H. S. Jones et al.* (Oxford: Clarendon, 1958 (1925)), p. 766).

146 Aristotle, *Poetics*, 1450a.33-35 (Fyfe).

147 Aristotle, *Poetics*, 1452a.10-20 (Fyfe).

148 Aristotle, *Poetics*, 1452a.23-25 (Halliwell).

suggests, is 'a change from ignorance to knowledge, leading to friendship or enmity, and involving matters which bear on prosperity or adversity'.[149] The best plots superimpose these two for a more memorable effect – and, as will be seen, some of Luke's *hodos* stories meet this requirement, combining recognition and reversal and building effective narratives.

Recognition can take different forms in a story and Aristotle identifies four types of recognition.[150] The simplest and uninventive is 'recognition through *tokens* [διὰ τῶν σημείων]', like birth marks, scars, etc. (*cf.* Odyssey's recognition by Euryclea, *Odyssey*, 19.415-505). The second type is *contrived* recognition, manufactured by the story-teller (αἱ πεποιημέναι) by 'false' or forced reasoning, παραλογισμός, external to the story and belonging to the poet, that is by means of letters, voice, etc. The third type of recognition is through *memory* (διὰ μνήμης) referring to things whose sight brings awareness. Finally, the fourth type of recognition is by *reasoning*, or sylogism (ἐκ συλλογισμοῦ), a 'second best' in relation to the complex plot based on recognition and reversal, where, as mentioned, narrative coherence results 'from the events themselves, where the emotional impact comes from a probable sequence'.[151]

The third element of plot is described by the concept of 'suffering' (πάθος; Fyfe's rendering: 'calamity'; Butcher: 'scene of suffering'; Halliwell: 'suffering'). According to Aristotle's definition 'calamity [suffering] is a destructive or painful occurrence, such as a death on the stage, acute suffering and wounding and so on [πάθος δὲ ἐστιν πρᾶξις φθαρτικὴ ἢ ὀδυνηρά, κτλ]'.[152] The most effective types of suffering are those where 'these calamities happen among friends, when for instance brother kills brother, or son father, or mother son, or son mother - either kills or intends to kill, or does something of the kind, that is what we must look for' (this vividly reminds one of Saul's conversion and persecution, Stephen's death, etc.).[153]

The fourth element of plot is the 'character' (ἦθος). Essential to a dramatic character is that it 'reveals [ethical] choice', τὴν

---
149 Aristotle, *Poetics*, 1452a.25-30 (Halliwell).
150 Aristotle, *Poetics*, 1454b.19-1455a.4.
151 Aristotle, *Poetics*, 1455a.16-20.
152 Aristotle, *Poetics*, 1452b.10-13 (Fyfe).
153 Aristotle, *Poetics*, 1453b.20-25 (Fyfe).

προαίρεσιν,¹⁵⁴ and people should be able to identify with such 'dispositions'. Thus, (a) dramatic characters should be 'good' (χρηστά; positive in intentions, although the outcome might be contrary to them), (b) be 'appropriate' (τὰ ἁρμόττοντα; building a *persona* that corresponds or harmonises to the common social prejudices, or perception); (c) be 'like' real life (τὸ ὅμοιον, corresponding to live cases, similar to reality, genuine, believable, credible); and (d) be 'consistent' (τὸ ὁμαλόν).¹⁵⁵

In the well-made tragedy the reversal of destiny should be caused by an inner, human 'flaw' of the main character, that leads him (her) downwards from prosperity into adversity (ἐξ εὐτυχίας εἰς δυστυχίαν). The nature of this Aristotelian 'flaw' has been greatly debated, yet it should not be identified with depravity but rather with a great human error, intellectual or moral (δι' ἁμαρτίαν μεγάλην) that makes the character both a toy of destiny and morally responsible.¹⁵⁶ Such a flaw is evidently present in Saul's life, before conversion, and in the disappointment of Cleopas and his companion. Jesus' suffering at the Passover, on the other hand, represents a descent into adversity on behalf of someone else's flaw or error, or sin, involving the force of divine destiny, *dei*.¹⁵⁷

---

154 Aristotle, *Poetics*, 1450b.5-9. Fyfe discusses προαίρεσιν as a technical term of Aristotle's ethics 'If character is to be revealed in a drama, a man must be shown in the exercise of his will, choosing between one line of conduct and another, and he must be placed in circumstances in which the choice is not obvious, i.e. circumstances in which everybody's choice would not be the same' (*Poetics*, 1450b.5-9, LCL, pp. 28-29, n. c). *Cf.* Aristotle in *Nicomachean Ethics*, 3.2.11: 'For it is our *choice* of good or evil that determines our character, not our *opinion* about good and evil' (it. mine). 'Choice' and 'will' appear clearly in Luke's post-Easter, *hodos* encounters, in the evangelistic dialogues.

155 Aristotle, *Poetics*, 1454a.16. Aristotle's comment shows his analytical genius: 'even if the original be inconsistent and offers such a character to the poet for representation, still he must be consistently inconsistent [ὅμως ὁμαλῶς ἀνώμαλον δεῖ εἶναι]' (*Poetics*, 1454a.25-30; Fyfe).

156 Aristotle, *Poetics*, 1453a.10-15. See Fyfe's comments, LCL, p. 46. On ἁμαρτία, see Golden, *Comic and Tragic Mimesis*, pp. 80-86.

157 M. L. Soards, 'The Historical and Cultural Setting of Luke-Acts', in E. Richard (ed.), *New Views on Luke-Acts* (Collegeville, MN: Liturgical, 1990), pp. 37, 42.

The Way and Hellenistic Mimesis 107

All these plot elements are interwoven in a complex texture of plot relations known as *complication* (τὸ δέσις) - if they belong to the first part of the story, and as *dénouement* (τὸ λύσις), if they belong to the last part.[158]

The Unity of Plot
A coherent plot is expected to integrate all its components to such an extent that if one of the incidents 'is displaced or removed, the sense of the whole is disturbed'.[159] This interdependence expresses the *unity of the plot*, which, as mimesis of one, unitary real action (οὕτω καὶ τὸν μῦθον, ἐπεὶ πράξεως μίμησίς ἐστι), should be itself a unitary and whole 'action' (μιᾶς τε εἶναι καὶ ταύτης ὅλης).[160] Plots, therefore, in tragedy or epic stories, 'should be constructed dramatically, that is around a single and complete action, with beginning, middle, and end', so that epic, by its unity should produce the expected delight.[161]

The main source for unity is not the character, and Aristotle notes that 'a plot is not unified, as some think, if built round an individual... [for] an individual performs many actions which yield no unitary action.'[162] The key is to select characteristic, unitary *actions* from the number of those that ever happened to a hero and build out of this selection the plot of a tragedy or of an epic story.[163] Such a unitary selection is fundamental for Luke's narrative art, as well. One of the best examples are Acts 9, 22, 26 where Luke selects the narrated events, or represents Saul's own selection of facts – in his speeches, so that each account of Saul's conversion comes with its own details, with its own unitary perspective.

---

158 Aristotle, *Poetics*, 1455b.25-30; also, Halliwell, *Aristotle. Mimesis*, p. 91, n. (d). Aristotle cautions that 'many poets handle the complication well, the dénouement badly: but constant proficiency in both is needed' (*Poetics*, 1456a.5-15; Halliwell).
159 Aristotle, *Poetics*, 1451a.30-35.
160 Aristotle, *Poetics*, 1451a.30-35; see, 1452a.2-4.
161 Aristotle, *Poetics*, 1459a.15-20 (Halliwell). Similarly, Kurz defines narrative criticism as the study 'of the plot of any narrative, including history, with a beginning, middle, and end' (*Reading Luke-Acts*, pp. 2-3).
162 Aristotle, *Poetics*, 1451a.15-20.
163 Aristotle, *Poetics*, 1451a.20-25.

Specifically, narrative unity involves the unity *of action, of time, and of space*. For tragedies such unity was reinforced by the specific limitations of theatrical representation to stay 'within a single revolution of the sun or close to it'; by contrast, epic was distinctively 'unlimited in time span' although its various scenes might be under certain constraints.[164] Such restrictions of time and space were expected not only for the Hellenistic theatre but also for literary parties such as the Greco-Roman *symposia*, which involved the reading aloud of literature, or for early Christian meetings where believers used to read extended parts of the biblical texts. The books of the NT, and in particular certain parts of Luke-Acts appear to have been designed for such reading (*cf.* Lk. 5:29-39; 7:36-50; 11:37-54; 14:1-24).[165]

Luke cares openly for the narrative unity of his stories, in terms of time and space. For example, Luke 24 gives the impression of one single day (Lk. 24:1, 23, 29, 33 and 36);[166] Saul's conversion gives the impression of taking place in just few days, (*cf.* Acts 9 and Galatians 1-2).

Finally, two other elements of tragedy contribute to its unity, its 'diction' (λέξις), and its argument or 'thought' (διανοία). 'Diction' is defined by Aristotle 'as expression through choice of words' [λέξιν εἶναι τὴν διὰ τῆς ὀνομασίας ἑρμηνείαν]', whose components 'are element, syllable, connective, noun, verb, conjunction, inflection, statement'.[167] Mastering *diction* means 'clarity and avoidance of banality',

---

164 Aristotle, *Poetics*, 1449b.9-14. He insists on the fact that 'the poet must remember to avoid turning a tragedy into an epic structure (by "epic" I mean with a multiple plot), say by dramatising the entire plot of the *Iliad*. In epic, because of its length, the sections take on an apt magnitude, but in plays it goes quite against expectations' (*Poetics*, 1456a.5-15; Halliwell).

165 A. N. Sherwin-White, *The letters of Pliny: A historical and social commentary* (Oxford: Oxford UP, 1966), p. 115: 'All classical literature was written to be read aloud, and the recitation is the logical development of the Symposium and the public performance of classical Greece' (*cf.* the discussion in P. J. J. Botha, 'Community and conviction in Luke-Acts', *Neot* 20 (1995), 145-165, esp. pp. 150-151; or Sterling, *Historiography*, p. 370, etc.).

166 Hickling, 'Emmaus', p. 29, n. 1; C. F. Evans, *Saint Luke* (London: SCM, 1990), p. 888.

167 Aristotle, *Poetics*, 1456b.20-25.

elegance and conviction being endangered by the use of loan words, metaphors, vowel lengthenings.[168] Similarly, 'thought' represents 'the capacity to say what is pertinent and apt [τὰ ἐνόντα καὶ τὰ ἁρμόττοντα]',[169] and it deals with the content and the form the argument ('proof, refutation, the conveying of emotions', the use of rhetoric style).[170] In this respect, Luke's style is well known for its wordplays, loan words, educated turns of phrase, and, for local colour, semitisms, direct and indirect speech, reports, convincing dialogues, all enhancing the unity and the literary dynamism of the story.

Hellenistic Historians and Mimesis

Although at home in literary works, in novels, compositional mimesis and literary style cannot be avoided by historians, either.[171] History writing can be seen, in fact, as a mimetic representation, yet in a different way than poetry

> The difference between the historian and the poet is not that between using verse or prose; Herodotus' work could be versified and would be just as much a kind of history in verse as in prose. No, the difference is this: that the one relates actual events [τὰ γενόμενα], [while] the other the kinds of things that might occur [οἷα ἂν γένοιτο]. Consequently, poetry is more philosophical [φιλοσοφώτερον] and more elevated than history [σπουδαιότερον; of graver import, Fyfe; see also in Halliwell, LCL, p. 59, n. (b)], since poetry relates more of the universal [τὰ καθόλου], while history relates particulars [τὰ καθ' ἕκαστον].[172]

History and poetry are contrasted in terms of object (the actual things - τὰ γενόμενα, and the particular - τὰ καθ' ἕκαστον, for history; the possible things - οἷα ἂν γένοιτο, and the general - τὰ καθόλου, for poetry; similarly, the mundane and less elevated matters, for history, *versus* mimesis of

---

168 Aristotle, *Poetics*, 1458a.15-20. The overuse of metaphors would turn the story into a 'riddle', the excess of loan words, into a 'barbarism'.
169 Aristotle, *Poetics*, 1450b.1-5.
170 Aristotle, *Poetics*, 1456a.35-40.
171 See Cook, *History Writing*; Gallie, *Philosophy*; Ricoeur, *Time*, vol. 1; H. White, *Metahistory: The Historical Imagination in Nineteenth-Century Europe* (Baltimore, MA: John Hopkins UP, 1973), etc.
172 Aristotle, *Poetics*, 1451b.5 (Halliwell).

elevated matters, σπουδαῖος, for poetry, and, in terms of general approach: philosophical *versus* unphilosophical.[173]

For most Hellenistic historians, however, writing history involved a philosophical and didactic emphasis, the goal of moral improvement. History writing aimed at providing significant examples, παραδείγματα, for people to emulate or to avoid.[174] Aristotle's contrast between history and poetry can be seen as a mild, balanced one for 'history is not absolutely disparaged: it is merely said to be less philosophic and worthwhile than poetry'.[175] His assessment is certainly less radical, for example, than that of Polybius for whom history writing should involve an applied, useful imitation of truth (χρήσιμον), while poetic representations are mainly aimed at delighting (τερπνόν).[176]

A study of the Hellenistic fashion of history writing strengthens the case for a stylistic overlap between the two genres (history and poetry), especially if one considers mimesis

---

173 G. Lüdemann quotes this passage of the *Poetics* to argue that Luke writes of 'things that might be', not of the 'actual things', so that Luke-Acts should be seen not as history but as imagination and faith, especially so in the Emmaus story, for example (*The Resurrection of Jesus: History, Experience, Theology* (London: SCM, 1994), p. 146). However, Aristotle is referring here to composition in terms of selection of facts and plot arrangement, rather than as betrayal of facts and fictional representation.

174 Diodorus Siculus, *Bibliotheca Historica*, 14.1.3.8, Plutarch, *Parallel Lives*, 11.19.5.16, Dion. Hal., *Roman Antiquities*, 4.25.6.2, 6.8.2.2, 11.13.3.4, Polybius, *Histories*, 7.11.3.1, etc. *Cf.* the discussion in Walbank, 'Profit or Amusement', p. 255.

175 G. E. M. de Ste. Croix, 'Aristotle on History and Poetry (*Poetics*, 9, 1451a.36-b.11)', in A. O. Rorty (ed.), *Essays on Aristotle's Poetics* (Princeton, NJ: Princeton UP, 1992), 23-32, esp. p. 29). A similar view has Torraca, *Duride*, p. 60.

176 In *Histories*, 2.56.11, Polybius argues that 'the object [τέλος] of tragedy is not the same as that of history but quite the opposite... the tragic poet should thrill and charm his audience [ἐκπλῆξαι καὶ ψυχαγωγῆσαι]... but it is the task of the historian to instruct and convince [διδάξαι καὶ πεῖσαι]'. However, the historian's duty is to entertain his audience, as well, the study of history should provide 'both benefit and pleasure', ἅμα καὶ τὸ χρήσιμον καὶ τὸ τερπνὸν ἐκ τῆς ἱστορίας ἀναλαβεῖν (*Histories*, 1.4.11).

in its historical development.¹⁷⁷ Thus, it has been suggested that Duris and others could have adopted a certain style for history writing under the influence of the *Poetics* yet in a way not intended by Aristotle, according to which history should 'compete with poetry for the quality of [τὰ] καθόλου [universal things] by adopting its means of presentation'.¹⁷⁸

The writings of the late Hellenistic historians such as Theopompus, Phylarchus, Theophorus, Duris, etc., reflect a changed perception of history, able to use the literary means of tragedy, or turn its accounts into a colourful, entertaining story (displaying a taste for 'des portraits individuels et une vision dramatique de l'histoire... l'effet esthétique et théâtral... la tendance au pathétique'), focused on persons not only on events, on their entire life as a vivid representation of a given epoch and of its morals.¹⁷⁹ Such a dramatic-artistic way of representing history is found increasingly significant for the assessment of Luke's own literary style, as his own manner of writing shares the some of the tendencies of these three Hellenistic historians.¹⁸⁰

THEOPOMPUS' MIMETIC STYLE

Theopompus has parted with the conservative tradition of Thucydides and Xenophon, and his manner of writing history has provided at the same time the model followed by many

---

177 *Cf.* 'i discepoli di Aristotele introdussero elementi innovativi nella dottrina del maestro, orientandola verso nuove problematiche e prospettive teoretiche' (Torraca, *Duride*, p. 60).
178 K. von Fritz, 'Bedeutung des Aristoteles', p. 85; Lesky, *History*, p. 765. Duris of Samos, flourished aroung 257 BC and wrote a biography of Agathocles of Syracuse, a treatise on tragedy, a history of Macedonia, and other works, many of them lost, surviving in fragments and quotations (*cf.* Cicero, *Letters to Atticus*, 6.1; Plutarch, *Pericles*, 28.2.6-3.5, Strabo, *Geography*, 1.3.19.11-15; see E. Schwartz, 'Duris', *RE*, vol. 5 (1905), col. 1853-1856; Walbank, 'History and Tragedy', *Historia* 9 (1960), pp. 216-234. For fragments of his works, see F. Jacoby, *Die Fragmente der griechischen Historiker*, vol. 2, Zeitgeschichte (Berlin: Weidmann, 1926), pp. 115-131; J. G. Hulleman, *Duridis Samii quae supersunt*, Utrecht: Bosch, 1841; C. Müller, *Fragmenta Historicorum Graecorum* (Paris: Didot, 1885), vol. 2, 466-488.
179 Pédech, *Trois Historiens*, pp. 9, 253.
180 Witherington, *Acts of the Apostles*, pp. 24-39. Cf. B.L. Ullman, 'History and Tragedy', *TAPA* 73 (1942), 25-53.

subsequent historians (especially by Duris and Phylarchus).[181] As Pédech notes, following the models of Herodotus in the use of sources and travel, of Hecateus in erudition and geographical information, and of Hellanicos in mythology, Theopompus' writings often have a pronounced geographic and ethnographic character.[182] In particular, he focused on the role of the individual, not of the city-state, as the main agent of history.[183] Polybius reproached him, for example, for having narrated Greek history centred on Philip, instead of presenting Philip as part of the larger history of Greece: 'it would have been much more dignified and fairer to include Philip's achievements in the history of Greece than to include the history of Greece in that of Philip'.[184] Despite this criticism, however, with Theopompus narration makes room for dramatic scenes and 'acts'. As Walbank notes, he was the first to use πράξεις as 'the acts of...', 'a historical account of somebody's life'.[185]

---

181 Pédech, *Trois Historiens*, p. 8: 'Théopompe marque une rupture avec la tradition de Thucydide, à laquelle se rattachent Xénophon, Philistos et l'Anonyme d'Oxyrhynchos'.
182 Pédech, *Trois Historiens*, pp. 251-252.
183 Pédech, *Trois Historiens*, pp. 8, 253.
184 Polybius, *Histories*, 8.11.3-4. Polybius' charges are rather severe: Theopompus changes the approach to his subject-matters in his work, and even the object of his study. For example, on Philip, see Polybius, *Histories*, 8.9.1-10.6, who accuses Theopompus of inconsistency: he starts by claiming that 'Europe had never produced such a man' yet soon, he fills his book with stories about Philip's cowardice, effeminacy, shamelessness, cruelty, etc. Polybius is 'amazed at the extravagance of this writer' (*Histories*, 8.9.5.4: τὴν ἀτοπίαν τοῦ συγγραφέως), for 'using language which contradicts his statement of the object he had in writing' (*Histories*, 8.10.1-2). For a thorough assessment of Theopompus' writing, *cf.* M. A. Flower, *Theopompus of Chios: History and Rhetoric in the Fourth Century BC* (Oxford: Clarendon, 1994), pp. 148-183; G. S. Shrimpton, *Theopompus the Historian*, Montreal: McGill-Queen's UP, 1991; Pédech, *Trois Historiens*, p. 248.
185 F. W. Wallbank, in Pédech, *Trois Historiens*, p. 248. As Pédech comments 'il a ouvert à l'historiographie des voies nouvelles. Il a créé l'histoire psychologique, celle qui s'attache à la peinture des hommes...' (p. 252). M. A. Flower notes that in writing history 'Theopompus was undoubtedly influenced by the emphasis given to individuals in epideictic and comiastic literature. Like Ephorus, he took an interest in life-style (δίαιτα or βίος), which seemed largely irrelevant to earlier

PHYLARCHUS' MIMETIC STYLE

Phylarchus' style was specifically sensationalist, and, as Polybius characterised it, saturated with 'random and careless statements'.[186] Polybius criticises his attempts at arousing 'pity and sympathy' [εἰς ἔλεον ... καὶ συμπαθεῖς] in a way peculiar 'to tragedy, but not to history'.[187] He has a penchant towards 'bringing horrors vividly before our eyes', stories like 'clinging women with their hair dishevelled and their breasts bare', 'crowds of both sexes together with their children and aged parents weeping and lamenting as they are led away to slavery', the torturing to death of the ex-tyrant Aristomachus of Argos, the recounting of catastrophes (περιπέτειαι, 'reversals') for the sake only of dramatic effect, often without other clear motifs or aims.[188]

Nevertheless, with this kind of Hellenistic historians, the gap between history and tragedy became increasingly smaller. As Quintilian writes, history is seen as having a right to use the means and the aims of poetic prose

> Est enim (historia) proxima poetis et quodam modo carmen solutum, et scribitur ad narrandum, non ad probandum, totumque opus non ad actum rei pugnamque praesentem, sed ad memoriam posteritatis et ingenii famam componitur.[189]

DURIS' MIMETIC STYLE

Duris needs to be mentioned, in particular, as the Hellenistic historian whose work has generated a complex discussion of the role of mimesis in the historian's accounts. In a famous fragment from *Macedonica*, he criticised his predecessors, Theopompus and Ephorus, according to the custom, for their shortcomings in using mimetic techniques

---

historians' (Flower, *Theopompus*, 150; see fragments F 49, 62, 105, 114, 121, etc.).
186 Polybius, *Histories*, 2.56.3.
187 Polybius, *Histories*, 2.56.7-8.
188 Polybius, *Histories*, 2.56.8-10, 2.56.13.4-14.1; *cf.* Walbank, 'Profit or Amusement', pp. 259-260.
189 Quintilian, *Institutionis Oratoriae*, 10.1.31.3-8.

Ἔφορος δὲ καὶ Θεόπομπος τῶν γενομένων πλεῖστον ἀπελείφθησαν· οὔτε γὰρ μιμήσεως μετέλαβον οὐδεμιᾶς οὔτε ἡδονῆς ἐν τῷ φράσαι, αὐτοῦ δὲ γράφειν μόνον ἐπεμελήθησαν.[190]

His understanding of mimesis is, however, difficult to assess. Τῶν γενομένων πλεῖστον ἀπελείφθησαν has been translated in various ways: 'Sie haben nicht Geschichte zu schreiben verstanden'; [191] 'they cut themselves off from the past';[192] 'Éphore et Théopompe sont de beaucoup inférieurs aux autres écrivains.'[193] N. G. Wilson translates 'Ephorus and Theopompus quite failed to do justice to events. They had no talent for faithful reporting or making narrative agreeable, and were only interested in writing'.[194]

The central idea of Duris' criticism seems to be, however, not so much a parting with the tradition, as rather a failure to keep up with more recent developments. It is interesting to note that in Suda's *Lexicon*, Ephorus' style is said to have been simple, flat and without vigour: ὁ μὲν γὰρ Ἔφορος ἦν τὸ ἦθος ἁπλοῦς, τὴν δὲ ἑρμηνείαν τῆς ἱστορίας ὕπτιος καὶ νωθρὸς καὶ μηδεμίαν ἔχων ἐπίτασιν, and, at the same time, the style of Theopompus was too bitter and of bad taste, ὁ δὲ Θεόπομπος τὸ ἦθος πικρὸς καὶ κακοήθης.

---

190 Duris, *Fragmenta* 2a, 76 (F 1.2).
191 See F. Blass, *Die attische Beredesamkeit* (Leipzig: Teubner, 1982), vol. 2, p. 409, n. 3 (as cited in Torraca, *Duride*, pp. 5-6).
192 M. L. W. Laistner, *The Greater Roman Historians* (Berkeley, CA: University of California, 1974), p. 8 (cf. Torraca, *Duride*, pp. 5-6).
193 R. Henry, *Photius: Bibliothèque* (Paris: Belles Lettres, 1960), vol. 2, p. 176.
194 N. G. Wilson, *Photius: The Bibliotheca*, a selective transl. with notes by N. G. Wilson (London: Duckworth, 1994), pp. 158-162, esp. p. 160 (cf. Photius, *Bibliotheca* 121a-b).
195 Suda, Ἔφορος, in *Lexicon epsilon*, 3953.2-5. Cf. Polybius, *Histories*, 8.10.1-2: ταύτην δὲ τήν τε πικρίαν καὶ τὴν ἀθυρογλωττίαν (bitter feeling and lack of restraint). Such an assessment questions the interpretation that Duris' γράφειν emphasizes a 'bare narration of facts', or 'bare' history-writing (Walbank, Schwartz) and would rather point to his psychologising, moralistic style (Flower). Especially that Photius is quite positive, as well: 'Duris is far inferior to them in his handling of precisely the aspects which he criticises... he was not justified in criticising either of them' (*Bibliotheca*, 121b). Other historians, however, seemed to have contributed to this 'hatred of Theopompus': it grew throughout the whole of Greece after Anaximenes imitated his

This shows the complexity of the quotation above: what does Duris mean by his criticism of their γράφειν, or art of writing, or style? It has been suggested that he imputes to them their exacerbated attention to the γραφικὴ λέξις (the *epideictic* style, used in written accounts, which had different requirements and goals from, say, the more lively, open debate style, ἀγωνιστικὴ λέξις, the style of spoken oratory).[196] According to Strasburger, in contrast with Plutarch's traditional style of recording facts or legends, Duris prefers a more modern style and criticises Ephorus' and Theopompus' accounts for being neither truthful representations of life (μίμησις), nor leading to artistic *pleasure* (ἡδονῆς).[197]

Therefore, it is difficult to attain a 'correct' rendering of this tension between simple and entertaining style, between sensationalist descriptions and correct representations. One could suggest, however, the following dynamic translation

> Ephorus and Theopompus have fallen short of modern standards: they have neither given proper place to mimesis, nor to a pleasant literary description, and cared only for a stylish sensationalist recording.[198]

---

style and wrote an abusive work on Athenians, Lacedaemonians and Thebans (Pausanias, *Description of Greece*, 6.18.5).

196 Aristotle, *Rhetoric*, 3.12.1-2.

197 H. Strasburger, *Die Wesensbestimmung der Geschichte durch die antike Geschichtsschreibung* (Wiesbaden: Steiner, 1966), p. 79. Theopompus' descriptions involved vivid impressions and his style, deemed 'unpleasant', prompted strong reactions and disputes.

198 'Stylish' could imply careful writing, at least in Theopompus' case, not only sensationalism, as in Phylarchus' case. Apparently, they did not ignore undiscriminately the received rules on word choice, rhythm, sounds, diction, clarity (*cf.* λέξεως δὲ ἀρετὴ σαφῆ καὶ μὴ ταπεινὴν εἶναι, Aristotle, *Poetics*, 22.1458a.15-25; Dion. Hal., *Composition*, 16-20). In this respect, it is difficult to harmonise Duris' unfriendly assessment with Dionysius' praise for their style in *Composition*, 23.1-49, where Ephorus and Theopompus are examples of the polished, rhythmed style (23.1: ἡ δὲ γλαφυρὰ καὶ ἀνθηρὰ σύνθεσις..., 23.45: τοὺς ἐν ταύτῃ πρωτεύσαντας καταριθμήσασθαι..., 23.49: δὲ τῶν πολλῶν' Ἔφορός τὲ καὶ Θεόπομπος). This translation above follows Meister and Pédech, here, in their attempt to preserve the tension between these historians' interest in style and their failure on further stylistic grounds (Pédech, *Trois Historiens*, pp. 370-371; *cf.* K. Meister, *Historische Kritik bei Polybios* (Wiesbaden: Steiner, 1975), pp. 109-122).

Of course, one of the main difficulties here is raised by the link between μιμήσεως, ἡδονῆς and ἐν τῷ φράσαι: is ἐν τῷ φράσαι linked logically to μιμήσεως, or to ἡδονῆς? Some authors supported the first variant,[199] while for others, μιμήσεως and ἡδονῆς are two interdependent concepts and Duris used imitation in Aristotle's sense as a reproduction (mimesis) in words (ἐν τῷ φράσαι) which brings the pleasure (ἡδονῆς) of understanding.[200]

Yet, the crux of the problem still remains: what does Duris understand by historical mimesis? According to C. W. Fornara, μίμησις here is 'an imitation of the emotion aroused by history', much as in Phylarchus' stories, emphasizing the human surprise at the workings of Fate (Fortune, *Tyche*).[201] According to this sensationalist interpretation, Duris' mimesis comes close to meaning *vivid representation*, and this is how the majority of scholars have understood it.[202] V. Gray has suggested a different reading, however, arguing that Duris' mimesis is most likely used with the meaning found in later writers such as Demetrius, Dionysius and Longinus. This kind of mimesis refers to an appropriate imitation of characters and situation, a representation 'true to nature'.[203]

---

199 E. Schwartz, 'Duris', *RE*, vol. 5 (1905), col. 1855. For him Ephorus and Theopompus were preoccupied with the exposition of facts not with their artistic representation and the associated language was not appealing to the reader.

200 P. Scheller, 'De hellenistica historiae conscribendae arte', Leipzig University (1911), PhD thesis, p. 69 (as cited by Torraca, *Duride*, p. 6).

201 C. W. Fornara, *The Nature of History in Ancient Greece and Rome* (Berkeley, CA: University of California, 1983), pp. 122-126.

202 Walbank, 'History and Tragedy', pp. 216-234; *idem*, 'Profit or Amusement', p. 258. R. B. Kebric argues that behind sensationalism there lies a moral purpose (*In the Shadow of Macedon: Duris of Samos* (Wiesbaden: Steiner, 1977); as cited by Walbank, 'Profit or Amusement', p. 259). As seen in Polybius' assessment, Duris and Phylarchus were perceived as authors for whom the historian was allowed to attract his readers with unusual and hyperbolical details (unlike Tacitus, for example), with 'wonder-tales, travellers' yarns, prodigious births, scandalous customs love-intrigues, elaborate costumes', etc. (Walbank, 'Profit or Amusement', p. 259).

203 V. Gray, 'Mimesis in Greek Historical Theory', *AJPh* 118 (1987), 467-486; K. Meister, *Polybios*, pp. 109-126; also Walbank, in his more recent studies (Walbank, 'Profit or Amusement', p. 259).

Pédech, also, writes that for Duris 'la μίμησις est une représentation concrète, quasi picturale de la réalité',[204] - which is reminiscent of Plato and Plutarch (cf. Plutarch's comparison between painting and history, one working with colours, the other with words).[205] By way of parenthesis, the metaphor of painting has also been used to describe Luke's style, his mixing of the artistic with the discordant recalling the style of an impressionist painter.[206] One finds it, as well, in Aristotle, where poetic mimesis is similar to painting, and the poet is a mimetic artist, like a painter or any other image-maker (ἐστι μιμητὴς ὁ ποιητὴς ὡσπερανεὶ ζωγράφος ἢ τις ἄλλος εἰκονοποιός).[207] The imagery of painting is also echoed in the requirement that the stories' characters should be ὅμοιον and ὁμαλόν (genuine and consistent).[208]

In particular, Pédech draws attention to fragment F 89, where Duris used the term ἐκμιμεῖσθαι. Commenting on *Iliad*, 21.234-248 (the overflow of Scamander in the pursuit of Achilles, as a mad flooding tide tumultuously sweeping the shore, and everything on it: cattle, people, trees, etc.), Duris argues that such imagery provides an accurate idea (ἔννοιαν) of the real event.[209] In conclusion, for Pédech 'l'objet de la μίμησις est de faire naître cette ἔννοια, qui doit produire une

---

204 Pédech, *Trois Historiens*, p. 371.
205 Plutarch, *De gloria Atheniensium*, 3.347a3-c. Plato uses the metaphor of mirror images and the illustration of painting, as well (*Rep*. 596d).
206 Evans, *Luke*, p. 42; Cadbury, *Making*, p. 334; Goulder, *Luke*, vol. 1, p. 231.
207 Aristotle, *Poetics*, 1460b.5-10; περί ζωγράφων in Diog. Laertius, *Lives*, 1.38.
208 Aristotle, *Poetics*, 1454a.15-20.
209 Duris, *Fragmenta* 2a, 76 (F 89.5): ταῦτα διὰ τὸ τὴν ἐν τοῖς κήποις ὑδραγωγίαν ἐκ μιμεῖσθαι λανθάνει πῶς ἀναγιγνώσκοντας, ὥστε μηδεμίαν ἔννοιαν λαμβάνειν πρὸς ὃ πεποίηκε. Duris favoured a mimesis that conformed to the historical facts yet allowed for poetical license in representation, as well. Homer's story of Achilles' confrontation with the Scamander river has descriptive force and his personification of the river does not obscure the devastating effects of the flooding. The passage is excellent description, yet it does not amount to history writing.

peinture ressemblante et une impression forte'.²¹⁰ Duris' emphasis on historical representation appears to advocate an *accurate* yet *dramatic* impression of the real world.²¹¹

Hellenistic Mimesis and Luke's Journey Models

Apart from *cultural, literary, and historical mimesis*, Luke's journey stories had another important resource, the Hellenistic novels with their adventures and ideology. Novelistic literature and its reflections in the LXX and in the Greco-Roman legends, provided Luke with major illustrations of literary mimesis at work.

The Journey Motif in Hellenistic Novels

As Pervo notes, whereas 'historical monographs with convincing affinities to Acts are difficult to identify... novels that bear likeness to Acts are... relatively abundant'.²¹²

Literary parallelism with the Hellenistic novels became more attractive for the New Testament scholars when it was shown that a previously late dating for novel authorship, in general, from the fourth-sixth century AD onwards,²¹³ needs to be amended to an earlier one, which starts from about 100 BC with the *Ninus Romance*, continues with Chariton's *Callirhoe* (25 BC - AD 50), with Iamblichus' *Babyloniaka* (approx. second century AD) and goes as late as Heliodorus' *Ethiopika* and Philostratus' *The Life of Apollonius of Tyana* (third - fourth century AD).²¹⁴

---

210 Pédech, *Trois Historiens*, p. 372. *Cf.* Pédech's definition of ἡδονῆς: 'l'ἡδονή... c'est essentiellement un plaisir esthétique, qu'une narration fidèle... L'historie est donc avant tout une peinture'.

211 *Cf.* Torraca's assessment: 'La mimesi di Duride è l'imitazione della realtà secondo le regole e i procedimenti delle opere destinate alla scena: il lettore deve essere compartecipe degli avvenimenti narrati come lo spettatore a teatro.' (*Duride*, p. 70).

212 Pervo, *Profit*, p. 137 (see also, pp. 101, 102, 111).

213 E. Rohde, *Der griechische Roman und seine Vorläufer*, W. Schmidt (rev) (Leipzig: Breitkopf, 1914 (1876)).

214 See Pervo, *Profit*, p. 87; S. P. and M. J. Schierling, 'The Influence of the Ancient Romance on Acts of the Apostles', *The Classical Bulletin* 54 (1978), 81-88; J. R. Morgan, 'Introduction', in J. R. Morgan and R. Stoneman (eds.), *Greek Fiction. The Greek Novel in Context* (London: Routledge, 1994), 1-12; B. E. Perry, *The Ancient Romances: A Literary*

The earlier romances placed their plots in plausible historical contexts, linking them to important figures of the past or important events (*Ninus, Callirhoe*, the fragmentary *Metiochus and Parthenope*), whereas the later ones broke free of the influence of history writing and came closer to the literary and stylistic interests of the Second Sophistic (AD 70-300).[215]

Culturally, the novel genre dominated the centre of the Mediterranean world and developed during a stable and prosperous period, when the Hellenistic East had recovered from the ravages of early Roman imperialism, and when 'the parochialism of the polis was no longer dominant'.[216] The literary environment was rather Hellenised than Hellenic,[217] a multiracial one: for example, of the novelists whose works have been preserved, such as Heliodorus, Lucian and Iamblichus who were Syrians, and Achilles Tatius who was a native of Alexandria.[218]

As novels were the product of a cosmopolitan society on the move, economically flourishing, militarily active and socially mobile,[219] the voyage motif - already a major literary theme in Greek literature[220] - became one of the most cherished plot

---

Historical Account of Their Origins (Los Angeles, CA: University of California, 1967); B. P. Reardon, *The Form of Greek Romance* (Princeton, NJ: Princeton UP, 1991); idem, *Collected Ancient Greek Novels* (Berkeley, CA: University of California, 1989).

215 Morgan, 'Introduction', p. 5; Chariton, *Callirhoe*, G. P. Goold (tr.) (Cambridge, MA: Harvard UP), 1995, p. 15; T. Hägg, *The Novel in Antiquity* (Oxford: Blackwell, 1983); Pervo, *Profit*, pp. 81-114, 115. On Second Sophistic, see A. Lesky, *History*, pp. 383, 829-845.
216 Pervo, *Profit*, pp. 111-112.
217 Pervo, *Profit*, p. 110.
218 Morgan, 'Introduction', p. 7.
219 Pervo, *Profit*, p. 111.
220 *Cf.* that 'tales of adventure, love, and travel are present in the earliest literature of Greece', *i.e.* the *Iliad* and especially the *Odyssey* (Schierling, 'Influences', p. 81). Popular traditions often associated the figure of an important leader with a story of successful journeying, *cf.* Moses, Joshua, in the OT; Xenophon and his return to Greece - in *Anabasis*, Alexander the Great and his wars, Caesar's *Bellum Gallicum*, etc. (K. Berger, *Theologiegeschichte des Urchristentums: Theologie des Neuen Testament* (Tübingen: Francke, 1994), p. 707).
Luke's accounts betray a good knowledge of voyaging in the

lines in popular literature. Novels or romances have even been defined as 'a fictional tale of adventure, usually written in prose, and most often involving love and travel'.[221] Nicetos Eugemianus, a Byzantine novelist, describes merrily the novel genre in the following suggestive words

> Flight, wandering, captures, rescues, roaring seas,
> Robbers and prisons, pirates, hunger's grip;
> Dungeons so deep that never sun could dip,
> His rays at noon-day to their dark recess,
> Chained hands and feet; and, greater heaviness,
> Pitiful partings. Last the story tells
> Marriage, though late, and ends with wedding bells.[222]

As an example, Chariton's *Callirhoe* comes close to certain features of Luke's journeys in Acts and fits the story line mentioned above: numerous adventures and final 're-wedding bells' (an incredible *re-union* after the marriage proper took place at the beginning of the dramatic plot).[223] These adventures happened during a series of eventful journeys in

---

Mediterrane sea, as well as a good knowledge of journey literature, *cf.* S. M. Praeder, 'Acts 27:1-28:16. Sea Voyages in Ancient Literature and the Theology of Luke-Acts', *CBQ* 46 (1984), 683-706, esp. p. 705.

221 Pervo, *Profit*, pp. 88-90; Perry, *Ancient Romances*, p. 28; Schierling, 'Influence', p. 81. Not all novels include both themes, of love and travel: *Daphnis and Chloe* lacks travel, *The Story of Apollonius King of Tyre* lacks a love plot, etc. Travel, still, occurs in almost all the romances: by land and by ship, in Chariton's *Callirhoe*; floating down the Nile tied to a cross, in Xenophon's *An Ephesian Tale*; on the open sea in a coffin, in *Apollonius King of Tyre*, etc. Generally, romances were all 'written about adventure incurred while traveling' (Schierling, 'Influence', pp. 81, 82).

222 Nicetos Eugemianus, cited by Schierling, 'Influence', p. 81. A great number of the Hellenistic novels, surviving often only in fragments, have been preserved due to the Byzantine love for literature (*cf.* 9th century, the *Bibliotheca* of Photius, the patriarch of Constantinopolis, *ca.* AD 820-891).

223 *Cf.* Goold's commentary on Chariton, *Callirhoe*, LCL, pp. 1, 10-12, 23: E. Rohde dated it in sixth century AD, yet for W. Schmidt it was written 'at [the] latest towards the end of the first century BC'. Linguistically, it belongs to the period 25 BC - AD 50, while historically, the action seems placed sometime between 404-332 BC (*op.cit.*, pp. 10-12).

the Mediterranean area, from Syracuse to Babylon, through Miletus and Cyprus, and back (cf. Acts) and started with Callirhoe's survival after a severe injury inflicted by her jealous husband Chaereas.[224] Saved by the pirates, she sails with them, remarries in Miletus, and journeys to Babylon to king Artaxerxes' court where is captured by the sieging army, where her ex-husband serverd. Finally, they meet in an interesting *recognition* scene, and the story ends happily with a re-marriage back at Syracuse.[225]

In this literary context, not only Acts, but also Luke's gospel has been seen as conforming 'to the pattern of Hellenistic literature, in which the story of the travelling teacher or wonder-worker was a favourite theme'.[226] Acts' story line was seen as supported by the idea of a Mediterranean voyage, a 'geographical expansion of the Gospel message from Jerusalem "to the end of the earth" (1.8)'.[227]

Voyages, in conclusion, being 'integral to the plot of both Acts and Greek romance' can provide 'a good starting point for

---

224 Apparent deaths, with their sensational, dramatic effect are characteristic of romances (Schierling, 'Influence', p. 83). Schierling mentions several examples: Apollonius' wife suffers apparent death at childbirth but is revived by a physician (*Apollonius King of Tyre*); Anthia, in Xenophon of Ephesus' *An Ephesian Tale*, survives poisoning by taking less than the lethal dose; in Pseudo-Lucian's, *The Ass*, a sleeping potion is happily mistaken for poison (*op.cit.*, p. 84; cf. in Reardon, *Collected*, the works of Anonymous, *Apollonius King of Tyre*, G. N. Sandy (tr.), pp. 736-772; Xenophon of Ephesus, *An Ephesian Tale*, G. Anderson (tr.), pp. 125-169; Pseudo-Lucian, *The Ass*, J. P. Sullivan (tr.), pp. 589-618).
225 G. Sandy suggests that the ancient Greek fiction was written especially for women ('New Pages of Greek Fiction', in J. R. Morgan and R. Stoneman (eds.), *Greek Fiction. The Greek Novel in Context* (London: Routledge, 1994, 130-145, p. 133). For example, according to Photius, Antonius Diogenes dedicated the work 'to his learned sister Isidora' (Reardon, *Collected*, p. 781; Sandy, *op.cit.*, p. 134).
226 W. L. Knox, *Hellenistic Elements*, esp. pp. 12-13.
227 L. Alexander, 'In Journeying Often": Voyaging in the Acts of the Apostles and in Greek Romance', in C.M. Tuckett (ed.), *Luke's Literary Achievement: Collected Essays*, JSNT Supplement Series 116 (Sheffield: Sheffield Academical, 1995), 17-50, esp. p. 22.

a comparative analysis of Acts and the Greek novels'.[228] Such parallels allow the reader to perceive not only geography as an opportunity for entertaining writing, but also history as literature, highlighting the importance of the plot and of journeying as major factors of narrative coherence.[229]

In this way, the Hellenistic novel constitutes an important resource for Luke's cultural and geographical perspective

> The novels, products of this [Hellenized, Greco-Roman] oikoumenē, often set their action precisely where Christianity first took root and flourished: Barnabas' Antioch, Paul's Tarsus, John's Ephesus, Mark's Alexandria, Polycarp's Smyrna. But the point of comparison is not mere propinquity, for the novels provide an extensive, concrete, and coherent account of the traditional culture of the New Testament world.[230]

This genre represents a convenient model for Luke's stories: it does not force upon the text any strict structure; it reflects the hybrid variety of the Hellenistic environment (no single *lex operis*),[231] and still provides a well defined literary model (similar plots, literary dependence).[232] As an objection, however, L. Alexander argued that the voyage plot in Acts differs from the plot of romance: thus, the NT hero is not a single individual but a collective entity (the Church) or a rhetorical entity (the Word); and the journeying movement in the NT is centrifugal, illustrating expansion, not the 'outward-and-return structure of the novels'.[233] Luke's *hodos* stories give

---

228 Alexander, 'Journeying', pp. 17-18; *cf.* R. F. Hock, 'The Greek Novel', in D. E. Aune (ed.), *Greco-Roman Literature and the New Testament* (Atlanta, GA: Scholars, 1988), 127-146, esp. pp. 138-139.
229 L. Alexander suggests that Luke-Acts were written according to the literary technical convention of *autopsia* (*Preface*, p. 37), often used 'in connection with the verification of the pieces of information from or about distant *places*' (*op.cit.*, pp. 35, 36-37).
230 Hock, 'Greek Novel', p. 139. See V. K. Robbins, 'Rhetoric and Culture: Exploring Types of Cultural Rhetoric in a Text', in Porter and Olbricht (eds.), *Rhetoric*, 443-463, pp. 443, 447, 453.
231 Pervo, *Profit*, pp. 98, 101, cf. 87-90.
232 Pervo, *Profit*, p. 90. *Cf.* Morgan's notes 'the similarity of the title of Lollianus' *Phoinikika* to that of canonical romances like *Ephesiaka*, *Babyloniaka*, or *Aithiopika* suggests that they might have been viewed as closely related, if not identical, forms' ('Introduction', p. 6).
233 Alexander, 'Journeying', p. 22; Schierling, 'Influence', p. 82.

certain grounds for disagreement, however, since Philip or Saul, or Cleopas are journeying as *individuals*, not collective characters. As well, Paul's missionary journeys are notorious for their return-and-report pattern, since he always comes back to Antioch and Jerusalem for reports.

The Journey Motif in Jewish Literature

As evidence that Luke uses traditional Jewish sources, not only Hellenistic patterns, one needs to consider the OT journey and encounter models and those in the Apocrypha.[234] A short review will confirm that at the level of the LXX material many stories conformed to the compositional features recommended by Aristotle (evidence of cultural influence - for the newer stories, and of general literary skills - for the earlier ones) providing Luke with both scriptural parallels and inspiring literary models.

OLD TESTAMENT MODELS

The OT provides a number of important literary models for Luke's journey and encounter motif (*cf.* L. Brodie, H. Gunkel, E. Reinmuth). Among these are the divine hospitality and revelation stories like Genesis 18:1-15 (three divine visitors meet Abraham and share a meal together), Genesis 19:1-23 (two angels visited Lot prompting him to a journey out of Sodom; they can turn people blind, ἐπάταξαν ἀορασίᾳ ἀπὸ μικροῦ ἕως μεγάλου, v. 11); the leadership encounter in Joshua 5:13-6:6 (Joshua and the commander of the army of the Lord, a story which parallels the divine commissioning of Moses, Exod. 3:1-4:18); Balaam's unexpected 'on the road' encounter with the Lord's angel - which, again, includes the sight motif and the recognition element (Num. 22:21-36). A journey

---

234 See F. Bovon, 'Herman Gunkel, Historian and Exegete of Literary Forms,' in F. Bovon and G. Rouiller (eds.), *Exegesis: Problems of Method and Exercises in Reading (Genesis 22 and Luke 15)* (Pittsburgh: Pickwick, 1978), 124-142; E. Reinmuth, *Pseudo-Philo und Lukas* (Tübingen: Mohr, 1994); E. V. McKnight, *Meaning in Texts: The Historical Shaping of a Narrative Hermeneutics* (Philadelphia, PA: Fortress, 1978). Other scholars, find such parallels far-fetched, *cf.* the dispute Haenchen vs. Windisch (Haenchen, *Acts*, p. 327, H. Windisch, 'Die Christusepiphanie vor Damaskus (Act. 9, 22, und 26) und ihre religionsgeschichtlichen Parallelen', *ZNW* 31 (1932), 1-23).

encounter with an uplifting effect occurs in Hagar's story (Gen. 16:6-15, it has a dialogue, a recognition event, a restoration scene).[235] A complex example, also, is the ascension of Elijah during a journey together with Elisha (2 Kgs. 2:8-15).[236] This last story does not only include a complex reversal (περιπέτεια with recognition, ἀναγνώρισις), but it includes a transition scene, as well, that of a handing over of the prophetic ministry for a new stage in the history of Israel.

Such stories are also important for Luke's 'on the road' journey paradigm for their emphasis on the *individual*, in contradistinction to, for example, the model of the Exodus journey which emphasizes the journey of a whole people.

Also, in these Jewish journeys one can note a certain 'problematisation' (*cf.* 'complication', τὸ δέσις).[237] Many OT journeys begin, in fact, with 'a problem, a question, or a crisis', with a 'fall' or an upset which demands critical attention. Journeying starts often in a dramatic context, from the need for 'a search for a solution, a "way" out (i.e., an ex-odus, ec-stacy, hope)'.[238]

JEWISH HELLENISTIC NOVELS

The problematisation present in the Jewish Hellenistic novels is actually the feature which differentiates them most from Greek novels and takes them closer to Greek drama

> The sense of a threat is increased, the point of conflict is sharpened and the scope of the action is limited and turned inward upon one or two protagonists who bear the burden of their extended family, and by extension, of Jews in general.[239]

---

235 Alsup, *Post-resurrection*, pp. 246-248, 252-258.
236 L. Brodie, 'Luke as an Imitation and Emulation of the Elijah-Elisha Narrative,' in E. Richard (ed.), *New Views on Luke and Acts* (Collegeville, MN: Liturgical, 1990), 78-85; *idem*, 'The Departure for Jerusalem (Luke 9:51--56) as rhetorical imitation of Elijah's departure for the Jordan (2 Kgs. 1:1-2:6)', *Bib* 70 (1989), 96-109, esp. pp. 53-55 and P. A. van Stempvoort, 'Interpretation', 30-42.
237 Aristotle, *Poetics*, 1455b.25-30.
238 Navone, *Theology of Story*, p. 55.
239 L. M. Wills, 'The Jewish Novellas', in J. R. Morgan and R. Stoneman (eds.), *Greek Fiction: The Greek Novel in Context* (London: Routledge, 1994), 223-238, p. 224; *cf.* also Pervo, *Profit*, pp. 119-121.

This strengthening of the suffering element of the plot (πάθος) corresponds to the general realism and dramatism of the biblical tradition (*cf.* Auerbach), and has allowed Jewish novels to contribute in a specific way to the literary genre of Hellenistic novel. Apart from this enhanced perception of conflict they manifest a preference for journeying as an opportunity for new experiences and wisdom, as in Ben Sirach or in Philo,[240] as well as for journeying as a means of *individual salvation, delivery,* and *reversal of fate.*

Tobit's Journey and Encounter

The novel-like story of Tobit's healing is usually seen by NT scholarship as a major LXX parallel of Luke's account of Saul's recovery of sight (*cf.* Tob. 11:7-18).[241] Yet, this story, aimed at vindicating a righteous Jew (6:1-9; 7:1; 11:1-6),[242] is also an interesting example of a plot built around a divinely guided journey.

The Way metaphor appears at the beginning of the story: as a righteous person Tobit walked 'in the ways of truth and righteousness' all the days of his life (ὁδοῖς ἀληθείας, 1:3). The

---

240 As N. Calduch-Benages notes, Ben Sirach, a Jewish Hellenistic writer, emphasizes well 'el valor profundamente pedagógico de los viajes' ('Elementos de inculturación helenista en el libro de Ben Sira: los viajes', *EstB* 54/3 (1996), 289-298). *Cf.* Sirach 8:16; 26:12; 31:9-17; 36:2; 42:3; 51:13; Prov. 26:17. A similar idea is found in Philo, where the novice is advised to travel by land and sea, and learn new things (*De Ebrietate*, 158.6-7: κἂν εἰ πεζεύειν καὶ πλεῖν δεῖ, γῆς καὶ θαλάττης ἄχρι τῶν περάτων ἀφικνεῖται, ἵνα ἴδῃ τι πλέον ἢ ἀκούσῃ καὶ νότερον, etc.). Plato opens advises the wise inspector to go in search of the few talented 'divinely inspired men' that a nation happens to have (θεῖοί τινες, οὐ πολλοί) being ready to take a voyage of enquiry by land and sea (κατὰ θάλατταν καὶ γῆν ζητεῖν) and find them (*Laws*, 951b.5-c.4).
241 *Cf.* Boismard, *Actes*, vol. 2, pp. 186-187.
242 A Jewish romance, dated around 200-180 BC, and written with a didactic and entertaining aim, without apocalyptic flavour or messianic emphases. *Cf.* I. Nowell, 'Tobit', in R. E. Brown, J. A. Fitzmyer, R. E. Murphy (eds.), *The New Jerome Biblical Commentary (NJBC)* (London: Chapman, 1993), 568-571; J. D. Thomas, 'The Greek Text of Tobit', *JBL* 91 (1972) 463-471; F. Zimmermann, *The Book of Tobit* (N.Y.: JAL, 1958); P. Deselaers, *Das Buch Tobit: Studien zu seiner Entstehung, Komposition und Theologie* (Freibourg: Freibourg Universitätsverlag, 1982).

background of the story is marked by adversity and suffering (Tobit is punished for his defiance in burying the bodies of the poor Jews in Nineveh). Struck by persecution and poverty he sends his son Tobias in a journey to Media to recover a sum of money. Tobias is helped by Raphael, an angel whom he does not recognise (οὐκ ἔγνω ὅτι ἄγγελος τοῦ θεοῦ ἐστιν, 5:4), yet whom he hires as a guide 'acquainted with the way' (ἐπίστῃ τὴν ὁδὸν πορευθῆναι, 5:6-8). The end brings with it restoration, the healing of Tobit and the wedding of Tobias (11:14-18). Raphael as a divine guide mediates God's blessing and restoration and discloses his identity only at the end (12:11-22, a recognition scene), when ascending to heaven (ἰδοὺ ἐγὼ ἀναβαίνω πρὸς τὸν ἀποστείλαντά με... καὶ ἀνέβη, 12:20; *cf.* the sight motif in 12:21, καὶ οὐκέτι ἠδύναντο ἰδεῖν αὐτόν).[243] The significance of this story does not reside in providing a parallel to Saul's experience, only: it also constitutes evidence of a journey plot with dramatic elements (encounter, appearance / disappearance) and its special appeal for a Jewish Hellenistic audience.

Heliodorus' Encounter

Like the previous story this legend (2 Macc. 3:1-40) has often been mentioned as a parallel, even source, to the account of Saul's conversion and healing.[244] Windisch gives a thorough discussion of their various points of similarity and contrast.[245] His conclusion, reiterated by many NT scholars afterwards, is that the Heliodorus legend is an inspirational parallel for the Damascus story, rather than a source (again the idea of mimetic paradigms).[246]

The background of the story (Aristotle's 'complication') is one of malicious accusations. Following Simon's plot to discredit the high priest Onias, Heliodorus is sent by Seleucus

---

243   *Cf.* the theme of recognition at a meal in Tob. 12:9, reminiscent of Lk. 24:41-43.
244   Haenchen, *Acts*, p. 326 (quoting A. Drews and F. Smend). Written *ca.* 120 BC, at an earlier date than 1 Macc., 2 Macc. was composed apparently, in its first form, by Jason of Cyrene, a Jew educated in Jewish orthodoxism as well as in Hellenistic rhetoric (N. J. McEleney, '1-2 Maccabees', *NJBC*, 421-446, esp. p. 423).
245   Windisch, 'Die Christusepiphanie', pp. 1-9, esp. pp. 3-5, 7.
246   Windisch, 'Die Christusepiphanie', p. 8; *cf.* Haenchen, *Acts*, p. 327.

IV Philopator to Jerusalem to confiscate the Temple treasure (2 Macc. 3:8, 13), under the pretext of an *inspection journey* in Coele-Syria and Phoenicia.[247]

The reversal point of this story is the moment when Heliodorus, ready to leave Jerusalem, has a vision, or rather an epiphany, in which a golden armoured horseman appears, his horse striking at Heliodorus (ὤφθη γάρ τις ἵππος etc., 2 Macc. 3:25 [LXX]). Two young men 'splendidly dressed' appear to him (προσεφάνησαν αὐτῷ) and scourge him thoroughly, causing him to fall to the ground (a suffering scene)[248], plunged into deep darkness (2 Macc. 3:26 [LXX], *cf.* Saul's blindness).

When the high priest offers a sacrifice on Heliodorus' behalf the two angelic young men appear again (ἐφάνησαν, 2 Macc. 3:32) to restore Heliodorus. Finally, they 'vanish out of sight' (ἀφανεῖς ἐγένοντο, 2 Macc. 3:34 [LXX]; *cf.* ἄφαντος ἐγένετο, Lk. 24:31),[249] and Heliodorus returns convinced that God himself will defend the Temple and its treasure (2 Macc. 3:38-40). This epiphanic vocabulary of appearance and disappearance (ἐφάνησαν, or ἀφανεῖς ἐγένοντο) provides one of the most important LXX parallels to the Emmaus disappearance of Jesus (*cf.* ἄφαντος ἐγένετο, Lk. 24:31) and to the disappearance of Philip who is 'taken away' by the Holy Spirit (πνεῦμα κυρίου ἥρπασεν τὸν Φίλιππον, Acts 8:39).

The Journey Motif and Its Greco-Roman Models

Luke's cultural environment includes the Greco-Roman legends as well and they have an important paradigmatic potential for his mimetic writing. In terms of plot, two main non-biblical legends seem to be the most important pagan parallels to Luke's post-Easter encounters, the legend of

---

247 In 4 Macc. 4:1-14 it is Apollonius not Heliodorus who leaves with this mission.
248 ἄφνω δὲ πεσόντα πρὸς τὴν γῆν," Macc. 3:27 [LXX]; *cf.* Acts 9:4, καὶ πεσὼν ἐπὶ τὴν γῆν.
249 For ἄφαντος, see, for example, Euripides, *Orestes*, 1496 ('but vanished was Zeus' daughter!... gone wholly from sight', ἐγένετο διαπρὸ δωμάτων ἄφαντος); also, *Helen*, 606 ('gone is thy wife - into the folds of air wafted and vanished! hid in heaven's depths', βέβηκεν ἄλοχος σὴ πρὸς αἰθέρος πτυχὰς ἀρθεῖσ' ἄφαντος· οὐρανῷ δὲ κρύπτεται, A. Way). See, also, Vergil, *Aeneid*, 9.656-658.

Romulus and the martiry of Apollonius.[250] Furthermore, the fable of Hercules at the cross-roads, a story in which Heracles reaches the age of maturity and has to choose between two 'ways' (or manners) of life, personified by two goddesses, Ἀρετή and Κακία is one of the most influential leadership and ethical choice paradigm in antiquity. [251]

THE ROMULUS LEGEND

As Ehrhardt notes, the Romulus legend 'was an adaptable, migrant myth',[252] being mentioned by several authors, among which Plutarch, Dionysius from Hallicarnassus, Ovid, Tit Livius, etc.[253] Plutarch mentions other similar appearance and disappearance stories, as well, such as that of Aristeas the Proconnesian, and the disappearances of the bodies of Cleomedes the Astypalaean and of Alcmene.[254] His stance is, however, rationalistic, for he questions ironically the possibility of bodily survival or resurrection.[255] In particular, Romulus' legend reminds one of the Emmaus story, with its encounter scene.[256]

---

250 Guillaume, *Luc interprète*, p. 86 .
251 Michaelis, 'ὁδός', p. 43. The fable is traced back to Prodicus, the Sophist, and is recounted in Xenophon, *Memorabilia*, 2.1.21-34. The idea of emancipation of youth through such experiences, occurs in Plato, as well (Navone, *Theology of Story*, p. 98).
252 Ehrhardt, 'Disciples', p. 195.
253 Johnson, *Luke*, p. 398; see, on Romulus' legend, Dion. Hal., *Roman Antiquities*, 2.63.1-4; Ovid, *Fasti*, 2.357-388 (February stories); also Livius, *Ab Urbe Condita*, 1.16; 1.40.3; Ennius, *Annals*, 1.110-115 (including the famous 'Romulus in caelo cum dis genitalibus aeuom degit'; *cf.* Cicero, *Tusculan Disputations*, 1.28; Vergil, *Aeneid*, 6.763), etc.
254 Plutarch, *Romulus*, 28.1-7; *cf.* Ehrhardt, 'Disciples', pp. 194-195; and Guillaume, *Luc interpréte*, p. 87; Alsup, *Post-Resurrection*, pp. 224-238.
255 Plutarch, *Romulus*, 28.6-7; *cf. Romulus*, 28.8.1-3: 'We must not, therefore, violate nature by sending the bodies of good men with their souls to heaven'.
256 Dionysius has Ascanius as witness, a man of blameless reputation, while Plutarch introduces Julius Proculus: 'one of the patricians, a man of noblest birth, and of most reputable character, a trusted and intimate friend of Romulus himself' (Plutarch, *Romulus*, 28.1.1-3). In Luke's gospel, a similarly credible Roman centurion witnesses Jesus' death and testifies that Jesus was a righteous man (Lk. 23:47).

He saw Romulus departing from the city fully armed and that, as he drew near to him, he heard him say these words: 'Julius, announce to the Romans from me, that the genius to whom I was allotted at my birth is conducting me to the gods, now that I have finished my mortal life, and that I am Quirinius'.[257]

In Plutarch's account, the encounter with the divine Romulus is narrated at the precise moment when the historian has expressed certain dark doubts about the whole story of deification.[258] Tension of a different type, however, is also present in Luke's account, in the form of the conflict between Jesus and the Jewish leaders, a general bitter skepticism on the part of the disciples (Lk. 24:18-24). Luke's story, however, is told in a much more positive manner.[259]

The two stories share at least two formal features: (a) a common emphasis on journeying - 'like Romulus, Jesus is leaving the city where he had been a πάροικος' (Lk. 24:18);[260] and (b) a recognition scene - 'just as the identity of Romulus is established by his armour, so Jesus is recognized by his breaking of the bread (Lk. 24:30).'[261] Alsup gives a longer, comprehensive list of correspondences.[262]

Apart from these points of formal correspondence one should note that Romulus' encounter is set 'on the road' - the locus of

---

257 Dion. Hal., *Roman Antiquities*, 2.63.4.
258 Plutarch, skeptical, notes the rumours, as well, see *Romulus*, 27.5.5-6.1: 'some conjectured that the senators... fell upon him and slew him, then cut his body in pieces, put each a portion into the folds of his robe, and so carried it away'; *cf.* 27.8.1-7. Similarly, Dionysius (Dion. Hal., *Roman Antiquities*, 2.63.3).
259 If Plutarch is 'a trained rhetor and a skeptic', for Ehrardt 'the author of the Emmaus story was a devout believer' (Ehrhardt, 'Disciples', p. 195). Luke's style, by contrast, is fresh, direct, emotional, bringing a dramatic change in the lives of the disciples (Guillaume, *Luc interprète*, p. 87; Johnson, *Luke*, p. 398).
260 Ehrhardt notes that 'Plutarch's report makes an effort to emphasize that this departure is not to be regarded as ominous' (Ehrhardt, 'Disciples', p. 195). By contrast, Jesus' departure from Jerusalem as well as the mentioning of Emmaus seem to be of ominous significance (see A. A. Just).
261 Ehrhardt, 'Disciples', p. 195.
262 Alsup, *Post-Resurrection*, p. 234. See the Introduction.

divine guidance.²⁶³ Part of the narrative 'complication' (δέσις) of the story, and also of its *dénouement* (λύσις) is the political dimension of the appearance and of Ascanius' (or Julius') report to the Senate (Luke also uses political connotations in the final report to the Eleven, *cf.* Lk. 24:32-35, and, in Saul's case, in Barnabas' presentation of Saul to the Twelve, Acts 9:27). Consistently, Luke's *hodos* reports are intended to justify a new vision and to validate a new direction in the life of the church (Lk. 24:24; 26). Such overtones are entirely consistent with Luke's general interest in the political case of the Messiah Jesus.²⁶⁴

The theme of divine intervention with special messengers and special messages, is often part of Luke's plot lines, as well. For example, in Peter's delivery from prison (Acts 12:6-17), a miraculous escape takes place in the presence of an angel, then a double recognition, and finally a sudden departure.²⁶⁵ In the account of Herod's death (Acts 12:20-24), Luke tells a story which echoes somehow Romulus' divine appearance: dressed in resplendent royal robes,²⁶⁶ Herod accepts praise to himself as to a god (θεοῦ φωνὴ καὶ οὐκ ἀνθρώπου), and is suddenly struck with a quick death (*cf.* a reversed plot in Acts 28:4-6, where Paul, for not having died at the viper's bite, is regarded as divine).²⁶⁷ Luke proves here a certain predilection for this motif of establishing whether somebody is or is not

---

263 Guillaume, *Luc interprète*, p. 86; Plutarch has ὡς ὁδὸν αὐτῷ βαδίζοντι ‘Ρωμύλος (*Romulus*, 28.1). In Dionysius' account, the road setting is implicit, ἔφη παραγιγνόμενος ἐξ ἀγροῦ (*Roman Antiquities*, 2.63.3).
264 For a comprehensive discussion of this aspect, see M. J. Borg, *Conflict, Holiness & Politics in the Teachings of Jesus* (Lewiston, NY: Mellen, 1984); R. J. Cassidy, and P. J. Scharper (eds.), *Political Issues in Luke-Acts* (Maryknoll, NY: Orbis, 1983).
265 Robinson, 'Place', p. 483.
266 Josephus says he was dressed in 'shining silver', *Jewish Antiquities*, 19.8.2.
267 This type of plot is present in several stories: *cf.* Jesus and the two disciples on the Emmaus road (Lk. 24); Paul and Barnabas taken for Jupiter and Mercur, in Lystra (Acts 14:12; *cf.* C. Gempf, 'Mission and Misunderstanding: Paul and Barnabas in Lystra (Acts 14:8-20)', in A. Billington, T. Lane, and M. Turner (eds.), *Mission and Meaning: Essays Presented to Peter Cotterell* (Carlisle: Paternoster, 1995), 56-69); Paul and the jailer, in Philippi (Acts 16:31); Paul and the barbarians of Malta (Acts 28:3).

divine, which apparently reflects a Hellenistic cultural paradigm, a literary and theological *topos* turned into apologetical instrument.

APOLLONIUS AND HIS 'MARTYRDOM'

Often mentioned by the later Fathers of the Church, Apollonius is presented in the Hellenistic literature of the time as a prophet of insight and supernatural powers.[268] The extraordinary fact of his life, as the legend says, is that being condemned by Domitian he dared the emperor to find his body, and at that very moment he disappeared.[269] There are multiple variant stories about Apollonius' death (as happening in Ephesus, in Lindus, Crete, etc.),[270] and generally they hold that he continued to appear to friends (like Damis and Demetrius), acquaintances, or to unbelievers (in the cave of Puteoli, in a public library in Tyana, etc.).[271] Most often in these appearances, bearing a certain similarity to Jesus' Easter encounters in Luke-Acts, Apollonius' message is one of hope and encouragement about the reality of the human soul and its existence after death.[272]

Apparently, however, rather than being relevant as a source of inspiration for Luke, the legend of Apollonius represents a

---

[268] Apollonius, a famous Neo-Pythagorean miracle worker, lived approx. 1st century AD, in Tyana, Cappadocia, and Philostratus' biography, written at the request of princess Iulia, made him famous as a Christ-like figure. *Cf.* M.-J. Lagrange, 'La vie d'Apollonios par Philostrate', *RB* 41 (1937), 5-28; Lagrange, 'Les légendes pythagoriciennes et l'évangile', *RB* 40 (1936), 482-511; A. Ehrhardt, 'Disciples', pp. 195-201; Guillaume, *Luc interpréte*, pp. 88-89.

[269] Guillaume, *Luc interpréte*, p. 88; Ehrhardt, 'Disciples', p. 197. A partially similar story is the 'martyrdom' of Peregrinus, who, having been a Christian prior to his conversion to Cynicism, 'disappeared' or burned himself to death at the Olympic Games, in AD 165 (Lucian, *Peregrinus*, 20-41, esp. 36)

[270] Philostratus, *Apollonius*, 8.5.51-56. The issue, was, again, the disappearance of the body. In Plutarch's story of Romulus 'there was no body, or part of it, or a remnant of his clothes to tell the story' (*Romulus*, 27.5.3-4). Luke takes care that his reader 'sees' first Jesus' dead body laid in the tomb (Lk. 23:55), and only then is he confronted with the resurrection and with its evidence.

[271] Philostratus, *Apollonius*, 8.31.

[272] Philostratus, *Apollonius*, 8.31.1-3.

case of NT influence on Hellenistic vision literature.[273] The story has a syncretistic look, reflecting the fact that Julia Mammaea, Philostratus' patron until AD 202, worshipped Apollonius along with Jesus, Abraham and Orpheus.[274] Christian apologists such as Lactantius and Arnobius referred to Apollonius, arguing that Jesus cannot be compared to him, at all.[275] Going beyond the apologetical debate, the NT accounts of Jesus and the legend of Apollonius illustrate together the major importance of the appearance paradigm. In a way, also, Luke might be considered a precursor of later Christian apologists, his concerns, however, being about Jesus' authority, the sacraments of the Church, apostolic authority, mission, etc.

HERACLES' DIVINE DESTINY

Michaelis mentions the legend of Heracles at the forks of Virtue and Vice as one of the important parallels to the Way motif in the NT.[276] Often referred to in relation to Matthew's 'two ways' parable, this legend is analysed here as an 'on the road' encounter with a heavenly being, a story involving the Greco-Roman motif of a young man's ethical challenge at the crossroads.[277]

---

[273] Flavius Philostratus, the Athenian, lived approx. AD 170 - 245, at Athens (Rome:, and moved to Tyre after the death of Julia Domna (AD 202). On historical priority and literary influence in relation to the NT, see Ehrhardt, 'Disciples', p. 198; E. Norden, *Agnostos Theos* (Stuttgart: Teubner, 1956), pp. 35, 45, 332, 337; Guillaume, *Luc interprète*, p. 88; Lagrange, 'Légendes', pp. 13-14.

[274] Guillaume, *Luc interprète*, p. 89; Ehrhardt, 'Disciples', pp. 199-120.

[275] Lactantius, *Divinarum Institutionum*,5.3. Arnobius, *Adversus Nationes*, 1.52; cf. Ehrhardt, 'Disciples', p. 198). F. C. Baur regarded it as a piece of consciously and intentionally anti-Christian polemic (F. C. Baur, *Apollonius von Tyana und Christus: Beitrag zur Religionsgeschichte der Ersten Jahrhunderth nach Christus*, E. Zeller (rev), (Hildesheim: Olms, 1966), mentioned by Ehrhardt, 'Disciples', pp. 198-199).

[276] Michaelis, 'ὁδός', p. 46.

[277] This motif of the 'young man's choice at the crossroads' is present, for example, in Plato, *Laws*, 799c.3-d.3: 'νέος... καθάπερ ἐν τριόδῳ γενόμενος καὶ μὴ σφόδρα κατειδὼς ὁδόν, κτλ.' Xenophon uses the Heracles parable as an illustration for Aristippus, a young man who wanted to avoid in life the extremes of slavery and deceitful power:

The Way and Hellenistic Mimesis

In a moralistic vein, the legend emphasizes the moment when 'the young, now becoming their own masters, show whether they will approach life by the path of virtue or the path of vice (εἴτε τὴν δι' ἀρετῆς ὁδὸν τρέψονται ἐπὶ τὸν βίον εἴτε τὴν διὰ κακίας)'.[278]

Reminiscent of Luke's theme of retreat into secluded places for the sake of prayer and teaching, or rest, Heracles goes into quiet places, as well (ἐξελθόντα εἰς ἡσυχίαν), to ponder his *hodos* decisions (ποτέραν τῶν ὁδῶν τράπηται, *cf.* ποίαν ὁδὸν ἐπὶ τὸν βίον τράπῃ).[279] The divine intervention takes the form of an encounter and a dialogue with the two goddesses of Vice and Virtue. The goddess of Vice (Κακία) promises him 'the pleasantest and the easiest road (τὴν ἡδίστην τε καὶ ῥᾴστην ὁδόν)',[280] a 'short and easy way to happiness' while Virtue's road to joy is pictured as a 'hard and long road' (ὡς χαλεπὴν καὶ μακρὰν ὁδὸν ἐπὶ τὰς εὐφρονσύνας ἡ γυνή σοι αὕτη διηγεῖται- ἐγὼ δὲ ῥᾳδίαν καὶ, βραχεῖαν ὁδὸν ἐπὶ τὴν αὐδαιμονίαν ἄξω σε).[281] The goddess of Virtue (Ἀρετή) stresses that, if he takes the road that leads to her (εἰ τὴν πρὸς ἐμὴ ὁδὸν τράποιο), she will communicate faithfully to him the divine things (ἀλλ' ἧπερ οἱ θεοὶ διέθεσαν τὰ ὄντα διηγήσομαι μετ' ἀληθείας).[282]

In one of the variant forms, Dio Chrysostomus introduces Hermes as having to choose between the road leading to true

---

'Nay, replied Aristippus, for my part I am no candidate for slavery; but there is, as I hold, a middle path in which I am fain to walk (ἀλλ' εἶναι τίς μοι δοκεῖ μέση τούτων ὁδός). That leads neither through rule nor slavery, but through liberty, which is the royal road to happiness.' (Xenophon, *Memorabilia*, 2.1.11.1-12.3). Virtue as the ability to find and keep the middle way is also one of the great themes of Aristotle's *Nicomachean Ethics*. The definition of virtue in *Nicomachean Ethics*, 2.6.15-16 emphasizes the idea of a balanced 'mean' between excesses.

278 Xenophon, *Memorabilia*, 2.1.21.7-8.
279 Xenophon, *Memorabilia*, 2.1.21.8-9, *cf.* 2.1.23.4-5.
280 Xenophon, *Memorabilia*, 2.1.23.6.
281 Xenophon, *Memorabilia*, 2.1.29.1-30.1.
282 Xenophon, *Memorabilia*, 2.1.27.4-5; 2.1.27.9-28.2. A similar concern for truthful exposition appears in Luke's prologue dedicated to Theophilus, *cf.* the use of διήγησις and the πᾶσιν ἀκριβῶς καθεξῆς σοι γράψαι (Lk. 1:1, 4). The introduction to διήγησις is important: it should win the audience but not overwhelm their critical judgement (*cf.* how Virtue emphasizes this 'I will not deceive you by a pleasant prelude', οὐκ ἐξαπατήσω δέ σε προοιμίοις ἡδονῆς, 2.1.27.8).

Royalty or to that leading to Tyranny. The path leading to royal virtues was safe, broad, and certain (ἀσφαλῆ καὶ πλατεῖαν, thus, people journeyed on it safely); the other was narrow, crooked and difficult (σκολιὰν καὶ βίαιον), that is dangerous, many having lost their lives on the path (the meaning of this parable is opposite to Jesus' story: safety is to be found on the good, broad road, while danger threatens one's life, on the narrow road).[283] The two goddesses are called differently, too, the blessed Royalty, child of Zeus (μακαρία δαίμων Βασιλεία),[284] and Tyranny (Τυραννίδα).[285]

Similar two-road imagery, associated with a discussion of the ethical way to happiness, is used in Diogenes' letters to Hicetas and to Monimus (the two roads to happiness).[286] These different versions of basically one and the same story: a decision at the crossroads, in the presence of a guide, and constitute important evidence of the mimetic literary mobility of this 'choice at the crossroads' paradigm. The essence of the story remains the same, yet the setting, the main character, and the nature of the guide (human or divine) are subject to change.

The Heraclean legend was very influential in Greco-Roman world, it represented a major model in the Hellenistic education of rulers.[287] As Julian put it, Heracles was

---

283 Dio Chrysostomus, *Discourses*, 1.67.5-9.
284 Dio Chrysostomus, *Discourses*, 1.73.
285 Dio Chrysostomus, *Discourses*, 1.78.
286 See 'Diogenes to Hicetas' and 'Diogenes to Monimus', in Malherbe, *Cynic Epistles*, pp. 131-133, 155-159.
287 Dio Chrysostomus, *Discourses*, 4.31.1-5: 'men of old called those persons "sons of Zeus" [Διὸς παῖδας ἐκάλουν] who received the good education [τῆς ἀγαθῆς παιδείας] and were manly of soul [τὰς ψυχὰς ἀνδρείους], having been educated after the pattern of the great Heracles [πεπαιδευμένους ὡς Ἡρακλέα ἐκεῖνον]'. Diogenes Laertius, *Lives*, 6.70-71, presents Heracles as a model, as well (R. Höistad's emphasizes that this 'cannot be accidental', *Cynic Hero and Cynic King: Studies in the Cynic Conception of Man* (Uppsala: Bloms, 1948), p. 56). As a divine figure Heracles provides assistance to those in need, brings charms against diseases, drives evil ways, keeps death aside (*Orphica, Hymni* 12, in *The Orphic Hymns*, A. N. Athanassakis (tr.) (Missoula, MT: Scholars, 1977); pp. 21-23). Höistad draws attention that such a portrait indicates a major cultural and religious transformation of Heracles' perception under Stoic and Cynic idealism. Homer's Heracles,

considered 'the greatest example [παράδειγμα]' of the Cynic lifestyle.[288] Luke's choice for the 'way' setting as the locus for a test of faith and missionary direction appears thus construed on an important Hellenistic paradigm of education and this observation raises once more the issue of the political profile of Theophilus.

The importance of the Heraclean traditions led some scholars even to the hypothesis that the primitive records of 'proto-Matthew' and 'proto-Mark' were dependent on them.[289]

---

the earliest reference, is portrayed as violent and primitive (E 392* Λ 601* Φ 24). See, the hymn *To Heracles the Lion-hearted*, in Hesiod's *Homeric Hymns* (the work of the Ionic School of Epic poetry), 15.6-7, and the pseudo-Homeric fragments in *Vita Herodotea*, 456; *Certamen*, 111 (*cf.* Höistad, *Hero*, pp. 22-23).

288 Julian, *Orations*, 6.187c.6: 'it was he who bequeathed to mankind the noblest example of this mode of life [τούτου τοῦ βίου παράδειγμα]'. The mature Heracles was pictured as skilled in prophecy and proficient in logic (Plutarch, *De E apud Delphos,* 387d), and was associated by some with eloquence and dialectic (Lucian, *Hercules,* 4.8-5.5). Heracles' paradigm gave hope that through toil and suffering humans can attain divinity. Jesus' resurrection, however, would point to a different perspective: he is not a model to follow, but a supreme Lord to obey (*cf.* A. George in *Études*, p. 282: 'Jésus "Seigneur" plutôt que "Roi"'). For a more detailed discussion of this paradigm, see D. Aune, 'Heracles and Christ: Heracles Imagery in the Christology of Early Christianity', in D. L. Balch, E. Ferguson, W. A. Meeks (eds.) *Greeks, Romans and Christians: Essays in Honour of Abraham J. Malherbe* (Minneapolis, MN: Fortress, 1990), 3-19.

289 T. Birt, *Aus dem Leben der Antike* (Leipzig: Teubner, 1922[2]); F. Pfister, 'Herakles und Christus', *Archiv für Religionswissenschaft* 34 (1937), 42-60. D. Aune describes Pfister's approach, however, as a 'most bizarre attempt to link the figure of Heracles to that of Jesus' ('Heracles and Christ', p. 11; *cf.* J. Fink, *Bildfrömmigkeit und Bekenntnis: das Alte Testament, Herakles und die Herrlichkeit Christi an der Via Latina in Rom* (Köln: Böhlau, 1978), p. 95; B. Berg, 'Alcestis and Hercules in the Catacomb of Via Latina', *VigChr* 48 (1994), 213-234). Archaeological findings support, however, this connection. Room N of the Via Latina complex of catacombs has a Christian picture of Heracles holding Kerber aside and freeing Alcestis (4th AD). In another example, Samson was depicted in the guise of Heracles in the frescoes of the Via Latina (*cf.* M. Simon, 'Remarques sur la Catacombe de la Via Latina', *Le Christianisme antique et son contexte religieux* 108/9 (Stuttgart: Hiersemann, 1988), 286-296; *cf.* Augustine, *De Civitate Dei*, 18.19, according to whom Samson was known to the Gentiles as 'Heracles').

More probable, however, would appear the hypothesis of A.J. Toynbee.[290] After looking at a number of Hellenistic saviour figures, he concludes that the Gospels contain 'a considerable number and variety of elements which have been conveyed to them by the stream of "folk memory"'.[291]

Mimesis, Journeying and Ideology

One of the main functions of mimesis, that of representation, had an important application in the geographical and historical literature of the Roman empire. In Luke's world this type of literature was often associated with ideology. Geography and history were by themselves ways of rationalising the world, of building an interpretation of the horizontal and vertical space and of accounting for the diversity of people in the world.[292] The two tended to be seen together, at least at the level of popular perception.[293]

Therefore, it is not an exaggeration to say that Jews learned geography 'in conjunction with their study of the Bible, just as Greeks learned geography from their study of Homer'.[294]

---

290 A. J. Toynbee, *A Study of History* (Oxford: Oxford UP, 1939), vol. 6, pp. 376-539.

291 Toynbee, *Study*, vol. 6, p. 457. M. Simon labelled Toynbee's theory as 'the hypothesis of spontaneous imitation through the channel of popular tradition' (M. Simon, *Hercule et le Christianisme* (Paris: Belles Lettres, 1955, p. 63). Aune coined a similar phrase, in 'Heracles and Christ', p. 19. For the parallel Heracles-Christ, see also W. L. Knox, 'The "Divine Hero" Christology in the New Testament', *HTR* 41 (1948), 229-249, p. 233). Some of the 'important and vital functions' of Heracles as a Hellenistic saviour were seen 'as applicable to Jesus to an even greater extent than they were to Heracles' (Aune, 'Heracles and Christ', p. 19, esp. pp. 12-14).

292 Geographical symbolism supplies the worshipper with the specific metaphors that accompany special places (high mountain, symbolic trees, unsettled sea, level places, etc.; *cf.* M. Eliade, *Patterns in Comparative Religion* (London: Sheed and Ward, 1958); *idem*, *Cosmos and History: The Myth of the Eternal Return* (N.Y.: Harper, 1959).

293 As L. Alexander notes, in such circles *historia* often involved geographical information and the writing of books (Plautus, *The Two Menaechmuses*, 234-248, *cf.* Alexander, *Preface*, p. 38).

294 J. M. Scott, *Paul and the Nations: The Old Testament and Jewish Background of Paul's Mission to the Nations with Special Reference to the Destination of Galatians* (Tübingen: Mohr, 1995), p. 3; *idem*, 'Luke's

Geographical findings, therefore, old and new, were often rationalised in the Judaic tradition, being interpreted according to a 'biblical map'.²⁹⁵ As a result, the Hebrew world view offered, a *static* perspective while Greek ethnography shared a *dynamic* view: 'the Jews could mechanically transfer an old name to some new people [see, Kition, Kettim, Kittim: Phoenician colony in Cyprus, Greeks, Romans]' whereas the Greeks, more interested in the actual development, thought that 'nations continued to be formed through expansion and division'.²⁹⁶ After Alexander the Great, however, these different perspectives displayed clear signs of reciprocal influence.²⁹⁷

Apart from reflecting on the historical consequences of their biblical stories, one particular way of Jewish authors to show their interest in geography and ideology was the development of the apocalyptic literature. Preoccupied, by definition, with the issues of global history and the final judgement of the world, apocalypses were very often written from ideological perspective. For example, 1 Enoch's message and argument are presented, for the most part of it, during a special journey of the author to the allegorical extremities of the earth, to the 'luminaries' of heaven, to the regions of the dead, and to the world of angels, during which Israel's land and the history of

---

Geographical Horizon', in D. W. G. Gill and C. Gempf (eds.), *The Book of Acts in Its Graeco-Roman Setting* (Carlisle: Paternoster, 1994), 483-544. Geography and ideology often intermingled creatively in the literature of the ancient Greece, as can be seen in the case of Polemo of Ilium (approx. 400 BC; author of *The Athenian Acropolis, Spartan Cities, Settlements in Italy and Sicily, Guidebook to Troy, The Sacred Way* – i.e., that from the sanctuary at Eleusis to Athens), or Pausanias (*Description of Greece*, AD 160-180; *cf.* Casson, *Travel*, pp. 294, 298-299).

295 *Cf.* P. S. Alexander, *The Toponymy of the Targumim, with Special Reference to the Table of Nations and the Boundaries of the Land of Israel*, D.Phil. thesis (Oxford: Oxford UP, 1974), pp. 11-17 (as cited by Scott, *Paul and the Nations*, p. 4).

296 E. J. Bickerman, 'Origines Gentium', *CPh* 47 (1952) 65-81, esp. pp. 77-78. At a different level, in terms of general view on history, the Greek thought was characterized as static, and the Hebrew, as dynamic (T. Boman, *Das hebräische Denken im Vergleich mit dem griechischen* (Göttingen: Vandenhoeck, 1983⁷).

297 Scott, 'Horizon', p. 521, n. 60.

the Hebrew heroes are being reinterpreted according to an enriched typological key.[298] In terms of ideology, Enoch's geographical adventure becomes a pretext for delineating a developed theology of judgement and reward.[299]

As for the Romans, for practical reasons, their imperial ideology was well integrated with the subject of journeying and exploring the world

> Roman writers did not attempt to make original contributions to scientific cartography, but rather sought to adapt Greek conceptions to the service of the Roman state. For the Romans, maps of the world were valued insofar as they were geopolitical and useful for propaganda and administration.[300]

In this ideological context, it is plausible that Luke wrote his accounts from a specific integrated geographical-ideological scheme.[301] His writing is aggressive in style (adopting journeys as its literary paradigm), culture (spreading the gospel in the Greek cities) and geographical conception (going as far as to 'the ends of the earth', or to Rome, the capital city of the

---

298 S. Bigger, 'Symbol and Metaphor in the Hebrew Bible' in S. Bigger (ed.), *Creating the OT* (Oxford: Blackwell, 1989), pp. 64-65. The story of Enoch's journeys in heavens and in the underworld has 'no close parallel in the Hebrew scriptures', although it does not follow strictly the model of foreign, non-biblical sources. Glasson considered that '1 Enoch 1-36 is a Jewish *nekyia*' (a hero's trip in the underworld, in Greek mythology). He admits, however, that 'it takes us beyond the Greek context' (T. F. Glasson, *Greek Influence in Jewish Eschatology* (London: SPCK, 1961), pp. 8-10; J. Collins, *Apocalyptic*, pp. 43-45). Also, Bauckham confirmed Himmelfarb's argument that these 'tours of hell' were not simply borrowed from pagan sources but were developed within Jewish apocalyptic traditions (Bauckham, 'Visions of Hell', p. 376; see M. Himmelfarb, *Tours of Hell*). For the text of 1 Enoch, see E. Isaac, 'A New Translation and Introduction to 1 (Ethiopic Apocalypse of) Enoch', in J. H. Charlesworth (ed.), *The OT Pseudepigrapha* (London: Darton, 1983), vol. 1, 5-89; M. A. Knibb, *The Ethiopic Book of Enoch* (Oxford: Oxford UP, 1982); J. T. Millik and M. Black, *The Books of Enoch* (Oxford: Clarendon, 1976); H. F. D. Sparks, '1 Enoch', in H. F. D. Sparks (ed.), *The Apocryphal OT* (Oxford: Oxford UP, 1984).
299 Millik, *Enoch*, p. 39; Bauckham, 'Visions of Hell', pp. 356, 359. *cf.* Wifall, 'The Sea of Reeds as Sheol', *ZAW* 92 (1980), pp. 325-332.
300 Scott, 'Horizon', pp. 487-488.
301 Praeder, 'Sea Voyages', p. 684.

Roman empire); as Alexander notes, through his journey accounts Luke 'storms' the ideological fortress of Greco-Roman world

> Luke structures his narrative in such a way that his hero is presented as 'invading' Greek cultural territory: first the 'hidden' ports of the Aegean, then the 'Greek sea' itself. It is as daring in its way as the paintings of the Iseum, and potentially - at least for the Greek reader - much more disturbing.[302]

In time, such incipient theological readings of geography have been continued by the literary developments of subsequent Christianity. Some of the most interesting testimonies come, for example, from the area of religious and pilgrimage maps. Thus, St. Jerome is attributed a number of maps of the *Holy Land*, where sites and landscape are accompanied by Christian comments.[303] Similarly, the mosaic map from the church of St. John at Madaba (*ca*. AD 541-565) is considered a world 'celebration' of the Christian religion.[304] Christian maps started to be regarded as graphical companions and illustrations to religious themes like 'salvation' and 'peregrination'.[305]

Supplementing his skills as a historian, and his literary talent at composing a 'well-planned' story, Luke the novelist and the ideologist proved he had a 'vision and the means to express it', the vision that 'the world be Christianized'.[306] More

---

302 Alexander, 'Journeying', pp. 38-39. Alexander's assessment reminds of Eusebius, *Proof*, 3.5.114d.1-2 'Let us go to other foreign lands, and overturn all their institutions', and *idem*, 3.5.115c.5-7 'Can anyone persuade himself that poor and unlettered men could make up such stories, and form a conspiracy to invade the Roman Empire?'
303 Manuscript copy of Jerome's *Holy Places*, made about AD 1150, kept at British Library Add. 10. 049.
304 C. D. Smith, 'Geography or Christianity? Maps of the Holy Land before AD 1000' in *JTS* 42 (1991), 143-152, esp. pp. 149-150.
305 Smith, 'Geography or Christianity?', p. 152.
306 Pervo, *Profit*, p. 138. J. Roloff disagrees with such a suggestion (*Die Kirche im Neuen Testament* (Göttingen: Vandenhoeck, 1993), p. 211). For A. Nobbs this vision has been fulfilled and, soon, in the 6th century, the historical model offered by Acts lost its relevance because of the final union between the empire and the church (A. Nobbs, 'Acts and Subsequent Ecclesiastical Histories', in B. W. Winter and A. D. Clarke

than adopting certain literary models, Luke's mimetic style displays the marks of a daring ideologising tendency. He imitates and challenges the imperial ideology of the Roman state with the width and the scope of his Christian journeys.

(eds.), *The Book of Acts in Its Ancient Literary Settings* (Carlisle: Paternoster, 1993), 153-162; p. 162).

CHAPTER 3

The Way and Synoptic Mimesis

After looking at the definition of mimesis, in the second chapter, and at a number of literary sources and models that Luke had in the LXX and in the Hellenistic literature, as well, the reader is better equipped now for assessing Luke's representation of sources. One of the most natural contexts for such a quest is the synoptic environment of the NT, itself. Lukan mimesis will be, thus, considered in relation to Mark's and Matthew's *hodos* material, and, next, this will be followed by a discussion of Luke's formal choices in his own *hodos* stories.

The grounds for such a comparison is provided by the observation that the Way motif in the synoptic gospels is supported by a common series of *hodos* texts, reiterated by all the three gospels in a very similar sequence.

(a) the ministry of John the Baptist (Mt. 3:3; Mk. 1:23; Lk. 3:5-6)
(b) the Commissioning of the Twelve (Mt. 10:5-10; Mk. 6:6-13; Lk. 9:1-10)
(c) the parable of the Sower (Mt. 13:1-23; Mk. 4:1-20; Lk. 8:4-21)
(d) the healing of a blind person (Mt. 20:29-34; Mk. 10:46-52, Lk. 18:35-43)
(e) the triumphal entry (Mt. 21:1-8; Mk. 11:1-11; Lk. 19:28-47)
(f) the taxes rendered to Caesar (Mt. 22:15-22; Mk. 12:13-17; Lk. 20:21-26).[1]

These references, together with other specific *hodos* stories of Luke, are evidence of a different types of journey notes, complementary to the Lukan *Reisenotizen* discussed earlier in chapter one. Together they represent an important, complex textual framework for Luke's general motif of the Way, despite

---

[1] The succession of these pericopes is almost identical in the three gospels, save for a few inversions (as in the commissioning of the Twelve which comes earlier in the narrative line of Matthew and is doubled in Luke by the Commissioning of the 70/72; Lk. 10:1-23).

their heterogeneous character (prophecies, parables, miracles, wisdom teaching, historical accounts, etc.).

Luke's Representation of Mark and Matthew

Before any comparison is being brought into discussion, one needs to emphasise that the main synoptic hypothesis adopted in this study is the hypothesis of Markan priority. It seems remarkable that, while this is just one of the main synoptic hypotheses used in Lukan studies,[2] quite a few authors from the ranks of those who defend alternative approaches would concede that 'such other material as Luke had remains secondary and supplementary to his Markan source' and that 'Mark was Luke's primary and respected source'.[3] For the sake of a better understanding of Luke's mimetic interaction with the synoptic authors, we will explore, yet, as well, the possibility of Luke's use of Matthew (avoiding, at the same time, the complex issue of Luke's possible interaction with Q).[4] Luke's specific emphases on the *hodos* theme and on the post-Easter encounters will be placed, thus, in the context of Mark's and Matthew's presentation of this motif.

Mark's Use of the Way Motif

Apart from Luke's theology of the Way, Mark's corresponding motif is one of the most discussed motifs of the NT, always under close scrutiny and subject to many debates. From the

---

2   *Cf.* Marshall, *Gospel,* p. 30; C.A. Evans, 'Source', pp. 17-45, etc.
3   E. Franklin, *Luke: Interpreter of Paul, Critic of Matthew* (Sheffield: Sheffield Academical, 1994), p. 368: 'the influence of Mark was all embracing in Luke and determined the overall shape and outlook of the third Gospel' (p. 367). See also F. Neirynck, 'La Matière Marcienne dans l'Évangile de Luc', in Neirynck (ed.), *L'Évangile de Luc* (Leuven: Leuven UP, 1989), p. 157: 'Ceux qui, comme B. C. Butler et A. Farrer, ont contesté l'existence de la source Q, ne nient pas pour autant la dépendance de Luc envers Marc'.
4   *Cf.* M. D. Goulder, 'On Putting Q to the Test', *NTS* 24 (1978), 218-234; idem, *Goulder,* Luke (vols. 1-2); A. M. Farrer, 'On Dispensing with Q', in D. E. Nineham (ed.), *Studies in the Gospels: Essays in Memory of R. H. Lightfoot* (Oxford: Blackwell, 1955), 55-86; M. S. Goodacre, *Goulder and the Gospels: An Examination of a New Paradigm* (Sheffield: Sheffield AP, 1996); see his web page www.bham.ac.uk./theology/q as well as that of S. Carlson, www.mindspring.com/scarlson/synopt.

very beginning, thus, one is met with the hermeneutical dilemma whether and when the Way should be seen as figure of speech or as a neutral geographical setting only. For some an absolute distinction is 'impossible' or even 'unnecessary,'[5] while for others, *he hodos* should be more often translated as 'road' not as 'way', or 'the way', in order to 'avoid unintended theological connotations associated with the "way"'.[6] This distinction has become a blurred one, in time, in many of the available Markan studies, since authors such as D. Rhoads and D. Michie have emphasized that settings have, always, a special contribution to the meaning of a narrative

> The settings of a story provide the context for the conflicts and for the actions of the characters. That context is often quite integral to the story, for settings can serve many functions essential to the plot.[7]

---

5   E. S. Malbon, *Narrative Space and Mythic Meaning in Mark* (Sheffield: JSOT, 1991), pp. 59-60. Malbon's definition of the 'way' sees it as a 'common biblical metaphor for courses of nature, modes of human and divine conduct, attitude, habit, custom, undertaking, plan, purpose, fate, and the like'. In Mark one finds *he hodos* as a *path* or a *road* (4:4, 15; 10:46), a *journey* (6:8; 10:17), a *system of doctrine* and a *way of life* (12:14).

6   R. H. Gundry, *Mark: A Commentary on His Apology for the Cross* (Grand Rapids, MI: Eerdmans, 1993), p. 442.

7   D. Rhoads and D. Michie, *Mark as Story: An Introduction to the Narrative of a Gospel* (Philadelphia, PA: Fortress, 1982), p. 63. Settings (spatial, temporal and social) help to reveal characters, determine conflict, or provide structure for the story (*cf.* the general discussion in M. A. Powell, *What is Narrative Criticism? A New Approach to the Bible* (London: SPCK, 1990), p. 70; also, S. Chatman, *Story and Discourse: Narrative Structure in Fiction and Film* (Ithaca, NY: Cornell UP, 1978), p. 141; for the significance of settings in the NT, see C. W. Hedrick, 'What is a Gospel? Geography, Time and Narrative Structure', in *PRS* 10 (1983), 255-268; E. S. Malbon, 'Narrative Criticism: How Does the Story Mean?', in J. C. Anderson, and S. Moore (eds.), *Mark and Method: New Approaches in Biblical Studies* (Minneapolis, MN: Fortress, 1992), 23-49). An example of a setting's theological implications in the Synoptic gospels is E. K. Wefald's study, 'The Separate Gentile Mission in Mark: A Narrative Explanation of Markan Geography, The Two Feeding Accounts and Exorcisms', *JSNT* 60 (1995), 3-26, esp. p. 9.

There is another reason, however, for which Mark's *hodos* settings should be analysed as a meaningful series. Save for a few skeptics like P. J. Achtemeier, W. H. Kelber and R. M. Fowler, the majority of NT scholars seem to agree that one of the key elements that make the Markan narrative as a whole cohere is its geography. This has to do with Mark's influential model of a three-parts gospel: Jesus' ministry in Galilee and around it (Mk. 1-8:26), Jesus' Journey to Jerusalem (Mk. 8:27-11:1), and, finally, Jesus' Passion and Resurrection in Jerusalem (Mk. 11-16),[8] yet, it involves more than that.

MARK'S SCHEME OF *HODOS* TEXTS

Setting a standard with his *hodos* scheme, Mark's series of *hodos* texts starts with the presentation of John the Baptist (Mk. 1:2-3; *cf.* Mal. 3:1, and Is. 40:3), a pericope with Christological implications and of programmatic importance.[9] He creates a parallel between 'your way', in Mark 1:2, and 'the way of the Lord' in Mark 1:3, setting a Christological perspective to his *hodos* texts (Luke has a similar intervention in Lk. 3:4-6, modifying Mark's emphases).[10]

Some of Mark's most eloquent examples of metaphorical use of the 'way' as a setting and as a symbol are found in the parable of the Sower (Mk. 4:4; 4:15), and in the Pharisees' and Herodians' interpellation of Jesus in relation to Caesar's tax (Mk. 12:14). Apart from that, setting references such as Mark 2:23; 4:4, 15; 6:8; 8:3, 27; 9:33, 34; 10:17, 32, 46, 52, are most often understood as part of Mark's intention to communicate a deeper meaning of the way, yet in a less spectacular manner.[11]

---

8 Wefald, 'Gentile Mission', p. 5. Also, see F. Neirynck, *Duality in Mark: Contribution to the Study of the Markan Redaction in Mark*, Louvain: Louvain University, 1988; B. van Iersel, 'De Betekenis van Markus vanuit zijn topografische Structuur', *TvT* 22 (1982), 117-138; B. Standaert, *L'Évangile selon Marc: Composition et genre littéraire* (Zevenbergen: Brugge, 1978); B. van Iersel, *Mark. A Reader-Response Commentary* (Sheffield: Sheffield Academical, 1998); D. B. Peabody, *Mark as Composer* (Macon, GA: Mercer UP, 1987), etc.
9 J. Marcus, The Way of the Lord: Christological Exegesis of the Old Testament in the Gospel of Mark (Edinburgh: T&T Clark, 1993), p. 12.
10 Marcus, *Way*, p. 37.
11 Gundry remains, however, a skeptic, *cf. Mark*, pp. 101, 457, 570, 573. According to him the 'on the road' setting in Mk. 10:32-33 implies simply 'open country' (p. 570). In 10:32-33 and that 11:8-9 simply

Mark's special emphasis on Jesus' main poles of activity, Galilee and Judaea, transfers implicitly a special significance to the 'space between' and to its series of *hodos* events.¹² The *hodos* notes come 'naturally' and provide an interpretation of this intermediary space so that the narrative sequence may cohere: (a) 1:14-8:26 Jesus is in Galilee; (b) 8:27-10:52 he is on the way to Jerusalem (8:31; 9:31; 10:32-33); (c) 11:1-15:41 Jesus is in Jerusalem.¹³

Although few in number, the correspondences between Mark's *hodos* series and Jesus' Passion notes convey clearly the idea of a journey to the Cross (*cf.* Mk. 9:31-32, 10:31-32). In these *Reisenotizen* the disciples are memorably portrayed as following Jesus 'full of fear', οἱ δὲ ἀκολουθοῦντες ἐφοβοῦντο (Mk. 10:32) and 'afraid to ask', ἐφοβοῦντο αὐτὸν ἐπερωτῆσαι (Mk. 9:32); this reiteration of 'fear' indicates Mark's mimetic sensationalism, similar to that noted by Auerbach in Peter's denial, and to Aristotle's idea of *katharsis* through intense emotions and through fear.

THE SYMBOLICAL SETTING OF PETER'S CONFESSION

One of the major tests of Mark's symbolic use of the Way setting has been his account of Peter's Confession. Since the story includes an 'on the road' setting, ἐν τῇ ὁδῷ ἐπηρώτα τοὺς μαθητὰς αὐτοῦ (*cf.* Mt. 16:13; Lk. 9:18), A. Stock concluded that 'the Way motif is definitely a Markan element', for 'both Matthew and Luke consistently eliminate the references'.¹⁴ The Confession context is important for it transfers its narrative centrality to Mark's *hodos* theme: in all structural schemes suggested for Mark 'the breakdown usually comes in the subdivision of 1:1-8:26 and 8:27-16:8', and so, Mark 8:27 represents the 'turning point' of the gospel.¹⁵

---

highlights a physical succession, a frontward-backward movement in a line of pilgrims not the way to Passion, 'a purely mundane meaning' (p. 573).

12 A. Stock, *The Method and Message of Mark* (Wilmington, DE: Glazier, 1989), pp. 26, 230-231.
13 Stock, *Method*, pp. 231-232.
14 Stock, *Method*, p. 235.
15 R. A. Guelich, *Mark 1-8:26* (Dallas, TX: Word, 1989), p. xxxvi; F. G. Lang, 'Kompositionsanalyse des Markusevangeliums', *ZTK* 74 (1977),

Peter's Confession represents a significant landmark for the gospel's geography: For example, Mark's references to the wilderness,[16] the mountain and the sea occur almost exclusively before Mark 8:27, while his mention of the 'way' goes beyond this turning point.[17] For U. Mauser, the significance of this landmark is that the proclamation in the desert, characteristic for the first part of the gospel, makes room now for 'the way through the desert', in the second part, a way that ends on the Cross, in a grave.[18] Both stages of Jesus' ministry are marked by an 'uninterrupted confrontation with the devil's might', yet, at the end of the story, this takes the form of a deadly experience.[19] By way of comparison, however, if John the Baptist ends his desert ministry in death, Jesus' sacrifice is continued by resurrection and he takes the people of God out of the old age, into the new one.[20]

The narrative centrality of Peter's Confession creates, as well, the context for Mark's reference to Philip's Caesarea. This setting was interpreted as a crucial occasion for the Markan Jesus to put aside his Messianic secrecy in a non-Jewish place,[21] at the beginning of his journey to Jerusalem, presenting himself as a king and a leader who remains loyal to

---

1-24; M. D. Hooker, *The Gospel According to St. Mark* (London: Black, 1991), pp. 200-201.

16 U. Mauser, *Christ in the Wilderness: The Wilderness Theme in the Second Gospel and its basis in the Biblical Tradition* (London: SCM, 1963), p. 132. For him 'the phrase ἔρημος τόπος is typically Marcan' (p. 104).

17 Mauser, *Wilderness*, pp. 142, 128. Cf. E. Best, *Following Jesus: Discipleship in the Gospel of Mark* (Sheffield: JSOT, 1981), pp. 15-18; W. H. Kelber, *The Kingdom in Mark: A New Place and a New Time* (Philadelphia, PA: Fortress, 1974), pp. 67-85, esp. pp. 67-70.

18 Mauser, *Wilderness*, pp. 132, 142.

19 Mauser, *Wilderness*, p. 132.

20 Mauser, *Wilderness*, p. 148.

21 W. Schmithals, *Das Evangelium nach Markus* (Würzburg: Echter, 1979), vol. 2, p. 387; Wefald, 'Gentile Mission', p. 25. For J. Marcus the Markan Jesus uses 'the way' Christologically, to communicate his divinity (Marcus, *Way*, p. 41; R. Otto, *The Kingdom of God and the Son of Man: A Study in the History of religion* (Boston, MA: Starr King, 1957), p. 103).

his mission.²² One of the special roles of Mark's geographical notes is, thus, to balance the theme of the Messianic secret.²³

However, dedicated to his hypothesis that, basically, Mark's composition is simple and not elaborate, R. Gundry objected to the integration of this *hodos* setting as part of Jesus' journey to the Cross. According to him, Jesus cannot be 'journeying towards his Passion', here, since he travels north from Bethsaida rather than south to Jerusalem.²⁴ Now, indeed, Mark's narrative does alternate between North and South, between Galilean and Judaean territory: Jesus travels from Galilee (Mk. 1:16-7:23) to the north and east (Mk. 7:24-9:29, *cf.* 9:30-52) then to the Transjordan (Mk. 10:1-52) and finally to Jerusalem (Mk. 11:1-16:8). As regards Jesus' symbolic – and redactional – journey, Mark communicates, however, a different overall structure, a linear one, and Philip's Caesarea, together with Peter's Confession can be regarded as the starting point of one great, revelational and last journey of Jesus to Jerusalem, to his Passion.

THE WAY IN MARK AND ITS CIRCULAR STRUCTURES

One of the most important arguments in favour of Mark's redactional intervention in favour of his Way motif is drawn from the evidence of his chiastic constructions with *he hodos*. This compositional tendency can be noted at the level of individual accounts as well as at the level of the whole book.²⁵

---

22   Bas van Iersel, *Reading Mark* (Edinburgh: T&T Clark, 1989), pp. 125-126. For Gundry, yet, Mark's geographical εἰς τὰς κώμας Καισαρείας, is an ambiguous expression reflecting in fact the 'region of Caesarea', as in Matthew (εἰς τὰ μέρη Καισαρείας τῆς Φιλίππου); *cf.* the hypothesis of J. Carmignac, for whom a Jewish phrase like 'into the borders of...' (בצפונות) was misread as 'into the villages of...' (בכפרות). J. Carmignac, 'Studies in the Hebrew Background of the Synoptic Gospels [Mistranslations, Verbal Plays, Visual Omissions, Synoptic Variants: Lk. 1:70-71, 78; Mk. 4:19, 5:13, 9:23, 9:49; *et permulti alii loci*...', *ASTI* 7 (1970), 64-93, p. 82, as cited by Gundry, *Mark*, p. 441.
23   G. Strecker, *Theologie des Neuen Testaments* (Berlin: Gruyter, 1996), pp. 364-367.
24   Gundry, *Mark*, p. 442: '"The way" is simply the road on which an event takes place as Jesus and others travel between localities, whatever the direction or destination of their travel'.
25   B. van Iersel, 'De Betekenis van Markus', pp. 117-138; Malbon, *Narrative Space*, p. 60; V. Taylor, *The Gospel According to St. Mark*

For example, the story of the Sower (Mk. 4:1-20; Mt. 13:1-23; Lk. 8:4-18) is told in an *inclusio* formula - *cf.* Mark 4:4, 15, preserved in all the three Synoptic gospels. Another Markan *inclusio* is present in the Bartimaeus' healing episode (Mk. 10:46, 52; ἐκάθητο παρὰ τὴν ὁδόν - ἠκολούθει αὐτῷ ἐν τῇ ὁδῷ). Stylistic repetition of *hodos* is also present in the case of the disciples' dispute about authority (Mk. 9:33, 34).

At the gospel's level, present on both sides of Mark 8:27, the *hodos* series has a structuring effect and creates a conceptual framework for the story,[26] leading to the idea of a comprehensive overall *hodos* chiasmus.[27] As a more refined model, in contrast with its well known three-part division of the gospel, Mark's gospel can be seen as a narrative in five parts characterised by five major localities: the *wilderness* (1:2-13), *Galilee* (1:14-8:26), the *way* (8:27-10:32), *Jerusalem*

(London): Macmillan, 1969), pp. 106-113; J. Gnilka, *Das Evangelium nach Markus (1,1-8,26)* (Zürich: Benziger, 1978), pp. 30-32; C. E. B. Cranfield, *The Gospel According to Saint Mark* (Cambridge: Cambridge UP, 1963, p. 14. For literary structures in Mark, see van Iersel, *Mark*, pp. 69-86, 125, 273-274, 347-350, and Danove, *Mark's Story*, p. 90. As regards Luke's chiastic structures, see R. Meynet, *Quelle est donc cette Parole? Lecture "rhétorique" de l'Evangile de Luc (1-9,22-24)* (Paris: Cerf, 1979), 2 vols.; *idem, Avez-vous lu saint Luc? Guide pour la rencontre* (Paris: Cerf, 1990); *idem, L'Evangile selon saint Luc: Analyse rhétorique* (Paris: Cerf, 1988), 2 vols.; J.-N. Aletti, *L'art de raconter Jésus-Christ: L'écriture narrative de l'évangile de Luc* (Paris: Seuil, 1989).

26 Rhoads and Michie, *Mark as Story*, p. 64 (*cf.* Malbon, *Narrative Space*, p. 68). A somewhat biased, yet thorough discussion of Mark's redaction of his *hodos* texts can be found in Gundry, *Mark*, p. 442. For J. Schreiber *hodos* is usually redactional in Mark (J. Schreiber, *Theologie des Vertrauens: eine redactionsgeschichtliche Untersuchung des Markus evangeliums* (Hamburg: Furche, 1967), pp. 190-191). E. Best has a similar view: for him Mk. 2:3, 4:4, 14-15, 11:8, 12:14 represent traditional usage, whereas Mk. 6:8 and 8:3 are redactional - 'it is principally in 8:27-10:52 that the word [*hodos*] is used redactionally' (Best, *Following Jesus*, p. 17, n. 8).

27 Stock, *Method*, p. 25 (see *idem*, 'Chiastic Awareness and Education in Antiquity', *BTB* 14 (1984), 23-22). J. Lambrecht noted chiastic structures in Mk. 4 and Mk. 13 ('Parables in Mk 4', *TvT* 15 (1975), 26-43; see *idem, Die Redaktion der Markus-Apokalypse: Literarische Analyse und Structuruntersuchung* (Rome: PBI, 1967).

(11:1-15:41), and the *tomb* (15:42-16:8).[28] Such a concentric structure would not only describe symbolically Jesus' ministry in its essential parts, yet also was suitable for reading at one sitting, for example as a Christian Passover Haggadah.[29]

Placed at the centre of this chiasmus the Way section has been seen as the *key* of the entire gospel,[30] and Mark's *hodos* terminology as having the potential to elucidate both the structure and the major themes of the gospel.[31] The section is replete with information and narrative structures and, for example, includes three overlapping series of triads which contribute to the general narrative coherence of the gospel: (a) Jesus' Passion predictions (Mk. 8:31; 9:31; 10:32f), (b) the disciples' failure to understand Jesus' plans (Mk. 8:32-33; 9:32; 10:35-41), and (c) Jesus' messianic teaching (Mk. 8:34-8; 9:35-7; 10:42-5). The whole section is built as a chiastic or *inclusio* structure with the ἐν τῇ ὁδῷ phrase occurring in Mark 8:27-10:52.[32]

THE WAY AS A CONTROLLING PARADIGM

For some NT scholars, for example, like J. Marcus, it would be 'no exaggeration' to assess that 'the way of Jesus' or 'the way of the Lord' represents more than one major theme in Mark's Gospel and, instead, it stands as 'the *controlling* paradigm for his interpretation of the life of his community'.[33] As such, the Markan motif of the Way is essentially linked to the hermeneutics of the Kingdom and of the Wilderness, of the New Exodus, and plays an important role of narrative mediation for Mark's topographical space.

The Way and Mark's Interest in the New Exodus

For W. H.. Kelber, the Way motif provides the theme of entrance into the kingdom of God (Mk. 9:47; 10:15, 23-25), and

---

28 See Iersel, *Mark*, p. 87.
29 D. Daube, 'The Earliest Structure of the Gospel', *NTS* 5 (1958), 174-187; A. Stock, 'A Christian Passover Haggadah?', *Liturgy* (COSO) 18 (1984), 3-13 (cited by Stock, *Method*, p. 14).
30 Stock, *Method*, p. 230.
31 Swartley, 'Structural Function', pp. 73-86.
32 Swartley, 'Structural Function', p. 75.
33 Marcus, *Way*, p. 47. italics mine.

is essential in the hermeneutical tradition of Deuteronomy.[34] W. Swartley notes that Jesus' ministry is portrayed in Mark as 'the ὁδός to the kingdom of God'.[35] For him the synoptic gospels, in their bipolar structure of Galilee and Jerusalem 'reflect the northern and southern settings of the origins and development of Israel's faith traditions', of the Exodus - as liberation, of the Torah - as holy instruction, and of the way-conquest - as a journey into God's heritage and victory against sinful and rebellious nations'.[36]

For J. Marcus, however, the Central Section of Mark's Gospel, 'is not, as Kelber and Swartley would have it, about the *human way to* the βασιλεία – to his kingdom [*i.e.*, the Exodus] but rather about *God's way* which *is* his βασιλεία, his own extension of power'.[37] According to this messianic perspective 'Jesus' "way" is painted in the familiar biblical colours of the Deutero-Isaian "way of the Lord"' (*i.e.* the New Exodus).[38] Thus, Mark 4, 8-9 with its references to the way and to the themes of blindness and understanding, *cf.* βλέπειν, ὁρᾶν, ἀκούειν, γιγνώσκειν, συνίειν, εἰδεῖν, νοεῖν (Mk. 4:12-13, 10:46-52),[39] should be interpreted within this Isaianic emphasis on a final restoration (*cf.* Is. 6:9; דרך and מסלול, in Is. 35:8, and the theme of transformed wilderness).[40]

Structuralist Approaches to Mark's Way Motif
Inspired by the symmetry of Mark's composition and by this centrality of the journey to Jerusalem, structuralist studies have suggested that the Way functions in Mark as an important mediating symbol - both as a 'myth' and as a 'parable'. As a paradigm of stability (expressed through the

---

34 W. H. Kelber, 'Kingdom and Parousia in the Gospel of Mark', University of Chicago (1970), PhD thesis, p. 109; also his book, *Kingdom* (*cf.* Best, *Following Jesus*, pp. 15-18).
35 Swartley, 'Structural Function', pp. 78-79.
36 Swartley, *Scripture Traditions*, p. 271.
37 Marcus, *Way*, p. 33, italics mine.
38 Marcus, *Way*, p. 40. As noted, such readings assume an audience of 'biblically literate Christians' (pp. 45-46).
39 Watts, *Influence*, pp. 108-112.
40 Watts, *Influence*, pp. 106-109; also, *cf.* 'Consolation', pp. 31, 33, 44-47, 59.

concept of *myth*) and of change (understood as *parable*),[41] the 'way' would ensure the passage between *the old* and *the new*, the mediation between death and salvation, between chaos and order. For E. Malbon, Mark's narrative unwinds progressively this tension between stability and change, between the earth's chaos and the heavenly order, between the sacred and the profane, through the symbol and imagery of journeying.[42] Mark's geography can thus be organized with the help of a number of spatial opposites grouped into three categories of hierarchical relations - the *geopolitical* (geographical regions, cities, towns); the *topographical* (sea, wilderness, mountains); and the *architectural* (houses, synagogues, the temple).[43]

order	chaos
heaven	earth
land	sea
Jewish homeland	foreign lands
Galilee	Judaea
isolated areas	inhabited areas
house	synagogue
Jerusalem environs	Jerusalem proper
Mt. Olives	Temple
tomb	mountain

The Way

---

41 Malbon, 'Mark: Myth and Parable', BTB 16 (1986), 8-17, p. 10. For Malbon 'myths are the agents of stability, fictions the agents of change'. She uses F. Kermode's and J. D. Crossan's sets of concepts here, myth and fiction, and, respectively, myth and parable (*cf.* F. Kermode, *The Sense of an Ending: Studies in the Theory of Fiction* (London: Oxford UP, 1966), p. 39; J. D. Crossan, *The Dark Interval: Towards a Theology of Story* (Niles: Argus, 1975), pp. 9, 50-63, 124-126). In essence, Kermode's polar model uses a static concept - myth (a vision of the world) which interacts with a dynamic concept - fiction (a challenge to this vision). On the relation between myth *vs.* parable, see Powell, *Narrative Criticism*, pp. 76-77.
42 Malbon, *Narrative space*, p. 2; *idem*, 'Mark', pp. 10.
43 Malbon, *Narrative Space*, p. 8; *cf.* Powell, on Malbon, in *Narrative Criticism*, pp. 76-77. Iersel, as well, notes these Markan parallelisms, *cf. Mark*, p. 485; also p. 87).

According to Malbon, the spatial and conceptual mediation takes place progressively, so that the opposition between the Jewish homeland and foreign lands is mediated by Jesus' ministry in the area of the Sea of Galilee; the opposition between Galilee and Judaea is mediated by the Road to Jerusalem; and, finally, the Jerusalem area, as an unstable environment leading to confrontation and death, is left without any mediatory elements.[44] The Way, or the Road, as a 'final mediation', does not signal simply another place or setting in Mark's topography, according to Malbon, but rather 'a way between places, a dynamic process of movement'.[45] Jesus' movement from the wilderness (1:12-13) to the city underlies the entire Markan story, which is framed by parallel references to the Way.[46] At the same time, during this mediation, the Way defines a new world, that is, the world of discipleship.[47] Mark's microcosm is dominated by the idea of journeying, leadership and discipleship: 'John prepares the way, Jesus leads the way, the disciples are called to follow on the way'.[48] The Markan Jesus is particularly bonded to this mediatory 'space between' which includes the symbols of the Way, of the mountain, and of the Sea of Galilee.[49]

From a textual point of view, although this structuralist perspective confirms much of the previous research, it has a major shortcoming since it relies quite heavily on a major exegetical constraint: this symmetry of mediation depends on Mark's shorter ending, focused on the empty tomb (Mk. 16:8).[50] This raises some questions on its relevance for the other synoptic gospels, for Luke, for example, since the

---

44 Malbon, *Narrative Space*, pp. 46-48.
45 Malbon, *Narrative Space*, p. 104.
46 Malbon, *Narrative Space*, p. 68: 'Between these two poles [Mk. 1:1-2; Mk. 16:7], further references to the way occur throughout the sequence, and thus a significant cluster is presented between 8:27 and 11:9'.
47 Malbon, 'Mark', p. 10.
48 Malbon, *Narrative Space*, p. 71. As a parable or representation of God, Jesus is the supreme mediation of the narrative tension in the gospels (*cf.* J. R. Donahue, 'Jesus as the Parable of God in the Gospel of Mark', *Int* 32 (1978), 369-386)).
49 Malbon, *Narrative Space*, p. 167.
50 With Mk. 16:9-20 in view, there would be 'no movement and no mediation', only an illogical return to the first opposition, Heaven *vs.* Earth, through Ascension (Malbon, *Narrative Space*, p. 105).

narrative structures of Luke transcend the limits of the gospel via literary correspondence, overarching parallels and echoed paradigms, and go beyond Luke 24, over into the book of Acts, across the literary and theological bridge of Jesus' Ascension (although, to be sure, journeying has a mediatory role there, as well, as a narrative support for Jesus' ministry and that of the disciples, in Luke-Acts).[51]

Matthew's Use of the Way Motif

Since the debate concerning Luke's sources is an on-going one, in relation to the Synoptic problem,[52] it seems appropriate to consider, in principle, the possibility of Luke's interraction with Matthew,[53] as well, while still allowing for Markan priority (*cf.* D. Chapman, A. M. Farrer, M. D. Goulder).[54]

---

51 Apart from classics like H.J. Cadbury or R. C. Tannehill, this correspondence is acknowledged by many other commentators, such as G. Muhlack, W. Radl, S.M. Praeder, etc., *cf.* section 4.1.1 of the present study, notes 1-9, 12. In spite of their arguments, M. C. Parsons holds a different view in *The Departure of Jesus in Luke-Acts: The Ascension Narratives in Context* (Sheffield: Sheffield Academical, 1987), arguing in favour of 'loosening the hyphen' in Luke-Acts (p. 24).

52 F. S. Spencer, 'Acts and Modern Literary Approaches', in B. C. Winter and A. D. Clarke (eds.), *The Book of Acts in Its Ancient Literary Setting* (Carlisle: Paternoster, 1993), 381-414, esp. pp. 385-386.

53 W. R. Farmer, *The Synoptic Problem. A Critical Review of the Problem of the Literary Relationships Between Matthew, Mark and Luke* (New York: Macmillan, 1964), idem, 'The Present State of the Synoptic Problem', in J. B. Tyson, R. P. Thompson, and T. E. Phillips (eds.), *Literary Studies in Luke-Acts: Essays in Honor of Joseph B. Tyson* (Macon, GA: Mercer UP, 1998) 11-36, etc.

54 Franklin, *Luke: Interpreter*, p. 367: 'the shape and the contents of Luke's Gospel are best explained on the supposition that Luke knew Matthew's Gospel as well as Mark's'. He suggests, further, that for Luke Matthew's revision of Mark was 'right in conception but wrong in its overall execution' (p. 371). For Goulder Luke has modified Matthew creatively around AD 90 (*Luke*, vol. 1, pp. 22-23). Bovon disagrees with him for this would assign to Luke 'a degree of freedom and creativity that is incompatible with the respect for tradition that Luke claims for himself' ('Studies in Luke-Acts: Retrospect and Prospect', *HTR* 85 (1992), 175-196, p. 178; 179). According to Ravens, Luke's was dissatisfied with Matthew's views on the obsolesence of the Law and the sacrificial system, since he favoured a 'reunited Israel under Jesus Messiah, the new Davidic king' (*Restoration*, p. 255, *cf.* pp. 213-246).

Such an approach is worth contemplating having in view the increasingly richer literature on this subject. Of particular value, in this context, is the redactional commentary of J. McNicol, D. L. Dungan and D. B. Peabody on Luke, written from a consistent neo-Griesbachian perspective.[55] According to them, Luke used a cyclic sequential parallelism to Matthew in his own exposition of Christianity's beginnings, a technique which seems to follow the literary recommendations of Lucian of Samosata, according to whom historians should write a 'progressive, well-proportioned narrative', knowing 'how to begin, how to arrange his material, the proper proportions for each part, what to leave out, what to develop, what it is better to handle cursorily, and how to put the facts into words and fit them together'.[56]

JESUS' JOURNEY TO JERUSALEM IN MATTHEW

Thus, it has been suggested that Luke follows Mark's sense of movement,[57] while he combines it with Matthew's emphasis on teaching, repeatedly breaking, for this purpose, Matthew's discourses.[58] This hypothesis would account for the mixed nature (teaching and journeying) of Luke's journey section (Lk. 9-19), which otherwise remains a puzzle and a threat to Luke's claims of compositional order.[59] In this respect, such a double redaction hypothesis, such as that of E. Franklin, is to be preferred to J. Drury's radical statement that in Luke 9:51-18:14 'the only certain answer' is 'that he [Luke] is not editing Mark' and that this section is made of 'Matthean material

---

55 J. McNicol, D. L. Dungan and D. B. Peabody, Luke's use of Matthew: Beyond the Q impasse. A demonstration by the research team of the international institute for gospel studies (Valley Forge, PA: Trinity, 1996).
56 Lucian, *How to Write History*, 6.6-10 (K. Kilburn); *cf.* McNicol, *Luke's Use*, pp. 13-24, 31-32; *cf.* J. Dupont, 'La question du plan des Actes des Apôtres à lumière d'un texte de Lucien de Samosate', *NovT* 21 (1979), 220-231.
57 *Cf.* Denaux, 'Delineation', p. 361. With two exceptions, Mark 6:46-8:27 (the *great omission*) and the *great interpolation* (Lk. 9:51-18:14; *cf.* the *small interpolation* of Lk. 6:20-8:3 and Lk. 19:1-27).
58 Franklin, *Luke: Interpreter*, p. 372. McNicol, *Luke's Use*, p. 38.
59 Franklin, *Luke: Interpreter*, p. 328.

mixed with his own',[60] or of 'Q' origin, plus specifically Lukan material, arranged in Deuteronomic order.[61]

One of the possible objections against relating Luke's journeying section to that of Matthew could be the fact that the latter is barely noticeable. However, although structuring Matthew is a difficult task,[62] there is some evidence for a journey scheme there.[63] Its starting point is slightly vague, since Jesus' decision to go to Jerusalem is recorded as early as 16:21 (Peter's Confession), yet the actual leaving of Galilee takes place at 19:1. Then, the journey proper covers a span of only two chapters and a half, between 19:1-21:16, similar to Mark 9-10. There is enough room, still, for some essential *hodos* texts and events, such as the second announcement of Jesus' Passion (Mt. 20:17-19), the healing of the blind man (Mt. 20:29-34), the Jerusalem entry (Mt. 21:1-8), etc. The end of the Matthean journey is similar to that of Mark, with the observation than Matthew stresses more the conflict between

---

[60] Drury, *Tradition and Design*, pp. 138-139. H. Baarlink provides a comparative table of mixed Markan and Matthean (Q) material in Luke's Jerusalem Journey ('Die Zyklische Struktur von Lukas 9:43b-19:28', *NTS* 38 (1992), 481-506, esp. p. 490). At the extremities of his journey section Luke has Markan material (Lk. 9:43-10:26-28; Mk. 9:31-41, 10:1; 12:28-34; Lk. 18:18-19:28, Mk. 10), while at the centre part (Lk. 10:29-17:37) alternates systematically Lukan and Q material.

[61] The lectionary-liturgical reading model that follows the text order of Deuteronomy has been argued in principal by Drury, Evans, and Goulder (J. Drury, *Tradition and Design*, p. 140; C. F. Evans, 'The Central Section of Saint Luke's Gospel', in D. E. Nineham (ed.), *Studies in the Gospels: Essays in Memory of R. H. Lightfoot* (Oxford: Blackwell, 1955), 37-53; M. D. Goulder, *The Evangelists' Calendar*; also 'Paschal Liturgy in the Johannine Church,' unpublished paper, read to the St. John Seminar of *SNTS* at Göttingen on 27 August 1987, as mentioned in Goodacre, *Goulder*, p. 295).

[62] Hagner notes Matthew's 'many "broken patterns"', that he has 'no grand overall structure', only an 'alternation of narrative and discourse' (Hagner, *Matthew 1-13* (Dallas, TX: Word, 1993, p. liii). See F. V. Filson, 'Broken Patterns in the Gospel of Matthew', *JBL* 75 (1956), 227-231; M. M. Thompson, 'The Structure of Matthew: A Survey of Recent Trends', *SBT* 12 (1982), 195-238.

[63] D. J. Verseput, 'Jesus' Pilgrimage to Jerusalem and Encounter in the Temple: A Geographical Motif in Matthew's Gospel', *NovT* 36/2 (1994), 105-121, esp. p. 120. See, also, McNicol, *Luke's Use*, p. 151.

Jesus and the people of Jerusalem.⁶⁴ In contrast, Luke would emphasize Jerusalem's importance as a site for Jesus' appearances after Resurrection, omitting the usual reference to Galilee.⁶⁵ He avoids the confrontational ending of Matthew (Jesus *vs.* Jewish leaders), although conflict still lurks in the background of the Emmaus journey and is present, as well, in Jesus' lament over the city (Lk. 13:31-35).

MATTHEW'S OWN *HODOS* SCHEME: A CHIASMUS?

Matthew is obviously fond of the *hodos* imagery since he introduces a unique series of *hodos* stories in his gospel

The journey of the Magi (Mt. 2:12)
The reference to Galilee of the Gentiles (Mt. 4:15, *cf.* Is. 9:1-2)
The pericope of the Two Ways and Two Gates (Mt. 7:13-14)⁶⁶
The parable of the Two Sons (Mt. 21:28-32)

---

64   Verseput, 'Pilgrimage', p. 116; *cf.* McNicol, *Luke's use*, p. 38.
65   Swartley, *Scripture Traditions*, pp. 39-43. For Mark and Matthew Jerusalem is the city of a deadly enmity (Lohmeyer, *Galiläa and Jerusalem*, pp. 26, 34), and Galilee represents a New Jerusalem for this is where 'in the time of Mark the authentic future lies' (Kelber, *Kingdom*, p. 139) for it is a representative place for Gentile mission (*cf.* Mt. 4:15; see R. H. Lightfoot, *The Gospel Message of St. Mark* (London: Oxford UP, 1952), pp. 106-116; C. F. Evans, 'I Will Go Before You Into Galilee', *JTS* n.s., 5 (1954), 3-18; S. Freyne, 'The Geography, Politics, and Economics of Galilee and the Quest for the Historical Jesus', in B. Chilton and C. A. Evans (eds.), *Studying the Historical Jesus* (Leiden: Brill, 1994), 75-121).
66   *The Community Rule* (1QS) presents a similar contrast between the two ways of Light and of Darkness (1QS 3:20-25, 3:25-4:5); see *The Epistle of Barnabas*, 18.1a-21.9b: ὁδοὶ δύο εἰσιν διδαχῆς καὶ ἐξουσίας, ἥ τε τοῦ φωτὸς καὶ ἡ τοῦ σκότους (2nd century AD). Matthew's reference is reminiscent of Jn. 14:5-6, both allowing a conceptual overlap of ἡ ὁδός and ἡ ζωή imagery (*cf.* P. Bonnard, *L'Évangile selon St. Matthieu* (Genève: Fides, 1982), p. 102). Bonnard notes in this respect that Matthew's 'way' is not a spiritualised, dualistic concept (as at Qumran), nor a moralistic one (as in the *Didache*), or Christological (as in John). Matthew emphasizes the literal sense: one has to know how to search and find the truth, how to embark on a solitary quest or journey for truth (*op. cit.*, p. 103; this personalised perspective corresponds to some of Luke's emphases and to Hellenistic models, as well). On Mt. 7:14-15 he argues that 'l'opposition fondamentale, qui domine toute la péricope est celle des mots πολλοί – ὀλίγοι' (*op.cit.*, p. 103).

Apart from that, the *hodos* setting is used at times as a specific detail to enhance the local colour of the account (*cf.* Mt. 8:28-34, the healing of the two demon-possessed men; Mt. 21:18-22, the judgement of the fig-tree). Although unevenly distributed, Matthew's *hodos* texts are grouped into two large sections, Matthew 2-13 (Jesus' ministry in Galilee) and Matthew 20-22 (the triumphal entry section). Outside these two groups the *hodos* setting is seldom mentioned (*cf.* Mt. 15:29-39) and, for example, even the parable of the Sower is told in a static setting, by the sea (Mt. 13:1, next to Jesus' lodgings, ἐξελθὼν ὁ 'Ιησοῦς τῆς οἰκίας ἐκάθητο παρὰ τὴν θάλασσαν, *cf.* the οἰκία theme in Matthew). By contrast, in Luke, this parable is told in the context of Jesus' dynamic journeying (Lk. 8:1, 4-21).

This chiastic arrangement is supported by Matthew's pair of blindmen healing stories (Mt. 9:27-31 and 20:29-34). Also, the Matthean motif of 'righteousness' present in Matthew 3-6,[67] goes quiet in the middle part of the gospel and re-emerges at the end in connection with the *hodos* theme, as the 'way of righteousness' (ἐν ὁδῷ δικαιοσύνης, Mt. 21:32).[68] Finally, there comes the traditional account about the tax rendered to Caesar which raises ironically the issue of ἡ ὁδός τοῦ θεοῦ (Mt. 22:16). The *hodos* stories support, thus, the hypothesis of a chiastic structure of Matthew,[69] and highlight the synoptic variety of journey notes.

---

67 The mention of 'righteousness' at Jesus' baptism, Mt. 3:15 - πληρῶσαι πᾶσαν δικαιοσύνην, is followed by the δικαιοσύνη series in the Matthean 'blessings' (Mt. 5:6; 5:10; 5:20). Later, Matthew refers to righteousness in Mt. 6:1; 33, and after this only at the end of the Gospel (Mt. 21:32).

68 Strecker, *Theologie*, pp. 385-411, analyses Matthew's theology as *Der Weg der Gerechtigkeit*, despite the presence of other topological motifs, as well, like the οἰκία motif (Mt. 8:14; 9:10, 28, 32; 13:36; 17:25, etc.). See also Strecker, *Der Weg der Gerechtigkeit: Untersuchung zur Theologie des Matthäus* (Göttingen: Vandenhoeck, 1966).

69 An overall symmetrical structure was attributed to Matthew by the J. C. Fenton, 'Inclusio and Chiasmus in Matthew', *Studia Evangelica*, vol. 1 (Berlin: Akademie, 1959), 174-179; C. H. Lohr, 'Oral Techniques in the Gospel of Matthew', *CBQ* 23 (1961), 403-435; H. B. Green, 'The Structure of Matthew's Gospel', *Studia Evangelica*, vol. 4 (Berlin: Akademie, 1965), 47-59; P. Gaechter, *Die literarische Kunst im Matthäus-Evangelium* (Stuttgart: Katholisches Bibelwerk, 1966); and

Luke's Representation of the Way Motif

After this succint review of Mark's and Matthew's *hodos* stories, Luke's representational style should result from the way he interacts with his sources, by expanding them, adding to them, or editing out certain themes, by reshaping them according to his own emphases and theology. Along with such aspects of Lukan style, one expects to uncover, as well, certain elements of his mimetic philosophy.

LUKE'S REPRESENTATION OF MARK'S JOURNEY MOTIF

Luke's representation of Mark's journey motif is complex, involving the reshaping of the Central Section and the redefining of some of Mark's themes such as the themes of prophecy, mission, prayer, wilderness, miracles, teaching and seeing, Jesus' messiahship, etc.

Luke's Expansion of Mark's Journey Section

One of the best examples of Luke's creative imitation of Mark is the inflation of Jesus' journey to Jerusalem, with its elaboration of Mark's journeying notes. Thus, Mark's journey section, two chapter long (*cf.* Mk. 8:27-10:32) has a ten chapter correspondent in Luke 9:18-19:27. At the same time, Luke's journey vocabulary seems more comprehensive, employing terms like πορεύομαι, πορεία, ἐγγίζω, ὁδεύω, ὁδοιπορέω, ὁδοιπορία, ἔρχομαι.[70] He associates with this journey scheme a richer series of geographical notes which includes occasional withdrawals into secluded places (ἐν τόπῳ τινί, κατὰ μόνας, etc.), the repeated mention of towns and villages (Lk. 9:12,

---

H. J. B. Combrink, 'The Structure of the Gospel of Matthew as Narrative', *TynB* 34 (1983), 61-90. In Hagner's views, however, although 'such a structure is in some ways appealing', one in fact can 'only speculate whether such a structure was really in the evangelist's mind' (Hagner, *Matthew 1-13*, p. lii).

70 Πορεύομαι is a preferred verb for Luke, part of 'the most important editorial schema of the gospel', the journey motif (Dillon, *Eye-Witnesses*, p. 89). It occurs in Luke approx. 50 times, in Acts 39 times, *vs.* approx. 33 times in the rest of NT (Dillon's analysis). As Cadbury emphasizes this preference is reflected most probably in the Lukan expansion of Mark's journey theme (*cf.* συμπορεύονται ὄχλοι in Mk. 10:1 and Lk. 14:25, while the verb occurs elsewhere in the NT only two more times, Lk. 7:11; 24:15 (Cadbury, *Style*, pp. 110, 177-178).

The Way and Synoptic Mimesis   159

πορευθέντες εἰς τὰς κύκλῳ κώμας καὶ ἀγροὺς καταλύσωσιν, 13:22, καὶ διεπορεύετο κατὰ πόλεις καὶ κώμας διδάσκων, etc.) which contextualises the story in the local landscape.[71]

Luke's Extra-Emphasis on Isaiah
Such an emphasis can be noted in various texts. For example, Luke's interest in Jesus' messianity and in the historical matter of prophetic succesion causes him to elaborate on the ministry of John the Baptist (Lk. 1:17; 1:76-79, 3:1-7, 7:27; cf. Mk. 1:2-3, Mt. 11:10). Thus, Mark's traditional text (1:2-3) is expanded in three different sections (Lk. 1:76, 79; 3:4-6; 7:27), and Luke 3:4-6 uses Mark 1:2-3 but adds an universalistic ending: ὄψεται πᾶσα σὰρξ τὸ σωτήριον τοῦ θεοῦ (cf. Is. 40:4-5).

In similar way, the evangelist has an intervention with Christological significance in Luke 3:4-6. Instead of using simply Mark's τὰς τρίβους τοῦ θεοῦ ἡμῶν, 'the paths of our God', which corresponds to the LXX and MT texts - לֵאלֹהֵינוּ (Mk. 1:2-3), he reformulates it as τὰς τρίβους αὐτοῦ, 'his paths' referring thus to a divine Jesus rather than to Yahweh's visitation.[72]

Concerning the Christological harmonisation of κύριος in Luke 3:4-6 with that of Luke 1:17 and 76-79 (esp. v. 76),[73] it is not clear whether Zechariah himself thought of the lord Messiah in Luke 1:17, 76-79, in the same way as Elizabeth did in Luke 1:43 (ἡ μήτηρ τοῦ κυρίου), or rather of God, the Lord. An argument in favour of messianic interpretation in these texts can be adduced from the use of κύριος in *The Testament of Levi*, 2:11; 4:4; *The Testament of Simeon*, 6:5. However, as Marshall points out, in such later works as these 'this usage may be Christian'.[74]

---

71 There is also, a certain contrast in the relative number of πόλις references: Matthew: x22; Mark: x7; Luke: x25; Acts: x32; of κώμη: Matthew: x4; Mark: x7; Luke: x12; Acts: x1 (cf. their links with κηρύσσω and πορεύομαι, as well).

72 J. Nolland, *Luke 1-9:20* (Dallas, TX: Word, 1989), p. 143; cf. Marcus, *Way*, p. 12.

73 The ἑτοιμάσαι ὁδοὺς αὐτοῦ in Lk. 1:76, 'to prepare his ways', is dependent on Mal. 3:1, yet the plural ὁδοὺς seems an influence from Is. 40:3-4, echoed as well in Mk. 1:2-3 (Nolland, *Luke 1-9:20*, pp. 88-89).

74 Marshall, *Gospel*, p. 93; see also, Nolland, *Luke 1-9:20*, pp. 143-145, on Lk. 3:4-6, and p. 337, on Lk. 7:27; and C. H. Dodd, *According to the*

Further, Luke appears to be a critical and thoughtful user of the LXX references to the 'way'. In Luke 3:4-6 he uses the plural, 'the rough ways', αἱ τραχεῖαι, whereas the LXX uses the singular, and in presenting the Lord's spiritual reform, he prefers the term ὁδοὺς λείας, 'smooth ways' instead of the LXX choice of πεδία 'level places' (*cf*. Lk. 3:5 καὶ αἱ τραχεῖαι εἰς ὁδοὺς λείας - Is. 40:4 [LXX], καὶ ἡ τραχεῖα εἰς πεδία). Through such a usage he might allude to the missionary journeys of the Church in Acts, as well as to the enlargement of God's kingdom to the 'ends of the world'. It is noticeable, also, that Luke's choice of words tends to reserve *positive* messianic connotations and a universalistic perspective for the Way.

Luke's Missionary Emphases

Another instance of Luke's multiplication of *hodos* stories is his use of *two* commissioning pericopes (Lk. 9:1-6, 10; 10:1-23; *cf*. Mk. 6:6-13). On the one hand, this is a Lukan emphasis on the disciples' proclamation (Mk. 6:8, Lk. 9:3, 10:4; a case of narrative redundancy), and, on the other hand, these stories communicate the emergence of Gentile evanghelism.

Indeed, in Luke 9:1-6, Jesus commissions the Twelve in correspondence to the number of the tribes of Israel (*cf*. Lk. 22:30) while the Seventy (seventy-two, in variant, Lk. 10:1; 10:1-12),[75] correspond to the traditional number of nations in the world (the Table of Nations). The same sequence of numbers is implied at Pentecost, twelve apostles (Acts 1:26; 2:14) and seventy nations (*cf*. Acts 2:5).[76] Similar concerns seem to be reflected in Luke 24:46-47 and Acts 1:8, where Jesus explains the nature of his disciples' mission as one

---

Scriptures: The Substructure of the New Testament Theology (London: Nisbet, 1952), p. 80).

75 *Cf. Textual Commentary*, p. 150. The symbol of '70' is 'an established entity in the Septuagint and in Christian tradition' (p. 151).

76 Scott, 'Horizon', pp. 524-543; *idem, Paul and the Nations*, pp. 5-121. The tradition that humanity is made up of 70 nations originates in the Table of Nations in Genesis 10, which provides a list of the nations descending from Noah's sons and who have re-populated the Earth (Gen. 46:27, Exod. 1:5, Deut. 10:32, Deut. 32:8 MT; 1 Chr. 1:1-2:2; Ezek. 38-39; Dan. 11; Is. 66:18-20; in Scott, *Paul and the Nations*, pp. 5-14; *cf.* also *The Book of Jubilees*, 8-9; *Sibylline Oracles*, 3; Josephus, *Antiquities*, 1.120-147, etc.).

which involves going 'to all the nations' (εἰς πάντα τὰ ἔθνη).⁷⁷ However, although this is a major theme in Acts, Luke is only alluding to it, here, in his gospel.⁷⁸

Stylistically, Luke's presentation of the Commissioning of the Twelve is more dramatic in comparison with Mark's corresponding pericope. Instead of indirect, simple narration of Jesus' command as in Mk. 6:8, καὶ παρήγγειλεν αὐτοῖς ἵνα μηδὲν αἴρωσιν (cf. Plato's ἁπλῆι διηγήσει, Rep. 392d), Luke presents it as direct speech (cf. Plato's διὰ μιμήσεως), creating a new occasion to impersonate Christ: 'take nothing, greet no one... stay there, leave, etc.' (Lk. 9:3-6, 10:3-13).

Editing Out Mark's *Hodos* Clauses

Luke's mimetic interests led him in certain cases to edit out Mark's *hodos* references, even if he used Mark's stories as such or chose to duplicate them. Two main constant interests of Luke can be noted here: one for a special *solemnity of action*, the other for a special *positive presentation of Christ*.

This is the case of Luke's *two* accounts about the disciples' quarrel over authority (Lk. 9:46-48; 22:4; cf. only one account in Mk. 9:33-34; a case of narrative multiplication, or literary redundancy) and in the presentation of the *two* questions about eternal life (Lk. 10:25-28; 18:18-23 - see a possibly third Lukan account of this type, in a *hodos* setting, at Lk. 9:57-58, καὶ πορευομένων αὐτῶν ἐν τῇ ὁδῷ εἶπέν τις πρὸς αὐτόν, ἀκολουθήσω σοι, κτλ.; cf. Mk. 10:17-27; Mk. 12:28-34).⁷⁹

The disciples' dispute over authority is presented by Luke without Mark's dynamism. Mark uses the *hodos* setting twice and introduces the scene through Jesus' direct speech, Mark 9:33-34, τί ἐν τῇ ὁδῷ διελογίζεσθε - πρὸς ἀλλήλους γὰρ διελέχθησαν ἐν τῇ ὁδῷ τίς μείζων. Luke *omits* the 'on the road'

---

77 According to D. L. Matson, the missionary pattern in Acts is taken from the commissioning of the Seventy / Seventy-two (*Household Conversion Narratives in Acts: Pattern and Interpretation* (Sheffield: Sheffield Academical, 1996), p. 185).
78 E. J. Schnabel, 'Jesus and the Beginnings of the Mission to the Gentiles', in J. B. Green and M. Turner (eds.), *Jesus of Nazareth: Lord and Christ. Essays on the Historical Jesus and New Testament Christology* (Carlisle: Paternoster, 1994), 37-58, pp. 46-47.
79 On Luke's tendency to use pairs of accounts, cf. Morgenthaler's 'rule of two', in *Geschichtsschreibung*, vol. 1 (*Gestalt*), pp. 96, 134, etc.

setting, and, instead of Mark's dynamic verbs (διελογίζεσθε, διελέχθησαν), he uses *nouns*: διαλογισμός in Luke 9:46, and φιλονεικία in Luke 22:24 - introducing the main scene with Mark's vocabulary yet in the indirect narrative mode (Lk. 9:46, εἰσῆλθεν δὲ διαλογισμὸς ἐν αὐτοῖς, τὸ τίς ἂν εἴη μείζων αὐτῶν, and 22:24 - ἐγένετο δὲ καὶ φιλονεικία ἐν αὐτοῖς, τὸ τίς αὐτῶν δοκεῖ εἶναι μείζων), which gives the scene a certain solemnity, similar to that of Greek dialogues between a master and his disciples (Plato also preferred the indirect style in narration). At the same time, there is evidence for a higher Lukan Christology: Jesus' intervention comes 'not *via* an initial questioning but in terms of his awareness of their thoughts'.[80] For Luke, a *theios aner* Jesus would not need to engage a dialogue to find out people's thoughts or to understand things happened in the past.

A similarly more refined and solemn atmosphere is met in Luke's two reports on *how one can inherit eternal life* (Lk. 10:25-28, 18:18-23), where Luke omits Mark's journey setting in Mark 10:17 (ἐκπορευομένου αὐτοῦ εἰς ὁδὸν).[81] Mark's use of the numeral εἷς as undefinite pronoun (Mk. 10:17, cf. εἷς τῶν γραμματέων, Mk. 12:28) is replaced by Luke with more specific and status-conscious nouns like νομικός (religious expert in the Law), and ἄρχων (ruler, leading official) and the characters ask questions in an official, more solemn way (ἀνέστη ἐκπειράζων, he raised up, asking, etc. Lk. 10:25, cf. ἐπηρώτησέν τις αὐτὸν ἄρχων, the official asked him, Lk. 18:28).

Luke tends to use a *high*-er mimetic mode, and often he includes parables or accounts about persons of high status (*cf.* the Ethiopian's story; the visit to Paulus, the proconsul of Crete, etc.).[82] In Luke, Jesus is not so much a μῖμος τῶν ἀτιμήτων, as in Mark (*cf.* Lücking's study), a representative of the poor, but rather one who often finds himself surrounded by people with a certain special social status. Comparatively,

---

80 Nolland, *Luke 9:21-18:34*, p. 51. In Lk. 24:24:13-25, however, Jesus had more questions.
81 In terms of sources Lk. 10:25-28 is drawn upon Mk. 12:28-34, which Mark sets in the Temple, and Lk. 18:18-23 on Mk. 10:17-27. For Luke both 10:25-28 and 18:18-23 are introduced by a question about inheriting eternal life, Lk. 18:18, Lk. 10:17 (*cf.* Mk. 12:28, and Mk. 10:17). These two episodes provide a remarkable *inclusion* in Luke.
82 Frye, *Anatomy*, p. 162; Hedrick, *Parables*, pp. 54-55.

Mark's report seems hurried and lacks the composed presentation of Luke: 'one having run in order to kneel, asked him', προσδραμὼν εἷς γονυπετήσας αὐτὸν ἐπηρώτα αὐτόν (Mk. 10:17). Also, Luke's reconstruction reflects his interest in dialogues or debates (*cf*. Lk. 24:13-35; Acts 8:25-40, 9:1-31; the Areopagus debate, Acts 17:16-34, etc.).

Through such stories Luke interferes with Mark's dynamic scheme of Jesus' journeying 'in full motion' towards Jerusalem, by creating a series of contrasting *static* scenes set, though, as 'on the road' encounters. This feature has been noted, for example, by D. Senior

> Luke does not present Jesus as a man in perpetual motion. He inserts into this long expanse of the Gospel (9:51-19:41) many of Jesus parables and discourses. The most important instructions on discipleship are also found here. Thus at the same time Jesus is 'on the road' the narrative seems curiously static.[83]

D. Mínguez highlights a similar contrast in Acts 8:25-40, where the desert (a static element) is being challenged by a dynamic evangelistic vision, expressed through a transformed journey.[84]

In some of Mark's *hodos* texts turned into static scenes, Luke emphasizes the revelation given through that special event. For example, in the Passion announcement in Luke 18:31 (*cf*. Mk. 10:32). Mark presents a narrator's impersonal yet dynamic picture of Jesus leading the disciples in their way to Jerusalem (ἦσαν δὲ ἐν τῇ ὁδῷ ἀναβαίνοντες εἰς Ἱεροσόλυμα) which contrasts strongly with Jesus taking them aside (καὶ παραλαβὼν πάλιν τοὺς δώδεκα, Mk. 10:32). Luke's setting is a rationalised and coherent, a more personalized scene. Jesus takes the disciples aside from the beginning, and his

---

83 D. Senior, *The Passion of Jesus in the Gospel of Luke* (Wilmington, DE: Glazier, 1989), p. 38.

84 D. Mínguez, 'Hechos 8:25-40. Análisis estructural del relato', *Bib* 57 (1976), 169-191). Luke develops a dynamic succession of contrasting static and dynamic settings, a series of journeying and retreat episodes. See Morgenthaler's alternating scheme in *Geschichtsschreibung* vol. 1, p. 163; *idem*, in *Lukas und Quintilian*, pp. 351-352.

revelational, evangelistic dialogue with the Twelve is longer than the one preserved in Mark (Lk. 18:31-33).[85]

Another important example of editing out Mark's *hodos* references is Luke's story of Jesus' healing of a blind person, where Luke mentions only one *hodos* setting out of Mark's two references (Lk. 18:35-43; Mk. 8:22-26; 10:46-52).[86] The healing takes place not when Jesus and his disciples 'were leaving Jericho', as in Mark, but 'as Jesus approached Jericho' (Lk. 18:35). Instead of simply following Mark's emphasis on discipleship - καὶ ἠκολούθει αὐτῷ ἐν τῇ ὁδῷ (Mk. 10:52), Luke's agenda dictates here a doxological ending with combined Christological and discipleship-related implications, καὶ ἠκολούθει αὐτῷ δοξάζων τὸν θεόν (Lk. 18:43). The messianic identity of the healer is emphasized better, in this way, and this reveals again the summary-oriented mind of Luke, who needs to comment somehow on the outcome of the encounter. Through its changed ending, the story communicates a sense of narrative progression turning itself into an introduction of the next account of Zacchaeus' conversion.[87] Luke's mimetic representation builds thus on the *introductory* and *transition character* of these *hodos* journey stories.

Luke's mimetic principles of representation are evident, then, in his selection and reshaping of the *miraculous feeding* pericope, as well, that is the feeding of the 5,000 (Lk. 9:10-17). In this variant the final report does not mention the *hodos* setting, reflecting Mark 6:30-44, which omits it, as well (by contrast, Mk. 8:1-10, the feeding of the 4,000 includes a *hodos* setting; see Mt. 15:29-39).

Jesus' portrait and the significance of the ending appear to have been major factors in Luke's decision for this selection. Thus, Mark 6:30-44 has a graphic presentation of Jesus' thanksgiving prayer (Mk. 6:41, ἀναβλέψας εἰς τὸν οὐρανὸν εὐλόγησεν καὶ κατέκλασεν τοὺς ἄρτους), followed immediately by a retreat to the mountain for prayer (Mk. 6:46; *cf.* Lk. 9:16,

---

85 Luke emphasizes παραλαβών as a characteristic of Jesus ministry (Lk. 9:10, 28). Mark uses it only once, in Mk. 10:32, in an ἐν τῇ ὁδῷ setting (Lk. 18:31). Matthew uses παραλάβω six times, but not with this ministry-related meaning (Mt. 1:20, 2:13, 20).

86 Mk. 10:46, 52. Luke keeps only the initial reference to the 'way' (Lk. 18:36).

87 Marshall, *Gospel*, pp. 692-693.

ἀναβλέψας εἰς τὸν οὐρανὸν εὐλόγησεν αὐτούς). By contrast, although Jesus' thanksgiving is also mentioned in Mark 8:6, it appears in a less graphic way (εὐχαριστήσας ἔκλασεν καὶ ἐδίδου τοῖς μαθηταῖς αὐτοῦ).

At the same time, in Mark 8:1-10 Jesus feels compassion toward the crowds yet, he himself suggests that they be dismissed (Mk. 8:3, 9). As a whole, the narrative is framed by the danger of perishing 'on the road', an ἀπολύσω - ἀπέλυσεν chiasmus (Mk. 8:3, 9).

Apparently, such an association of the Way with Jesus' dismissal did not promote a positive image of the Way, nor of Jesus. Therefore, Luke modifies the emphasis in Mark 6:30-44 and presents the sending home of the people as being the disciple's initiative, not of Jesus. In Luke's account Jesus is the compassionate Lord who corrects his disciples and suggests a meal and a time of rest for the people instead of a mere dismissal (Mk. 6:35-37). While Mark frames his story with the 'dismissing the multitudes' theme, using an ἀπόλυσον chiasmus (cf. Mk. 6:36, ἀπόλυσον αὐτούς, Mk. 6:45b, αὐτὸς ἀπολύει τὸν ὄχλον), Luke edits this motif out and keeps a positive emphasis on the Way (people travelling with Jesus discover his messianic identity and the dismissal is mentioned only once, at the beginning, Lk. 9:12).

Although not a *hodos* story, Luke's account of the sea storm provides another instance of similar redactional emphases (Lk. 8:22-26; cf. Mk. 4:35-41; and 6:45-53). Here Luke leaves aside Mark 6:45-53, where Jesus walks on the sea and is mistaken for a ghost (a possible 'on the lake' encounter), in favour of Mark 4:35-41. From this mimetic - redactional perspective, Mark 6:45-53, did not provide the ideal setting for teaching and revelation or for ethical choice - while Mark 4:35-41 did.

Stylistic Differences and Thematic Integration

In some of these *hodos* pericopes Luke intervenes stylistically in rephrasing the details and reshaping the story. For example, such an instance is the Commissioning of the Twelve (Mk. 6:6-13; Lk. 9:1-6, 10). Luke's journey motif becomes more specific: Mark's εἰς ὁδόν is mentioned here as εἰς τὴν ὁδόν, 'on *the* journey'. This emphasis did not go unnoticed by NT commentators and, for example, Marshall writes that 'Luke's addition of the article with ὁδός may be due to Q, 10:4, or perhaps indicate that one particular journey is in mind'.[88]

In another, more complex example, the theme of *wilderness* is transformed by Luke, this time in the reverse, for he is not associating it with a literary motif as theologically profound as Mark's.[89] Whereas in Mark the wilderness represents *par excellence* the site of temptation and suffering,[90] in Luke there is no such special meaning for ἔρημος τόπος (Mk. 1:35, 45; 6:31; 6:32, 35; *cf.* only Lk. 4:42; 9:12).[91] Luke's account of the feeding miracle, for example, does not retain Mark's use of ὁδός nor of ἔρημος (*cf.* Lk. 9:10-17; Mk. 6:30-44). For Luke ἔρημος represents rather the territory that includes the lower Jordan valley.[92] Luke's Jesus takes his disciples aside

---

[88] Marshall, *Gospel*, p. 352; also, Nolland, *Luke 1-9:20*, p. 427. H. R. Stein considers that this 'first missionary journey' of the Twelve 'was a rehearsal for their future mission as witnesses to Jesus throughout the world' (*cf.* Luke 24:46-48; Acts 1:8; in *Luke* (Nashville, TN: Broadman, 1992), p. 269). The Lukan addition in 9:1 ('power', δύναμιν) foreshadows the future empowerment at Pentecost (J. Achtemeier, 'The Lucan Perspective on the Miracles of Jesus: A Preliminary Sketch', *JBL* 94 (1975), 547-62; J. Ernst, *Das Evangelium nach Lukas* (Regensburg: Pustet, 1977), p. 285, Bock, *Luke 1:1-9:50* (Grand Rapids, MI: Baker, 1994), p. 813).

[89] Mauser, *Wilderness*, p. 148.

[90] Mauser, *Wilderness*, pp. 123, 128, 145.

[91] Mauser, *Wilderness*, p. 104.

[92] Mauser, *Wilderness*, p. 147; R. W. Funk notes than of the important meanings of ἔρημος in the Synoptics was that associated with the ministry of John the Baptist, that is 'Bethany beyond the Jordan which lies in the lower Jordan valley on the east bank, and Aenon near Salim, especially if it is the one located southeast of Shechem' ('The Wilderness', *JBL* 78 (1959), 205-214, p. 210). According to Mauser, Luke's use of the wilderness references in 1:80, 3:1-6, 4:4-6, would support such a view. As regards the simpler meaning of the term, Funk notes that 'ὁ ἔρημος τόπος was developed as alternative to nominal ἔρημος just because the latter had acquired definite geographical connotations. "A wilderness place" is always indefinite in the NT and means the country in contrast to the town' (*op.cit.*, p. 213; *cf.* Lk. 4:42; 9:12). It is interesting to note Eusebius' assessment of the desert and the ministry of John the Baptist, 'He [God] has transferred the glory of Jerusalem to the desert of Jordan, since, from the times of John, the ritual of holiness began to be performed not at Jerusalem but in the desert' (Eusebius, *Proof*, 9.6.432b.11-c.3).

(παραλαβὼν αὐτοὺς... κατ' ἰδίαν), yet not to a significant 'desert place' but to a down to earth location, to Bethsaida (Lk. 9:10).

Where Luke's story lacks in geographical dramatism, he makes up for it by establishing literary links with other more dramatic theological themes. Mark's motif of retreat and his wilderness theme are being transformed, thus, in Luke's gospel, in relation to other motifs such as the theme of prayer in seclusion or on the mountain, or of Jesus' teaching in private (Lk. 5:16, cf. Mk. 1:35; Lk. 10:23; cf. Mk. 6:30; Lk. 5:16, cf. Mk. 1:35; Lk. 10:23, cf. Mk. 6:30).

The *theme of prayer*, in particular, is well represented in Luke. The disciples need to understand that they *must* pray always, τὸ δεῖν πάντοτε προσεύχεσθαι (Lk. 1:1; cf. the connection with the larger δεῖ theme of Luke-Acts: the necessity of Jesus' Passion - Lk. 9:22; 17:27; 24:7, of testimony - Lk. 4:43; or the necessity of suffering for Christ, in Acts 9:16; 14:22, etc.). Jesus prays on a mountainside before choosing the Twelve (Lk. 6:12-16; cf. Mk. 3:13-19). Also, at the Transfiguration (Lk. 9:28-36; Mark omits, cf. Mk. 9:2-8).[93]

Even Peter's Confession (Lk. 9:18-28) can be regarded as part of this series of prayer texts set in an 'off the way' environment (cf. Lk. 9:18, εἶναι αὐτὸν προσευχόμενον κατὰ μόνας, Mk. 8:27-32 does not mention prayer).[94] Jesus' teaching on prayer is given in a similar context of retreat in 'a certain place' (Luke 11:1, ἐν τόπῳ τινὶ προσευχόμενον).[95]

It may be noted that Luke joins the motif of journey with that of retreat and prayer, especially when he has in view a messianic revelation. Thus, Jesus prays after the return of the 70/72 disciples from their missionary journey (Lk. 10:21-23; see that Mk. 6:30-32 does not mention prayer). Luke 24:13-35

---

93 For Luke the mountain is 'a place for retreat to be with God' (Nolland, *Luke 1-9:20*, p. 269). There is an exception, however, in Lk. 4:42-44, as a parallel to Mk. 1:35 (*op.cit.*, pp. 215-216).
94 Peter's Confession, Lk. 9:18-28; cf. Mk. 8:27-30. 'Luke does keep the implied privacy from the crowds' (Nolland, *Luke 1-9:20*, p. 452). The wilderness and the retreat places are in Luke a way station 'a place of waiting and preparation for the next stage' (cf. Lk. 1:80; 3:2; 4:1; 5:16, in Nolland, *Luke 1-9:20*, p. 215).
95 Nolland, *Luke 9:21-18:34*, p. 612; cf. the correspondence with Lk. 9:18. According to Nolland, Luke has a 'disproportionate fondness' for both terms.

mentions the journeying and the disciples' rest, in Emmaus, as well as their prayer. Journeying and a time for meditation and prayer come together in Damascus (Acts 9:9, 18). Luke's prayer theme offers numerous points of contact with his *hodos* scheme, even earlier in the narrative, as in Zechariah's *hodos* quotations from Malachi 3:1, 4:2 and Isaiah 9:2; 59:8; 60:1-2 (ὁδοὺς αὐτοῦ, εἰς ὁδὸν εἰρήνης), mentioned in a context of prayer (praise song).

In the context of the disciples' misunderstanding motif in Luke 9, and of Jesus' revelation, Jesus' movements are noticeably *slowed down* in Luke's representation. Journeying with Jesus makes room for the Transfiguration and for the Great Confession, as occasions of revelation in secluded places, in static scenes. At the level of Luke's global structure, the narrative flows between three major *static* sections

> The Jerusalem stories of Nativity (Lk. 1-3),
> The Transfiguration and Confession scenes (Lk. 9)
> The Jerusalem stories of Jesus' Passion and Resurrection
> (Lk. 19-24).

Luke's representational triad (revelation, prayer, retreat scene) occurs again in Luke 9 (the Transfiguration) and Luke 24 (the Ascension) in the special setting of the mountain, the two stories finding themselves in a special narrative correspondence. As the mountain reflects the idea of divine presence (cf. Acts 1:1-12),[96] both texts are based on a Deuteronomistic imagery,[97] and both mention heavenly beings, a manifestation of light, witnesses, etc.[98] Messianic tension is present in both in the fact that, while Luke 9 gradually takes the reader into a deeper and mysterious concealment of Jesus' Passion, Luke 24 moves him gradually out of puzzlement to

---

96 J.G. Davies, *Ascended*, pp. 42, 187; *cf.* Talbert, *Patterns*, p. 64, n. 19; Just, *Feast*, pp. 16-20.

97 Moessner, 'Luke 9:1-50: Luke's Preview of the Journey of the Prophet Like Moses of Deuteronomy', *JBL* 102 (1983), 575-605; also, in Moessner, *Lord*.

98 Just, *Feast*, p. 20; J.H. Davies, 'The Purpose of the Central Section of St. Luke's Gospel', in F. L. Cross (ed.), *Studia Evangelica*, vol. 2 (Berlin: Akademie, 1964), pp. 164-169; J.G. Davies, 'Prefiguration', pp. 229-33.

openness and understanding, and this is representative of Luke's 'theological geography'.[99]

In conclusion, Luke's representation of Mark's motif of the Way includes various techniques. He keeps some *hodos* material and edits out some, he rationalises and personalises Mark's accounts, aiming at a positive perception of the Way as a messianic motif. He also integrates into his journey motif other specific themes of his, such as *prayer* or *revelation* in secluded places, evangelistic dialogues, solemn scenes and slowed down movements, or the use of high status characters.

LUKE'S REPRESENTATION OF MATTHEW'S *HODOS* TEXTS

This is a rather difficult and quite speculative entreprise, yet worth doing for the sake of exploring from an alternative synoptic perspective, Luke's mimetic style. An assessment of Luke's representation of Matthew's motif of the Way should take into consideration at least three main issues: their related editing of Mark's *hodos* texts (the synoptic threefold tradition), Luke's omission of some important *hodos* passages of Matthew's (a subject which raises the question whether Luke has, actually, known Matthew's gospel, at all), and the nature of their structural and narrative parallelisms.

Parallel Editing of the Synoptic Tradition

In a number of places, both Luke and Matthew adopt a similar line of redaction of Mark's passages. For example, in editing the 'Isaianic Gospel' of the Way, both display a similar tendency to expand Mark's *hodos* series and emphasize the ministry of John the Baptist. Both add extra OT references concerning the coming of the Messiah (Is. 40:3; Mt. 3:3; Mk. 1:2-3; Lk. 3:5-6): Matthew adds Isaiah 9:1-2 (Mt. 4:15), while Luke adds the prayer or praise song of Zechariah (Lk. 1:76, 79; cf. Is. 9:2, 40:3, 58:8, 60:1-2; Mal. 3:1). As well, both add an extra testimony concerning John the Baptist (Mt. 11:10; Lk. 7:27).

There are, also, other instances, when they edit differently Mark's *hodos* references. For example, Matthew 20:17-19 follows Mark 10:32-34 and places the Passion announcement in a *hodos* setting, whereas Luke, on the contrary, emphasizes

---

99 Just, *Feast*, p. 22.

Jesus' awareness of the coming Passion at the expense of Mark's journey indicators (Lk. 18:31-34).

Luke's Omission of *Hodos* Passages

The issue here is how Luke, if he knew Matthew, has come to edit out some large and famous *hodos* passages such as (a) the journey of the Magi to Bethlehem (Mt. 2:1-23), (b) the reference to the Galilee of Gentiles (Mt. 4:15), and (c) the Two Ways sayings of Jesus (Mt. 7:13-14). Admitting that the following analysis is forced too often to rely on the argument from absence, it is important, however, to see that such omissions can still be coherently explained in line with Luke's theological tendencies as known from his redaction of Mark.

The *Two Ways* parables can be regarded as Q material since they have a parallel in Luke's pericope about the narrow door (Lk. 13:22-31; ἀγωνίζεσθε εἰσελθεῖν διὰ τῆς στενῆς θύρας, Lk. 13:24, etc.). Luke keeps the idea of challenge (στενή, enhanced by ἀγωνίζεσθε),[100] yet does not preserve the mention of ἡ πύλη and ἡ ὁδός (the gate and the way). If the text belongs to the Q source, one cannot be sure of its original form. Matthew might have modified it to include these elements, as well. The second important element in the saying is the opposition ὀλίγοι - πολλοί (few - many), preserved by both Matthew and Luke (Mt. 7:13-14; Lk. 13:23). However, instead of building on the idea of the *two ways* and on the contrast ὀλίγοι - πολλοί, like Matthew, Luke elaborates on the *door concept* (ἡ στενὴ θύρα; ἀποκλείσῃ τὴν θύραν; κρούειν τὴν θύραν, Lk. 13:24-25; *cf.* Mt. 25:10, ἐκλείσθη ἡ θύρα; also Lk. 11:7). Matthew's contrast ὀλίγοι - πολλοί becomes in Luke a repeated contrast between the first and the last, οἱ πρῶτοι - οἱ ἔσχατοι (Lk. 13:30). Whereas Matthew highlights the choice, Luke is more

---

100 A similar emphasis on the element of *constraint* occurs in the parable of the Great Banquet, Mt. 22:10, συνήγαγον πάντας οὓς εὗρον, and Lk. 14:23, καὶ φραγμοὺς καὶ ἀνάγκασον εἰσελθεῖν. As a testimony to the Lukan taste for contrasts 'dans Luc ces invités insolites sont d'un genre plus misérable mais moralement plus rassurant', although they contradict, for example, the Qumran qualifications for the holy congregation (Bonnard, *St. Matthieu*, p. 320, on Mt. 22:8-9, 10). The mention of necessity (ἀνάγκη), is apparently a Lukan preference, along with δεῖ (5 times in Luke-Acts: Lk. 14:18, 23; Lk. 21:23; Acts 10:24; 13:46), Matthew uses it only once (Mt. 18:7).

judgemental of the Jews and presents a total inversion of priority.[101] For some reason, Luke is not attracted by the idea of choosing between two different ways. The way is not so much a matter of choice, in Luke, as it is in itself an important *locus* for essential ethical and theological choices. As well, the plural 'ways' is kept as a reference to missionary ministry, as a sign of the Lord's coming.

Next, the reference to the Galilee 'by the way of the sea' (Mt. 4:15), related to Gentiles, is surprisingly missing from Luke, especially if he knew Isaiah and tended to emphasize his message (and, also, if he used Matthew). However, it could have been omitted by Luke on the grounds that caused him to leave out Mk. 6:46-8:27 (the Great Omission), as well, i.e., his particular focus on Jewish mission in the Gospel.

Finally, it is difficult to understand why Matthew's account of the Magi's visit (Mt. 2:1-23) does not find its way into Luke's gospel. The Lukan motifs of journeying, worshipping and joy at the birth of the Messiah are all present there. However, whereas Luke builds an idyllic picture of Jerusalem in Luke 1-3 (and this feature of Luke's prologues is well known), Matthew's atmosphere is on the whole, rather grim, dramatic, emphasizing the rejection of Messiah. For Luke, rejection is a theme to be mentioned rather at the end of the gospel.[102] The issue of rejection and suffering occurs at the beginning of the gospel only in a very subtle, indirect way (*cf.* Simon's prayer, Luca 2:34-35). Another possible reason for Luke's omission of this pericope could be Luke's Jewish particularism.[103] One could suggest that the evangelistic, Gentile emphases in the

---

101 J. O. York, *The Last Shall Be First: The Rhetoric of Reversal in Luke* (Sheffield: Sheffield Academical, 1991).
102 J. L. Ray, *Narrative Irony in Luke-Acts: The Paradoxical Interaction of Prophetic Fulfillment and Jewish Rejection* (Lewiston, NY: Mellen, 1996), p. 8.
103 Cadbury is the first (1927) to call attention to Luke's Jewish particularism (*Making*, p. 254). Similar views are hold by Jervell, Sanders, Wilson (*cf.* Wilson, *Gentiles*, pp. 29-56). For R. Maddox, Luke, unlike the other evangelists 'has no need to fit into the Gospel a theme [like Gentile evangelism] which he plans to set forth at length in a second volume' (*The Purpose of Luke-Acts* (Edinburgh: T&T Clark, 1982), p. 55; see also Dollar, *Exploration*, pp. 39, 43-44, 57, etc.).

story of the three Magi are reserved by Luke for the Ethiopian conversion in Acts (Acts 8:25-40).[104]

Hodos Chiasmus in Matthew and in Luke

While Luke keeps together the parables of the adversary and of the Great Banquet, at the heart of his Central Journey (Lk. 12:58-59; 14:15-24), between the two questions concerning the inheriting of eternal life (Lk. 10:25-28; 18:18-23), Matthew places them at the beginning and, respectively, at the end of his gospel (Mt. 5:25, 22:1-14).

Luke centralizes ethical challenge and encloses it with a discipleship *inclusio*: it comes after a series of three Lukan specific *hodos* texts (how to follow Jesus, Lk. 9:57-58; the commissioning of the 70/72, Lk. 10:1-23, and the Good Samaritan, Lk. 10:30-37), and it is followed, immediately, by Jesus' questions about discipleship (Lk. 14:25-33) and the parable regarding the 'salt or soil' quality of Israel (Lk. 14:34-35). This centralization of ethical challenge in Luke 12-14, highlights, in fact, the chiastic structure of Luke 9-19, which, as suggested by other studies, is centred on Jesus' lament over Jerusalem (Lk. 13:33-35).[105] Goulder, Talbert, Bailey,

---

104 Both main characters are figures with royal connections, from a distant country. In both stories Jerusalem is a town of contradictions and inner division (the Magi look for the Messiah in the royal palace, the Eunuch looks for salvation in the Temple). While the journey of the Magi is placed at the beginning of the Gospel as a sign of the universalistic perspectives of Matthew; a similar function has in Acts the Ethiopian's story. The Magi return on another road full of joy (Mt. 2:12; Mt. 2:10), the Ethiopian returns full of joy after his encounter with Philip (Acts 8:39). Yet there are important differences, too: the Magi set out because of Jesus, not because they wanted to worship at the Temple; they had only the Star - and no Scripture is mentioned; they do not use any Philip-like figure to interpret the meaning of signs (although they consult Herod's scribes); they bring gifts to Jesus, while the Eunuch receives a message and baptism; the Ethiopian could be regarded as a disfigured functionary, while the Magi are, as far as we know, whole and independent.

105 Walker, *Jesus and the Holy City*, p. 62; H. L. Egelkraut, *Jesus' Mission to Jerusalem: A Redaction-Critical Study of the Travel Narrative in the Gospel of Luke, Lk 9:51-19:48* (Frankfurt: Lang, 1976), p. 198; H. Baarlink, 'Struktur', pp. 487-490, gives one of the few detailed schemes of this chiasmus available in Lukan studies.

Blomberg, and Franklin agree that Luke's journey narrative 'falls into two parts with the conclusion of the first coming at the end of chapter thirteen.'[106] Matthew and Luke share, thus, the idea of an overall structural chiasmus, yet they construct it differently. While Matthew organizes his narrative into a large global ethical chiasmus, Luke's centralizes the challenge and relies on a revelation chiasmus in Luke 9 - Luke 24.[107]

Luke's Journey Motif in Luke-Acts

The second part of this journey into Luke's mimetic representation is focused on studying his literary style by assessing his *own hodos* accounts. For convenience, the *hodos* references are divided into three distinct groups: (a) the *hodos* occurences in Luke's Infancy narratives (including its thematic

---

106 Franklin, *Luke: Interpreter*, p. 337. Talbert acknowledges a division point at 13:33. For Bailey the 'Jerusalem Document' breaks at 13:35 although he observes a circular structure within 13:22-35, as well. Goulder regards 13:21 as the ending of the first half of the narrative, for it is here that Luke's full use of Matthew comes to an end (Goulder, 'The Chiastic Structure of the Lucan Journey', in F. L. Cross (ed.), *Studia Evangelica*, vol. 2 (Berlin: Akademie, 1964), 195-202; Blomberg, 'Midrash', pp. 233-247; Bailey, *Poet and Peasant*, p. 82). Franklin, similarly, suggests a break at 13:35 (Franklin, *Luke: Interpreter*, p. 338, n. 1). One of his arguments is the parallelism between the parable of the Good Samaritan and the story of the Pharisee and of the tax collector (Lk. 10:25-37; 18:9-14). Further support is adduced from the parallelism between the parables of the importunate claimants (Lk. 11:5-8; 18:1-8) and those of the girded loins and of the dishonest steward (Lk. 21:13-21; 16:18-31; Franklin, *op.cit.*, p. 337), or as well, from Lk. 9:37-62, 18:31-34 (shortcomings in discipleship); Lk. 9:51-56, Lk. 19:1-10 (receiving Jesus and his disciples); Lk. 10:25-28 and Lk. 18:18-23 (inheriting eternal life); Lk. 10:29-37 and Lk. 17:11-19 (the Samaritan); Lk. 12:52-53, 14:25-27, 18:28-30 (loss and restoration of family unity); Lk. 11:1-3 and Lk. 18:1-14 (prayer).
107 Just, *Feast*, p. 22 (also, pp. 16, 20). After Lk. 9 there is a gradual descending into silence and concealment of the Passion and Resurrection; with Lk. 24 the narrative builds up, Christologically, towards the Ascension. Marshall, however, is not very convinced of such a chiasm 'without doing some violence to the text' (Marshall, *Gospel*, p. 402). Fitzmyer, as well, disagrees with Talbert (Fitzmyer, *Luke I-IX*, p. 97), and states that 'it is impossible to detect a structure in this account' (p. 825).

and literary links with Acts); (b) Luke's Central Section (highlighting Luke's own *hodos* stories and their literary structure); and, finally (c) the Emmaus *hodos* encounter, seen as a journey story beyond the landmark of Jerusalem and of Jesus' Passion.

The Journey Motif and the Infancy Narratives

Luke's *hodos* motif has a special place in the Infancy gospel. Apart from the well known Isaianic prophecy at the beginning of John's ministry, in Luke 3:5-6), Luke adds other similar references: Zechariah's prayer, Luke 1:76 - ἑτοιμάσαι ὁδοὺς αὐτοῦ,[108] Luke 1:79 - κατευθῦναι τοὺς πόδας ἡμῶν εἰς ὁδὸν εἰρήνης; reiterations on John the Baptist (Lk. 7:27).

The entire Nativity section in Luke is marked by the motifs of 'journeying' and 'sojourning'.[109] Thus, Mary travels from Galilee to Judah to visit Elizabeth (Lk. 1:39-56), Joseph and Mary embark on a journey from Nazareth to Bethlehem in Judaea (2:1-7), and the shepherds travel to Bethlehem from the hills of Judaea (Lk. 2:8-20). As well, Joseph and Mary travel to Jerusalem twice, once for Mary's purification (2:22-39) and once for the Passover and, probably, for Jesus' *bar-mitzvah* (2:41-51). In this last instance, the *hodos* mention in Luke 2:44 (ἦλθον ἡμέρας ὁδόν) does not carry any deep metaphorical meaning, yet it contributes to the general impression of movement, characteristic of times of prophetic fulfillment. This period has an idyllic outlook emphasized later, as well, by Jesus' picture as a young prodigy, a theme with Hellenistic connotations.[110]

---

108 Nolland, *Luke 1-9:20*, p. 88. *Cf*. Lk. 1:76, καὶ σὺ δέ, παιδίον, προφήτης ὑψίστου κληθήσῃ· προπορεύσῃ γὰρ ἐνώπιον κυρίου ἑτοιμάσαι ὁδοὺς αὐτοῦ. Lk. 1:79 adds 'will guide our feet into the path of peace' (*cf*. Ps. 13:3 [LXX, Ps. 14:3]; Ps. 107:14; Is. 9:2; 41:3; 58:8; 59:8, 9; 60:1-2). This quotation is not paralleled in Mk. 1:2-3.

109 Moessner, *Lord*, p. 294.

110 Cicero's birth is announced by the appearance of a phantom to his nurse (φάσμα δοκεῖ) foretelling 'that her charge would be a great blessing to all the Romans' (Plutarch, *Cicero*, 2.1.4-6). Further, Luke's portrayal of Jesus the boy and of his brilliance in understanding is closely paralleled by that of Cicero 'his natural talent shone out clear and he won name and fame among the boys, so that their fathers used to visit the schools in order to see Cicero with their own eyes and

The special dynamics of the Nativity contributes to its prefatory role.[111] Luke introduces here his paradigm of 'divine visitation', and comes back to it, later, in Jesus' journey to Jerusalem and in the Emmaus encounter.[112] Even from the Infancy narratives, this theme is coherently supported by the role of the Spirit as a divine character.[113]

One can note, further, a significant *linguistic correspondence* between these Infancy texts and the other *hodos* accounts in Luke-Acts which emphasizes common Lukan authorship and the same representational vocabulary and vision.[114] For example, the language of amazement and eye-witnesses, in Saul's conversion, ἐξίσταντο δὲ πάντες οἱ ἀκούοντες (Acts 9:21) is found also in Luke 2:47; the divine intervention through angels, ἄγγελος δὲ κυρίου - in Acts 8:26, and also in Luke 1:11, 2:9 (*cf.* Mt. 1-2); the reference to Israel, υἱῶν τε ᾽Ισραήλ - in Acts 5:21, 7:37, 9:15, 10:36, also in Luke 1:16. The noun ὀπτασία, vision, is not found in the NT elsewhere but in Luke 1:22, in the Emmaus road encounter (Lk. 24:23), and in 2 Cor. 12:1. Apart from the stereotyped expression in the 'Lord's prayer', the adjective οὐράνιος occurs only in Luke 2:13 and in

---

observe the quickness and intelligence in his studies' (*Cicero*, 2.2.5-9; *cf.* McNicol, *Luke's Use*, p. 68).

111 Robinson, 'Place', p. 483. For a general discussion, *cf.* Minear, 'Birth Stories', p. 121.

112 D. McBride, *Emmaus: The Gracious Visit of God According to Luke* (Dublin: Dominican, 1991), pp. 30, 49-54. Apart from the Exodus paradigm and Isaiah's Judgement model of God's visit, he mentions other OT parallels, as well: a visit which creates new life (1 Sam 2:21); brings salvation (Ps. 106:4); achieves liberation (Exod. 4:31); calls sinners to account (Hos. 9:7); wins the victory for God's people (Zeph. 2:7); punishes enemies (Jer. 46:21); represents the care of a good shepherd (Ezek. 34), *cf.* McBride, *op.cit.*, pp. 6, 3-29.

113 W. Shepherd, *The Narrative Function of the Holy Spirit as Character in Luke-Acts* (Atlanta, GA: Scholars, 1994), p. 251.

114 Boismard and Lamouille, in their multiple-redactor hypothesis, assign these correspondences to 'Luke': 'Act II [*i.e.* 'Luke'] offre des contacts thématiques et littéraires très étroits avec l'évangile de l'enfance de Lc; nous pourrons en conclure que le même auteur, pour nous Luc, a écrit l'évangile de l'enfance et le niveau II des Actes des apôtres' (Boismard, *Actes*, vol. 3, p. 14). For them 'Act I' is a pre-Lukan redactor, *ca.* AD 50 (an original document coming from Peter), 'Act II' comes from 'Luke', *ca.* AD 80, and 'Act III' is a post-Lukan redactor, *ca.* AD 90 (*cf.* vol. 1: *Introduction - Textes*).

Acts 26:19, in the description of Saul's commissioning. In these texts, also, Luke prefers the form ʹΙερουσαλήμ to that of ʹΙηροσολύμα (Lk. 2:25, 38, 41, 43, 45; *cf.* Lk. 24:13, 24:18; 24:33; 24:47; 24:52; Acts 1:8; 1:12; 1:19; 8:27; 9:2; 9:26, etc).[115]

Another thematic correspondence between these texts is the occurrence of the *two witnesses* motif (Lk. 2:25-38, Anna and Simeon; Cleopas and his companion, Lk. 24:4; Moses and Elijah, Lk. 9:30,32; two angels, Acts 1:10; etc., *cf.* Morgenthaler's 'rule of two').[116]

Lastly, journeying in this section is integrated, as in the whole of Luke-Acts, with the themes of physical or intellectual impairment or with healing, as a result of faith or lack of it. For example, the story of Zechariah's numbness (Lk. 1:20-22) has its counterparts in the intellectual blindness of Cleopas and his companion (Lk. 24:16),[117] in Paul's blindness and his recovery (Acts 9:8-9), in Elymas' blindness (Acts 13:4-12), etc.[118]

Jesus' Journey to Jerusalem and Its Hodos Stories

In spite of several thematic approaches to Luke's Central Section, in the last decades, none has interpreted it in terms of Lukan mimesis. Lukan researchers, so far, suggest that nothing much can be said about this passage where a loose theology is associated to a loose geography.[119] By contrast, one can discover more of its message by looking at its form and its structure through the lens of mimetic representation.

---

115 Boismard, *Actes*, vol. 3, pp. 14-17.
116 Morgenthaler, *Geschichtsschreibung*, vol. 1 (*Gestalt*), p. 96.
117 The motif of intellectual and physical sight is found in Greek and Hellenistic philosophers, as well, for example, in Plato. He says, in relation to mimesis, that 'it often happens that the dimmer vision sees things in advance of the keener' (Plato, *Rep.* 595; *cf. Rep.* 596a4; see also Murray, *Plato on Poetry*, p. 190; Lee, *Plato, The Republic*, pp. 360-361). Plato develops further this sight motif with the theory of forms (ἰδέαι), the metaphor of imitation of nature as through a mirror, etc.
118 On the OT theme of disobedience and blindness, see Watts, 'Consolation', pp. 31-59.
119 Baum, *Lukas*, p. 380.

THE MEANING OF LUKE'S CENTRAL SECTION

The theological significance of Luke's journey section is controlled by its *teaching* content and by its *Passion* perspective.[120] In terms of material, Luke crams here much of his specific stories,[121] and shapes the story line into three similarly built parts (19:51-13:21; 13:22-17:10; 17:11-19:27; all sections integrate the motifs of journeying, teaching, specific parables, characteristic table fellowship, etc.). The link between teaching and journeying is a subtle one, and Luke sustains it by various literary techniques (for example, F. J. Matera suggests that majority of Jesus' instruction is given at *specific points* of changes of time and place: Lk. 9:51, 56; 10:17, 38; 11:1, 14, 37, 53; 21:1, 13:10, 22; 14:1, 25; 51:1; 17:11; 18:31; 18:35; 19:1, 28, 29, 37, 41, 45).[122]

According to Kümmel's *redactional classification*[123] one can note seven different types of interpretations for Luke 9-19: (a) as an account of Jesus' preparation and commissioning of his disciples;[124] (b) as parallel to the teachings of Deuteronomy;[125]

---

120 The massive presence of didactic material led J. Schneider to the hypothesis that Luke 9-19 has a primarily parenetic purpose (J. Schneider, 'Zur Analyse des lukanischen Reisenberichtes', in J. Schmidt and A. Vögtle (eds.), *Synoptischen Studien* (Münich: Karl Zink, 1953), 207-229; cf. Swartley, *Scripture Traditions*, p. 128, note 91). Green notes that 'only 9:51-56; 11:14-16; 13:10-13; 14:1-6; 17:11-19; and 18:35-43 contain material other than sayings'. The teaching element is used 'to solidify the relation between disciples and master', to encourage people to serve together with Jesus for the fulfilment of God's plan (Green, *Theology*, p. 104). W. Grundmann suggests that the journey is built on the Lukan theme of the 'the teacher in the face of death'. Jesus journeys to suffer and he utters vital teaching for his disciples (Grundmann, *Lukas*, p. 198; idem, 'Fragen der Komposition des lukanischen "Reiseberichts"', *ZNW* 50 (1959), 252-271, p. 254).
121 Bock, *Luke 1:1-9:50*, p. 23. See also B. Reicke, 'Instruction and Discussion in the Travel Narrative', in K. Aland (ed.), *Studia Evangelica* (Berlin: Akademie, 1959), vol. 1, 206-216; Goulder, 'Chiastic Structure', pp. 195-202.
122 F. J. Matera, 'Jesus' Journey to Jerusalem (Luke 9.51-19.46): A Conflict with Israel', *JSNT* 51 (1993), 57-77, pp. 60, 62; p. 76, n. 38.
123 W. G. Kümmel, *Introduction to the New Testament* (London: SCM, 1975), pp. 141-147.
124 J. Schneider, D. Gill, W. C. Robinson, S. Brown.
125 C. F. Evans, D. Moessner.

(c) as a teaching series focused on the debate with Jesus' opponents;[126] (d) as a journey model of Jesus' awareness of his Passion,[127] or (e) as a compositional device uniting Jesus' actual journey to his Passion with his messianic teachings;[128] (f) as an effective Christian metaphor of the history of redemption seen as 'the Way';[129] (g) an anticipation of Jesus' ascension;[130] (h) as a picture of the Jewish and Samaritan dilemma of choosing between listening to Jesus and rejecting him;[131] or (i) as a retrospective composition of Luke, narrating Jesus' journey to Jerusalem by analogy to Paul's later and similarly tragic journey to the Judaean capital.[132]

From a *literary perspective*, D. Moessner mentions four thematic strands in the assessment of this Lukan section. The first is the *theological-Christological* approach, according to which Jesus' journey to Jerusalem is 'a viable symbol of a distinctive phase in the unfolding dynamic of the *Heilsgeschichte*', the authoritative journey of the king Messiah along with Jesus' awareness of his suffering as a path to glory.[133] The second is the *ecclesiastical-functional* approach, which considers that the coherence of Luke's central section is due to a 'useful parallel between Jesus' journeying and the church's present journeys'.[134] Thirdly, the *literary-aesthetical* approach, uncovers a distinct literary structures like chiasmus, analogy to Deuteronomy, lectionary cycles, etc. In this case, the story's literary coherence is achieved through artistic means for 'Jesus still journeys to Jerusalem, but he does so through a carefully conceived artistic pattern', a journey 'frozen' in a literary structure.[135] The fourth is the *traditional-logical* approach, according to which the Jerusalem

---

126 B. Reicke, I. H. Marshall, F. J. Matera.
127 J. C. O'Neill, H. Conzelmann, S. Schulz.
128 W. Grundmann, A. George, M. L. Strauss.
129 W. C. Robinson.
130 J. H. Davies, H. Flender, G. Lohfink, M. Parsons.
131 F. Schütz.
132 G. Bouwman, *cf.* Kümmel, *Introduction*, pp. 141-142.
133 H. Conzelmann, J. H. Davies, C. F. Evans, J. A. Fitzmyer, W. C. Robinson, F. Schütz, C. H. Talbert (Moessner, *Lord*, p. 24).
134 W. Grundmann, E. Lohse, P. von Osten-Sacken, B. Reicke, J. Schneider, F. Stagg.
135 K. E. Bailey, J. Drury, C. F. Evans, M. D. Goulder, A. Guilding, R. Morgenthaler, C. H. Talbert, L. T. Johnson.

The Way and Synoptic Mimesis 179

journey is an intrinsic sequence of the earlier gospel tradition, a 'convenient scaffolding for a great mass of heterogeneous traditions' which does not follow a perceptible chronological sequence).¹³⁶

In a more compact summary F. J. Matera suggests that two main aspects have been emphasized in the study of Luke's Jerusalem journey, the *Christological* aspect and the *ecclesiological* one.¹³⁷

Closer to the present study's perceptions, however, is M. Miyoshi's classification, who notes two types of Lukan journey studies, based on whether the emphasis in interpreting the Jerusalem journey has been laid on (1) the journey indicators, *Reisenotizen*,¹³⁸ or (2) on Luke's specific theology of journeying, die *Theologie der Stoffe im Reisebericht*.¹³⁹

The present study takes into account the various, different types of journey stories in Luke 9-19 ('journey within a journey' stories, recognition accounts, journey parables, etc.), and suggests that such short paradigmatic accounts in Luke-Acts (*hodos* stories, trial and arrest narratives, prison delivery stories, etc.) are evidence of a constant style and provide a fresh point of view for the assessment of Luke's theology of the

---

136 J. Blinzler, G. Ogg, E. E. Ellis, J. N. Geldenhuys, I. H. Marshall, V. Taylor, R. P. B. Rigaux, L. Girard (in Moessner, *Lord*, p. 24).
137 Matera, 'Jesus' Journey to Jerusalem', esp. pp. 58-59. At p. 59, n. 9, he mentions that among those seeing Luke's purpose as primarily Christological are H. Conzelmann, *Luke*; J. H. Davies, 'Central Section', pp. 164-69; W. Grundmann, 'Fragen', pp. 252-271; P. von Osten-Sacken, 'Zur Christologie des lukanischen Reiseberichts', *EvT* 33 (1973), 476-496. Alternatively, other scholars view Luke's purpose as more ecclesiological, focusing on salvation history, discipleship or the church's mission (*cf.* D. Gill, 'Observations', pp. 199-221; B. Reicke, 'Instruction and Discussion', pp. 206-216; M. Miyoshi, *Anfang*; Robinson, 'Travel Narrative', pp. 20-31; J. Schneider, 'Reisenberichtes', pp. 207-229; G. W. Trompf, 'La section médiane de l'évangile de Luc: l'organisation des documents', *RHPR* 53 (1975), 141-154; G. Sellin, 'Komposition, Quellen und Funktion des lukanischen Reiseberichtes (Lk. 9:51-19:28)', *NovT* 20 (1978), 100-135).
138 H. Conzelmann, W. C. Robinson, E. Lohse, G. G. Gamba, W. Grundmann, A. Denaux, J. H. Davies, D. Gill.
139 J. Schneider, B. Reicke, C. F. Evans, G. Bligh, M. D. Goulder, D. Moessner, X. Meeüs, F. Gils (as cited by Miyoshi, *Anfang*, pp. 2-5).

Way. Luke's journey is perceived, therefore, as a *'literary motif that functions with specific narrative roles'*.[140]

LUKE'S NOVEL-LIKE, SHORT JOURNEY ACCOUNTS

The journey theme, already acknowledged as being essential to the message of Luke-Acts,[141] is specifically illustrated, then, through this series of *hodos* accounts, which display remarkable literary dynamism and surprising novel-like features.

Stopped on the Way, a Discipleship Sub-Theme

The first Lukan specific *hodos* text in this section is Luke 9:57-58. Paralleled by Matthew 8:18-22, yet without a mention of the 'way' there, this passage shares the traditions of Mark's report on the rich young man and his question about eternal life (Mk. 10:17-27). Luke 9:57 uses two specific journey-related terms, *hodos* and *porevo*, in the context of discipleship, *akoloutheo*: καὶ πορευομένων αὐτῶν ἐν τῇ ὁδῷ εἶπέν τις πρὸς αὐτόν, ἀκολουθήσω σοι ὅπου ἐὰν ἀπέρχῃ.[142] A similar story appears in Luke 18:18-23, yet without an explicit *hodos* setting. This type of early Christian tradition singles out Jesus as a teacher often stopped on the road with a request for a word of Torah wisdom or for healing. Alternatively, Jesus would stop others 'on the road' or during a journey, with the purpose of teaching and discipling (*cf.* Lk. 9:59-62; esp. Lk. 9:59, Lk. 9:60). Apart from its OT or Hellenistic tradition, the pattern of instruction 'on the way' is profoundly characteristic of Jesus' ministry, and this may have influenced the collective

---

140 Swartley, *Scripture Tradition*, p. 129, n. 94; *cf.* also, Denaux, 'Delineation', p. 367.

141 Navone writes 'Jesus travels from Galilee to Jerusalem to accomplish what his disciples will communicate in their journey from Jerusalem to the ends of the earth (Rome) in the Age of the Church (Luke-Acts).. Even his [Jesus'] parables recount travel stories (*e.g.* the Prodigal Son)' (Navone, *Theology of Story*, p. 54).

142 Next to ἡ ὁδός, πορεύομαι with its cognates has been seen as a *'terminus technicus'* linking together several Lukan themes and waving them into the 'fabric of faithful discipleship' (Gill, 'Observations', p. 214).

memory concerning the later post-resurrection appearances or encounters.[143]

Multiple Commissionings of the Disciples

Luke was fond of recording different variants of Jesus testimonies, or to shape them, as literature, and thus one finds in his gospel not only the commissioning of the Twelve (Lk. 9:1-6, 10) but in addition, that of the Seventy disciples, as well (Lk. 10:1-23). It has been argued that in Luke 9:1-6 Jesus commissions the Twelve in correspondence to the number of the tribes of Israel (*cf.* Lk. 22:30). The Seventy (*cf.* the seventy-two variant for Lk. 10:1; 10:1-12),[144] would then correspond to the traditional number of nations in the Table of Nations. Similar concerns are present in Luke 24:46-47 and Acts 1:8, where the disciples' mission involves going 'to all the nations' (εἰς πάντα τὰ ἔθνη). The same sequence of numbers is implied at the Pentecost, twelve apostles (Acts 1:26; 2:14); and seventy nations (*cf.* Acts 2:5).[145] Luke manifests here an interesting tendency towards gematria, with parallels only in Matthew.

Journey Parables: Meeting Half-Dead Travellers

Among Luke's specific *hodos* texts, one of the most celebrated is Jesus' parable of *the Good Samaritan* (Lk. 10:30-37).[146] This challenging story of Jesus is set by Luke[147] on the road *down* to Jericho, leading *away* from Jerusalem (ἄνθρωπός τις

---

143 Dunn, Christianity in the Making, ch. 8.3-8.6.
144 For Metzger '72' should be preferred as the *lectio difficilior* (Metzger, *Textual Commentary*, p. 150).
145 Scott, 'Horizon', pp. 483-544; *cf.* pp. 524-543; *idem, Paul and the Nations*, pp. 5-121.
146 W. O. E. Oesterley, *The Gospel Parables in the Light of their Jewish Background* (London: SPCK, 1936), pp. 166-168; B. B. Scott, *Hear Then the Parable: A Commentary on the Parables of Jesus* (Minneapolis, MN: Fortress, 1989), p. 194, cf. idem, *Re-Imagine the World: An Introduction to the Parables of Jesus* (Santa Rosa, CA: Polebridge, 2002), pp. 55-64; R. W. Funk, 'The Good Samaritan as Metaphor', in J. D. Crossan (ed.), *Semeia 2: The Good Samaritan* (Missoula, MT: Scholars, 1974), 74-81; etc.
147 J.P. Meier, 'The Historical Jesus and the Historical Samaritans: What Can Be Said?', *Biblica* 81 (2000) 202-32, is utterly in favor of its genuine character. Dunn shares this position, yet discerns later layers of interpretation, as well (Dunn, *Jesus Remembered*, p. 538).

κατέβαινεν άπό 'Ιερουσαλήμ εις 'Ιεριχώ και λησταις περιέπεσεν, Lk. 10:30; ιερεύς τις κατέβαινεν εν τη όδώ, v. 31; Σαμαρίτης δέ τις όδεύων ήλθεν, v. 33).

Its plot starts in a strikingly similar way to the common folk-tale of 'The Grateful Dead Man', usually cited as a parallel for Tobit's journey. According to this story, a traveller comes upon the corpse of a man killed by robbers and buries him; later on in his journey, he meets a stranger - the dead man's spirit who befriends him and helps him in his travels in return his earlier kindness. Often this help includes a happy-ending marriage of the traveller with a woman whom he delivered from a troublesome spirit.[148] In the Good Samaritan parable the popular parallel goes only half way through the story, and this would have been enough rhetorically, to startle Luke's audience (or Jesus' original listeners). The particular format of Luke's story shows that the Samaritan continues to take care of the attacked man and pays for any further expense, instead of being himself rewarded for his services.

As far as the plot is concerned, the story displays a series of dramatic 'return points'. A first reversal of action, of a negative nature, is provided by the robbers' attack. This violence takes place in a journeying setting, and fits well Aristotle's requirements of a suffering scene: an Israelite brother attacks an Israelite brother, leaving him nearly dead. Luke's description is dramatic, sensationalist: he 'fell into the hands of robbers, who stripped him, beat him, and went away, leaving him half dead [λησταις περιέπεσεν... εκδύσαντες... πληγάς επιθέντες... αφέντες ημιθανή]' (Lk. 10:3). The man's fortunes are thus completely reversed from happiness to disaster.

After the traveller's journeying is interrupted, the road turns into a setting of further trial and testing (v. 31, εν τη όδώ, is paralleled in v. 32, by κατά τον τόπον). This is the second reversal, of positive nature, when the Samaritan comes on the same road as a providential saviour and helps the half-dead victim. The dramatic tension reaches a high level for this

---

148 Wills, 'Jewish Novellas', pp. 231-232. Another story has been suggested, as well, as a model for Tobit's plot, namely 'The Monster In The Bridal Chamber' (S. Thompson, *The Folktale* (N.Y.: Dryden, 1946); see I. Nowell, 'Tobit', in R. E. Brown, J. A. Fitzmyer, R. E. Murphy, *The New Jerome Biblical Commentary* (London: Chapman, 1993), pp. 568-571).

change of fate does not come through expected channels (*cf.* the priest and the Levite, Lk. 10:31-32). The recognition of the benefactor's identity, a Samaritan, was in itself a reason for ethnic and religious tension. Luke's final emphasis highlights the man's restoration and the Samaritan's complete care for his fellow traveler. Luke's Jesus expects his audience to perceive this dramatic challenge and leads them to a clear conclusion (Lk. 10:36-37).

Journey Parables: the Prodigal Son's Adventures
In Jesus' parable of the Prodigal Son (Lk. 15:11-32), the reader encounters to a greater degree the elements of the Hellenistic novel. The departure to a distant foreign land has all the spicy details and the adventure characteristic to Greek novels: a long journey, the pride and courage of youth, the attraction of wealth and its short-lived existence, the perils of dissolute living, the drama of final restoration, etc. All hint to romance in a way that contradicts previous assessments of Luke, according to which this genre is entirely alien to Luke-Acts, and in general, to Jewish novellas (Lk. 15:13-14).[149]

The journey plot includes a turning point which takes place in a 'discovery' moment and is expressed through a language of decision ('raising up' and the 'journeying back', ἀναστὰς πορεύσομαι πρὸς τὸν πατέρα μου, Lk. 15:18). The moment of decision comes in spite of the distance and of the apparently irretrievable loss of status (a scene of suffering, of *pathos*). The young man rehearses mentaly his future apologetic dialogue with his father and the return includes the scene of an encounter 'on the way', a moment of recognition and greeting,

---

149 Wills draws attention that 'the two most noteworthy characteristics of the Greek novel, love and travel, are lacking in Jewish novellas' ('Jewish Novellas', p. 235). Motifs that raise the interest of a Jewish audience are 'not conjugal love, threatened by separation, but the extended family ties of Judaism, threatened by evil' (*op.cit.*, p. 235). S. P. and M. J. Schierling would emphasize that Luke-Acts, still, includes the love of God, yet this is not a particulary strong argument (Schierling, 'Influence', p. 86). The story of the Prodigal Son, however, shows that Luke was no stranger to the romantic features of the Hellenistic novels (a life of partying and love, bankruptcy, an adventure conveniently placed in a foreign, distant, unnamed land).

followed by celebration.¹⁵⁰ Characteristic of Luke, the *dénouement* includes a meal of fellowship, a feast of restoration.¹⁵¹ At the end, the happy father provides a summary (a report to his elder son), through which Jesus communicates to his audience the essence of the story.¹⁵²

Zacchaeus' Encounter: Journeying, Sojourning, and Salvation
Another illustration of Luke's interest in significant encounters during a journey is the account of Zacchaeus' conversion, although the specific *hodos* setting is missing (Lk. 19:1-10). However, the account starts with an unmistakable emphasis on journeying, καὶ εἰσελθὼν διήρχετο τὴν ʼΙεριχώ (Lk. 19:1), ὅτι ἐκείνης ἤμελλεν διέρχεσθαι (v. 4), ἦλθεν ἐπὶ τὸν τόπον (v. 5), εἰσῆλθεν καταλῦσαι (19:7), ἦλθεν γὰρ ὁ υἱὸς τοῦ ἀνθρώπου (v. 10).

Luke's integration of themes links journeying with the 'necessity' or 'must do' motif – the δεῖ motif (Lk. 19:5b, σήμερον γὰρ ἐν τῷ οἴκῳ σου δεῖ με μεῖναι), a theme related not only to Jesus' Passion (Lk. 9:22; 17:25; 24:7, 26) but also to other

---

150 In an interesting parallel scene, when Chaereas and Callirhoe return to Syracuse, Hermocrates, her father, hastens to the ship and embraces his daughter (Chariton, *Callirhoe*, 8.6.8). When Daphnis' true identity is found out, his brother Astylos runs to greet him and hugs him (Longus, *Daphnis and Chloe*, 4.23.1; *cf.* 2.30.1; 4.36.3). This Lukan detail conforms 'to a social convention of how people greeted those they had long supposed had died' (Luke 15:22-25; *cf. Daphnis and Chloe*, 2.30-37; 4.26; Luke 15:25-32, *Daphnis and Chloe*, 4.24.3-4; as discussed in Hock, 'Greek Novel', p. 140).
151 Navone notes that *'Home, homelessness* and *homecoming* are implied in biblical travel stories' (Navone, *Theology of Story*, p. 58). Christ' own travel story is 'a paradigm of homecoming' (p. 60). The meals or the baptisms at the end of so many Lukan stories have a similar meaning of restoration.
152 Luke, with literary skill phrases out the moralistic comment through the mouth of his characters, instead of repeating it himself (Goulder, *Luke*, vol. 1, p. 103). Although the *Oratio Recta* repetition is a common feature in Luke, one can find it in Mark and in Matthew, as well (Goodacre, *Goulder*, pp. 239-242).

missionary aspects in Luke-Acts, and to the motif of table fellowship (cf. Lk. 2:49; 4:43; 13:16; 19:5; Acts 3:21).[153]

Continuing the compositional emphases of the preceding story in the narrative (the blind man's healing), the motif of 'seeing' is also present here, with restoration connotations. Thus, Zacchaeus tries hard to *see* Jesus, καὶ ἐζήτει ἰδεῖν τὸν Ἰησοῦν (v. 3), ἵνα ἴδῃ αὐτόν (v. 4), although he is not blind but only 'impaired' due to his short height. With great artistic skill Luke uses the reciprocal construction, and Jesus *sees* Zacchaeus as well, ἀναβλέψας ὁ Ἰησοῦς (v. 5), and even more, the crowds *saw* their encounter and murmured against it, καὶ ἰδόντες πάντες διεγόγγυζον (v. 7). At the end of the story, Zacchaeus surprises everyone with his generous way of celebrating Christ, '*Look*, half of my wealth...!' ἰδοὺ τὰ ἡμίσιά μου τῶν ὑπαρχόντων (v. 8), a happy ending which fully corresponds with the way Luke highlighted earlier the joy of Zacchaeus at the news that Jesus will enter his house (χαίρων, v. 6, cf. the Ethiopian's story, Acts 8:39).

Luke uses a thematic 'seeking' *inclusio* here, καὶ ἐζήτει ἰδεῖν (v. 3), and ζητῆσαι καὶ σῶσαι (v. 10), with clear soteriological implications, and between these two remarks the story displays a dramatic reversal. Zacchaeus sought to see Jesus (v. 3), but finally the reader realises that Jesus is the one who sees people and seeks to save the lost (v. 10).

One has to note another characteristic of Luke's style, that Messiah removes social barriers to make salvation available to all (Luke 19:9),[154] and thus, Zacchaeus overcomes the disadvantage of his short stature and that of the large crowd standing between him and Jesus (v. 3), as well as that of his notoriety. The final restoration is sealed by a fellowship meal (Lk. 19:5-7). Furthermore, Jesus explains his actions to the revolted crowd in short a Lukan summary (report).

These emphases are enhanced by the particular position of this conversion story in Luke's narrative: 'the strategic

---

153 R. C. Tannehill, 'The Story of Zacchaeus as Rhetoric: Luke 19:1-10', in V. K. Robbinson (ed.), *Semeia 64: The Rhetoric of Pronouncement* (Missoula, MT: Scholars, 1994), 201-211, esp. pp. 204-205.

154 Matson, *Household*, p. 73. For some instead of a salvation story (conversion) this is more a vindication story of Zacchaeus as a son of Abraham (J. A. Fitzmyer, A. C. Mitchel and R. C. White). *Cf.* Swartley, *Scripture Traditions*, pp. 91-93.

placement of this story at the conclusion of the journey to Jerusalem suggests that it is in some way definitive for Jesus' ministry on the pages of Luke'.[155]

The Emmaus Story: A Journey Beyond Jerusalem

Jesus' appearance to the two disciples on the Emmaus road is certainly one of Luke's most significant additions to the synoptic series of journey notes and accounts (Lk. 24:13-35). Reflecting Luke's general tendencies, the importance of the Emmaus journey derives from its *transitional* features, and from its *redactional* emphasis on *journeying* and *theological challenge*. As part of the *hodos* triad discussed in the present work, it clearly displays the features of Luke's post-Easter encounter paradigm and illustrates his compositional principles.

MIXED MOTIFS AND LITERARY CONTINUITY

The Emmaus story has been regarded as a continuation of Luke's more general journey motif.[156] Its characteristics have led certain scholars to see it as a transitional story, connecting the previous journey of Jesus to Jerusalem (Lk. 9-19) with the post-Easter period. It certainly shares a similar 'travel and discussion' format (*journey* and *didache*),[157] and the teaching contributes to the understanding of the passion mystery and of Jesus' messianic identity.[158] For Guillaume, this feature of 'proclamation "on the road"' (l'instruction kérygmatique "in via"') is the essential point of the whole account.[159]

A highly polished narrative, the Emmaus account reflects Luke's integration of different motifs and themes, and ensures a strong retrospective relation, through links with motifs such

---

155 Matson, *Household*, p. 70.
156 Green, *Theology*, pp. 102-103; Bock, *Luke 9:51-24:53*, p. 1909.
157 Dillon, *Eye-Witnesses*, pp. 90, 113, 134. Similar observations are made in Just, *Feast*, p. 58; Green, *Theology*, p. 102.
158 Dillon, *Eye-Witnesses*, p. 113, n. 127; p. 149; *cf.* Conzelmann, *Luke*, pp. 57-60; 197-198. The misunderstanding of Jesus' identity and the journey motif 'serve to explain each other' (Dillon, *op.cit.*, p. 198, n. 1; see also B. Reicke, 'Instruction and Discussion in the Travel Narrative', in K. Aland (ed.), *Studia Evangelica* (Berlin: Akademie, 1959), vol. 1, 206-216).
159 Guillaume, *Luc interprète*, p. 92.

as the restoration motif, the table fellowship motif, the kingdom of God motif, the prayer motif, the sight motif, etc.[160] Some of the motifs are looking forwards, announcing major themes in Acts: the proof from scripture motif, the report to the apostles, the encounter motif, etc. In particular, the table fellowship scene has strong eucharistic connotations, and as such it challenges the normal Passover paradigm, announcing the time of the Church

> For if the Emmaus meal is proleptic of the meal fellowship of the early Christian communities, then the location of the Emmaus meal is also proleptic of the primary geographical location where meal fellowship will be celebrated in the Church, i.e. outside Jerusalem.[161]

At the same time, one can note that the two disciples do not belong to the select circle of the Eleven, and this is a foretaste of the shared and team-styled ministry of the Christians in Acts.[162]

THE REDACTIONAL CHARACTER OF THE STORY

Both Schubert and Dillon concluded that Luke took the initial story of the 'Emmaus *appearance*'[163] and fashioned it into an 'Emmaus *journey*'.[164] They suggest that the original story was 'an older and simpler Emmaus tradition', thought to have

---

160 Just, *Feast*, p. 220.
161 Just, *Feast*, p. 51, italics mine. If for Israel the Passover was the most significant meal, here, in Emmaus, from a resurrection perspective, Luke challenges the established geographical and religious codes of Judaism.
162 Just, *Feast*, pp. 53-54. The two appear to belong to the group of οἱ λοιποί, not from the Eleven (Lk. 24:9). The apostles persevere in faith, while the two disciples need to be rebuked and brought back (Brown, *Apostasy*, p. 75; *cf.* Creed, *Luke*, p. 294). J. D. M. Derrett, however ('The walk to Emmaus (Lk 24,13-35): the lost dimension', *EstB* 54/2 (1996), 183-193, esp. pp. 185-186, n. 7), considers that they are 'from them' ἐξ αὐτῶν (Lk. 24:13), from the apostles (Lk. 24:10-11).
163 Schubert characterises it as 'an appearance-story which was dominated wholly and exclusively by the motif of a recognition scene which is so familiar from ancient mythology, legend and literature' (P. Schubert, 'The Structure and Significance of Luke 24', in W. Eltester (ed.), *Neutestamentliche Studien für Rudolf Bultmann* (Berlin: Töpelmann, 1957), 165-186, p. 174).
164 Dillon, *Eye-Witnesses*, p. 140; also pp. 133-134.

included verses 13, 15b, 16, 28-31,[165] and to have ended with v. 31 'a very effective and truly dramatic climax of the recognition appearance'.[166] This hypothesis seems well supported by the distinct Lukan character of the vv. 32-35 (*cf.* the use of ἐξηγέομαι, Lk 24:35, *cf.* Acts 10:8; 15:12, 14; 21:19; Jn. 1:18; ἐν τῇ κλάσει τοῦ ἄρτου, Lk. 24:35, Acts 2:42; uniquely Lukan; διήνοιγεν, v. 32; *cf.* Lk. 2:23; 24:45; Acts 16:14; 17:3).[167] The unexpected yet impressive inversion between the *hodos* reports in 24:33-35 (the announcement of the apostles comes first, ὄντως ἠγέρθη ὁ κύριος καὶ ὤφθη Σίμωνι, v. 34, and then the report of Cleopas, ἐξηγοῦντο, in v. 35), provides supplementary evidence that Luke carefully composes the end of this story, using the reports and their *hodos* formulation (vv. 32, 35) in a 'subtle, yet highly deliberate' way.[168] In addition, it has been argued that the story had a 'natural ending' at v. 32, since on their return the two disciples could not have entered the gates of Jerusalem for they 'were closed at sunset'[169] (however, if Emmaus was situated at 160 stadia away from Jerusalem, they had enough time to travel and be back at dawn). Emmaus itself is not presented as the hometown of Cleopas or of his companion and the place they stopped could well have been but a station for a night before going to their homes.[170]

---

165 Schubert, 'Structure', p. 174.
166 Schubert, 'Structure', pp. 172, 170.
167 Marshall, *Gospel*, p. 900; Fitzmyer, *Luke X-XXIV*, pp. 1555-1556. L. M. Maloney emphasizes that Lk. 24:32-35 introduces a major narrative pattern, the report to the apostles ('*All that God had Done with Them*': *The Narrative of the Works of God in the Early Christian Community as Described in the Acts of the Apostles* (N.Y.: Lang, 1991), pp. 37-38).
168 Fitzmyer, *Luke X-XXIV*, p. 1558. 'The Walk to Emmaus is a highly-finished literary composition' and the marks of Luke's vocabulary and interests are present in all the sections of the story (Dodd, 'Appearances', p. 13). The *hodos* report is peculiarly Lukan and paradigmatic for his encounters on the way, so that it is probable that he intervened here, modifying the initial emphases of the traditional account.
169 Ehrhardt, 'Disciples', p. 182. Lk. 24:13 has two variant readings ἑξήκοντα and ἑκατὸν ἑξήκοντα, almost equally attested.
170 Goulder, *Luke*, vol. 2, p. 781. He favours Qalonieh as Luke's Emmaus (four miles from Jerusalem) for as an inn it might have been a familiar gathering point (p. 784). This makes the return to Jerusalem even more

JOURNEYING AND LEXIS

The journey motif pervades the whole of the Emmaus story and is particularly well reflected at the level of Luke's *lexis* (diction and vocabulary, repetition, alliteration). Thus, the two disciples journey to Emmaus (ἦσαν πορευόμενοι, Lk. 24:13).[171] Jesus joins them in their journey (ἐγγίσας συνεπορεύετο αὐτοῖς, Lk. 24:15), and asks about their debate on the road (περιπατοῦντες, Lk. 24:17). Jesus' appearance is serene, within the limits of normality (unexpectedly so, given the nature of the subject), reminding one of the appearance of Romulus to Ascanius, with the exception that Jesus is not recognised.[172]

Once arrived in Emmaus, Jesus impersonates the innocent traveller, as if he wanted to continue his journey, αὐτὸς προσεποιήσατο πορρώτερον πορεύεσθαι (Lk. 24:28; *cf.* the use of προσεποιήσατο, the alliteration in ο and ω, with rhetorical resonance).[173] The memory of the events that had just

---

dramatic: the two disciples were braced for a long journey, yet they changed their mind. Derrett favours a similar hypothesis: 'for all three it was a πατάπαυσις, lodging, in a metaphorical as well as a literal sense, since they have closed (*cf.* Lk. 6:40) so fruitful a journey with its unique intellectual experience (*cf.* Prov. 29:17; Lk. 6:40)'. Rest and inheritance are associated in Deut. 12:9; Is. 63:14, 25:19; 1 Sam. 63:14, *cf.* Derrett, 'Walk', p. 190, n. 35. See, also, the idea of a messianic banquet in Robinson, 'Place,' pp. 485-486.

171 Πορεύομαι is often used by Luke in his introductions. It appears, for example, with his specific introductory formula καὶ ἐγένετο ἐν τῷ plus a finite verb, in Lk. 7:11, Lk. 10:38, and Lk. 17:11 (Cadbury, *Style*, pp. 59, 106; *cf.* Fitzmyer, *Luke I-IX*, pp. 119-120; *Luke X-XXIV*, p. 1563; Dillon, *Eye-Witnesses*, p. 89). The use of καὶ ἐγένετο and καὶ ἰδοὺ could reflect in chapter twenty-four Luke's desire to imitate 'the character of a narrative that is about heavenly beings (angels) in 24:4 and the Messiah in 24:15' (Just, *Feast*, p. 59).

172 Dion. Hal., *Roman Antiquities*, 63.4. Appearances could also be frightful, *cf.* *The Apparition*, a fragment where the main character could see an appearance like a 'god advancing with a shadowy form and having a mournful and frightening visage', ἑώρα θεόν τινα σκοτισίῳ προϊόντα εἴδει καὶ πενθικὴν καὶ φρικώδη ἔχοντα ὄψιν (*Apparition*, 8-12, in S. A. Stephens and J. J. Winkler (eds.), *Ancient Greek Novels: The Fragments. Introduction, Text, Translation, and Commentary* (Princeton, NJ: Princeton UP, 1995), 409-415, esp. pp. 412-413).

173 The high presence of Lukanisms emphasizes the redactional, compositional intervention of the author: καὶ ἰδοὺ - 24:13; temporal notices, like ἐν αὐτῇ τῇ ἡμέρᾳ - 24:13; αὐτῇ τῇ ὥρᾳ - 24:33; ἦσαν

happened warms their hearts so intensely, οὐχὶ ἡ καρδία ἡμῶν καιομένη ἦν [ἐν ἡμῖν], that the two disciples mention the 'on the road' theme twice, first, in an indirect summary, ὡς ἐλάλει ἡμῖν ἐν τῇ ὁδῷ, ὡς διήνοιγεν ἡμῖν τὰς γραφάς (in Lk. 24:32); and secondly, in the final report to the Eleven, ἐξηγοῦντο τὰ ἐν τῇ ὁδῷ κτλ. (Lk. 24:35).[174]

A comparison with the OT texts emphasizes as well the journey character of the story. In its first part, the Emmaus account has been described as a 'journey encounter',[175] while

---

πορευόμενοι - 24:13, periphrastic part. with εἰμί - καιομένη ἦν - 24:32; ᾗ ὄνομα ᾽Εμμαοῦς - Septuagintalism (cf. similar expressions in Lk. 1-2, τὸ ὄνομα αὐτῆς ᾽Ελισάβετ; καλέσεις τὸ ὄνομα αὐτοῦ ᾽Ιωάννην; ᾗ ὄνομα Ναζαρεθ; τὸ ὄνομα αὐτοῦ ᾽Ιησοῦν, etc.); the use of καὶ αὐτοί, αὐτός - unstressed (Lk 24:14, 25, 28, 31, 35); πρὸς ἀλλήλους - πρὸς + acc. (Lk. 24:14, 17b, 18, 25, 32); καὶ ἐγένετο ἐν τῷ + dat. (Lk. 24:15, 30); ἀποκριθεὶς... εἶπεν (Lk. 24:18); ὀνόματι (LK. 24:18); ἐν αὐτῇ ἐν ταῖς ἡμέραις ταύταις (Lk. 24:18); τὰ περὶ (Lk. 24:19); ἀνὴρ προφήτης (Lk. 24:19; also, Lk. 5:8; 11:32; Acts 1:11, 16; 2:14, 22, 29, 37; 3:12, 14; 5:35, etc.); δυνατὸς ἐν - (Lk. 24:19; Acts 7:22; 18:24); the hyperbolic use of πᾶς: παντὸς τοῦ λαοῦ (Lk. 24:19); σὺν πᾶσιν τούτοις τρίτην ταύτην ἡμέραν (Lk. 24:21); ἐπὶ πᾶσιν οἷς ἐλάλησαν οἱ προφῆται (Lk. 24:25); οἱ ἄρχοντες (Lk. 24:20); τινες (Lk. 24:22); ἀρξάμενος (Lk. 24:27, 33); absolute use of ὑποστρεφεῖν - ὑπέστρεψαν (Lk. 24:33); τοὺς ἕνδεκα (Lk. 24:33; 24:9); ἐν τῇ κλάσει τοῦ ἄρτου (Lk. 24:35; uniquely Lukan), etc. For more comprehensive lists of Lukanisms, see Guillaume, *Luc interprète*, pp. 69-76; Fitzmyer, *Luke X-XXIV*, pp. 1555-1556.

174 Tannehill (*The Narrative Unity of Luke-Acts: A Literary Interpretation* (Philadelphia, PA: Fortress), 1986), vol. 1, p. 279) notes that this summary 'gives the conversation on the road equal importance with the recognition at the meal'. For Guillaume 'l'essentiel du récit n'est d'aillleurs pas dans la "reconnaissance" de Jésus, mais dans l'instruction kérygmatique en même temps que dans la fraction du pain, symbole d'une signification plus profonde' (*Luc interprète*, p. 95).

175 E. Reinmuth, *Pseudo-Philo und Lukas* (Tübingen: Mohr, 1994), pp. 177-181. Together with Alsup, Zwiep, Seidensticker, he favours the presence of OT connections in the Emmaus story, in contrast with the opinion that the journey encounter reflects a Greco-Roman paradigm (Gunkel, Windisch, Ehrhardt, Betz, Bultmann, Grundmann, Guillaume, etc.). Reinmuth highlights, as well, the similarity between Lk. 24:13-26 and LAB 35-36 (Pseudo-Philo's *Liber Antiquitatum Biblicarum*). The two accounts share a common literary pattern: 'Reisesituation, fremden Reisebegleiter (*angelus Domini*), Dialog,... Belehrung,... Akt der sakramentalen Gemeinschaft, etc.' (Reinmuth, *Pseudo-Philo*, p. 179). This pattern witnesses how appealing was this

the second part is dominated by the motif of a 'heavenly rapture' or miraculous disappearance,[176] a motif that reminds of the Elisha-Elijah paradigm.[177]

RECOGNITION AND HELLENISTIC PARALLELS

The meaning of the journey is particularly highlighted in the recognition scene at the breaking of the bread. Reflecting Luke's Christological agenda, the scene is exquisitely narrated as a 'divine' recognition, since the disciples' eyes are opened to know him, αὐτῶν δὲ διηνοίχθησαν οἱ ὀφθαλμοὶ καὶ ἐπέγνωσαν αὐτόν (Lk. 24:31).[178]

The combination between recognition and reversal of journey makes the meal scene a memorable one (for Aristotle the finest recognition is 'that which occurs simultaneously

---

story model for Hellenistic redactors and religious narrators during the intertestamental period.

176 The disappearance event has been interpreted by Ehrhardt as an indication of Hellenistic Christology (Ehrhardt, 'Disciples', p. 185; also, n. 2; cf. Euripides, Orestes, 1496; Helen, 606; Vergil, Aeneid, 9.656-658, etc.). For him, as well, the αὐτὸς εἶπεν in Lk. 24:25 represents an allusion to the Pythagorean αὐτὸς ἔφα, emphasizing Jesus' divine authority.

177 Reinmuth, Pseudo-Philo, pp. 178-179. On the Elijah-Elisha traditions in Luke, see T. L. Brodie, 'Towards unravelling Luke's use of the Old Testament: Luke 7:11-17 as an imitation of 1 Kings 17:17-24', NTS 32 (1986), 247-267, pp. 261-262; idem, 'The Departure for Jerusalem (Luke 9:51-56) as rhetorical imitation of Elijah's departure for the Jordan (2 Kgs. 1:1-2:6)', Bib 70 (1989), 96-109; C. A. Evans, 'The Function of the Elijah / Elisha Narratives in Luke's Ethic of Election', in C. A. Evans and J. A. Sanders (eds.), Luke and Scripture: The Function of Sacred Tradition in Luke-Acts (Minneapolis, MN: Fortress, 1993), 70-83; R. J. Miller, 'Elijah, John, and Jesus in the Gospel of Luke', NTS 34 (1988), 611-622. M. Prior, as well, argues for the presence of Elisha-Elijah paradigms in the Ascension account (Jesus the Liberator: Nazareth Liberation Theology (Luke 4:16-30) (Sheffield: Sheffield Academical, 1995), chapter six).

178 The divine blinding of the eyes (ἐκρατοῦντο, v. 16; an instance of passivum divinum) followed by a final recognition (διηνοίχθησαν, v. 31) is a sequence characteristic to Luke. The sight motif is present as well in Lk. 19:42, νῦν δὲ ἐκρύβη ἀπὸ ὀφθαλμῶν σου (Guillaume, Luc interprète, p. 177), in Lk. 2:30, ὅτι εἶδον οἱ ὀφθαλμοί μου τὸ σωτήριόν σου.

with reversal').[179] Through recognition, the two disciples are restored to fellowship with the other apostles (Lk. 24:34-35; 36-50).

An almost perfect case of cultural relevance, the similarity of the Emmaus recognition scene to other such scenes in the Greek novels, can be illustrated by two specific examples. A first parallel is the recognition scene between Chaereas and Callirhoe (a story written between 25 BC - AD 50, contemporary to Luke). Their story is the story of two spouses separated by terrible adventures, who come together at the end of a long and periplous journey (during a siege, Chaereas captures the town of Aradus, and finds his wife amid the prisoners). The encounter scene describes how, getting near her, Chaereas felt his heart strangely stirred and was seized with excitement (ἐταράχθη τὴν ψυχὴν καὶ μετέωρος ἐγένετο) although he did not know she was his former wife (cf. the disciples' 'burning hearts', in their 'premonition' on the Emmaus road).[180] Proper recognition takes place, later, when Chaereas starts *speaking*: 'While he was still speaking, Callirhoe recognised his voice and uncovered her face [ἔτι λέγοντος ἡ Καλλιρόη γνωρίσασα τὴν φωνὴν ἀπεκαλύψατο]'.[181]

Another captivating novel parallel is the recognition or, rather, mis-identification by voice and appearance, found in Iamblichus, *Babyloniaka*,[182] a later story than Luke-Acts, yet relevant through its play on the theme of death and return to life. Here, an Aphrodite priestess believes she saw her dead son Tigris alive, risen from the dead, 'recognising' him by the way he speaks and looks (ἤδη γάρ σε γινώσκω, καὶ ὧν εἶπας ἀκούσασα καὶ ὄψιν ἰδοῦσα), while she was actually beholding another young man, Rhodanes.[183] The real recognition scene is delayed, here, however, since Rhodanes and Sinonis, his young female companion, continued for a time to play the roles of

---

179 Aristotle, *Poetics*, 1452a.25-30; 1455a.15.
180 Chariton, *Callirhoe*, 8.1.7.
181 Chariton, *Callirhoe*, 8.1.8.
182 A story written most probably in sec. 2, AD; cf. Iamblichus, *A Babylonian Story* (or *Babyloniaka*), trans. G. N. Sandy, in Reardon (ed.), *Collected*, pp. 783-797.
183 Iamblichus, *Babyloniaka*, 75b.41, in Stephens and Winkler, *Fragments*, 179-241, esp. pp. 210-211; Rhodanes and Sinonis are mistaken for Tigris brought back as a hero by Aphrodite.

Tigris and Aphrodite, taking advantage of the *naiveté* of the islanders.[184] By contrast, Cleopas and his companion do not recognise Jesus (ἐπέγνωσαν) by his voice or by his appearance.[185] The prolonged dialogue on the road enhances the narrative suspense. Also, just before the actual recognition at the meal (Lk. 24:30), Luke indulges a little longer in the theatrical features of his story: after Jesus is mistaken for a stranger, παροικεῖς, who wants to join the journey (Lk. 24:18), now, Jesus pretends he wants to journey further (a mimesis or imitation of journeying? *cf.* Lk. 24:28).[186] The plot displays a remarkable internal symmetry: Jesus had joined the two disciples as a stranger, and now wants to journey further, still as a stranger. The comparison with Romulus' appearance is valid for this part of the Emmaus account, as well, yet one has to remark that the mystery surrounding Jesus is certainly deeper: his identity remains still hidden at this point of the story.

At the end of this analysis of Luke's journey stories in the Synoptic context, one can identify a few of his artistic rules for historic representation. For example, Luke has a tendency towards presenting the Way in a positive manner, with positive connotations. His editing of Mark's *hodos* scheme integrates Mark's geographical and theological themes with his own Lukan ones (*cf.* prayer and revelation in secluded places). Luke personalises and rationalises many of Mark's

---

184 Stephens and Winkler, *Fragments*, p. 194.
185 Derrett notes that the OT Yahweh hides his face, in his revelations, and rather makes his voice heard (Exod. 33:14, 23; Num. 12:8 and Tgg. Exod. 33:11; Mal. 3:16-17; *cf.* 'Walk', p. 188). Similarly, C. F. Evans, *Resurrection and the New Testament* (London: SCM, 1970), p. 66. As regards ὤφθη, often met in LXX, Luke's 'sight' theme seems to reflect Hellenistic influence and an anti-Docetic approach (Talbert, *Literary Patterns*, p. 114).
186 A similarly playful indecision is intentionally emphasized by Luke in his famous series of reversals that can be found in the plot line of the Malta episode. The barbarians think successively that Paul is a lawless person (φονεύς): bitten by a viper it seems that the goddess of 'righteousness' does not want him alive (ἡ δίκη ζῆν οὐκ εἴασεν; Acts 28:4); soon, they change their mind for he survives: therefore, Paul must be a god (αὐτὸν εἶναι θεόν, Acts 28:6). Discovery by reasoning is again present here, creating a playful suspense.

hodos accounts, favouring an alternance of dynamic *hodos* events with *static, solemn* scenes, where *high status* characters stop and question Jesus on essential issues pertaining to salvation. The *transition* potential of Luke's *hodos* stories is obvious , as in the case of blind Bartimaeus' healing which serves as introduction to the restoration of Zacchaeus, and, as well, is evident in the Emmaus story, looking at the various motifs woven in the account.

Specifically, this survey of the synoptic *hodos* texts of the NT has highlighted that within the limits of his Central Section and even beyond it, Luke includes journey stories and paradigms of his own such as the parable of the Good Samaritan, of the Prodigal Son, the account of Zacchaeus' restoration, and the Emmaus encounter. It cannot be overlooked that these stories reflect well Aristotle's requirements for the well-written plot (significant encounters, recognition scenes, turning points and reversals of destiny, suffering scenes or suffering narrative backgrounds, restorational endings - meals, feasts, dialogues, care and assistance, restitution, significant summaries or reports).

Such evidence for a complex Lukan paradigm of journeying constitutes the foundation of this study's further research into the literary anatomy and narrative function of Luke's post-Easter 'on the road' encounters that constitutes the subject of the fourth chapter.

CHAPTER 4

The Post-Easter Paradigm

The evidence so far confirms that Luke's 'on the road' encounters share more than a few formal correspondences. They are part of a larger Lukan collection of events set 'on the road' or during a journey, all displaying a similar type of plot line, in close correspondence with Aristotle's rules for the well-told story and reflecting a specific form of Luke's journey paradigm. Their literary and theological significance reflects the transitional characteristics of their narrative context, that is, of Luke 24 – Acts 1 and, respectively, Acts 8-9, and their own literary 'anatomy'.

Literary Unity and Transition in Luke 24 - Acts 1

In the background of this journeying paradigm is Luke's fondness for narrative repetition and internal parallelism, a subject that has been researched in-depth by NT scholarship.[1] The study of narrative parallelism in Luke-Acts has its roots in the Tübingen School, in the works of F. C. Baur, M. Schneckenburger and E. Zeller (tendency criticism).[2] Later, influential contributions came from H. J. Cadbury, R. Morgenthaler (literary criticism), C. H. Talbert, H. Flender, G. Muhlack, W. Radl, G. Trompf (redaction criticism), and M. D. Goulder (typological criticism).[3] Talbert's discussion of the

---

1 *Cf.* S. M. Praeder, 'Jesus-Paul, Peter-Paul, and Jesus-Peter Parallelisms in Luke-Acts: A History of Reader Response', *SBL Sem.Pap.*, 1984, 23-49, p. 38.
2 F. C. Baur, *Paul the Apostle of Jesus Christ: His Life and Work, His Epistles and His Doctrine* (London: Williams, 1875); M. Schneckenburger, *Über den Zweck der Apostelgeschichte* (Bern: Fischer, 1841); E. Zeller, *The Acts of the Apostles*, 2 vols. (London: Williams, 1875-1876).
3 Apart from the classical studies of Cadbury (*Style; Making*), Morgenthaler (*Geschichtsschreibung*, vols. 1-2), or Talbert (*Patterns*) relevant discussions can be found in Flender, *Luke*, chapter one; G. Muhlack, *Die Parallelen im Lukasevangelium und in der*

literary *architecture* of Luke-Acts has been particularly relevant.[4] He emphasized that Luke and Acts are built on corresponding patterns which reflect the classical Greco-Roman symmetry in composition.[5] The cultural continuity between Luke-Acts and its Hellenistic environment became, thus, even more apparent.[6]

Subsequently, literary repetition in Luke-Acts has been analysed extensively from various angles as a mark of style or literary fashion, yet rather at a macro-narrative level, and

Apostelgeschichte (Frankfurt: Lang, 1979); W. Radl, *Paulus und Jesus im lukanischen Doppelwerk: Untersuchungen zu Parallelmotiven im Lukasevangelium und in der Apostelgeschichte* (Bern: Lang, 1975); G. W. Trompf, *The Idea of Historical Recurrence in Western Thought: From Antiquity to the Reformation* (Berkeley, CA: University of California, 1979); Praeder, 'Parallelisms', pp. 23-39. See also, J. B. Green, 'Internal repetition in Luke-Acts: contemporary narratology and Lucan historiography', in B. Witherington, III (ed.), *History, Literature and Society in the Book of Acts* (Cambridge: Cambridge UP, 1996), 283-299.

4   For Talbert narrative criticism is complementary to redaction criticism, since the latter has 'no concern for formal patterns as such' except if the literary arrangement is found to be 'theologically motivated' (Talbert, *Patterns*, p. 8, *cf.* p. 5). See, e.g., Haenchen's too brief mention of Luke's *technique of repetition* (*Acts*, p. 357).

5   Talbert mentions symmetrical structures in Homer's *Iliad* and *Odyssey*, the writings of Thucydides, the *Odes* of Horace, particularly Vergil's *Aeneid* and Diogenes Laertius' *Lives* (Talbert, *Patterns*, pp. 67-82, 125-136; *cf.* C. Whitman, *Homer and the Heroic Tradition* (Cambridge: Cambridge UP, 1953); G. E. Duckworth, *Structural Patterns and Proportions in Vergil's Aeneid* (Ann Arbor, MI: University of Michigan, 1962); H. R. Rawlings, III, *The structure of Thucydides' History* (Princeton, NJ: Princeton UP, 1981), pp. 5-6). This issue is also addressed, in part, by W. J. McCoy, 'In the shadow of Thucydides', in Witherington III (ed.), *History, Literature*, 3-32. On the rhetorical balance of Luke-Acts see Talbert, *Patterns*, pp. 22, 26, 29, 48; *cf.* also, C. Clark, 'Parallel Lives: The Relation of Paul to the Apostles in the Lucan Perspective', London Bible College, Brunel University (1996), PhD thesis.

6   Talbert, *Patterns*, pp. 7-8. Luke's correspondences are, in part, an 'appropriation of the antiquity's custom of recapitulating an earlier book at the beginning of the next' (*Patterns*, p. 64, n. 18; as examples, see Diodorus Siculus, *Bibliotheca Historica*, 1.42; 2.1; 3.1, etc.; Josephus, *Antiquities*, 8.1.1; 13.1.1; 14.1.1; 15.1.1, etc.; Polybius, *Histories*, 2.1; 4.1; 3.1; etc.).

frequently restricted to the patterns of Acts.[7] Luke's use of narrative repetition is evident in the notorious reiterations of Saul's commissioning (Acts 9, 22, 26), of Cornelius' conversion (Acts 10-12), and of the 'apostolic decree' (Acts 15:20-21; 15:28-29; 21:23-25). Luke's Gospel has its own examples, such as the commissioning of the Twelve and of the Seventy / Seventy-two; the literary correspondences in the Nativity stories, etc. Using the language of communication theories this reiteration has been described as literary redundancy,[8] or multiplication of narrative,[9] or as themes with variations, the latter coming closer to this study's views on Luke's hodos encounters. These themes are 'privileged *loci* for exploring Luke's method and meaning',[10] and essential for the main plot lines of Luke-

---

7   D. Marguerat, 'Saul's Conversion (Acts 9, 22, 26) and the Multiplication of Narrative in Acts', in C. M. Tuckett (ed.), *Luke's Literary Achievement: Collected Essays* (Sheffield: Sheffield Academical, 1995), 129-155, p. 130. Luke is restricted in his gospel by the authority of his synoptic predecessors, while in Acts he is an 'author at liberty' (C. K. Barrett, *Luke the Historian in Recent Study* (London: Epworth, 1961), p. 27; Dibelius, *Studies*, p. 2).

8   *Cf.* R. D. Witherup, 'Functional Redundancy in the Acts of the Apostles: a Case Study', *JSNT* 48 (1992), 67-86; and *idem*, 'Cornelius Over and Over Again: "Functional Redundancy" in the Acts of the Apostles', *JSNT* 49 (1993), 45-66; R. C. Tannehill, 'The Composition of Acts 3-5: Narrative Development and Echo Effect', *SBL Sem.Pap.* 1984, 217-240, esp. pp. 237-240. On the expansion of symbols, Tannehill refers to E. K. Brown, *Rhythm in the Novel* (Toronto: University of Toronto, 1950), *cf.* Tannehill, 'Composition', p. 229.

9   Marguerat, 'Conversion', pp. 129-155. This dialectic 'of similarity and dissimilarity' allows the reader to note '*both* continuity *and* displacement, change *and* identity' (Marguerat, p. 132). For the general theory of literary redundancy *cf.* Marguerat's bibliography (R. Alter, *The Art of Biblical Narrative* (London: Allen, 1981), pp. 88-113; M. Sternberg, *The Poetics of Biblical Narrative: Ideological Literature and the drama of Reading* (Bloomington, IN: Indiana UP, 1987); pp. 365-440; G. W. Savran, *Telling and Retelling: Quotation in Biblical Narrative* (Bloomington, IA: Indiana UP, 1988); and S. Bar-Efrat, *Narrative Art in the Bible* (Sheffield: Sheffield Academical, 1989), pp. 211-216, etc.).

10 D. Hamm, 'Paul's Blindness and its Healing: Clues to Symbolic Intent (Acts 9; 22 and 26)', *Bib* 71 (1990), 63-72, p. 63. See also, *idem*, 'Sight to the Blind: Vision as Metaphor in Luke', *Bib* 67 (1986), 457-77.

Acts.¹¹ As expanding symbols in the narrative they create an effect of literary dynamism and unity.¹²

The Narrative Context of Luke 24 - Acts 1

The two major sections of Luke-Acts, Jesus' journey to Jerusalem (Lk. 9:51-19:44), and the missionary journeys of the early church (Acts 19:21-28:31),¹³ are connected through the pivot of Jesus' Ascension¹⁴ which is a culmination of the resurrection appearances¹⁵ and a major illustration of Luke's

---

11   Marguerat, 'Conversion', p. 131. *Cf.* the parallells between Jesus and the Church, Lk. 1:1-8:56 and Acts 1:1-12:17; Jesus and Paul (Lk. 9:51-19:28; Acts 19:21-21:17); the trials of Jesus and of Paul (Lk. 23:4-47; Acts 23:9-27:43) (pp. 15-17), Transfiguration and Ascension, Lk. 9:1-34 and Acts 1:1-12 (Talbert, *op.cit.*, pp. 15-17; and p. 64, n. 19; J.G. Davies, *Ascended*, pp. 42, 187). See also Moessner, '"The Christ Must Suffer": New Light on the Jesus-Peter, Stephen, Paul Parallels in Luke-Acts', *NovT* 28/3 (1986), 220-256; idem, '"The Christ Must Suffer", The Church Must Suffer: Rethinking the Theology of the Cross in Luke-Acts', *SBL Sem.Pap.* 1990, 165-195; Cadbury, *Making*, p. 233; Flender, *Luke*, p. 20; Fitzmyer, *Luke X-XXIV*, p. 1559, etc.
12   Tannehill, 'Composition', pp. 240, 229. Prior, *Liberator*, pp. 53-56.
13   D. M. Stanley, 'Paul's Conversion in Acts: Why the Three Accounts?', *CBQ* 15 (1953), 315-338, esp. pp. 320-321. Instead of choosing Peter as a parallel character to Jesus, Luke focuses on Paul in Acts (Stanley, p. 322; *cf.* F. V. Filson, 'The Journey Motif in Luke-Acts', in W. W. Gasque and R. P. Martin (eds.), *Apostolic History and the Gospel: Biblical and Historical Essays Presented to F. F. Bruce on His 60th Birthday* (Grand Rapids, MI: Eerdmans, 1970), 68-77, esp. p. 70).
14   It has a *transition function*, for it *connects* and *transfers* the plot lines (Dillon, *Eye-Witnesses*, p. 267). By contrast, Parsons emphasizes that Jesus' Ascension separates Luke from Acts (*Departure*, pp. 24-25, 63, 198-199). *cf.* also E. Franklin, 'The Ascension and the Eschatology of Luke-Acts', *SJT* 23 (1970), 191-200; idem, *Christ the Lord* (London: SPCK, 1975); V. Larranaga, *L'Ascension de Notre-Seigneur dans le Nouveau Testament* (Rome: PBI, 1938); P.A. van Stempvoort, 'The Interpretation of the Ascension in Luke-Acts', *NTS* 5 (1958-59), 30-42; Lohfink, *Die Himmelfahrt Jesu* (München: Kösel, 1971); B. K. Donne, *Christ Ascended* (Exeter: Paternoster, 1983); J. Maile, 'The Ascension in Luke-Acts', *TynB* 37 (1986), 29-59, etc.
15   Resurrection is central in Luke-Acts (H. D. Buckwalter, *The Character and Purpose of Luke's Christology* (Cambridge: Cambridge UP, 1996), *cf.* p. 118, *cf.* p. 102).

emphasis on Jerusalem.[16] The Easter narratives have a pivotal role in Luke-Acts,[17] and the Ascension represents its narrative and theological 'hinges'.[18] In this context, *journeying further* with Good News as a message, has a transition role, as well, and in the process, it challenges the Jewish traditional emphasis on *Jerusalem's centrality*.[19]

JERUSALEM'S CENTRALITY AND ITS CHALLENGE

Jerusalem's centrality is transparent in Luke's gospel and provides an essential link with the past, with 'the "arché" of the Church',[20] reflecting the nationalistic pride of the first century Judaism(s). For Jews Jerusalem was *the* holy city, a major metropolis and fatherland

> I should speak now of the Holy City [τῆς ἱεροπόλεως] the things I ought to. This city, as I said, is my homeland, the capital not of the Judaean territory [μητρόπολις δὲ οὐ μιᾶς χωρας ᾽Ιουδαίας] only but of many others, for it has sent colonies, in time, to neighbouring countries, etc.[21]

Such statements were not without biblical support. For example, Isaiah 1:26 states in similar words God's promise to Jerusalem 'And I will restore your judges as at the first, and your counselors as at the beginning. Afterward you shall be called the city of righteousness, the faithful city [LXX: πόλις

---

16   Jesus does not return to Galilee after resurrection for the Way must start again 'from Jerusalem' (Lk. 24:47; Acts 1:8; *cf.* Navone, 'Three Aspects', p. 119; Robinson, 'Travel Narrative', pp. 23-24, 27; Walker, *Jesus and the Holy City*, p. 57).
17   Guillaume, *Luc interprète*, p. 7.
18   Franklin, 'Ascension', pp. 191-200; *idem, Christ the Lord*, pp. 29-41; Prior, *Liberator*, pp. 24, 53-56. The Ascension joins the *missio ad Judaeos* with the one *ad gentes* (Prior, *Liberator*, pp. 55-56). Lk. 1-2 and Acts 1-2 are seen as 'vehicles of the evangelist's theology, rather than statements of history' (Talbert, *Patterns*, p. 49).
19   Walker, *Jesus and the Holy City*, p. 58. Jerusalem is the 'central bearings on which the double work swivels' (Wilson, *Gentiles*, p. 95; *cf.* Walker, *op.cit.*, p. 58, n. 5).
20   Conzelmann, *Luke*, p. 133. Jerusalem is a 'Raumsymbol für die Kontinuität zwischen Jesu und der Kirche' (Lohfink, *Himmelfahrt*, p. 263).
21   King Agrippa I to Gaius, in Philo, *Embassy to Gaius*, 276-329, esp. 281.1-5: (my translation; *cf.* Scott, 'Horizon', pp. 489-450).

δικαιοσύνης, μητρόπολις πιστὴ Σιων]' (RSV).²² Similarly central was the Temple in Jerusalem and the oracular primacy of Scripture, whose restoration was regarded as symbolic of the Messiah's age.²³ The whole Mediterranean context was characterized by such a craving for national centres: the Samaritans assigned a similar centrality to Mt. Garizim, the Greek themselves had at Delphi, their own centre or 'omphalos of the earth'; the Romans had Rome.

Thus, Luke's reader would not be surprised to see in Luke 24 – Acts 1 so many references to Jerusalem and will understand the special significance of the city (Lk. 24:13, 24:18; 24:33; 24:47; 24:52; Acts 1:8; 1:12; 1:19). He might raise an eyebrow, though, at Luke's use of two spellings for Jerusalem, that is Ἱεροσόλυμα and Ἱερουσαλήμ.²⁴ It has been suggested that Ἱεροσόλυμα stands for a geographical, profane meaning, and Ἱερουσαλήμ, for a sacral, hebraising one;²⁵ or that Luke use *Ierousalēm* in Jewish contexts and *Hierosolyma* in non-Jewish contexts. A third explanation holds that *Ierousalēm* could indicate narrative material dealing with the apostles, while *Hierosolyma* highlights stories dealing with Paul and Hellenists. The grammatical hypothesis notes that

---

22 See also, Is. 2:2: 'the nations will stream to the highest mountain, the mountain of Zion'. The geographical boundaries after the flood were seen as unmovable, *cf.* MT Deut. 32:8 and *Jubilees* 8:12-21 (Shem received 'the middle of the earth', with Mount Zion 'in the midst of the navel of the earth'; see Scott, 'Horizon', pp. 507-509.)
23 Scott, 'Horizon', pp. 498-450; Hastings, *Prophet and Witness*, p. 176.
24 D. D. Sylva 'Ierousalēm and Hierosolyma in Luke-Acts', *ZNW* 74 (1983), 207-221; also, Morgenthaler, *Lukas und Quintilian*, p. 345-351, who compares Jerusalem with Troy and Rome. A comprehensive discussion of the two names of Jerusalem can be found in J. Rius-Camps, *El Camino de Pablo a la Mission de los Paganos: Commentario Liguistico y Exegetico a Hch.13-28* (Madrid: Cristianidad, 1984), pp. 19-22; I. de la Potterie, 'Les deux noms de Jérusalem dans l'Évangile de Luc', *RSR* 69 (1981), 57-70; and *idem*, 'Les deux noms de Jérusalem dans les Actes des Apôtres', *Bib* 63 (1982), 153-187; R. Schütz, 'Ἱερουσαλήμ und Ἱεροσόλυμα im Neuen Testament', *ZNW* 11 (1910), 169-87; G. M. Gomez, 'Jerusalén-Jerosólima en el vocabulario y la geografía de Lucas', *RCatT*, 7 (1982), 131-186, p. 174, etc.
25 W. Ramsay, 'Professor Harnack on Luke' (II), *Expositor* 3 (1907), 97-124, pp. 110-112; A. von Harnack, *The Acts of the Apostles* (London: Williams, 1909), pp. 76-82.

Hierosolyma is declinable thus used with prepositions, while in all other cases Luke uses the undeclinable form, *Ierousalēm*.²⁶ Lastly, *Hierosolyma* has been seen as an intratextual etymological key for *Ierousalēm*, an emphasis on the city seen as a 'holy Salem'.²⁷

In this last sense, Morgenthaler notes that 'Hierosolyma was a *hiera polis*', a holy city.²⁸ Luke's preference for the other form,' Ιερουσαλήμ, city of peace, would indicate, according to him, a retrospective idealisation of the past, similar to the way in which the old city of Troy was idealised as past history by Homer and Vergil ('holy Ilion', 'holy Troia', *cf.* ἐπεὶ Τροίης ἱερὸν πτολίεθρον ἔπερσεν, in *Odyssey*, 1.2). The ideal of a new Troy led Aeneas into his journey for the founding of Rome 'tendimus in Latium... illic fas regna resurgere Troiae' (*Aeneid*, 1.205). By way of comparison, Luke's use of *Ierousalēm* (Lk. 24:1, 33; Acts 8:27, 9:2, 21, 26, etc.) would emphasize the recent siege and the fall of Jerusalem (a subtle *vaticinium ex eventu*).²⁹

The challenge to Jerusalem's centrality is evident, however, in the Ascension account, which takes place actually on the Mt. of Olives, outside the capital (Lk. 24:50; Acts 1:12).³⁰

> The Mount of Olives, not Jerusalem, is the geographical 'hinge' of Luke-Acts. If (as argued above) Jesus' departure to the Mount of Olives was theologically significant for Luke, then the fact that Luke-Acts is 'centred' on an event just outside Jerusalem's walls may also be important.³¹

Luke 9:51 has already prepared the reader to the idea that the actual destination of Jesus' journeying is his ἀνάλημψις,

---

26 Sylva, 'Ierousalēm', pp. 208-210.
27 Sylva, 'Ierousalēm', pp. 210-211; 214, 219.
28 Morgenthaler, *Lukas und Quintilian*, p. 354.
29 Morgenthaler, *Lukas und Quintilian*, p. 346.
30 Mark's later ending does not mention the site (Mk. 16:19). Matthew places it on a mountain in Galilee (Mt. 28:16).
31 Walker, *Jesus and the Holy City*, p. 81, *contra* M. Hengel, 'The Geography of Palestine in Acts', in R. Bauckham (ed.), *The Book of Acts in Its Palestinian Setting* (Carlisle: Paternoster, 1995), 27-78, p. 46, and G. Lohfink, *Himmelfahrt*, p. 264.

the Ascension, not Jerusalem.³² The change of paradigm is enhanced through the movement *into* (εἰς) and *out* (ἀπό) from Jerusalem, in the Emmaus account, and through the famous Emmaus meal.³³

Narrative Unity and Transition in Luke 24

Indeed, the Emmaus encounter plays an important function, as well, at the heart of Luke's last chapter. Luke 24, as a whole, displays interesting transitional features in terms of literary style and of narrative devices (one can see, here, at work an interesting temporal contraction doubled by a spatial divergence).³⁴

For such reasons, the Emmaus story has often been described as 'a gem of the narrative art'.³⁵ It functions as a meeting point of several literary and theological motifs of Luke, such as journey, fulfilment of prophecy, recognition and hospitality.³⁶ At the same time, it serves as an introduction for the series of Jesus' appearances (to the two disciples, to Simon - v. 34, to the Eleven - vv. 36-49, at the Ascension), and for Luke's motif of proof-from-prophecy, and lays the foundation for the later qualifications for apostolic ministry.³⁷

In particular, in the context of the proof-from-prophecy motif in Luke 24,³⁸ the Emmaus story plays an controlling role.³⁹ Its

---

32 Jesus' Ascension is announced in Lk. 9:51 (τὰς ἡμέρας τῆς ἀναλήμψεως αὐτοῦ), in relation to his journeying to Jerusalem (πορεύεσθαι εἰς Ἰερουσαλήμ), see Talbert, *Patterns*, pp. 114-115; see p. 122, n. 20.
33 Dillon notes the special significance in Acts of the dialectic *to Jerusalem / from Jerusalem* (Dillon, *Eye-Witnesses*, p. 93).
34 For Ehrhardt it is 'unwise to regard the whole of Luke 24 as one unit' (Ehrhardt, 'Disciples', pp. 182, 193). The Emmaus account is for him 'a self-contained, and originally independent story' (*op.cit.*, p. 183).
35 Schubert, 'Structure', p. 168.
36 Robinson, 'Place', p. 481.
37 Schubert, 'Structure', pp. 169-170, 172-173. The Emmaus account provides 'an emotionally satisfying bridge between the shock of absence (the tomb) and the shock of full presence' (Johnson, *Luke*, pp. 398): θαυμάζων τὸ γεγονός, Lk. 24:12; ὡμίλουν πρὸς ἀλλήλους, 24:14; πτοηθέντες δὲ καὶ ἔμφοβοι, 24:37; etc.
38 Schubert, 'Structure', pp. 176-178; McBride, *Emmaus*, pp. 202-203. The *evangelium quadraginta dierum* became a major theme of the early Christian mysticism. In some of the Apocrypha the risen Lord continues to teach for longer periods (Ehrhardt, 'Disciples', p. 185).

internal chiasmus extends into a controlling circular structure for the whole of Luke 24,[40] organised around the fundamental core of the Easter proclamation, 'they say he lives!', οἱ λέγουσιν αὐτὸν ζῆν (Lk. 24:23b).[41]

TEMPORAL CONTRACTION AND NARRATIVE UNITY

According to Aristotle, as one can recollect, unity of *action* was more important for the tragic plot than unity of *character* and this implied a careful selection of events and an appropriate length of the show, or of the story.[42]

In this context, one cannot help noting that in Luke 24 the reader meets a 'carefully constructed *time-framework*', a unitary *temporal* scheme that is 'one of Luke's devices for bringing out the theological significance of the events recounted'.[43] Luke uses a series of time notes which

---

39 McBride, *Emmaus*, p. 205; Dillon, *Eye-Witnesses*, p. 133. The themes of recognition and Scripture connect the post-Easter events and determine their rhetorical dialectic (J. Plevnik, 'The Eyewitnesses of the Risen Jesus in Luke 24', *CBQ* 49 (1987) 90-103, p. 95). They link together the Emmaus story with the Eleven's encounter (Lk. 24:13-35; Lk. 24:36-53). The parallelism between the two accounts is discussed in Marshall, *Gospel*, p. 890, and Hickling, 'Emmaus', pp. 24, 28, who notes here a compositional *diptych* (Hickling, p. 21).

40 Nolland, *Luke 18:35-24:53*, p. 1199. He suggests an elaborate concentric structure of Lk. 24 built around the Emmaus story (p. 1207).

41 Nolland, *Luke 18:35-24:53*, pp. 1203, 1207; similarly, Guillaume, *Luc interprète*, p. 7, and Just, *Feast*, p. 56; Green, *Luke*, pp. 841-842. The centre of the chiasmus, the famous testimony 'he lives' (v. 23b; Green, *op.cit.*, pp. 842-843), is supported by the repeatet use of καὶ ἰδοὺ in Lk. 24:4; 13, 49. Stylistically, Metzger agrees with this reading (*Textual Commentary*, pp. 188-189). See also Bock, *Luke 9:51-24:53*, p. 1907; A. Plummer, *A Critical and Exegetical Commentary on the Gospel According to Saint Luke* (Edinburgh: T&T Clark, 1981 (1896)), p. 551. καὶ ἰδοὺ introduces, in general, Christological episodes, like in Lk. 9:30-32 (Ehrhardt, 'Disciples', pp. 182-183; Just, *Feast*, pp. 16-20. Davies, 'Central Section', pp. 164-169; Davies, 'Prefigurement', pp. 229-233).

42 *Cf.* Aristotle, *Poetics*, 1449b.9-20; 1451a.15-35; 1459a.15-20, and section 2.2.2 of the present study. Length limitations and structured reading were present in the early worship as well (*cf.* Lk. 5:29-39; 7:36-50; 11:37-54; 14:1-24). On reading aloud at various meetings in antiquity see Sterling, *Historiography*, p. 370; Botha, 'Community', pp. 150-151; Sherwin-White, *The letters of Pliny*, p. 115.

43 Dillon, *Eye-witnesses*, p. 14.

emphasizes the gradual coming of the resurrection *day*, one single and superlative day of glorious manifestation of Jesus' messiahship: the *day* of Preparation (Lk. 23:54), the first *day* after the sabbath, at dawn (Lk. 24:1); the *day* of resurrection (v. 24:7), on that same *day* - the Emmaus encounter (v. 23; *cf.* the evening, v. 29; the very *hour*, v. 33).

According to this scheme the whole of Luke 24 gives the impression of having happened on *one single day*,[44] an observation which prompted different interpretations. For some authors the 'one day' interval is a hint that a new creation takes place at the resurrection.[45] Thus, it signals a parallel between Luke 24 and Genesis 1, focusing on the eighth day - the first of the new creation and the day of the resurrection.[46] The time notes at Luke 24:1, 23, 29, 33 and 36, speak certainly of Luke's artistry in setting the temporal frame of his stories in a way that confers unity of composition to his accounts.[47]

For others, closing the gospel story on a pure chronological note, in Luke 24, could have thrown the composition off balance, emphasizing a time-table instead of an event that transcends history.[48]

This contraction of the temporal scheme into a shorter period is one of Luke's effective means for achieving narrative

---

44 Hickling, 'Emmaus', p. 29.
45 Ellis, *Luke*, p. 276.
46 Just, *Feast*, p. 41.
47 Hickling, 'Emmaus', p. 29, n. 1; also, Evans, *Luke*, p. 888. Just explains the temporal contraction and the lack of time-notes after Emmaus (only one occurrence of ἕως in Lk. 24:49), by the fact that time is redefined in Lk. 24, a new aeon has started and any reference to the old one is irrelevant (*Feast*, p. 50). Like Hellenistic writers, Luke uses suggestive, ambiguous, or abrupt endings (W. F. Brosend II, 'The means of absent ends', in B. Witherington III (ed.), *History, Literature*, 348-362, esp. p. 360). *Cf.* as well, Acts 28, and Mk.16, in D. Marguerat, 'The End of Acts (28:16-31) and the Rhetoric of Silence', in Porter and Olbricht (eds.), *Rhetoric*, 74-89; J. L. Magness, *Sense and Absence: Structure and Suspense in the Ending of Mark's Gospel* (Atlanta, GA: Scholars, 1986).
48 Leaving aside the mentioning of the forty days, in the present form the story has no temporal gap between the gospel and its epilogue (Parsons, *Departure*, pp. 194-195; Tannehill, *Narrative*, vol. 1, pp. 298-301).

unity.⁴⁹ Luke's style is not monochrome, however, for he would not avoid the idea of expanding the temporal scheme, either, when narrative or theological reasons make it necessary. In Acts 1:3, he highlights the fourty days between Jesus' resurrection and his Ascension, a period he did not mention in Luke 24.⁵⁰ Apart from providing further historical detail, this period has, as well, Christological implications, for example it emphasizes a Moses-Jesus parallel.⁵¹

Luke 24 remains, further, the space where Luke overlaps with apparent easiness different, yet concurring, temporal frameworks (Luke 24:13-35). There is a striking contrast between the narrated time (*extradiegetic*, characteristic of the main narrative plot line) and the two disciples' perception of time in the Emmaus story (*intradiegetic*, characteristic of their own situation).⁵² Cleopas and his companion live their own

---

49 A similar temporal contraction takes place in Saul's account between his journey to Damascus and his visit to Jerusalem (Acts 9:19b, 23, 26; Gal. 1:17-20). For another example, consider the healing of the blind man in Bethany, Lk. 8:22-26, which involves a 'studied rearrangement of the events constitutive of the account' (Green, *Luke*, p. 337).

50 For some authors, it might be possible that the Ascension account in Acts reflects Luke's later, better access to information (Kurz, *Reading Luke-Acts*, p. 21).

51 P. H. Menoud, 'Pendant quarante jours', in W. C. van Unnik (ed.), *Neotestamentica et Patristica* (Leiden: Brill, 1962), 148-156; *cf.* the discussion in Zwiep, *Ascension*, pp. 1-25.

52 For this terminology (*diegetic, intradiegetic*, etc.), see R. W. Funk, *The Poetics of Biblical Narrative* (Sonoma, CA: Polebridge, 1988), pp. 154-155. Modifying the terminology of S. Rimmon-Kennan (*Narrative Fiction: Contemporary Poetics* (London: Methuen, 1983)), Funk suggests three types of narrators: the *hyperdiegetic* (extradiegetic, for Rimmon-Kennan) - who narrates from without the story; the *intradiegetic*, who narrates events from within the story (he is a diegetic character in the narrative of the extradiegetic narrator); and the *hypodiegetic* - who recapitulates or tells a past story in the intradiegetic's narrative (*cf.* J. H. McDonald, 'Rhetorical Issue and Rhetorical Strategy in Luke 10:25-37 and Acts 10:1-11:18', in Porter and Olbricht (eds.), *Rhetoric*, 59-73). McDonald gives a good illustration of these narrators in Acts, in the case of Cornelius' vision (*op.cit.*, p. 68, n. 14). Thus, the author of Acts is a 'hyperdiegetic' narrator (Acts 10:1-8), Cornelius' recounting of the event to Peter is 'intradiegetic' (Acts 10:30-33), while his recounting of the event later, within Peter's own

time line, characterized by disappointment and counting the days back to the Friday of the Crucifixion: 'it is now the third day' τρίτην ταύτην ἡμέραν (Lk. 24:21).[53] Once arrived in Emmaus, they feel acutely that the day came to an end, πρὸς ἑσπέραν ἐστιν καὶ κέκλικεν ἤδη ἡ ἡμέρα (Lk. 24:29).[54] Meanwhile, the reader and the narrator knew all the time that this is the first day of prophetic fulfilment, *the* day of resurrection! These two contrasting frameworks intersect at their high point when the disciples recognise Jesus. The narrative and temporal progression focuses, finally, on the very hour of their return to Jerusalem, αὐτῇ τῇ ὥρᾳ (Lk. 24:33, a Lukanism).[55]

SPATIAL DIVERGENCE AND NARRATIVE TRANSITION

The transition role of the Emmaus journey can be seen, as well, as a result of Luke's use of two different spatial-frameworks centred on Jerusalem.[56] Journeying or returning to Jerusalem is juxtaposed to the theme of leaving the capital,[57] and both create an evident narrative tension in the story. The two disciples, indeed, are journeying, but there is a general feeling that they move in the wrong direction.[58]

The significance of the distance between Jerusalem and Emmaus has been much debated (30, 63, 160 stadia).[59] For

---

account in Jerusalem (Acts 11:13-14) is 'hypodiegetic', *i.e.* a report about a report.

53   R. Meynet notes perceptively this cheerless view of time: 'Pour Cléopas et son compagnon Jésus est mort. Et ils portent la mort avec eux, dans leurs paroles et sur leurs visages sombres. Avec leur maître leur espérance aussi est morte.' (*L'Évangile selon saint Luc*: *Analyse rhétorique* (Paris: Cerf, 1988), vol. 2, p. 243).

54   The stylistic and temporal unity of the chapter is evident: to the setting 'early at dawn' in Lk. 24:1 corresponds the 'evening' when 'the day is now nearly over' in Lk. 24:29.

55   Just, *Feast*, p. 49.

56   McBride, *Emmaus*, p. 24. Although Jerusalem is visited by God, it fails to acknowledge the visitation (Lk. 19:42-44).

57   Dillon, *Eye-Witnesses*, p. 93, n. 65.

58   McBride, *Emmaus*, p. 124 (Lk. 13:33). Thus 'giving the pull of Jerusalem in Luke's theology it can be said that the two disciples are going in the wrong direction' (p. 124).

59   For Just the meal outside Jerusalem points out to the centrifugal thrust of the story (Just, *Feast*, pp. 50-51). Emmaus has been assigned various locations: Qalonieh (30 stadia, or four miles from Jerusalem);

some, Luke's details are 'sufficient to establish clearly that the meal was taken well outside the boundaries of the city'.[60] For others, Emmaus is just another part of Jerusalem.[61] In fact, we have here two different Lukan spatial perspectives

> Luke's placement of the first post-resurrection meal *outside Jerusalem* is a significant part of his table fellowship matrix and his geographical perspective. The meals of the new age that are founded on the death and resurrection of Christ will now be celebrated as much outside as within Jerusalem'.[62]

Literary Unity and Transition in Acts 8:26-9:31

The other two *hodos* stories illustrated by this paradigm, Saul's encounter with Jesus and Philip's evangelization of the Ethiopian eunuch, function in Acts 8-9, a section with similar characteristics to those of Luke 24. These two chapters display narrative unity, contrasting spatial and temporal frameworks, linguistic unity. The unitary character of this narrative pivot is enhanced by the landmark nature of Saul's encounter and of Cornelius' conversion (Acts 10-12).

Literary Coherence and Unity in Acts 8:26-9:31

One of the main reasons for the narrative unity of Acts 8:26-9:31 is the special mimetic relation between the accounts of Saul's encounter and of the Ethiopian's conversion. They share several features, prefigured before them by the Emmaus encounter. This kind of relation has not been directly

---

El-Qubeibeh (63 stadia); and Amwas (160 stadia). The longer the distance, the more difficult the one day return journey; however, the disciples may have returned the second day (Goulder, *Luke*, vol. 2, p. 781).

60 Just, *Feast*, p. 50. See also Bock, *Luke 9:51-24:53*, p. 1908; Fitzmyer, *Luke X-XXIV*, p. 1561; Dillon, *Eye-Witnesses*, pp. 87-88; Wanke, *Emmauserzählung*, pp. 37-43; Marshall, *Gospel*, p. 892.

61 For Lohfink Emmaus is nothing else but a reference to the Jerusalem area (Lohfink, *Himmelfahrt*, pp. 207-208, 264). Similarly, Green, *Luke*, pp. 844-845, n. 12. Bock looks cautiously both to Jerusalem and to the historical detail (*Luke 9:51-24:53*, pp. 1908-1909). For Guillaume not the actual geography is important 'ce qui compte, c'est la vision de foi' (*Luc interprète*, p. 109).

62 Just, *Feast*, p. 221.

described in the secondary literature as 'mimetic', yet Luke's repeated use of the same literary paradigms highlights the presence of some clear mimetic principles.

NARRATIVE UNITY

In Acts 8-9, Philip's and Saul's ministries are presented *via* a consistent parallelism. Thus, they both proclaim the Messiah Jesus (ἐκήρυσσεν αὐτοῖς τὸν Χριστόν; Philip in Samaria, Acts 8:5, *cf.* 8:35, εὐηγγελίσατο αὐτῷ τὸν Ἰησοῦν; and Paul, after conversion, in Damascus, Acts 9:20, ἐκήρυσσεν τὸν Ἰησοῦν), and they both preach about Jesus' name (περὶ τοῦ ὀνόματος Ἰησοῦ Χριστοῦ, Acts 8:12; 9:15, 27-29).[63]

Further, Saul's story 'engulfs' Philip's evangelism between his mention in Acts 8:1-3 and in 9:1ff. In Acts 8:3 Saul is ravaging the church, ἐλυμαίνετο τὴν ἐκκλησίαν, and, again, in 9:1 he breathes destruction against the disciples of the Lord, ἐμπνέων ἀπειλῆς καὶ φόνου εἰς τοὺς μαθητὰς τοῦ κυρίου. This *inclusio* suggests that Philip's story represents a sort of parenthetical, introductory missionary account to Paul's major experience. It also relates Philip's portrait and mission to that of Paul (Philip is mentioned independently in Acts 6:5, then in this Pauline *inclusio*, Acts 8:5-8:40, and later in Acts 21:8, again in relation to Paul).[65]

In terms of spatial relations, as in Luke 24, Luke emphasizes in Acts 8-9 the tension between journeying 'from' and 'to' Jerusalem (Acts 8:1-3, 9:2, 9:26, 28). In particular, the structure of Acts 9:1-31 is built with the help of double chiastic reference to Jerusalem, centred on Saul's call.[66]

---

63   Tannehill, *Narrative*, vol. 2, p. 115. The references to the 'name' of Jesus tend to cluster in Acts 2-5 and 8-9.
64   This ἐλυμαίνετο is a NT *hapax*. In LXX, see Ps. 80:14. Boismard highlights a possible parallel between Saul and the old Assyrian threat: 'comme jadis les Assyriens ou les Chaldéens, Paul "ravage" l'église, qui est le nouveau peuple de Dieu', and the fact that in both situations God saves and restores his people (*Actes*, vol. 2, pp. 120-124, esp. p. 122).
65   Barrett, *Acts*, vol. 1, p. 421; Plümacher, *Schriftsteller*, p. 91.
66   Rather than considering that Acts 9:19b-22 belongs to the next section, that is, with vv. 23-31, and thus forming a new independent unit in Acts 9:19a-31, this study supports the view that Acts 9:1-31 as a literary unit fits well the picture of Luke's compositional intervention. Acts 9:1-31, as a unitary pericope, involves a complete reversal cycle of Saul's life (*cf.* Zmijewski, *Apostelgeschichte*, p. 370).

In terms of temporal frameworks, Luke compresses the temporal gaps for the sake of narrative dynamism. For example, Acts 9:26-28 gives the impression that Saul's journey to Jerusalem has taken place some time *soon* after Paul's commissioning (*cf.* Gal. 1:18). Luke telescopes this journey to Jerusalem and for the sake of narrative unity presents a more compact story.[67]

The way time and space frameworks are built can vary even in relation to one and the same story. For example, in the first account of Saul's encounter, the story is presented according to a three day long time span, and three places are mentioned as important: Jerusalem, the road, and Damascus (Acts 9). Later in Acts 22, Luke mentions only the road and the Temple, as settings, and a single time reference, the encounter at noon. Finally, Acts 26 mentions only a single time reference, at noon, and one spatial location, 'on the road'. Characters can be portrayed differently, as well. For example, narrative concerns make Ananias to gradually disappear from the scene, in Acts 9, 22, 26.[68]

LINGUISTIC AND THEMATIC UNITY

The connected recurrences of πορεύομαι and ὁδός in Acts 8-11 (Acts 8:27, 31, 36; 9:3, 11, 15, 17, 21) remind of 'the familiar journey motif throughout Luke-Acts',[69] on the one hand, yet, at the same time, they represent essential material for Luke's *hodos* paradigm.

Particularly in Acts 8:26-9:31, Luke emphasizes the *hodos* setting in a uniquely emphatical manner. From a total of twenty-two specific references to the 'way' (*hodos*) in Acts, in its twenty-eight chapters, it is remarkable that there are six such mentions only in chapter eight and nine, considerably more than the average in the rest of Acts (for example, there is no mention of *hodos* in Cornelius' accounts, Acts 10-12).[70] This

---

67 Boismard, *Actes*, vol. 2, p. 186, Dunn, *Acts*, p. 117.
68 S. Reymond, 'Paul sur le chemin de Damas (Ac. 9, 22 et 26). Temps et space d'une expérience,' in *NRT* 118 (1996), 520-538, esp. p. 533.
69 Spencer, *Philip*, p. 133; *cf.* Filson, 'Journey', pp. 68-77; Moessner, *Lord*, pp. 26-33; R. F. O'Toole, 'Philip and the Ethiopian Eunuch (Acts 8:25-40)', *JSNT* 17 (1983), 25-34, pp. 29-31.
70 After this relatively dense presence of *hodos* in chapters eight and nine, the 'way' motif is present with only one mention per story or per

high concentration illustrates well Luke's mimetic emphasis on a specific *lexis* of transition.

As a whole, Acts 8-9 is characterised by Luke's creative variations on the Way theme. So, after the 'way' occurs in the angel's command to Philip (Acts 8:26), it provides the setting for the Ethiopian's baptism (Acts 8:36), as well as for the jubilant ending of the story (Acts 8:39). Then, it also occurs in implicitly, in the connotations of the Ethiopian's need for a guide (Acts 8:31, τις ὁδηγήσει με)[71] and in the metaphorical reference to Christians seen as 'those... being of the Way' (Acts 9:2, τινας... τῆς ὁδοῦ ὄντας). Finally, it is used with paradigmatic meaning in Ananias' dialogue with Paul (Acts 9:17, Ἰησοῦς ὁ ὀφθείς σοι ἐν τῇ ὁδῷ ᾗ ἤρχου), and in Barnabas' report to the apostles, on Paul's behalf (Acts 9:27, ἐν τῇ ὁδῷ εἶδεν τὸν κύριον καὶ ὅτι ἐλάλησεν αὐτῷ), and with apologetic meaning, with reference to those who witnessed Paul's experience, during his journey, οἱ συνοδεύοντες (Acts 9:7). This unusually rich mention of *hodos* represents a special literary connection between Philip's and Saul's narratives, on the one hand, and it also reminds of the *hodos* emphasis in the Emmaus story. In both cases it becomes an important characteristic of the literary and theological transition after Jesus' resurrection.

The literary play on the theme of journeying happily *versus* journeying dangerously (and being persecuted) is exquisite. The *hodos* motif of Acts 8:26-9:31 casts the happy journeying of the Ethiopian eunuch in a remarkable contrast with Saul's

---

chapter, in general, the only exception being the double mention of the 'way' in Acts 18:25-26.

71 G. Ebel, 'ὁδός', *NIDNTT* vol. 3, 935-943, p. 936 'Anyone who does not know the way needs a *hodēgos* (not before Polybius), a leader to guide him and to show him the way (*hodēgeō*, Aeschylus onwards)', and, also, *hodēgeō* occurs, as well 'in the context of the journey of the soul to heaven'. D. Mínguez notes as well the presence of a polivalent ὁδηγεῖν in the Ethiopian story ('Hechos 8:25-40', pp. 180-181). See *Wisdom*, 9:11, 10:10-17; *The Testament of Judah*, 14:1; 19:1; *The Testament of Gad* 5:7; *Didache*, 3:2-6 (*cf.* Bultmann, 'Mandäischen und manichäischen Quellen', p. 134; E. Hennecke, *Neutestamentliche Apocryphen*, vol. 2: *Apostolisches Apokalypsen und Verwandtes* (Tübingen: Mohr, 1964), pp. 297-372, esp. pp. 368, 371-372; G. Schneider, *Die Apostelgeschichte* (Freiburg: Herder, 1980), vol. 1, p. 504, n. 48).

The Post-Easter Paradigm   211

persecution of Christians, which appears thus as exceedingly violent. The contrast continues, ironically, with the fact that Saul's journey to Damascus is itself under threat. The Road to Damascus becomes the locus of his existential challenge, much as he would have liked to make it a threat for those who 'belonged to the Way'. This thematic play witnesses, again, in favour of Luke's remarkable literary skills.

Further, one should note the massive presence of πορεύομαι constructs in Acts 8-9 (Acts 8:26, 27, 39; 9:3, 11, 15, 31, *cf*. Lk. 24:13, 28), εἰσπορευόμενος καὶ ἐκπορευόμενος (Acts 8:3; 9:28).[72] The combined semantic contribution of ὁδός and πορεύομαι constructs, to which one could add the ἔρχομαι derivatives (ἔρχομαι, Acts 8:40; προσέρχομαι, 8:29; διέρχομαι, 8:40, 9:32; εἰσέρχομαι, 9:6, 12, 17; συνέρχομαι, 9:39), covers an extensive list of references in Acts 8-9,[73] communicating an atmosphere of dynamism, a progressive mode forward which D. Mínguez would call 'the way of Philip', *el camino de Felipe*, as opposed to a certain apostolic rigidity concerning evangelism.[74]

This type of dynamic journeying is highlighted further by the repeated prophetic commissioning 'rise up and go', constructed with ἀνίστημι and πορεύομαι, such as ἀνάστηθι καὶ πορεύου, or with ἀνάστηθι καὶ ἔρχομαι, addressed to Philip, to Ananias and to Saul, *cf*. Acts 8:26 ἀνάστηθι καὶ πορεύου, Acts 9:11 ἀναστὰς πορεύθητι, and Acts 9:6, ἀνάστηθι καὶ εἴσελθε.[75]

---

72 Lindijer, 'Creative', p. 77. The Lukan formula ἐπορεύετο γὰρ τὴν ὁδόν has Hellenistic counterparts in Joshua 3:4 [LXX], Xenophon, *Anabasis*, 2.2.11.1; 3.1.6.3; Josephus, *Antiquities*, 1.282 (see Schneider, *Apostelgeschichte*, vol. 2, p. 506, n. 76).

73 D. Mínguez, 'Hechos 8:25-40', pp. 178-179. This semantic domain includes ὁδηγεῖν, ἀναβαίνειν, καταβαίνειν, ὑποστρέφειν, διέρχεσθαι, προσέρχεσθαι, προστρέχειν, and a certain role has the interplay of the prepositions ἀπό and εἰς (p. 179).

74 Mínguez, 'Hechos 8:26-40', p. 186.

75 Boismard, *Actes*, vol. 3, p. 120. See the parallel between Paul's vision (Acts 9:3-6, 8-9) and the vision of Ezekiel (Ezek. 1-3; *cf*. Ezek. 1:26, 27, 28; Ezek. 2:1; Ezek. 3:22). Ezek. 3:22 has: ᾽Ανάστηθι καὶ ἔξελθε εἰς τὸ πεδίον, καὶ ἐκεῖ λαληθήσεται πρὸς σέ, and Acts 9:6 has: ἀνάστηθι καὶ εἴσελθε εἰς τὴν πόλιν, καὶ λαληθήσεταί σοι ὅ τί σε δεῖ ποιεῖν. Ezek. 3:23 runs: καὶ ἀνέστην καὶ ἐξῆλθον εἰς τὸ πεδίον, and Acts 9:8, ἠγέρθη δὲ Σαῦλος ἀπὸ τῆς γῆς... χειραγωγοῦντες δὲ αὐτὸν εἰσήγαγον εἰς Δαμασκόν (Boismard, *Actes*, vol. 2, pp. 122-124). For Boismard, the parallel between Ezekiel and Saul emphasizes Saul's later vehement message

This command, indicating divine authority, urgency of situation and human obedience – with prophetic connotations (cf. its occurrence in Gen. 19:15, 22:3, 24:10, etc.; Jon. 1:2, 3:1, and in later LXX literature such as Tob. 8:10, 1 Esd. 9:1, etc.), has a high incidence in Luke-Acts in comparison with the rest of the NT, and in particular in Acts 8-10.

The 'rise up' command, however, is not used only of Saul or Ananias, in Acts 8-9, but also in Peter's case, as well, although from a different perspective. For example, Peter commands Aeneas to stand up, Acts 9:34, ἀνάστηθι καὶ στρῶσον σεαυτῷ; similarly, he raises Tabitha from the dead, Ταβιθά, ἀνάστηθι, in Acts 9:40, and asks Cornelius to stop kneeling before him, ἀνάστηθι καὶ ἐγὼ αὐτὸς ἄνθρωπός εἰμι, Acts 10:20. God himself commands Peter, in the table vision, to rise and eat, ἀναστάς, Πέτρε, θῦσον καὶ φάγε, Acts 10:13, and determines him to go to Cornelius' house in Acts 10:20, ἀλλὰ ἀναστὰς κατάβηθι καὶ πορεύου σὺν αὐτοῖς (cf. when Peter goes to rise up Tabitha, ἀναστὰς δὲ Πέτρος συνῆλθεν αὐτοῖς, Acts 9:39). Through such a formula Peter is portrayed as a man of action, ready to carry on the divine commands. The two verbs, πορεύομαι and ἀνίστημι, become thus marks of Luke's mimetic representation, effective in creating a dynamic atmosphere of action and change, of God's direct and implicit intervention through the word of his servants.

The linguistic homogeneity of these chapters and their journey emphases can be seen, further, in Luke's use of πορεύομαι and ἐγγίζειν, another Lukan generic formula. It has been met twice in the Emmaus story, when Jesus joins his disciples 'on the road' ἐγγίσας συνεπορεύετο αὐτοῖς (Lk 24:15), and when he simulates his further journeying, ἤγγισαν εἰς τὴν κώμην οὗ ἐπορεύοντο, καὶ αὐτὸς προσεποιήσατο πορρώτερον πορεύεσθαι (Lk. 24:28). This 'drawing near' represents the actual setting of Saul's encounter, as well, ἐν δὲ τῷ πορεύεσθαι ἐγένετο αὐτὸν ἐγγίζειν τῇ Δαμασκῷ (Acts 9:3), and a similar formula occurs in Philip's evangelization of the Ethiopian, πρόσελθε καὶ κολλήθητι τῷ ἅρματι τούτῳ. προσδραμὼν δὲ ὁ Φίλιππος, κτλ. (Acts 8:29-30). Apparently, this is one of Luke's preferred methods of preparing the atmosphere for a significant miracle (cf. the healing of the blind which takes

---

against the Jewish rejection of Jesus (Ezek. 2:3-8; 3:9, 26-27; 12:2-3, 9, 25, etc.; op.cit., p. 124).

place while Jesus was getting near Jericho: ἐγένετο δὲ ἐν τῷ ἐγγίζειν αὐτὸν εἰς ' Ιεριχώ, Lk. 18:35).[76]
At the same time, the linguistic unity of Acts 8:26-9:31 involves a special relationship with Luke's Infancy narratives (cf. ἐπέρχεσθαι ἐπί, in Luke 1:35, Acts 1:8 and Acts 8:24; ἐξίσταντο δὲ πάντες οἱ ἀκούοντες, in Acts 9:21 and Luke 2:47; ἄγγελος δὲ κυρίου, in Acts 8:26; Luke 1:11; 2:9, cf. Mt. 1-2),[77] suggesting that Luke uses a specific language of transition and divine intervention in Luke 1-3 and in Acts 8-9.

Saul's Encounter as Narrative Landmark

The transition characteristics of Acts 8:26-9:31 need a more detailed assessment. Internal unity is important, yet one needs to highlight the distinction between Acts 8-9 from Acts 10-12 (Cornelius' conversion), and the relation between Acts 8-9 and Luke 24 - Acts 1 (the Ascension).

THE NATURE OF PAUL'S VISION

Although Paul himself does not provide a detailed description of the nature of Christ's appearance to him (cf. 1 Cor. 15:1-8),[78] through his emphatic repetition of ὤφθη he communicates that his encounter enjoys a similar status to that of other appearances of Jesus to his disciples (ὤφθη Κηφᾷ... ὤφθη πεντακοσίοις ἀδελφοῖς... ὤφθη ' Ιακώβῳ... ὤφθη κἀμοί, vss. 5-8).[79] The crucial question, however, is whether Luke considers

---

76 Boismard, *Actes*, vol. 3, p. 128. Mark has this account while Jesus leaves Jericho.
77 This relation is characteristic of the 'Acts II' level of redaction, i.e. characteristic to Luke (ca. AD 80), according to Boismard, *Actes*, vol. 1, and vol. 2, pp. 13-17. The *hodos* report and the emphases on Jerusalem, visions, etc. reflect Luke's redaction (cf. *Actes*, vol. 3, pp. 14-17, 135).
78 W. L. Craig, 'From Easter to Valentinus and the Apostles' Creed Once More: A Critical Examination of James Robinson's Proposed Resurrection Appearance Trajectories', *JSNT* 52 (1993), 19-39, p. 24. Accordingly, the ἐκτρώματι ('untimely born' NRSV) in 1 Cor. 15:8 has been interpreted by some as 'a tacit recognition of the apparent divergence in form' (Alsup, *Post-Resurrection*, p. 84). In fact, this clause - ὡσπερεὶ τῷ ἐκτρώματι ('as to an aborted one'), does not imply a deeper contrast than the other antithesis ἔσχατον δὲ πάντων ('the last of all'), which has, actually, a strong inclusivist meaning.
79 Cf. H. W. Bartsch, 'Inhalt und Funktion des urchristlichen Osterglaubens,' in H. Temporini and W. Haase (eds.), *Aufstieg und*

this appearance, as well, as an Easter christophany or as a less important vision (*cf.* Acts 26:19 τῇ οὐρανίῳ ὀπτασίᾳ).[80]

To an important degree, the nature of Saul's vision is related to the meaning of the forty days passed between Jesus' resurrection and his Ascension. For Conzelmann, for example, this represents a period which discriminates between the resurrection appearances and the later heavenly appearances which 'are of a different kind, for they establish no relationship with the Lord in the special sense that the Resurrection appearances do'.[81] For Alsup, also, Paul's vision is utterly different from the gospel appearances and these differences 'are so categorical that two distinct traditional origins are undoubtedly to be sought'.[82] Borgen even argued that Luke de-materialised the appearance to Paul so that his sub-apostolic status might be even more obvious.[83]

Luke's choice of terms might prove a useful guide in this assessment, however. The vision of the Macedonian, for example, is a presented as a dream at night (ὅραμα διὰ [τῆς] νυκτός, Acts 16:9-10). At night, too, Peter encounters an angel of the Lord who delivers him (ἄγγελος δὲ κυρίου διὰ νυκτός, Acts 5:19). Cornelius sees an angel of the Lord during the day, yet his experience is, again, presented in terms of ὅραμα, a vision: εἶδεν ἐν ὁράματι φανερῶς, κτλ. Acts 10:3, 22, 11:13; 12:7-9). Paul sees an angel in a vision at night, in Acts 27:22-24 (παρέστη γάρ μοι ταύτῃ τῇ νυκτί... ἄγγελος). In this context, Luke's choice for τῇ οὐρανίῳ ὀπτασίᾳ, a heavenly vision, in Acts 26:18, the third presentation of Saul's encounter, stands in marked contrast to the aforementioned instances of ὅραμα;

Niedergang der Römischen Welt: Geschichte und Kultur Roms inn Spiegel der Neuren Forschung (II.25.1) (Berlin: Gruyter, 1982), 794-890, esp. pp. 805, 811-819, 836-843.

80 Zwiep, *Appearance*, pp. 161, 173.
81 Conzelmann, *Luke*, p. 203; see also Lohfink, *Conversion*, p. 25. Alsup argues that there is an unbridgeable gap between the gospels' anthropomorphic epiphanies and Jesus' 'heavenly' appearance to Saul.
82 Alsup, *Post-resurrection*, p. 84.
83 P. Borgen, 'From Paul to Luke', *CBQ* 31 (1969), 168-182, p. 180 (*cf.* Acts 9 and 1 Cor. 15:1-11). See also Evans, *Resurrection*, pp. 55-56; C. W. Hedrick, 'Paul's Conversion / Call: A Comparative Analysis of the Three Reports in Acts', *JBL* 100 (1981), 415-432, esp. pp. 430-431.

only παρέστη of Acts 27:22 enjoys a similar position, yet the latter takes place at night.⁸⁴
Luke leads his readers, thus, to think of this appearance as of a special *christophany* not a vision. The lexical difference (ὅραμα *vs.* ὀπτασία) combined with the contrast between the day setting of the Damascus' encounter and the night settings of the majority of the other visions (save Peter's threefold vision of a meal) emphasizes the higher degree of 'reality' in this theophany.⁸⁵
Its special nature, further, is highlighted by the contrast between heavenly light *versus* day light, as a further element of theophanic manifestation (Exod. 24:15; Ps. 27:1; 29:7; 78:14; 97:1; Is. 9:2; 42:16; 60:1, 20; Ezek. 1:4; Micah 7:8, *cf.* Xenophon, *Cyropaideia*, 4.2.15).⁸⁶
Luke is not very precise about the physical phenomena of the heavenly light, φῶς ἐκ τοῦ οὐρανοῦ, and the voice, φωνή (Acts 9:3),⁸⁷ and Haenchen might be right that he 'shows a certain thoughtlessness',⁸⁸ yet, still, the author emphasizes

---

84 G. Lüdemann, in *Early Christianity according to the Traditions in Acts* (Minneapolis, MN: Fortress, 1989), p. 112, notes that 'vv. 3-9 do not report a *horama* but a christophany'.
85 D. M. Stanley, 'Paul's Conversion in Acts: Why the Three Accounts?', *CBQ* 15 (1953), 315-338, p. 332. Loisy draws attention to the difference between Saul's experience and a vision at night 'ce fut donc autre chose qu'un rêve ou une illusion nocturne' (Loisy, *Les Acts de Apôtres* (Paris: Nouvry, 1920), p. 815; reprinted (Frankfurt: Minerva, 1973), cited in Stanley, p. 332, n. 58).
86 Barrett, *Acts*, vol. 1, p. 449. For Zmijewski Saul's vision was a theophany, since light is the traditional environment for such an experience. All these (indirect) signs point out towards a christophany (*Apostelgeschichte*, p. 378).
87 *Cf.* M. W. Meyer, 'The light and voice on the Damascus Road', *Forum* 2 (1986), 27-35.
88 Haenchen, *Acts*, p. 321, n. 7. *Cf.* Acts 9:7, the companions were 'hearing the voice yet [were] not seeing anyone'; Acts 22:9, they 'saw the light yet could not hear the voice speaking to me', and Acts 26:13, 'I saw a light from heaven... brighter than the sun, shining around me and my companions' (NRSV). Luke uses alternatively the verb ἀκούω with the noun in accusative, ἤκουσεν φωνήν (9:4; ἤκουσα φωνήν in Acts 26:14) and in the genitive ἀκούοντες... τῆς φωνῆς (9:7; *cf.* ἤκουσα φωνῆς in Acts 22:7), apparently without any distinction intended (Conzelmann, *Acts*, p. 71, and Haenchen, *Acts*, pp. 322-323; *cf.* 4 Macc. 3:27; Deut. 4:12). However, Acts 22:9 appears to emphasize a difference, in the idea that

through certain details that this appearance was witnessed as 'real'. In particular, one notes the presence of Saul's journey companions, οἱ συνοδεύοντες (Acts 9:4), who function as major witnesses in the narrative.[89] Luke insists then, lexically, that they *saw* that something happened, ὁράω (ὀφθείς, εἶδεν; Lk. 24:34; Acts 9:12, 17, 27; Acts 26:16), in contrast with the LXX emphasis on 'hearing', in the OT theophanies.[90] According to Barrett, two other elements point out in the direction of a classical theophany, Saul's falling to the ground and the enigmatic dialogue with Jesus.[91]

On the whole, even the defenders of a firm theological *hiatus* between the Resurrection appearances and the Damascus road encounter agree that Saul's encounter comes close to the gospel resurrection appearances, both as an exception and a confirmation of the Ascension limit.[92]

---

    the sound they heard was not understood (τὴν δὲ φωνὴν οὐκ ἤκουσαν τοῦ λαλοῦντός). On the difference between ἀκούω with the Accusative (hear and understand) or with the Genitive (hear without understanding), *cf.* G. Steuernagel, 'Akoyontes tes phones [Apg. 9:7]: Ein Genitiv in der Apostelgeschichte', *NTS* 35 (1989) 619-24; R. Bratcher, 'Akouō in Acts 9:7 and 22:9', *ExpTim* 7 (1959-1960), 243-245; H. R. Moehring, 'The verb akouein in Acts 9:7 and 22:9', *NovT* 3 (1959), 88-99).

89 Haenchen, *Acts*, p. 322; Polhill, *Acts*, p. 235, etc.

90 In an OT-like epiphany it is expected that hearing would take precedence over seeing (Michaelis, 'ὁράω, εἶδον, βλέπω', *TDNT*, vol. 5, 315-382). Seidensticker (*Auferstehung*, p. 36), suggests that Paul saw himself as one of OT prophets who had similar *Lichtglanz* epiphanies, of a visionary δόξα-*Herlichkeit* type (Is. 6:1, Ezek. 1:4-3:16, Exod. 19:16-19). G. O'Collins stresses as well that 'unlike the OT prophets, the apostolic witnesses to Easter typically saw the risen Lord rather than heard his word' (*Christology: A Biblical, Historical and Systematic Study of Jesus* (Oxford: Oxford UP, 1995), pp. 92-93). See also, G. Kittel's article 'ἀκούω', *TDNT*, vol. 1, pp. 216-225. Luke's vision accounts come somewhere between those of the Hellenistic mystery religions, where revelation is mainly a *seeing* event, and those of the OT revelation where revelation is almost entirely a *hearing* experience (Stanley, 'Paul's Conversion', p. 331, n. 54).

91 Barrett, *Acts*, vol. 1, p. 450.

92 Zwiep, *Appearances*, p. 173. *Cf.* also Talbert *Luke and the Gnostics: An examination of Lukan purpose* (Nashville, NY: Abingdon, 1966), pp. 17-32.

The Easter appearances close with the risen Christ's ascension. Neither the vision of Stephen and Ananias nor the experience of Paul's companions on the Damascus road modify this pattern of no christophanies after the Ascension. The only (partial) *exception* is the appearance to Paul himself.[93]

The material connection between the appearances and the resurrection sets a *temporal limit to the appearances* which, while *extended* by the special time of the Damascus experience, is not removed.[94]

SAUL'S CALL AND CORNELIUS' CONVERSION

As the two accounts display obvious similarities, scholars have seen them as two related, major conversion stories.[95] According to Witherup, both accounts pair up the central characters in a similar way. A major figure (Saul, Peter) is destined to foster the movement of the gospel to the Gentiles, and a minor figure 'disappears from the narrative' at the end of the story (Ananias, Cornelius). Structurally, the narrative argument is strengthened in both stories by the motif of a double heavenly vision.[96] The course of the events is essentially altered by divine intervention, of the ascended Jesus in the first, of the Holy Spirit, in the second.[97]

The vocabulary of these two stories has several points of contact, significant words like 'heavens' (Acts 9:3; 10:11), 'earth' (Acts 9:4; 10:11), 'voice' (Acts 9:4; 10:13), and 'rise up' (Acts 9:6; 10:13). For H.-S. Kim, the similarity includes even a *Reisemotiv*, the ὁδοιπορούντων in Acts 10:9, and the 'getting near the city', τῇ πόλει ἐγγιζόντων, or the ἀναστὰς κατάβηθι καὶ πορεύου σὺν αὐτοῖς, in Acts 10:20.[98]

---

93 O'Collins, 'Luke on the Closing of the Easter Appearances', in G. O'Collins and G. Marconi (eds.), *Luke and Acts* (N.Y.: Paulist, 1993), 161-166, esp. p. 166, italics mine.
94 Michaelis, 'ὁράω', *TDNT*, vol. 5, p. 359, n. 212, italics mine.
95 Witherup, 'Cornelius', pp. 63-34.
96 Kim, *Geisttaufe*, p. 188; G. Stählin, *Die Apostelgeschichte* (Göttingen: Vandenhoeck, 1970), p. 149; P.-G. Müller, 'Die "Bekehrung" des Petrus. Zur Interpretation von Apg. 10:1-11:18', *HerKor*, 28 (1974), 372-375, p. 374.
97 Kim, *Geisttaufe*, p. 188: in both stories there is, structurally, an interval (*eine Diastase*) between the divine intervention and the divine confirmation of the new direction.
98 Kim, *Geisttaufe*, p. 188.

Apart from this, the literary repetition of Cornelius' story has a strong local character, being confined to Acts 10-11, with a summary in Acts 15:7-9. By contrast, the repetition of Saul's story has a more general character. Luke repeats it in three different places in Acts (Acts 9, 22, 26).[99]

Although it displays the characteristics of a missionary introduction, from the perspective of a *hodos* appearance Saul's encounter rather looks backwards, putting an end to a previous persecution and signaling the end of the Easter appearances; by contrast, Cornelius' story is more future oriented, officially opening the Gentile period in the life of the Church.

CORNELIUS'S CONVERSION AND THE ETHIOPIAN'S CHALLENGE

The plot discontinuity between Acts 9 and Acts 10, is further highlighted by the contrast between the Cornelius' story and that of the Ethiopian.

The Community Difference

At this level the contrast between Cornelius' conversion and that of the Ethiopian is shaped as a contrast between an individual and a community. Cornelius' conversion stands as representative for all the Gentiles who would repent, while the Ethiopian's is more private, less public and less publicized.[100]

---

99 For many commentators, Acts 9 is a conversion story, while Acts 22, 26, represent call / commissioning accounts (*cf.* J. B. Polhill, *Acts* (Nashville, TN: Broadman, 1992, p. 503, n. 163). After, P. J. Munck (*Paul and the Salvation of Mankind* (London: SCM, 1959); *idem*, *The Acts of the Apostles* (Garden City, NY: Doubleday, 1967), K. Stendahl has argued decisively, that Saul' experience should be seen rather as a call (commissioning) story than a conversion (*Paul Among Jews and Gentiles* (London: SCM, 1977), pp. 8-16. For an alternative view, see G. Lohfink, *Conversion*, p. 29; J. G. Klein, *Die Zwölf Apostel: Ursprung und Gehalt einer Idee* (Göttingen: Vandenhoeck, 1961). Intermediary approaches of this issue are suggested by C. Burchard, *Der dreizehnte Zeuge: Traditions- und kompositionsgeschichtliche Untersuchung zu Lukas' Darstellung der Frühzeit des Paulus* (Göttingen: Vandenhoeck, 1970), and K. Löning, *Die Saulustradition in der Apostelgeschichte* (Münster: Aschendorff, 1973).
100 Barrett, *Acts*, vol. 1, p. 492, see p. 421; *cf.* A. Weiser, 'Tradition und lukanische Komposition in Apg 10.36-43', in J. N. Aletti *et al.* (eds.), *A*

Cornelius is an insider: a Roman God-fearer known to the community (Acts 10:2). On the contrary, the Eunuch is an outsider: he journeys from afar and needs to travel back, and there are no other references to him in Acts.

Cornelius' baptism becomes a matter of public notoriety, while the Ethiopian's conversion, on the contrary, is known only to Philip and to the Eunuch himself, of course, to the reader. The Ethiopian's story represents a breakthrough, as well, yet of a quieter sort.[101] It functions rather as a development of Philip's mission and as an introduction to Saul's calling.

Cornelius' conversion, on the other hand, can be perceived as a major step forward in the process of proclaiming the gospel to the Gentiles, 'a definite advance on the story of the Ethiopian'.[102] Saul's missionary commissioning, as an apostle to the Gentiles, is placed, thus, between two Gentile conversion stories: a strange, unexpected conversion of a rich travelling Ethiopian, and a bold, foreseeable and traceable conversion of Cornelius, one of the pious Romans living in Palestine.

Contrasting Religious Portraits

The contrast between Acts 8-9 and Acts 10-12 comes clearly to the front in the comparison of the Ethiopian's and Cornelius' religious identity. The issue is, again, one of precedence and authority: who is the most radical figure of the two, who is the better representative of pagan or Gentile believers, who is to have converterd and what is his place in Luke's narrative?

According to Barrett, the Ethiopian is the more radical, since he could not have been a Jew by birth (Acts 8:27) neither could he, as an eunuch, have become a proselyte.[103] However,

---

Cause de l'Évangile: Études sur les Synoptiques et les Actes (Paris: Cerf, 1985), 757-768; Stählin, *Apostelgeschichte*, p. 149.

101 Cf. J. B. Polhill, 'The Hellenist Breakthrough: Acts 6-12', *RevExp* 71 (1974), 475-486. Alternatively, the Ethiopian's account could be seen as part of a longer series of challenging actions of the Spirit (Polhill, *Acts*, p. 227: 'The *Spirit* was the radical').

102 Barrett, *Acts*, vol. 1, p. 421.

103 Barrett, *Acts*, vol. 1, p. 420; Spencer has a similar view (*Philip*, p. 172). Alternatively, the Ethiopian should be regarded as a 'God-fearer'. However, if there is a distinct possibility that the original, pre-Lukan

for Boismard, interested to note the levels of Lukan and pre-Lukan redaction, there are certain echoes of the New Exodus theme in Acts 8 (*cf.* Is. 35) and so, the pre-Lukan, Petrine eunuch could have been a proselyte 'un païen sympathisant du judaïsme'; while 'Luke' (or Act II), would have considered him with certainty 'un Juif en exil auprès de la reine d'Éthiopie'.[104]

Taking into consideration the complex social profile of the Ethiopian eunuch as regards race, class, and gender, or his lack of scripture understanding,[105] his portrait appears to be rather that of an exotic African, a 'God-fearing' foreigner from 'the ends of the earth'.[106] Looking for religious integration he

---

story introduced the Ethiopian as a God-fearer, Luke's emphases are less clear-cut. As Spencer notes 'by avoiding "God-fearer" language in Acts 8 which he used in 10:2, 22 (*cf.* v. 35), Luke effectively distanced Philip's convert from Cornelius and other Gentile Christians' (*op.cit.*, p. 163; see M. Wilcox, 'The God-fearers in Acts: A Reconsideration', *JSNT*, 13 (1981), 102-122, p. 108; K. G. Kuhn, 'προσήλυτος', *TDNT*, vol. 6, pp. 730-743). It is difficult to assess the Ethiopian's status from the absence of φοβούμενος or σεβόμενος τὸν θεόν in Acts 8, however, for his journey to Jerusalem, for worship, may imply the opposite (Spencer, *op.cit.*, p. 165; *cf.* Josephus, *Antiquities*, 3.318-319; *Wars*, 6.426-427).

104 Boismard, *Actes*, vol. 2, p. 181.
105 F.S. Spencer, 'The Ethiopian and his Bible: A Social-Science Analysis', *BTB* 22 (1992), 155-165, p. 155. G. Schneider highlights three main characteristics of the Ethiopian as a *dramatis persona*: (1) physical disability; (2) social prominence (δυνάστης, *cf.* Gen. 50.4 [LXX]); (3) sympathy towards Jews and their religion (*Apostelgeschichte*, vol. 1, p. 501, in Zmijewski, *Apostelgeschichte*, p. 362). Generally, Lukan scholarship has noted in this account (1) the geographical aspect, as the gospel reaches for the first time an African; (2) the sociological, as the story narrates the transition from rejection to acceptance; (3) the social-cultural, since he is a man of means (here Barrett disagrees, *Acts*, vol. 1, p. 426, for 'the ἅρμα was certainly not the most luxurious kind of vehicle'); and (4) the religious, since he is not a proselyte, nor a full Gentile, nor a Jew (Zmijewski, *Apostelgeschichte*, pp. 361-363; Spencer, *Philip*, p. 185).
106 Spencer, 'Ethiopian', p. 155; *cf.* C. J. Martin, 'A Chamberlain's Journey and the Challenge of Interpretation for Liberation', in K. G. Cannon and E. Schüssler-Fiorenza (eds.), *Semeia 47: Interpretation for Liberation* (Missoula, MT: Scholars, 1989), 105-135.

apparently faced rejection due to his foreign identity and to his physical impairment (cf. κωλύω).[107]
There is a difficulty, however, in interpreting εὐνοῦχος as an allusion to physical disability.[108] Some scholars, such as B.R. Gaventa or W. Willimon, alternate between acknowledging a physical impairment, and thus the eunuch is a pagan, a Gentile at the limits of acceptability,[109] and a secondary, interpretable feature, a social position more than a disability - and then the Ethiopian is not such an extreme person, but primarily a general symbol of 'all those from earth's end who, unlike Jerusalem Jews, will receive the gospel'.[110]
The best supported case, though, is that for a physical meaning of 'eunuch' in Acts 8:27.[111] There is overwhelming evidence regarding the deviant, despised connotations of εὐνοῦχος in the ancient Mediterranean world.[112] It would be

---

107 Spencer, 'Ethiopian', p. 161: the Ethiopian experiences a dramatic change of status, from 'a marginal God-fearer to a full-rights member of the people of God' (eunuchs in antiquity 'belonged to the most despised and derided group of men' - cf. G. Petzke, 'εὐνοῦχος', in H. Balz and G. Schneider (eds.), Exegetical Dictionary of the New Testament (Grand Rapids, MI: Eerdmans, 1991), vol. 2, 80-81; L. Hug, 'Eunuchen', in A. F. Pauly, G. Wissowa et al (eds.), Real-Encyclopädie der klassichen Altertumswissennschaft, Supp. vol. 3, cols. 449-455; L. H. Gray, 'Eunuch', Encyclopedia of Religion and Ethics (Edinburgh: T&T Clark, 1912), vol. 5, 579-585). The case for physical connotations of εὐνοῦχος is supported by several observations. Luke often refers to public figures beset by some bodily 'defect' (Naaman, in Lk. 4:27; Jairus and Publius have suffering relatives, Lk. 7:2-3; 8:41-42; Acts 28:7-8). From this perspective εὐνοῦχος and δυνάστης are tautologic (Acts 8:27). Often a male servant of a female royal figure was castrated (Spencer, Philip, p. 166).
108 P. de Meester, "'Philippe et l'eunuque éthiopien" ou "Le baptême d'un pèlerin de Nubie"?', NRT 103 (1981), 360-374, p. 363 (cf. Spencer, Philip, pp. 131-133).
109 Gaventa, From Darkness, p. 104.
110 Gaventa, From Darkness, p. 123. Spencer notes a similar incertitude at W. Willimon (Spencer 'Ethiopian', p. 156).
111 Spencer, 'Ethiopian', p. 156.
112 For Hermotimus, a high office eunuch at the court of king Xerxes (Herodotus, History, 8.104-106), castration is 'the wickedest trade on earth' [ἔργων ἀνοσιωτάτων], and he plans it as revenge against those who crippled him, a 'no man, a thing of nought' [ἀντ' ἀνδρὸς... τὸ μηδὲν εἶναι]. Bagoas, a eunuch interested in philosophy, learns from Diocles

difficult to avoid these connotations, in Luke's world, for a Greek reader, and Luke stresses the term repeatedly (8:32, 34, 36 and 39).[113]

It follows that the Ethiopian is not only a 'very strong representative of foreignness within a Jewish context',[114] or a God-fearer, but also he represents a character much 'more remote from the people of God than Cornelius', and his conversion marks 'an even more radical stage in the rise of the Gentile mission that Peter's visit to Caesarea'.[115] The Ethiopian eunuch is a 'better representative of the gospel's reach "to the end of the earth" than Cornelius is',[116] but a less suitable one for a next step in the missionary ministry of the church; a more extreme case than Cornelius yet of lesser public notoriety: a *prelude* to Cornelius' conversion,[117] an *Vorspiel*,[118] or *Auftakt*.[119]

This whole discussion about the religious identity of the Ethiopian raises another issue, too, the comparison between Philip and Peter. Usually, scholars who reject the Ethiopian's identification as a paradigmatic Gentile motivate this by 'the disturbance this would cause to a prior conclusion: that the narrator intends to present Peter as the initiator of the

---

that he cannot have access to such science 'since he was a eunuch; such people ought to be excluded,... a eunuch was neither man nor woman but something composite, hybrid, and monstrous, alien to human nature' (Lucian, *The Eunuch*, 6.3-15; A. Harmon). Titus allowed eunuchs at the palace, yet Domitian had officially banned castration throughout the empire (*cf.* Gray, 'Eunuch', 579-585). Josephus and Philo nurtured similar prejudices against eunuchs, particularly so against transvestites. Josephus calls them 'infanticides' (*Antiquities*, 4.290-91); Philo refers to them as 'androgynes', 'men who pervert their sex and effeminate their appearance' (*Special Laws*, 1.325, my translation).

113 Dollar, *Exploration*, p. 147.
114 Tannehill, *Narrative*, vol. 2, p. 108.
115 Barrett, *Acts*, vol. 1, p. 420.
116 Tannehill, *Narrative*, vol. 2, pp. 134-135.
117 Conzelmann, *Acts*, p. 67.
118 O. Bauernfeind, *Kommentar und Studien zur Apostelgeschichte* (Tübingen: Mohr, 1980), p. 123; Schneider, *Apostelgeschichte*, vol. 1, p. 498.
119 Plümacher, *Schriftsteller*, p. 90.

Gentile mission in the story of Cornelius' conversion'.[120] Haenchen notes, for example, that

> [Luke] cannot and did not say that the eunuch was a Gentile; otherwise Philip would have forestalled Peter, the legitimate founder of the Gentile mission! For that reason Luke leaves the eunuch's status in a doubtful light.[121]

For others, Luke is not interested in contrasting Peter with Philip, but intends to show that 'the incorporating of the Gentiles into the Church without subjecting them to the law originated neither with Paul, nor with Peter, but with God'.[122] The more radical variant of this stance is that Luke wants to emphasize how every 'new step is taken by someone other than the apostles, and the apostles must then catch up with events that are happening independently of them'.[123] However, Luke takes quite definite steps to clear the stage and to emphasize that the fundamental changes in the missionary agenda of the Church are brought by God through the apostles in Jerusalem (cf. Philip's evangelism is not any longer reported, after this event; in Acts 15, Peter stands up first, v. 7, then Barnabas and Paul, v. 12, and the Peter has the final word).

Narrative Independence

Apart from such attempts at rationalising the narrative sequence of the Ethiopian's, Saul's, and Cornelius' stories, it has been argued that the Ethiopian's conversion finds itself in a certain narrative isolation, by virtue of its independent nature. For example, Plümacher argued that, despite Luke's efforts at integrating it narratively, the Ethiopian's account remains to be seen just as a loose episode 'äußerlich als Episode'.[124] Barrett disagrees with the idea of such a narrative

---

120 Tannehill, *Narrative*, vol. 2, p. 110.
121 Haenchen, *Acts*, p. 314.
122 Dibelius, 'Conversion', p. 122.
123 Tannehill, *Narrative*, vol. 2, p. 110. However, Peter has a primary role in Cornelius' story: he finds himself, unwillingly, in the avantgarde of Gentile evangelism.
124 Plümacher, *Schriftsteller*, p. 91.

isolation, on the grounds that Luke returns later in Acts to mention again Philip the Evangelist (Acts 21:8-9).[125]

However, the Ethiopian's conversion does not seem 'at home' in Luke's literary environment. For Haenchen, this story comes from an independent tradition (the Hellenistic tradition of the Seven) where it had a foundational inaugurating character for the Gentile mission, which it lost in Luke-Acts, because Luke did not want to jeopardize Peter's apostolic authority.[126] From a divinely guided first-ever conversion of a Gentile, the Ethiopian's story becomes a prefiguring, unofficial beginning, a low-key step in a longer process, 'an edifying story'.[127] According to such a view, Luke takes the initial prominent and independent story of the Ethiopian's tradition and paints it with the less contrasting colours of intermediarity, characteristic of a half-Jewish, half-Gentile portrait, of a '"Zwischenbereich" zwischen Judentum und Heidentum'.[128]

The truth is that in Luke's narrative logic Cornelius' conversion cannot be regarded as 'a causal factor in a sequence of events that moves toward the end of the earth', nor as a '"stepping-stone" between the conversion of the Samaritans and the Gentiles'.[129]

> Temporal relations between the Cornelius episode and the preceding stories of Philip and Saul are very vague, and no causal sequence is indicated... Peter does not react to Cornelius in light of what has already happened to Philip and Saul. [...] The conversion of the Ethiopian was a private and isolated event that had no effect. The conversion of Cornelius has consequences in the following narrative, as the reference back to it in Acts 15 makes clear.[130]

---

125 Barrett, *Acts*, vol. 1, p. 421; *cf.* Acts 21:8-9.
126 Haenchen, *Acts*, p. 315.
127 Haenchen, *Acts*, p. 316.
128 Schneider, *Apostelgeschichte*, vol. 1, p. 498; *cf.* Zmijewski, *Apostelgeschichte*, p. 361.
129 Tannehill, *Narrative*, vol. 2, p. 107. Similarly, Polhill considers that the Ethiopian is a *Gentile* eunuch, a most challenging combination 'a radical step for a Jew, even for a Hellenist Jew like Philip' (*Acts*, p. 227).
130 Tannehill, *Narrative*, vol. 2, pp. 113, 137. However, the Ethiopian's conversion remains one of the narrative gems of Acts. And it still has an important narrative role: creates the background for courageous,

Hodos Encounters and Narrative Transitions

Moessner's journey scheme for Luke-Acts, with its transition pivots in Luke 9 and Acts 6-9, comes closest to this model. However, in view of the present findings, one could imagine a narrative scheme with other two transition pivots, both based on the *hodos* motif present in Luke 24 and Acts 8:26-9:31.[131]

Anticipation	Fulfilment of history of salvation	Extension
Galilee	Jerusalem	Rome
Luke 1:1——Luke 24—————Acts 8:26-9:31——— 28:31		
hodos transition	*hodos* transition	
Galilee → Jerusalem	Jerusalem → Rome	

The Church story: from Jerusalem to the ends of the world

Morgenthaler's geographical scheme of journeys and Jerusalem-set scenes in Luke-Acts is also close to the present observations on the structural implications of a journeying plus encounter paradigm. He notes, for example, four major Jerusalem scenes and three main journeys in Luke-Acts, with the last (to Rome) breaking the symmetry:[132]

I. Jerusalem scene	Luke 1:5-4:13
I. Journey to Jerusalem	4:14-19:44
II. Jerusalem scene	19:45-24:33
III. Jerusalem scene	Acts 1:4-7:60
II. Journey (missionary)	8:1-21:17
IV. Jerusalem scene	21:18-26:32
III. Journey to Rome	27:1-28:31

The *hodos* scheme suggests a similar outline, where static scenes of special revelation (Lk. 1-3; 9:1-50; 20-23; Acts 1:13-7;

Spirit guided, and effective evangelism. It seems to answer the question 'how far can go the Gospel?' and the answer is 'as wildly far as the Ethiopian eunuch, both geographically and socially'.
131 *Cf.* Moessner, *Lord*, pp. 296-297, 304-305;
132 Morgenthaler, *Lukas und Quintilian*, pp. 353, 351-352; *idem*, *Geschichtsschreibung*, vol. 1, p. 163.

Acts 10-12) alternate with journey sections (Lk. 4:1-8:56; 9:51-19:44; Lk. 24 - Acts 1:12; Acts 13-28). Between Luke 24 - Acts 1 and Acts 8:26-9:31 comes Acts 1:13-7 as a section marked by quieter, background variations of Luke's journey motif (the Pentecost account and the pilgrimage theme, Acts 2:1-41; Stephen's speech and Israel's wanderings, Acts 7:1-53; and Acts 8:1-4 - the scattering of the Christians across Palestine). One could suggest a modified narrative scheme for Luke-Acts where revelation and journeying is controlled by two important transition sections, Luke 24-Acts 1, and Acts 8-9:

Luke 1-3   **Revelation**: The Nativity hodos stories
4:1-8:56   The journeys of the Galilean ministry
9:1-50   **Revelation**: Messiah's journey to the Cross
9:51-19:44   Jesus' journey to Jerusalem
19:45-23   **Revelation**: Resurrection in Jerusalem
Lk. 24 - Acts 1:12 *Post-Resurrection Transition*
Acts 1:13-7   **Revelation**: Pentecost, Pilgrims in Jerusalem
Acts 8:26-9:31   *Pre-Gentile Evangelistic Transition*
10-12   **Revelation**: The beginning of Gentile mission
13-28   The *Acta Pauli* (missionary journeys)

At the end of this analysis, one has to acknowledge that despite all these arguments, not everything in Luke-Acts is journey, or journeying story; however, the above mentioned compositional schemes highlight the important role of the *hodos* references in the narrative coherence of Luke-Acts. Luke's encounter paradigm functions in well-defined contexts, with specific linguistic, thematic and structural features, and brings a specific contribution to the advance of the overall plot, to the completion of the Gospel's journey from Jerusalem to Rome.[133]

---

133 The geography of Luke's journey accounts in Acts leads to Rome (W. L. Knox, *The Acts of the Apostles* (Cambridge: Cambridge UP, 1948), p. 55; *cf.* Morgenthaler, *Lukas und Quintilian*, p. 340. However, both capitals, Jerusalem and Rome, are not really surrendering to the Gospel 'Rom kommt im Lukastext wirklich nicht besser weg als Jerusalem' (*cf.* Morgenthaler, *Lukas und Quintilian*, p. 349). The 'ends of the world' remain unnamed, and still aimed at, while journeying itself shares something of the missionary goal, as a setting of special revelation, of challenge and of change of existential paradigms.

The Anatomy of Luke's On the Road Paradigm

Since the literary context in which Luke's *hodos* paradigm functions has been discussed, as well as the main cultural references that need to be checked in terms of cultural relevance and Lukan source, one could look now in greater detail at the paradigm itself. The following discussion aims to shed new light on the way the *hodos* encounters share a common structure, by referring to Aristotle's plot rules and by emphasizing Luke's literary intervention.

The Emmaus Meal as Sacramental Ending

This a major point of *hodos* parallelism since the other two encounters end with a sacramental scene, i.e. baptism. J. Dupont has argued in favour of a sacramental meaning of the Emmaus meal from the premise of this parallelism itself.[134] The eucharistic significance of the Emmaus meal has been particularly well noted in the liturgical readings of the story, such as that of R. Orlet, who allows a later dating of Luke.[135] His interpretation has won numerous adherents, with multiple, nuanced readings.[136]

However, the eucharistic meaning of this meal has been acknowledged by others only as a '*relation* to the Eucharist', with no clear reflection of 'the *mode* of a primitive eucharistic celebration'.[137] The objection seems valid, and D. Bock argued, for example, that 'although there is breaking of bread and

---

134 J. Dupont, 'Meal', pp. 105-121. B. P. Robinson argues against such views for 'recognition by the eunuch precedes his baptism, whereas in the Emmaus story the recognition does not occur until the breaking of the bread' ('Place', p. 483). Here Luke seems to have a combined recognition-reversal scene in a sacramental evironment.
135 R. Orlet, 'An Influence of the Early Liturgy Upon the Emmaus Account', *CBQ* 21 (1959), 212-219, esp. pp. 216-217.
136 H. D. Betz, 'The Origin and Nature of Christian Faith According to the Emmaus Legend (Luke 24:13-32', *Int* 23 (1969), pp. 32-46, p. 38; see also Marshall, *Gospel*, p. 898). X. Léon-Dufour shares a similar view, highlighting the prophetic significance of Jesus' participation in the Emmaus meal (*Sharing the Eucharistic Bread*, p. 124, cited in Just, *Feast*, p. 234). As well, Guillaume writes that the essential emphasis of the story is on the 'breaking of the bread', rather than on recognition (*Luc interprète*, p. 95).
137 Fitzmyer, *Luke X-XXIV*, p. 1560.

thanksgiving, [the Emmaus meal] is not a eucharist, especially given the absence of wine'.[138] Since meals occur frequently in Luke-Acts ('simple' meals - Lk. 7:36; 11:37; 14:1; feasts - 5:29, miraculous provisions - 9:16, cultic meals - 22:14, weddings - 14:8-9, and the eschatological banquet - 12:37; 13:29), Bock accepts only the idea of a simple meal and of a resurrection fellowship.[139] A similar view is espoused by Nolland according to whom 'there is no sense in which Luke is claiming that Jesus celebrated a communion service with these disciples'.[140]

While acknowledging Luke's special use of κλάω (to break), authors such as Alsup and especially Green have stressed instead of eucharistic connotations that the 'breaking of the bread' (v. 35) highlights an important link of this meal with the Miraculous Feeding of the 5000 (Lk. 9:12-17). For Green, in particular, this supersedes the possible link between the Emmaus meal and the Last Supper: 'Not coincidentally, the feeding of the thousands itself possesses revelatory significance within the Lukan narrative, leading from misconception to correct perception of Jesus' identity as Messiah (Lk. 9:7-20)'.[141] According to Danker and Derrett the Emmaus meal has the connotations of a divine banquet.[142]

Derrett's article calls for particular attention, since his interpretation associates two distinct motifs, the *sight* theme

---

138 Bock, *Luke 9:51-24:53*, p. 1903, n. 1.
139 Bock, *Luke 9:51-24:53*, p. 1919. B. P. Robinson suggests the meal 'speaks of how Christ is to be encountered and recognised not in one special kind of Christian meal but wherever and whenever Christians break bread together' ('Place', p. 494).
140 Nolland, *Luke 18:35-24:53*, pp. 1208-1209. The theme of hospitality to strangers (φιλοξενία) as a sign of brotherly love (φιλαδελφία), a major Christian theme, is only one of Luke's several motifs in the Emmaus story (Grassi, 'Emmaus', pp. 463-465, esp. p. 465; *cf.* R. Orlet, 'Liturgy' pp. 212-219; on how this Christian custom was perceived by the Greco-Romans and by Jews alike, see W. L. Lane, *Hebrews 9-13* (Dallas, TX: Word, 1991, p. 511, and J. Thurén, in *Das Lobopfer der Hebräer: Studien zum Aufbau und Anliegen von Hebräerbrief 13* (Åbo: Åbo Akademi, 1973), 49-247, p. 209).
141 Green, *Luke*, p. 843; *cf.* Alsup, *Post-Resurrection*, p. 199, and Robinson, 'Place', 487-494.
142 F.W. Danker, *Jesus and the New Age: According to Saint Luke, A New Commentary on the Third Gospel* (Philadelphia, PA: Fortress, 1988), pp. 394-395. Derrett, 'Walk', pp. 190-193.

and the *meal* or the *banquet* motif. According to him, the Emmaus meal has a restoration, covenantal meaning. Luke's reference to ὤφθη, 'see', and 'eating and drinking' are seen as signs of the covenant, Exodus 24:10-11, as reminders of Israel's experience of Mt. Sinai.[143] That he has an eucharistic interest here transpires from his language, for example, from his significant parallelism in Luke 22:19 and Luke 24:30

Luke 22:19: καὶ λαβὼν ἄρτον εὐχαριστήσας ἔκλασεν καὶ ἔδωκεν αὐτοῖς λέγων, Τοῦτό ἐστιν τὸ σῶμά μου τὸ ὑπεὺμῶν διδόμενον·

Luke 24:30: καὶ ἐγένετο ἐν τῷ κατακλιθῆναι αὐτὸν μετ' αὐτῶν λαβὼν τὸν ἄρτον εὐλόγησεν καὶ κλάσας ἐπεδίδου αὐτοῖς.[144]

The imperfect ἔκλασεν is used only here by Luke (Lk. 22:19), yet it occurs in the rest of the NT in 1 Corinthians 11:24 with a clear eucharistic meaning, and, as well, in Matthew 15:36, 26:26 and Mark 8:6, 14:22.

Two other instances when Luke mentions the breaking of the bread have also been associated with the Eucharist, as well. One is Acts 20:11 (*cf.* Luke's note that 'on the first day of the week' they met 'to break bread', κλάσαι ἄρτον, Acts 20:7) and the other, more disputed, is a meal of encouragement, Acts 27:35. Taken during the shipwreck, just a few hours before seeing the land, this has also been interpreted, by authors like Wanke, as an allusion to the Eucharist.[145]

Cleopas and his companion report emphatically that their recognition of Jesus happened at the breaking of the bread, ἐν τῇ κλάσει τοῦ ἄρτου (Lk. 24:35). This Lukan phrase appears only here and in the more developed context of church worship in Acts 2:42.[146] In this case, B. P. Robinson's comment, that 'Luke has no interest in the place of the Eucharist as such in

---

143 Derrett, 'Walk', pp. 191, 193; Jesus disappears from sight when his participation in the new covenant is clear; also p. 193, n. 55: Deut. 6:5, 7; *Sifre Deuteronomy*, 34; '*Avôt de Rabbi Nathan* (B) 35.
144 J. H. Neyrey, 'Luke 24:13-35, "The Risen Shepherd"', in J. H. Neyrey (ed.), *Resurrection Stories*, Wilmington, DE: Glazier, 1988, 38-49, p. 41. See Fitzmyer, *Luke X-XXIV*, p. 1568, on Lk. 22:19, 9:16.
145 J. Wanke, 'κλάω', *EDNT*, vol. 2, 295-296, esp. p. 296. J. Behm has a different view ('κλάω', *TDNT*, vol. 3, 726-743). For him the ancient custom (Jer. 16:7; Lam. 4:4) has no cultic connotations even in the NT.
146 Boismard, *Actes*, vol. 3, pp. 18-19.

the life of the Church, but considerable interest in the Last Supper',[147] could indicate that Luke's emphases are being left aside or that, at the same time, one has to acknowledge too fine a distinction, that would highlight either a very early Lukan Gospel, and (or) a very untheologically minded Luke.

Given the early character of the scene, its sacramental connotations would appear as more probable, if Luke's intervention and interests are seen as better represented in the text, or more probable, too. In this respect, NT scholarship remarked two main areas of Lukan redaction: (a) the original account had stressed only the appearance element yet Luke turned it into a journey story (Dillon, Schubert); and (b) the original account followed the model of OT epiphanies, yet Luke decided to use, with apologetic intention, the Hellenistic language of a *theios aner* appearance (Ehrhardt).[148]

It seems plausible, then, that the original story had referred only to a famous recognition meal, after the Resurrection, while Luke, later, has emphasized specifically, the proof from Scripture, the *theios aner* connotations, and the eucharistic parallels.[149] His focus on recognition, on the opening of eyes at

---

147 Robinson, 'Place', p. 494.
148 Ἄφαντος is used in classical Greek of disappearing gods (Euripides, *Helen*, 606: βέβηκεν ἄλοχος σὴ πρὸς αἰθέρος πτυχὰς ἀρθεῖσ' ἄφαντος· οὐρανῷ δὲ κρύπτεται 'gone is thy wife - into the folds of air wafted and vanished! hid in heaven's depths', etc.; A. Way); cf. Fitzmyer, *Luke X-XXIV*, p. 1568). Ehrhardt is critical of the hypothesis of the OT 'divine tramp' motif as present in the NT (vs. Gunkel; Ehrhardt, 'Disciples', p. 194). The theme of divine encounters has rather a Hellenistic origin (Guillaume, *Luc interprète*, pp. 89-90; Gempf, 'Mission', 56-69). For Ehrhardt in the Emmaus story the reader is faced with an '*epiphaneia* to wanderers than of a wanderer' (vs. Gunkel). The language used - ἄφαντος ἐγένετο (v. 31), seems to belong to the technical terminology of pagan religion, related to an ἐπιφανής (Ehrhardt, pp. 184-185). Since ἄφαντος it is a *hapax legomenon* in the NT, and is unknown to the Septuagint (so Ehrhardt; however, see 2 Macc. 3:32 ἐφάνησαν, 3:34, ἀφανεῖς ἐγένοντο) Ehrhardt notes that 'linguistically we are faced in our story with material which is alien to biblical diction' (Ehrhardt, p. 185; similarly Guillaume, *op.cit.*, p. 89; Grundmann, *Lukas*, p. 447; cf. Euripides, *Orestes*, 1494; *Helen*, 605; Vergil, *Aeneid*, 9.657, 2 Macc. 3:34). The overpowering of human sight (Lk. 24:16, 31), has 'no parallel in the Gospels' (Ehrhardt, p. 184).
149 Grundmann, *Lukas*, p. 442.

'the breaking of the bread' and on the disappearance of Jesus, his special emphasis on ἐν τῇ κλάσει τοῦ ἄρτου (Lk. 24:34-35), while the entire OT argument together with the encounter itself are mentioned simply as 'the things happend on the road', τὰ ἐν τῇ ὁδῷ,[150] represent important evidence of a Lukan eucharistic reading of the original account.

The Hodos Paradigm

Up until now, the paradigm transpiring from these three stories has been interpreted in two major ways. Scheffler has regarded them as 'fictitious' creations aimed at encouraging a persecuted community. Lindijer has suggested a *hodos* series instead, even if he has referred only to the Emmaus and the Gaza road accounts. Building further on their insights, the present thesis argues that this encounter paradigm is a literary form focused on the evangelistic 'creativity' of those non-apostolic ministers who have continued Jesus' mission, and as such, it is based on the centrality of two major scenes: the recognition and the restoration scene.

THE RECOGNITION SCENE

'Recognition' or 'discovery', a progress in knowledge (in the form of ἐπιγινώσκειν, in Lk. 24) is clearly a key concept of the Emmaus story, coming at pivotal points, at the beginning (v. 16), the climax (v. 31), and the conclusion (v. 35) of the pericope.[151] This has led to the idea of a 'sight and recognition' chiasmus of Luke 24:16, 31a.[152]

One can even identify two types of recognition in the Emmaus account: an ironical *non*-recognition (misidentification) at the beginning,[153] and a sacramental or meal-

---

150 *Cf.* Guillaume, *Luc interprète*, p. 95. Tannehill, *Narrative*, vol. 1, p. 279. Such a complex plot model, with two climaxes, as suggested in this study, provides a better fitting narrative pattern for interpreting the Emmaus encounter.
151 Dillon, *Eye-Witnesses*, p. 104.
152 Just, *Feast*, pp. 64-68.
153 Kurz, *Reading Luke-Acts*, p. 143; *cf.* Joseph and his brothers in Gen. 44:18-45:3. C. Hickling notes in a similar vein that 'the Emmaus story is the ironical story of a long misidentification, a *non-recognition* story' ('The Emmaus Story and its Sequel', in S. Barton and G. Stanton (eds.), *Essays in Honour of Leslie Houlden* (London: SPCK, 1994), 21-33, esp.

related recognition at the end of the story.[154] This narrative complexity highlights two mechanisms of recognition: one by argument or dialogue, and one by divine mysterious intervention, during the sacramental meal.

As regards the Ethiopian's story, this account does not include a proper 'recognition' scene, nor an epiphany.[155] However, it has a recognition dialogue focusing on Jesus' identity as Yahweh' Servant (Isaiah 53:7-8). The Ethiopian experiences an evangelistic messianic 'discovery' or 'furthering of knowledge', a general, Scripture mediated recognition of Jesus' messianic identity.[156]

Next, the recognition scene is obvious in Saul's encounter, and more subtle, too. The persecutor encounters an unexpected vision and finds himself under pressure to recognise the identity of the one who speaks to him (ἤκουσεν φωνὴν λέγουσαν αὐτῷ, Acts 9:4; cf. ὧν εἶπας ἀκούσασα καὶ ὄψιν ἰδοῦσα,[157] and γνωρίσασα τὴν φωνὴν ἀπεκαλύψατο[158]). Aristotle ranked recognition by voice among the contrived category and lower types,[159] yet Luke's scene has here a different foundation: this is a recognition by inference or logical argument, by dialogue, a 'recognition by reasoning', ἐκ συλλογισμοῦ.[160] For us, this type of dialectic discovery of Jesus the Lord secures the narrative coherence of the story by connecting the encounter as such with the proof-from-prophecy argument. In general, Luke's OT allusions take two

---

pp. 23-24, italics mine). Παροικεῖς strengthens the contrast of non-recognition: he is the saviour, and still plays the πάροικος, a foreigner who does not know what has happened.

154 R. Schnackenburg, *Jesus in the Gospels. A Biblical Christology* (Louisville, KY: John Knox, 1995), p. 186; Schubert, 'Structure', p. 172, etc.

155 Guillaume, *Luc interprète*, p. 92.

156 Aristotle, *Poetics*, 1452a.25-30: 'a "discovery", as the terms itself implies, is a change from ignorance to knowledge, producing either friendship or hatred in those who are destined for good fortune or ill' (Fyfe).

157 Iamblichus, *Babyloniaka*, 75b.41.

158 Chariton, *Callirhoe*, 8.1.8.

159 Aristotle, *Poetics*, 1454b.31.

160 Aristotle, *Poetics*, 1455a.4; 1455a.20.

complementary forms, explicit and implicit, and both of the are present in Luke's *hodos* paradigm.¹⁶¹

Pattern

The recognition dialogues are well structured, displaying a dialectic pattern: (a) question; (b) counter-question; (c) explanation (*cf.* Zmijewski, Morgenthaler). Since the Easter *kerygma* is paradigmatic in Luke-Acts, the evangelistic dialogue tends to display, also, a standard form.

Thus, Luke 24:17-19 displays a complex dialogue scheme: 'a dialogue begins, questions are put and answered to, problems are expressed'.¹⁶² Jesus asks τίνες οἱ λόγοι οὗτοι οὓς ἀντιβάλλετε πρὸς ἀλλήλους (Lk. 24:17), and Cleopas answers with a counter-question Σὺ μόνος παροικεῖς Ἰερουσαλὴμ καὶ οὐκ ἔγνως τὰ γενόμενα ἐν αὐτῇ ἐν ταῖς ἡμέραις ταύταις (Lk. 24:18),¹⁶³ and is addressed himself a leading counter-question, Ποῖα (Lk. 24:19). There follows a double explanation section: first the summary of the Passover events and of Jesus' ministry provided by the disciples (Lk. 24:20-24) then Jesus' explanation of the Scripture (Lk. 24:25-27).

In Philip's evangelisation of the Ethiopian, the dialogue takes, as well, the question and counter-question form, as a *Frage-Gegenfrage* structure, or *Rede-Gegenrede Schema* (although not as developed as in the Emmaus account).¹⁶⁴ The dilectic nature of the dialogue is evident in various instances: the eunuch has the opportunity to ask two questions; Philip's

---

161 Spencer, *Philip*, p. 132; Lindijer, 'Creative', pp. 80, 82.
162 Lindijer, 'Creative', p. 83.
163 Fitzmyer, *Luke X-XXIV*, p. 1564, notes that *paroikein* often meant 'to inhabit a place without citizenship, dwell as a resident alien', and was also used 'of temporary visitors (which would suit the sojourn of a Passover pilgrim)'. For parallels to this rhetorical question, see Cicero, *Pro Milone* 12.33: 'An vero, iudices, vos soli ignoratis, vos hospites in hac urbe versamini...?'; or in *Pro Rabirio Perduellionis*, 10.28.9-11: 'Are you such a stranger to this city (*hospes es huiusce urbis*), so ignorant of our traditions and our custom, as not to know this, till we get the impression that you are a visitor in a foreign country (*peregrinari in aliena civitate*), not a magistrate in your own?'.
164 Zmijewski, *Apostelgeschichte*, pp. 381, 363, 372.

first inquiry can be described, as well, as a dialectical question open to two answers.¹⁶⁵

Aware of Jesus' divinity, Saul addresses Jesus as κύριος (Acts 9:5) and his 'recognition' reaction is helped by both the implicit and explicit message of the speaker. Lohfink suggests that Paul realises Jesus' Lordship for he is addressed in an OT fashion (*cf.* Acts 9:4-6, Gen. 46:2f, Exod. 3:4-10), with a characteristic divine call in three parts: λέγω... τίς εἶ... ἐγώ εἰμι (*cf.* the dialogue format). Jesus' statement has a biblical ring, a biblical format 'Jesus muß biblisch reden... an Stelle von ἐγώ εἰμι ὁ θεός... heißt es dort ἐγώ εἰμι ' Ἰησοῦς'.¹⁶⁶ However, the overall structure of the dialogue (1) address, or call; (2) answer with counter-question; (3) introduction with charge, does not come necessarily from the LXX, but is more general, for it also occurs in *Joseph and Aseneth*, 14, and *The Testament of Job*, 3, and thus Luke uses here a 'narrative schema'.¹⁶⁷

Lexis and Dramatisation

The recognition context allows in Luke's *hodos* paradigm for a special dramatisation of the dialogue. In Saul's encounter this takes the form of theatrical *mis-en-scène*. Questioning takes place while Saul is fallen to the ground (πεσὼν ἐπὶ τὴν γῆν, Acts 9:4) and Jesus' presentation is marked by suspense (his identity is disclosed only at the second intervention, Acts 9:5). A lengthier dialogue takes place between Jesus and Ananias (Acts 9:10-16), this time in a dream: the threatening heavenly appearance (*cf.* Acts 26:19, τῇ οὐρανίῳ ὀπτασίᾳ) is here contrasted with a more friendly dialogue ἐν ὁράματι (Acts 9:10). The 'vision within vision' element, Acts 9:12, is interwoven with the actual commissioning of Ananias, which is a 'journey within a journey' story, this superimposition of narrative structures being characteristic of Luke's style.

---

165 Aristotle, *On Interpretation*, 11.10-13: 'If therefore the dialectical question is a request for an answer, *i.e.* either for the admission of a premiss or for the admission of one of two contradictories', etc. (E. M. Edghill).
166 Lohfink, 'Darstellungsform', p. 256.
167 Lüdemann, *Early Christianity*, p. 110. For a criticism of Lohfink see Burchard, *Dreizehnte Zeuge*, p. 88.

The dialogue between Jesus and Ananias, as well, has a dialectic form (commission, v. 10; objection, v. 13; re-commission, v. 15). Not only is the double vision theme effective here, as often mentioned, but also the double dialogue plays a special role. Jesus is dramatically portrayed as a king, one who uses intermediaries, commissioners with a mission to heal and baptise future commissioners. Luke's *hodos* stories involve often such a high status emphasis, a high mimetic mode.

In both the Emmaus account and in that of Philip's evangelism the encounter with the stranger is narrated as a dramatic scene with a skilful introduction. Jesus introduces himself through a polite question, τίνες οἱ λόγοι οὗτοι οὓς ἀντιβάλλετε πρὸς ἀλλήλους περιπατοῦντες (Lk. 24:17). Philip intervenes and offers his help through an attractive wordplay (paronomasia), ἆρά γε γινώσκεις ἃ ἀναγινώσκεις- (Acts 8:30).[168] In admitting his need for guidance the Ethiopian uses a polite and polished Greek, πῶς γὰρ ἂν δυναίμην ἐὰν μή τις ὁδηγήσει με - (Acts 8:31), the only Lukan example of ἂν with the optative in the apodosis.[169] Moreover, the Ethiopian asks a specific theological question with a δέομαι σου (Acts 8:34) 'a polite way of introducing a request' (*cf*. Acts 21:39; Lk. 8:38; Gal. 4:12)'.[170]

Consequently, Philip starts to expound the Scriptures and proclaims Jesus, ἀρξάμενος ἀπὸ τῆς γραφῆς ταύτης εὐηγγελίσατο αὐτῷ τὸν Ἰησοῦν (Acts 8:35). The verb ἄρξομαι has the connotations of elevated debate; it can be found as an introduction to intellectual arguments (Plato, *Rep*. 596a5: 'Shall we then, start the inquiry at this point by our customary procedure?', βούλει οὖν ἐνθένδε ἀρξώμεθα ἐπισκοποῦντες, ἐκ τῆς εἰωθυίας μεθόδου;).

The rhetorical qualities of these explanations are again highlighted in Luke 24:32, where Jesus sets the disciples' hearts 'on fire' (οὐχὶ ἡ καρδία ἡμῶν καιομένη ἦν;). The two

---

168 Bruce remarks, as well, the literary use of ἆρά γε (*Acts*, p. 226).
169 In the NT koine the future indicative ὁδηγήσει tended to be used for the aorist subjunctive ὁδηγήσῃ, the classical construction (Bruce, *Acts*, p. 226). See also, on ὁδηγήσει, Schneider, *Apostelgeschichte*, vol. 1, p. 504, n. 48 (Jn. 16:13; *Wisdom*, 9:11, 10:10-17; *The Testament of Judah*, 14.1; 19.1; *The Testament of Gad*, 5.7; *Didache*, 3.2-6).
170 Bruce, *Acts*, p. 227.

disciples are 'convinced, delighted, and enabled to respond vigorously - for that is what καιομένη implies'.[171]

Part of Luke's mastery of diction (*lexis*) comes from his rhythmed alliterated constructions. One can find a higher frequency of rhythmical *clausulae* wherever Luke's compositional intervention is at work, and especially so in his speeches.[172] For example, the Emmaus account includes its memorable μεῖνον μεθ᾽ ἡμῶν | ὅτι πρὸς ἑσπέραν ἐστιν | καὶ κέκλικεν ἤδη ἡ ἡμέρα (Lk. 24:28; *cf.* the alliteration in η, ι and ν). Similar use of rhythm and even rhyme is present in Acts 9:6, ἀλλὰ ἀνάστηθι καὶ εἴσελθε εἰς τὴν πόλιν | καὶ λαληθήσεταί σοι ὅ τί σε δεῖ ποιεῖν, or in Acts 9:17, Σαοὺλ ἀδελφέ, ὁ κύριος ἀπέσταλκέν με | Ἰησοῦς ὁ ὀφθείς σοι ἐν τῇ ὁδῷ ᾗ ἤρχου | ὅπως ἀναβλέψῃς καὶ πλησθῇς πνεύματος ἁγίου.[173]

Luke uses good rhythm and balanced constructions in his dialogue scenes or speech sections and, usually, these constructions occur at the beginning of the dialogue, as part of the *captatio benevolentiae*. Apart from inevitable Semitisms (ᾗ ὄνομα Ἐμμαοῦς, Lk. 24:1; τὴν καλουμένην Εὐθεῖαν, Acts 9:11; or Ἀνάστηθι καὶ πορεύου, Acts 8:26, Ἀναστὰς πορεύθητι, Acts

---

171 Derrett, 'Walk', p. 189, *cf.* n. 28.
172 F. Siegert, 'Mass Communication', 42-58, esp. p. 50. See, Lk. 14:24 and 14:33; Acts 24:2-8. A more detailed analysis of Luke's prose rhythm could contextualise better his Hellenistic (we suggest, Asianist) style. Siegert notes that 'prose rhythm thus is one of the means for structuring texts which have been labelled "oral typesetting"' (Siegert, *op.cit.*, p. 48; see also H. v.D. Parunak, 'Oral Typesetting: Some uses of Biblical Structure', *Bib* 62 (1981), 153-69; F. Blass, *Die Rhythmen der asianischen und römischen Kunstprosa* (Leipzig: Deichert, 1905), etc.).
173 Rhythm and assonance amounting to rhyme can be found in other Lukan passages, as well, for example in Lk. 22:67-68. Knox notes that Luke presents Jesus' refusal in four short and well-balanced clauses: ἐὰν ὑμῖν εἴπω, | οὐ μὴ πιστεύσητε· ἐὰν δὲ ἐρωτήσω, | οὐ μὴ ἀποκριθῆτε. Another example is the language of the penitent thief in Luke 23:41. Luke breaks in v. 41 into 'fine Greek prose, with *good rhythm* [emph. mine] καὶ ἡμεῖς μὲν δικαίως, | ἄξια γὰρ ὧν ἐπράξαμεν ἀπολαμβάνομεν· | οὗτος δὲ οὐδὲν ἄτοπον ἔπραξεν, a contrast with μέν and δέ, a cretic with the last long syllables resolved to end the second clause, with a double assonance ἄξια, ἐπράξαμεν, and ἀπολαμβάνομεν, ἔπραξεν, and a cretic with both syllables resolved and a trochee to end the third clause' (Knox, *Some Hellenistic Elements*, pp. 10-11).

9:11), Luke's Greek constructs here an elevated atmosphere, well suited to this type of divine encounter.

RECOGNITION AND THE ARGUMENT FROM SCRIPTURE

The mimetic analysis of Luke's recognition has to do, as well, with the argument, or 'thought' (διανοία) of his representations. The issue is whether Luke builds a coherent argument at the level of the OT quotations in each story, and if there is detectable, noticeable development of his OT citations in this threefold series.

As a rule, the introduction of the stranger (*cf.* dialectical dialogue) is followed by an argument from Scripture which corrects an initial misinterpretation of the prophetic texts. If in the Emmaus' story the two disciples had the wrong messianic expectation, and if the Ethiopian does not understand the prophet Isaiah and this prompts the argument from Scripture and Prophets (*cf.* the use of γραφή, γραφαί in Lk. 24:27, 32 and Acts 8:32, 35; and of προφῆται, προφητῶν in Lk. 24:25, 27; Acts 8:28, 30, 34),[174] Saul's lack of understanding receives a different treatment, yet its characteristic lack of OT references has there a Christological significance.[175]

The OT Argument in the Emmaus Encounter

The recourse to Scripture in the Emmaus account is part of Luke's major motif of prophecy fulfilment.[176] There is a special correspondence between the OT emphases at the beginning and at the end of Luke's gospel, in this respect.[177] At the same time, the proclamation lines present in Jesus' exegesis in Luke 24:19b-27, are re-used in Acts 2:22-36; 3:13-26; 4:8-12; 5:29-32;

---

174 In Acts 8:34 the Ethiopian asks 'as the ideal non-Christian reader should but only the Christian reader can' (Conzelmann, *Acts*, p. 63). Luke's phrasing denotes hermeneutical skills (Zmijewski, *Apostelgeschichte*, p. 364).
175 Just, *Feast*, pp. 70-71.
176 Schubert, 'Structure', p. 176; Guillaume, *Luc interprète*, p. 78. *Cf.* D. L. Bock, 'The Use of the Old Testament in Luke-Acts: Christology and Mission', *SBL Sem. Pap.* (Atlanta, GA: Scholars), 1990, 494-511.
177 Robinson, 'Place', pp. 481-497; esp. p. 483; *cf.* Schubert, 'Structure', p. 179; Boismard, *Actes*, vol. 3, pp. 14-17.

10:36-43; 13:17-41.[178] In the Emmaus recognition scene Luke uses an implicit as well as an explicit type of proof-from-scripture argument, setting up a model for the other two stories.

In the Emmaus story Jesus' *direct* or *explicit* argument from prophecy is conducted *via* an emphatic mention of *all* of the OT scriptures (Lk. 24:25, ἐπὶ πᾶσιν οἷς ἐλάλησαν οἱ προφῆται, and Lk. 24:27, ἀρξάμενος ἀπὸ Μωϋσέως καὶ ἀπὸ πάντων τῶν προφητῶν... ἐν πάσαις ταῖς γραφαῖς). This repetition of the 'all' syntagm is not accidental, and has 'a polemical ring', with two major implications in reaffirming the authority of the OT.[179]

First, Luke points to the exhaustive nature of Jesus' messianic claim, and in this light 'it was Jewish ignorance that had caused the death of Christ'.[180] Then he addresses an encouragement to the Christians who, according to Ehrhardt 'in spite of being dissatisfied with the use of synagogal *testimonia* for the Messiah Jesus, refused to spiritualize, and eventually evaporate, the use of the Old Testament in the Church'.[181]

The Christological dialogue in the Emmaus story brings into focus as well the issue of what kind of Messiah Jesus was: 'a prophet mighty in deed and word before God and all the people' (Lk. 24:19), expected to bring redemption to Israel (λυτρόομαι, Lk. 24:21), an Exodus-like liberation.[182] Yet, while the Exodus motif was well rooted in the hopes of Palestinian and Hellenistic Jews in the first century AD one still needs to

---

178 Guillaume, *Luc interprète*, pp. 122-127.
179 Ehrhardt, 'Disciples', p. 188. Although Mt. 11:13 and Jn. 1:45 use a similar phrase ('all the prophets and the law', πάντες γὰρ οἱ προφῆται καὶ ὁ νόμος) 'this coupling of the *Tôrah* and the *Nebî'îm* is really Lucan in the NT' although the phrase occurs in Palestinian literature, as well (QS 1:3; 4QDibHam 3:12; 1QS 8:15-16; CD 5:21-6:1; 6QD 3:4 (Fitzmyer, *Luke X-XXIV*, p. 1567). For Bock the emphatic 'all' (ἐπὶ πᾶσιν) is an indication of 'much OT teaching on this' (Bock, *Luke 9:51-24:53*, p. 1916).
180 Ehrhardt, 'Disciples', p. 191.
181 Ehrhardt, 'Disciples', p. 192. For Ehrhardt the Emmaus account stands for a Lukan emphasis on 'the continuation of the Old Testament in the Catholic Church' (p. 193).
182 R. H. Fuller, *The Formation of the Resurrection Narratives* (London: SPCK, 1972), p. 110; Robinson, 'Place', pp. 481-497, 482; Moessner, *Lord*, p. 325.

ask whether Luke did not have in view here some other, more recent, yet also influential Septuagintal texts. According to the present study, the *implicit references* to the Scripture, i.e. LXX, in the Emmaus encounter are linked to the Maccabeean traditions, to their call for national independence and obedience to the Law. Luke 24 is related to Maccabeean literature in two main ways, both implicit: firstly, through its mention of 'Emmaus' as a site, involving its historical significance, and secondly through certain linguistic and theological correspondences.[183]

In the hypothesis of a Luke less acquainted with Palestine and more with the LXX, one could argue that his 'Emmaus' is the one placed in the valley of Ajalon, a witness of victorious Maccabeean battles (' Αμμαοῦς, in 1 Macc. 3:40, 57; 4:1-15; 9:50).[184]

---

183 For Lohfink, Dillon, McBride, and others, Emmaus is simply part of Jerusalem, a home of the two disciples, and thus, the significance of the journey fades away (Lohfink, *Himmelfahrt*, p. 264; McBride, *Emmaus*, p. 123). The whole incident would emphasize, then, the importance of Jerusalem (G. R. Osborne ('Resurrection', in J. B. Green, S. McKnight, and I. H. Marshall (eds.), *Dictionary of Jesus and the Gospels* (Leicester: Intervarsity, 1992), 673-688, pp. 681-683). If Emmaus is used for its own resonance, then Luke might well have thought of a special meaning, distinct from the desire to be just, simply, historically accurate.

184 As mentioned already, the most plausible sites for Emmaus are *Qalonieh* (30 stadia), *Qubeibeh* (63 stadia), *Amwas* (160 stadia). *Qalonieh* offers the best variant in terms of a distance that can be easily walked twice in 24 hours (Bock, *Luke 9:51-14:53*, p. 1908; Goulder, *Luke*, vol. 2, p. 784). *Qubeibeh*, a village seven-eight miles north-west of Jerusalem, is not attested in the early tradition but appears as 'Emmaus' in 'Privilegio di Baldovino', around AD 1114. The main argument in favour of *El-Qubeibeh* is its correspondence with the accepted ἑξήκοντα reading of 24:13 (McBride, *Emmaus*, p. 123). Wettstein, Griesbach, Nestlé, Aland, prefer the reading ἑξήκοντα in Lk. 24:13 (save A. Merk in *Novum Testamentum Graece et Latine*). The best attested variant, archaeologically, is *Amwas* ('Imwas, or Nicopolis), located at a distance of twenty miles from Jerusalem, 160 stadia (R. North and P. J. King, 'Biblical Archeology', in R. E. Brown, J. A. Fitzmyer, R. E. Murphy (eds.), *The New Jerome Biblical Commentary* (London: Chapman, 1993), 1196-1218; p. 1218). The place is supported by the ancient Palestinian tradition (ℵ K* Θ Π 079vid 1079* syrpal arm Eusebius Jerome Sozomen). See also the comprehensive analysis of the

This 'Emmaus' represented a strategic place in defending Jerusalem.[185] It was a fortress of similar importance on the west of Jerusalem as Jericho was on the east.[186] In the war of AD 70, the Roman legions finally converged on Jerusalem from Jericho and Emmaus.[187]

'Emmaus' thus, had a certain political resonance, related to victorious battles and returns to Jerusalem, to great military speeches. For example, the army of Judas the Maccabee camped at 'Emmaus' and he encouraged his troops there (1 Macc. 3:57-58). It is in this place that the Israelites remembered God's salvation at the Red Sea, μνήσθητε ὡς ἐσώθησαν οἱ πατέρες ἡμῶν ἐν θαλάσσῃ ἐρυθρᾷ (1 Macc. 4:9), and cried that God may 'favour us and remember his covenant with our fathers and crush this army before us today. Then all the Gentiles will know that *there is one who redeems and saves Israel*', καὶ γνώσονται πάντα τὰ ἔθνη ὅτι ἔστιν ὁ λυτρούμενος καὶ σῴζων τὸν Ἰσραήλ (1 Macc. 4:10-11, RSV). After victory they praised God for 'Israel had a great deliverance that day', ἐγενήθη σωτηρία μεγάλη τῷ Ἰσραήλ ἐν τῇ ἡμέρᾳ ἐκείνῃ (1 Macc. 4:24-26, RSV).[188]

There is a surprising linguistic correspondence between Luke 24:21 and 1 Macc. 4:10-11, pointing to the importance of

---

two major readings - σταδίους ἑξήκοντα (60 stadia) and ἕκατον ἑξήκοντα, in Guillaume, *Luc interprète*, pp. 97-98). Despite the distance from Jerusalem, Amwas still represents for an appreciable number of scholars the best choice for Emmaus (P. F.-M. Abel, *Les livres des Maccabées* (Paris: Gabalda, 1949); idem, *RB* 34 (1925), 347-367; equally so, Dalman, Bouwman, Finegan, Wanke - however, not Dillon, *Eyewitnesses*, p. 88, n. 51). Marshall accepts it, as well (Marshall, *Gospel*, p. 892).

185 J. A. Goldstein, *I Maccabees* (Garden City, NY: Doubleday, 1976), pp. 259-260; D. Bally, *The Geography of the Bible. A Study in Historical Geography* (London: Lutterworth, 1958, p. 145.
186 J. W. Hunkin, 'I & II Maccabees' (London: SPCK, 1928; pp. 126-158; esp. p. 138; Guillaume, *Luc interprète*, pp. 101-105.
187 Strabo, *Geography*, 16.2.40-41 (Ἰερικοῦς, cf. Goldstein, *I Maccabees*, pp. 265-266). He suggests that Judas and his men sang hymns beginning with 'Give thanks to unto the Lord', a formula used, for example, in 1 Chr. 16:8-36; 2 Chr. 20:21; Pss. 106, 107, 108, 136 (p. 265). The Davidic connotations are reminiscent of 1 Sam. 19:5; 2 Sam. 23:10, 12, and 1 Chr. 11:14 (p. 266).
188 Josephus, *Wars*, 6.1.6; 2.3.

the liberation theme ἡμεῖς δὲ ἠλπίζομεν ὅτι αὐτός ἐστιν ὁ μέλλων λυτροῦσθαι τὸν Ἰσραήλ (24:21), a Lukan phrase not paralleled in the rest of the NT. The two disciples' concept of redemption appears to be a political one, implying 'freedom from Roman tyranny through a "messianic" deliverer' (cf. Acts 7:35, where Moses is called 'ruler and deliverer', ἄρχοντα καὶ λυτρωτήν; the two disciples journeying to Emmaus were expecting an *alter* Moses after the model of Judas, the Maccabee).[189] The Emmaus setting with its implicit connotations helps Luke to highlight the contrast between Jesus and the Maccabeean messianic paradigms, supporting Jesus' argument from Scripture concerning his identity and messianic ministry (cf. Acts 21:28, as well).

OT Citation in the Ethiopian's 'On the Road' Encounter

Luke's argument in this *hodos* account is famous for its explicit mention of the prophet Isaiah (cf. Is. 53:7-8; Acts 8:32-33) and for identifying Jesus with the Servant.[190] It has been suggested that Luke associates the paschal theme of the sacrificed lamb with the baptism motif, strengthening the idea of restoration.[191]

Regarding the actual text, Boismard argues that the initial version of the story contained 27b, 28a, 29-31, 35-36a, 39a.e and that it mentioned the name of Isaiah only in Acts 8:30, where Philip hears the Ethiopian reading from the prophet's book. The repetition in Acts 8:28 and the actual passage in

---

189 Jesus is called ἀνὴρ προφήτης δυνατὸς ἐν ἔργῳ καὶ λόγῳ (v. 19) a Lukan phrase reminding of Luke 5:8, ἀνὴρ ἁμαρτωλός; Acts 6:5, Στέφανον, ἄνδρα πλήρης πίστεως καὶ πνεύματος ἁγίου; Acts 18:24, Ἀπολλῶς... ἀνὴρ λόγιος, δυνατὸς ὢν ἐν ταῖς γραφαῖς. Referring to Jesus as a 'prophet mighty in deed and word', the two disciples failed to remember the OT aspect of the messianic *rejection* (Just, Feast, p. 198; see also, Fitzmyer, *Luke X-XXIV*, p. 1564). Cleopas and his companion explain their hope to see Israel delivered from the Romans, based on both OT (Isa 41:14; 43:14; 44:22-24) and Maccabean history (1 Macc. 4:11; echoed in Pss. Sol. 9:1).
190 Luke uses this text to describe Jesus' life as that of a slaughtered lamb. This is the first explicit identification of the suffering Servant with Jesus in Acts, although the identification has already been implied in 3:13, 3:26; 4:27, 30 (see the discussion on παῖς, in Bruce, *Acts*, p. 227).
191 *Cf.* 1 Cor. 5:7. The cathecumens received baptism during the Passover night (Boismard, *Actes*, vol. 2, p. 182).

Acts 8:32-33, thus, would represent the intervention of the Lukan author proper (*cf.* Acts II).[192] This is an interesting hypothesis for according to it the same Luke who was fond of using OT prophecy has added the *hodos* emphases in vv. 39b, 36a, emphasizing thus the Isaianic motif of a New Exodus.[193]

Since this is a matter of implicit LXX allusions, one has to admit that the presence of other mentions of Isaiah, in Luke-Acts, favour the conclusion that Luke knew more of the context of this quotation. For example, he alludes to Isaiah 52:13 (the Servant's exaltation) in Acts 3:13 and he quotes Isaiah 53:12 in Luke 22:37 - as being fulfilled in the person of Jesus.[194]

It could be suggested in this context, although this is an argument 'from silence', that Luke quotes Isaiah in a context-sensitive manner, deliberately playing down the idea of the Servant's death for 'the sins of his people' for his quotation of Isaiah 53:7-8 ends short of Isaiah 53:8b, ἀπὸ τῶν ἀνομιῶν τοῦ λαοῦ μου ἤχθη εἰς θάνατον.[195] As Dillon remarks, Isaiah 53:7b-8c is 'cut off tantalizingly short of the Isaian Servant's death'

---

192 Boismard, *Actes,* vol. 2, pp. 179-182; vol. 3, pp. 121-126; vol. 1, *Introduction.*

193 Boismard, *Actes,* vol. 3, p. 122. The desert (αὕτη ἐστιν ἔρημος) characterises the road rather than the city for 'the road plays a more important part in the narrative than the city: If Philip had taken the wrong road... he would have missed the Ethiopian' (Bruce, *Acts,* p. 225; *cf.* Strabo, *Geography,* 16.2.30 concerning the city of Gaza, left desert when destroyed by Jannaeus: μένουσα ἔρημος). For Boismard, Luke (Acts II) has added the *hodos* setting in 8:26, modelling the testimony into a text which parallels Is. 53:1-10 (see *Actes,* vol. 2, pp. 179-182). The themes of Is. 35:1-10 (the symbolical images of the road, the desert, the water, and the motif of rejoicing) are present in the Emmaus story, as well (*Actes,* vol. 2, p. 180-181; the story of the Ethiopian has three mentions of *hodos* in 26, 36 and 39c, as does Is. 35:8). Isaiah stresses in particular that none of those journeying on the Holy Road through the desert would go astray, not even a fool (Is. 35:8).

194 Bruce, 'Philip and the Ethiopian', *JSS* 34 (1989), 377-387, esp. p. 382.

195 The hypothesis that Luke used a whole OT book as hermeneutical key for a citation has raised certain questions. Did the first century rabbis, for example, practice such an exegesis ? Juel implies a negative answer (D. Juel on Strauss, *Davidic Messiah,* p. 298). At the same time, if shorter sections were considered as specialised teaching on Messianic subjects, then would be need for further quotation, if the meaning was traditionally clear.

(Is. 53:8d), and 'such cropping is not accidental' (cf. the following, underligned text).[196]

Isaiah ⁵³⁶ πάντες ὡς πρόβατα ἐπλανήθημεν, ἄνθρωπος τῇ ὁδῷ αὐτοῦ ἐπλανήθη· καὶ κύριος παρέδωκεν αὐτὸν ταῖς ἁμαρτίαις ἡμῶν. ⁵³:⁷ Καὶ αὐτὸς διὰ τὸ κεκακῶσθαι οὐκ ἀνοίγει τὸ στόμα· <u>ὡς πρόβατον ἐπὶ σφαγὴν ἤχθη καὶ ὡς ἀμνὸς ἐναντίον τοῦ κείροντος αὐτὸν ἄφωνος οὕτως οὐκ ἀνοίγει τὸ στόμα αὐτοῦ.</u> ⁵³:⁸ <u>ἐν τῇ ταπεινώσει ἡ κρίσις αὐτοῦ ἤρθη· τὴν γενεὰν αὐτοῦ τίς διηγήσεται· ὅτι αἴρεται ἀπὸ τῆς γῆς ἡ ζωὴ αὐτοῦ, ἀπὸ</u> τῶν ἀνομιῶν τοῦ λαοῦ μου ἤχθη εἰς θάνατον.[197]

As A. George notes 'it is truly remarkable that Luc was able to find and quote from Is. 53. exactly that almost unique passage which speaks about the death of the Servant without mentioning its relation to the sins of the people'(cf. Is. 53:4, 6, 9-12 LXX).[198] Similarly, Dillon comments that 'Luke's "theology of the cross" does not include atonement for sins'.[199]

The usual interpretation of this omission is that Luke's theology of Jesus' death is rather a *theologia gloriae*, which interprets the death of Jesus as the prerequisite for Jesus' entrance into glory (see Lk. 24:26-27) and less of a *theologia crucis*, which sees Jesus' death as atonement or expiatory sacrifice for our sins (see Acts 20:28)'.[200]

---

196 Dillon, 'Acts of the Apostles', in R. E. Brown, J. A. Fitzmyer, R. E. Murphy (eds.), *The New Jerome Biblical Commentary* (London: Chapman, 1993), 722-767, p. 743. A. George notes, as well, that 'il est frappant qu'il [Luke] ne reproduise pas le dernier stique d'Isa. 53:8' (*Études*, p. 195).
197 If the initial account included only vv. 27b, 28a, 29-31, 35-36a, 39a (Boismard, *Actes*, vol. 2, pp. 179-182; vol. 3, pp. 121-126) then Luke's citation introduces selectively Is. 53:6b-7. Luke's text, underligned, allows a less emphatic view on atonement doubled by increased universalism.
198 George, *Études*, p. 195.
199 Dillon, 'Acts', p. 743; cf. G. Voss, *Die Christologie der lukanischen Schriften in Grundzuegen* (Bruges: Brouwer, 1965), p. 130.
200 Cf. J.H. Neyrey, *The Passion According to Luke: A Redaction Study of Luke's Soteriology* (Toronto: Paulist, 1985), p. 213, n. 3. Käsemann argued in favour of a Lukan *theology of glory* (*Essays on New Testament Themes* (Philadelphia, PA: Fortress, 1964), pp. 92-93), while Barrett defended the presence of a *theologia crucis* ('Theologia Crucis - in Acts?', in C. Andersen, *Theologia Crucis-Signum Crucis* (Tübingen: Mohr, 1979), 73-84; cf. K. Löning, 'The Circle of Stephen and Its

However, Luke's omission of the prophet's 'death for sins' (*cf.* Is. 53:5, 8b) can be related to his known universalistic perspective on the Gospel. Had Luke continued the quotation with the Isaianic τοῦ λαοῦ μου (Is. 53:8b) or had he started it earlier with ἄνθρωπος τῇ ὁδῷ αὐτοῦ ἐπλανήθη· καὶ κύριος παρέδωκεν αὐτὸν ταῖς ἁμαρτίαις ἡμῶν (Is. 53:6), the emphasis would have unfortunately fallen on the prophet's message for his own Jewish people. As things are, the focus is on Jesus' messianic identity, and on the Ethiopian's access to its universal benefits.[201]

By avoiding to mention the specific address to Israel, λαοῦ μου, and her wanderings (τῇ ὁδῷ... ἐπλανήθη) Luke's argument maintains a cautious ambiguity (the unity of 'thought', *cf.* Aristotle's διανοία). He keeps the Way as a positive symbol,[202] and prepares its later use in the singular in the commissioning

---

Mission', in J. Becker (ed.), *Christian Beginnings: Word and Community from Jesus to Post-Apostolic Times* (Louisville, KY: Knox, 1993), 103-131, p. 112). For a general discussion of the issue, see W. G. Kümmel, 'Luc en Accusation dans la Théologie Contemporaire', in F. Neirynck (ed.), *L'Évangile de Luc* (Leuven: Leuven UP, 1989), 93-109; Conzelmann, *Luke*, p. 201; D. E. Aune, 'Greco-Roman Biography', in D. E. Aune (ed.), *Greco-Roman Literature and the New Testament* (Atlanta, GA: Scholars, 1988), 107-126; F. Bovon, *Luc le Théologien: Vingt-cinq ans de recherches (1950-1975)* (Paris: Delachaux, 1988), pp. 175-181. Recently, D. Ravens has argued that a pro-Jewish Luke saw "repentance" as an available and sufficient means for the salvation of the Jews (μετάνοιαν εἰς ἄφεσιν ἁμαρτιῶν, Lk. 3:3, 24:47* Acts 2:38, 5:31), and, hence, he could not emphasize Jesus' death as atonement (*Restoration*, chapters four and five).

201 According to a positive interpretation of αἴρεται (Acts 8:33; *cf.* W. Radl, 'αἴρω', *EDNT*, vol. 1, p. 41), it can mean 'lift up', 'carry', 'take' (*vs.* negative connotations, as in 'remove', or 'destruction', 'death', *cf.* Lk. 23:18). Therefore, after his suffering the Servant is exalted or vindicated, 'lifted up', as a reference to Jesus' ascension - Lk. 24:51; Acts 1:2, 9-11 (Spencer, *Philip*, p. 176; D. Juel, *Messianic Exegesis: Christological Interpretation of the Old Testament in Early Christianity* (Philadelphia, PA: Fortress, 1988), p. 128). In this case, the Ethiopian eunuch goes through a status transformation in his union with Christ 'from a marginal God-fearer to a full-rights member of the people of God' (Spencer, 'Ethiopian', p. 161).

202 *Cf.* Luke's Christological emphasis in editing Mark's Feeding Miracle, and his eschatological challenge in relation to Matthew's (Q's) parable of the Two Ways.

of Saul (cf. Acts 9:2, etc.). The offence of having already described an Ethiopian *eunuch* who is received into the people of God seemed sufficiently challenging for the moment; there was no need to accuse the whole Israel of wandering (ἐπλανήθη).

The Implicit Argument From Scripture in Saul's Encounter
Characteristic of Saul's *hodos* encounter is the fact that Luke uses no obvious quotation of Scriptures. This comes as a surprise, since he later mentions the prophets, even if laconically, in Peter's evangelism of Cornelius (Acts 10:43, πάντες οἱ προφῆται μαρτυροῦσιν ἄφεσιν ἁμαρτιῶν λαβεῖν διὰ τοῦ ὀνόματος αὐτοῦ). In the *hodos* series, therefore, Saul's encounter 'on the road' represents an anti-climax of Luke's explicit references to OT. There are, apparently, two possible explanations for such an omission (a) Luke did not want to interfere with the original lack of OT references; or (b) Luke had here a different theological emphasis (he tells the story three times emphasizing Saul's commission and the need for a Gentile mission). The story, however, makes use, arguably, of OT *implicit* references. On the one hand, such an OT allusion is already part of Luke's style; on the other hand, the Pauline source itself seems to have encouraged it (cf. Rom. 2:1, Phil. 3:5).

A first reflection of OT style can be found in the *double calling*, the Hebrew Σαοὺλ Σαούλ (Acts 9:4).[203] Saul's counter-question acknowledges the special divine character of his interlocutor (Τίς εἶ, κύριε; Acts 9:5).[204]

The recent emphasis in Lukan studies on Davidic Christology,[205] allows, furthermore, to reconsider here an older theory regarding the possibility of a second LXX allusion. As early as 1932, H. Windisch has noted the possibility of an implicit narrative connection between Saul, the persecutor of

---

203 Lohfink, *Conversion*, pp. 61-64, 72. Jesus commissions like the OT Yahweh, ἀνάστηθι καὶ εἴσελθε, cf. Jonah 1:1; 3:1. This language, yet, was at the same time characteristic of the first century preaching (Munck, *Paul*, p. 29; idem, *Acts*, p. 82; Hedrick, 'Paul's Conversion / Call', pp. 415-432).
204 Barrett, *Acts*, vol. 1, p. 450.
205 Cf. Strauss, *Messiah*; C. Burger, *Jesus als Davidssohn: eine traditiongeschichtliche Untersuchung* (Göttingen: Vandenhoeck, 1970).

the Messiah, and Saul, the late king of Israel, the persecutor of David, the future king.²⁰⁶

Following Windisch's argument, one can suggest that from the perspective of Luke's *hodos* paradigm Acts 9 and 1 Sam. 24 are related through a number of relevant correspondences. Both stories emphasize the *hodos setting* (ἐπὶ τῆς ὁδοῦ, 1 Sam. 24:4 [LXX]; and καὶ ἀνέστη Σαουλ καὶ κατέβη εἰς τὴν ὁδόν, 1 Sam. 24:8 [LXX]). Both stories involve a *persecution dialogue*, David's call stops king Saul from pursuing him (*cf.* Jesus' call stops Saul's journeying). Both stories involve the pursuing of a righteous hero, the throne-inheritor (διώκεις - καταδιώκεις). David's question to Saul raises the issue of persecution and murder: καὶ νῦν ὀπίσω τίνος σὺ ἐκπορεύῃ, βασιλεῦ Ἰσραήλ - ὀπίσω τίνος καταδιώκεις σύ; (1 Sam. 24:15 [LXX]). A similar question is addressed later, ἵνα τί τοῦτο καταδιώκει ὁ κύριός μου ὀπίσω τοῦ δούλου αὐτοῦ (1 Sam. 26:18 [LXX]).

To this persecution dialogue one could add the issue of the proverb mentioned in Acts 9:5-6 (*cf.* Acts 26:14, 'It hurts you to kick against the goads', NRS). The closest Jewish parallel seems to be *Pss. Sol.* 16:4: 'he jabbed me as a horse is goaded to keep it awake, my saviour and protector at all times saved me'.²⁰⁷ and generally, this Lukan saying is seen as a puzzling Greek-sounding proverb,²⁰⁸ completely lacking in Hebrew and Aramaic parallels.²⁰⁹ The general assumption is that Luke (or Paul) added this saying because they wanted to suit the speech to a royal audience and highlight the divine constraint of the commissioning.²¹⁰

---

206 Windisch, 'Christusepiphanie', p. 20, argues in favour of such a parallel between Paul and king Saul. A Davidic parallel is rather implicit here than explicit.
207 R. B. Wright (tr.), in J. H. Charlesworth (ed.), *The OT Pseudepigrapha*, vol. 2, p. 665.
208 Euripides, *Bacchanals*, 794: πρὸς κέντρα λακτίζοιμι θνητὸς ὢν θεῷ (...kick against the pricks, man raging against God).
209 Lohfink, *Conversion*, p. 77. For B. Witherington the proverb reflects 'a *Greek*, not Jewish, idiom, and it meant "It is fruitless to struggle against God, or against one's destiny"' (Witherington, 'Editing the Good News: some synoptic lessons for the study of Acts', in B. Witherington, III (ed.), *History, Literature*, 324-347, p. 341; *cf.* A. Vogeli, 'Lukas und Euripides', *TZ* 9 (1953), pp. 415-438).
210 Witherington, 'Editing', p. 341.

It would be interesting to note that there is a long tradition for quoting proverbs in a debate or persecution dialogue. The first parallel is David's quotations in front of Saul 'as the ancient proverb says, "Out of the wicked comes forth wickedness"'(NRSV) (1 Sam. 24:14), or 'he has come out to seek my life, like one who hunts a partridge in the mountains', (1 Sam. 26:20). One could mention other OT parallels, such as Jotham's address to the people of Shechem (Judg. 9:1-21), etc. The problem, however, is that the parable is not part of Acts 9, it has been translated and introduced here, by Erasmus, from Acts 26:14 (Basel, 1516).[211]

This recognition dialogue with its allusions to the royal persecution narratives in the LXX would help a Jewish reader to perceive the Davidic character of Jesus. It makes room, also, for Luke's emphasis that the ascended Jesus uses his 'divine voice' and substitutes himself for the authority and message of the OT Scriptures. Jesus is a Yahweh-like royal figure who commissions Ananias and Saul, who utters prophecies about the fate of his servant in the same way in which the OT Scriptures prophesied about him, concerning his suffering and exaltation.

The adversative ἀλλά (Acts 9:6) announces a definitive break in the course of Saul's life,[212] and the command to rise up (ἀνάστηθι) and to wait to be told what he is expected to do, λαληθήσεταί σοι ὅ τί σε δεῖ ποιεῖν, has its counterpart in the declaration of Acts 9:15-16 σκεῦος ἐκλογῆς ἐστίν... ἐγὼ γὰρ ὑποδείξω αὐτῷ ὅσα δεῖ αὐτὸν ὑπὲρ τοῦ ὀνόματός μου παθεῖν. Thus, δεῖ ποιεῖν and δεῖ παθεῖν prefigure prophetically Saul's new destiny and express, as well, Jesus' divine authority.

The contrast between the implicit and explicit use of LXX is important as an intra-paradigmatic variation, in the context of Luke's *hodos* encounters. Luke uses the paradigm to emphasize the idea of a divinely guided Christianity, in continuing development and progress.

---

211 Metzger, *Textual Commentary*, p. 362.
212 Barrett, *Acts*, vol. 1, p. 451; he paraphrases 'you have been persecuting me, but that is to end now'. N. Turner, however, would not stress as much the adversative meaning as the connective one (Turner, in J. H. Moulton (ed.), *A Grammar of New Testament Greek*, vol. 3 'Syntax' (Edinburgh: T&T Clark, 1963), p. 330).

Thus, one can note here a series of fine similarities and distinctions. The resurrected Jesus uses the OT argument in the Emmaus story in a way similar to his earlier earthly ministry. Philip follows Jesus' example and presents the gospel with a similar emphasis on the OT (Lk. 24:27, Acts 8:34; Lk. 24:27, 32, Acts 8:35; Lk. 24:27, Acts 8:35), and Saul, after his conversion, proved as well from Scriptures that Jesus is the son of God (Acts 9:20; 22; 27, 28). However, Jesus' relation to the OT is changed after his Ascension. If before the Ascension, the risen Jesus refers back to the authority of the Scriptures, in Emmaus, in Saul's story the voice of the ascended Jesus speaks with the full authority of the word of God.

This internalisation or personalization of the meaning of proofs-from-prophecy shows that Luke allows for a certain gradual change in his theological emphases. A high Christology gradually takes control over the story, as it did over history, as well, and the hodos encounters are witnesses to this transformation.

RECOGNITION, *PATHOS* AND MIMETIC CHARACTERS

Apart from recognition as a plot element of major importance, it can be argued that Luke's mimetic representation of his *hodos* encounters also includes the *motif of suffering*. Quite a number of NT scholars have noted the presence of recognition in Luke's *hodos* encounters, yet the background of these stories is dominated by the presence of a suffering motif, in Aristotelian sense, taking the form of Jesus' supreme sacrifice at the Passover, of the Eunuch's physical disability, and of Saul's persecution and malice. Over against this background Luke's characters have to take ethical and faith-related decisions.

Story Characters and Their Ethical Choices

The issue of *ethical choice* is one of Luke's characteristic emphases in his short journey stories. It can be noted, for example, in the parable of the Good Samaritan, where he takes the decision to interrupt his journey and help a fellow human in need. The young man in the parable of the Prodigal Son takes a fundamental decision to return home and ask for his father's forgiveness. Similarly, Zacchaeus decides to do everything in his power to see Jesus, and then he gives away half of his wealth as a sign of his restoration. This emphasis is reminiscent, also, of the 'way' as a special setting for ethical challenges in Hellenistic literature (*cf.* the parable of Heracles at the crossroads, and the *Cynic Epistles*, in chapters two and three).

Similarly, when the two disciples journeying on the Emmaus road meet a divine Jesus in disguise, they soon find themselves before a decision to reconsider the Scriptures in a new way. Later, their insistence that Jesus would stay with them is clearly the result of a positive decision concerning his interpretation of the prophets.

This positive thrust has a comedy-related tendency, in contrast to Greek tragedy, and is closer to the style of the Hellenistic novels. Luke's characters do not sink to the depth of misfortune and disbelief, as a result of their fatal 'flaw' (ἁμαρτία). They are restored through their interaction with the risen Jesus. The 'blinding' of the two disciples on the Emmaus road does not imply a fatal course on their actions, like Hera's madness descending on Heracles, or like Oedip's murder. Luke's stories could better be described as reversed 'could-have-been' tragedies.[213]

The Ethiopian is also given a choice: to accept or not the help of a stranger who could explain the Scriptures to him; and later, to ask or not for baptism. In both situations, he meets the challenge and he experiences a transformation of status and a change in destiny..

The most dramatic situation, however, is that of Saul. He is almost forced to surrender, the Lord leaves so little room for choice. Is the main theme of his story the punishment of a persecutor (*cf.* the story of Heliodorus, 2 Macc. 3:1-40) or the call of a future missionary? According to our *hodos* paradigm, this brings together three different episodes (1. the encounter, Acts 9:1-9; 2. the reversal of life and ministry at Damascus, Acts 9:10-25; and 3. the reiteration of the reversal at

---

213 See, for example, Hedrick, *Parables*, pp. 54-55, on Via's discussion of comedy: the 'low mimetic realistic tragedy' moves downward toward loss and catastrophe, and the 'low mimetic realistic comedy' moves upward toward happy-ending and prosperity. Golden notes that the double plot of comedy involves the rewarding of the good and the punishment of the bad, in other words restoration and justice (Golden, *Tragic and Comic Mimesis*, p. 92).

Jerusalem, Acts 9:26-31), the theme of reversal and restoration has precedence over that of punishment. Saul's 'on the road' experience leads him to an ethical, theological choice as well: he rises and is baptised, ἀναστὰς ἐβαπτίσθη (Acts 9:18), and then preaches Jesus' name in Damascus and in Jerusalem, ready for the forthcoming mission.

If Luke emphasizes the happy ending of his *hodos* encounters, one can ask further whether his characters are 'appropriate' and 'credible' (see chapter two, on Aristotle). Here, Luke's ethnographic and historical details contribute considerably to the portrait of his main characters. The contextualisation of the two disciples (name: Cleopas, journey to Emmaus, time of day: evening, date: the third day from Jesus' crucifixion), or of the eunuch (Ethiopian, from queen Candace's court, treasurer, journeying on the road down to Gaza, using a chariot, reading aloud), or of Saul's story (letters from priests, continuation of persecution, mention of Jerusalem and of Damascus, the street called Straight, the house of Judah, Saul by name, Ananias, Barnabas, etc.) all present them as perfectly contextualised, credible personages, living in a Hellenistic Palestine.

According to our mimetic model, however, there is another character in the story: the Lord himself. His presence does not surprise the reader in the same way it surprises the actual heroes of Luke's accounts. He is a sort of extradiegetic character: he comes into the story and leaves, at will, in these post-Easter encounters, and even the narrator is not able to justify the movements of this character. Hence, a certain feeling of mystery accompanies these accounts and creates a reaction of awe. Philip acts according to the same paradigm, his role being an extradiegetic one: he approaches the Ethiopian unexpectedly to the Ethiopian (yet, the reader knows already the details of this visit), akin to an appearance, he disappears suddenly (in contrast to the Ethiopian, the reader learns about Philip's final destination). This correspondence between Jesus' and Philip's actions, as extradiegetical characters, strengthens the view that Luke pays attention here to a special narrative paradigm.

The Emmaus Encounter and Jesus' Suffering

In the Emmaus account the suffering motif can be mentioned mainly in relation to Jesus' Passion. For Luke this passion is divinely ordained, part of God's plan of salvation (ἔδει παθεῖν τὸν Χριστόν; Lk. 24:25-27),[214] as a preliminary stage before the glorification of the Messiah.[215] It is remarkable, in this context, that God's will or plan (ἡ βουλή τοῦ θεοῦ) is used by Luke 'similarly to the way Hellenistic historians speak of a divine principle of order or fate' (such as τύχη, εἱμαρμενη, γνώμη, ἀνάγκη).[216]

However, next to these themes in the background of this story, one notes also the disciples' suffering, as well, as they are troubled at the thought of Jesus' definitive death. This suffering is dramatically highlighted by theatrical details, for Luke presents the disciples stopping and looking sad, 'long faced', ἐστάθησαν σκυθρωποί (Lk. 24:17).

For Luke, however, Christ's suffering was not only a historical reality and a good dramatical detail to mention, but also an opportunity to discuss the increasingly more debated issue of the death of the wise. In an age when Socrates asserts that 'those who pursue philosophy aright study nothing but dying and being dead',[217] when Plato accepts voluntary death in certain conditions,[218] and when Seneca's famous *70th*

---

214 Tannehill, *Narrative*, vol. 1, p. 284. *Cf.* E. Tiedke and H.-G. Link, 'δεῖ', *NIDNTT* vol. 2, 664-666; R. Morgenthaler, 'ἀνάγκη', *NIDNTT* vol. 2, 663-664. For C. H. Cosgrove 'Δεῖ is therefore a typical Lukan vehicle for describing the necessity that God's plan, as expressed in Scripture, be fulfilled' ('The Divine Δεῖ in Luke-Acts. Investigations into the Lukan Understanding of God's Providence', *NovT* 2 (1984), pp. 168-191, esp. p. 174; see also, Moessner, 'The "script" of the Scriptures in Acts: suffering as God's plan (βουλή) for the world for the "release of sins"', in B. Witherington III (ed.), *History, Literature*, 218-250).
215 Ehrhardt, 'Disciples', p. 188.
216 Moessner, 'Script', pp. 221-222.
217 Plato, *Phaedo*, 64a.7-8; *cf.* J. A. Droge and J. D. Tabor, *A Noble Death: Suicide and Martyrdom Among Christians and Jews in Antiquity* (San Francisco, CA: Harper, 1992), pp. 20, 21; D. E. Aune, 'Human Nature and Ethics in Hellenistic Philosophical Traditions and Paul: Some Issues and Problems', in T. Engberg-Pedersen (ed.), *Paul in His Hellenistic Context* (Edinburgh: T&T Clark, 1944, 291-312.
218 Plato, *Laws*, 873c. According to this discussion of principles, death is acceptable to Plato if God allows times of necessity or compulsion (*anangke*): (a) at the *polis*' orders; (b) during a calamity (suffering); and (c) in a shameful situation (Droge and Tabor, *Noble Death*, p. 22).

Epistle is a panegyric to the freedom of death,[219] and the deaths of Socrates and of Cato of Utica (95-46 BC) were particularly influential as models,[220] Luke's *hodos* encounters made good literature and interesting philosophy with their discussion of Jesus' suffering. For, even if Jesus' death becomes a model for persecuted Christians (*cf.* Stephen, Acts 7; Paul's journey to Jerusalem, Acts 20:7ff.), the force of the model resides in the continuation of life in a heavenly place, through resurrection, not in a reason for voluntary death (*cf.* the impact of this teaching in Athens, Acts 17:31-32).[221]

As a literary technique, this contrast between Jesus' death and the discovery of his resurrection draws its force from a series of logical pairs of intense dramatism, such as journey and teaching *versus* meal and revelation, argument about the

---

219 *Cf.* 'the wise man will live as long as he ought, not as long as he can', Seneca, *Epistle*, 70.4-5; *cf. Epistle*, 17.9; 77.5-20. Condemned by Nero in the spring of AD 65, Seneca died of his own hand 'voluntariam mortem' (Tacitus, *Annals*, 15.60-64; Cassius Dio, *Roman History*, 62.25). However, as Tacitus remarked on the forced suicide of Asiaticus (during the reign of Claudius, AD 47), his freedom consisted only of the *means* of his death (Tacitus, *Annals*, 11.3; *cf.* Droge and Tabor, *Noble Death*, p. 29).

220 One can even speak about a *fascination with death* of the Greco-Roman culture in the first century AD, prompted by the aura of voluntary death in legend and in life, by an admiration for theatrical gestures, and by a disregard of the physical body (*cf.* A. D. Nock, *Conversion: the old and the new in religion from Alexander the Great to Augustine of Hippo* (Oxford: Clarendon, 1933, p. 198). For example, Cicero admired the self-inflicted death of Seneca (Cicero, *Tusculan Disputations*, I.40-42). Similarly, Cato decided to fall in his sword after a night of reading Plato's *Phaedo* (Plutarch, *Cato the Younger*, 70.1.2-6.9; *cf.* Droge and Tabor, *Noble Death*, p. 29). According to Cicero, 'Cato departed from life with a feeling of joy in having found a reason for death (*ut causam moriendi*) [...] For the whole life of the philosopher, as the same wise man says, is a preparation for death (*commentation mortis est*)' (*Tusculan Disputations*, I.30.74.1-12). The list of Greek personalities who chose to inflict death on themselves, in various manners, is considerably longer (Droge and Tabor, p. 29).

221 C. H. Talbert argued that Luke presents Jesus as a moral model or martyr ('Martyrdom in Luke-Acts and the Lukan Social Ethic', in R. J. Cassidy (ed.), *Political Issues in Luke-Acts* (Maryknoll, NY: Orbis, 1983), pp. 99-110; and in 'The Way of the Lukan Jesus: Dimensions of Spirituality', *PRS* 8 (1982), 237-249.

significance of death *versus* the experience of resurrected life, non-recognition *versus* recognition, and the joy of understanding Jesus' identity energises the disciples with that superhuman strength to journey back to Jerusalem, on the same night.

Philip's Encounter: Suffering Prophet and Rejoicing Eunuch
In the second example, Luke portrays the Ethiopian as one uncertain to whom the prophet was referring in Isaiah 53:7-8, where the servant of the Lord is said to be taken to the slaughter like a lamb (ὡς πρόβατον ἐπισφαγὴν ἤχθη), and made to suffer the humiliation of injustice (ἐν τῇ ταπεινώσει [αὐτοῦ] ἡ κρίσις αὐτοῦ ἤρθη).[222]
The πάθος motif seems to be expressed here in two different, yet convergent ways. First, Luke quotes Isaiah in a context-sensitive manner, playing down the Servant's death for the 'sins of his people'.[223] As Bruce observed, in the Ethiopian's story one could deduce 'a theology of suffering, possibly of redemptive suffering, but hardly of vicarious suffering'.[224]

---

222 Spencer, 'Ethiopian', p. 158. As mentioned, αἴρω could mean 'eliminated', 'removed' or 'taken up', 'lifted' or 'raised' in the positive sense of reward, of glorification, vindication or reinstatement. In his monograph, Spencer stresses that ὅτι αἴρεται ἀπὸ τῆς γῆς ἡ ζωὴ αὐτοῦ (Acts 8:33) 'calls to mind the peculiarly Lukan account of Jesus' ascension into heaven' (Lk. 24:51; Acts 1:2, 9-11; *Philip*, p. 176; *cf.* Juel, *Messianic Exegesis*, p. 128). However, in an earlier article, Spencer suggested, plausibly, that Luke implies an Eunuch-specific reading of the Isaiah passage, so that τὴν γενεὰν αὐτοῦ τίς διηγήσεται was understood by the Ethiopian as a denied procreation ('Ethiopian', p. 158). If, however, the connotations of *genea* are positive instead of negative, expressing *exultation* not *lamentation*, then the text may refer to the Ethiopian's joy at being included in the people of God, as a result of Jesus' exaltation (*Philip*, pp. 178-180; Roloff, *Apostelgeschichte*, p. 141; Haenchen, *Acts*, p. 312; E. Kränkl, *Jesus der Knecht Gottes* (Regensburg: Pustet, 1972), p. 115).
223 Dillon, 'Acts', p. 743; George, *Études*, p. 195.
224 Bruce, *Acts*, p. 382. Marshall sums up this view of Luke noting that 'In the Servant... we see the supreme case of a person who goes to suffering by the will of God and is subsequently vindicated by God... there is no evidence that he has positively evaluated the Servant concept in terms of redemptive suffering' (Marshall, *Luke, Historian*, p. 172).

Secondly, the Ethiopian can identify himself with the suffering and the shame of the Prophet, not only from a universal perspective but from the perspective of his impairment, as well (this is one of the ways mimesis functions). If εὐνοῦχος in Acts 8:27 refers to physical impairment, then the Isaiah pericope read by the Ethiopian (Is. 53:7-8, in Acts 8:32-33) provides a further illustration of suffering, πάθος, which overlaps with the suffering characteristic of the prophet.

Spencer argues consistently that Luke replaced the emphasis on the servant's death and on its atoning efficacy by 'highlighting instead the element of ταπεινώσεις (vv. 7-8a)',[225] with its negative connotations of 'oppression', 'degradation', 'humiliation' and 'debasement'.[226] A reading that accepts castration among the connotations of the Ethiopian's story corresponds well with the honour and shame code of the first-century Mediterranean culture, and with the suffering message of Isaiah 53.[227] Physiological masculinity was related to male social identity and reputation.[228] The Eunuch finally gains a positive perspective on life by being given a new

---

225 Spencer, *Philip*, p. 175.
226 R. Leivestad, 'Ταπεινός-ταπεινόφρων', *NovT* 8 (1966), 36-47. Leivestad argues that ταπεινώσεις had a secular negative meaning - humiliation as debasement, not a positive and theological one (humility or meekness) as in the later forms of ταπεινός and ταπεινόφρων.
227 For Spencer and others, Luke is 'patently immersed in the honor / shame culture of his day' ('Ethiopian', p. 158). See also, D. B. Gowler, 'Characterization in Luke: A Socio-Narratological Approach', *BTB* 19 (1989), 54-62, 1989, esp. pp. 58-60.
228 D. D. Gilmore, 'Introduction: the Shame of Dishonor', in D. D. Gilmore (ed.), *Honor and Shame and the Unity of the Mediterranean* (Washington, DC: American Anthropological Association, 1987), 2-21, p.10; B. J. Malina, *The New Testament World: Insights from Cultural Anthropology* (Atlanta, GA: John Knox, 1981), pp. 25-50; D. Daube, 'Shame Culture in Luke', in M. D. Hooker and S. G. Wilson (eds.), *Paul and Paulinism: Essays in Honor of C. K. Barrett* (London: SPCK, 1982), 355-372.

Saul, the Persecutor, and the Suffering of Christians

status, i.e., a place in the new people of God.[229] These positive endings are characteristic of Luke.[230]

Perhaps the most dramatic, theatrical expression of the suffering motif in Luke's *hodos* encounters, an essential part of Luke's mimesis of persecution, is to be found in the account of Saul's encounter with the risen Christ. The correspondence with Aristotle's views is striking, since he says that 'tragedy must seek... cases where the sufferings occur within relationships, such as brother and brother... when the one kills (or is about to kill) the other'.[231]

The suffering motif is present, first, implicitly, in the background, since the reader is already informed about Stephen's death assisted by Saul (Acts 7:58, 8:1). Acts 8:3 is echoed and enhanced by Acts 9:1. In this way events from without the encounter proper participate in the general motif of suffering. This is reminiscent of the way 'complication' (τὸ δέσις) works, comprising 'events outside the play, and often some of those within it'.[232]

The encounter continues with an explicit reference to suffering in Luke's straightforward statement regarding Saul's threat to Christians, ὁ δὲ Σαῦλος ἔτι ἐμπνέων ἀπειλῆς καὶ φόνου. The accusation is reiterated by Ananias' response to Jesus, Acts 9:13, ὅσα κακὰ τοῖς ἁγίοις σου ἐποίησεν ἐν Ἰερουσαλήμ. The suffering inflicted by Paul on his fellow Jews (Israelite brothers) reaches a climax in Jesus' accusation of Paul, where he identifies himself with the persecuted ones,

---

229 Lindijer, 'Creative', p. 80.
230 *Cf.* Haenchen, in Schneider, *Apostelgeschichte*, vol. 1, p. 508, n. 91, on χαίρων (Lk. 15:5; 19:6; Col 2:5. *Cf.* χαίροντες, in Lk. 19:37; Acts 5:41; Rom. 12:12; 1 Cor. 7:30; 2 Cor. 6:10).
231 Aristotle, *Poetics*, 1453b.15-20.
232 Aristotle, *Poetics*, 1455b.25-30.
233 Klein, *Zwölf Apostel*, pp. 114-144. In a detailed exegesis of Paul's violent persecution, Klein argues that Luke 'spotlights' Paul as one who 'does to his victims the worst that one man can do to another' (p. 126). If so, the purpose of Luke's portrait is a tendentious 'degradation' of Paul's ministry in his earlier years (p. 144). Wilson offers a comprehensive critique of this view, disagreeing with Klein's exaggerated contrast between Paul's and Luke's reconstruction of his earlier years (*Gentiles*, pp. 157-160).

τί με διώκεις, and Ἰησοῦς, ὃν σὺ διώκεις (Acts 9:4-5). Conversion and change seem not enough to absolve Saul of his guilt: the disciples continued to be afraid of him, πάντες ἐφοβοῦντο αὐτὸν μὴ πιστεύοντες ὅτι ἐστιν μαθητής (Acts 9:27).

The motif of suffering is, then, present in Paul's personal life. The first reference would be his blindness, and later in the text, Jesus announces Saul of further future suffering as a missionary, Acts 9:16, ὅσα δεῖ αὐτὸν... παθεῖν (cf. Acts 9:6, δεῖ ποιεῖν). Further, Saul is in danger of being killed by the Jews in Damascus for his preaching (Acts 9:23, ἀνελεῖν) and, when he escapes to Jerusalem, he again is in danger of being killed by the Jews in Jerusalem (ἀνελεῖν, Acts 9:28). In Acts 9:1-31 the rich lexical variety of the journey motif is matched by the lexical variety of the threat and suffering motif: ἐμπνέων ἀπειλῆς and φόνου (v. 1), δεδεμένους ἀγάγῃ (vv. 2, 21), διώκεις (v. 5), οὐδὲν ἔβλεπεν (v. 8), μὴ βλέπων, καὶ οὐκ ἔφαγεν οὐδὲν ἔπιεν (v. 9), ὅσα κακὰ... ἐποίησεν (v. 13), παθεῖν (v. 16), πορθήσας (v. 21), ἀνελεῖν (v. 23, 29), ἀνέλωσιν (v. 24), ἐφοβοῦντο αὐτὸν (v. 26).

The Reversal and Restoration Act

One should note the simultaneous presence of reversals (περιπέτεια) and recognition (ἀναγνώρισις) as characteristic of the superior type of plot, the complex one, in Aristotle's terms, which provides a solid foundation for the overturn of fortune (μετάβασις) between prosperity and adversity.[234] In fact, this narrative transformation has a reverse nature in Luke's paradigm: the positive endings of the post-Easter encounters indicate a lighter genre than tragedy, closer to novels and to comedy.[235] More dramatic is Saul's story, where the persecutor

---

234 Aristotle, *Poetics*, 1452a.10-15.
235 *Cf.* the definition of tragedy in chapter six of the *Poetics* 'tragedy, then, is mimesis of an action which is elevated, complete, and of magnitude... through pity and fear accomplishing the katharsis of such emotions', δι' ἐλέου καὶ φόβου περαίνουσα τὴν τῶν τοιούντων παθημάτων κάθαρσιν (*Poetics*, 1449b.25-30). *Tractatus Coislinianus*, or the *Anonymous On Comedy*, provides a comparable definition of comedy adapting word for word Aristotle's definition of tragedy in the Poetics: '...through pleasure and laughter effecting the purgation of the like emotions' (L. Cooper, *An Aristotelian Theory of Comedy* (Oxford: Blackwell, 1924), pp. 224-286).

becomes the persecuted, and good fortune turns into a series of lynching attempts.

There are two important narrative relations to be noted here, the relation between recognition and reversals in Luke's paradigm, and the role of 'reversal', as such, both as a change in direction and in the characters' destiny. The first involves a geographical point of return, the idea of journeying. For example, in the Emmaus story the disciples return to Jerusalem and Emmaus represents such a point of return (*Wendepunkt der Geschichte*).[236] Similarly, the Damascus road encounter is a point of return for Saul's journeying in Acts 9. Concerning the second narrative relation, reversal affects a character's destiny, and the Ethiopian's conversion and Saul's commission display such a 'hinge' transformation at baptism.[237] One could note, however, a third dimension of reversal in Luke, as well, the theme of the divine δεῖ, ἀνάγκη (see Aristotle 'necessity', κατὰ τὸ ἀναγκαῖον).[238]

A TWO *FOCI* PLOT: TEACHING AND SACRAMENTS

Schubert was among the first scholars to draw attention to the existence of multiple climaxes in Luke's journey encounters. According to him Luke uses several 'high points' in the Emmaus story: a climax in the recognition scene (Lk. 24:31), and an earlier one, in Jesus' proof-from-prophecy explanation.[239] Just makes a similar observation, concluding that 'the teaching together with the breaking of the bread form the climax of Luke's Gospel'.[240] Yet, how can such a double climax be explained, in terms of narrative?

As mentioned before, the three Lukan post-Easter journey encounters end with a similar emphasis on a restoration into fellowship, illustrated by a sacramental act. Such a plot development can be described as *linear progression* with a

---

236 F. Schnider and W. Stenger, 'Beobachtungen zur Struktur der Emmausperikope (Lk. 24:13-35)', *BZ* 16 (1972), 94-114, esp. p. 113.
237 Lindijer, 'Creative', p. 85.
238 Aristotle, *Poetics*, 1452a.23-24.
239 Schubert, 'Structure', pp. 172-174; in a generalisation, he even writes that the climax of the Emmaus story 'occupies the whole of the story (vss. 13-31) with the exception of verses 13, 15b, 16, 28-31. These few verses are the only parts left of the "original"' (p. 174).
240 Just, *Feast*, p. 219.

sacramental climax (LP-SC). Yet, at the same time, a different plot line is at work, based on the encounter and its representative feature, the evangelistic dialogue. The encounter element is placed at the centre of the narrative and has often been seen as generating a chiastic organisation of the plot (EC, *encounter chiasmus*).

Sometimes, NT commentators have argued that the restoration event itself (the sacramental act) is at the centre of a chiastic structure and controls the story (SC, *sacramental chiasmus*). Usually scholars take sides on this issue, opting either for a sacramental or for an encounter chiasmus. Better than favouring one of the two climax models, it could be suggested, instead, that Luke's composition keeps in balance these two important plot elements, the recognition and the restoration scenes, in a double climax structure, which fits the literary recommendations of Aristotle's *Poetics*.

Encounter, Teaching and Table Fellowship at Emmaus

Emmaus itself turns from an end-point (*Endpunkt*) of the journey into a return-point of the story (*Wendepunkt*).[241] From a starting point, Jerusalem becomes the final destination of journeying. The Emmaus meal (vv. 28-31) is at the centre (vv. 12-27, journeying *from* Jerusalem; vv. 32-35, *to* Jerusalem; a chiasmus of type SC, sacramental).[242] For others, the proclamation in Luke 24:23c is the core of the Easter message (a chiasmus of type EC, evangelistic dialogue).[243]

v. 13	ἐν αὐτῇ τῇ ἡμέρᾳ ἦσαν πορευόμενοι εἰς κώμην...
v. 14	ὡμίλουν πρὸς ἀλλήλους περὶ πάντων κτλ.
v. 15	καὶ ἐγένετο ἐν τῷ ὁμιλεῖν αὐτοὺς
	καὶ συζητεῖν καὶ αὐτὸς Ἰησοῦς
	ἐγγίσας συνεπορεύετο αὐτοῖς,
v. 23c	οἳ λέγουσιν αὐτὸν ζῆν
v. 31b	καὶ αὐτὸς ἄφαντος ἐγένετο ἀπ' αὐτῶν

---

241 Schnider and Stenger, 'Struktur', p. 113.
242 *Cf.* Guillaume, *Luc interprète*, p. 75, n. 2. Such schemes have been suggested by X. Léon-Dufour, *Resurrection and the Message of Easter* (London: G. Chapman, 1974), pp, 200ff., and Schnider and Stenger, 'Struktur', pp. 103-112.
243 Nolland, *Luke 18:35-24:53*, pp. 1199, 1203, 1207; Guillaume, *Luc interprète*, p. 75; also Green, *Luke*, pp. 842-843.

v. 32 καὶ εἶπαν πρὸς ἀλλήλους
v. 33 ἀναστάντες αὐτῇ τῇ ὥρᾳ ὑπέστρεψαν εἰς Ἰερουσαλήμ

The presence of evangelistic teaching at the centre would rather support a linear progression of the story with a sacramental ending (LP-SC). J. H. Neyrey has suggested a composite scheme (a chiasmus of combined EC-SC type, *i.e.* evangelisation-sacrament type).[244]

v. 12	(a) Journey from Jerusalem
v. 15	(b) evangelistic dialogue takes place
v. 15	(c) Jesus appears
v. 16	(d) the disciples' eyes are closed
v. 17-27	(e) Jesus' initiative: (teaching)
v. 28-30	(e') Jesus' initiative: (feeding)
v. 31a	(d') the disciples' eyes opened
v. 31b	(c') Jesus disappears
v. 32	(b') evangelistic dialogue remembered
v. 33	(a') Journey back to Jerusalem

For Neyrey the meaning of the story resides in its centre 'where Jesus takes the pastoral initiative to teach *and* feed'.[245] The story indicates a complex continuity of Jesus' ministry after resurrection, through his apostles (*cf.* Nolland, Lindijer). Luke anticipates the later ecclesial transformations by letting the reader know that (a) it is not to the apostles that Jesus ministers here; (b) it is not in Jerusalem that he made himself known at the first meal; and, finally, that (c) this is the first time when Jesus argues directly and apologetically from the OT Scriptures in support of his messianic ministry.

Evangelism and Baptism in the Ethiopian's Story

As seen, two major events compete here for narrative centrality: the teaching 'on the way' and the sacramental act of

---

244 J. H. Neyrey, 'Luke 24:13-35 "The Risen Shepherd"', in J. H. Neyrey (ed.), *Resurrection Stories* (Wilmington, DE: Glazier, 1988), 38-49, p. 39.
245 Neyrey, 'Luke 24:13-35', p. 39, italics mine.

baptism.[246] The centrality of teaching is emphasized by the antithesis between mystery and comprehension, ignorance and revelation (vv. 25, 40).[247] This chiasmus is supported by the Spirit *inclusio* (vv. 29, 39),[248] by the evangelism motif (*cf.* v. 25 - εὐηγγελίζοντο; v. 35 - εὐηγγελίσατο; v. 40 - εὐηγγελίζετο), and by the journey motif (vv. 25, 40), etc.[249] Spencer makes a fine (probably too subtle) distinction, placing the citation of Isaiah 53:7-8 (J) at the centre of the chiasmus

v. 25	A. ὑπέστρεφον εἰς Ἱεροσόλυμα,
	B. πολλάς τε κώμας τῶν Σαμαριτῶν
	C. εὐηγγελίζοντο
v. 26	D.ἐλάλησεν πρὸς Φίλιππον
	E. πορεύου... ἐπὶ τὴν ὁδὸν
v. 27	F. Καὶ ἰδοὺ ...εὐνοῦχος
v. 29	G. εἶπεν δὲ τὸ πνεῦμα τῷ Φιλίππῳ,
v. 31	H. ἀναβάντα καθίσαι σὺν αὐτῷ.
v. 32	I. ἡ δὲ περιοχὴ τῆς γραφῆς
vv. 32-35	J. Is. 53.7-8: citation
v. 35	I' ἀπὸ τῆς γραφῆς ταύτης
v. 39	H' ἀνέβησαν ἐκ τοῦ ὕδατος
	G' πνεῦμα κυρίου ἥρπασεν τὸν Φίλιππον
	F' καὶ οὐκ εἶδεν αὐτὸν οὐκέτι ὁ εὐνοῦχος
	E' ἐπορεύετο γὰρ τὴν ὁδὸν αὐτοῦ
v. 40	D' Φίλιππος δὲ εὑρέθη εἰς Ἄζωτον·
	C' εὐηγγελίζετο
	B' τὰς πόλεις πάσας
	A' τοῦ ἐλθεῖν αὐτὸν εἰς Καισάρειαν.

---

246 *Cf.* though, Mínguez, 'Hechos 8:25-40', pp. 168-191; O'Toole, 'Philip', pp. 25-29; P. de Meester, '"Philippe et l'eunuque éthiopien" ou "Le baptême d'un pèlerin de Nubie"?', *NRT* 103 (1981), pp. 366-367; Schneider, *Apostelgeschichte*, vol. 1, p. 498; Lindijer, 'Creative', pp. 80-81; Spencer, *Philip*, pp. 131-133.
247 Mínguez, 'Hechos 8:25-40', pp. 171, 178; *cf.* Spencer, *Philip*, p. 143.
248 Mínguez, 'Hechos 8:26-40', p. 176. O'Toole points out that Mínguez left undiscussed circular arrangements like those marked by ἀναβαίνειν (Acts 8:31, 39), γραφή (Acts 8:32, 35), and ἀνοίγειν (Acts 8:32, 35; O'Toole, 'Philip', p. 27).
249 Spencer places Is. 53.8-8 at the centre, *cf.* Spencer, *Philip*, p. 132.

The Post-Easter Paradigm 261

Mínguez has stressed the centrality of evangelism, rather than the presence of a *hodos inclusio*. Accordingly, O'Toole criticised him for focusing on εὐαγγελίζεσθαι and not on the central place of πορεύεσθαι and ὁδός.[250] This shortcoming is even more puzzling given that Mínguez himself highlighted the significance of the way (*hodos*) motif, which, allowing for a *static versus dynamic hodos* contrast, represents the profound generative matrix for the narrative coherence of Acts 8:26-40, 'el camino de la fecundidad', 'the path of (spiritual) fruitfulness', the path of productiveness.[251]

As an alternative to Mínguez's emphasis on evangelism, O'Toole and J. Dupont argued for the centrality of baptism.[252] For O'Toole the structure of the story takes the shape of a geographic *inclusio* (the journey) with the baptism as its core.[253] He, thus, suggests a sacrament-centred structure (chiasmus of type SC, yet he does draw any chiastic scheme explicitly; *cf.* Guillaume's structural scheme).

vv. 25-35 journey from Jerusalem, evangelistic dialogue
vv. 36-38 river baptism by the road (sacrament)
vv. 39-40 journey to Ethiopia (final *hodos* emphasis)

Yet, if Luke's purpose is to show that 'Philip acts like Jesus',[254] then, by comparison with the first half of the Emmaus story (*cf.* Lk. 24:13-35 // Acts 8:26-40) one should suggest a similar circular structure

v. 34 dialogue: the Ethiopian seeks guidance,
v. 35 Philip's evangelistic explanation
v. 36 dialogue: the Ethiopian asks for baptism
v. 38 climax: baptism and changed journey

---

250 O'Toole, 'Philip', p. 28.
251 Mínguez, 'Hechos 8:26-40', p. 183.
252 J. Dupont, 'Meal', p. 120, says that baptism is 'the conclusion and the climax of the passage'. O'Toole argues, also, that 'whether the unit be Acts 8-9:18 or Acts 8-12, the general context of Acts 8:25-40 suggests that Luke emphasizes divine intervention and baptism' (O'Toole, 'Philip', p. 30- see pp. 28-33).
253 O'Toole, 'Philip', pp. 27, 30, 31. *Cf.* Dupont, 'Meal', p. 120: 'The story of the Ethiopian eunuch is the story of his baptism; the whole story leads to baptism'.
254 O'Toole, 'Philip', p. 32.

Extending this observation, one notes a linear narrative progression that starts with a double commissioning (Acts 8:26-29; v. 26: ἀνάστηθι καὶ πορεύου, v. 29: Πρόσελθε καὶ κολλήθητι), and continues with evangelisation at its centre (Acts 8:30-35). This ensures the moment of recognition and reaches a sacramental climax in the act of baptism (Acts 8:36-38), where the reversal of status and expectations takes place. The *dénouement* presents the two men emphatically parting their ways (Acts 8:39-40).

Encounter, Baptism, and a New Call for Saul
In terms of structure, the textual limits of the story can be defined in three ways: (1) Acts 9:1-19a, the journey story ends with Saul's baptism; (2) Acts 9:1-22, it ends with Saul's preaching in Damascus; (3) Acts 9:1-31, it includes the full story, ending with the return to Jerusalem. Within the limits of the first variant, Acts 9:1-19a, the story has a reversal point in the encounter with the risen Christ, and a final restoration climax in the baptismal sacrament.[255]

vv. 1, 2	journey set up: Paul's leaves Jerusalem with an agenda against the Hodos people,
v. 3a	journey setting: as a leader, accompanied by soldiers,
vv. 4-6	the revelational dialogue the miraculous blinding,
vv. 7-8	journey setting: incapacitated, led by his companions
vv. 18, 19a	journey end: at Damascus; he regains sight, and is baptised; Ananias' hodos summary.

---

[255] Löning, *Saulustradition*, pp. 62-63; Schneider, *Apostelgeschichte*, vol. 2, pp. 18-31. They see the first part of Saul's story as made of two sections: 1-9 and 10-19a (Löning, p. 63; Schneider, p. 18). Löning notes a narrative correspondence between the two: 'der Verfolger / einer der Verfolgten; wird engegen seiner Absicht / wird unerwarted; durch eine Vision in seiner Annäherungsbewegung / durch eine vision zur Annäherung an den Verfolger; Zum Stillstand gebracht / in Bewegung gesetzt.' For him the symmetry is fully redactional, and emphasizes the change of life course due to the divine intervention (*op.cit.*, p. 63).

The Post-Easter Paradigm 263

According to the second variant, Acts 9:1-22 is the pericope that can be regarded as an independent literary unit,[256] and it allows for a concentric structure, as well.[257] An argument in favour of this textual division is the pivotal character of the temporal note in Acts 9:23, ὡς δὲ ἐπληροῦντο ἡμέραι ἱκαναί ('after some time had passed', NRSV). If this stands for the three years mentioned by Paul in Galatians 1:17-20, before which he did not visit Jerusalem and did not see any of the apostles, such a division would correspond to the natural course of events.

Thirdly, it can be argued, as well, that the Lukan account of Saul's conversion includes the whole of Acts 9:1-31 as a unitary text, starting in Jerusalem and ending with Saul's return to the same locality yet in an entirely different situation (the persecutor becomes the persecuted one, the arch-enemy of the Church becoming a minister of the Word).

Rather than considering that Acts 9:19b-22 belongs to the next section, and together with vv. 23-31 forms another independent unit (Acts 9:19a-31),[258] one could argue that Acts 9:1-31 is a self-consistent unitary passage, displaying credible marks of Luke's compositional intervention. The reversal cycle in Saul's life is complete. According to this variant of the story, the central events are Saul's baptism and the recovering of sight, as a restoration climax. Then, the two corresponding halves can be interpreted as *Acta Pauli* - before baptism, and *Acta Pauli* - after his baptism.[259]

9:1-3, 7   (a) Jerusalem: violent persecution of the Way, credentials from the high priest;
9:4-8   (b) journeys as leader, vision and blinding; journeys incapacitated

---

256 Löning, *Saulustradition*, pp. 43-48; Zmijewski, *Apostelgeschichte*, p. 370, mentions here, as well, J. Roloff, F. Mußner, R. Pesch, K. Kliesch.
257 R. Pesch, *Die Apostelgeschichte* (Neukirchen: Neukirchener, 1986), vol. 1, p. 298.
258 This correlation is favoured by O. Bauernfeind, A Wikenhauser, E. Haenchen, H. Conzelmann, G. Schneider, A. Weiser, G. Schille, etc. (*cf.* Zmijewski, *Apostelgeschichte*, p. 370).
259 Zmijewski, *Apostelgeschichte*, p. 370. For him Acts 9:19b-31 is 'Das erste Wirken des Saulus in Damaskus und Jerusalem' with two stages (a) 19b-22; and (b) 23-30 (p. 385). In v. 31 Luke makes a summary, a 'zwischenbilanz' (Roloff, *Apostelgeschichte*, p. 157).

9:9	(c) blinded, he waits in Damascus
9:10-18	(d) the Lord answers
9:19-22	(c') sight is regained, baptism; Paul preaches in Damascus; Ananias' *hodos* summary
9:23-26	(b') reversal of persecution and of journey from Damascus back to Jerusalem
9:27-30	(a') Jerusalem as destination and departure point for new journeys: new credentials, from Barnabas; (9:27; Barnabas' *hodos* report - second summary)

One supplimentary argument for the literary unity of Acts 9:1-31, according to the *hodos* perspective of the present thesis, is the double 'way' *inclusio* which involves the motif of Saul's changed credentials (vv. 1, 27).[260] Barnabas' summary reflects Luke's inclination to regard this as an alternative end of the account. The whole of Acts 9:1-31 displays an interesting circular structure based on the Way motif

9:1-9	(A) Paul, the persecutor of the Way
9:10-25	(B) Paul, the persecuted Christian (Damascus)
9:26-31	(C) Paul, the persecuted preacher of the Way

The first two sections (A) and (B) allow for a chiastic (reversal) parallelism.[261] The last two sections (B) and (C) are perfect parallels, save the *hodos* report in (C), and include the hesitation of the disciples (Ananias, v. 13-14; the disciples in Jerusalem, v. 26); the reassurance motif (the Lord, v. 15-16 and Barnabas, v. 27); Paul's preaching (in Damascus, v. 20-22; in Jerusalem, v. 28b-29a); the plots deviced by the Jews in order to kill Paul (in Damascus, v. 23-24; in Jerusalem, v. 29b); Paul's escape (from Damascus to Jerusalem, v. 25; from Jerusalem to Tarsus, v. 30).[262] All the three subunits (A, B, C) are based on a recognition event (Jesus and Paul, Paul and the

---

[260] The apostles are for Luke 'die Quelle aller legitimität' (Haenchen, *Apostelgeschichte*, p. 324; Schneider, *Apostelgeschichte*, vol. 2, p. 34).

[261] Löning, *Saulustradition*, pp. 62-63; Schneider, *Apostelgeschichte*, vol. 2, pp. 18-31.

[262] D. Gill, 'The Structure of Acts 9', *Bib* 55 (1974), 546-548. At that time, Gill's observation brought a new perspective. However, it has not been discussed at length in other subsequent studies.

disciples) and on a reversal of destiny (from Jewish persecutor to Jewish Christian, from Christian evangelist to a persecuted minister). The overall scheme displays a reversal pattern.

THE FINAL *HODOS* REPORTS

Apart from its role in supporting a chiastic structure, the 'way' setting is remarkable through its part in Luke's final summaries. The question is what kind of reason or message, literary or theological, is Luke attaching to these end-reports.

The Two-Pronged Report of Emmaus

In one of the first mentions of this narrative feature, Dillon has drawn attention to the particular form of this *hodos* summary, presented by Luke in a two clauses format. According to him, Luke 24:35 provides special closure to the story, an essential recapitulation

> A succinct, two-pronged conclusion to the whole pericope. Indeed, τὰ ἐν τῇ ὁδῷ and ὡς ἐγνώσθη ἐν τῇ κλάσει τοῦ ἄρτου recapitulate the entire passage in its two components, the travellers' dialogue and the meal scene.[263]

Another perspective on this summary is that of a 'report to the apostles', a trend which starts with the Emmaus account and continues in a long series of similar reports in Acts (Lk. 24:33-35; Acts 4:23-31; 11:1-18; 12:11-17; 14:26-28; 15:1-35; 21:15-20a).[264] Luke's redaction is present in particular in the mention of the Eleven (vs. 33) and in the report, ἐξηγοῦντο.[265]

---

263 Dillon, *Eye-Witnesses*, p. 103.
264 Maloney, *'All that God'*, pp. 189-190; the series of reports has been remarked earlier by other commentators, *e.g.* Marshall, *Gospel*, p. 900. For Maloney, Luke uses a 'common basic [narrative] model, which we may with justice call the form "report to the community"' (Maloney, *'All that God'*, pp. 189-190). The pattern includes the arrival of the messengers, the presence of the apostles, and the report itself, and can be met with various degrees of completeness in Lk. 24:33-35 (the arrival/assembly stages are telescoped in one sentence); Acts 4:23-31; Acts 11:1-18 (the report receives its most extended statement; the assembly is not present); Acts 12:11-17; Acts 14:26-28 (the most compact of the scenes); Acts 15:1-35 (the most complex of the pericopes); Acts 21:15-20a (has all the elements of the pattern). In our

Fitzmyer regards the double use of ἐν τῇ ὁδῷ (vv. 32, 35) as a supplementary emphasis on the 'geographical setting' in which Christ instructs his disciples about the meaning of Scripture (the theme of 'in via teaching').[266] As Jesus gives his 'final and supreme instruction' about his destiny in such a setting this represents a 'subtle, yet highly deliberate' Lukan use of the *hodos* motif, one 'not to be missed'.[267] In its first occurrence, the *hodos* report takes a reflexive form, intensely affective and personal (Luke 24:32)

Οὐχὶ ἡ καρδία ἡμῶν καιομένη ἦν ἐν ἡμῖν
    ὡς ἐλάλει ἡμῖν ἐν τῇ ὁδῷ,
    ὡς διήνοιγεν ἡμῖν τὰς γραφάς.

Its phrasing has rhetorical connotations: καιομένη ἦν ('was burning', periphrastic construction with καίομαι, καίω, old Attic - 'to burn', here metaphorically) was used as a descriptive of rhetorical conviction.[268] Διήνοιγεν (*cf.* 24:31a διηνοίχθησαν οἱ ὀφθαλμοί, 24:45 διήνοιξεν αὐτῶν τὸν νοῦν, also Lk. 2:23, Acts

---

analysis, however, the emphasis falls on the *hodos* report of the disciples.
265 Schubert, 'Structure', pp. 170, 172; Marshall noted as well the Lukan character of this ending (*Gospel*, p. 900). For Bock the reference to the Eleven 'raises the issue of Luke's relationship to John 20:24-29. If all the Eleven were at the gathering noted by Luke, then why was Thomas not convinced until a week later (John 20:24-29)?' (*Luke 9:51-24:53*, p. 1920). For him, also, the report (ἐξηγοῦντο, translated as 'explication') plays a lesser role (p. 1921). However, Maloney translates it with 'report' and points out that ἐξηγέομαι is a Lukan term found again at Acts 15:12, 14 and 21:19; its cognate διηγέομαι is used at Acts 12:17, ἐκδιηγέομαι at Acts 15:3 (Maloney, '*All That God*', pp. 38-39).
266 Fitzmyer, *Luke X-XXIV*, p. 1558.
267 Fitzmyer, *Luke X-XXIV*, p. 1558. Just remarked as well, the double use of the ἐν τῇ ὁδῷ, without, however, elaborating on its significance (Just, *Feast*, p. 60).
268 The expectation was that a good speaker should set his audience 'on fire' (Derrett, 'Walk', p. 189). Thus, Cicero, *Brutus*, 80.276.9, refers to 'incitaret anima'; in 80.278.4-5, good rhetoric creates 'dolor', 'ardor animi', 'perturbatio animi', 'inflammares nostros animos'; *de Oratore* 2.45.188.10: 'incendere iudicem', etc.; *cf. The Testament of Napthali*, 7.4; Jer. 20:9; Ps. 38:14 [LXX]). See Marshall, *Gospel*, pp. 898-899; Guillaume, *Luc interprète*, p. 69.

16:14; 17:3) is a Lukanism, part of Luke's sight and understanding motif. As can be seen, the first summary is focused on the rhetorical event, the evangelistic dialogue 'on the road' (ἐλάλει, διήνοιγεν) with Jesus' supernatural power of conviction. By contrast, the second one takes the form of a report (ἐξηγοῦντο) to the Eleven in Jerusalem (Lk. 24:34-35)

ἐξηγοῦντο
  τὰ ἐν τῇ ὁδῷ
  καὶ ὡς ἐγνώσθη αὐτοῖς ἐν τῇ κλάσει τοῦ ἄρτου

Here Luke highlights the element of recognition (ἐγνώσθη corresponds chiastically with Lk. 24:16 μὴ ἐπιγνῶναι) and the report's emphasis changes: the encounter and the explanations of the road are referred to, simply, as τὰ ἐν τῇ ὁδῷ, while the things remembered specifically are the 'breaking of bread', the eucharistic meal.

The Final *Hodos* Reference in the Ethiopian's Encounter

If Philip is called at the beginning of the story to go on a desert road,[269] Luke reiterates the *hodos* setting by framing the final part of the account in a special 'way' *inclusio*. The road setting specifically borders the event of baptism. However, one has to note that the previous explanation of the gospel is also framed between two significant journey interruptions. At the first stop

---

269 'At noon', or 'going south' (Acts 8:26); or on a road going to Gaza 'which is desert' (Spencer, *Philip*, p. 156). Κατὰ μεσημβρίαν can either mean 'toward the south' or 'about noon', yet, for Spencer 'the case for the temporal meaning appears stronger'. The only other New Testament usage (Acts 22:6) refers to 'midday', in the context of travel. Most of the LXX instances suggest 'noon-time', as well and, as in 1 Kgs. 18:26-29 (Elijah at Mt. Carmel), this specific time points to an hour of divine testing (Spencer, *Philip*, p. 136; see Unnik, 'Befehl', pp. 328-329; Gaventa, *From Darkness*, pp. 101-103). It can be suggested that in association with the idea of a 'desert road', the heat of the noon time is one of Luke's hermeneutical keys for the event. μεσημβρία and ἔρημος convey the idea of loneliness and of obedience at a time of testing. The road is depopulated, abandoned - it is at noon, and yet Philip runs to meet a stranger. For M. S. de Toca, Luke is intentionally ambiguous, referring probably to the Queen of the South, *cf.* Lk. 11:31, βασίλισσα νότου (M. S. de Toca, 'πορεύου κατὰ μεσημβρίαν (Hch 8:26)', *EstB* 55 (1997), 107-115).

the Ethiopian invites Philip to explain the Gospel (Acts 8:29-30). At the second stop he has the opportunity to accept the Gospel and to be baptised, a possibility he realises 'while journeying along the road' (ὡς δὲ ἐπορεύοντο κατὰ τὴν ὁδόν, 8:36).²⁷⁰ At the end of the Ethiopian's baptism, Luke places the second end-mention of *hodos* (the third in the account), after Philip's disappearance, when the eunuch continues *his way full of joy*, ἐπορεύετο γὰρ τὴν ὁδὸν αὐτοῦ χαίρων (Acts 8:39). The Lord has transformed this journeying home of the Ethiopian: he is no longer just a Jewish proselyte or a god-fearer, he has become a fully accepted member of the Way (*cf.* Acts 9:2).

For Mínguez the final *hodos* emphasis in the Ethiopian's story contrasts with the previous apostolic lack of evangelistic horizon. By comparison with the conservative ways of the apostles, the way of Philip is a progressive way.²⁷¹ His suggestion is interesting, having in view that of all the three *hodos* encounters, only Philip's evangelisation does not include a *hodos* report to the Twelve. However, the special place of the apostles in Luke's volumes would not encourage such an interpretation which implies a lack of agreement between the evangelistic agenda of Philip and that of the apostles (*cf.* in Samaria, Philip's evangelism is fully approved by the Twelve).

Through his omission of a report to the Twelve in this story, Luke creates, however, an evangelistic suspense, for this act of gospel proclamation is bolder than the previous interaction with the Samaritans. With accomplished literary skill, and great theological precaution, Luke introduces step by step the issue of Gentile evangelism: first he introduces the Ethiopian's story, then Paul and his commissioning, and thirdly Peter, the

---

270 On κωλύω, see Spencer, *Philip*, pp. 184. The main interpretations of Luke's use of κωλύω here have to do with baptism (a primitive baptismal liturgy, as in Cullmann, *Baptism in the New Testament* (London: SCM, 1950), pp. 71-80) and with Jewish cultic prevention from Temple worship (*cf.* Is. 43:6 [LXX] with its 'do not withhold', μὴ κώλυε; see A. W. Argyle 'Concerning κωλύειν', *ExpTim* 67 (1955-1956), p. 17). Spencer rightly notes that the Judaism known to Luke 'prevented' (κωλύω, Acts 8:36) the full acceptance of eunuchs (*Philip*, pp. 171, 182).

271 Mínguez, 'Hechos 8:25-40', p. 186.

one who, with undented apostolic authority, 'inaugurates' officially the new ministry towards the Gentiles.

In this sense, Acts 8:26-9:31 provides a proper introduction to the developments in Acts 10-12. *In Acts 8:26-9:31, Philip's ministry and Saul's journey are presented by Luke as a thematic unit focused on the challenges and opportunities of the Way, evidence that the hodos motif inspires Luke to literary innovation.*

Saul's New Credentials and His *Hodos* References

Luke's insistence upon a two clause *hodos* summary resurfaces in the account of Saul's encounter. In its first occurrence, the *hodos* flash-back is part of Ananias' introduction to Saul (Acts 9:17), which emphasizes the authority of the Lord Jesus as the one who 'shows himself' (ὁ ὀφθείς) and the one 'who sends' (ἀπέσταλκεν)

Σαοὺλ ἀδελφέ, ὁ κύριος ἀπέσταλκέν με,
᾿Ιησοῦς ὁ ὀφθείς σοι ἐν τῇ ὁδῷ ᾗ ἤρχου.

Luke emphasizes here (a) the essential theophany character of this encounter (ὁ ὀφθείς σοι, using *passivum divinum*), (b) the actual journey setting (ἐν τῇ ὁδῷ) and (c) indirectly, the theme of obedience *versus* resistance to the Lord, *via* an ironic contrast between Ananias' obedience and Saul's initial violent campaign. The whole report centres on the significance of Jesus' identity and authority (ὁ κύριος,... ὁ ὀφθείς, apodosis with aorist participle). Further, Luke's redaction confronts the reader with an implicit contrast between Paul and *his* way, ἐν τῇ ὁδῷ ᾗ ἤρχου, and Christians who belonged to the Way, τῆς ὁδοῦ ὄντας (9:2).

As in the Emmaus account, the *hodos* summary occurs a second time, in the form of a developed evangelistic report to the Eleven (Acts 9:27).

διηγήσατο αὐτοῖς
    πῶς ἐν τῇ ὁδῷ εἶδεν τὸν κύριον
    καὶ ὅτι ἐλάλησεν αὐτῷ,
    καὶ πῶς ἐν Δαμασκῷ ἐπαρρησιάσατο
    ἐν τῷ ὀνόματι τοῦ ᾿Ιησοῦ.

In terms of format, Barnabas carefully mentions (διηγήσατο, narrates) two major credentials in Paul's favour (a) the experience on the way (the vision and the dialogue, εἶδεν and ἐλάλησεν) and (b) the complete change in Saul's life, who has turned into an evangelist (*cf.* the Emmaus' two-pronged report). Alternatively, one can see here a three clause statement: (a) Paul saw the Lord while he was 'on the road' (πῶς ἐν τῇ ὁδῷ εἶδεν τὸν κύριον), and (b) the Lord spoke to him (καὶ ὅτι ἐλάλησεν αὐτῷ), and (c) subsequently Paul started a genuine and successful preaching ministry in Damascus, proclaiming 'the name of Jesus' (ἐν Δαμασκῷ ἐπαρρησιάσατο ἐν τῷ ὀνόματι τοῦ Ἰησοῦ).[272]

Concerning the author of the report, the text suggests that Barnabas is the main subject: he is concerned with Paul (ἐπιλαβόμενος αὐτόν), he takes him to the apostles (ἤγαγεν) and reports (διηγήσατο) - however, the report could also be attributed to Saul (διηγήσατο, aor. ind. 3rd. pers. sing. of διηγέομαι, can stand for both). In this variant, Luke emphasized here Paul's subordination to the Twelve (see Acts 15; and the priority of Peter in the evangelisation of Gentiles, Acts 10-12). There is again a contrast between Acts 9:1-2 and Acts 9:27, possibly ironic, that highlights the substitution of Paul's relation to the priests with his subordonation to the apostles. If Barnabas made the report, the contrast is rather about the Jewish and the new Christian credentials of Paul (persecution letters from the priests, yet new preaching credentials to and from the apostles) highlighting the complete change, or reversal in Paul's life.

The hodos summaries, as a Lukan motif, represent a skilful way of providing an ending to the post-Easter encounters and a dynamic introduction to Gentile evangelism. They constitute important evidence of Luke's compositional art and of his ability to interwave motifs, to use narrative 'complication' (δέσις) and *dénouement* (λύσις).

They do not emphasize only Luke's fondness for what has happened 'on the road' (encounter and dialogue). They also illustrate his interest in the credentials and the dynamics of

---

272 Bruce prefers here the variant ὅ τι instead of majority reading ὅτι for 'it comes more naturally between the two πῶς clauses, constituting with them a third indirect question in one sequence' (Bruce, *Acts*, p. 243).

the missionary ministry, and in the issue of evangelistic restoration through sacraments.

If on the one hand these stories reflect a continuation of Luke's Way motif in the Gospel (*cf.* Jesus' journey to Jerusalem), on the other, the *hodos* reports highlight the authority of the apostles and the need for apostolic validation of all the major events in the life of the Church. In particular, Jesus' appearances and the Gentile evangelistic initiative needed to be understood and validated for the Church by the Twelve apostles. This was an important emphasis for the emerging Gentile church, an important foundation for its relation with the Jewish Christian community.

These reports are also an illustration of the transformation undergone by the Easter *hodos* kerygma. From a setting of an encounter with the risen Jesus, leading to a joyous announcement of the resurrection (the Emmaus encounter), the *hodos* setting becomes a symbol of God's initiatives towards the Gentiles (the Ethiopian's conversion), and finally a locus of far reaching missionary perspectives (proclamation to new peoples, to kings, promises of success, warnings of persecution; in Saul's conversion). Luke's representation of encounters allows us to note the transformation of the meaning of the Way motif: from an Isaianic reference to the Way of the Lord (the New Exodus), it becomes a resurrection symbol, then an evangelistic symbol, associated with a representation of Christianity itself. From a purely collective symbol it has become the locus of a personal, existential adventure with God.

These reports have not exhausted the multiple meanings of the Way motif in Luke-Acts. Paul's mission provides new perspectives which will require further study. For the time being, it has been showed that Luke's theology of the Way represents more that Jesus' journey to Jerusalem, and that mimetic (*i.e.* compositional) approaches are a valuable scholarly means for understanding Luke's style and theology.

Conclusions

Starting from the observation that Luke's post-Easter encounters display a series of formal correspondences, this assessment has gone a step further, building on the ideas of C. H. Dodd and C.H. Lindijer by using the literary insights of Aristotle's *Poetics*. Basically, this analysis has been built on two premises: (1) these accounts should be regarded as *hodos* encounters, and not just as post-Easter appearances (thus, they are integrated into Luke's major literary and theological motif of the Way); and (2) their literary correspondences should be analysed according to the terms of Hellenistic mimesis, that is, with the representation concepts explained by the Hellenist and Greek historians and literary theorists (*cf.* Aristotle, Duris, Theopompus, Ephorus). The results can be listed under two headings: *The relevance of mimesis for Luke's Journey motif* and *The narrative coherence of Luke's journey stories*.

The Relevance of Mimesis for Luke's Journey Motif

Formally, these 'on the road' encounters display with sufficient clarity, within the limits of topical variety and literary creativity, one and the same pattern that conforms well to Aristotle's recommendations for the 'well-made' or 'well-represented' plot. Luke's literary environment (historiography, novel-writing, tragedy, the epic genre) provides many examples, some of considerable interest, of such well-planned plots involving climactic recognitions and reversals of fate. By comparison, one notes Luke's awareness of Hellenistic literary taste, and also, his literary creativity and his theological and philosophical principles.

This assessment of Luke's literary representation of sources and of reality has constantly referred to Aristotle's categories of plot composition, for their clarity and literary insight (even if his *Poetics* is oriented primarily towards an analysis of tragedy, and its views are not cited directly in Hellenistic literature). The appropriateness of this discourse is based on the fact that Aristotle's work represented a synthesis of a larger, on-going discussion, and that his views on compositional mimesis are echoed indirectly in a number of other authors; also, his treatise provides a useful point of comparison with many other, and later Hellenistic authors, who treated the subject in a different manner.

In particular, Luke's literary paradigm for his post-Easter encounters provides a special place for the *hodos* symbolism (the 'way' as a setting and as major reference in the final lines of the story), includes a journey encounter that plays a special narrative and theological role of transition, and builts the story plot according to the mimetic requirements presented in Aristotle's *Poetics* and in other literary treaties. The main findings of the present study can be summarized in the following 10 observations

1. The post-Easter encounter paradigm displays a central 'recognition' or 'discovery' scene (ἀναγνώρισις), an unexpected encounter 'on the road' provided by divine initiative.
2. The recognition moment has a complex dialectic structure involving a question and counter-question dialogue. Luke's dialogues display a strong Christological emphasis reflecting both his sources and his specific theology, which involves explicit and implicit LXX references. The arguably implicit references to Isaiah 35, 53; 1 Maccabees 4; or 1 Samuel 24, 26 reflect the messianic conceptions of Luke's time (Davidic, Mosaic, Maccabeean): the risen Jesus is the prophesied Messiah, the ascended Jesus has the absolute authority of Yahweh, of Yahweh's word in the Scriptures. Luke's recognitions correspond well to Aristotle's recognition by reasoning (ἐκ συλλογισμοῦ).
3. The background of the three encounters can be understood in terms of Aristotle's pre-climactic conflicts, known as 'complication' (δέσις), centred in Luke's case on Jesus' Passion. It involves a suffering motif (πάθος) centred on Jesus' individual death, but also reflects its collective significance, and includes, as well, the personal suffering of the main story characters, alleviated by their encounter with Jesus. According to Luke's social and national emphases, Jesus' Passion is perceived as a violent, unjust, disappointing and dividing event for the entire Jewish people. Such an official rejection of Jesus and of his teaching is reminiscent of Plato's views of cultural censorship and military supervision of all religious and artistic innovation, of philosophical and artistic mimesis. The Gospel is represented, thus, in terms of

a challenge for the Hellenistic city and its citizens, as an opportunity for cultural and religious *renaissance*.
4. The reversal event (περιπέτεια) present in all three Lukan stories mentioned above is assimilated to a 'homecoming' or restoration ending, featuring an act with sacramental connotations (a meal with eucharistic connotations: Lk. 24:30-31; a baptism: Acts 8:36-38; Acts 9:18). The presence of reversals combined with recognitions highlights the existence of a *complex plot*, a compositional feature highly approved by Aristotle.
5. The paradigm plot ends with a variation on the recognition theme, a departure of the messenger (or disappearance) and a replacement of his physical presence with a lasting spiritual insight. The latter is connected with the general literary and prophetic motif of 'sight and understanding', resulting in a joyous new vision and ministry. This personalisation of restoration has been interpreted as a testimony to Luke's art of *dénouement* (λύσις).
6. In terms of diction (λέξις) the vocabulary used by Luke is rich and well suited to the subject matter. In particular, the vocabulary related to the theme of suffering is rich in concepts and imagery, constituting a major compositional element next to the journey vocabulary. The composition is balanced, for the inevitable 'barbarisms' associated with Luke's OT citations and allusions (LXX imitation) are parallelled by an obvious attempt by Luke to write a polite, cultured, well rhythmed story (*cf.* particularly in the introductory sections of the Christological dialogues).
7. The characters of the accounts, for which the Aristotelian term is τὰ ἤθη (a semantic extension for [moral] 'characteristics', 'habits' *cf. Poetics*, chapters six and fifteen, *e.g.* 1450a.37, 14450a.5-10, etc., preferred by Aristotle to the more specialised term, τὸ πρόσωπον) are portrayed as being on 'their way', journeying, experiencing an unexpected restoration from a previously wrong or irrelevant course of life. This type of plot corresponds to the Hellenistic stories where the road or the journey were frequently used as an opportunity for divine encounters and for moral decisions. Similarly, Luke's *hodos* encounters involve the intervention of a divine character such as the risen Jesus or his Spirit, or his angel or messenger, essential participants in the transformation (μετάβασις).
8. The 'on the road' setting is emphatically mentioned at the end of the story in the form of a *hodos* report (the Emmaus account and Saul's encounter) or of a narrative re-iteration of setting (the

Ethiopian's evangelisation), *cf.* Luke 24:32, 35; Acts 8:39; 9:17; 27. These reports or reiterations provide a specific introduction or transition to the next accounts: the Emmaus 'road' report introduces the encounter of the Eleven with the risen Jesus; the Ethiopian's happy journey down the Gaza road introduces the issue of 'those belonging to the Way' in Acts 9:1 and of Saul's journey(s) (persecution and call); the Damascus *hodos* reports introduce (a) the new preaching journeys of Paul and the issue of his relation with the apostles, and (b) Peter's apostolic, groundbreaking evangelistic journeys (the Cornelius episode, etc.).

9. The narrative and theological unity of these journey encounters is emphasized by Luke's method of designing different and overlapping spatial and temporal frameworks. Distances and periods of time are contracted or expanded in order to suit the narrative dynamics and to support the main narrative emphases. This liberty in presentation does not always coincide with the characteristics of the initial event. It reflects rather Luke's mimetic understanding of literary representation. Luke 24 gives the impression of all happening in one day, although it covers more than that in its actual temporal length. The Emmaus road encounter is explicitly presented as taking place within the span of one evening, although it involves a supper at night and the return to Jerusalem, later, an event that could rather take place the next day, since the city gates would be closed at sunset. Different accounts related to Saul's commissioning, such as his encounter with the risen Jesus, his healing in Damascus, his early preaching in Damascus and his fleeing in a basket, as well as his later testimony in Jerusalem and his subsequent departure to Tarsus, are brought together in one single story which emphasizes the reversal of his destiny. The reader is given the impression of a unitary series of events taking place during a relatively short period of time. Time and space are seen from a special hermeneutical perspective as well as in the case of the Ethiopian's conversion. Luke takes, apparently, an initially independent evangelistic story, and places it in a literary context of mission and persecution that chases the first Christians away from Jerusalem. Functioning as a transition narrative between Stephen's death and Saul's call, the story prepares the reader, together with Saul's conversion, for the later 'official' beginning of Gentiles' evangelisation through the conversion of Cornelius. The literary effect emphasizes the dynamic nature of these journeys and of Christianity as the Way.

10. The argument of Luke's *hodos* encounters (διανοία) is Christological and evangelistic in nature, affirming the significance of Jesus' death (of universal value and not a model for others such as Cato's, Socrates', or Seneca's deaths), of his resurrection and ascension, and of his divine lordship. The ideology of the disciples' journey has to do rather with Jesus' evangelistic programme to the farthest corners of the earth, than with the actual model of Jesus' journey to Jerusalem. In the process, Jerusalem's centrality is challenged as well as that of Rome, implicitly. The scene is set thus for a new *hodos* paradigm: people's lives are challenged and changed through personal encounters with Jesus' gospel 'on the road'.

This study submits that Luke's art of emplotment can best be characterised as a mixture of drama, novel, Hellenistic historiography and comedy. This can be seen in the positive endings of his stories, in the element of adventure and the legendary details, in his care for the historical and geographical texture of his narrative. Such an observation confirms and further contextualises the findings of C. H. Dodd, R. Pervo, D. O. Via and R. W. Funk, who have highlighted, as well, the complex, tragic and comic nature of many of Luke's parables.

In particular, such a combination of literary features was characteristic of the Hellenistic historians (*cf.* Duris, Theopompus, Ephorus, Phylarchus, etc.), who used personalised and dramatised representations of reality, a mimesis designed to communicate historical facts and to delight or impress the audience. Luke, therefore, can be compared with these authors not only as a Hellenistic historian himself, but also from the point of view of style and of literary mimesis, as a Hellenistic writer who is fond of vivid descriptions and the personalisation of events.

The merits of the present study reside, thus, in combining this reconsideration of Luke as a Hellenistic historian with a nuanced view of him as Hellenistic mimetic author, at a moment when in the area of NT studies the majority of commentators have emphasized Luke's mimesis rather as an imitation of the Septuagint's style and content. These mimetic features indicate that Luke's approach to his sources was literarily and philosophically motivated, as well, not only ideologically oriented or theologically focused.

The Narrative Coherence of Luke's Journey Stories

This book's contention is that Luke's theology of the Way should be based on more than just the redactional *Reisenotizen* of Jesus' journey to Jerusalem, or the teaching and journeying format of Jesus' ministry, important as they are. One can identify, for example, a 'journey within a journey' phenomenon in Jesus' journey to Jerusalem (J. Navone), journey stories such as the parable of the Good Samaritan, the account of Zacchaeus' conversion, the parable of the Prodigal Son. These stories, together with the post-Easter *hodos* encounters, reflect a different literary paradig and a particular, specific interest of Luke in the journeying motif. Their main action is an important encounter set 'on the road', leading to restoration, to a personalised, positive reversal of destiny. The main characters in these stories are Jesus, the subject of the 'recognition', and an evangelized person, a convert (the roles may be redistributed, i.e. an evangelist and the evangelized person). The encounter is initiated by a divine person (the angel or the Spirit of the Lord, or the risen Jesus himself).

This new paradigm is not focused on a collective personage, such as the Church or the disciples, who benefits from these encounters, but rather on a journeying individual who experiences salvation (restoration) in the context of personal adventure. Such a story line comes close to the typical novel plot and could appeal in special way to the first century reader, displaying a great apologetic and evangelistic potential.

Through such stories Luke continues to provide and defend a positive meaning for the Way, in agreement with his use of *hodos* in the singular in Luke-Acts, and in consonance with his representational emphases in the Gospel, with his redaction of Mark (when mentioned together, Jesus and the Way are presented in a positive manner). Luke's special events set 'on the way' do not lead to setbacks, failures, sudden terminations of journeying or of life, but represent as many opportunities for evangelistic progress and restoration.

On account of their characteristics, these stories are able to function effectively in the narrative transition and contribute to the literary coherence of Luke-Acts. The gospel of Luke and the book of Acts, on the one hand (*cf.* Luke 24 - Acts 1), and the two halves of Acts, on the other hand (*cf.* Acts 8-9), are thus connected through similar challenging encounters 'on the road', in addition to other great Lukan motifs (Ascension, Pentecost, Persecution, Mission).

Luke 24 ensures the gospel's finale through a thematic and paradigmatic transition to the themes and motifs of Acts. Acts 8-9 reiterates this paradigm and introduces the Gentile mission (Acts 10-12) and the later missionary journeys of Paul (Acts 13-28). Both sections have a similar transition profile, based on *hodos* encounters and significant *hodos* reports. While the *hodos* setting connects the resurrection stories with the main journey of the gospel, Jesus' journey to Jerusalem, the *hodos* reports relate these post-Easter challenges to the validating authority of the Lord and of the church, one of the main themes of Acts.

In essence, the post-Easter *hodos* paradigm communicates a model of divine encounter that can be perceived both as good literature and as challenging theology. Confronting the reader with Jesus' resurrection and with his supreme lordship, the *hodos* post-Easter encounter has, in Luke's representation, an evangelistic character and is more open to popular emulation than Jesus' journey to Jerusalem. Its individual ethos, reversal and restoration thrusts do not communicate a collective Exodus-like paradigm, but rather a contemporary adventure and an emphasis on individual salvation, available to Jews and Gentiles alike. It allows the reader to perceive Luke, the evangelist, as an educated writer, a talented storyteller, a sensible communicator, a profound, bold, creative and inspiring theologian of the early Church, an author profoundly marked by the idea of meeting the resurrected Jesus in a life changing encounter, during one's journey through life.

Bibliography

Primary Resources

Aelianus, *Historical Miscellany (Varia Historia)*, translation and notes by N. G. Wilson, LCL (London: Harvard University Press, 1997)
Abel, P.F.-M., *Les livres des Maccabées* (Paris: Éditions J. Gabalda, 1949)
Aristotle, *De Arte Poetica* (Leipzig: B.G. Teubner Verlag, 1878)
—, *Poetics*, in E. Bekker (ed.), *Aristotelis Opera* (Berlin: W. de Gruyter, 1960), vol. 2
—, *Poetics*, S. Halliwell (tr.), LCL (earlier LCL version, tr. by W.H. Fyfe) (Cambridge, MA: Harward University Press, 1995)
—, *The Art of Rhetoric*, J.H. Freese (tr.), LCL (London: W. Heinemann, 1982)
—, *The Nicomachean Ethics*, H. Rackham (tr.), LCL (London: W. Heinemann, 1982 (1926))
Kassel, R., *Aristotelis. De Arte Poetica Liber*, Oxford Classical Texts (Oxford: Clarendon Press, 1965)
Charlesworth, J.H., (ed.), *The Dead Sea Scrolls: Hebrew, Aramaic, and Greek Texts with English Translations. Rule of the Community and Related Documents* (Tübingen: J.C.B. Mohr, 1994), vol. 1
—, *The Dead Sea Scrolls: Hebrew, Aramaic, and Greek Texts with English Translations. Damascus Document, War Scroll, and Related Documents* (Tübingen: J.C.B. Mohr, 1995), vol. 2
Chariton, *Callirhoe*, G.P. Goold (tr.), LCL (Cambridge, MA: Harvard University Press, 1995)
Cicero, *Tusculan Disputations*, J.E. King (tr.), LCL (London: W. Heinemann, 1950)
—, *Pro Rabirio Perduellionis*, H.G. Hodge (tr.), LCL (London: W. Heinemann, 1959)
Dionysius of Halicarnassus, *The Roman Antiquities*, E. Cary (tr.), LCL (London: W. Heinemann, 1978)
—, *On Literary Composition*, in *The Critical Essays*, S. Usher (tr.), LCL (London: W. Heinemann, 1985), vol. 2
—, *On the Style of Demosthenes*, in *The Critical Essays*, S. Usher (tr.), LCL (London: W. Heinemann, 1974)
Dio Chrysostomus, J.W. Cohoon (tr.), LCL (London: W. Heinemann, 1961), 5 vols.
Diogenes Laertius, *Lives of Eminent Philosophers*, R.D. Hicks (tr.), LCL (London: W. Heinemann, 1979)
Ennius, *Annals*, E.H. Warmington (tr.), in *The Remains of Old Latin*, LCL

Bibliography

Eusebius of Caesarea, *The Proof of the Gospel (Demonstratio Evangelica)*, W.J. Ferrar (tr.), Translations of Christian Literature, Series 1 (Greek Texts) (London: Macmillan, 1920)

Euripides, A.S. Way (tr.), LCL (London: W. Heinemann, 1987), 4 vols.

Goldstein, J.A., *I Maccabees, A New Translation with Introduction and Commentary by J. A. Goldstein*, The Anchor Bible (Garden City, NY: Doubleday, 1976)

Herodotus, *History of the Greek and Persian War*, A.D. Godley (tr.), LCL (London: W. Heinemann, 1981), 4 vols.

Hesiod, *The Homeric Hymns and Homerica*, H.G. Evelyn-White (tr.), (London: W. Heinemann, 1982)

Homer, *Iliad*, A.T. Murray (tr.), LCL (London: W. Heinemann, 1988, (1976))

—, *Odyssey*, A.T. Murray (tr.), LCL (London: W. Heinemann, 1980, (1976))

—, *Homeri Opera*, ed. and notes by Th.W. Allen, SCBO (Oxford: Clarendon Press, 1974)

Isaac, E., 'A New Translation and Introduction to *1 (Ethiopic Apocalypse of) Enoch*', in J.H. Charlesworth (ed.), *The OT Pseudepigrapha* (London: Darton, Longman & Todd, 1983), vol. 1

Isocrate, *To Demonicus*, G. Norlin (tr.), LCL (London: W. Heinemann, 1980)

Josephus, *Jewish Antiquities*, R. Marcus (tr.), LCL (London: W. Heinemann, 1966)

—, *Against Apion* (Contra Apionem), H.St.J. Thackeray (tr.), LCL (London: W. Heinemann, 1966)

Knibb, M. A., *The Ethiopic Book of Enoch* (Oxford: Oxford University Press, 1982)

Longinus, *On the sublime*, W.H. Fyfe (tr.), rev. by D. Russel, LCL (London: W. Heinemann, 1995)

Lucian of Samosata, *How to Write History*, in *The Works of Lucian*, K. Kilburn (tr.), LCL (Harvard: Harvard University Press, 1958)

Millik, J.T., and M. Black, *The Books of Enoch* (Oxford: Clarendon Press, 1976)

Pausanias, *Description of Greece*, W.H. Jones (tr.), LCL (London: W. Heinemann, 1918-1935), 5 vols.

Pindar, *The Odes of Pindar*, J. Sandys (tr.), LCL (London: Harvard University Press, 1989)

—, *Pindari Carmina cum Fragmentis* (pars I-II), in H. Maehler (ed.) (Leipzig: B.G. Teubner Verlag, 1987-1989)

Philostratus, *The Life of Apollonius of Tyana*, F.C. Conybeare (tr.), LCL (Harvard: Harvard University Press, 1989, (1912))

Plato, *The Republic*, P. Shorey (tr.), LCL (London: W. Heinemann, 1982, (1987))

Lee, D., *Plato, The Republic*, introduction, notes by D. Lee (tr.), (London: Penguin, 1987²)

—, *The Laws*, R.G. Bury (tr.), LCL (London: W. Heinemann, 1984)
—, *Phaedrus*, H.N. Fowler (tr.), LCL (London: W. Heinemann, 1982)
—, *Ion*, W.R.M. Lamb (tr.), LCL (London: W. Heinemann, 1975)
—, *Timaeus*, R.G. Bury (tr.), LCL (London: Harward University Press, 1989)
Plautus, *The Two Menaechmuses*, P. Nixon (tr.), LCL (London: W. Heinemann, 1951)
Plutarch, *Parallel Lives*, B. Perrin (tr.), LCL (London: W. Heinemann, 1982)
Polybius, *The Histories*, W.R. Paton (tr.), LCL (London: W. Heinemann, 1979-1980)
Prigent, P., *Épître de Barnabé. Introduction, traduction et notes* (Greek text edited and presented by R. A. Kraft), Sources Chrétiennes (172) (Paris: Éditions du Cerf, 1971)
Quintilianus, *Institutionis Oratoriae*, tr. and notes by M. Winterbottom, SCBO (Oxford: Clarendon Press, 1970), 2 vols.
Xenophon, *Memorabilia*, E.C. Marchant (tr.), LCL (London: W. Heinemann, 1979)
Zeitlin, S., *The First Book of Maccabees*, S. Tedesche (tr.), introduction and commentary by S. Zeitlin (N.Y.: Harper and Brothers, 1950)
The Orphic Hymns, A.N. Athanassakis (tr.), (Missoula, MT: Scholars Press, 1977)

*

Nestle-Aland, *Novum Testamentum Graece 27th Ed.* (Stuttgart: Deutsche Biblegesellschaft, 1993, (1898))
Aland, K., and M. Black, M. Martini, B. M. Metzger, A. Wigren (eds.), *The Greek New Testament* (Stuttgart: United Bible Societies, 1993)
Elliger, K. and W. Rudolph (eds.), *Biblia Hebraica Stuttgartensia* (Stuttgart: Deutsche Bibelgesellschaft, 1990)
Rahlfs, A., (ed.), *Septuaginta* (Stuttgart: Deutsche Bibelgesellschaft, 1935)

Selective Bibliography

Aarde, A. van, 'Narrative Point of View: An Ideological Reading of Luke 12:35-48', *Neotestamentica* 22 (1988), 235-52

Achtemeier, J., 'The Lucan Perspective on the Miracles of Jesus: A Preliminary Sketch', *Journal of Biblical Literature* 94 (1975), 547-562.

Albertz, M., 'Zum Formgeschichte der Auferstehungsberichte', *Zeitschrift für die neuetestamentlische Wissenschaft* 21 (1922), 259-269

Alexander, L., '"In Journeying Often": Voyaging in the Acts of the Apostles and in Greek Romance', in C.M. Tuckett (ed.), *Luke's Literary Achievement: Collected Essays*, JSNT Supplement Series 116 (Sheffield: Sheffield Academic Press, 1995), 17-50

—, *The Preface to Luke's Gospel: Literary Convention and Social Context in Luke 1:1-4 and Acts 1:1* (Cambridge: Cambridge University Press, 1993)

Alexander, P.S., *The Toponymy of the Targumim, with Special Reference to the Table of Nations and the Boundaries of the Land of Israel*, D.Phil. thesis (Oxford: Oxford University, 1974)

Aletti, J.-N., *L'art de raconter Jésus-Christ: L'écriture narrative de l'évangile de Luc* (Paris: Éditions des Seuil, 1989)

Alsup, J.E., *The Post-resurrection Appearance Stories of the Gospel Tradition: A History-of-Tradition Analysis with Text-Synopsis* (London: SPCK, 1975)

Argyle, A.W., 'O. Cullmann's Theory Concerning κωλύειν', *Expository Times*, 67 (1955-6), 17

Auerbach, E., *Mimesis: The Representation of Reality in Western Literature*, W.A. Trask (tr.), (Princeton NJ: Princeton University Press, 1953)

Aune, D.E., 'Heracles and Christ. Heracles Imagery in the Christology of Early Christianity', in D.L. Balch, E. Ferguson, W.A. Meeks (eds.), *Greeks, Romans and Christians: Essays in Honour of Abraham J. Malherbe* (Minneapolis, MN: Fortress Press, 1990), 3-19

Avenarius, G., *Lukians Schrift Zur Geschichtsschreibung* (Meisenheim: Glan, 1956)

Baarlink, H., 'Die Zyklische Struktur von Lukas 9:43b-19:28', *New Testament Studies* 38 (1992), 481-506

Bachmann, M., *Jerusalem und der Tempel: Die geographisch-theologischen Elemente in der lukanischen Sicht des jüdischen Kultzentrums*, BWANT 109 (Stuttgart: Kohlhammer, 1980)

Bailey, K.E., *Poet and Peasant: A Literary-cultural Approach to the Parables in Luke* (Grand Rapids, MI: Eerdmans, 1976)

—, *Through Peasant Eyes* (Grand Rapids, MI: Eerdmans, 1980)

Bailie, G., *Violence Unveiled: Humanity at the Crossroads* (N.Y.: Crossroads, 1995)

Bally, D., *The Geography of the Bible: A Study in Historical Geography* (London: Lutterworth Press, 1958)

Balz, H., and G. Schneider, *Exegetical Dictionary of the NT* (Grand Rapids, MI: Eerdmans, 1991), vol. 2

Barrett, C.K., 'Theologia Crucis - in Acts?', in C. Andersen (ed.), *Theologia Crucis - Signum Crucis* (Tübingen: J.C.B. Mohr, 1979), 73-84

—, *The Acts of the Apostles: A Critical and Exegetical Commentary*, ICC (Edinburgh: T&T Clark, 1994)

—, *Luke the Historian in Recent Study* (London: Epworth, 1961)

Bartsch, H.W., 'Inhalt und Funktion des urchristlichen Osterglaubens', in H. Temporini and W. Haase (eds.), *Aufstieg und Niedergang der römischen Welt: Geschichte und Kultur Roms in Spiegel der neuren Forschung*, vol. II.25.1 (Berlin: W. de Gruyter, 1982), 794-890

Bauckham, R., 'Early Jewish Visions of Hell', *Journal of Theological Studies* 41 (1990), 355-85

Bauernfeind, O., *Kommentar und Studien zur Apostel-geschichte*, WUNT 22 (Tübingen: J.C.B. Mohr, 1980)

Baur, F.C., *Paul the Apostle of Jesus Christ: His Life and Work, His Epistles and His Doctrine* (London: Williams & Norgate, 1875)

Baum, A.D., *Lukas als Historiker der Letzten Jesusreise* (Wuppertal: R. Brockhaus Verlag, 1993)

Beardslee, W.A., 'What is It About? Reference in New Testament Literary Criticism', in E.S. Malbon and E.V. McKnight (eds.), *The New Literary Criticism and the New Testament*, JSNT Supplement Series 109 (Sheffield: Sheffield Academic Press), 1994, 367-86.

Becker, O., *Das Bild des Weges und verwandte Vorstellung im frühgriechischen Denken* (Berlin: Weidmann Verlag, 1937)

Berg, B., 'Alcestis and Hercules in the Catacomb of Via Latina', *Vigilae Christianae* 48 (1994), 213-34.

Berger, K., *Theologiegeschichte des Urchristentums: Theologie des Neuen Testament* (Tübingen: Francke Verlag, 1994)

Best, E., *Following Jesus: Discipleship in the Gospel of Mark* (Sheffield: JSOT Press, 1981)

Betz, H.D., 'The Origin and Nature of Christian Faith According to the Emmaus Legend (Luke 24:13-32)', *Interpretation* 23 (1969), 32-46

—, *Hellenismus und Urchristentum: Gesammelte Aufsätze* (Tübingen: J.C.B. Mohr, 1990)

Blass F., *Die Rhythmen der asianischen und römischen Kunstprosa (Paulus, Hebräerbrief, Pausanius, Cicero, Seneca, Curtius, Apuleius)* (Leipzig: A. Deichert, 1905)

Blomberg, C.L., 'Midrash, Chiasmus, and the Outline of Luke's Central Section', in R.T. France and D. Wenham (eds.), *Gospel Perspectives:*

Studies in Midrash and Historiography (Sheffield: JSOT Press, 1983), 217-61

Bock, D.L., 'The Use of the Old Testament in Luke-Acts: Christology and Mission', *SBL Seminar Papers* 1990, 494-511

—, *Luke 1:1-9:50*, Baker Exegetical Commentary on the NT, ECNT 3a (Grand Rapids, MI: Zondervan Press, 1994)

—, *Luke 9:51-24:53*, Baker Exegetical Commentary on the NT 3b (Grand Rapids, MI: Baker Books, 1996)

—, *Proclamation from Prophecy and Pattern: Lucan Old Testament Christology* (Sheffield: Sheffield Academic Press, 1987)

Boismard, M.-É and A. Lamouille, *Les Actes Des Deux Apôtres*, Études Bibliques 12 (Paris: Éditions J. Gabalda, 1990)

Bonnard, P., *L'Évangile selon St. Matthieu* (Genève: Labor et Fides, 1982².

Borg, M.J., *Conflict, Holiness & Politics in the Teachings of Jesus* (Lewiston, NY: E. Mellen Press, 1984)

Bosch, D.J., *Transforming Mission: Paradigm Shifts in Theology of Mission*, ASMS 16 (Maryknoll, NY: Orbis Books, 1996[10])

Botha, P.J.J., 'Community and Conviction in Luke-Acts', *Neotestamentica* 20/2 (1995) 145-65

Bovon, F., 'Studies in Luke-Acts: Retrospect and Prospect', *Harvard Theological Review* 85, 2 (1992), 175-96

Bovon, F., *Luc le Théologien: Vingt-Cinq Ans de Recherches (1950-1975)* (Paris: Delachaux, 1978)

Braumann, G., 'Das Mittel der Zeit', *Zeitschrift für die neuetestamentlische Wissenschaft* 54 (1963), 117-45.

Bratcher, R., 'Akouō in Acts 9:7 and 22:9', *ExpTim* 7 (1959-1960), 243-245.

Moehring, H.R., 'The verb akouein in Acts 9:7 and 22:9', *Novum Testamentum* 3 (1959), 88-99

Breech, J., *The Silence of Jesus: The Authentic Voice of the Historical Man* (Philadelphia, PA: Fortress Press), 1983

Brink, C.O., *Horace: On Poetry. The 'Ars Poetica'* (Cambridge: Cambridge University Press, 1971)

Brodie, T.L., 'Greco-Roman Imitation of Texts as a Partial Guide to Luke's Use of Sources', in C.H. Talbert (ed.), *Luke-Acts: New Perspectives from the SBL Seminar* (N.Y.: Crossroads, 1984), 17-46

—, 'Luke 7:36-50 as an Internalization of 2 Kings 4:1-37: A Study of Luke's Rhetorical Imitation', *Biblica* 64 (1983), 457-85

—, 'Towards unravelling Luke's use of the Old Testament: Luke 7:11-17 as an imitation of 1 Kings 17:17-24,' *New Testament Studies* 32 (1986), 247-67

—, 'Luke as an Imitation and Emulation of the Elijah-Elisha Narrative,' in E. Richard (ed.), *New Views on Luke and Acts* (Collegeville, MN: The Liturgical Press, 1990), 78-85

—, 'The Departure for Jerusalem (Luke 9:51-56), as rhetorical imitation of Elijah's departure for the Jordan (2 Kgs. 1:1-2:6)', *Biblica* 70 (1989), 96-109

—, 'The accusing and stoning of Naboth (1 Kgs. 21:8-13) as one component of the Stephen text (Acts 6:9-14; Acts 7:58a)', *Catholic Biblical Quarterly* 45 (1983), 417-32

—, *Luke the Literary Interpreter: Luke-Acts as a Systematic Rewriting and Updating of the Elijah-Elisha Narrative in 1 and 2 Kings* (Rome: Pontifical Bible Institute, 1987)

Brosend, W. F., II. 'The Means of Absent Ends', in B. Witherington III (ed.), *History, Literature and Society in the Book of Acts* (Cambridge: Cambridge University Press, 1996), 348-62

Brown, E.K., *Rhythm in the Novel* (Toronto: University of Toronto Press, 1950)

Brown, R.E., 'Jesus and Elisha', *Perspective* 12 (1971), 85-104

Brown, S., *Apostasy and Perseverance in the Theology of Luke* (Rome: Pontifical Bible Institute, 1969)

Bruce, F.F., 'Philip and the Ethiopian', *Journal of Semitic Studies* 34/2 (1989), 377-87

—, *The Book of Acts* (Grand Rapids, MI: Eerdmans, 19880.

Buckwalter, H.D., *The Character and Purpose of Luke's Christology*, SNTS 89 (Cambridge: Cambridge University Press, 1996)

Bultmann, R., 'Die Bedeutung der neuerschlossenen mandäischen und manichäischen Quellen für das Verständnis der Johannesevangeliums', *Zeitschrift für die neuetes-tamentlische Wissenschaft* 24 (1925), 100-146

—, *The History of the Synoptic Tradition* (Oxford: B. Blackwell, 1963)

Burchard, C., *Der dreizehnte Zeuge: traditions- und kompositionsgeschichtliche Untersuchung zu Lukas, Darstellung der Frühzeit des Paulus* (Göttingen: Vandenhoeck & Ruprecht, 1970)

Bywater, I., *Aristotle on the Art of Poetry* (Oxford: Oxford University Press, 1909)

Cadbury, H.J., *The Making of Luke-Acts* (London: Macmillan, 19582)

—, *The Style and Literary Method of Luke* (Cambridge: Harvard University Press, 1920)

Calduch-Benages, N., 'Elementos de Inculturación Helenista en el Libro de Ben Sira: Los Viajes', *Estudios Bíblicos* 54/3 (1996), 289-98

Cambier, J., 'Le voyage de S. Paul à Jerusalem en Act. 9:26ss. et le schema missionnaire theologique de St. Luc', *New Testament Studies* 8 (1962), 249-57

Carmignac, J., 'Studies in the Hebrew Background of the Synoptic Gospels [Mistranslations, Verbal Plays, Visual Omissions, Synoptic Variants: Lk. 1:70-71, 78; Mk. 4:19; 5:13; 9:23; 9:49; et permulti alii loci...', *ASTI* 7 (1970), 64-93

Cassidy, R.J., and P.J. Scharper (eds.), *Political Issues in Luke-Acts* (Maryknoll, NY: Orbis Books, 1983)
Casson, L., *Travel in the Ancient World* (Baltimore, MA: John Hopkins University Press, 1994 (1974))
Castelvetro, L., *Poetica d'Aristotele vulgarizzata e sposta* (Basilea: Pietro de Sedabonis (Peter Perna), 1576 (1570))
—, *Castelvetro on the Art of Poetry: an abridged translation of Lodovico Castelvetro's Poetica d'Aristotele vulgarizzata e sposta*, introduction and notes by Andrew Bongiorno, Medieval and Renaissance Texts and Studies 29 (Binghamton, NY: State University of New York, 1984)
Chatman, S., *Story and Discourse: Narrative Structure in Fiction and Film* (Ithaca, NY: Cornell University Press, 1978)
Clark, A.C., 'Parallel Lives: The Relation of Paul to the Apostles in the Lucan Perspective', PhD thesis, London Bible College, Brunel University London (1996)
Collins, J.J. *The Apocalyptic Imagination* (N.Y.: Crossroads, 1983)
Combrink, H.J.B., 'The Structure of the Gospel of Matthew as Narrative', *Tyndale Bulletin* 34 (1983), 61-90
Conzelmann, H., 'Zur Lukasanalyse', *Zeitschrift für Theologie und Kirche* 49 (1952), 16-33
—, *The Acts of the Apostles* (Philadelphia, PA: Fortress Press, 1963)
—, *Die Apostelgeschichte* (Tübingen: J.C.B. Mohr, 1972)
—, *An Outline of the Theology of the New Testament* (London: SCM Press, 1969)
—, *The Theology of Saint Luke* (London: Faber & Faber, 1960)
Cook, A., *History Writing: The theory and practice of history in Antiquity and in Modern Times* (Cambridge: Cambridge University Press, 1988)
Craig, W. L., 'From Easter to Valentinus and the Apostles' Creed Once More: A Critical Examination of James Robinson's Proposed Resurrection Appearance Trajectories', *Journal for the Study of NT* 52 (1993), 19-39
Cranfield, C.E.B., *The Gospel According to Saint Mark*, Cambridge Greek New Testament Commentary (Cambridge: Cambridge University Press, 1963)
Creed, J.M., *The Gospel According to Saint Luke* (London: Macmillan, 1930)
Crites, S., 'The Narrative Quality of Experience', *Journal of the American Academy of Religion* 39 (1971), 291-311
Croix, G.E.M. de St., 'Aristotle on History and Poetry (*Poetics*, 9.1451a.36-b.11)', in A.O. Rorty (ed.), *Essays on Aristotle's Poetics* (Princeton, NJ: Princeton University Press, 1992), 23-32
Crossan, J.D., 'Structuralist Analysis and the Parables of Jesus. A Reply to D.O. Via, Jr. "Parable and Example Story: A Literary-Structuralist Approach"', in R.W. Funk (ed.), *Semeia 1: A Structuralist Approach to the Parables* (Missoula, MT: Scholars Press, 1974), 192-221

—, *In Parables: The Challenge of the Historical Jesus* (London: Harper and Row, 1973)
—, *The Dark Interval: Towards a Theology of Story* (Niles: Argus, 1975)
Cullmann, O., *Baptism in the New Testament* (London: SCM Press, 1950)
—, *Salvation in History* (London: SCM Press, 1967)
Curtis, A.H.W., 'Theological Geography', in R.J. Coggins and J.L. Houlden (eds.), *A Dictionary of Biblical Interpretation* (London: SCM Press, 1990), 687-90
Danker, F.W., *Jesus and the New Age: According to Saint Luke, A New Commentary on the Third Gospel*, rev. and exp., (Philadelphia, PA: Fortress Press, 1988 (1972))
Danove, P.L., *The End of Mark's Story: A Methodological Study*, BIS 3 (Leiden: E.J. Brill, 1993)
Daube, D., *The New Testament and Rabbinic Judaism* (N.Y.: Arno, 1973)
—, 'Shame Culture in Luke', in M.D. Hooker and S.G. Wilson, *Paul and Paulinism: Essays in Honor of C.K. Barrett* (London: SPCK, 1982), 355-72
Davies, J.G., 'The Prefigurement of the Ascension in the Third Gospel', *Journal of Theological Studies* 6 (1955), 229-33
—, *He Ascended Into Heaven: A Study in the History of Doctrine* (London: Lutterworth, 1958)
Davies, J.H., 'The Purpose of the Central Section of St. Luke's Gospel', in F.L. Cross (ed.), *Studia Evangelica*, vol. 2, Texte und Untersuchungen zur Geschichte der altchristlichen Literatur 87 (Berlin: Akademie Verlag, 1964), 164-69
Denaux, A., 'The Delineation of the Lucan Travel Narrative Within the Overall Structure of the Gospel', in C. Focant (ed.), *The Synoptic Gospels: Source Criticism and the New Literary Criticism* (Leuven: Leuven University Press, 1993), 357-92
—, 'Old Testament Models for the Lukan Travel Narrative: A Critical Survey', in C.M. Tuckett (ed.), *The Scriptures in the Gospels*, BETL 81 (Leuven: Leuven University Press, 1997), 271-305
Derrett, J.D.M., 'The Walk to Emmaus (Lk. 24:13-35), The Lost Dimension', *Estudios Bíblicos* 54 (1996), 183-93
Derrida, J. *La Dissémination* (Paris: Éditions des Seuil, 1972)
Detweiler, R., 'Introduction: from chaos to legion to chance: the double play of apocalyptic and mimesis', in R. Detweiler and W. Doty (eds.), *The Daemonic Imagination: Biblical Text and Secular Story* (Atlanta, GA: Scholars Press, 1990), 1-26.
Dibelius, M., 'The Acts of the Apostles in the Setting of the History of Early Christian Literature', in H. Greeven (ed.), *Studies in the Acts of the Apostles* (London: SCM Press, 1956), 192-206
—, 'The Conversion of Cornelius', *Studies in the Acts of the Apostles* (London: SCM Press, 1956), 108-22

—, 'Paul in the Acts of the Apostles', *Studies in the Acts of the Apostles* (London: SCM Press, 1956), 207-14
—, 'Style Criticism of the Book of Acts', M. Ling, in H. Greeven (ed.), *Studies in the Acts of the Apostles* (London: SCM Press, 1956), 1-26
—, *From Tradition to Gospel* (London: Nicholson, 1934)
Diefenbach, M. *Die Komposition des Lukasevangeliums unter Berücksichtigung antiker Rhetorikelemente*, FTS 43 (Frankfurt: J. Knecht, 1993)
Dillon, D.J., 'Easter Revelation and Mission Program in Luke 24:46-48', in D. Durken (ed.), *Sin, Salvation and the Spirit* (Collegeville, MN: The Liturgical Press, 1979), 240-70
—, 'Acts of the Apostles', in J.A. Fitzmeyer, R.E. Brown, R.E. Murphy (eds.), *The New Jerome Biblical Commentary* (London: G. Chapman, 19932), 722-67
—, *From Eye-Witness to Ministers of the Word: Tradition and Composition in Luke 24* (Rome: Pontifical Bible Institute, 1978)
Dodd, C.H., *According to the Scriptures: The Substructure of the New Testament Theology* (London: Nisbet, 1952)
—, 'The Appearances of the Risen Christ: An Essay in Form-criticism of the Gospels', *Studies in the Gospels: Essays in Memory of R.H. Lightfoot* (Oxford: Oxford University Press, 1957), 9-35
Dollar, H.E., *A Biblical-Missiological Exploration of the Cross-Cultural Dimensions in Luke-Acts* (Lewiston, NY: E. Mellen Press), 1993
Donahue, J.R., 'Jesus as the Parable of God in the Gospel of Mark', *Interpretation* 32 (1978), 369-86
—, *The Gospel in Parable: Metaphor, Narrative and Theology in the Synoptic Gospels* (Philadelphia, PA: Fortress Press, 1988)
—, 'Redaction Criticism: Has the Hauptstrasse Become a Sackgasse?' in E.R. Malbon and E.V. McKnight (eds.), *The New Literary Criticism and the New Testament*, JSNT Supplement Series 109 (Sheffield: Sheffield Academic Press, 1994), 25-57
Dongel, J.R., *'The Structure of Luke's Gospel'*, PhD thesis Union Theological Seminary, Virginia (1991)
Donne, B.K., *Christ Ascended* (Exeter: Paternoster Press, 1983)
Dömer, M., *Das Heil Gottes: Studien zur Theologie des lukanischen Doppelwerkes* (Bonn: Hanstein, 1978)
Dormeyer D., *The New Testament Among the Writings of Antiquity*, The Biblical Seminar 55 (Sheffield: Sheffield Academic Press, 1998)
Droge, J.A., and J.D. Tabor, *A Noble Death: Suicide and Martyrdom Among Christians and Jews in Antiquity* (San Francisco, CA: Harper, 1992)
Drury, J., *Tradition and Design in Luke's Gospel: A Study in Early Christian Historiography* (London: DLT, 1976)
—, *The parables in the Gospels: history and allegory* (London: SPCK, 1985)

Duckworth, G.E., *Structural Patterns and Proportions in Vergil's Aeneid* (Ann Arbor, MI: University of Michigan Press, 1962)

Dudley, D.R., *A History of Cynism* (Hildesheim: G. Olms, 1967 (1937))

Dunn, J.D.G., *The Acts of the Apostles, Epworth Commentaries*, (Peterborough: Epworth Press, 1996)

—, *Christianity in the Making, Jesus Remembered*, vol. 1, (Grand Rapids, MI: Eerdmans, 2003)

Dupont, J., 'The Meal at Emmaus', in P. Benoit, J. Delorme and M.E. Boismard (eds.), *The Eucharist in the New Testament* (London: G. Chapman, 1964), 105-21

—, 'Les Pèlerins D'Emmaüs (Luc 24:13-35)', in *Miscellanea Biblica B Ubach*, Scripta et Documenta (1), (Montserrat: Benedictine Abbey, 1953), 349-74

—, 'Le Repas d'Emmaüs', *Lumen Vitae* 31 (1957), 77-92

—, 'La question du plan des Actes des Apôtres à lumière d'un texte de Lucien de Samosate', *Novum Testamentum* 21 (1979), 220-31

—, *The Salvation of the Gentiles* (N.Y.: Paulist Press, 1979)

Duris, 'Fragmenta', in C. Müller (ed.), *Fragmenta Historicum Graecorum, II* (Paris: Firmin Didot, 1885), 466-88

—, 'Fragmente', in F. Jacoby (ed.), *Die Fragmente der Griechischen Historiker, II A, Kommentar (Berlin: Weidmann Verlag, 1926), 115-31*

Edwards, R.A., 'The Redaction of Luke', *Journal of Religion* 49 (1969), 392-405

Egelkraut, H.L., *Jesus', Mission to Jerusalem: A Redaction-Critical Study of the Travel Narrative in the Gospel of Luke, Lk. 9:51-19:48* (Frankfurt: Peter Lang, 1976)

Ehrhardt, A. 'The Disciples of Emmaus', *New Testament Studies* 10 (1963), 182-201

Eisenman, R.H. and M. Wise, *The Dead Sea Scrolls Uncovered* (Shaftesbury: Element, 1992)

Eliade, M., *Cosmos and History: The Myth of the Eternal Return*, W.R. Trask (N.Y.: Harper, 1959 (1954))

—, *Patterns in Comparative Religion*, R. Sheed (London: Sheed and Ward, 1958)

Ellis, E.E., *The Gospel of Luke* (London: Marshall, Morgan, and Scott, 19742)

Ernst, J., *Das Evangelium nach Lukas*, Regensburger Neues Testament 3 (Regensburg: F. Pustet Verlag, 1977)

Esler, P.F., *Community and Gospel in Luke-Acts: The Social and Political Motivations of Lucan Theology* (Cambridge: Cambridge University Press, 1987)

Evans, C.A., 'Source, Form and Redaction Criticism: The 'Traditional', Methods of Synoptic Interpretation', in S.E. Porter and D. Tombs (eds.),

Bibliography

Approaches to the New Testament Study, JSNT Supplement Series 120 (Sheffield: Sheffield Academic Press, 1995), 17-45

—, 'The Function of the Elijah/Elisha Narratives in Luke's Ethic of Election', *Luke and Scripture: The Function of Sacred Tradition in Luke-Acts* (Minneapolis, MN: Fortress Press, 1993), 70-83

Evans, C.F., 'The Central Section of Saint Luke's Gospel', in D.E. Nineham (ed.), *Studies in the Gospels: Essays in Memory of R.H. Lightfoot* (Oxford: B. Blackwell, 1955), 37-53

—, 'I Will Go Before You Into Galilee', *Journal of Theological Studies n.s.* 5 (1954), 3-18

—, *Resurrection and the New Testament* (London: SCM Press, 1970)

—, *Saint Luke* (London: SCM Press, 1990)

—, 'Speeches in Acts', in A. Descamps and R. P. A. de Halleux (eds.), *Mélanges Bibliques en hommage à R.P. Béda Rigaux* (Gembloux: Éditions Duculot, 1970), 287-302

Fackre, G., 'Narrative Theology. An Overview', *Interpretation* 37 (1983), 340-352

Farrer, A.M., 'On Dispensing with Q', in D.E. Nineham (ed.), *Studies in the Gospels: Essays in Memory of R.H. Lightfoot* (Oxford: B. Blackwell, 1955), 55-80

Feiler, P.F., '*Jesus the Prophet: The Lucan Portrayal of Jesus as the Prophet Like Moses*', PhD thesis, Princeton Theological Seminary (1986)

Fenton, J.C., 'Inclusio and Chiasmus in Matthew', in K. Aland (ed.), *Studia Evangelica*, vol. 1, Texte und Untersuchungen zur Geschichte der altchristlichen Literatur 73 (Berlin: Akademie Verlag, 1959), 174-179

Ferrary G.R.F., 'Plato and Poetry', in G.A. Kennedy (ed.), *The Cambridge History of Literary Criticism*, vol. 1: *Classical Criticism* (Cambridge: Cambridge University Press, 19953), 92-148

Filson, F.V., 'Broken Patterns in the Gospel of Matthew', *Journal of Biblical Literature* 75 (1956), 227-31

—, 'The Journey Motif in Luke-Acts', in W. W. Gasque and R.P. Martin (eds.), *Apostolic History and the Gospel: biblical and historical essays presented to F. F. Bruce on his 60th birthday (Grand Rapids, MI: Eerdmans, 1970)*, 68-77

Fitzmyer, J.A., *The Gospel According to Luke I-IX*, Anchor Bible (28) (Garden City, NY: Doubleday, 1981)

—, *The Gospel According to Luke X-XXIV*, Anchor Bible 28A (Garden City, NY: Doubleday, 1985)

—, *Luke the Theologian: Aspects of His Teaching* (London: G. Chapman, 1989)

Flender, H., *Saint Luke: Theologian of Redemptive History* (London: SPCK, 1967)

Flower, M.A., *Theopompus of Chios: History and Rhetoric in the Fourth Century BC* (Oxford: Clarendon Press, 1994)

Fink, J., *Bildfrömmigkeit und Bekenntnis: das Alte Testament, Herakles und die Herrlichkeit Christi an der Via Latina in Rom* (Köln: Böhlau Verlag, 1978)

Finn, T.M., 'The God-fearers Reconsidered', *Catholic Biblical Quarterly* 47 (1985), 75-83

Focant, C., 'Introduction', in C. Focant (ed.), *The Synoptic Gospels: Source Criticism and the New Literary Criticism* (Leuven: Leuven University Press, 1993), 3-8

Fornara, C.W., *The Nature of History in Ancient Greece and Rome*, Eidos Studies in classical kinds (Berkeley, CA: University of California Press, 1983)

Forster, E.M., *Aspects of the Novel* (London: W. Clowes, 1974)

Franklin, E., *Luke: Interpreter of Paul, Critic of Matthew*, JSNT Supplement Series 92 (Sheffield: Sheffield Academic Press, 1994)

—, 'The Ascension and the Eschatology of Luke-Acts', *Scottish Journal of Theology* 23 (1970), 191-200

—, *Christ the Lord* (London: SPCK, 1975)

Freeland, C.A., 'Plot Imitates Action: Aesthetic Evaluation and Moral Realism in Aristotle's Poetics', in A.O. Rorty (ed.), *Essays on Aristotle's Poetics* (Princeton, NJ: Princeton University Press, 1992), 111-32

Frei, H., 'The "Literal Reading" of Biblical Narrative in the Christian Tradition: Does It Stretch or Will It Break?', in F. McConnell (ed.), *The Bible and the Narrative Tradition* (N.Y.: Oxford University Press, 1986), 36-77

—, *The Eclipse of Biblical Narrative: A Study in Eighteenth and Nineteenth Century Hermeneutics* (New Haven, CT: Yale University Press), 1974

Freyne, S., 'The Geography, Politics, and Economics of Galilee and the Quest for the Historical Jesus', *Studying the Historical Jesus* (Leiden: E.J. Brill, 1994), 75-121

—, *Galilee, Jesus, and The Gospels: Literary Approaches and Historical Investigations* (Philadelphia, PA: Fortress Press, 1988)

Friedrich, G., 'Die Gegner des Paulus im 2 Korintherbrief', in M. Hengel O. Betz, and P. Schmidt (eds.), *Abraham unser Vater: Juden und Christen im Gespräch über die Bibel*, AGJU 5 (Leiden: E.J. Brill, 1963), 200-201

Fritz, K. von., 'Die Bedeutung des Aristoteles für die Geschichtsschreibung', in *Histoire et Historiens dans l'Antiquité*, Entretiens de la Fondation Hardt 4 (Genève: Vandoeuvres, 1956 (1948)), 85-145

Frye, N., *The Anatomy of Criticism: Four Essays* (Princeton, NJ: Princeton University Press, 1959)

Fuller, R.H., *The Formation of the Resurrection Narratives* (Philadelphia, PA: Fortress Press, 1980 (1971))

Funk, R.W., 'The Good Samaritan as Metaphor', in J.D. Crossan (ed.), *Semeia 2: The Good Samaritan* (Missoula, MT: University of Montana, 1974), 74-81

Funk, R.W., R.W. Hoover and *The Jesus Seminar, The Five Gospels: The Search for the Authentic Words of Jesus* (N.Y.: Macmillan, 1993)

Gaechter, P., *Die literarische Kunst im Matthäus-Evangelium* (Stuttgart: Katholisches Bibelwerk, 1966)

Gallie, W.B., *Philosophy and Historical Understanding* (N.Y.: Schoken, 1958)

Garrett, S., *The Demise of the Devil: Magic and the Demonic in Luke's Writing* (Minneapolis, MN: Fortress Press, 1989)

Gasque, W.W., *A History of the Criticism of the Acts of the Apostles* (Tübingen: J.C.B. Mohr, 1975)

Gaventa, B.R., 'From Darkness to Light: Aspects of Conversion in the New Testament' (Philadelphia, PA: Fortress Press, 1986)

Gebauer, G., and C. Wulf, *Mimesis: Culture. Art. Society* (Berkeley, CA: University of California Press, 1995) (German ed., *Mimesis: Kultur. Kunst. Gesellschaft* (Reinbeck: Rowohlt, 1992))

Gellrich, J.M., 'Figura, Allegory and the Question of History', in Lerer S. (ed.), *Literary History and the Challenge of Philology: The legacy of Erich Auerbach* (Stanford, CA: Stanford University Press, 1996), 107-123

Gelzer, T., 'Klassizismus, Attizismus und Asianismus', in H. Flashar (ed.), *Le Classicisme à Rome aux 1ers siècles avant et après J.-C.*, Entretiens sur l'Antiquité Classiques 25 (Genève: Vandoeuvres, 1979), 1-41

—, 'Towards a Theology of Acts: Reading and Rereading', *Interpretation* 42 (1988), 146-57

Gempf, C., 'Acts', in D.A. Carson, R.T. France, et. al. (eds.), *New Bible Commentary* (Leicester: InterVarsity Press, 19944), 1066-1107

—, 'Mission and Misunderstanding: Paul and Barnabas in Lystra (Acts 14:8-20)', in T. Lane, A. Billington, and M. Turner (eds.), *Mission and Meaning: Essays Presented to Peter Cotterell* (Carlisle: Paternoster Press, 1995), 56-69

Genette, G. *Narrative Discourse* (Ithaca, NY: Cornell University Press, 1980)

George, A., *Études sur l'Oeuvre de Luc* (Paris: Éditions J. Gabalda, 1978)

—, 'La royauté de Jésus', in A. George (ed.), *Études sur l'oeuvre de Luc* (Paris: Éditions J. Gabalda, 1978), 257-82

—, 'La royauté de Jésus selon l'évangile de Luc' *Science et Esprit* 14 (1962), 57-62

Gilchrist, J.M., 'The Historicity of Paul's Shipwreck', *Journal for the Study of NT* 61 (1996), 29-51

Gill, D., 'Observations on the Lukan Travel Narrative and Some Related Passages', *Harvard Theological Review* 63 (1970), 199-221

Gill, D., 'The Structure of Acts 9', *Biblica* 55 (1974), 546-48

Gilmore, D.D., 'Introduction: The Shame of Dishonor', in D.D. Gilmore (ed.), *Honor and Shame and the Unity of the Mediterranean* (Washington, D.C.: American Anthropological Association Press, 1987), 2-21

Girard, L., *L'Évangile des voyages de Jésus, ou la section 9:51-18.14 de Saint Luc* (Paris: Éditions J. Gabalda, 1951)

Girard, R., *Deceit, Desire, and the Novel* (Baltimore, MA: John Hopkins University Press, 1965)

—, *Violence and the Sacred* (Baltimore, MA: John Hopkins University Press, 1979)

—, *Things Hidden since the Foundation of the World* (Stanford, CA: Stanford University Press, 1987)

—, *A Theater of Envy* (Oxford: Oxford University Press, 1991)

—, '"The ancient trail trodden by the wicked": Job as scapegoat', in A. J. McKenna (ed.), *Semeia 33: René Girard and Biblical Studies* (Missoula, MT: Scholars Press, 1985), 13-41

Glasson, T.F., *Greek Influence in Jewish Eschatology* (London: SPCK, 1961)

Gnilka, J., *Das Evangelium nach Markus (1:1-8:26)*, EKNT 1 (Zürich: Benziger, 1978)

Golden, L., *Aristotle on Tragic and Comic Mimesis* (Atlanta, GA: Scholars Press, 1992)

Goldhill, S., *The Poet's Voice: Essays on Poetics and Greek Literature* (Cambridge: Cambridge University Press, 1991)

Gómez, G.M., 'Jerusalén-Jerosólima en el Vocabulario y la Geografía de Lucas', *Revista Catalana de Teologia* 7 (1982), 131-86

Goodacre, M.S., *Goulder and the Gospels: An Examination of a New Paradigm*, JSNT Supplement Series 133 (Sheffield: Sheffield Academic Press, 1996)

Goodman, N., *Languages of Art: An Approach to a Theory of Symbols* (Indianapolis, IN: Bobbs-Merrill, 1969)

Goodman, P., *The Structure of Literature* (Chicago, IL: University of Chicago, 1964)

Goppelt, L., 'Das Osterkerygma Heute', in L. Goppelt (ed.), *Christologie und Ethik: Gesamte Aufsatze zum Neuen Testament* (Göttingen: Vandenhoeck, 1968), 79-101

Goulder, M.D., 'The Chiastic Structure of the Lukan Journey', in F. L. Cross, *Studia Evangelica*, vol. 2, Texte und Untersuchungen zur Geschichte der altchristlichen Literatur 87 (Berlin: Akademie Verlag, 1964), 195-202

—, 'On Putting Q to the Test', *New Testament Studies* 24 (1978), 218-234

—, *The Evangelist's Calendar* (London: SPCK, 1979)

—, *Luke: A New Paradigm* (Sheffield: Sheffield Academic Press, 1989)

—, *Type and History in Acts* (London: SPCK, 1964)

Gowler, D.B., 'Characterization in Luke: A Socio-Narratological Approach', *Biblical Theology Bulletin* 19 (1989), 54-62

Graß, H., *Ostergeschehen und Osterberichte* (Göttingen: Vandenhoeck & Ruprecht, 19704)
Grassi, J.A., 'Emmaus Revisited (Luke 24:13-35 and Acts 8:26-40)', *Catholic Biblical Quarterly* 26 (1964), 463-65
Green, H.B., 'The Structure of Matthew's Gospel', *Studia Evangelica*, vol. 4, Texte und Untersuchungen zur Geschichte der altchristlichen Literatur 102 (Berlin: Akademie Verlag, 1965), 47-59
Green, J.B., 'The Demise of the Temple as "Culture Center", in Luke-Acts: An Exploration of the Rending of the Temple Veil', *Revue Biblique* 101 (1994), 495-515
—, 'Internal Repetition in Luke-Acts: Contemporary Narratology and Lucan Historiography', in B. Witherington III (ed.), *History, Literature and Society in the Book of Acts* (Cambridge: Cambridge University Press, 1996), 283-299
—, *The Theology of the Gospel of Luke* (Cambridge: Cambridge University Press, 1995)
—, *The Gospel of Luke*, NICNT (Cambridge: Eerdmans, 1997)
Grundmann, W., *Das Evangelium nach Lukas* (Berlin: Evangelische Verlaganstalt, 19612)
Guelich, R.A., *Mark 1-8:26*, WBC 34A (Dallas, TX: Word Books, 1989)
Guillaume, J.-M., *Luc interprète des anciennes traditions sur la résurrection de Jésus*, Études Bibliques (Paris: Éditions J. Gabalda, 1979)
Gundry, R.H., 'The Essential Physicality of Jesus', Resurrection According to the New Testament', in J.B. Green and M. Turner (eds.), *Jesus of Nazareth: Lord and Christ. Essays on the Historical Jesus and New Testament* (Carlisle: Paternoster Press, 1994), 204-19
—, *Mark. A Commentary on His Apology for the Cross* (Grand Rapids, MI: Eerdmans, 1993)
Haenchen, E., *The Acts of the Apostles* (Oxford: B. Blackwell, 1971)
—, *Der Weg Jesu: eine Erklärung des Markus-evangeliums und der kanonischen Parallelen* (Berlin: W. de Gruyter, 1968)
Hagner, D.A., *Matthew 1-13*, WBC 33A (Dallas, TX: Word Books, 1993)
Halliwell, S., *Aristotle's Poetics* (London: Duckworth, 1986)
Hamm, D., 'Acts 3:1-10: The Healing of the Temple Beggar as Lucan Theology', *Biblica* 67 (1986), 305-19
—, 'Paul's Blindness and Its Healing: Clues to Symbolic Intent (Acts 9; 22 and 26)', *Biblica* 71 (1990), 63-72
—, 'Sight to the Blind: Vision as Metaphor in Luke,' *Biblica* (1986), 457-77
Hamerton-Kelly, R.G., 'A Girardian interpretation of Paul: rivalry, mimesis and victimage in the Corinthian correspondence', in A. J. McKenna (ed.), *Semeia 33: René Girard and Biblical Studies* (Missoula, MT: Scholars Press, 1985), 65-81

Hansen, W., *Antology of Ancient Greek Popular Literature* (Bloomington, IN: Indiana UP, 1998)
Harnack, A., *The Acts of the Apostles* (London: Williams & Norgate, 1909)
Hasel, G., *New Testament Theology: Basic Issues in the Current Debate* (Grand Rapids, MI: Eerdmans, 1993 (1978))
Hastings, A., *Prophet and Witness in Jerusalem: A Study of the Teaching of Saint Luke* (London: Longmans, Green & Co., 1958)
Haya-Prats, G., *L'Esprit Force de l'Église* (Paris: Éditions du Cerf, 1975)
Havelock, E.R., *Preface to Plato* (Cambridge, MA: Harvard University Press, 1963)
Hedrick, C.W., 'What is a Gospel? Geography, Time and Narrative Structure', *Perspectives of Religious Studies* 10 (1983), 255-68
—, *Parables as Poetic Fictions: The Creative Voice of Jesus* (Peabody, MA: Hendrickson, 1994)
—, 'Paul's Conversion/Call: A Comparative Analysis of the Three Reports in Acts', *Journal of Biblical Literature* 100 (1981), 415-32
Hemer, C. J. *The Book of Acts in the Setting of Hellenistic History* (Tübingen: J.C.B. Mohr, 1989)
Hengel, M. 'The Geography of Palestine in Acts', in R. Bauckham (ed.), *The Book of Acts in Its Palestinian Setting*, BAIFCS 3 (Carlisle: Paternoster Press, 1995), 27-78
—, *Between Jesus and Paul: Studies in the Earliest History of Christianity* (London: SCM Press, 1983)
Hennecke, E., *Neutestamentliche Apocryphen, vol. 2: Apostolisches Apokalypsen und Verwandtes* (Tübingen: J.C.B. Mohr, 19643)
Henry, R., *Bibliothèque [par] Photius*, texte établi et traduit par R. Henry (Paris: Belles Lettres, 1960)
Hickling, C., 'The Emmaus Story and Its Sequel', in S. Barton and G. Stanton (eds.), *Essays in Honour of Leslie Houlden* (London: SPCK, 1994), 21-33
Himmelfarb, M., *Ascent to Heaven in Jewish and Christian Apocalypses* (Oxford: Oxford University Press, 1993)
—, *Tours of Hell: Apocalyptic Form in Jewish and Christian Literature* (Philadelphia, PA: State University of Pennsylvania Press, 1983)
Hock, R.F., 'The Greek Novel', in D.E. Aune (ed.), *Greco-Roman Literature and the New Testament*, SBL Sources for Biblical Scholars (21) (Atlanta, GA: Scholars Press, 1988), 127-146
Holtz, T., *Untersuchungen über die Alttestamentlichen Zitate bei Lukas* (Berlin: Akademie Verlag, 1968)
Höistad, R. *Cynic Hero and Cynic King: Studies in the Cynic Conception of Man* (Uppsala: C. Bloms, 1948)
Hooker, M.D., *The Gospel According to St. Mark*, Black's NT Commentaries (London: A&C Black, 1991)

Hull, W.E., 'A Structural Analysis of the Gospel of Luke', *Review and Expositor* 64 (1967), 421-25

Hutton, J., *Aristotle's Poetics*, transl., introduction and notes, by J. Hutton (N.Y.: W.W. Norton, 1982)

Iersel, B., van, 'De Betekenis van Markus Vanuit Zijn Topografische Structuur', *Tijdschrift voor Theologies* 22 (1982), 117-38

—, *Mark: A Reader-Response Commentary*, W.H. Bisscheroux (tr.), JSNT Supplement Series 164 (Sheffield: Sheffield Academic Press, 1998)

Innes, D.C., 'Longinus: Structure and Unity', in J.G.J. Abbenes, S.R. Slings, I. Sluiter (eds.), *Greek Literary Theory After Aristotle: A collection of papers in honour of D.M. Schenkeweld* (Amsterdam: Amsterdam University Press, 1995), 111-24

Ireland, D.J., *Stewardship and the Kingdom of God: An Historical, Exegetical and Contextual Study of the Parable of the Unjust Steward in Lk. 16:1-3* (Leiden: E.J. Brill, 1992)

Isaac, B., 'Bandits in Judaea and Arabia', *Harvard Studies in Classical Philology* 88 (1984), 171-203

Jáuregui, J.A., 'Historiografía y teología en Hechos. Estado de la investigación desde 1980', *Estudios Bíblicos* 53 (1985), 97-123

Jaeger, W., *The Theology of the Early Greek Philosophers: The Gifford Lectures 1936* (Oxford: Clarendon Press, 1947)

—, *Early Christianity and Greek Paideia* (Cambridge, MA: Harvard University Press, 1961)

Jervell, J., 'Retrospect and Prospect in Luke-Acts Interpretation', *SBL Seminar Papers* 1991, 383-403

—, 'The Church of Jews and Godfearers', in J.B. Tyson (ed.), *Luke-Acts and the Jewish People* (Minneapolis, MN: Augsburg Press, 1988), 11-20

Johnson, L.T., *The Gospel of Luke*, Sacra Pagina Series (3) (Collegeville MN: The Liturgical Press, 1991)

Joubert, S.J., 'The Jerusalem Community as Role-Model for a Cosmopolitan Christian Group. A Socio-Literary Analysis of Luke's Symbolic Universe,' *Neotestamentica* 29/1 (1995), 49-59

Juel, D., *Luke-Acts* (London: SCM Press, 1983)

—, *Messianic Exegesis: Christological Interpretation of the Old Testament in Early Christianity* (Philadelphia, PA: Fortress Press, 1988)

Just, A.A., Jr. *The Ongoing Feast: Table Fellowship and Eschatology at Emmaus* (Collegeville MN: The Liturgical Press, 1993)

Kebric, R., *In the Shadow of Macedon: Duris of Samos*, (Hist. Einzelschr. 29), (Wiesbaden: Steiner, 1977)

Kelber, W.H., *The Kingdom in Mark: A New Place and a New Time* (Philadelphia, PA: Fortress Press, 1974)

Kennedy, G.A., *The Art of Persuasion in Greece* (Princeton, NJ: Princeton University Press, 1963)

—, *The Art of Rhetoric in the Roman World (300 BC - AD 300)* (Princeton, NJ: Princeton University Press, 1972)

—, *Classical Rhetoric and its Christian and Secular Tradition* (London: C. Helm, 1980)

—, *New Testament Interpretation through Rhetorical Criticism* (London: University of North Carolina Press, 1984)

Kermode, F., *The Sense of an Ending: Studies in the Theory of Fiction* (London: Oxford University Press, 1966)

Kilgallen, J.J., 'Persecution in the Acts of the Apostles', *Luke and Acts* (N.Y.: Paulist Press, 1993), 143-60

Kim, H.-S., *Die Geisttaufe des Messias: eine kompositionsgeschichtliche Untersuchung zu einen Leitmotiv des lukanischen Doppelwerks* (Berlin: Peter Lang, 1993)

Kingsbury, J.D., *Matthew as Story* (Philadelphia, PA: Fortress Press, 19882)

Klein, J.G., *Die zwölf Apostel: Ursprung und Gehalt einer Idee* (Göttingen: Vandenhoeck & Ruprecht, 1961)

Lerer S. (ed.), *Literary History and the Challenge of Philology: The legacy of Erich Auerbach* (Stanford, CA: Stanford University Press, 1996)

Knox, J., *Some Hellenistic Elements in Primitive Christianity* (London: Oxford University Press, 1944)

Knox, W.L., 'The "Divine Hero" Christology in the New Testament', *Harvard Theological Review* 41 (1948), 229-249.

—, *The Acts of the Apostles* (Cambridge: Cambridge University Press 1948)

Kodell, J., 'The Theology of Luke in Recent Study', *Biblica* 1 (1971), 115-144.

Koester, H., *History, Culture, and Religion of the Hellenistic Age*, Series Hermeneia (Philadelphia, PA: Fortress Press, 1980)

Kosman, A., 'Acting: Drama as the Mimēsis of Praxis', in A.O. Rorty (ed.), *Essays on Aristotle's Poetics* (Princeton, NJ: Princeton University Press, 1992), 51-72

Kraabel, A.T., 'The Disappearance of the "God-fearers"', *Numen* 28 (1981), 113-26

Kränkl, E., *Jesus der Knecht Gottes* (Regensburg: F. Pustet Verlag, 1972)

Kremer, J., *Pfingstbericht und Pfingstgeschehen: eine exegetische Untersuchung zu Apg. 2:1-13* (Stuttgart: Katholisches Bibelwerk, 1973)

Kurz, W.S., 'Hellenistic Rhetoric in the Christological Proof of Luke-Acts', *Catholic Biblical Quarterly* 42 (1980), 171-95

—, 'Narrative Approaches to Luke-Acts', *Biblica* 68 (1987), 195-220

—, *Reading Luke-Acts: Dynamics of Biblical Narrative* (Louisville, KY: Westminster Press, 1993)

Kümmel, W., *Introduction to the New Testament* (London: SCM Press, 1975)

—, *The Theology of the New Testament* (London: SCM Press, 1975)

Lagrange, M.-J., 'Les légendes pythagoriciennes et l'évangile', *Revue Biblique* 40 (1936), 481-511
—, 'La vie d'Apollonios par Philostrate', *Revue Biblique* 41 (1937), 5-28.
Lambrecht, J., 'Parables in Mk. 4', *Tijdschrift voor Theologie* 15 (1975), 26-43.
—, *Die Redaktion der Markus-Apokalypse, Literarische Strukturuntersuchung* (Rome: Pontifical Bible Institute, 1967)
Lane, W.L., *Hebrews 9-13*, WBC 47B (Dallas, TX: Word Books, 1991)
Lang, F.G., 'Kompositionsanalyse des Markusevangeliums', *Zeitschrift für Theologie und Kirche* 74 (1977), 1-24.
Larranaga, V., *L'Ascension de Notre-Seigneur dans le Nouveau Testament* (Rome: Pontifical Bible Institute, 1938)
Lévi-Strauss, C., 'The Story of Asdiwal', in E. Leach (ed.), *The Structural Study of Myth and Totemism*, ASAM 5 (London: Tavistock, 1967), 1-47
—, 'The Structural Study of Myth', *Journal of American Folklore* 68 (1955), 428-44
Leivestad, R., 'Ταπεινός-ταπεινόφρων', *Novum Testamentum* 8 (1966), 36-47
Lesky, A., *A History of Greek Literature* (London: Methuen, 1966)
Levine, B., 'René Girard on Job: the question of the scapegoat', in A. J. McKenna (ed.), *Semeia 33: René Girard and Biblical Studies* (Missoula, MT: Scholars Press, 1985), 125-33
Levoratti, A.J., 'La lectura no sacrificial del evangelio en la obra de René Girard', *Revista Bíblica* 47 (1985), 159-76
Lieu, J., '"The Parting of the Ways": Theological Construct or Historical Reality?', *Journal for the Study of NT* 56 (1994), 101-19
Lightfoot, R.H., *The Gospel Message of St.Mark* (London: Oxford University Press, 1952)
Lindijer, C.H., *De Armen en de Rijken bij Lucas* (The Hague: Boekecentrum, 1981)
—, *Handelingen van de Apostolen, vol. 1: Van Jerusalem naar Antiochië (hfsk 1-12)*, A.F.J. Klijn (ed.), De Prediking van het Nieuwe Testament (Nijkerk: Callenbach, 1975)
—, *Handelingen van de Apostelen, vol. 2: Door*, A.F.J. Klijn (ed.), De Prediking van het Nieuwe Testament (Nijkerk: Callenbach, 1979)
—, 'Two Creative Encounters in the Work of Luke. Luke 24:13-35 and Acts 8:26-40', in F.J. Lijn, T. Baarda, and W.C. van Unnik (eds.), *Miscellanea Neotestamentica, Supplement to Novum Testamentum*, vol. 48 (Leiden: E.J. Brill, 1978), 77-86
Litke, W.D., *'Luke's Knowledge of the Septuagint: A Study of the Citations in Luke-Acts'*, PhD thesis, McMaster University, Canada (1993)
Lohfink, G., *Die Himmelfahrt Jesu* (Münich: Kösel, 1971)
—, *The Conversion of Saint Paul* (Chicago, IL: Franciscan Herald Press, 1976)

Lohmeyer, E., *Galiläa und Jerusalem* (Göttingen: Vandenhoeck & Ruprecht, 1936)

Lohr, C.H., 'Oral Techniques in the Gospel of Matthew', *Catholic Biblical Quarterly* 23 (1961), 403-35

Lohse, E., 'Lukas als Theologe der Heilsgeschichte', in *Die Einheit des Neuen Testaments: exegetische Studien zur Theologie des Neuen Testaments* (Tübingen: Vandenhoeck & Ruprecht, 1973), 145-164.

Löning, K., 'The Circle of Stephen and Its Mission', in J. Becker (ed.), *Christian Beginnings: Word and Community from Jesus to Post-Apostolic Times* 103-31, (Louisville, KY: Westminster Press, 1993)

—, *Die Saulustradition in der Apostelgeschichte* (Münster: Aschendorff, 1973)

Louw, J.P., and E.A. Nida, *Greek-English Lexicon of the New Testament Based on Semantic Domains* (N.Y.: United Bible Societies, 1988-1989)

Lücking, S., *Mimesis der Verachteten. Eine Studie zur Erzählweise von Mk. 14:1-11*, Stuttgarter Bibelstudien 152 (Stuttgart: Katholisches Bibelwerk, 1992)

Lüdemann, G., *Early Christianity According to the Traditions in Acts. A Commentary*, J. Bowden (Minneapolis, MN: Fortress Press, 1989)

—, *Paul, Apostle to the Gentiles* (London: SCM Press, 1984).

—, *Paulus, der Heidenapostel* (Göttingen: Vandenhoeck & Ruprecht, 1980)

Lüderitz, G., 'Rhetorik, Poetik, Kompositionstechnik im Marcusevangelium', in H. Canzik (ed.), *Markus-Philologie*, WUNT 33 (Tübingen: J.C.B. Mohr, 1984), 165-203

Lyonnet, S., '"La Voie", dans les Actes des Apôtres', in J. Delorme, and J. Duplacy (eds.), *La Parole de Grâce: Études Lucaniennes à la Mémoire d'Augustin George* (Paris: Recherches de Science Religieuse, 1981), 149-64

MacDonald, D.R., *Mimesis and Intertextuality in Antiquity and Christianity. Studies in Antiquity and Christianity* (Harrisburg, PA: Trinity Press International, 2001)

Maddox, R., *The Purpose of Luke-Acts* (Edinburgh: T&T Clark, 1982)

Magness, J.L., *Sense and Absence: Structure and Suspense in the Ending of Mark's Gospel* (Atlanta, GA: Scholars Press, 1986)

Maile, J. 'The Ascension in Luke-Acts', *Tyndale Bulletin* 37 (1986), 29-59

Malbon, E.S., 'Mark: Myth and Parable', *Biblica* 16 (1986), 8-17

—, 'Narrative Criticism: How Does the Story Mean?', in S. Moore and J.C. Anderson (eds.), *Mark and Method: New Approaches in Biblical Studies* (Minneapolis, MN: Fortress Press, 1992), 23-49

—, *Narrative Space and Mythic Meaning in Mark* (Sheffield: JSOT Press, 1991 (1986))

Malherbe, A.J., *Social Aspects of Early Christianity* (Philadelphia, PA: Fortress Press, 1983²)

Maloney, L.M., *"All That God Had Done with Them": The Narrative of the Works of God in the Early Christian Community as Described in the Acts of the Apostles*, American University Studies, Series 7, Theology of Religion 91 (N.Y.: Peter Lang, 1991)

Marcus, J. *The Way of the Lord: Christological Exegesis of the Old Testament in the Gospel of Mark* (Edinburgh: T&T Clark, 1993)

Marguerat, D., 'The End of Acts (28:16-31) and the Rhetoric of Silence', in S.E. Porter and T.H. Olbricht (eds.), *Rhetoric in the New Testament: Essays from the 1992 Heilderberg Conference*, JSNT Supplement Series 90 (Sheffield: Sheffield Academic Press, 1993), 74-89

—, 'Saul's Conversion (Acts 9, 22, 26) and the Multiplication of Narrative in Acts', in C.M. Tuckett (ed.), *Luke's Literary Achievement: Collected Essays*, JSNT Supplement Series 116 (Sheffield: Sheffield Academic Press, 1995), 129-55

Markus, R.A., 'How on Earth Could Places Become Holy? Origins of the Christian Idea of Holy Places', *Journal of Early Christian Studies* 2/3 (1994), 257-71

Marshall, I.H., 'Luke and His "Gospel"', in P. Stuhlmacher (ed.), *Das Evangelium und die Evangelien*, WUNT 28 (Tübingen: J.C.B. Mohr, 1983), 289-308

—, *The Gospel of Luke: A Commentary on the Greek Text* (Exeter: Paternoster Press, 1992 (1978))

—, *Luke: Historian and Theologian* (Exeter: Paternoster Press, 1970)

Martin, C.J., 'A Chamberlain's Journey and the Challenge of Interpretation for Liberation', in K. G. Cannon and E. Schüssler-Fiorenza (eds.), *Semeia 47: Interpretation for Liberation* (Missoula, MT: Scholars Press, 1989), 105-35

Marxen, W., 'Die Auferstehung als historisches und als theologisches Problem', in W. Marxen. *Die Bedeutung der Auferstehungbotschaft für den Glauben an Jesu Christus* (Gütersloh: Delling and Geier, 19686)

Matera, F.J., 'Jesus', Journey to Jerusalem (Luke 9:51-19:46) A Conflict with Israel', *Journal for the Study of NT* 51 (1993), 57-77

Mauser, U., *Christ in the Wilderness: The Wilderness Theme in the Second Gospel and Its Basis in the Biblical Tradition*, SBT (London: SCM Press, 1963)

McCoy, W.J., 'In the Shadow of Thucydides', in B. Witherington III (ed.), *History, Literature and Society in the Book of Acts* (Cambridge: Cambridge University Press, 1996), 3-32

McBride, D., *Emmaus: The Gracious Visit of God According to Luke*, (Dublin: Dominican Publications, 1991)

McCasland, S.V., 'The Way', *Journal of Biblical Literature* 77 (1958), 220-230

MacCormack, S., 'Loca Sancta: The Organization of Sacred Topography on Late Antiquity', in R. Ousterhout (ed.), *The Blessings of Pilgrimage* (Urbana, IL: University of Illinois Press, 1990), 6-40

McCown, C.C., 'The Geography of Jesus' Last Journey to Jerusalem', *Journal of Biblical Literature* 51 (1932), 107-29

—, 'The Geography of Luke's Central Section', *Journal of Biblical Literature* 58 (1938), 51-56

—, 'Gospel Geography: Fiction, Fact and Truth', *Journal of Biblical Literature* 60 (1941), 1-25

McDonald, J.I.H., 'Rhetorical Issue and Rhetorical Strategy in Luke 10:25-37 and Acts 10:1-11:18', in S.E. Porter and T.H. Olbricht, *Rhetoric and the New Testament: Essays from the 1992 Heidelberg Conference*, JSNT Supplement Series 90 (Sheffield: Sheffield Academic Press, 1993), 59-73

McNicol, J., D.L. Dungan and D.B. Peabody, *Luke's Use of Matthew: Beyond the Q Impasse. A Demonstration by the Research Team of the International Institute for Gospel Studies* (Valley Forge, PA: Trinity Press International, 1996)

Mealand, D.L., 'Hellenistic Historians and the Style of Acts', *Zeitschrift für die neuetestamentlische Wissenschaft* 82 (1991), 42-66

—, 'Luke-Acts and the Verbs of Dionysius of Halicarnassus', *Journal for the Study of NT* 63 (1996), 63-86

—, 'The Phrase "Many Proofs" in Acts 1,3 and in Hellenistic Writers', *Zeitschrift für die neuetestamentlische Wissenschaft* 80 (1989), 134-35

Meeks, W.A., *The First Urban Christians: The Social World of the Apostle Paul* (New Haven, CT: Yale University, 1993)

Meister, K., *Historische Kritik bei Polybios*, Palingenesia 9 (Wiesbaden: Steiner, 1975)

Melberg, A., *Theories of Mimesis* (Cambridge: Cambridge University Press, 1995)

Menoud, P.H., 'Pendant Quarante Jours', W.C. van Unnik (ed.), *Neotestamentica et Patristica*, Festschrift O. Cullmann (Leiden: E.J. Brill, 1962), 146-56

—, 'Le Plan des Actes des Apôtres', *New Testament Studies* 1 (1954), 44-51

Menzies, R.P., *The Development of Early Christian Pneumatology With Special Reference to Luke-Acts* (Sheffield: Sheffield Academic Press, 1991)

—, *Empowered for Witness: The Spirit in Luke-Acts*, JPT (6) (Sheffield: Sheffield Academic Press, 1994)

Metzger, B.M., *A Textual Commentary on the Greek Testament* (London: UBS, 1971)

Meynet, R. *Quelle est donc cette Parole? Lecture "rhétorique" de l'Evangile de Luc (1-9, 22-24)* (Paris: Éditions du Cerf, 1979)

—, *Avez-vous lu saint Luc? guide pour la rencontre* (Paris: Éditions du Cerf, 1990)

—, *L'Evangile selon saint Luc: Analyse rhétorique* (Paris: Éditions du Cerf, 1988)

Mink, L.O., 'History and Fiction as Modes of Comprehension', in R. Cohen (ed.), *New Directions in Literary History* (Baltimore, MA: John Hopkins University Press, 1974), 104-24

Mínguez, D. 'Hechos 8:25-40. Análisis Estructural del Relato', *Biblica* 57/2 (1976), 169-91

Michaelis, W. *Die Erscheinungen des Auferstandenen* (Basel: Heinrich Majer, 1944)

Miller, R.J., 'Elijah, John, and Jesus in the Gospel of Luke', *New Testament Studies* 34 (1988), 611-22

Minear, P.S., 'Luke's Use of the Birth Stories', in L.E. Keck and J.L. Martyn (eds.), *Studies in Luke-Acts* (London: SPCK, 1968), 113-30

Miyoshi, M., *Der Anfang des Reiseberichtes Lk. 9:51-10:24, eine redaktionsgeschichtliche Untersuchung*, AnBib (60) (Rome: Biblical Institute Press, 1974)

Moehring, H.R., 'The verb akouein in Acts 9:7 and 22:9', *Novum Testamentum* 3 (1959), 88-99

Moessner, D.P., '"The Christ Must Suffer": New Light on the Jesus-Peter, Stephen, Paul Parallels in Luke-Acts', *Novum Testamentum* 28/3 (1986), 220-56

—, 'Luke 9:1-50: Luke's Preview of the Journey of the Prophet Like Moses of Deuteronomy', *Journal of Biblical Literature* 102 (1983), 575-605

—, '"The Christ Must Suffer", The Church Must Suffer: Rethinking the Theology of the Cross in Luke-Acts', *SBL Seminar Papers*, 1990, 165-95

—, *Lord of the Banquet: The Literary and Theological Significance of the Lukan Travel Narrative* (Minneapolis, MN: Fortress Press, 1989)

—, 'The "Script" of the Scriptures in Acts: Suffering as God's Plan ($\beta o \upsilon \lambda \acute{\eta}$) for the World for the "Release of Sins",' in B. Witherington III (ed.), *History, Literature and Society in the Book of Acts* (Cambridge: Cambridge University Press, 1996), 218-50

Mohm, S., *Untersuchungen zu den historiographischen Anschauungen des Polybios*, Dissertation (Saarbrücken, 1977)

Morgan, J.R., 'Introduction', in J. R. Morgan and R. Stoneman (eds.), *Greek Fiction: The Greek Novel in Context* (London: Routledge, 1994), 1-12

Moltmann, J., *The Way of Christ: Christology in Messianic Dimensions* (London: SCM Press, 1990)

Morgenthaler, R., *Die lukanische Geschichtsschreibung als Zeugnis: Gestalt und Gehalt der Kunst des Lukas*, 2 vols., (Zürich: Zwingli Verlag, 1948-1949)

—, *Lukas und Quintilian. Rhetorik als Erzählkunst* (Zürich: Gotthelf Verlag, 1993)

Most, W.G. 'Did St. Luke Imitate the Septuagint?' *Journal for the Study of NT* 15 (1982), 30-41

Moulton, W.F., and A.S. Geden, *Concordance to the Greek Testament: According to the Texts of Westcott and Hort, Tischendorf and the English Revisers*, H.K. Moulton (rev. 5th ed) (Edinburgh: T&T Clark, 1993)

Moxnes, H., 'Social Relations and Economic Interaction in Luke's Gospel: A Research Report,' in *Luke-Acts: Scandinavian Perspectives* (Göttingen: Vandenhoeck & Ruprecht, 1991), 58-75

Muhlack, G., *Die Parallelen im Lukasevangelium und in der Apostelgeschichte*, TW 8 (Frankfurt: Peter Lang, 1979)

Munck, J., *The Acts of the Apostles* (Garden City, NY: Doubleday, 1967)

—, *Paul and the Salvation of Mankind* (London: SCM Press, 1959)

Murray, P., *Plato on Poetry: Ion, Republic 376e-398b, Republic 595-608b* (Cambridge: Cambridge University Press, 1996)

Müller, P.-G. 'Die "Bekehrung" des Petrus. Zur Interpretation von Apg. 10:1-11:18', *Herder-Korrespondenz* 28 (1974), 372-75

Navone, J., 'The Journey Theme,' *Bible Today* 58 (1972), 616-19

—, 'Three Aspects of the Lucan Theology of History', *Biblical Theology Bulletin* 3 (1973), 115-32

—, *Towards a Theology of Story* (Slough: St. Paul, 1977)

—, 'Narrative Theology and Its Uses: A Survey', *Irish Theological Quarterly* 52/3 (1986), 212-30

Naumann, W., 'Review of Auerbach, Mimesis', *Modern Philology* 45 (1947/48), 211-12

Neirynck, F., *Duality in Mark: Contribution to the Study of the Markan Redaction in Mark* (Louvain: Louvain University Press, 1972)

Neyrey, J., *The Passion According to Luke: A Redaction Study of Luke's Soteriology*, N.Y. (Toronto: Paulist Press, 1985)

—, 'Luke 24:13-35 "The Risen Shepherd"', in J.H. Neyrey (ed.), *Resurrection Stories* (Wilmington, DE: M. Glazier, 1988), 38-49.

Nicolet, C., *Space, Geography and Politics in the Early Roman Empire* (Ann Arbor, MI: University of Michigan Press, 1990)

Nobbs, A., 'Acts and Subsequent Ecclesiastical Histories', in B.W. Winter and A.D. Clarke (eds.), *The Book of Acts in Its Ancient Literary Settings*, BAIFCS 1 (Carlisle: Paternoster Press, 1993), 153-62

Nock, A.D., *Conversion: the old and the new in religion from Alexander the Great to Augustine of Hippo* (Oxford: Clarendon Press, 1933)

Nola, M., 'Towards a Positive Understanding of the Structure of Luke-Acts', PhD thesis, Aberdeen University (1987)

Nolland, J., *Luke 18:35-24:53*, WBC 35C (Dallas, TX: Word Books, 1993)

—, *Luke 1-9:20*, WBC 35a (Dallas, TX: Word Books, 1989)

—, *Luke 9:21-18:34*, WBC 35b (Dallas, TX: Word Books, 1993)

Norden, E., *Agnostos Theos* (Stuttgart: B.G. Teubner Verlag, 1956)
Nowell, I., 'Tobit', in J.A. Fitzmeyer, R.E. Brown, R.E. Murphy (eds.), *The New Jerome Biblical Commentary* 19932), 568-71
O'Collins, G., 'Luke on the Closing of the Easter Appearances', in G. O'Collins and G. Marconi (eds.), *Luke and Acts* (N.Y.: Paulist Press, 1993), 161-66
—, *Christology: A Biblical, Historical and Systematic Study of Jesus* (Oxford: Oxford University Press, 1995)
O'Toole, R.F., 'Philip and the Ethiopian Eunuch (Acts 8:25-40)', *Journal for the Study of NT* 17 (1983), 25-34
Oesterley, W.O.E., *The Gospel Parables in the Light of Their Jewish Background* (London: SPCK, 1936)
Ogg, G., 'The Central Section of the Gospel According to St. Luke', *New Testament Studies* 18 (1971), 39-53
Ong, W.J., 'Mimesis and the Following of Christ', *Religion and Literature* 26 (1944), 73-77
Osborne, G.R., *The Resurrection Narratives: A Redactional Study* (Grand Rapids, MI: Baker Books, 1984)
Parsons, M.C., *The Departure of Jesus in Luke-Acts: The Ascension Narratives in Context* (Sheffield: Sheffield Academic Press, 1987)
Parunak, H.D., 'Oral Typesetting: Some uses of Biblical Structure', *Biblica* 62 (1981), 153-69
Peabody, D.B., *Mark as Composer*, New Gospel Studies 1 (Macon, GA: Mercer University Press, 1987)
Pédech, P., *Trois Historiens Méconnus: Théopompe - Duris - Phylarque*, Collection d'Études Anciennes 119 (Paris: Belles Lettres, 1989)
Perrin, N., 'The Wredestrasse Becomes the Hauptstrasse: Reflections on the Reprinting of the Dodd Festschrift', *Journal of Religion* 46 (1966), 296-300
Perry, B.E., *The Ancient Romances: A Literary Historical Account of Their Origins. Sather Lectures 1951* (Los Angeles: University of California Press, 1967)
Pervo, R.I., *Profit with Delight: The Literary Genre of the Acts of the Apostles* (Philadelphia, PA: Fortress Press, 1987)
Pesch, R., *Die Apostelgeschichte*, EKKNT 5.1 (Neukirchen: Neukirchener Verlag, 1986)
Petersen, N.R., *Literary Criticism for New Testament Critics*, GBS (Philadelphia, PA: Fortress Press, 1978)
Pfister, E., 'Herakles und Christus', *Archiv für Religionswissenschaft* 34 (1937), 42-60
Plevnik, J., 'The Eyewitnesses of the Risen Jesus in Luke 24', *Catholic Bible Quarterly* 49 (1987), 90-103

Plummer, A., *A Critical and Exegetical Commentary on the Gospel According to Saint Luke* (Edinburgh: T&T Clark, 1981 (1896))

Plümacher, E., *Lukas als hellenistischer Schriftsteller: Studien zur Apostlegeschichte*, Studien zur Umwelt des Neuen Testament 9 (Göttingen: Vandenhoeck & Ruprecht, 1972)

Polhill, J.B., 'The Hellenist Breakthrough: Acts 6-12', *Review and Expositor* 71 (1974), 475-86

—, *Acts*, NAC 26 (Nashville, TN: Broadman Press, 1992)

Porter, S.E., 'Literary Approaches to the New Testament: From Formalism to Deconstruction and Back', in S.E. Porter and D. Tombs (eds.), *Approaches to NT Studies*, JSNT Supplement Series 120 (Sheffield: Sheffield Academic Press, 1995), 77-128

Porter, S.E., and T.H. Olbricht (eds.), *Rhetoric and the New Testament: Essays from the 1992 Heidelberg Conference*, JSNT Supplement Series 90 (Sheffield: JSOT Press, 1993)

Potterie, I. de la, 'De Compositione Evangelii Marci', *Verbum Dei* 44 (1966), 166.

Powell, M.A., *What is Narrative Criticism? A New Approach to the Bible* (London: SPCK, 1990)

Praeder, S.M., 'Jesus-Paul, Peter-Paul, and Jesus-Peter Parallelisms in Luke-Acts: A History of Reader Response', *SBL Seminar Papers*, 1984, 23-49

—, 'Luke-Acts and the Ancient Novel', *SBL Seminar Papers*, 1981, 269-92

Preminger, A., Golden, L. et. al. *Classical Literary Criticism. Translations and Interpretations* (N.Y.: F. Ungar, 1974)

Prigent, P., *Épître de Barnabé. Introduction, Traduction et Notes. Texte Grec établi et présenté par R.A. Kraft*, Sources Chrétiennes 172 (Paris: Éditions du Cerf, 1971)

Prior, M., *Jesus the Liberator: Nazareth Liberation Theology (Luke 4:16-30)*, The Biblical Seminar 26 (Sheffield: Sheffield Academic Press, 1995)

Rackham, R.B., *The Acts of the Apostles* (London: Methuen, 1901)

Radl, W., *Paulus und Jesus im lukanischen Doppelwerk: Untersuchung zu Parallelmotiven im Lukasevangelium und in der Apostelgeschichte*, Bern: Peter Lang, 1975)

Rapske, B.M., 'Acts, Travel, and Shipwreck', in D.W.J. Gill and C. Gempf (eds.), *The Book of Acts in Its Graeco-Roman Setting*, BAIFCS 2 (Carlisle: Paternoster Press, 1994), 1-47.

Ravens, D., *Luke and the Restoration of Israel*, JSNT Supplement Series 119 (Sheffield: Sheffield Academic Press, 1995)

Ray, J.L., *Narrative Irony in Luke-Acts: The Paradoxical Interaction of Prophetic Fulfillment and Jewish Rejection*, Mellen Biblical Series 48 (Lewiston, NY: E. Mellen Press, 1996)

Reinmuth, E., *Pseudo-Philo und Lukas* (Tübingen: J.C.B. Mohr, 1994)

Repo, E., *Der 'Weg' als Selbstbezeichnung des Urchristentums: eine traditions-geschichtliche und semasiologische Untersuchung*, Annales Academiae Scientiarum Fennicae, Ser. B, Tom 132.2 (Helsinki: Suomalainen Tiedeakatemia, 1964)

Resseguie, J.L., 'Interpretation of Luke's Central Section (Luke 9:51-19:44) Since 1856', *Studia Biblica et Theologica* 1-5 (1971-5), 3-36

Reymond, S., 'Paul sur le Chemin de Damas (Ac. 9, 22 et 26), Temps et Space d'une Expérience', *Nouvelle Revue de Theologie* 118 (1996), 520-38

—, *L'Experience du chemin de Damas: Approche narrative d'une expérience spirituelle*, Diplôme de spécialisation en science biblique, (Lausanne: Université de Lausanne, 1993)

Rhoads, D., and D. Michie, *Mark as Story. An Introduction to the Narrative of a Gospel* (Philadelphia, PA: Fortress Press, 1982)

Richard, E., 'Luke - Writer, Theologian, Historian: Research and Orientation of the 1970's', *Biblica* 13 (1983), 3-15

Ricoeur, P., *Time and Narrative*, K. McLaughlin and D. Pellauer (trans.), vol. 1 (Chicago, IL: University of Chicago Press, 1984)

—, 'Interpretative Narrative', in R. Schwartz (ed.), *The Book and the Text: The Bible and Literary Theory* (Cambridge: B. Blackwell, 1990), 237-57

—, 'The Narrative Function', in W.A. Beardslee (ed.), *Semeia 13: The Poetics of Faith. Essays Offered to A.N. Wilder* (Missoula, MT: Scholars Press, 1978), 177-202

Riesner, R., 'James' Speech (Acts 15:13-21), Simeon's Hymn (Luke 2:29-32) and Luke's Sources', in J.B. Green and M. Turner (eds.), *Jesus of Nazareth: Lord and Christ. Essays on the Historical Jesus and New Testament Christology* (Grand Rapids, MI: Eerdmans, 1994), 263-80

Rimmon-Kenan, S., *Narrative Fiction: Contemporary Poetics* (London: Methuen, 1983)

Ritoók, Z., 'Some Aesthetic Views of Dio Chrysostom and Their Sources', in J.G.J. Abbenes, S.R. Slings, I. Sluiter (eds.), *Greek Literary Theory After Aristotle: A Collection of Papers in Honour of D.M. Schenkeweld*, (Amsterdam: Amsterdam University Press, 1995), 125-34

Ringe, S.H., 'Luke 9:28-36: The Beginning of an Exodus', in M.A. Tolbert (ed.), *Semeia 28: The Bible and Feminist Hermeneutics* (Missoula, MT: Scholars Press, 1983), 83-99

—, *Luke*, Westminster Bible Companion Series (Louisville, KY: Westminster Press, 1995)

Rius-Camps, J., 'Cuatro paradigmas del Pentateuco refundidos en los Hechos de los apóstoles', *Estudios Biblicos* 53 (1995), 25-54

—, *El Camino de Pablo a La Mission de Los Paganos: Commentario Liguistico y Exegetico a Hch.13-28* (Madrid: Ediciones Cristianidad, 1984)

Robbins, V.K., 'Rhetoric and Culture: Exploring Types of Cultural Rhetoric in a Text', in S.E. Porter and T.H. Olbricht (eds.), *Rhetoric and the New*

Testament: Essays from the 1992 Heidelberg Conference, JSNT Supplement Series 90 (Sheffield: JSOT Press, 1993), 443-63
—, *Jesus the Teacher: A Socio-Rhetorical Interpretation of Mark* (Minneapolis, MN: Fortress Press, 19922)
—, 'By Land and by Sea: The We-Passages and Ancient Sea Voyages,' in C.H. Talbert (ed.), *Perspectives on Luke-Acts* (Edinburgh: T&T Clark, 1978), 215-42
—, 'Oral, Rhetorical, and Literary Cultures: A Response', in J. Dewey (ed.), *Semeia 65: Orality and Textuality in Early Christian Literature* (Missoula, MT: Scholars Press, 1995), 75-91
—, 'Socio-Rhetorical Criticism: Mary, Elizabeth and the Magnificat as a Test Case', in E.S. Malbon and E.V. McKnight (eds.), *The New Literary Criticism and the New Testament*, JSNT Supplement Series 109 (Sheffield: Sheffield Academic Press, 1994), 164-209
—, *The Tapestry of Early Christian Discourse: Rhetoric, Society and Ideology* (London: Routledge, 1996)
Robinson, B.P., 'The Place of the Emmaus Story in Luke-Acts', *New Testament Studies* 30 (1984), 481-97
Robinson, W.C. 'The Theological Context for Interpreting Luke's Travel Narrative', *Journal of Biblical Literature* 79 (1960), 20-31
—, *Der Weg des Herrn: Studien zur Geschichte und Eschatologie im Lukas Evangelium. Ein Gespräch mit Hans Conzelmann* (Hamburg: Bergstedt, 1964)
Rohde, E., *Der griechische Roman und seine Vorläufer*, W. Schmidt (rev. 3rd ed.) (Leipzig: Breitkopf & Härtel, 1914)
Roloff, J., *Die Apostelgeschichte* (Göttingen: Vandenhoeck & Ruprecht, 1981)
—, *Die Kirche im Neuen Testament*, GNT 10 (Göttingen: Vandenhoeck & Ruprecht, 1993)
Romm, J.S., *The Edges of the Earth in Ancient Thought. Geography, Exploration, and Fiction* (Princeton, NJ: Princeton University Press, 1992)
Rostagni, A., 'Aristotele e l'Aristotelismo Nella Storia Dell'estetica Antica', *Studi Italiani di Filologia Classica* 2 (1922), 1-147
Rydberg, L., *Fachprosa, vermeintliche Volkssprache und Neues Testament*, SGU 5 (Uppsala: Academia, 1967)
Ryken, L., *Words of Life: A Literary Introduction to the New Testament* (Grand Rapids, MI: Baker Books, 1987)
Rutgers, L., 'Archeological Evidence for the Interaction of Jews and non-Jews in Late Antiquity', *The American Journal of Archaeology* 96 (1992), 101-18
Safrai, S., 'Pilgrimage to Jerusalem at the End of the Second Temple Period', *Studies on the Jewish Background of the New Testament* (Assen: Van Gorcum, 1974), 184-215

Sanders, J.T., *The Jews in Luke-Acts* (London: SCM Press, 1987)
Satterthwaite, P.E., 'Acts Against the Background of Classical Rhetoric', in B.W. Winter and A.D. Clarke (eds.), *The Book of Acts in Its Ancient Literary Setting*, BAIFCS 1 (Carlisle: Paternoster Press, 1993), 337-80
Scheffler, E.H., 'Emmaus - a Historical Perspective', *Neotestamentica* 23 (1989), 251-67
Schierling, S.P., and M.J. Schierling, 'The Influence of the Ancient Romance on Acts of the Apostles', *The Classical Bulletin* 54 (1978), 81-88
Schille, G., *Die Apostelgeschichte des Lukas* (Berlin: Evangelische Verlaganstalt, 1984)
Schleiermacher, F.D.E., *Luke - A Critical Essay (Über die Schriften des Lukas: Ein kritischer Versuch)*, transl. and critical apparatus by C. Thirwall, Schleiermacher studies and translations 13 (Lewiston, NY: E. Mellen Press, 1993)
Schmidt, K.L., *Der Rahmen der Geschichte Jesu: literarkritische Untersuchungen zur ältesten Jesusüberlieferung* (Berlin: Trowitzsch, 1919)
Schmithals, W., *Die Apostelgeschichte des Lukas* (Zürich: Theologischer Verlag, 1982)
—, *Einleitung in die drei ersten Evangelien* (Berlin: W. de Gruyter, 1985)
—, *Das Evangelium nach Markus*, ÖTKNT 2 (Würzburg: Echter, 1979)
Schnabel, E.J., 'Jesus and the Beginnings of the Mission to the Gentiles', in J.B. Green and M. Turner (eds.), *Jesus of Nazareth: Lord and Christ. Essays on the Historical Jesus and New Testament Christology* (Carlisle: Paternoster Press, 1994), 37-58
Schnackenburg, R., *Jesus in the Gospels: A Biblical Christology*, O.C. Dean (Louisville, KY: John Knox Press, 1995) (*Die Person Jesu Christi im Spiegel der vier Evangelien* (Freiburg: Herder, 1993))
Schneckenburger, M., *Über den Zweck der Apostelgeschichte* (Bern: Fischer, 1841)
Schneider, G., *Die Apostelgeschichte* (Freiburg: Herder, 1980)
Schneider, J., 'Zur Analysen des lukanischen Reisenberichtes', in J. Schmidt and A. Vögtle (eds.), *Synoptischen Studien* (Münich: K. Zink, 1953), 207-29
Schnider, F., and W. Stenger, 'Beobachtungen zur Struktur der Emmausperikope (Lk. 24:13-35)', *Biblische Zeitschrift* 16 (1972), 94-114
Schonfield, H., *The Essene Odyssey: The Mystery of the True Teacher and The Essene Impact on the Shaping of Human Destiny* (Shaftesbury: Element, 19933)
Schubert, P., 'The Structure and Significance of Luke 24', in W. Eltester (ed.), *Neutestamentliche Studien für Rudolf Bultmann* (Berlin: Töpelmann, 19572), 165-86

Schwartz, E., 'Duris,' in A. F. Pauly, G. Wissowa *et al* (eds.), *Real-Encyclopädie der klassischen Altertumswissenschaft (RE)*, vol. 5, (1905), col. 1853-56

Schweiker, W., 'Sacrifice, interpretation, and the sacred: the import of Gadamer and Girard for religious studies', *Journal of the American Academy of Religion* 55 (1987), 791-810

Shrimpton, G.S., *Theopompus the Historian* (Montreal: McGill-Queen's University Press, 1991)

Scott, B.B., *Hear Then the Parable. A Commentary on the Parables of Jesus* (Minneapolis, MN: Fortress Press, 1989)

Scott, J.M., 'Luke's Geographical Horizon', in D.W. Gill, and C. Gempf (eds.), *The Book of Acts in Its Graeco-Roman Setting*, BAIFCS 2 (Carlisle: Paternoster Press, 1994), 483-544

—, *Paul and the Nations: The Old Testament and Jewish Background of Paul's Mission to the Nations with Special Reference to the Destination of Galatians*, WUNT 84 (Tübingen: J.C.B. Mohr, 1995)

Seeley, D., *Deconstructing the New Testament*, Biblical Interpretation Series 5 (Leiden: E.J. Brill, 1994)

Segovia, F., 'The Journey(s) of Jesus to Jerusalem. Plotting and Gospel Intertextuality', in A. Denaux (ed.), *John and the Synoptics*, BEThL 101 (Leuven: Leuven University Press, 1992), 535-41

Seidensticker, P., *Der Auferstehung Jesu in der Botschaft der Evangelisten*, StBSt 26 (Stuttgart: Katholisches Bibelwerk, 1967)

Sellin, G., 'Komposition, Quellen und Funktion Des Lukanischen Reiseberichtes (Lk. 9:51-19:28)', *Novum Testamentum* 20 (1978), 101-35

Senior, D., 'The Foundations for Mission in the New Testament', in D. Senior and C. Stuhlmueller, *The Biblical Foundations for Mission* (Maryknoll, NY: Orbis Books, 1983), 141-32

—, *The Passion of Jesus in the Gospel of Luke* (Wilmington, DE: M. Glazier, 1989)

Shepherd, W., *The Narrative Function of the Holy Spirit as Character in Luke-Acts* (Atlanta, GA: Scholars Press, 1994)

Sherwin-White, A.N., *The letters of Pliny: A historical and social commentary* (Oxford: Oxford University Press, 1966)

Sibinga, J.S. 'Acts 9:37 and other cases of ellipsis obiecti', in T. Baarda, A. Hilhorst, G.P. Luttikuizen, A.S. van der Woude (eds.), *Text and Testimony. Essays on New Testament and Apocryphal Literature in Honor of A.F.J. Klijn* (Kampen: J.H. Kole, 1988), 242-46.

Siegert, F., 'Mass Communication and Prose Rhythm in Luke-Acts', in S.E. Porter and Th.H. Olbricht, *Rhetoric and the New Testament: Essays from the 1992 Heildelberg Conference*, JSNT Supplement Series 90 (Sheffield: JSOT Press, 1993), 42-58.

Simon, M., 'Remarques sur la Catacombe de la Via Latina', in *Le Christianisme antique et son contexte religieux* 108/9 (Stuttgart: A. Hiersemann, 1988), 286-96.

Smith, C.D., 'Geography or Christianity? Maps of the Holy Land Before AD 1000', *Journal of Theological Studies* 42 (1991), 143-52.

Smith, J.Z., *Drudgery Divine: On the Comparison of Early Christianities and the Religions of Late Antiquity* (Chicago, IL: University of Chicago Press, 1990)

—, *Map is not territory: studies in the history of religions* (Leiden: E.J. Brill, 1978)

—, *To take place: toward theory in ritual* (Chicago, IL: University of Chicago Press, 1992)

Snodgrass, K., 'Streams of Tradition Emerging from Isaiah 40:1-5 and Their Adaptation in the New Testament', *Journal for the Study of NT* 8 (1980), 24-45

Sparks, H.F.D., 'The Semitisms of Luke's Gospel', *Journal of Theological Studies* 44 (1943), 129-38

—, 'The Semitisms of the Acts', *Journal of Theological Studies NS* 1 (1950), 16-28

Spencer, F.S., 'Acts and Modern Literary Approaches', in B.W. Winter, and A.D. Clarke (eds.), *The Book of Acts in Its Ancient Literary Setting*, BAIFCS 1 (Carlisle: Paternoster Press, 1993), 381-14

—, 'The Ethiopian and His Bible: A Social-Science Analysis', *Biblical Theology Bulletin* 22 (1992), 155-65

—, *The Portrait of Philip in Acts* (Sheffield: Sheffield Academic Press, 1992)

Stagg, F., *Book of Acts: The Early Struggle for an Unhindered Gospel* (Nashville, TN: Broadmann Press, 1955)

Standaert, B., *L'Évangile selon Marc: Composition et genre littéraire* (Zevenbergen: Brugge, 1978)

Stanley, D.M., 'Paul's Conversion in Acts: Why the Three Accounts?' *Catholic Biblical Quarterly* 15 (1953), 315-38

Stählin, G., *Die Apostelgeschichte* (Göttingen: Vandenhoeck & Ruprecht, 1970)

Steck, O.H., *Israel und das Gewaltsame Geschick der Propheten* (Neukirchen-Vluyn: Neukirchener Verlag, 1967)

Stein, H.R., *Luke*, NAC 24, (Nashville, TN: Broadman Press, 1992)

Stempvoort, P. van, 'The Interpretation of the Ascension in Luke-Acts', *New Testament Studies* 5 (1958-59), 30-42

Stendahl, K., 'The Apostle Paul and the Introspective Conscience in the West', *Harvard Theological Review* 56 (1963), 199-215

—, *Paul Among Jews and Gentiles* (London: SCM Press, 1977)

Stephens, S.A., and J.J. Winkler (eds.), *Ancient Greek Novels: The Fragments. Introduction, Text, Translation, and Commentary* (Princeton, NJ: Princeton University Press, 1995)

Sterling, G.E., *Historiography and Self-Definition. Josephos, Luke-Acts, and Apologetic Historiography* (Leiden: E.J. Brill, 1992)

Steyn, G.J., 'Intertextual Similarities Between Septuagint Pretexts and Luke's Gospel', *Neotestamentica* 24 (1990), 229-45

—, 'Luke's Use of MIMHSIS? Re-opening the Debate', in C. M. Tuckett (ed.), *The Scriptures in the Gospels* (Leuven: Leuven University Press, 1997), 551-57

Stock, A., *The Method and Message of Mark* (Wilmington, DE: M. Glazier, 1989)

Strauss, M.L., *The Davidic Messiah in Luke-Acts: The Promise and Its Fulfillment in Lukan Christology*, JSNT Supplement Series 110 (Sheffield: Sheffield Academic Press, 1995)

Strasburger, H., *Die Wesensbestimmung der Geschichte durch die antike Geschichtsschreibung*, Stizungsberichteder der Wiss. Gesselschaft an der J. W. Goethe Universität 5 (Wiesbaden: Steiner, 1966)

Strecker, G., and F.W. Horn (Bearbeiter), *Theologie des Neuen Testaments*, (Berlin: W. de Gruyter, 1996)

Streeter, B.H., *The Four Gospels. A Study of Origins* (London: Macmillan, 1961 (1927))

Swartley, W.M., *Israel's Scripture Traditions and the Synoptic Gospels* (Peabody: Hendrickson, 1994)

—, 'The Structural Function of the Term 'Way' (Hodos) in Mark's Gospel', in W. Klassen (ed.), *The New Way of Jesus: Essays Presented to Howard Charles* (Newton, KA: Faith and Life Press, 1980), 73-86

Talbert, C.H., 'Martyrdom in Luke-Acts and the Lukan Social Ethic', in R.J. Cassidy (ed.), *Political Issues in Luke-Acts* (Maryknoll, NY: Orbis Books, 1983), 99-110

—, *Literary Patterns, Theological Themes and the Genre of Luke-Acts* (Missoula, MT: Scholars Press, 1974)

—, *Luke and the Gnostics: An Examination of Lukan Purpose*, (Nashville, TN: Abingdon Press, 1966)

—, *Reading Luke: A Literary and Theological Commentary on the Third Gospel* (N.Y.: Crossroads, 1982)

Tannehill, R.C., 'The Story of Zacchaeus as Rhetoric: Luke 19:1-10', in V.K. Robins (ed.), *Semeia 64: The Rhetoric of Pronouncement*, (Missoula, MT: Scholars Press, 1994), 201-11

—, The Composition of Acts 3-5: Narrative Development and Echo Effect, *SBL Seminar Papers*, 1984, 217-40

—, *The Narrative Unity of Luke-Acts: A Literary Interpretation*, vol. 1: *The Gospel According to Luke* (Philadelphia, PA: Fortress Press, 1986)

—, *The Narrative Unity of Luke-Acts: A Literary Interpretation*, vol. 2: *The Acts of the Apostles* (Philadelphia, PA: Fortress Press, 1990)

Taylor, J.E., *Christians and the Holy Places: The Myth of Jewish-Christian Origins* (Oxford: Clarendon Press, 1993)

Taylor, V., *The Gospel According to St.Mark* (London: Macmillan, 19698)

Thompson, M.M., 'The Structure of Matthew: A Survey of Recent Trends', *Studia Biblica et Theologica* 12 (1982), 195-238

Thurén, J., *Das Lobopfer der Hebräer: Studien zum Aufbau und Anliegen von Hebräerbrief 13* (Åbo: Åbo Akademi, 1973)

Toca, M.S. de, 'Πορεύου κατὰ μεσημβρίαν (Hch. 8:26)', *Estudios Bíblicos* 55 (1997), 107-15

Tolbert, M.A., *Sowing the Word: Mark's World in Literary-Historical Perspective* (Minneapolis, MN: Fortress Press, 1989)

Torraca, L., *Duride Di Samo: La Maschera Scenica Nella Storiografia Ellenistica* (Salerno: P. Laveglia, 1988)

Tracy, D., *The Analogical Imagination* (N.Y.: Crossroads, 1981)

Travers, M., 'Luke', in L. Ryken and Tremper Longmann III (eds.), *A Complete Literary Guide to the Bible* (Grand Rapids, MI: Zondervan, 1993)

Trocmé, E., *Le 'Livre des Actes', et l'Histoire* (Paris: Presses Universitaires de France, 1957)

Trompf, G.W., *The Idea of Historical Recurrence in Western Thought: From Antiquity to the Reformation* (Berkeley, CA: University of California Press, 1979)

—, 'La section médiane de l'évangile de Luc: L'organization des documents', *Revue de l'Histoire et de Philosophie Religieuses* 53 (1975), 141-54

Turner, M., *Power from on High: The Spirit in Israel's Restoration and Witness in Luke-Acts*, JPT Supplement Series 9 (Sheffield: Sheffield Academic Press, 1996)

Turner, N., *A Grammar of New Testament Greek*, vol. 4: *Style* (Edinburgh: T&T Clark, 1976), 56-57

—, 'The Quality of the Greek of Luke-Acts', in J.K. Elliot (ed.), *Studies in New Testament Language and Text* (Leiden: E.J. Brill, 1976)

Tyson, J.B., 'Conflict as a Literary Theme in the Gospel of Luke', in W.R. Farmer (ed.), *New Synoptic Studies: The Cambridge Gospel Conference and Beyond* (Macon, GA: Mercer University Press, 1983), 303-30

—, 'Jews and Judaism in Luke-Acts: Reading as a Godfearer', *New Testament Studies* 41 (1995), 16-38

Unnik, W.C., van 'Der Befehl an Philippus', *Sparsa Collecta: The Collected Essays of W. C. van Unnik*, vol. 1 (Leiden: E.J. Brill, 1973), 328-39

Vermes, G., *The Dead Sea Scrolls in English* (Sheffield: JSOT Press, 19954)

—, 'The "Son of Man" Debate', *Journal for the Study of NT* 1 (1978), 19-32

Vernant, J.-P., 'Myth and Tragedy', in A.O. Rorty (ed.), *Essays on Aristotle's Poetics* (Princeton, NJ: Princeton University Press, 1992), 33-50.

Verseput, D.J., 'Jesus', Pilgrimage to Jerusalem and Encounter in the Temple: A Geographical Motif in Luke's Gospel', *Novum Testamentum* 46/2 (1994), 105-121

Via, D.O., *The Parables: Their Literary and Existential Dimension* (Philadelphia, PA: Fortress Press, 1967)

Vinson, R.B., 'A Comparative Study of the Use of Enthymemes in the Synoptic Gospels', in D.F. Watson (ed.), *Persuasive Artistry: Studies in NT Rhetoric in Honour of George A. Kennedy*, JSNT Supplement Series 50 (Sheffield: JSOT Press, 1991), 119-41

Volz, P., *Die Eschatologie der jüdischen Gemeinde im neutestamentlichen Zeitalter* (Hildesheim: G. Olms, 1966 (1934))

Voss, G., *Die Christologie der lukanischen Schriften in Grundzügen* (Paris: Desclée de Brouwer, 1965)

Walaskay, P.W., *"And So We Came To Rome": The Political Perspective of St. Luke* (Cambridge: Cambridge University Press, 1983)

Walbank, F.W., 'History and Tragedy', *Historia* 9 (1960), 216-34

—, 'Profit or Amusement: Some Thoughts on the Motives of Hellenistic Historians'. in G. Schepens and E. de Keysen, H. Verdin (eds.), *Purposes of History: Studies in Greek Historiography from the 4th to the 2nd Centuries B.C. Proceedings of the International Colloquium, Leuven 24-26 May, 1988*, Studia Hellenistica 30 (Leuven: Leuven University Press, 1990), 253-66

Walker, P.W.L., *Jesus and the Holy City: New Testament Perspectives on Jerusalem* (Grand Rapids, MI: Eerdmans, 1996)

—, *Holy City, Holy Places? Christian Attitudes to Jerusalem and the Holy Land in the Fourth Century*, Oxford Early Christian Studies (Oxford: Clarendon Press, 1990)

—, (ed.), *Jerusalem Past and Present in the Purposes of God* (Croydon: Deo Gloria Trust, 1992)

Wallace M.I., and Th.H. Smith (eds.), *Curing violence* (Sonoma, CA: Polebridge, 1994)

Wanke, J., *Die Emmauserzählung: Eine redactions-geschichtliche Untersuchung zu Lk. 24:13-35*, Erfuhrter Theologische Studien 31 (Leipzig: St. Benno, 1973)

Watts, R.E., 'Consolation or Confrontation? Isaiah 40-55 and the Delay of the New Exodus', *Tyndale Bulletin* 41.1 (1990), 31-59

—, 'The Influence of the Isaianic New Exodus on the Gospel of Mark', PhD thesis, Cambridge University (1990)

Watson, F., 'Literary Approaches to the Gospels. A Theological Assessment', *Theology* March/April 1996, 124-33

—, *Text, Church and World: Biblical Interpretation in Theological Perspective* (Edinburgh: T&T Clark, 1994)

Wefald, E.K., 'The Separate Gentile Mission in Mark: A Narrative Explanation of Markan Geography, The Two Feeding Accounts and Exorcisms', *Journal for the Study of NT* 60 (1995), 3-26

Weinert, F.D., 'Luke, the Temple and Jesus' Saying About Jerusalem's Abandoned House (Luke 13:34-35)', *Catholic Biblical Quarterly* 44 (1982), 68-76

—, 'The Meaning of the Temple in Luke-Acts', *Biblical Theology Bulletin* 11 (1981), 85-89

Weiser, A., 'Tradition und Lukanische Komposition in Apg. 10:36-43', in J.N. Aletti, *at. al.* (eds.), *A Cause de l'Évangile: Études sur les Synoptiques et les Actes* (Paris: Éditions du Cerf, 1985), 757-68

Wenham, J.W., 'Synoptic Independence and the Origin of Luke's Travel Narrative', *New Testament Studies* 27 (1980-1981), 509-10

Wette, W.M.L., *Kurzgefasstes exegetisches Handbuch zum Neuen Testament: kurze Erklärung der Evangelien des Lukas und Markus*, 2 vols. (Leipzig: Weidemann, 18463).

Wilckens, U., 'The Tradition-history of the Resurrection of Jesus', in C.F.D. Moule (ed.), *The Significance of the Message of the Resurrection for Faith in Jesus Christ* (Naperville, IL: Allenson, 1968), 51-76

—, *Resurrection, Biblical Testimony to the Resurrection. An Historical Examination and Explanation* (Atlanta, GA: John Knox, 1978)

—, *Auferstehung. Das biblische Auferstehungszeugnis historisch Untersucht und Erklärt* (Gütersloh: Gütersloh Taschenbuch, 1974 (1970))

Wifstrand, A., *L'Eglise Ancienne et la Culture Grécque*, trans. by L.-M. Dewailly (Paris: Éditions du Cerf, 1962)

Wilcox, M., 'The God-fearers in Acts: A Reconsideration', *Journal for the Study of NT* 13 (1981), 102-22

Wilken, R.L., *The Land Called Holy* (New Haven, CT: Yale University Press, 1992)

Williams, R.R., *The Acts of the Apostles* (London: SCM Press, 1953)

Wills, L.M., 'The Jewish Novellas', in J.R. Morgan and R. Stoneman (eds.), *Greek Fiction. The Greek Novel in Context* (London: Routledge, 1994), 223-38

Wilms, G.H., 'Deuteronomic Traditions in St. Luke's Gospel', PhD thesis, Edinburgh University (1972).

Wilson, S.G., *The Gentiles and the Gentile Mission in Luke-Acts* (Cambridge: Cambridge University Press, 1973)

Wilson, N.G., *Photius, The Bibliotheca*, a selective translation and notes by N.G. Wilson (London: Duckworth, 1994)

Windisch, H., 'Die Christusepiphanie vor Damaskus (Act. 9, 22, und 26) und Ihre religionsgeschichtlichen Parallelen', *Zeitschrift für die neuetestamentliche Wissenschaft* 31 (1932), 1-23.

Witherington, B. III., 'Editing the Good News: Some Synoptic Lessons for the Study of Acts', in B. Witherington III (ed.), *History, Literature and Society in the Book of Acts* (Cambridge: Cambridge University Press, 1996), 324-47

—, *The Acts of the Apostles. A Socio-Rhetorical Commentary* (Carlisle: Paternoster, 1998)

Witherup, R.D., 'Cornelius Over and Over Again: "Functional Redundancy" in the Acts of the Apostles', *Journal for the Study of NT* 49 (1993), 45-66

—, 'Functional Redundancy in the Acts of the Apostles: A Case Study', *Journal for the Study of NT* 48 (1992), 67-86

Wojcik, J., *The Road to Emmaus: Reading Luke's Gospel* (West Lafayette, IN: Purdue University Press, 1989)

Woodruff, P., 'Aristotle on Mimēsis', in A.O. Rorty (ed.), *Essays on Aristotle's Poetics* (Princeton, NJ: Princeton University Press, 1992), 73-95

York, J.O., *The Last Shall Be First: The Rhetoric of Reversal in Luke* (Sheffield: Sheffield Academic Press, 1991)

Zeller, E., *The Acts of the Apostles* (London: Williams & Norgate, 1875-1876)

Ziegler, K., 'Tragödia', in A. F. Pauly, G. Wissowa *et al* (eds.), *Real-Encyclopädie der Klassischen Altertumswissenschaft (RE)*, vol. 6, A 2 (1937), cols. 1899-2075

Zmijewski, J., *Die Apostelgeschichte* (Regensburger Neues Testament (Regensburg: F. Pustet Verlag, 1994)

Zwiep, A.W., *The Ascension of the Messiah in Lukan Christology*, Supplements to Novum Testamentum 87 (Leiden: E.J. Brill, 1997)

Indexes

Index of General Terms

A

adventure: 121, 139, 183, 271, 277, 278; and novels, 120, 121; contemporary, individual, 279; heroic achievements, 52; journey symbol, 50; maritime, 29; models, 118; of Callirhoe, 192; of the Prodigal Son, 183; with God, 271
alliteration: 189, 236, *See* style
anagnorisis: 86, 104, 105, 124
anangke: 251, 257, *See* fate
antithesis: 260, *See* opposites, contrast
appearance: 11, 12, 13, 14, 16, 17, 19, 94, 128, 131, 132, 187, 191, 213, 215, 217, 251, 271, 273
archaism: 82, *See* Atticism
argument: 97, 109, 231, 232, 233, 237, 241, 276, *See* Scripture, thought, unity of action
art: 23, 24, 78, 90, 91, 94, 99, 108, 115, 185, 193, 202, 271, 275, 277, *See* style, mimesis, representation
ascension: 46, 66, 124, 178, 198, 199, 201, 214, 217
Atticism: 78, 79, 82, 267, *See* archaism, imitation
audience: 19, 23, 93, 182, 183, 184, 247, 277
author: Luke, 277; as collective author, 175, 242; educated, 78; Hellenistic, 86, 96; of reports, in Luke-Acts, 270; rhetor, theologian, 81
authority: 148, 161, 178, 212, 238, 247, 248, 269, 271, 274

B

baptism: 8, 210, 219, 242, 257, 260, 261, 262, 263, 264, *See* sacrament, restoration
blind, blindness: 124, 141, 150, 155, 164, 176, 185, 194, 213, 249, *See* sight motif, suffering, restoration

Bread: 191, 228, 229, 231, 257, 267, *See* eucharist, fellowship, restoration

C

call: divine, 234, 250; OT double call, 245, 246; Philip's call, 267; Saul's, 219, 246, 276, *See* conversion
causal: 104, 107, 224
central: Central Section, 41, 43, 194; Emmaus story, 203; evangelism, 261; recognition, 274; vision, 9
centrality: 41, 69; Jerusalem's, 70, 201; narrative, 145, 146; the Ethiopian's, 260; the Temple's, 200; theological, 13
centre: chiastic, 258; dramatic, 15; Jerusalem, 206; meaning, 259; narrative, 258; of Acts 9, 208; of Saul's conversion, 32; outside Jerusalem, 201
centrifugal: 123, 207, *See* centrality
change: challenging journeys, 99; discipleship paradigms, 64; from ignorance to knowledge, cf. recognition, 105; in destiny and journey, 257; in destiny and status, of Ethiopian, 250; in Jesus relation to the OT, 248; in meaning of the way, 69; in perceiving history, 111; instruction at points of change, 177; *metabasis*, 105; *metabole*, 105; of fate, in The Good Samaritan parable, 183; of fortune, reversal, 105; of journey paradigms, 70; of life, Saul, 262; of person, *via* mimesis, 93; of Saul's life, 270
character: literary - better than living humans, 101; credible, in Luke, 250; decisions, in Luke, 248; destiny, 257; destructive interference, 93; dramatic, 106; extradiegetic, 250, 251; flaw, 106; genuine, 117; high status, 194;

idealised, in tragedy, 101; imitation of characters, 117; in tragedy, 85, 103; plot element, 104, 106; proselyte, 222; restored, in Luke, 249; rich, 100; Saul, main character, 32; settings, 143; subject to change, 134; suitable, 96; the Lord, 250; the Spirit, 31, 175; toy of destiny, 107; unity of character, 203

chiasmus: composite, 259; encounter, 258; evangelistic, 258; *hodos* structures, in Mk., 147, 148, 149; journey based, in Lk. 24, 203; recognition by sight, 47; sacramental, 258, 261

choice: 56, 170, 250; ethical, 54, 55, 106, 134, 165, 171, 249, *See* decision; linguistic, 79, 109; of Ethiopian, 249; of mimetic media, 101; of paradigm, 135; theological, 250

climax: 82; Emmaus' meal, 188, 257; Ethiopian's baptism, 262; multiple, 257; Saul's baptism, 262; Saul's persecution, 256

coherence: compositional, 82; literary, 84; narrative, 105, 122, 149, 226, 233, 261; of real events, 104

comedy: 20; comic nature, 277; Peter's betrayal, 90; restoration, 249, 256, 277; reversed tragedy, 249; vs. tragedy, 101

complex: dialogue, 233; plot, 105, 107; recognition, 232

complication: *desis*, 107, 124, 130, 255, 271

composition: Aristotle, 23; creativity, 83; elements, 40; Emmaus' story, 14; Hellenistic rules, 19; Lukan, 29, 78, 154; Lukan art, 271; Lukan structure, 57; Luke's Central Section, 57, 178; Markan, 150; mimesis, 75, 109; Saul's story, 263; structure, 85; techniques, 85; unity, 66

compression: of time periods, mimesis, 74; temporal, 209

conflict: dramatic, 125

continuity: cultural, between Luke-Acts and Hellenistic environment, 196; of Jesus' ministry, 259; of journeying and Emmaus, 186; of Luke's journey motif, 27; of plot, discontinuity between Acts 9-Acts 10, 218; of redemption; Robinson, W.C., 64, 65

contraction: temporal, 202, 204

conversion: Cornelius', 7, 197; Ethiopian's, 3, 17, 31, 46, 48, 172, 207, 224; Hellenistic stories, 17; Lydia's, 6; parallels, Emmaus, Ethiopian, Saul, 248, 257, 271; parallels, Ethiopian vs. Cornelius, 219, 222, 224; parallels, Ethiopian vs. Saul, 123, 276; parallels, Saul vs. Cornelius, 217; Samaritans' and Gentiles', 224; Saul's, 5, 31, 127, 208, 256; Zacchaeus', 164, 184

crisis: the core of a plot complication, *desis*, 124

crossroads: decision, 55, 133, 134; Heracles, 55

D

delight: dialogue on the Emmaus road, 236; history and literature, 111; Luke's history style, 277; of art, mocked by Plato, 93; of dramatic art. *See* pleasure

dénouement: *lysis*, 107, 130, 184, 262, 271

destination: Jerusalem, 40; Temple, 41

destiny: *dei* motif, suffering *pathos*, 248; instruction *in via*, 266; reversals, 194, 257, 265, 276, 278; Saul's, Cleopas', 107; tragic, major fall, 106

dialogue: 5, 270; christological, 238, 275; complex, 233; debates, 163; dialectic, 234; Emmaus, 98; evangelistic, 1, 258, 260; Heracles, 133; Lukan, 83; master-disciples, 162; on the road, 267; questions, 274; reasoning, 233; recognition,

Indexes

232, 247; revelational, 164; scenes, 237; suspense, recognition, 193
dianoia: 85, 103, 109, 237
diction: Aristotle's mimesis; choice of words, 109; *lexis*, 103; linguistic unity, 109; clarity, choice of vocabulary, 78; Lukan style; atticism, 79; Emmaus vocabulary, 48, 189; Ethiopian's rethoric, 235; Philip's style, 235; rhythm, 236; vocabulary, 78; Markan style, 85
disappearance: 16, 18, 275, *See* appearance, encounter, vision; Elisha-Elijah, 191; Emmaus, 231; Ethiopian's, 268; Heliodorus legend, Emmaus, 128; Hellenistic legends, 128; Philip's, 32, 47, 128
disciple: apostasy and the Way, 68; commissioning of the 12-70, 181; discipleship paradigms, 64, 68; disputes, 148, 161; Emmaus; disappointment, 241; disciples vs. apostles, 69; fear motif, 256; following vs. perseverance, 68; *hodos* challenges, 172; Jesus; as a model, 66; cares, 168; following, 164; leads, 163; journeying paradigm, 71, 152, 180; *katharsis*, 103; mission, 160; persecutions, 63; place in narrative, 205; recognition, 192; restoration, 192, 249; reversal, 265; suffering motif, *pathos*, 251; teaching *in via*, 266; understanding motif, 149
discovery. *See* recognition, *anagnorisis*
drama: dramatic climax in Emmaus, 188; drama and history, 111, 113; drama and Jewish novels, 125; drama and sensationalism, 115; dramatic; details, in Emmaus, 251; dialogue, of Saul, 234; journeying, 124; plot components, 104; return points, 182; scene, for Ethiopian, 235; situation, of Saul, 250; stories in OT, 125; Incarnation, 91; Luke and Hellenistic drama, 21; Luke's interest, 15; mimesis, novels, history, 73; OT dramatism, 89; Peter's betrayal, 90; Plato's mimesis, 83; the Prodigal Son's drama, 183; recognition scene, 15; the Good Samaritan's, 182; tragedy, in Saul's story, 255, 256

E

emotion: emotion and intellect, 102; emotion and tragedy, 105; emotional impact, 105; emotions and history, 116
emplotment: Luke's techniques, 277
emulation: 82; of popular stories. *See* imitation, mimesis
enactment: 15; mimesis, 74, 101, *See* impersonation
encounter: in Acts 8-9, 207; Jewish Hellenistic models, 125; Lukan encounters, 27; Lukan specific; Emmaus, 190; Philip and the Ethiopian, 253; of the Prodigal Son, 183; Saul and Jesus, 255; Zacchaeus, 184; Lukan specific encounters; thiefs, priests, Samaritans, 181; OT models, 124
ending: confrontational (in Matthew), 155; doxological, 164; happy, 185, 210, 250; positive, 8, 255, 256, 277; restorational, 194, 275; sacramental, 1, 259; universalistic, 159
entertaining: history, 110, 111; stories, 28; style, 115, 122
epiphany: christophany; Saul, 214; Saul, *horama*, 215; Heliodorus, 127; post-Easter, 32
ethos: 103, 104
eucharist: 267, etc.; alluded to, 227, 231, 275; eucharistic connotations and miraculous feeding, 228; eucharistic reading, 231; the Last Supper, 230
expansion: centrifugal, 123; geographical, 43, 122; geographical, radiating, 70; of pattern, 14

external: symbols of the way, 35
eyesight. See sight motif, blindness

F

fate: *anangke, tyche, gnome, eimarmene*; 251; of innovators, 98; reversals, 125, 183, 273; sensationalism and history, 116
fear: 23, 102; God-fearer; Cornelius, 7, 219; Ethiopian, 7, 222, 268
feast: Eleusis, 51
feel: compassion, 165; hearts burning, 103; loss, 15; mystery, 250
fellowship: apostles, 192; feast, 184; meal, 184, 185, 187; restoration, 258; resurrection, 228; table fellowship, 207
fiction: mimesis, 74; novels, 120; representation, 83
figura: interpretation; figural, 87, 144; figural, Melberg, A., 90; mimesis; figural, 88
final: bells, 121; destination, 39; recognition, 31; report, 9, 130, 190; restoration, 183, 185
flaw: of character, 106; of Saul, 107
focus: double focus; challenges, opportunities, 269; evangelistic dialogue, 267; Jesus' messianity, 244; Journey motif; Reisenotizen, 56; legend; on Jesus, 32; of encounters, 231; of history; on persons, 111; on *hodos* accounts, 173; on Jesus' debates, 178; on Palestine, 58; on return, 206; on Septuagint imitation, 76; recognition, 231
foreign: actors, 97; cultural inspectors, 97; Ethiopian, 220, 222; foreigner; baptism, 8; respect, 85; lands, 151, 183; performers, 85
framework: conceptual, for Peter's Confession, 148; narrative, 14, 67; spatial; two different, in Acts 8-9, 208; two different, in Lk. 24, 206; temporal; different types in Acts 8-

9, 209; different types in Lk.24, 205; different types, in Lk. 24, 203

G

genre: appearance, 11, 17; appearance, OT related, 18; development, types, 18; Hellenistic novel, 119, 122, 125; Luke's literary environment, 273; mixt tragedy-comedy, Saul's story, 256; overlap, history and poetry, 111; romance, in Luke 15, 183; special, new, Peter's betrayal, 90

H

hinge: geographical, of Luke-Acts, 201; theological, in Luke-Acts, 199; transformation, baptism, 257
history: and Luke, as historian, 117, 277; and mimesis, 73, 109; Duris, 116; and objectivity, 71; and philosophy, 110; and poetry, 110, 111; and redemption, 178; and theology, in Luke, 4; and tragedy, 113; and truth, 110; as literature, 122; benefit and pleasure, 25; drama of Incarnation, 91; Hellenistic, 111; idealised, 201; of literature, 75; of redemption; as a journey, 65; continuity, 71; three stages, 59, 64; of salvation; individual, 67; of tradition, 18; transcended, 204; vs. salvation, 71; writing, 83, 84, 85, 119; Duris, *117*; Phylarchus, *113*; Polybius, 112; Theopompus, 112

I

idealised: characters, 101; cities, history, 201; reports, 28
ideology: geography, 138; geopolitical, 139; in 1 Enoch, 139; literature, 277; of Roman Empire, 140; of the disciples, 277

Indexes

imagery: Eleusinian, 51; Hellenistic, 50; life as a journey, 54; New Exodus, 46; of painting, 117; Scamander and Achilles, 117; two-roads, 134; wilderness, 150
imitation: accurate vs. creative, 95; challenge of ideology, 140; creative, 101; emulation, 82; hybrid model, 82; instinctive, 100; literary, 19; of form, of content, 19; plot and life, 103; literary dependence, 122; mimesis, 73, 74; of biblical style, 76; of emotion, 116; of Hellenistic models, 81; of LXX, 74, 277; of master's way, 62; of OT, 30; of OT appearances, 16; of reality, 82; of reality, Markan, 90; of truth, 110; of vocabulary, structure, themes, 80; pleasure of understanding, 116; representation, 75; rhetorical, of famous authors, 82; serious, elevated, Plato, 96; similarity, 75
impairment: 221; physical, 254
impersonation. *See* enactment; dramatic, in Plato, 83; enactment, dialogue, 93; Jesus as traveller, 189; Luke's speeches, 96; vs. plain narrative, 93; vulgar, for Plato, 83
inclusio: discipleship *inclusio*, in Luke, 172; geographic, journey, 261; hodos; in Ethiopian's conversion, 261, 268; in Mark, 164; in Saul's conversion, 264; in Acts 8-9, 208; in Mark, 148; Spirit, in Philip's call, 260; Zacchaeus, in Luke, 185
indirect: style; direct speech, in Luke, 161; direct style, in Luke, 96; in Mark, 162; plus direct speech, Homer, 93; preferred by Plato, 83
innovation: artistic and religious, 274; Christians, as innovators, 98; literary, 269; strangers, 97
inspector: cultural; corrupted ideas, 98; inspection journey, of Heliodorus, 127; of foreign cultures, in Plato, 97
instruction: at points of change, in Luke, 177; of the Spirit, in Acts 8,

10, 8; on discipleship, on the road, 163; on Scripture, on the road, 266; proclamation, on the road, 186; solemn, 16; Torah, 150
intellectual: arguments, 235; blindness; Cleopas, 176; Elymas, 176; Paul, 176; error, or ethical, 107; katharsis, 102
internal: chiasmus, 203; connotations of the way, 35, 37; OT quotations, 81; proof from prophecy, 248; symmetry, 193
irony: in Luke, 171; Ananias and Saul, 269; Emmaus misrecognition, 232; Saul is under threat, 211; Saul send to Tarsus, 270; in Plato, 92; on Caesar's tax, 157

J

Jerusalem: Jerusalem and Troy, 201; Jerusalem-type, appearances, 12; Jesus' journey to Jerusalem, 59, 62; journey types; in and out from Jerusalem, 202
journey: continuity, Robinson, 64; different types of journeys, 29; discipleship, 66; divinely guided, 66; drama, 124; founding empires, 201; from Nazareth to Rome, 66; happy journey, persecution journey, 211; idealised; destination, 39; Exodus, 35; Jesus' journey to Jerusalem, 40; ideology, 137; in OT, 124; journey scheme, in Matthew, 157; journey within journey, 235; lexical variety, 256; mimesis of journeying, in Emmaus, 193; missionary, 198; mixed, heterogenous material, 142; motif, 59; motif, in Luke, 158, 174; multiplicity, Flender, 71; notes, 29; of cultural, evangelistic, 99; of Heliodorus, 127; of the Prodigal Son, romantic, 183; of Tobit, 126; patterns, in Luke, 178; pilgrimage, 226; revelation, 226; reversal of destiny and of journey, 192;

Samaritan's and the Grateful Dead Man, 182; scheme, in Matthew, 155; significance, in Luke, 177; slowed down, in Luke, 168; teaching, in Emmaus, 186; telescoped, Acts 9, 209; to Jerusalem, 65; transition character, in Luke, 164; transition role, in Luke 24 - Acts 1, 199; transitions in Luke-Acts, 225; two types, in Luke, 179

joy: from narrative, 24; joyful endings, 8; joyous restoration, 179; of resurrection, 271; of Rhoda, 10; of understanding Jesus, 253; of Zacchaeus, 185; road to joy and virtue, 134; the Ethiopian's, 103; the Ethiopian's, 268

judgement: of fig-tree, 157; of God, 38; of Jews, 171; solemn, 42; theology of judgement, 139

K

katharsis: 23, 102, 103, 256

kerygma: Easter, 233; *hodos* kerygma, 271; kerygmatic appearances, 13; kerygmatic paradigms, 28; post-Easter, 9

L

lexis: 103, 109, 189, 236; of transition, 210

literature: apocalyptic, 139; Hellenistic parallels, 16, 30; Hellenistic, and ethics, 249; history, 122; innovation, in Luke-Acts, 269; Jewish, and archaisms, 82; voyage motif, 120

liturgical: reading; Central Section, 154; Emmaus, 227

M

map: biblical, 137; Christian maps, 140; of the Holy Land, 140; world maps and ideology, 139

martyr: Jesus, 40

meal: at the centre of Emmaus encounter, 258; Emmaus, 187, 227; eucharist, 187, 227, 228, 267, 275; fellowship, 187; in Luke-Acts, 228; motif, next to sight motif, 229; of encouragement, 229; of fellowship, 184; of recognition, 231; restoration, covenant, 229; sacramental, 232; scene, 265; recognition, in Emmaus, 192; significance, 98; theatre, drama, 193; three visions of Peter, 215; vs. teaching, 253

melopoiia: 103

metaphor: of painting; Luke's style, 117; the way, 32; connotations, 143; geographical, 34; Hellenistic, 50; inner life, 35; redemption, 178; the Sower parable, 144

mimesis: Aristotle; different from reality, 101; literary creativity, 84; of action, 84; painting, 117; plot, action, 103; positive, 99; definition, 73, 74; Duris, 116; vivid representation, 116; Heracles; crossroads paradigm, 134; in NT, 90; literary, 19, 73; Lukan; close to Aristotle, 85; dynamic action, 212; editing Mark, 161; high mimetic mode, 235; *hodos* paradigm, 207, 208; LXX, 76; of plot, 82; OT models, 123; rhetorical, 81; style and vocabulary, 75; thematic, 81; Markan, sensationalist, 145; *mimemata*, 74; of *hodos* encounters, 25; Plato; ambiguous, 92; imitation, inferior, 91; impersonation, 93; positive, in creation, 94; unethical, 93; similarity and dissimilarity, 75

mission: 10, 28; Luke's emphases, 160; of the Church, 198

model: Emmaus, 238; Heracles, 135; Jesus' journey, 66; Lk.24 for Acts 8-12, 9; Mark's Central Section, 58; Saul's encounter, 11 motif: baptism, 242; blindness, 46; encounters, 5; ethical choice, 54, 133; fear motif, 103; geographical, 11; heavenly vision, 217; *hodos*, 225, 266, 271; journey, 66; journeying hero, 54; meal, 229; New Exodus, 242; of heavenly rapture, 191; proof from prophecy, 202; retreat, 167; sight and understanding, 47; sight motif, 124; suffering, 48, 248; the Way, 2, 149, 261; two witnesses, 176; wandering, 33; Way and salvation, 67

N

narrative: centrality, 13; models, 19, 73; parallels, 10, 169, 195; structures, 80, 122, 152, 235, 264; function: mimesis in Mark, 86

O

opposites: in Emmaus; types, 260; the Way in Hellenism, 52, 53
opsis: 103
overlap: of different journey schemes, 27; of frameworks, spatial and temporal, 276; of genres - history and poetry, 111; of suffering, in Acts 8, 254; of temporal frameworks, in Lk. 24, 205; of triads, in Mark, 149

P

parable: dynamic, in Luke, 157; the Good Samaritan and mimesis, 85; Hellenistic parallels, the Prodigal Son, 183; Hellenistic parallels, the Good Samaritan, 181; Heracles legend, 133; imitation of reality, 84; of choice, Hellenistic, 55; of high status persons, in Luke, 162; recognition, in OT, 31; static, in Matthew, 157; the Sower and the way, 144; tragic-comic, in Luke, 277
paradigm: based on Emmaus story, 10; change, 70; discipleship, 64; divine visitation, 175; Elisha-Elijah, 191; ethical, 134, 135; hodos encounters, 208, 225, 231, 246; journey, 50, 124, 149, 179; kerygmatic, 28; mimesis, 84; on the road, 2; plot paradigm, 84; theios aner, 48
path: heroic, glorious paths, 52; middle path, *via media*, 55; of spiritual fruitfulness, 261; path of prosperity, 52; paths of God, 159; paths of virtue and vice, 133; the way, 35, 39; two paths to Acropolis, 56; ways of the Lord, 47
pathos, 104, 105, 248. See suffering.
pattern: christological dialogue, 233; Easter appearance, 217; expansion, Dodd, 14; in Luke, Talbert, 196; instruction on the way, 180; of travel, 87; recommended, Aristotle, 84; scapegoat, Girard, 88; sea voyage, shipwreck, 29; travelling teacher, 121; types, 178; unified story form, in Luke, 18
peripeteia: 104, 124. See adventure
persecution: context, for Luke, 4; destiny reversal, 265; *ecclesia pressa*, 59; Jesus, the Church, 256; of the Way, 264; Saul and David, 246
person: credible personages, 250; high status, 162; imitation changes person, 92, 93; personalisation, in Luke, 194; personalised; accounts, 169; meaning, 27; scene, 163; personified; vice, virtue, 128; providential, 183; suffering, 274; young, at crossroads, 55
pivot: Lk. 9, 24-Acts 1, 6-9, 8-9, 225; Lk. 9, Acts 6-9, 44; Lk.6, 24-Acts1, 8-9, 225
plot: coherent, 107; literary plot, 103, 104; plot coherence, 82; plot elements, 18; *peripeteia, anagnorisis, pathos, ethos*, 104;

texture, relations, 107; plot lines; complex, 256; legends and Luke-Acts, 128; Luke-Acts, 197; novels and Acts, 123; turning point, in Luke-Acts, 183; two *foci*, 258; plot, soul of tragedy, 103; simple and complex, 105; well constructed, 84, 103

praxis: 83, 100

progression: linear with sacramental climax, 262; narrative, 164, 206, 258

Q

question: at the crossroads, 55; complication, 124; counter-question, 233, 234; Lukan dialectic pattern, 233, 234, 246, 274; more solemn, in Luke, 162; open question, 234; rhetorical, 8

R

recognition: Aristotle, 104; Auerbach, 30; by memory, 105; by reasoning, 105; chiasmus, 47; contrived, by reasoning, 105; Heliodorus, 127; meal, bread breaking, 231; non-recognition, 32, 253; of Callirhoe, 121, 192; of Jesus, 31, 86; of Jesus, by Saul, 232, 234; of Jesus, in Emmaus, 191, 193, 230; of Odysseus, 31, 89; of Oedipus, 31; of Peter, 130; of the Prodigal Son, 184; of Raphael, 31; of Rhodanes and Sinonis, 193; of Romulus, 130; of Samaritan, 183; OT argument, 237, 247; OT examples, 124; reversal, 105, 256; scenes, 10, 13, 14, 15; through tokens or signs, 105; types, 105, 232

report: appearance reports, 11; author of reports, in Luke-Acts, 270; direct speech, 185; double, in Emmaus, 2; final *hodos* reports, 9, 265; final reports, summaries, 184; *hodos* reports, 130, 188, 266, 271; in Acts, 265; journey reports, 40; Lukan specific, 73; representation, 73; to the Eleven, 267, 270; to the Twelve, 6

reproduction. *See* mimesis

restoration: ending, 194, 275; ending, in Tobit, 126; feasting, 184; into fellowship, 258; Luke's constant style, 179; mark of Messia, 200; meal, in Emmaus, 229; of sight and redemption, 46; of the Ethiopian, 262; personalisation, 275; sacramental, 258, 271; the Prodigal Son, 183; the Good Samaritan's story, 183; Zacchaeus, 185

revelation: contrasted with ignorance, 260; in solitary places, 169; journeying, 87; messianic, 167; on the road, 9; scenes and journey stories, 226; teaching, 165; through dialogue, 164

reversal: change (*metabole*), 105; complex; *peripeteia* and *anagnorisis*, 124; of destiny; Saul, 250; of fortune; *metabasis*, 256; *peripeteia*, 104; point of return; *Wendepunkt*, 257; positive and negative, 182; recognition, 105; restoration, 262; reversal point; Heliodorus, 127

road: debates, dialogues, 189; encounters and Hellenistic models, 19; encounters and Luke's Way / Journey motif, 27; Heracles' roads, 134; Jesus as a teacher 'on the road', 180; journey paradigm, 124; the locus of revelation, 130

S

sacrament: baptism, of Saul, 262; baptism, of the Ethiopian, 260; Lukan compositional connotations, 230; sacramental acts, in the final, 6; sacramental chiasmus, 258; sacramental climax, 258; sacramental meal, Emmaus, 232 scheme: chiastic, 261, 263; composite, 259; compositional, 226; contraction, in Lk. 24, 204; different journey schemes, in Luke-Acts. *See* journey, structure, Jerusalem, temporal, spatial schemes, etc.; discrepancy, 61; geographical-temporal, 65; *hodos* scheme, in Luke, 194; *hodos* scheme, in Mark, 144; ideological, 139; *journey scheme, in Luke*, 59, 65, 158; journey scheme, in Luke-Acts, 225; of journeys and static scenes, 225; redaction of journey scheme, 163; static scheme, in Emmaus, 69; temporal schema, in Lk. 24, 203

sight: 5; motif, 47, 229, 275; OT, 124; recognition, 232; by memory, 105; recovery; Tobit, 125; restoration, 47, 263; understanding, 267

spatial: divergence, 202; frameworks, 207, 276; imagery, 69; mediation, 151; opposites, 151; relation to Jesus, 68; relations in Acts 8-9, 208

structure: chiasmus, in Mark, 149; chiastic structures, 265; dialectic structure, 234; dialectic, in Luke, 70; dynamic structure of plots, 104; invading journey, in Luke, 139; outward and return structure, in novels, 123; plots and structure, 104; structures and standards, 25; superimposition of structures, 235

style: Ephorus' style, flat, 114; Hellenist historians and Aristotle, 111; indirect style, 83; Luke and Atticism, 78, 79; Luke and *autopsia*, 80; Luke and Hellenistic style, 72; Luke and imitative style, 80; Luke and impressionist painting, 117; Luke and LXX style, 74, 76, 77; Luke and Theopompus' *praxeis*, 113; Luke's diction, 236; Luke's double calls, 245; Luke's mimetic style, 140; Luke's positive style, 249; Luke's superimpositions of journeys, 235; Mark's style, 90;
novels and entertaining, 122; NT style, popular, 90; of representation, mimetic, 88; Plutarch and Duris, 115; style and emulation of masters, 82; Theopompus' style, bitter, 114; Theopompus, Phylarchus, Ephorus, Duris; sensation and mimesis, 113; stylish recording, 115

suffering: Aristotle, *pathos*, 104, 105; Lukan motif, 248, 255; necessity of, the *dei* motif, 167; of brothers, due to Saul, 255; of Ethiopian, 221, 254; of Jesus, at Passover, 107; of Jesus, Emmaus, 251; of Jesus, in Isaiah prophecy, 254; of Jesus, in wilderness, 166; of Jesus, path to glory, 178; of Lord's Servant, 48; of the Prodigal Son, 183; of Saul, 256; of Saul, of Ethiopian, etc., 248; of the traveller to Jericho, 182; of Tobit, 126

symbol: external symbols, the way, 35; historical symbol, Exodus, 39; *hodos* setting, Peter's confession, 145; Jerusalem as a symbol, 178; of progressing evangelism, 271; of the Dioscuri, 87; of the Way, 144; symbolic convert, the Ethiopian, 7; the Ethiopian, 221; the Way, as a positive symbol, 245

T

table: of nations, 160, 181; table fellowship, 207, 259

teaching: in Lk. 9-19, 41; in private, 167; journey, 61; journeying, 278; meal, 253, 257; movement, in Luke, 154; on the way, 260, 266; revelation, 165. *See* instruction

temporal: compression, in Lk. 24 - Acts 1, 209; condition for apostleship, 65; contraction, 202; contraction, in Luke, 204; development in Luke-Acts, 66; emphasis, vs. geographical, in the Journey motif, 65; frameworks,

209; limit to appearances, 217; notes in Acts 9, 263; overlap of schemes, in Lk. 24, 205; progression, 206; scheme, expanding and contraction, in Lk. 24, 205; spatial dynamics, of Luke's Way motif, 66; spatial frameworks, 276; unitary temporal schema, in Lk. 24, 203

theatre: as play - and mimesis, 74; as play - and plot, 255; Hellenistic. *See* drama, plot, mimesis; *mis-en-scène*, 234

theophany: anthropomorphic, 16; essential, to Saul, 269. *See* epiphany.

tragedy: characters, 101; components of tragedy (*mythos, ethos, lexis, dianoia, opsis, melopoiia*), 103; efect of tragedy (emotions), 105; epic, tragedy, and mimesis, 20; history, Polybius, 113; history, Quintilian, 113; in Saul's story, 255; Luke's style. *See* drama, imitation, comedy, plot; Luke's style, comedy, 249; reversal of destiny, 106; tragic and comic, in Luke, 277; unity, 109

transition: features, in Emmaus story, 186; function of hodos stories, 164; in Luke 24, 206; journey stories, 199; nature, Bartimaeus, 194; pivot role, 225

typology: 1 Enoch, 138; Raphael typology in Lk. 24, 31; typological interpretation of the Way, 33

U

unity: narrative, 205; narrative, of Acts 8-9, 207; of action, of character, 203; of composition, 66; unified plot, 107; unified story form, 18; unitary actions, 108; unitary temporal scheme, 203

V

vision: dialogue, 270; double heavenly vision, 217; double vision theme, 235; encounters, 18; Heliodorus, 127; of Cornelius, 214; of Paul, Acts 27, 214; of Stephen, 217; of the Macedonian, 214; revelation, 87; Saul's vision, 214; vision within vision, 235

W

word: as rhetorical entity, 123; avoidance of obscurity, 109; choice of words, diction, 109; literature, mimesis in words, 116; Luke and loan words, 78; painting with words, 117; the way of the word, 69

wordplay: *hodos* encounters, 109; in Acts 8.30, 235

Index of Authors

A

Aletti, J.-N., 148, 219
Alexander, L., 80, 122, 123, 137, 139
Alexander, P.S., 137
Alsup, J.E., 11, 124, 214, 228
Alter, R., 81, 197
Auerbach, E., 31, 82, 125
Aune, D.E., 122, 136, 252

B

Baarlink, H., 155, 172
Bachmann, M., 42
Bailey, K.E., 41, 61, 172, 173, 178
Balz, H., 1, 221
Bar-Efrat, S., 197
Barrett, C.K., 7, 197, 209, 215, 219, 224
Bartsch, H.W., 214
Bauernfeind, O., 222, 264
Baum, A.D., 43, 57
Baur, F.C., 132, 195
Beardslee, W.A., 86
Becker, O., 50
Behm, J., 230
Berg, B., 135
Berg, W., 81
Berger, K., 120
Best, E., 146, 148, 150
Betz, H.D., 17, 27, 30
Bigger, S., 138
Birt, T., 136
Blass, F., 114, 236
Blomberg, C.L., 41, 44, 173
Bock, D.L., 45, 166, 177, 186, 207, 228, 237, 266
Boismard, M.-É., 6, 46, 125, 175, 211, 213, 220, 238, 242, 243
Bonnard, P., 157
Borg, M.J., 130
Borgen, P., 214
Bosch, D.J., 10
Botha, P.J.J., 108, 203, 204

Bovon, F., 50, 123, 153
Boyce, J.L., 88
Brant, J.A., 88
Bratcher, R., 215
Braumann, G., 64
Brink, C.O., 22
Brodie, T.L., 19, 74, 80, 81, 123, 124
Brosend, W.F., II, 204
Brown, E.K., 197
Brown, M.R., 51
Brown, S., 49, 64, 65, 67, 69, 70, 177
Bruce, F.F., 235, 254, 270
Buckwalter, H.D., 198
Bultmann, R., 29, 53, 81
Burchard, C., 218, 234
Bywater, I., 21

C

Cadbury, H.J., 27, 28, 29, 76, 82, 117
Calduch-Benages, N., 125
Carmignac, J., 147
Cassidy, R.J., 130
Casson, L., 51, 87, 137
Castelvetro, L., 20
Charlesworth, J.H., 36, 37, 138
Chatman, S., 144
Collins, J.J., 138
Combrink, H.J.B., 157
Conzelmann, H., 10, 27, 34, 41, 59, 63, 65, 68, 70
Cook, A., 75, 87, 109
Craig, W.L., 213
Cranfield, C.E.B., 148
Creed, J.M., 76, 78, 79, 187
Croix, G.E.M., de St., 110
Cullmann, O., 59
Curtis, A.H.W., 10

D

Danker, F.W., 229
Daube, D., 149, 255
Davies, J.G., 31, 168, 198

Davies, J.H., 42, 168, 179
Denaux, A., 27, 33, 42, 43, 44, 57, 154, 180
Denniston, J.P., 91
Derrett, J.D.M., 187, 188, 193, 229, 236, 239, 267
Derrida, J., 95
Deselaers, P., 126
Detweiler, R., 88
Dibelius, M., 27, 29, 32
Diefenbach, M., 76
Dillon, D.J., 3, 4, 48, 186, 187, 243, 253, 265, 266
Dodd, C.H., 14, 160, 273
Dollar, H.E., 10, 171, 222
Donahue, J.R., 57, 151
Dongel, J.R., 46
Donne, B.K., 198
Dormeyer, D., 80
Droge, J.A., 252, 253
Drury, J., 6, 154
Dungan, D.L., *See* McNicol, J.
Dunn, D.G.J., 8, 209
Dupont, J., 3, 154, 227, 261

E

Edwards, R.A., 71
Egelkraut, H.L., 61
Ehrhardt, A., 12, 48, 128, 230, 238, 252
Eichhorn, J.G., 57
Eisenman, R.H., 37
Eliade, M., 51, 137
Else, G.F., 83, 99, 100, 101
Ernst, J., 166
Esler, P.F., 7
Evans, C.A., 57, 191
Evans, C.F., 44, 117, 155, 156

F

Fackre, G., 82
Farmer, W.R., 153
Farrer, A.M., 142, 153
Fenton, J.C., 157
Filson, F.V., 45, 155, 198, 209
Fink, J., 136

Fitzmyer, J.A., 2, 43, 68, 188, 190, 228, 230, 233, 238, 266
Flender, H., 27, 64, 70, 198, 251
Flower, M.A., 112, 113
Fornara, C.W., 116
Forster, E.M., 84
Franklin, E., 142, 154, 173, 198
Freeland, C.A., 102
Freyne, S., 156
Fritz, K., 22, 111
Frye, N., 83, 85, 163
Fuller, R.H., 48, 239
Funk, R.W., 30, 166, 181, 205, 277

G

Gadamer, H.G., 75
Gallie, W.B., 104
Garrett, S., 68
Gasque, W.W., 10, 64
Gaventa, B.R., 7, 221, 267
Gebauer, G., 75, 88
Gempf, C., 131
Genette, G., 83
George, A., 135, 243, 253
Gilchrist, J.M., 87
Gill, D., 57, 179, 180, 265
Gilmore, D.D., 255
Girard, L., 57, 61
Girard, R., 88
Glasson, T.F., 39, 138
Gnilka, J., 148
Gogarten, F., 76
Golden, L., 20, 92, 93, 94, 99, 100, 102, 107, 249
Goodacre, M.S., 143, 153, 155, 184
Goodman, N., 101
Goodman, P., 84
Goppelt, L., 13
Goulder, M.D., 5, 10, 59, 60, 117, 153, 172, 173, 195
Gowler, D.B., 255
Graß, H., 12
Grassi, J.A., 3
Gray, V., 116
Green, H.B., 157
Green, J.B., 40, 60, 62, 177, 186, 228, 259

Grundmann, W., 48, 177, 179, 231
Guelich, R.A., 145
Guillaume, J.-M., 4, 5, 30, 47, 186, 199, 231, 258, 261
Gundry, R.H., 143, 144, 147, 148
Gunkel, H., 13, 123

H

Haenchen, E., 7, 39, 56, 73, 124, 196, 215, 223, 253
Hägg, T., 119
Hagner, D.A., 155, 157
Halliwell, S., 107
Hamm, D., 197
Hammerton-Kelly, R.G., 88
Hansen, W., 28
Harnack, A., 200
Hasel, G., 59
Hastings, A., 40, 200
Havelock, E.R., 93
Hedrick, C.W., 84, 104, 144, 163, 214, 245, 249
Heidegger, M., 75
Hemer, C.J., 27, 60
Hengel, M., 50, 61
Henry, R., 114
Himmelfarb, M., 39, 138
Hock, R.F., 122, 184
Höistad,R., 135
Holtz, T., 45
Hooker, M.D., 145
Hull, W.E., 57
Hulleman, J.G., 111

I

Iersel, B. van, 144, 147, 149, 151
Innes, D.C., 82
Isaac, E., 138

J

Jaeger, W., 27, 50, 53, 54
Jakoby, F., 112
Jáuregui, J.A., 60
Jervell, J., 7
Johnson, L.T., 6, 7, 47, 128, 202

Juel, D., 45, 243, 244, 253
Just, A.A., 3, 47, 168, 173, 186, 204, 232, 258

K

Kebric, R.B., 116
Kelber, W.H., 146, 150, 156
Kennedy, G., 79
Kennedy, G.A., 78, 82
Kermode, F., 152
Kim, H.S., 77, 218
Klein, J.G., 256
Knibb, M.A., 138
Knox, W.L., 76, 121, 136, 226, 236
Koester, H., 78, 79
Koller, H., 74
Kosman, A., 102
Kränkl, E., 253
Kremer, J., 3
Kümmel, W., 177, 244
Kurz, W.S., 31, 78, 84, 107, 205, 232

L

Laistner, M.L.W., 114
Lambrecht, J., 148
Lamouille, A., *See* Boismard, M.-E.
Lane, W.L., 228
Lang, F.G., 145
Langrange, M.J., 131
Larranaga, V., 198
Leivestad, R., 254
Léon-Dufour, X., 258
Lerer, S., 75
Lesky, A., 22, 111, 119
Levine, B., 88
Levoratti, A.J., 88
Lightfoot, R.H., 156
Lindijer, C.H., 2, 4, 5, 211, 231, 233, 255, 257, 260, 273
Litke, W.D., 45
Lohfink, G., 16, 198, 199, 234, 239, 245
Lohmeyer, E., 58, 154, 156
Lohr, C.H., 157
Lohse, E., 64, 65
Löning, K., 32, 244, 262, 263, 265

Lücking, S., 74, 85, 163
Lüdemann, G., 65, 66, 110, 215, 219, 234

M

MacCormack, S., 34
MacDonald, D.R., 19
Maddox, R., 171
Magness, J.L., 205
Maile, J., 198
Malbon, E.S., 86, 143, 144, 148, 151, 152
Malherbe, A.J., 55, 56
Maloney, L.M., 188, 266
Markus, R.A., 34, 35
Marquerat, D., 197
Marshall, I.H., 3, 30, 41, 64, 142, 160, 266
Martin, C.J., 221
Martin, R., 77
Matera, F.J., 179
Matson, D.L., 160, 161, 185
Mauser, U., 146
Mayer, E., 27
McBride, D., 3, 175, 202, 239
McCasland, S.V., 27, 35, 36, 38
McCown, C.C., 60
McCoy, W.J., 196
McDonald, J.H., 205
McEleney, N.J., 127
McKeon, R., 74, 82, 101
McKnight, E.V., 124
McNicol, J., 153, 154, 155, 156, 173, 174
Mealand, D.L., 79
Meister, K., 117
Melberg, A., 31, 75, 83, 88, 91, 95
melopoiia, 103
Menoud, P.H., 204
Menzies, R.P., 65
Metzger, B.M., 8, 160, 181
Meynet, R., 148
Michaelis, W., 133
Michie, D., *See* Rhoads, D.
Miller, R.G., 191
Millik, J.T., 139
Minear, P.S., 64

Mínguez, D., 163, 210, 261, 269
Mink, L.O., 104
Miyoshi, M., 41, 179
Moehring, H.R., 216
Moessner, D.P., 27, 44, 178, 209, 225
Morgan, J.R., 119, 121, 122
Morgenthaler, R., 71, 161, 163, 176, 201, 225
Muhlack, G., 195
Müller, C., 111
Munck, P.J., 245
Murray, P., 91

N

Naumann, W., 75
Navone, J., 27, 59, 65, 97, 124, 128, 180, 184, 199, 278
Neirynck, F., 142, 144
Neyrey, J.H., 229, 244, 259
Nobbs, A., 140
Nock, A.D., 253
Nolland, J., 159, 160, 162, 166, 167, 174, 203, 228
Norden, E., 132
Nowell, I., 126

O

O'Toole, R.F., 209
O'Collins, G., 216
Oesterley, W.O.E., 181
Ogg, G., 57
Ong, W.J., 88
Osborne, G.R., 239

P

Parsons, M.C., 198, 205
Parunak, H.D., 236
Peabody, D.B., 144, *See* McNicol, J.
Pédech, P., 22, 112, 117
Perry, B.E., 119, 120
Pervo, R.I., 48, 78, 118, 119, 122, 125, 140
Pesch, R., 263
Pfister, F., 136
Plevnik, J., 203

Plümacher, E., 76, 208, 222, 224
Plummer, A., 77, 203
Polhill, J.B., 3, 216, 218, 219, 224
Pope, M.H., 143
Powell, M.A., 144, 151
Praeder, S.M., 139, 195
Preminger, A., 20
Prior, M., 191, 199

R

Radl, W., 195, 244
Ramsay, W., 200
Rapske, B.M., 87
Ravens, D., 42, 153
Reinmuth, E., 81, 123, 190, 191
Repo, E., 27, 32, 33, 35, 38, 48, 49
Resseguie, J.L., 57
Rhoads, D., 143, 144, 148
Richard, E., 64, 80, 107, 124
Ricoeur, P., 83, 85, 101, 104, 109
Rimmon-Kennan, S., 205
Ringe, S.H., 43
Rius-Camps, J., 81
Robinson, B.P., 9, 130, 189, 202, 229, 230, 238, 239
Robinson, W.C., 27, 34, 64, 65, 66, 67, 199
Rohde, E., 118, 121
Roloff, J., 3, 7, 140, 254, 263
Rostagni, A., 21
Rydberg, L., 79

S

Safrai, S., 43
Samain, É., 46
Savran, G.W., 197
Scheffler, E.H., 2, 4, 231
Scheller, P., 116
Schierling, S.P., 119, 120, 121, 183
Schille, G., 7
Schleiermacher, F.D.E., 57
Schmidt, K.L., 28, 59
Schmidt, W., 121
Schmithals, W., 4, 146
Schnabel, E.J., 161
Schnackenburg, R., 232

Schneckenburger, M., 195
Schneider, G., 1, 210, 211
Schneider, J., 177, 179
Schnider, F., 257
Schonfield, H., 36, 37
Schubert, P., 187, 188, 202, 232, 237, 258, 266
Schwartz, E., 22
Schweiker, W., 88
Scott, B.B., 181
Scott, J.M., 137, 138, 160, 181
Selling, G., 179
Senior, D., 10, 163
Shepherd, W., 63, 175
Sherwin-White, A.N., 108, 203
Shrimpton, G.S., 112
Siegert, F., 236
Simon, M., 136
Smith, C.D., 34
Smith, J.Z., 35
Smith, T.H., 88
Soards, M.L., 107
Sparks, H.F.D., 77, 138
Spencer, F.S., 80, 153, 209, 220, 233, 253
Stagg, F., 41
Stählin, G., 217, 219
Standaert, B., 144
Stanley, D.M., 198, 215
Stempvoort, P.A., 31, 124, 198
Stenberg, M., 197
Stendahl, K., 218
Stenger, W., *See* Schnider, F.
Stephens, S.A., 189, 193
Sterling, G.E., 60, 108, 203, 204
Steyn, G.J., 19, 23, 73, 80, 81
Stock, A., 145, 148, 149
Strasburger, H., 115
Strauss, M.L., 27, 33
Strecker, G., 58, 147, 157
Swartley, W.M., 27, 42, 150

T

Talbert, C.H., 31, 60, 173, 195, 253
Tannehill, R.C., 6, 197, 231
Taylor, J.E., 35
Taylor, V., 148

Thompson, M.M., 155
Thompson, S., 182
Thurén, J., 228
Toca, M.S., 268
Tolbert, M.A., 56
Torraca, L., 22, 110
Toynbee, A.J., 136
Tracy, D., 84
Trocmé, E., 78
Trompf, G.W., 179, 195
Turner, N., 77

U

Ullman, B.L., 112
Unnik, W.C., 2, 8, 268

V

Vermes, G., 37
Verseput, D.J., 155, 156
Via, D.O., 84, 85, 104, 249, 277
Vinson, R.B., 78
Vogeli, A., 247
Volz, P., 39
Voss, G., 243

W

Walaskay, P.W., 43
Walbank, W.F., 24, 95, 113, 116, 117
Walker, P.W.L., 34, 42, 172, 199
Wallace, M.I., 89

Wanke, J., 3, 207, 229, 240
Watts, R.E., 33, 47, 150, 176
Wefald, E.K., 143, 144, 146
Weinert, F.D., 42
Weiser, A., 219
Wette, W.M.L., 57
Wifstrand, A., 79, 80
Wilamowitz-Moellendorff, U., 79
Wilckens, U., 11
Wilcox, M., 220
Wilken, R.L., 34
Wills, L.M., 125, 182, 183
Wilson, N.G., 114
Wilson, S.G., 171, 199, 256
Windisch, H., 124, 127, 246
Wisse, J., 79
Witherington, B., III, 24, 112, 247
Witherup, R.D., 197
Woodruff, P., 74, 92, 93, 94, 100
Wulf, C. *See* Gebauer, G.

Y

York, J.O., 171

Z

Zeller, E., 195
Ziegler, K., 95
Zmijewski, J., 8, 39, 215, 220, 224, 237
Zwiep, A.W., 13, 31, 81, 214

Paternoster Biblical Monographs
(All titles uniform with this volume)
Dates in bold are of projected publication

Joseph Abraham
Eve: Accused or Acquitted?
A Reconsideration of Feminist Readings of the Creation Narrative Texts in Genesis 1–3
Two contrary views dominate contemporary feminist biblical scholarship. One finds in the Bible an unequivocal equality between the sexes from the very creation of humanity, whilst the other sees the biblical text as irredeemably patriarchal and androcentric. Dr Abraham enters into dialogue with both camps as well as introducing his own method of approach. An invaluable tool for any one who is interested in this contemporary debate.
2002 / 0-85364-971-5 / xxiv + 272pp

Octavian D. Baban
Mimesis and Luke's on the Road Encounters in Luke-Acts
Luke's Theology of the Way and its Literary Representation
The book argues on theological and literary (mimetic) grounds that Luke's on-the-road encounters, especially those belonging to the post-Easter period, are part of his complex theology of the Way. Jesus' teaching and that of the apostles is presented by Luke as a challenging answer to the Hellenistic reader's thirst for adventure, good literature, and existential paradigms.
2005 */ 1-84227-253-5 / approx. 374pp*

Paul Barker
The Triumph of Grace in Deuteronomy
This book is a textual and theological analysis of the interaction between the sin and faithlessness of Israel and the grace of Yahweh in response, looking especially at Deuteronomy chapters 1–3, 8–10 and 29–30. The author argues that the grace of Yahweh is determinative for the ongoing relationship between Yahweh and Israel and that Deuteronomy anticipates and fully expects Israel to be faithless.
2004 / 1-84227-226-8 / xxii + 270pp

Jonathan F. Bayes
The Weakness of the Law
God's Law and the Christian in New Testament Perspective
A study of the four New Testament books which refer to the law as weak (Acts, Romans, Galatians, Hebrews) leads to a defence of the third use in the Reformed debate about the law in the life of the believer.
2000 / 0-85364-957-X / xii + 244pp

July 2005

Mark Bonnington
The Antioch Episode of Galatians 2:11-14 in Historical and Cultural Context
The Galatians 2 'incident' in Antioch over table-fellowship suggests significant disagreement between the leading apostles. This book analyses the background to the disagreement by locating the incident within the dynamics of social interaction between Jews and Gentiles. It proposes a new way of understanding the relationship between the individuals and issues involved.
2005 / 1-84227-050-8 / approx. 350pp

David Bostock
A Portrayal of Trust
The Theme of Faith in the Hezekiah Narratives
This study provides detailed and sensitive readings of the Hezekiah narratives (2 Kings 18–20 and Isaiah 36–39) from a theological perspective. It concentrates on the theme of faith, using narrative criticism as its methodology. Attention is paid especially to setting, plot, point of view and characterization within the narratives. A largely positive portrayal of Hezekiah emerges that underlines the importance and relevance of scripture.
2005 / 1-84227-314-0 / approx. 300pp

Mark Bredin
Jesus, Revolutionary of Peace
A Non-violent Christology in the Book of Revelation
This book aims to demonstrate that the figure of Jesus in the Book of Revelation can best be understood as an active non-violent revolutionary.
2003 / 1-84227-153-9 / xviii + 262pp

Robinson Butarbutar
Paul and Conflict Resolution
An Exegetical Study of Paul's Apostolic Paradigm in 1 Corinthians 9
The author sees the apostolic paradigm in 1 Corinthians 9 as part of Paul's unified arguments in 1 Corinthians 8–10 in which he seeks to mediate in the dispute over the issue of food offered to idols. The book also sees its relevance for dispute-resolution today, taking the conflict within the author's church as an example.
2006 / 1-84227-315-9 / approx. 280pp

Daniel J-S Chae
Paul as Apostle to the Gentiles
His Apostolic Self-awareness and its Influence on the Soteriological Argument in Romans
Opposing 'the post-Holocaust interpretation of Romans', Daniel Chae competently demonstrates that Paul argues for the equality of Jew and Gentile in Romans. Chae's fresh exegetical interpretation is academically outstanding and spiritually encouraging.
1997 / 0-85364-829-8 / xiv + 378pp

Luke L. Cheung
The Genre, Composition and Hermeneutics of the Epistle of James
The present work examines the employment of the wisdom genre with a certain compositional structure and the interpretation of the law through the Jesus tradition of the double love command by the author of the Epistle of James to serve his purpose in promoting perfection and warning against doubleness among the eschatologically renewed people of God in the Diaspora.
2003 / 1-84227-062-1 / xvi + 372pp

Youngmo Cho
Spirit and Kingdom in the Writings of Luke and Paul
The relationship between Spirit and Kingdom is a relatively unexplored area in Lukan and Pauline studies. This book offers a fresh perspective of two biblical writers on the subject. It explores the difference between Luke's and Paul's understanding of the Spirit by examining the specific question of the relationship of the concept of the Spirit to the concept of the Kingdom of God in each writer.
2005 / 1-84227-316-7 / approx. 270pp

Andrew C. Clark
Parallel Lives
The Relation of Paul to the Apostles in the Lucan Perspective
This study of the Peter-Paul parallels in Acts argues that their purpose was to emphasize the themes of continuity in salvation history and the unity of the Jewish and Gentile missions. New light is shed on Luke's literary techniques, partly through a comparison with Plutarch.
2001 / 1-84227-035-4 / xviii + 386pp

July 2005

Andrew D. Clarke
Secular and Christian Leadership in Corinth
A Socio-Historical and Exegetical Study of 1 Corinthians 1–6
This volume is an investigation into the leadership structures and dynamics of first-century Roman Corinth. These are compared with the practice of leadership in the Corinthian Christian community which are reflected in 1 Corinthians 1–6, and contrasted with Paul's own principles of Christian leadership.
2005 / 1-84227-229-2 / 200pp

Stephen Finamore
God, Order and Chaos
René Girard and the Apocalypse
Readers are often disturbed by the images of destruction in the book of Revelation and unsure why they are unleashed after the exaltation of Jesus. This book examines past approaches to these texts and uses René Girard's theories to revive some old ideas and propose some new ones.
2005 / 1-84227-197-0 / approx. 344pp

David G. Firth
Surrendering Retribution in the Psalms
Responses to Violence in the Individual Complaints
In *Surrendering Retribution in the Psalms*, David Firth examines the ways in which the book of Psalms inculcates a model response to violence through the repetition of standard patterns of prayer. Rather than seeking justification for retributive violence, Psalms encourages not only a surrender of the right of retribution to Yahweh, but also sets limits on the retribution that can be sought in imprecations. Arising initially from the author's experience in South Africa, the possibilities of this model to a particular context of violence is then briefly explored.
2005 / 1-84227-337-X / xviii + 154pp

Scott J. Hafemann
Suffering and Ministry in the Spirit
Paul's Defence of His Ministry in II Corinthians 2:14–3:3
Shedding new light on the way Paul defended his apostleship, the author offers a careful, detailed study of 2 Corinthians 2:14–3:3 linked with other key passages throughout 1 and 2 Corinthians. Demonstrating the unity and coherence of Paul's argument in this passage, the author shows that Paul's suffering served as the vehicle for revealing God's power and glory through the Spirit.
2000 / 0-85364-967-7 / xiv + 262pp

Scott J. Hafemann
Paul, Moses and the History of Israel
The Letter/Spirit Contrast and the Argument from Scripture in 2 Corinthians 3
An exegetical study of the call of Moses, the second giving of the Law (Exodus 32–34), the new covenant, and the prophetic understanding of the history of Israel in 2 Corinthians 3. Hafemann's work demonstrates Paul's contextual use of the Old Testament and the essential unity between the Law and the Gospel within the context of the distinctive ministries of Moses and Paul.
2005 / 1-84227-317-5 / xii + 498pp

Douglas S. McComiskey
Lukan Theology in the Light of the Gospel's Literary Structure
Luke's Gospel was purposefully written with theology embedded in its patterned literary structure. A critical analysis of this cyclical structure provides new windows into Luke's interpretation of the individual pericopes comprising the Gospel and illuminates several of his theological interests.
2004 / 1-84227-148-2 / xviii + 388pp

Stephen Motyer
Your Father the Devil?
A New Approach to John and 'The Jews'
Who are 'the Jews' in John's Gospel? Defending John against the charge of antisemitism, Motyer argues that, far from demonising the Jews, the Gospel seeks to present Jesus as 'Good News for Jews' in a late first century setting.
1997 / 0-85364-832-8 / xiv + 260pp

Esther Ng
Reconstructing Christian Origins?
The Feminist Theology of Elizabeth Schüssler Fiorenza: An Evaluation
In a detailed evaluation, the author challenges Elizabeth Schüssler Fiorenza's reconstruction of early Christian origins and her underlying presuppositions. The author also presents her own views on women's roles both then and now.
2002 / 1-84227-055-9 / xxiv + 468pp

Robin Parry
Old Testament Story and Christian Ethics
The Rape of Dinah as a Case Study

What is the role of story in ethics and, more particularly, what is the role of Old Testament story in Christian ethics? This book, drawing on the work of contemporary philosophers, argues that narrative is crucial in the ethical shaping of people and, drawing on the work of contemporary Old Testament scholars, that story plays a key role in Old Testament ethics. Parry then argues that when situated in canonical context Old Testament stories can be reappropriated by Christian readers in their own ethical formation. The shocking story of the rape of Dinah and the massacre of the Shechemites provides a fascinating case study for exploring the parameters within which Christian ethical appropriations of Old Testament stories can live.

2004 / 1-84227-210-1 / xx + 350pp

Ian Paul
Power to See the World Anew
The Value of Paul Ricoeur's Hermeneutic of Metaphor in Interpreting the Symbolism of Revelation 12 and 13

This book is a study of the hermeneutics of metaphor of Paul Ricoeur, one of the most important writers on hermeneutics and metaphor of the last century. It sets out the key points of his theory, important criticisms of his work, and how his approach, modified in the light of these criticisms, offers a methodological framework for reading apocalyptic texts.

2006 / 1-84227-056-7 / approx. 350pp

Robert L. Plummer
Paul's Understanding of the Church's Mission
Did the Apostle Paul Expect the Early Christian Communities to Evangelize?

This book engages in a careful study of Paul's letters to determine if the apostle expected the communities to which he wrote to engage in missionary activity. It helpfully summarizes the discussion on this debated issue, judiciously handling contested texts, and provides a way forward in addressing this critical question. While admitting that Paul rarely explicitly commands the communities he founded to evangelize, Plummer amasses significant incidental data to provide a convincing case that Paul did indeed expect his churches to engage in mission activity. Throughout the study, Plummer progressively builds a theological basis for the church's mission that is both distinctively Pauline and compelling.

2006 / 1-84227-333-7 / approx. 324pp

David Powys
'Hell': A Hard Look at a Hard Question
The Fate of the Unrighteous in New Testament Thought
This comprehensive treatment seeks to unlock the original meaning of terms and phrases long thought to support the traditional doctrine of hell. It concludes that there is an alternative—one which is more biblical, and which can positively revive the rationale for Christian mission.
1997 / 0-85364-831-X / xxii + 478pp

Sorin Sabou
Between Horror and Hope
Paul's Metaphorical Language of Death in Romans 6.1-11
This book argues that Paul's metaphorical language of death in Romans 6.1-11 conveys two aspects: horror and hope. The 'horror' aspect is conveyed by the 'crucifixion' language, and the 'hope' aspect by 'burial' language. The life of the Christian believer is understood, as relationship with sin is concerned ('death to sin'), between these two realities: horror and hope.
2005 / 1-84227-322-1 / approx. 224pp

Rosalind Selby
The Comical Doctrine
The Epistemology of New Testament Hermeneutics
This book argues that the gospel breaks through postmodernity's critique of truth and the referential possibilities of textuality with its gift of grace. With a rigorous, philosophical challenge to modernist and postmodernist assumptions, Selby offers an alternative epistemology to all who would still read with faith *and* with academic credibility.
2005 / 1-84227-212-8 / approx. 350pp

Kiwoong Son
Zion Symbolism in Hebrews
Hebrews 12.18-24 as a Hermeneutical Key to the Epistle
This book challenges the general tendency of understanding the Epistle to the Hebrews against a Hellenistic background and suggests that the Epistle should be understood in the light of the Jewish apocalyptic tradition. The author especially argues for the importance of the theological symbolism of Sinai and Zion (Heb. 12:18-24) as it provides the Epistle's theological background as well as the rhetorical basis of the superiority motif of Jesus throughout the Epistle.
2005 / 1-84227-368-X / approx. 280pp

Kevin Walton
Thou Traveller Unknown
The Presence and Absence of God in the Jacob Narrative
The author offers a fresh reading of the story of Jacob in the book of Genesis through the paradox of divine presence and absence. The work also seeks to make a contribution to Pentateuchal studies by bringing together a close reading of the final text with historical critical insights, doing justice to the text's historical depth, final form and canonical status.
2003 / 1-84227-059-1 / xvi + 238pp

George M. Wieland
The Significance of Salvation
A Study of Salvation Language in the Pastoral Epistles
The language and ideas of salvation pervade the three Pastoral Epistles. This study offers a close examination of their soteriological statements. In all three letters the idea of salvation is found to play a vital paraenetic role, but each also exhibits distinctive soteriological emphases. The results challenge common assumptions about the Pastoral Epistles as a corpus.
2005 / 1-84227-257-8 / approx. 324pp

Alistair Wilson
When Will These Things Happen?
A Study of Jesus as Judge in Matthew 21–25
This study seeks to allow Matthew's carefully constructed presentation of Jesus to be given full weight in the modern evaluation of Jesus' eschatology. Careful analysis of the text of Matthew 21–25 reveals Jesus to be standing firmly in the Jewish prophetic and wisdom traditions as he proclaims and enacts imminent judgement on the Jewish authorities then boldly claims the central role in the final and universal judgement.
2004 / 1-84227-146-6 / xxii + 272pp

Lindsay Wilson
Joseph Wise and Otherwise
The Intersection of Covenant and Wisdom in Genesis 37–50
This book offers a careful literary reading of Genesis 37–50 that argues that the Joseph story contains both strong covenant themes and many wisdom-like elements. The connections between the two helps to explore how covenant and wisdom might intersect in an integrated biblical theology.
2004 / 1-84227-140-7 / xvi + 340pp

Stephen I. Wright
The Voice of Jesus
Studies in the Interpretation of Six Gospel Parables
This literary study considers how the 'voice' of Jesus has been heard in different periods of parable interpretation, and how the categories of figure and trope may help us towards a sensitive reading of the parables today.
2000 / 0-85364-975-8 / xiv + 280pp

Paternoster
9 Holdom Avenue,
Bletchley,
Milton Keynes MK1 1QR,
United Kingdom
Web: www.authenticmedia.co.uk/paternoster

Paternoster Theological Monographs
(All titles uniform with this volume)
Dates in bold are of projected publication

Emil Bartos
Deification in Eastern Orthodox Theology
An Evaluation and Critique of the Theology of Dumitru Staniloae
Bartos studies a fundamental yet neglected aspect of Orthodox theology: deification. By examining the doctrines of anthropology, christology, soteriology and ecclesiology as they relate to deification, he provides an important contribution to contemporary dialogue between Eastern and Western theologians.
1999 / 0-85364-956-1 / xii + 370pp

Graham Buxton
The Trinity, Creation and Pastoral Ministry
Imaging the Perichoretic God
In this book the author proposes a three-way conversation between theology, science and pastoral ministry. His approach draws on a Trinitarian understanding of God as a relational being of love, whose life 'spills over' into all created reality, human and non-human. By locating human meaning and purpose within God's 'creation-community' this book offers the possibility of a transforming engagement between those in pastoral ministry and the scientific community.
2005 / 1-84227-369-8 / approx. 380 pp

Iain D. Campbell
Fixing the Indemnity
The Life and Work of George Adam Smith
When Old Testament scholar George Adam Smith (1856–1942) delivered the Lyman Beecher lectures at Yale University in 1899, he confidently declared that 'modern criticism has won its war against traditional theories. It only remains to fix the amount of the indemnity.' In this biography, Iain D. Campbell assesses Smith's critical approach to the Old Testament and evaluates its consequences, showing that Smith's life and work still raises questions about the relationship between biblical scholarship and evangelical faith.
2004 / 1-84227-228-4 / xx + 256pp

July 2005

Tim Chester
Mission and the Coming of God
Eschatology, the Trinity and Mission in the Theology of Jürgen Moltmann
This book explores the theology and missiology of the influential contemporary theologian, Jürgen Moltmann. It highlights the important contribution Moltmann has made while offering a critique of his thought from an evangelical perspective. In so doing, it touches on pertinent issues for evangelical missiology. The conclusion takes Calvin as a starting point, proposing 'an eschatology of the cross' which offers a critique of the over-realised eschatologies in liberation theology and certain forms of evangelicalism.
2006 / 1-84227-320-5 / approx. 224pp

Sylvia Wilkey Collinson
Making Disciples
The Significance of Jesus' Educational Strategy for Today's Church
This study examines the biblical practice of discipling, formulates a definition, and makes comparisons with modern models of education. A recommendation is made for greater attention to its practice today.
2004 / 1-84227-116-4 / xiv + 278pp

Darrell Cosden
A Theology of Work
Work and the New Creation
Through dialogue with Moltmann, Pope John Paul II and others, this book develops a genitive 'theology of work', presenting a theological definition of work and a model for a theological ethics of work that shows work's nature, value and meaning now and eschatologically. Work is shown to be a transformative activity consisting of three dynamically inter-related dimensions: the instrumental, relational and ontological.
2005 / 1-84227-332-9 / xvi + 208pp

Stephen M. Dunning
The Crisis and the Quest
A Kierkegaardian Reading of Charles Williams
Employing Kierkegaardian categories and analysis, this study investigates both the central crisis in Charles Williams's authorship between hermetism and Christianity (Kierkegaard's Religions A and B), and the quest to resolve this crisis, a quest that ultimately presses the bounds of orthodoxy.
2000 / 0-85364-985-5 / xxiv + 254pp

Keith Ferdinando
The Triumph of Christ in African Perspective
A Study of Demonology and Redemption in the African Context
The book explores the implications of the gospel for traditional African fears of occult aggression. It analyses such traditional approaches to suffering and biblical responses to fears of demonic evil, concluding with an evaluation of African beliefs from the perspective of the gospel.
1999 / 0-85364-830-1 / xviii + 450pp

Andrew Goddard
Living the Word, Resisting the World
The Life and Thought of Jacques Ellul
This work offers a definitive study of both the life and thought of the French Reformed thinker Jacques Ellul (1912-1994). It will prove an indispensable resource for those interested in this influential theologian and sociologist and for Christian ethics and political thought generally.
2002 / 1-84227-053-2 / xxiv + 378pp

David Hilborn
The Words of our Lips
Language-Use in Free Church Worship
Studies of liturgical language have tended to focus on the written canons of Roman Catholic and Anglican communities. By contrast, David Hilborn analyses the more extemporary approach of English Nonconformity. Drawing on recent developments in linguistic pragmatics, he explores similarities and differences between 'fixed' and 'free' worship, and argues for the interdependence of each.
2006 / 0-85364-977-4 / approx. 350pp

Roger Hitching
The Church and Deaf People
A Study of Identity, Communication and Relationships with Special Reference to the Ecclesiology of Jürgen Moltmann
In *The Church and Deaf People* Roger Hitching sensitively examines the history and present experience of deaf people and finds similarities between aspects of sign language and Moltmann's theological method that 'open up' new ways of understanding theological concepts.
2003 / 1-84227-222-5 / xxii + 236pp

July 2005

John G. Kelly
One God, One People
The Differentiated Unity of the People of God in the Theology of Jürgen Moltmann
The author expounds and critiques Moltmann's doctrine of God and highlights the systematic connections between it and Moltmann's influential discussion of Israel. He then proposes a fresh approach to Jewish–Christian relations building on Moltmann's work using insights from Habermas and Rawls.
2005 / 0-85346-969-3 / approx. 350pp

Mark F.W. Lovatt
Confronting the Will-to-Power
A Reconsideration of the Theology of Reinhold Niebuhr
Confronting the Will-to-Power is an analysis of the theology of Reinhold Niebuhr, arguing that his work is an attempt to identify, and provide a practical theological answer to, the existence and nature of human evil.
2001 / 1-84227-054-0 / xviii + 216pp

Neil B. MacDonald
Karl Barth and the Strange New World within the Bible
Barth, Wittgenstein, and the Metadilemmas of the Enlightenment
Barth's discovery of the strange new world within the Bible is examined in the context of Kant, Hume, Overbeck, and, most importantly, Wittgenstein. MacDonald covers some fundamental issues in theology today: epistemology, the final form of the text and biblical truth-claims.
2000 / 0-85364-970-7 / xxvi + 374pp

Keith A. Mascord
Alvin Plantinga and Christian Apologetics
This book draws together the contributions of the philosopher Alvin Plantinga to the major contemporary challenges to Christian belief, highlighting in particular his ground-breaking work in epistemology and the problem of evil. Plantinga's theory that both theistic and Christian belief is warrantedly basic is explored and critiqued, and an assessment offered as to the significance of his work for apologetic theory and practice.
2005 / 1-84227-256-X / approx. 304pp

Gillian McCulloch
The Deconstruction of Dualism in Theology
With Reference to Ecofeminist Theology and New Age Spirituality
This book challenges eco-theological anti-dualism in Christian theology, arguing that dualism has a twofold function in Christian religious discourse. Firstly, it enables us to express the discontinuities and divisions that are part of the process of reality. Secondly, dualistic language allows us to express the mysteries of divine transcendence/immanence and the survival of the soul without collapsing into monism and materialism, both of which are problematic for Christian epistemology.

2002 / 1-84227-044-3 / xii + 282pp

Leslie McCurdy
Attributes and Atonement
The Holy Love of God in the Theology of P.T. Forsyth
Attributes and Atonement is an intriguing full-length study of P.T. Forsyth's doctrine of the cross as it relates particularly to God's holy love. It includes an unparalleled bibliography of both primary and secondary material relating to Forsyth.

1999 / 0-85364-833-6 / xiv + 328pp

Nozomu Miyahira
Towards a Theology of the Concord of God
A Japanese Perspective on the Trinity
This book introduces a new Japanese theology and a unique Trinitarian formula based on the Japanese intellectual climate: three betweennesses and one concord. It also presents a new interpretation of the Trinity, a co-subordinationism, which is in line with orthodox Trinitarianism; each single person of the Trinity is eternally and equally subordinate (or serviceable) to the other persons, so that they retain the mutual dynamic equality.

2000 / 0-85364-863-8 / xiv + 256pp

Eddy José Muskus
The Origins and Early Development of Liberation Theology in Latin America
With Particular Reference to Gustavo Gutiérrez
This work challenges the fundamental premise of Liberation Theology, 'opting for the poor', and its claim that Christ is found in them. It also argues that Liberation Theology emerged as a direct result of the failure of the Roman Catholic Church in Latin America.

2002 / 0-85364-974-X / xiv + 296pp

Jim Purves
The Triune God and the Charismatic Movement
A Critical Appraisal from a Scottish Perspective
All emotion and no theology? Or a fundamental challenge to reappraise and realign our trinitarian theology in the light of Christian experience? This study of charismatic renewal as it found expression within Scotland at the end of the twentieth century evaluates the use of Patristic, Reformed and contemporary models of the Trinity in explaining the workings of the Holy Spirit.
2004 / 1-84227-321-3 / xxiv + 246pp

Anna Robbins
Methods in the Madness
Diversity in Twentieth-Century Christian Social Ethics
The author compares the ethical methods of Walter Rauschenbusch, Reinhold Niebuhr and others. She argues that unless Christians are clear about the ways that theology and philosophy are expressed practically they may lose the ability to discuss social ethics across contexts, let alone reach effective agreements.
2004 / 1-84227-211-X / xx + 294pp

Ed Rybarczyk
Beyond Salvation
Eastern Orthodoxy and Classical Pentecostalism on Becoming Like Christ
At first glance eastern Orthodoxy and classical Pentecostalism seem quite distinct. This ground-breaking study shows they share much in common, especially as it concerns the experiential elements of following Christ. Both traditions assert that authentic Christianity transcends the wooden categories of modernism.
2004 / 1-84227-144-X / xii + 356pp

Signe Sandsmark
Is World View Neutral Education Possible and Desirable?
A Christian Response to Liberal Arguments
(Published jointly with The Stapleford Centre)
This book discusses reasons for belief in world view neutrality, and argues that 'neutral' education will have a hidden, but strong world view influence. It discusses the place for Christian education in the common school.
2000 / 0-85364-973-1 / xiv + 182pp

Hazel Sherman
Reading Zechariah
The Allegorical Tradition of Biblical Interpretation through the Commentary of Didymus the Blind and Theodore of Mopsuestia
A close reading of the commentary on Zechariah by Didymus the Blind alongside that of Theodore of Mopsuestia suggests that popular categorising of Antiochene and Alexandrian biblical exegesis as 'historical' or 'allegorical' is inadequate and misleading.
2005 / 1-84227-213-6 / approx. 280pp

Andrew Sloane
On Being a Christian in the Academy
Nicholas Wolterstorff and the Practice of Christian Scholarship
An exposition and critical appraisal of Nicholas Wolterstorff's epistemology in the light of the philosophy of science, and an application of his thought to the practice of Christian scholarship.
2003 / 1-84227-058-3 / xvi + 274pp

Damon W.K. So
Jesus' Revelation of His Father
A Narrative-Conceptual Study of the Trinity with Special Reference to Karl Barth
This book explores the trinitarian dynamics in the context of Jesus' revelation of his Father in his earthly ministry with references to key passages in Matthew's Gospel. It develops from the exegeses of these passages a non-linear concept of revelation which links Jesus' communion with his Father to his revelatory words and actions through a nuanced understanding of the Holy Spirit, with references to K. Barth, G.W.H. Lampe, J.D.G. Dunn and E. Irving.
2005 / 1-84227-323-X / approx. 380pp

Daniel Strange
The Possibility of Salvation Among the Unevangelised
An Analysis of Inclusivism in Recent Evangelical Theology
For evangelical theologians the 'fate of the unevangelised' impinges upon fundamental tenets of evangelical identity. The position known as 'inclusivism', defined by the belief that the unevangelised can be ontologically saved by Christ whilst being epistemologically unaware of him, has been defended most vigorously by the Canadian evangelical Clark H. Pinnock. Through a detailed analysis and critique of Pinnock's work, this book examines a cluster of issues surrounding the unevangelised and its implications for christology, soteriology and the doctrine of revelation.
2002 / 1-84227-047-8 / xviii + 362pp

Scott Swain
God According to the Gospel
Biblical Narrative and the Identity of God in the Theology of Robert W. Jenson
Robert W. Jenson is one of the leading voices in contemporary Trinitarian theology. His boldest contribution in this area concerns his use of biblical narrative both to ground and explicate the Christian doctrine of God. *God According to the Gospel* critically examines Jenson's proposal and suggests an alternative way of reading the biblical portrayal of the triune God.
2006 / 1-84227-258-6 / approx. 180pp

Justyn Terry
The Justifying Judgement of God
A Reassessment of the Place of Judgement in the Saving Work of Christ
The argument of this book is that judgement, understood as the whole process of bringing justice, is the primary metaphor of atonement, with others, such as victory, redemption and sacrifice, subordinate to it. Judgement also provides the proper context for understanding penal substitution and the call to repentance, baptism, eucharist and holiness.
2005 / 1-84227-370-1 / approx. 274 pp

Graham Tomlin
The Power of the Cross
Theology and the Death of Christ in Paul, Luther and Pascal
This book explores the theology of the cross in St Paul, Luther and Pascal. It offers new perspectives on the theology of each, and some implications for the nature of power, apologetics, theology and church life in a postmodern context.
1999 / 0-85364-984-7 / xiv + 344pp

Adonis Vidu
Postliberal Theological Method
A Critical Study
The postliberal theology of Hans Frei, George Lindbeck, Ronald Thiemann, John Milbank and others is one of the more influential contemporary options. This book focuses on several aspects pertaining to its theological method, specifically its understanding of background, hermeneutics, epistemic justification, ontology, the nature of doctrine and, finally, Christological method.
2005 / 1-84227-395-7 / approx. 324pp

Graham J. Watts
Revelation and the Spirit
A Comparative Study of the Relationship between the Doctrine of Revelation and Pneumatology in the Theology of Eberhard Jüngel and of Wolfhart Pannenberg
The relationship between revelation and pneumatology is relatively unexplored. This approach offers a fresh angle on two important twentieth century theologians and raises pneumatological questions which are theologically crucial and relevant to mission in a postmodern culture.
2005 / 1-84227-104-0 / xxii + 232pp

Nigel G. Wright
Disavowing Constantine
Mission, Church and the Social Order in the Theologies of John Howard Yoder and Jürgen Moltmann
This book is a timely restatement of a radical theology of church and state in the Anabaptist and Baptist tradition. Dr Wright constructs his argument in dialogue and debate with Yoder and Moltmann, major contributors to a free church perspective.
2000 / 0-85364-978-2 / xvi + 252pp

Paternoster
9 Holdom Avenue,
Bletchley,
Milton Keynes MK1 1QR,
United Kingdom
Web: www.authenticmedia.co.uk/paternoster

July 2005